Problems of Moral Philosophy

Problems of Moral Philosophy

An Introduction to Ethics

THIRD EDITION

edited by
PAUL W. TAYLOR
Brooklyn College, City University of New York

Wadsworth Publishing Company, Inc.
Belmont, California

PRINTED IN THE UNITED STATES OF AMERICA
PRINTING (LAST DIGIT): 9 8 7 6 5 4 3 2 1

LIBRARY OF CONGRESS CATALOGING IN PUBLICATION
DATA

TAYLOR, PAUL W
  PROBLEMS OF MORAL PHILOSOPHY.

  INCLUDES BIBLIOGRAPHIES.
  1. ETHICS—ADDRESSES, ESSAYS, LECTURES.
I. TITLE.
BJ71.T3 1978   170'.8   77–16073
ISBN 0–534–00592–6

COVER BY LINDA ROBERTSON

Contents

Preface to the First Edition

This volume, which is a combination of textbook and anthology, is intended to serve as a clear and orderly introduction to the study of moral philosophy or ethics. The terms "moral philosophy" and "ethics" are here used interchangeably. They cover any systematic reflection about moral questions (that is, questions that require the making of moral judgments in answering them) and about meta-moral questions (questions about morality as a whole). The book is divided into nine chapters, each dealing with a basic problem of ethics. The textbook portion of the book consists of the introductory essays to the nine chapters. Their purpose is to set forth each problem in a way that will stimulate students to begin thinking about it themselves. Various conceptual distinctions are made in these introductions, and students may avoid some confusions in their thinking by keeping the distinctions in mind as they study the readings of a chapter.

The readings represent different positions developed by moral philosophers regarding each of the nine problems. In any one chapter will be found several contrasting positions, along with arguments defending or attacking the views set forth in each position. It is hoped that the student will come to understand moral philosophy as a dialogue carried on by those who seek clarity and truth through the uncompromising use of reason, disregarding the social acceptability or unacceptability of the conclusions. The student should be encouraged to participate in this dialogue and so engage in the actual practice of moral philosophy itself. The present volume has been designed to help bring this about.

Included at the end of each chapter is a list of additional readings that will extend the philosophical dialogue begun in the chapter. These supplementary readings have been chosen specifically with the idea that students might want to know about inexpensive, easily available paperback books that contain recent writing on the problem of the chapter. Although these lists are not meant as scholarly bibliographies, they can be used for assigning independent papers to students or as extra required reading for class discussion. Some of these books appear again and again on the lists; these are the books that cover all or most of the nine problems dealt with, and hence can be effectively used as companion works to the present volume. Perhaps the one paperback book that provides the best companion work is W. K. Frankena's *Ethics* (Prentice-Hall's Foundations of Philosophy Series).

Very good bibliographies on the various problems of ethics discussed in this volume may be found at the end of chapters in J. Hospers, *Human Conduct: An Introduction to the Problems of Ethics* (Harcourt, Brace and World, Inc.), and in R. B. Brandt, *Ethical Theory: The Problems of Normative and Critical Ethics* (Prentice-Hall, Inc.).

In teaching courses in ethics I have found that the ordering of the nine problems according to the present arrangement of chapters is an effective guide to the logical and coherent development of students' thinking in moral philosophy. The experience of other teachers, however, might indicate that a different order would be preferable. Taking this into account, I have tried to make each chapter independent of the others so that they can be taken up in any order. Two limitations must nevertheless be mentioned. The first is that the criticisms of utilitarianism contained in Chapter 5 do presuppose some familiarity with utilitarian ethics, which is the subject matter of Chapter 4. The second is that the introduction to Chapter 8, on "Intrinsic Value," makes some references to R. M. Hare's analysis of value judgments in Chapter 7. It is also possible in some instances to use the readings of one chapter in conjunction with those of another, in so far as they are concerned with one problem. No hard and fast lines can be drawn between certain problems when they overlap or when there are close logical connections between them. This is as it should be, for moral philosophy is a unified field of inquiry.

Finally, as is the case with any selection of readings in an anthology, there is always the possibility that the editor's choice of excerpts gives a distorted or misleading presentation of a philosophical argument. I have carefully tried to avoid this, but full responsibility for any such weakness rests with me. The complete work from which a reading has been taken should be consulted whenever a teacher or student wishes to understand it in the framework of its original context.

A book of this sort would not be possible without the cooperation of authors, editors, and publishers who were willing to make their work available for reprinting. I wish to express my sincere thanks to all who have so kindly granted me permission to include material in this volume.

I have also benefited from the comments of those who reviewed the selection of readings for this book and who made suggestions regarding the introductions. My apologies are due to certain of my colleagues at Brooklyn College with whom I share an office. They have had to put up with some inconveniences which my work on this book involved for them. For their courtesy, understanding, and patience I am very grateful.

I owe a large debt to my students at Brooklyn College who have participated in philosophical discussions with me. Their challenging questions and uncompromising search for unevasive answers have often led me to think out my own views more carefully. My students have also had an influence on this book in helping me to see what ethical problems were of basic concern to them and what kinds of confusions needed most to be avoided. In the courses in ethics I have taught, learning has indeed been a two-way process. For this I can only declare my heartfelt thanks to all my students.

PAUL W. TAYLOR

Preface to the Second Edition

In this edition I have tried to preserve the basic character of the book while making improvements both in the introductory essays and in the selection of readings. The principal changes are to be found in Chapters 7 and 9.

In Chapter 7 a greater emphasis has been placed on the current controversy over the logical connection between facts and value judgments. I have included in this chapter all the material from the work of Professor R. M. Hare, instead of having it appear in two separate chapters as was the case in the First Edition. Hare's "prescriptivism" can now be seen as a development out of the attack on naturalism begun by G. E. Moore. I have brought the contents of Chapter 7 up to date by including an example of Mrs. Philippa Foot's recent arguments against Hare's prescriptivism, along with a criticism of Mrs. Foot's position by Professors D. Z. Phillips and H. O. Mounce.

In Chapter 9 the whole concept of the rationality of morals is considered afresh. The nature of moral claims and their relation to self-interest are given a wider context for the student's reflection. Professor Rawl's well-known essay "Justice as Fairness" has been included for two reasons. First, it provides an analysis of the concept of justice which is directly relevant to the criticisms of utilitarianism raised in Chapters 4 and 5. Second, it attempts to show that moral obligation rests on the rational commitment of individuals to live in a moral community, where a moral community is conceived as a society in which each person is related to others by "the duty of fair play." The rationality of moral rules is further explored in Professor David Gauthier's study of morality and social advantage. The question "Why should I be moral?" is then seen to arise when neither considerations of fairness nor those of social advantage are allowed to count as reasons for an individual's being moral. Thus Professor Nielsen's discussion of the individual's quest for the justification of morality is given a more adequate background than was possible in the First Edition.

I have also brought up to date all the Supplementary Paperback Reading lists at the ends of chapters. In the past several years there has been a great increase in the number of high quality paperbacks published in the field of moral philosophy. I list below various paperbacks that could be used effectively as companion volumes to this book (in addition to W. K. Frankena's *Ethics*, mentioned in the Preface to the First Edition). All of the following are collections of essays:

R. Ekman, *Readings in the Problems of Ethics.* (Scribner's)
J. Feinberg, *Moral Concepts.* (Oxford University Press)

P. Foot, *Theories of Ethics*. (Oxford University Press)
J. Margolis, *Contemporary Ethical Theory*. (Random House)
J. J. Thomson and G. Dworkin, *Ethics*. (Harper and Row)

I wish to thank all those who have kindly given me the benefit of their thoughtful criticisms of both the introductory material and the selection of readings used in the First Edition. In addition, I am greatly indebted to the following persons, who made many helpful suggestions regarding changes that would be desirable in a Second Edition: Norman O. Dahl, University of Minnesota at Minneapolis; William E. Mann, Saint Olaf College; Thomas Regan, North Carolina State University at Raleigh; James P. Hawkins, Santa Monica College; John H. Tietz, Simon Fraser University; Joel Feinberg, the Rockefeller University; Romaine L. Gardner, Wagner College; and Joseph C. Burgess, the University of Santa Clara.

P. W. T.

Preface to the Third Edition

Chapters 10 and 11 have simply been added to the Second Edition, which otherwise remains unchanged. It is hoped that the broader coverage by the two new chapters will make the third edition of the book a more adequate introduction to ethics.

The following reviewers provided thoughtful suggestions to me in my work on the Third Edition: Elizabeth L. Beardsley, Temple University; Tom L. Beauchamp, Georgetown University; Donald Burrill, California State University, Los Angeles; William Parent, University of Santa Clara; and Paul Wheatcroft, Grossmont College.

P. W. T.

Problems of Moral Philosophy

1

WHAT IS

MORALITY?

Introduction

ETHICS AND MORALITY

Ethics may be defined as the philosophical study of morality. In order to understand the terms of this definition it is necessary to answer two questions: What is morality? What makes a study of morality a philosophical study? We shall examine two different answers to the first question in this chapter, and still other answers will be suggested by philosophers in later chapters. The subject matter of ethics may itself be considered one of the problems of ethics. Moreover, the question of what makes an inquiry into morality a philosophical one rather than, say, a scientific or historical one is also a matter of dispute. So we must realize that defining ethics as the philosophical study of morality provides only a general indication of its nature. With this in mind, however, the following remarks may prove useful as a way to approach the problems of ethics.

Morality has to do with right and wrong conduct and with good and bad character. Moral judgments are made not only about the actions that people do, but also about their motives or reasons for doing them and about their more general character traits. Thus we think that an action is wrong when a person violates a trust that another has placed in him, and we think an action is right if the person who does it is keeping a trust. We judge someone's motive to be bad when his aim in doing an act is to harm another and we judge it to be good when the aim is to help another. If one person is generally honest and another is hypocritical, we may judge that the first person is a good man or has good character because he is honest, and that the second is bad or has a bad character because he is a hypocrite.

In all such judgments of conduct, motives, and character traits, we are applying moral norms. A moral norm may be either a rule of conduct or a standard of evaluation. That is, it may be a requirement that anyone in certain circumstances ought to do a certain kind of action (for example, to treat another person fairly) or ought to refrain from doing a certain kind of action (for example, to refrain from telling a lie). Or the norm may be a standard of evaluation, which we refer to when we judge whether something is good or bad, desirable or undesirable, worthy or worthless. As applied to conduct, standards are used for judging how good or bad are the consequences of a person's actions. It is possible for the same *kind* of action to be wrong when it is done in one situation and right when it is done in another because in the first situation the consequences of doing an action of that kind are bad while the consequences of doing the same kind of action in the second situation are good. As an example, consider how an act of lying can be wrong in one case and right in another. If one person causes harm to come to someone else by telling a lie, we would ordinarily judge the action to be wrong. However, in the following situation we would probably judge the same kind of action (telling a lie) to be right: An American abolitionist who is protecting a runaway slave in the cellar of his house tells a lie when a suspicious neighbor questions him about runaway slaves. We have, then, two sorts of reasons why an action ought or ought not to be done: that the action is of a *kind* that is required or prohibited by a moral rule, and that the action will, in the given circumstances, have good or bad *consequences* as judged by a standard of evaluation.

Moral judgments of people's motives and character traits are made on the basis of standards of evaluation, not rules of conduct. Thus we judge a person to be morally admirable according to the degree to which he fulfills some ideal we accept of human excellence or virtue. And we think of a man as vicious, ignoble, or despicable in so far as he has motives and character traits we consider morally bad or undesirable. It is, of course, possible to judge that a man is a good man because he always strives to do actions that are required by moral rules of conduct and to refrain from actions forbidden by moral rules. But even in this case what is being judged directly is not the person's actions but his "will," that is, his aims, motives, and intentions in acting in certain ways.

It is important to notice that the rules of conduct and standards of evaluation used by someone in his moral judgments need not be the conventionally accepted norms of a society's established moral code. They may, instead, be norms which the individual has chosen for himself after having rejected, wholly or in part, the conventional morality of his society. But no matter whether a person has unreflectively absorbed a set of rules and standards from his social environment or has chosen them himself on the basis of critical reflection, he will implicitly refer to them whenever he judges the rightness or wrongness of his own or another's actions and the goodness or badness of his own or another's character. In so far as a person tries to live up to the rules and standards which he sincerely accepts, they become part of his "philosophy of life," guiding his choices and giving direction to his conduct. They determine his ultimate ends and ideals in life, and thereby provide the grounds for his deciding that some goals are more worth striving for than others.

When a stable set of rules and standards governs the choices and conduct of a large majority of people in a given society, we speak of the norms shared by a whole culture. Such norms are embodied in the society's customs, traditions, and laws. They define its moral outlook and give form to its whole way of life. Furthermore, they are backed up by social sanctions. This means that various sorts of approval and encouragement are given to those who try to live up to them, and various sorts of disapproval and discouragement are given to those who fail to conform to them. Sanctions may be of any degree of severity, ranging from smiles and frowns to economic rewards and physical punishment.

Now the question: What is morality? can be understood as asking for the characteristics by which a person's or society's moral norms can be distinguished from all its other norms. The question means: What is it that makes a standard a moral standard and a rule of conduct a moral rule? It should be noted that the word "moral" is here being contrasted with "nonmoral," not with "immoral." In other words, our question concerns how norms are to be classified or described. When, on the other hand, "moral" is contrasted with "immoral" (or "ethical" with "unethical"), we are concerned with evaluating a person or an action. In this second sense, a moral person or act is one that is judged to be morally good or right and an immoral one is one that is judged to be morally bad or wrong. In order to determine whether something is morally good or bad, right or wrong, we must refer to *moral* standards or rules, where "moral" is used in the first sense. That is, we must refer to standards or rules that belong to the category of morality, as distinct from such categories as law and etiquette. Now the question: What is morality? is the question: How do we know that any given standard or rule belongs to the category of morality?

THE CONCEPT OF MORALITY

In this chapter we are presented with two answers to the foregoing question. Thus the two readings may be seen as two ways of delimiting the subject matter of ethics, when "ethics" is understood as the philosophical study of morality. We have not yet explained what is involved in a philosophical study of morality, but before doing so it is a good idea to try to be clear about the concept of morality itself. This clarification is what our two readings are aiming at.

In the first reading Professor Ralph Barton Perry begins with an analysis of what a value judgment is. In his view, when we judge something to be valuable or good we are making an assertion that the something is an object of a positive interest. By "positive interest" he means any feeling, desire, or attitude that can be described as liking the object, preferring it over other things, approving of it, and being generally disposed to bring it about, protect it, hold on to it, and cherish it. Thus nothing can have value unless someone has this kind of feeling or attitude toward it. As soon as someone takes a positive interest in an object it is good, and it is good just because this interest is taken in it. A similar analysis is given of a negative value judgment (that something is bad, undesirable, evil, etc.). In this case we assert that someone has a negative interest in the object. By "negative interest" is meant any feeling, desire, or attitude that can be described as disliking the object, being against it, disapproving of it, or wanting to avoid or get rid of it.

This view of value judgments has been called "the interest theory of value" because it makes the value of an object depend on the presence of someone's positive or negative interest. An implication of this theory is that something is good because one likes it or approves of it; one does not like it or approve of it because it is good. After setting forth his theory, Professor Perry defends it against several objections that might be raised to it. He is then ready to present his account of the nature of morality.

According to his position, morality is one aspect of a civilization or culture. In order to know what aspect, it is necessary to distinguish moral values from nonmoral ones. The question here is not, What things are morally good? or, What is our moral duty? It is rather, What is meant by calling something morally good? or, How can we determine whether a duty is a moral one? Professor Perry's answer, in brief, is that the domain of morality is the area where interests are in conflict and there is an attempt to bring these conflicting interests into harmony. In order to clarify this basic idea, Professor Perry considers four conceptions of morality that he believes are one-sided or mistaken. After showing why and in what respects he thinks these are misconceptions of morality, he expounds his own view, and thus provides us with one way of distinguishing moral from nonmoral norms.

The second reading in this chapter, by Professor John Hartland-Swann, takes quite a different approach to the problem. He does not begin with a general theory of value, but instead tries to account for the different criteria employed by various cultures for differentiating a moral question from a nonmoral one. He shows how each of the following questions is considered by some societies to be moral and by others not to be moral: Ought I to marry one wife or two wives? Ought I to kill this hornet? Is incest a moral issue? Is it morally wrong, or morally neutral, to keep slaves provided you treat them kindly? After considering each question, Professor Hartland-Swann is prepared to suggest what makes a question a matter of morality for one society but not for another. His view may be summarized in the statement: "A moral matter is one concerned with those customs (social rules or norms) that are believed to be socially important in a given culture at a given time." The crucial concept here is that of "social importance," and Professor Hartland-Swann takes pains to explain what he means by it. Then he proceeds to examine the special authority that moral standards and rules have in a culture. He concludes his essay with a discussion of the kind of definition of morality he has offered.

WHAT IS ETHICS?

Let us return to our explanation of the nature and purpose of ethics. The term "moral philosophy" is often used as another name for ethics, when ethics is taken as the philosophical study of morality. We must now try to arrive at some answer to the question: What makes a study of morality a philosophical study? One way to approach this question is by contrasting the scientific study of morality with the philosophical.

We have seen that morality is a set of social rules and standards that guide the conduct of people in a culture. It is one aspect of a culture's whole way of life, and has a special importance to everyone who has been brought up within the framework of that way of life. When morality is understood in this way, we can see that it can be investigated on two different levels: that of the individual and that of society.

On the level of the individual, a person's morality includes his moral beliefs about what is right and wrong, the standards he uses in judging human motives and character, and the rules by which he tries to guide his life. When he fails to live up to his moral norms, he may experience the feelings of guilt and remorse. He may hold himself responsible or accountable for his own acts, just as he may hold others responsible for having done similar acts. Thus in certain circumstances he may take a moral attitude toward himself and others. His moral ideals may inspire him to strive to become a better man. He may even commit himself to carrying out his moral principles at some cost to his self-interest. It is clear, then, that if a person's morality were different, his whole experience of life would be different. He would not only behave differently, but would also have different thoughts, feelings, attitudes, and desires. In short, he would be a different kind of man.

Now since the morality of an individual is part of his experience of life, it can be studied empirically. His moral judgments can be accurately described, and their causes and effects investigated. A psychological explanation can be given to show why a particular person has the moral beliefs and attitudes he does have, and how his behavior is influenced by them. Psychologists can study the origin and growth of a man's conscience, and even relate his moral experiences to unconscious wishes, anxieties, and emotional conflicts of which he is unaware.

Similarly, on the level of society, empirical knowledge about morality can be sought and obtained. Anthropologists, sociologists, historians, and social psychologists have examined the various moral codes of different societies and of different epochs. They have studied the moral norms operating in different economic and social classes within a culture. They have observed and explained the presence of "deviants" in a society, whose norms are at variance with those generally accepted in the society. They have seen how moral rules and standards are related to the social structure and how they function in preserving a society's way of life. All these social aspects of morality are subject to the techniques of historical research, anthropological "field work," and sociological analysis.

Let us sum up this empirical knowledge of moral phenomena in the life of an individual and in the structure and functioning of a society as: *the scientific description and explanation of morality*. For convenience, we may call this scientific study of morality "descriptive ethics." We may now readily distinguish it from *the philosophical study of morality*. Philosophers are interested in morality for two basic purposes: a normative purpose and an analytic purpose. The first purpose is to show how it is possible to construct a consistent system of moral norms valid for all mankind. Many methods of philosophical thinking have been used to accomplish this purpose, and we shall become familiar with a number of them in this book. In all such cases, the philosopher is concerned with the question whether a rational ground of moral obligation can be established. He examines the ultimate foundations of morality in order to show that a certain set of moral standards and rules are finally justifiable. His aim is not to describe or causally explain what moral beliefs people have, but to inquire into their truth or falsity. As a result of his inquiry he hopes to answer the question: Is there a set of standards and rules which any rational person would be justified in adopting as guides to his life? Thus the philosopher seeks what might be called a conception of the good life for man as an ideal for all men to try to live up to.

Philosophical thinking carried on in a systematic way to accomplish this purpose is *normative ethics,* and constitutes one side of the philosophical study of morality. The other side is *analytic ethics* or *meta-ethics.* Here the philosopher's task is, first, to analyze the meaning of the terms used in moral discourse, and second, to examine the rules of reasoning (or methods of knowing) by which moral beliefs can be shown to be true or false. The first task of analytic ethics is a semantical one, the second a logical and epistemological one. We shall briefly consider each task in turn.

The aim of the first task is to explain precisely how such terms as "good," "right," "duty," and "ought" function in moral language. When people express their moral convictions, prescribe conduct, appraise character and motives, deliberate about what they ought or ought not to do, and evaluate what they and others have done, they are using moral language. Whether they are thinking out a moral issue for themselves or are discussing it with others, they are carrying on moral discourse. We learned the language of morals in our childhood, and we teach it to our own children when we try to bring them up morally. It is the job of philosophy to make a careful and thorough analysis of the meaning of the words and sentences that make up such language. The final aim is to achieve a full understanding of moral concepts (duty, virtue, responsibility, right action, etc.) and how they function in moral discourse. This first task of meta-ethics may be designated "conceptual analysis."

The second task of meta-ethics may be called "the analysis of the logic of moral reasoning." Here the philosopher's job is to make explicit the logical principles which are followed (or are intended to be followed) when people give moral reasons for or against doing an act, or when they try to justify their accepting or rejecting a moral judgment. Just as the philosophy of science attempts to show the logical structure underlying scientific method—the process whereby scientists verify their statements and support their theories by appeal to evidence—so analytic ethics attempts to show how moral beliefs can be established as true or false, and on what grounds anyone can claim to know they are true or false. As we shall see later, there is much dispute, not only about what methods of reasoning are to be used, but even about whether any method is possible at all. Thus the problem of analytic ethics is twofold. On the one hand is the question whether there is any such thing as moral truth or moral knowledge. On the other is the question: *If* there is such a thing, how can we gain it? This double aspect of analytic ethics may be brought out in the following list of questions, each pair of which is a way of expressing the basic twofold problem:

Is there a valid method by which the truth or falsity of moral beliefs can be established?	If so, what is this method and on what grounds does its validity rest?
Are moral statements verifiable?	If so, what is their method of verification?
Is there such a thing as knowledge of good and evil, right and wrong?	If so, how can such knowledge be obtained?
Is there a way of reasoning by which moral judgments can be justified?	If so, what is the logic of such reasoning?
Can we claim that the reasons we give in support of our moral judgments are good (sound, valid, acceptable, warranted) reasons?	If so, on what grounds can we make this claim? What are the criteria for the goodness (soundness, validity, etc.) of a reason?

Whenever anyone tries to answer these questions in a clear and orderly way, he is doing analytic ethics. We are now in a position to see a logical relation between analytic and normative ethics. Analytic ethics inquires into the *presuppositions* of normative ethics, in the following way. If a philosopher constructs a system of moral norms and claims that these norms are validly binding upon all mankind, he presupposes that there is a procedure whereby moral norms can be validated and that he has followed this procedure. He claims, in other words, to have moral knowledge and hence assumes that such knowledge is possible. Now it is precisely this assumption that is brought into question in analytic ethics. The very use of such words as "know," "true," "valid," and "justified" as applied to moral judgments is a problem for analytic ethics. Such words are used in normative ethics, but are not explicitly and carefully analyzed. Their analysis is just the task that meta-ethics sets for itself. It may therefore be argued that meta-ethics or analytic ethics is logically prior to normative ethics. Meta-ethical questions must first be answered before the complete development of a normative ethical system can be successfully achieved. It should be noted, however, that these two branches of ethics were not distinguished until midway in the twentieth century, so that the writings of moral philosophers before this time tend to cover both the problems of normative ethics and the problems of analytic ethics. In studying these writings it is always helpful to ask oneself, Is the philosopher making moral judgments and trying to show that they are justified, or is he examining what it means to claim that a moral judgment can be justified? In this way we can make clearer to ourselves exactly what questions the philosopher is trying to answer and so be better able to judge the soundness of his arguments.

We may sum up these introductory remarks about the nature of ethics in the following outline:

I. The Scientific Study of Morality (Descriptive Ethics)
Description and explanation of the moral life of man as manifested in any given individual's moral experience and in any given society's moral code.
II. The Philosophical Study of Morality
   A. Normative Ethics
   Inquiry into the rational grounds for justifying a set of moral norms for all mankind, and the rational construction of a system of such norms.
   B. Analytic Ethics or Meta-Ethics
      1. Conceptual analysis
      Semantical study of the meaning of words and sentences used in moral discourse.
      2. Analysis of the logic of moral reasoning
      Study of the methods by which moral judgments can be established as true or false, or whether any such method is possible at all.

CUSTOMARY MORALITY AND REFLECTIVE MORALITY

The ultimate purpose of normative and analytic ethics is to enable us to arrive at a critical, reflective morality of our own. Everyone is brought up with some set of moral beliefs, and every society has some moral code as part of its way of life. But an individual may either blindly accept the moral code of his society, or he may come to reflect upon it and criticize it. If he blindly accepts it, we may speak of his morality as "conventional" or "customary." Such an individual might well have strong moral convictions and might well be a good man in that he lives up to his norms. But he remains a child of his culture and lacks the ability to support his convictions by rational argument. Should he suddenly be confronted by others who have moral beliefs contradictory to his own and who hold them with as much certainty as he holds his own, he will feel lost and bewildered. His state of confusion might then turn into a deep disillusionment about morality. Unable to give an objective, reasoned justification for his own convictions, he may turn from dogmatic certainty to total scepticism. And from total scepticism it is but a short step to an "amoral" life—a life without any moral principles at all. Thus the person who begins by accepting moral beliefs blindly can end up denying all morality. Disillusionment and doubt can demoralize him, ultimately leading him to repudiate all moral ideals.

We can think of the process of moral growth as moving away from both complete dogmatism and complete scepticism. Neither of these conditions can provide reasons for or against moral beliefs. They are not the result of philosophical thought. One rests on blind faith in the authority of parents or society; the other is a reaction to deep emotional insecurity when intellectual certainty has been destroyed. The condition of moral maturity is the condition in which an individual has the capacity to be open-minded about his moral beliefs, defending them by reasoned argument when they are challenged and giving them up when they are shown to be false or unjustified. Of course it is possible for a person to conclude, on the basis of his own philosophical reflection about morality, that there is no valid method of reasoning by which moral beliefs can be justified or shown to be unjustified. That is, a person might come to think that all the meta-ethical questions placed on the left side of the foregoing list must be answered in the negative. But even here he will remain open-minded about his conclusions, always holding them tentatively and always willing to listen seriously to arguments on the other side.

Moral growth occurs, then, as the individual develops the capacity to reason about his moral beliefs. Instead of blindly adopting his society's moral code or being easily shocked by the moral systems of other cultures, he is able to think clearly, calmly, and coherently about any set of moral norms. He learns how to give good reasons for accepting and rejecting such norms, or else he learns the limits of moral reasoning, or why no such reasoning is possible. But whatever might be his conclusions, they are arrived at on the basis of his own reflection. He can then decide for himself what standards of evaluation and rules of conduct to commit himself to.

It is this sort of person—one who can think for himself and make decisions on the basis of his own thinking—who is the true individualist. Even if he ends up with moral norms that happen to be in general agreement with those of his society, they are of his own choosing so long as he can show why he thinks they are the norms he ought to follow. The process of critical reflection, however, will often lead a man to disagree with his society. In this case it is his critical reflection, not his disagreement, that makes him an individualist.

How can the shift from customary morality to reflective morality be accomplished? The answer lies in ethics, the philosophical study of morality. For ethics is nothing but the most systematic and thorough endeavor to understand moral concepts and to justify moral norms. Its supreme goal is to construct a moral order that can stand up to the critical scrutiny of reflective men. In so far as each of us tries to develop into a morally mature person, we are engaged in the practice of moral philosophy. We are striving to be clear and rational in our ethical thinking (the specific purpose of analytic ethics) and, if possible, to arrive at the principles of a universally valid moral system (the specific purpose of normative ethics). Thus ethics is not to be thought of merely as an intellectual game. It deals with the most vital issues we shall ever confront in practical life, and it alone can provide an adequate foundation for the moral growth of the individual.

RALPH BARTON PERRY
A Definition of Morality

THE DEFINITION OF VALUE IN TERMS OF INTEREST

•   •   •   •   •

The question "What does 'value' mean?" is not the same as the question "What things have value?" Though the two questions are often confused, the difference is evident when attention is called to it. The statement that "a sphere is a body of space bounded by one surface all points of which are equally distant from a point within called its center" is different from the statement that "the earth is (or is not) a sphere." The statement that peace is a condition in which societies abstain from the use of violence in settling their disputes, is different from the statement that the world is (or is not) now at peace. And similarly, a statement, such as is proposed below, of what value is, differs from the statement that peace is valuable.

If the second of each of these pairs of statements is to be definitive and accurate it is clearly advisable to have in mind the first. If, in other words, one is to know whether peace is or is not valuable, it is well to know what 'valuable' is: in other words, to know what it is that is stated about peace when it is stated that it is valuable. But while the question raised by the second statement depends on an answer to the question raised by the first, the two questions are not the same question. And it is the first question with which the present inquiry is primarily concerned. In other words, theory of value ascribes value to things only in the light of what 'value' means.

•   •   •   •   •

According to the definition of value here proposed, *a thing—any thing— has value, or is valuable, in the original and generic sense when it is the object of an interest—any interest*. Or, *whatever is object of interest is ipso facto valuable*. Thus the valuableness of peace is the characteristic conferred on peace by the interest which is taken in it, for what it is, or for any of its attributes, effects, or implications.

Value is thus defined in terms of interest, and its meaning thus depends on another definition, namely, a definition of interest. The following is here proposed: interest is *a train of events determined by expectation of its outcome*. Or, *a thing is an object of interest when its being expected induces actions looking to its realization or non-realization.* Thus peace is an object of interest when acts believed to be conducive to peace, or preventive of peace, are performed on that account, or when events are selected or rejected because peace is expected of them.

•   •   •   •   •

The word 'interest' is the least misleading name for a certain class of acts or states which have the common characteristic of *being for or against.* The expressions 'motor-affective attitudes' or 'attitudes of favor and disfavor' serve as its best paraphrases. 'Caring' and 'concern' are also convenient synonyms. The absence of interest is indifference, as when one says, 'It makes no difference to me,' 'I do not care,' or 'It is of no concern to me.' Indifference is to be distinguished from negative interest. Thus one speaks of not caring, or of its making no difference 'one way or the other,' implying that interest embraces both ways. It is especially significant to note that the words for which 'interest' is substituted come in pairs of opposites, which are not related simply as grammatical positives and negatives.

'Interest,' then, is to be taken as a class name for such names as 'liking'-'disliking,' 'loving'-'hating,' 'hoping'-'fearing,' 'desiring'-'avoiding,' and countless other kindred names. . . .

•   •   •   •   •

The charge that the definition is *circular* consists in pointing out that when a thing is affirmed to be good because it is an object of positive interest, it is always possible to raise the question of the goodness of the interest. Thus it is generally agreed that the goodness of drugs is questionable despite the intense craving of the addict; and it is usually concluded that the drug is bad because the craving is bad. It would seem to follow that in order that a thing shall be good it must be the object of a good interest, in which case 'good' is defined in terms of good.

But this objection loses its force altogether when it is recognized that an interest may itself possess value, positive or negative, by the application of the same definition as that which is applied to its object. While the craving does invest its object with positive value, the craving may be invested with negative value from the standpoint of other interests; and this second value may be considered as overruling the positive value owing to its taking the higher ground of health or morals. The appetitive goodness of the drug does not include or imply the hygienic or moral goodness of the appetite. There are two goods, one of which is, in some sense yet to be examined, superior to the other. In other words, the definition does not state that a thing is good only when it is the object of a good interest, but when it is the object of any interest, good or bad. When the interest is good, its object is thereby enhanced, but there is no circularity.

But in escaping circularity does one not fall into *contradiction?* Is it not contradictory to affirm that the same object is both good and bad? The charge of contradiction is lightly made and, as a rule, superficially examined. The important thing is to discover just what propositions would, and what propositions would not, be contradictory. It is sometimes supposed that the expression 'one man's meat is another man's poison' involves a contradiction. But there would be a contradiction only provided the same proposition was both affirmed and denied. Thus it would be contradictory to say that one man's meat was not that man's meat, or that another man's poison was not his poison. Meat to one man and poison to another are not contradictories, but are two different and consistent propositions.

By a kind of grammatical license the term 'contradiction' is sometimes applied to interests. Strictly speaking, interests do not contradict, but *conflict*. Only propositions contradict. But interests are sometimes allowed to borrow the contradictoriness or consistency of their objects when these are stated as propositions. Thus the interests in preserving and in destroying the life of the same individual are said to be contradictory, because the will of one can be expressed by the resolve 'he shall live' and the will of the other by the resolve 'he shall not live.' But to speak of interests themselves as contradictory is confusing and misleading. Two contradictories cannot both be true, but two conflicting forces can coexist.

To assert of the same object that it is good and that it is bad *seems* to be contradictory, because the two assertions are elliptical, that is, because of the omission of the axis of reference. It may seem to be contradictory to assert of the same body that it is 'above' and 'below' when one fails to specify *what* it is above and below. Similarly, it seems to be contradictory to say of the same thing that it is both good and bad when one omits to specify the interests from which it derives its goodness and badness. The interests being specified, there is no contradiction whatever in asserting that the same object is practically useful and aesthetically ugly, or that the same act is selfishly beneficent and socially injurious.

But is not contradiction escaped only by falling into *relativism?* Well, if one may be permitted a vulgarism, and so what? The word 'relativism' has a bad sound; even the word 'relativity,' despite its association with the latest physics, conveys a suggestion of philosophical untenability. But suppose that one substitute the more colorless word 'relational' and, instead of rejecting it as a fault, boldly affirm it as a merit; since it provides not only for value, but for ambivalence and multi-valence.

Many of the most familiar characteristics of things are relational. There is no disputing the fact that brother and son are relational characteristics. In other words, when one describes a man as a brother or a son, one states his relation to another human being. For any man, there is someone to whom he is related: 'God gives us relations.' So, according to the theory here proposed, when one describes a thing as good or bad one describes it in terms of its relation, direct or indirect, to a second thing, namely, an interest.

This, be it noted, is not the same as to say that one value is definable only by its relation to another *value,* which may or may not be the case. There is nothing in the relational view which forbids a thing's being conceived as absolutely valuable; that is, valuable regardless of the value of anything else.

There is only one kind of relativism which is epistemologically objectionable, and which is commonly known as 'vicious relativism.' The viciousness lies in its scepticism. It consists in the doctrine that all statements are elliptical unless they are introduced by the words 'it seems to me at this moment.' Were this the case I should not even be stating what I am saying now. I should say, 'it seems to me that it seems to me that it seems to me,' etc. *ad infinitum;* in which case I would never get to *what* seems to me, and I might as well have saved myself the trouble of making any statement at all.

Suffice it to say that the theory of value here proposed is no more relativistic in this vicious sense than any other theory, whe'her of value or of any other matter. The supposition that a relational theory of value is peculiarly vicious in its relativism rests on a confusion. It is mistakenly supposed that because objects derive their value, positive and negative, from interest it is implied that the interest from which they derive value is the interest of the knower or judge. This would mean that if I am to judge that an object possesses positive value to me *I* must like, desire, will, or love it. When, however, value is defined in terms of interest, then *any* interest will satisfy the definition; and if I observe that anyone else likes, desires, loves or wills a thing, then I am bound by the definition to judge it good. The evidence of its goodness or badness is the observable fact of interest, which is just as objective, and just as open to agreement, as any other fact of life or history.

• • • • •

THE MEANING OF MORALITY

Morality is something which goes on in the world; or, at any rate, there is something which goes on in the world to which it is appropriate to give the name of 'morality.' Nothing is more familiar; nothing is more obscure in its meaning. Moral science, moral philosophy, or moral theory consists in the investigation of this going on. . . .

If there is any doubt as to the correctness of this statement that morality is something that goes on in the world, and which appears in all societies and in all periods of history, it rests on an ambiguity. It may, indeed, be doubted whether moral ideals have ever been *realized* in any historic society: misanthropy, pessimism, cynicism, and the doctrine of original sin, have all challenged this claim. But it cannot be denied that morality exists as a *pursuit,* having its own ideal by which a certain kind of human success or failure is judged.

The emphasis on the ideal rather than its realization has led to the wide acceptance of the view that morality and having an ideal mean the same thing. Thomas Mann, in his *Magic Mountain,* had one of his characters, the brilliant and voluble Hans Castorp, propound the paradoxical opinion that morality is to be looked for not 'dans la vertue, c'est-à-dire, dans la raison, la discipline, les bonnes moeurs, l'honnêteté' but rather in their opposites—'le péché, en s'aban-donnant au danger, à ce qui est nuisible, à ce qui nous consume.'[1] A similar paradox is to be found in Nietzsche's view that morality lies 'beyond good and evil.' Later days have seen the rise of cults such as fascism, nazism, and bolshevism, which have derived their morale from their defiance of morality. If such confusions are to be avoided it is necessary to distinguish the qualities of fidelity, discipline, perseverance, and enthusiasm which lend vigor to *any* cult, from the specific content of the moral cult. One must be prepared to reject the edifying associations of the word 'ideal,' and recognize that ideals may be moral, immoral, or unmoral. Similarly, morality does not consist merely in having principles and scruples, but in the nature of that to which obligation is felt and sacrifice is made.

Morality can be initially identified by a set of terms used as predicates in moral judgments: terms such as 'ought,' 'duty,' 'right,' 'good,' 'virtue,' and their opposites. It is essential here, as in general theory of value, to distinguish between the predicates and that *of which* they are predicated. There are two questions: 'What is morally good?' and 'In what does moral goodness consist?' Moralists of the past have usually been concerned with the first of these questions, and have sought a summary answer. Thus the ancients reduced the virtues (the things held virtuous) to justice, temperance, courage, and wisdom; while the Christians reduced the duties (things held dutiful) to faith, hope, and love, and 'the two great commandments,' love of God and love of neighbor. The four ancient virtues were then reduced to justice or wisdom, and the Christian duties to love; or both were reduced to happiness.

When this line of thought arrives at a supreme generalization it tends to pass over into the second of the above inquiries, with which it is easily confused. When it is affirmed that only wisdom or justice is virtuous, or that the only duty is love, or that the only good is happiness, it is natural to equate the meaning of virtue, duty, and good with these unique exemplifications. Despite this natural presumption, however, there are two distant questions, and it would be impossible without redundancy to give the same answer to both; that would be to say 'virtue is virtuous,' 'duty is dutiful,' or 'goodness is good.' The first question is answered when the predicate of virtuousness, dutifulness, or good-ness, whatever it means, is assigned to a certain grammatical subject; the second question is answered when the predicate itself is analyzed or clarified. It is the second question and the discussions to which it gives rise that constitute the primary subject matter of moral theory.

It is an open secret at this stage of the discussion that morality takes conflict of interest as its point of departure and harmony of interests as its ideal goal. Before expounding this ideal it will be profitable to examine certain widespread misconceptions of morality which have lowered its prestige not only among

---

[1] Modern Library Edition, 1927, p. 430. [Castorp's opinion is that morality is to be looked for, not "in virtue, that is to say, in reason, discipline, good manners, honesty," but rather in their opposites—"in sin, recklessness, what is hurtful, what destroys us."—Ed. note.]

moral sceptics and cynics, but, to no inconsiderable extent, in the popular mind. It is one or more of these misconceptions that have given morality its bad name, as when Disraeli is reported to have said of Gladstone that he was 'a good man in the worst sense of the term.' Among these misconceptions there are four which lead all the rest: asceticism, authoritarianism, preceptualism, and utopianism.

These misconceptions of morality arise not from sheer blindness but from an exaggerated emphasis on some one of its aspects. Since these misconceptions are half-truths their correction throws light on the whole truth. Every solid entity can be approached from different sides, and its many-sidedness tends to escape knowledge through abstraction of one of its sides: the elevation is mistaken for the building. So morality, having many sides, yields distortions. But the one-sidedness can be explained by the many-sidedness—the misunderstandings can be understood.

The first and commonest of these misunderstandings is asceticism. Morality does not coincide with the inclination of the moment, or with any particular inclination. Owing to the fact that it requires inclinations to be overruled and disciplined, duty comes to be identified with *dis*inclination—with doing what one does not want to do or leaving undone what one wants to do. When this aspect of morality is erected into its supreme principle, the good life becomes a life 'against'—a substitution of negative for positive interests. Every interest which raises its head is regarded as an enemy, or at least a danger. This is what is known as *asceticism*.

The truth of the matter is precisely the opposite of this—namely, a life 'for,' the substitution of positive for negative interests. It is the original conflict, and not the moralization, of interests that multiplies negations. Morality is an organizing of interests in order that they may flourish. The denials derive their only *moral* justification from the affirmations for which they make room. The purpose of morality is the abundant life.

A second aspect of morality arises from the fact that men learn it from some authority—domestic, civil, social, or religious—which issues commands and enforces them. *Authoritarianism* is the name given to the view which identifies morality with the acceptance and obedience of authority; with uncritical acceptance, and passive obedience. But authority ceases to be an ultimate principle at the moment when attention is directed to the credentials of the authority and the motives by which acceptance and obedience are dictated. It then appears that the authority of the authority requires that it shall be powerful, or wise, or good; while obedience is dictated by fear, or the need of guidance, or by love and gratitude. In other words, authority ceases to be absolute, but rests on ulterior grounds which displace its sheer authoritativeness. And these ulterior grounds involve some idea of good: when governed by fear, the obedient subject himself 'knows what is good for him'; when governed by the need of guidance he assumes that the authority knows what is good for him; when governed by love he attributes goodness to the authority itself. Each good turns out to consist in interest—whether selfish interest, or self-interest, or disinterested benevolence.

Authoritarianism is the aspect which morality presents to dependence and immaturity. It is the morality of childhood—whether of the individual or of the group. The child learns morality at his mother's knee, or upon his father's. This childhood is never entirely outgrown. The parent is replaced by the policeman, ruler, or priest. Men are always in need of authority, and require to be controlled by the power, wisdom, and example of their betters. They have to be threatened, bribed, or seduced if they are to behave as the moral ideal requires. But this fact, important as it is for explaining the causes of human conduct, does not define the ideal itself; nor does it account for that mature phase of the moral life in which having understood the moral ideal men are persuaded to adopt it and to observe its requirements for the sake of its ideal end.

A third misconception of morality may properly be called *preceptualism*—morality as identified with a set of precepts. It is analogous to what in the realm of law is called 'legalism'—which is substituting the letter for the spirit or intent of the law. Moral organization like any organization requires its rules; which must be observed by the members if the purpose of the organization is to be served. Just as the law may be abstracted from its social utility and taken as an absolute, so the moral rules may be similarly abstracted.

The taboos and other customs which are unquestioningly accepted by social groups, are either arbitrary conventions resulting from accident, tradition, imitation, and habit, or can be traced to an apparent utility, formerly discovered by experience and subsequently forgotten. They are either quite indefensible, or defensible only in terms of the rediscovery and confirmation of their utility. When they are merely arbitrary conventions they cease, like fashions, to have any moral force; when their apparent utility is disproved and they are still taken seriously, they are called '*mere* taboos.'

Precepts are usually expressed, like the scriptural commandments, in the imperative voice. They assume the form of injunctions: 'thou shalt,' 'thou shalt not.' But while the grammatical voice is imperative, the real voice has disappeared: the 'stern daughter of the voice of God,' has become an orphan, retaining only the sternness. Commandments are left without a commander. The authority has faded until nothing is left of it but its utterances tinged with an echo of authoritativeness.

When precepts are thus explained they are not explained away. Morality continues to embrace positive and negative generalizations of action, such as justice, veracity, murder, theft, but instead of being taken as the ultimates of morality, shining in their own light, and having their force in themselves, they are seen to be the instruments by which the good life is achieved, as the rules of hygiene minister to personal or social health.

The fourth of the common misconceptions of morality arises from the gap which separates its ideal goal from its achievement. It is of its very nature that there should be such a gap, that the 'reach' *should* 'exceed the grasp,' but it is equally essential that the gap should be recognized and bridged. *Utopianism* stands for a divorce and not a gap. It does not mean that the ideal is too high, for all moral ideals are counsels of perfection, but that no route is plotted from the present actualities to or toward the remote ideal. It is this path, or series of steps, or chain of intermediaries, which makes the ideal, however exalted, a 'practical possibility.'

When the ideal is disconnected from the field of present action and transplanted to another world, it ceases to play its role of ideal-to-be-realized. Men then tend to be divided into two opposing camps, those who ignore the ideal through preoccupation with present action, and those who cease to be active in the practical sphere through dreaming the ideal. The first are the 'opportunists' who act without purpose or direction. Since they have no ideal by which to judge their shortcomings they become the servants of things as they are. The second, the utopians, tend to substitute the image of the ideal for its realization and to become 'visionaries.' Seeking to correct the myopia of the opposing camp they acquire the defect of presbyopia, and become so farsighted that they cannot deal with what lies about them. The moral life requires that men shall be able to shift their focus between the near and the far, and to engage in short-range segments of long-range endeavor.

The correction of these four misconceptions throws light on the true conception of morality. In order to promote an organized harmony of life men must limit and adjust interests without destroying them, submit to authority without slavishness, conform to rules for the sake of the end which these subserve, and seek the ideal goal through a succession of effective acts departing from the here and now.

Morality is man's endeavor to harmonize conflicting interests: to prevent conflict when it threatens, to remove conflict when it occurs, and to advance from the negative harmony of non-conflict to the positive harmony of coöperation. Morality is the solution of the problem created by conflict—conflict among the interests of the same or of different persons. The solution of the personal problem lies in the substitution for a condition of warring and mutually destructive impulses—a condition in which each impulse, being assigned a limited place, may be innocent and contributory. For the weakness of inner discord it substitutes the strength of a unified life in which the several interests of an individual make common cause together. The same description applies to the morality of a social group, all along the line from the domestic family to the family of nations.

Such a moralization of life takes place, insofar as it does take place, through organization—personal and social. This crucial idea of organization must not be conceived loosely, or identified with organism. In organism, as in a work of art, the part serves the whole; in moral organization the whole serves the parts, or the whole only for the sake of the parts. The parts are interests, and they are organized in order that they, the constituent interests themselves, may be saved and fulfilled.

When interests are thus organized there emerges an interest of the totality, or moral interest, whose superiority lies in its being greater than any of its parts —greater by the principle of inclusiveness. It is authorized to speak for all of the component interests when its voice is their joint voice. The height of any claim in the moral scale is proportional to the breadth of its representation. What suits all of a person's interests is exalted above what merely suits a fraction; what suits everybody is exalted above what merely suits somebody.

•   •   •   •   •

Morality conceived as the harmonization of interests for the sake of the interests harmonized can be described as a cult of freedom. It does not force interests into a procrustean bed, but gives interests space and air in which to be more abundantly themselves. Its purpose is to provide room. And ideally the benefits of morality are extended to all interests. Hence moral progress takes the double form, of liberalizing the existing organization, and of extending it to interests hitherto excluded. Both of these principles have important applications to the 'dynamics' of morality, or to the moral force in human history. The extension of moral organization is made possible by increase of contact and interaction, which, however, then multiplies the possibilities of conflict. Hence the peculiar destiny of man, whose ascent is rendered possible by the same conditions which make possible his fall. There can be no development of a unified personality or society without the risk of inner tensions; no neighborhood, nation, or society of all mankind, without the risk of war.

Morality as progressive achievement requires the integration of interests. They cannot be simply added together. If they are to compose a harmonious will that represents them all, they must be brought into line. At the same time, if such a will is truly to embrace them, which is the ground of its higher claim, they must themselves accept the realignment. Morality is an integration of interests, in which they are rendered harmonious without losing their identity. The procedure by which this is effected is the method of *reflective agreement*, appearing in the personal will, and in the social will.

Interests are integrated by reflection. In the creation of the personal will there occurs a thinking over, in which the several interests of the same person are reviewed, and invited to present their claims. Reflection overcomes the effects of forgetfulness and disassociation. It corrects the perspectives of time and immediacy, anticipating the interests of tomorrow, and giving consideration to the interests which at the moment are cold or remote. It brings to light the causal relations between one interest and another. From reflection there emerge decisions which fulfill, in some measure, the purpose of harmony: plans, schedules, quotas, substitutions, and other arrangements by which the several interests avoid collision and achieve mutual reinforcement.

The personal will which emerges from reflection is not, as has sometimes been held, merely the strongest among existing interests, prevailing after a struggle of opposing forces. It is not a mere survivor, other contestants having been eliminated. It does not intervene on one side or the other, but takes a line down the middle, analogous to the resultant or vector in a field of forces. It makes its own choices, and sets its own precedents. Its accumulated decisions, having become permanent dispositions, form a character, or unwritten personal constitution.

The achievement of such a personal will cannot be indefinitely postponed. The exigencies of life are imperative, and have to be met with whatever personal will can be achieved. There is always a dateline for action. Any given personal will is thus inevitably premature, provisional, and subject to improvement. But insofar as it is enlightened and circumspect this personal will is considered as finally justified, except insofar as it neglects the similar personal wills of others. Within the domain of its included interests it is a moral ultimate. The several interests which it embraces have no moral cause for complaint insofar as they have been given the opportunity of contributing to the purpose to which they are subordinate.

The relation of the personal will to the person's several interests is primarily one of government, overruling, or dominance. It serves as a check or censor called into play when any of the particular interests tends to exceed bounds. Like a sentinel it challenges each passing interest and requires it to show its credentials.

The similarity between the personal and social forms of the moral will must not be allowed to obscure their profound difference. It is true that as the personal will emerges from reflection so the social will emerges from communication and discussion. In both cases the emergent will represents a totality of interests, and achieves by organization a substitution of harmony for conflict. The difference lies in the fact that whereas the personal will is composed of sub-personal interests, the social will is composed of persons.

But while the social moral will is a will of persons, society is not a person. Excluding fictitious persons, corporate persons, legal persons, and every metaphorical or figurative use of the term, the only real person is that being which is capable of reflecting, choosing, relating means to ends, making decisions, and subordinating particular interests to an overruling purpose. It follows that there can be no moral will on the social level except as composed of several personal wills which are peculiarly modified and interrelated.

The ramifications of this fact pervade the whole domain of morality and moral institutions. It is echoed in all of those doctrines which exalt the person as an end in himself. It gives meaning to fraternity as the acknowledgment of person by fellow-persons. It gives to the individual man that 'dignity' of which we hear so much. It provides for that unique role of the person as thinker, judge, and chooser, which lies at the basis of all representative institutions, and determines the moral priority of individuals to society.

The creation of a social moral will out of personal wills depends on benevolence, that is, one person's positive interest in another person's interest. To be benevolent here means not that I treat you well so far as it happens to suit my existing interests to do so; my concern for your interests is an independent interest. Taking your desires and aversions, your hopes and fears, your pleasures and pains, in short, the interests by which you are actually moved, I act as though these interests were my own. Though I cannot, strictly speaking, *feel* your interests, I can acknowledge them, wish them well, and allow for them in addition to the interests which are already embraced within me. When you are at the same time benevolently disposed to my interests, we then have the same problem of reconciling the same interests, except that my original interests form the content of your benevolence and your original interests the content of mine.

In this pooling of interests I am ordinarily concerned that your benevolence shall actually embrace my original interests; and you are similarly concerned to accent yours. Each of us assumes that the other can safely be trusted to look out for his own. Assuming that each will be biased in favor of his own interests, the bias of each will tend to correct the bias of the other. Each will be the special pleader of his own interests, and his insistence on them will reinforce the other's weaker benevolence.

There will be a further difference. Your interests are best and most immediately served by you, and mine by me. I can for the most part serve you best by letting you serve yourself. The greater part of my benevolence, therefore, will take a permissive form. I will sometimes help you, but more often will abstain from hurting you; or will so follow my own inclinations as to make it possible for you also to follow yours; or accept your inclinations as setting a limit to mine.

No will is here introduced over and above the wills of the two persons, but since the two wills now represent the same interests, they will have achieved a community of end and a coöperative relation of means. In each person the new socialized purpose will have become dominant over his original interests. Neither will have become the mere means to the other since the common end is now each person's governing end. . . .

•   •   •   •   •

JOHN HARTLAND-SWANN
The Moral and the Non-Moral

. . . I want to draw attention to something which most of us realize, if somewhat vaguely, but the significance of which is often misunderstood. It is this. (i) What may be regarded as an example of moral (morally good) behaviour by community A, may be regarded as an example of immoral (morally bad) behaviour by community B. (ii) What may be a moral issue for community A, may be a non-moral issue for community B. (iii) What may be regarded

From John Hartland-Swann, *An Analysis of Morals* (1960). Reprinted by permission of George Allen and Unwin Ltd. (London).

as a morally good practice by community A at time t_1, may be regarded as a morally bad practice at time t_2 (say 100 years later) by that same community. (iv) What may be regarded as a non-moral issue by community A at time t_1, may be regarded as a moral issue by that same community (or their descendants) at time t_2.

• • • • •

To start the process of clarification, I propose to take four examples to illustrate the sociological points made above.

i. 'Ought I to Marry One Wife or Two Wives?'

Is this a moral or a non-moral issue? All orthodox Christians, and no doubt many non-Christians as well, would regard this as a distinctively moral issue, quite apart from legal sanctions against polygamy; and someone who, unbeknown to the law officers of the Crown, managed to possess two wives at the same time would tend to be condemned on moral grounds. (It is interesting to note, however, that opinion would be very divided as regards condemning a man who kept both a wife and a *mistress*—the example of Charles II is not perhaps to be discounted altogether here—and in countries like France moral disapproval would disappear to vanishing point.) For an orthodox Moslem, on the other hand, the original question would have no moral flavour whatever; for him, it would be a purely prudential issue, to be settled on grounds of expediency and most probably financial expediency.

Now issues of this kind have tended to worry . . . moral philosophers and particularly those who have been Christians with all the fixed views on this question which are part and parcel of the Christian way of life. Some writers on ethics—the more broadminded—have resorted, when faced with this issue, to something like this. In order not to condemn polygamy, which is so widely practised throughout the world, and not only by Moslems, they have said: 'Everyone agrees (i.e. *ought* to agree) that one ought not to be able to possess any woman or women one chooses; hence the Moslem is still acting morally, when he takes two or more wives, since he recognizes the 'sacred institution of marriage'; or perhaps: 'Granted it is our duty to promote the greatest happiness of the greatest number, it so happens that this can best be promoted in one community by a man having several wives and in another community by a man restricting himself to one.' Therefore, it might be urged, although the problem of marrying one or four wives appears to a Moslem to be a non-moral issue, and to a Christian a moral issue, a *moral* principle is involved in both cases, and it may be assumed that the discerning Moslem, like the discerning Christian, would fully subscribe to such a principle. Or, to put it slightly differently, both Moslem and Christian accept a 'higher' moral principle—'sacredness of marriage' principle or 'greatest-happiness' principle—under which both practices, monogamy and polygamy, can be legitimately and satisfactorily subsumed. There is something to be said for this argument, although for the moment it gets us nowhere. For to the Christian, however tolerant he may be towards mistress-keeping (and here the Anglo-Saxons are less flexible than the Latins), marrying more than one wife is *in itself* immoral; whereas to the Moslem it is not a moral issue at all—or, if you prefer, it is perfectly moral to do this.

It is worth noting that social anthropologists have been of great service to moral philosophers on points of this kind, although these services have rarely been appreciated by moral philosophers. But, whether appreciated or not, what the social anthropologists have shown, to some extent indirectly, is that you cannot evaluate or appraise any given practice or institution or behaviour-pattern, in any given community, *out of relation* to the multitude of other practices, institutions and behaviour-patterns which are common to that community. This means that if you wish to praise or censure, as morally desirable or undesirable, a particular practice or institution, you have got to take into account the whole way of life of the community concerned. This does not imply that you cannot praise or blame, from a moral point of view, a particular practice or institution; but it does imply that you have first to consider the whole way of life with which this practice or institution is supposedly integrated, and then decide whether it appears to further the purposes or ideals which this way of life presupposes. If it does further them, or accord with them, it is still open to you to criticize at the highest possible level—i.e. by calling in question the moral desirability of the way of life itself, presuming you can grasp it sufficiently well for this purpose. But all such criticism, in the end, will reduce to the fact that you do not subscribe, and do not want others to subscribe, to the principles or ends lying behind or comprising the way of life you are criticizing—to this and no more. . . .

ii. 'Ought I to Kill this Hornet?'
Is this a moral or a non-moral problem? To most if not all Western peoples this would be a purely prudential issue—and one to be solved without hesitation ('Yes: kill it if you can'). To a Jainist however—and there are millions of this sect in India and elsewhere—it would certainly be an immoral act to kill a hornet if this could possibly be avoided. Admittedly, the injunction against destroying life in any form is primarily accepted on religious grounds; but the contravention of a religious injunction, not only for Jainists but for most Christians too, is equally a moral misdemeanour. So the argument that a Christian does not accept Jainist religious injunctions gets us nowhere; for the Christian has his list of religious injunctions too, even if these usually differ from the Jainist's. The fact that it must be very difficult for an orthodox Jainist to carry out this particular injunction to the letter—since bacteria are killed when he boils his water—is nothing to the point; this is merely a practical difficulty which in no way diminishes the moral force of his non-killing rule. For him to kill a hornet is an immoral act, even if his considering it to be so stems from his religious beliefs. No piece of philosophical sophistication therefore—e.g. 'Jainism is mere superstition' or 'We ought to keep religion and morals separate'—can get around this fact. One may well hold the view—many do—that all or at least most of the world religions inculcate morally disastrous ideas—they certainly enjoin a lot of

conduct that increases human' misery; but this does not allow us to claim that certain types of behaviour are not regarded as immoral when we know very well that, by some at least, they are so regarded. We can say, if we like, that they *ought not* to be regarded as immoral; but to do that is to *prescribe* . . . a different way of life for another community.

iii. 'Is Incest a Moral Issue?'

The problem here is whether the practice of incest, which initially affects only two people although its possible consequences may affect many more, should be condoned as being morally neutral or deplored as being morally reprehensible. Generally, this practice has been regarded, for many years now, as very definitely a moral issue quite apart from the legal sanctions imposed on those caught indulging in it; and any such indulgence has aroused the strongest condemnation. That was why Shelley, who appeared as a dangerous iconoclast on this issue, could not find a theatre manager willing to stage his *Cenci*. To the ancient Egyptians, however, incest does not appear to have presented itself as a moral issue at all; and its practice was, as students of ancient history are well aware, more or less *de rigueur*[1] for any Pharaoh who happened to have a sister.

This is an interesting example since it concerns a practice about which many people today—including no doubt the lineal descendants of the ancient Egyptians, if there are any—feel strongly from a specifically moral point of view.[2] Moreover, this is just the sort of issue on which a moral philosopher is supposed to take a stand and make clear, once for all, whether he is merely a purely 'relativist' in morals or whether he can produce some 'objective' standard of conduct which will, automatically and irrevocably, stamp incest as morally damnable. There is however a deplorable confusion inherent in this implicit demand on the moral philosopher. As a man, or as a rational human being if you prefer, he will certainly be able to take a stand—which probably means that he will have subscribed to certain principles with which the practice of incest is either consistent or inconsistent. If there are moral principles—and we have not yet defined 'moral'—and incest is inconsistent with them, then, for him at least, incest will be morally reprehensible. But although he will naturally want others to share his views, he will not, *as* a moral philosopher, be able to offer the assurance that some people seek; he will not, that is, be able to declare, if he is honest, that moral philosophy 'says' you must not commit incest. Moral philosophy can say no such thing; for to put the matter shortly, moral philosophy analyzes but does not 'hand out' *oughts* and *ought-nots*.

iv. 'Is it Morally Wrong, or Morally Neutral, to Keep Slaves Provided You Treat Them Kindly?'

Now slavery is a complicated issue—it always has been—and there are gradations of slavery ranging from the position where the slave is the absolute property of

---

[1] [i.e., the proper thing to do.—Ed. note.]
[2] From a modern biological point of view the dangers of any kind of inbreeding—provided it is not indulged in too persistently—are held to be largely illusory.

his master, who may do what he likes with the slave, to the position where the possession of slaves carries with it very definite responsibilities and the master's 'rights' are closely regulated by law (as was the case in China until very recent times). Again, we all know how emotionally confused an argument about slavery can become when a Labour agitator starts talking about 'economic' slavery. In order to keep the issue under control therefore, the meaning of the word 'slave' in my query may be taken as 'a person whose liberty and whole way of life is subject to the unfettered control of his or her master'. It is perhaps worth noting, in passing, Aristotle's much discussed view about the status of slaves. For him (*Politics*, I, 2, 13–15, 1255 a) 'It is manifest . . . that there are cases of people of whom some are freemen and the others slaves by nature, and for these slavery is an institution both expedient and just'. Let us not argue with Aristotle, who in this matter was but the child of his age; let us rather take into consideration two much later conflicts of opinion on this point. First, there is the difference in opinion between, as we might elliptically put it, pre-Wilberforce and post-Wilberforce Britain. Prior to Wilberforce, or rather prior to the general acceptance of Wilberforce's views, it was regarded as morally permissible to keep slaves provided their skins were black; but it was immoral to make slaves of white men. Now however, in post-Wilberforce Britain, it is almost universally agreed that it is definitely immoral to keep slaves at all, even if you treat them kindly as many of the planters in the southern States of America did. Thus, previously slave-keeping aroused, among most people in Britain, no moral qualms provided the skins of the slaves were not white; whereas now, it is generally regarded as immoral to enslave anybody. If we switch our attention to Saudi Arabia, however, we find that, whether or not slaves are objects to be treated kindly, the bulk of the nation, or certainly the ruling classes, regard slave-keeping as perfectly moral—or maybe they regard it as a non-moral prudential issue, like the question of marrying one, two or more wives up to the Koranic limit. Yet the same Saudi Arabians might well regard the slave-labour camps of the Soviets as highly immoral institutions—as we do in the West. For it might be their opinion that an individual buying and possessing slaves is one thing; and that an impersonal State compelling men and women to be State-slaves is another.

To sum up briefly. The four examples cited and discussed have served to illustrate the sociological facts stated formally in the first paragraph of this section. Many issues are regarded as either morally significant or morally neutral, and many types of behaviour are regarded as either moral or immoral, according to local cultural conventions; and moral verdicts therefore differ in accordance with differing ways of life. There seem to be certain broad areas of agreement regarding what is a moral and what is a non-moral issue, and what is a moral and what is an immoral act; but even here such views are contingent: they could have been otherwise. It is quite possible to envisage a community where thieving had no moral stigma attached to it—only being caught doing it. Ancient Sparta came very near to this.

We are now in a position to come to grips with our problem. I shall start by making some dogmatic claims, which I shall then proceed to explain and justify.

i. Given one set of conditions, a sentence embodying either prescriptive or evaluative concepts may be moral, and given another set of conditions the *same* sentence may be non-moral. This applies whether the sentence is a question, or a judgment or expresses a principle.

ii. We cannot explain the concept of morality without (a) taking a brief glance at the etymology of the terms 'moral' and 'ethical' and (b) introducing the notion of 'social importance'.

iii. Moral rules (positive and negative prescriptions) possess a special authority which non-moral rules do not.

What I have claimed under (i) follows partly from what has been demonstrated earlier in the chapter and will be reinforced by what I have to say in connection with (ii). I shall therefore proceed to discuss my second claim.

•   •   •   •   •

First of all, it is clear enough that the terms 'moral' and 'ethical' respectively derive from Latin and Greek words meaning 'pertaining to *custom* or *customs*'. Anyone can reassure himself on this point by consulting a Latin dictionary and a Greek lexicon, or, if neither of these is handy, the Shorter Oxford English Dictionary. It remains true however that not all, and not even perhaps the majority of customs in any given community are regarded as moral, and their neglect or rejection immoral. It is customary, in most Western countries, to eat solid food with a knife and fork; but we do not call someone who fails to do this, preferring to use his fingers, immoral—although we might well condemn him in some milder way. If on the other hand we moved among the Indian community of Singapore, we should find that it is customary among many educated Indians to eat their food with their fingers; but they would certainly not condemn a fellow-Indian as immoral for choosing to eat with a knife and fork. Again, we sometimes find ourselves condemning as immoral certain customs, either among our own community or (as is more frequently the case) among foreign communities, which are regarded as either perfectly moral or perhaps morally neutral by those who practise them. Finally, we often become seriously perplexed when, with the utmost tolerance and impartiality, we try to decide which of the customs of some 'primitive' or non-literate people are to be classed as forming part of their moral code and which are to fall into some other classification. Professor John Ladd, in his most illuminating investigation and analysis of the ethics of the Navaho Indians, writes as follows:

A social interdiction holds up the consequence of being "shamed before others" if one is caught violating it. In this it resembles a "rule of etiquette" in our own culture, since the main reason for not putting food into one's mouth with a knife in our society is that it would bring shame to us and our family. This presents us with a dilemma: are we to regard social interdictions merely as rules of etiquette? or are they rules of morality? That this issue has not been faced squarely is to be seen by the rather arbitrary way in which most of these prescriptions are reported in the literature on the Navahos—sometimes one prescription is referred to as a rule of etiquette and another prescription which has the same basis is classed as a moral rule. (*The Structure of a Moral Code*, p. 248.)

It is clear, then, that it would be foolish to try to equate the customary with the moral. A simple piece of logical technique will serve to reinforce this point. It always makes sense to utter queries or comments like the following: 'I know it's the custom here, but is it moral?', or 'I gather that headhunting is an ingrained custom with this tribe, but don't you think it's a thoroughly beastly and immoral custom?' or 'I wonder if fornication is really immoral?—it's customary in some communities and condemned in others.' In short, despite the etymological origin of 'moral', it clearly does not mean, today at least, the same as 'customary' or 'consonant with custom'. What then is the significance of the apparent detachment of the 'moral' from the 'customary'?

Let us notice for a start that it is not so detached as we might at first think; simply because those actions or kinds of behaviour which are commonly regarded as moral, in any particular community, are not the unusual or the abnormal—on the contrary, they are the customary actions or kinds of behaviour, or, more precisely, those which have *become* customary. It is the general custom, in most communities, to tell the truth and refrain from lying, to keep and not break promises, to show kindness and not cruelty to other human beings, to protect the weak and aged, to show respect to parents and so on.

It is also however the custom in every community to do a lot of things—to eat food in certain ways, wear certain kinds of clothes, play certain kinds of games—none of which would be regarded as specifically moral by any member of the community concerned. What then is it that differentiates a moral from a morally neutral custom? To answer this will be to solve our problem. But the answer is a little complicated and has become overlaid with sophistication by some moral philosophers.

Let us return to actions or to behaviour in general—for moral judgments, whether prescriptive or simply evaluative, are either designed to guide or influence, or else to appraise, actual or potential behaviour, potential behaviour being taken to include such dispositions as motives and intentions. Now in primitive societies certain customs, and certain patterns of behaviour, came to be regarded as *more important* than others—more important because they directly affected the lives and happiness of all members of the tribe, or because they indirectly affected the tribe's security, food supply and general amenities. The observance of these customs, or the maintenance of these behaviour patterns, was therefore hedged about with taboos; and sanctions were imposed, of greater or lesser severity, for the neglect or violation of these taboos.

The appeal to the practice of 'taboo-ing' need not alarm the reader, even if it does savour of using the 'beastly habits of the heathen' to interpret civilized Western morality. 'Taboo' is a word of Polynesian origin and is, admittedly, merely an importation into English for which social anthropologists are mainly responsible. But it is nevertheless a useful word. For basically a 'taboo' is a prohibition of some kind, or, more technically, a negative prescription. And all communities, by whatever name they call them, do make use of prescriptions, positive of course as well as negative, in order to *regulate* their social life and thus ensure the maintenance of customs regarded as socially important. In the case of *very* important customs—i.e. customs considered absolutely vital to the continued existence and security of the community—explicit legal sanctions are imposed to cover cases of violation.

Of course, the actual importance attached to the violation of different customs has varied enormously, not only between different primitive communities, but equally between primitive and modern communities. Take for instance the custom of not killing a fellow human being in private revenge, the violation of which is termed homicide or murder. Homicide, except in self-defence, is generally visited, in any modern community, with the maximum penalty—either the death sentence or life imprisonment; but among primitive peoples, killing could frequently be atoned for by merely paying compensation to the dead man's relatives. But other 'crimes', which might have a lesser importance for us today or none at all—such as the violation of some ritualistic taboo which we regard as 'pure superstition'—may in the past have entailed the death penalty. There is an interesting modern parallel here in the case of Soviet Russia. The most heinous crime there is certainly not homicide if this means killing the successful peasant next door; it is 'anti-State' political activity, as defined by the clique in power—and it is this which incurs the most drastic penalties that can be imposed, not only against the offender but, likely as not, against his family as well.

But to return to our main theme. In cases where the infringed customs are considered very important, then the sanctions take the form of actual physical punishment—a fine, imprisonment or even the death penalty. Such infringements are covered by what we call the legal code of the community concerned. In other cases, where the custom infringed, though important, is considered less socially significant, the sanctions consist of overt blame or silent disapproval— which blame or disapproval is usually present, possibly in a more stringent form, in the case of infringements of customs whose violation brings the offender within the scope of legal sanctions.[3] In yet other cases, where the customs violated are deemed to have far less, if any, social significance, disapproval will be of a far milder nature. It is these three types of cases which crystallize out into legal offences, moral misdemeanours and lapses of etiquette. The trouble is however that what may be legally penalized in one community may only be morally condemned in another, and just mildly censured in yet another—according to the time and the place and the nature of the community or civilization concerned. Thus, to quote another example, sleeping with another man's wife was visited with imprisonment in republican Rome but is not so visited in Rome

---

[3] It is by no means the case, however, that we always blame people (i.e. morally condemn them) for breaking laws. If we think a certain law punishes a man merely for his ignorance of some regulation, regarded as trivial, we probably would not blame the man who is legally punished. And we sometimes even give our moral approval to people who break certain laws which we regard as morally misguided.

or the United States today, although it is so visited under United States *military* law.

Reflection on this point enables us to grasp two important facts, one obvious and the other not so obvious. First, it drives home the relativity of what is lawful and what unlawful and makes us healthily suspicious of anyone who declares that this or that is unlawful *in itself*. Secondly, it clears up a matter which has often troubled moral philosophers: the difference between mere disapproval and so-called moral disapproval. The latter is disapproval of something regarded as important in a more *socially* significant way than what is merely disapproved. If a man disapproves of a certain style of feminine attire, he would presumably not wish his approval to be regarded as moral disapproval; but if he disapproved of couples mating before marriage, the chances are that his disapproval *would* rank as moral disapproval. We must notice however that what one person may regard with mere disapproval, another may regard with moral disapproval—i.e. for him it *is* a socially significant matter and not just a matter of taste or preference. Again, what may arouse moral approval or disapproval at one time may easily, a few years later, arouse a different kind of approval or disapproval. Some of the plays of both Ibsen and Shaw aroused intense moral disapproval when they were first produced ('It's clearly reprehensible to write plays around venereal disease or prostitution'); whereas today those same plays (e.g. *Ghosts* and *Mrs. Warren's Profession*) are approved or disapproved, as they should be, on aesthetic grounds alone. The ancient Spartans did not morally disapprove of boys stealing provided they were not caught; the modern Navaho Indians too, while morally disapproving of stealing because it is *bahadzid* (dangerous and wrong), are nevertheless prepared to withhold censure if someone gets away with it; whereas Englishmen and Americans on the whole morally disapprove of stealing whether one gets away with it or not.

Morality then—despite the sophistications often favoured by moral philosophers and which we shall discuss in a moment—is, I suggest, the term or concept which refers to the keeping or violating of customs considered socially important —important in the mutual relations between man and man and between a man and his community. We tend to lose sight of this simply because moral rules (positive and negative prescriptions) appear to have an independent existence and special authority which exempt us from enquiring into their *raison d'être*; but we can easily remind ourselves of the origin of moral rules by referring their content to our current social values. It is true that in any given community, ancient or modern, it is not always easy to determine how much of its morality is freely accepted and how much imposed by some powerful body of elders or by social tradition. But this does not affect the status of the moral. The moral will turn out to be what is regarded, freely or by conditioning, as the socially important as regards conduct and dispositions. If I see a small child drowning in a canal, and I have a new suit on and am due to meet a friend in a few minutes, then, while it is important for me to preserve my suit and keep my appointment, it is much more important for me, if I have a moral sense, to rescue the child and save its life; for I recognize that this is a moral duty, i.e. that it is *socially* important. The fact that I may rescue the child purely out of a feeling of sympathy, and not even consider my moral duty, in no way weakens my analysis; for human sympathy is one of the factors responsible for maintaining that sort of conduct which most moral codes enjoin.

I come now to my third claim—that moral rules possess a special authority which non-moral rules do not.

Now morality expresses itself, so to speak, in rules—consisting of positive and negative prescriptions ('ought'-sentences) or even of straightforward imperatives, like the Ten Commandments. . . .

. . . Morality may also express itself—at a more sophisticated level—by declaring certain goals of conduct to be desirable or valuable in themselves; and this is where its evaluatory side comes in. Morality is thus regulative in principle: it enjoins or forbids, usually through positive or negative prescriptions, conduct which promotes or undermines the social equilibrium of the community; and this social equilibrium, it is believed, is kept in being by the maintenance and perpetuation of certain customary forms of behaviour. When we talk about 'morality' enjoining this or forbidding that, we must not be misled by this phrase; for it is always someone's, or some community's, morality which does the positive and negative prescribing: there is not some mysterious and impersonal 'morality' which hovers over all our heads issuing its particular ukases. Nevertheless, it is true that moral rules do have an impersonal and objective quality to which I shall refer later.

I come now to the question of moral authority. Suppose it was asked: 'Why do people in all or most communities tend, if not always to obey, at least to regard moral rules, or rather what they recognize to be such, as in some sense compulsive or endowed with a special authority?'

•   •   •   •   •

Let us follow Professor Ladd for a start:

. . . the two distinctive elements of this special moral authority are its presumed superiority and legitimacy. This means that the moral obligatoriness of an act is thought to be a consideration which is more overwhelming and demanding upon us than, say, the intense distaste we may have for doing it. Moral considerations are in this sense superior to non-moral ones. Moreover, the demands for superiority must be thought to be legitimate, for many sorts of actions make questionable demands of one sort or another upon us. In other words, these demands must be regarded as valid and binding. The conception of "legitimacy" introduces the elements of impersonality and objectivity . . .[4]

The criterion, then, which according to Professor Ladd enables us to distinguish a moral rule from, say, a rule of etiquette, is the *believed* superiority and legitimacy of the moral rule. In Professor Ladd's view, one of the advan-

[4] *Op. cit.*, p. 84. The concepts of 'superiority' and 'legitimacy' are more fully explained by Professor Ladd in later sections of his chapter entitled 'Moral Prescriptions'.

tages of this criterion, over the many other criteria that have been proposed by anthropologists, sociologists and philosophers, is that it is not ethnocentric, i.e., it applies to *all* communities, literate or nonliterate, who appear to have a moral code. I find this criterion congenial; and it ties up with what I have said earlier about morality referring to customs considered socially important; for it is the keeping and not violating of these customs which will appear to the majority as the superior obligation (superior to the obligation to stand up when ladies come into the room), and as the legitimate obligation (the one which cannot be lightly ignored on account of personal inclinations to avoid the task it may impose).

This criterion, however, as Professor Ladd well realizes, does not take us the whole way. For although these two properties of superiority and legitimacy may provide us with 'an analysis of the distinctively moral character of moral obligation',[5] nevertheless we must now determine what exactly is the obligatory character of the moral rules or prescriptions which form part of any moral code; we must, that is, consider the character of moral *obligation*.

. . . For our present purpose . . . it will suffice to take one type of prescription only, which can be exemplified in the sentence 'One ought always (or generally) to tell the truth'. We find this prescription embedded in most moral codes since truth-telling is generally regarded as a socially important custom. Now if, in answer to some query about conduct, I say 'One ought always to tell the truth', then, if I am talking sincerely, I imply that I have accepted (that I *subscribe to*) the *general* and *impersonal* principle which enjoins truth-telling always. And it is this subscription on my part which makes the principle authoritative for me and (in my view) for everyone else. There is no mysterious commander: I create the obligation for myself and others, so to speak, simply by subscribing to the principle which is itself impersonal. The principle or prescription gained its initial momentum, and thus became part of the moral code of the community, because it was regarded as socially important that the truth should be told; and it thus became both a superior and a legitimate prescription, as Professor Ladd would put it. If however I doubted its social value, I might well refuse to subscribe to it; and it would then have no 'special authority' for me. In fact, I do doubt its social value if the principle is qualified by 'always', although I subscribe to it if 'always' is replaced by 'generally'.

We can now see that there are three equally significant facets to any 'explanation' of morality. First, the notion of morality developed from the desire to maintain and safeguard socially important customs; secondly, the regulative prescriptions, designed to restrain people from violating these socially important customs, have a compulsive power because believed to possess a special authority; and thirdly, the prescriptions possessing this special authority, i.e. moral prescriptions, when subscribed to by an individual *oblige* him so to order his conduct as to do what they enjoin and refrain from doing what they prohibit.

[5] *Ibid.*

This follows from their logical structure; and although one can subscribe to a particular prescription and then do the reverse of what it prescribes, by so doing one is acting inconsistently.

Several vistas are now opened up. We see at once how it *comes about* that one type of conduct is called moral by one community, since its performance is regarded as socially important and its neglect or violation socially disastrous; and how it is that the same type of conduct is not called either moral or immoral by another community, since neither its performance nor its neglect are regarded as socially important. Thus we see why a practice such as incest was not deemed immoral by the ancient Egyptians; for, wisely or unwisely, they did not regard its avoidance as important from a social point of view. Again, we can now see—although there is a lot more to be said about this later—how the specifically 'immoral' can shade off into the 'naughty' or the 'unsportsmanlike', according to the degree of social importance attached to the type of conduct in question by the particular individual concerned. Less than justice has been done to the richness of our moral vocabulary by most writers on ethics.

There is another point we must now consider. Frequently enough individuals hold opinions which differ, sometimes radically, from those held by other individuals, or by the community at large, as to whether a certain act or class of actions is moral, immoral or morally neutral. This might lead us to infer that when I myself for instance differ in this way from an acquaintance, or from my community, by claiming a certain act to be morally neutral which my acquaintance or the community claims to be immoral—that in such a case I am merely claiming, in effect, that the doing of such an act is simply not a matter of social importance from *my* point of view. I am claiming this of course; but my use of the phrase '*morally* neutral' implies a good deal more. For moral claims are expressed by means of 'ought'-sentences—they take the form of prescriptions. And if I subscribe to a prescription—as I do if I utter it sincerely—then I *logically* imply that it holds good for everyone else as well as myself—or at least for everyone in my particular community.

Hence, if I say 'This act (specifying it) ought not to be regarded as either moral or immoral', I am in effect saying that it ought to be regarded as not socially important by *everyone*, including of course myself. Arguments about the immorality versus the moral harmlessness of homosexuality usefully illustrate this point.

Similarly, if I hold some practice to be immoral, which the community or my verbal opponent regards as morally neutral—spending one's whole life just piling up money, for example—then, by claiming such a practice to be immoral, I am not only condemning it myself—I am implying that, owing to its social importance (more accurately, the social importance of its avoidance), it ought to be condemned by everyone. In other words, however individualistic or even eccentric my views on morality may appear, by *using* the words 'moral' or 'immoral', or the expression 'morally neutral', I imply that the action, or principle of conduct, to which one or the other of these epithets is applied, is in fact and objectively either socially important or not socially important. Once again, a reference to the Latin progenitor of the English word 'moral' is useful; for 'custom', except in the special usage such as 'It is my custom to smoke a cigar before breakfast', is a word that applies to what a particular society or community does.

Put at its simplest, we may say that when I argue with someone, or argue implicitly with the norms of my community, on what I call moral issues, I am in effect arguing about issues which are either (a) generally regarded as socially important or (b) ought, in my opinion, to be regarded as socially important. Thus, if I say 'It's really *immoral* to paint in that way', and I am not joking or being precious, then I imply that such a type of painting is to be condemned, not on account of its failing to appeal to my aesthetic taste, but because in my view it is socially important for it not to be produced. Similarly, if I were to argue that wife-beating is not a moral issue at all, then I would be arguing to the effect that it is *not* a socially important matter whether or not one beats one's wife.[6] One would not get very far with this view in either Britain or the United States today, but in Czarist Russia it would probably have been quite happily accepted, from highest to lowest, from the Czarina down to the female serf.

If the foregoing analysis is sound, then we have our answer to the basic question posed at the outset of the chapter—in that we can now see what it is that differentiates the moral from the non-moral whether problems or issues, judgments or principles or ends are at stake. And we can test our theory without much difficulty.

Suppose someone regards truth-telling and promise-keeping as moral issues; and suppose he asks himself why he and the community at large regard truth-telling and promise-keeping as moral issues, and choosing a motor car and playing cricket as non-moral issues. Provided he does not make an appeal to a religious authority of some sort, what answer can he give himself, if he thinks it out, other than to admit that truth-telling and promise-keeping derive their moral status from their preponderant social importance? Notice carefully that the question 'Is truth-telling a moral issue?' is quite different from the question 'Why should I tell the truth?' The answer to the second question depends on whether or not I have subscribed to the general moral prescription 'One ought always (or generally) to tell the truth'—and if I have subscribed to that principle, then I am *logically* bound to tell the truth unless the situation is such as to enable me to invoke another general principle which I deem to absolve me from truth-telling in this particular case. Nevertheless, when a person subscribes to such principles as 'The truth ought generally to be told', or 'Promises made ought generally to be kept', he is in effect subscribing to such principles just

---

[6] Professor L. J. Russell has sent me an interesting comment on this point. 'I'm not sure that wife-beating wouldn't have been regarded as a husband's moral duty, in places where it was practised. For example, in the sixteenth century in Elizabethan England, it was a husband's duty to chastise his wife if she didn't behave: he was expected to train her, and beating was regarded as an important means of doing this. (Generally the girl married young, while the man was very much older.)'

because—even if he has forgotten this or never even knew about it—such principles have acquired or been endowed with a special authority on account of their being about issues of great social importance.

At the same time—as earlier arguments have been designed to show—there is nothing which is 'intrinsically' or 'unconditionally' or 'absolutely' moral —or immoral; what is moral, or immoral, depends on the degree of social importance attached to its performance, or avoidance, by some particular community at some particular time and in some particular place. Or, where there is a divergence between individual and community moral appraisals, what is moral or immoral depends, so far as the individual is concerned, on what *he* regards as socially important and thus considers ought to be regarded as socially important by the community, or perhaps by humanity as a whole. That there is a large measure of agreement concerning what is to be regarded as socially important (to do or not to do) in the sphere of human conduct is something which is obvious. It is also something for which we may be thankful; for the general stability of social life depends on a widespread agreement—which is never however a universal agreement—that certain principles are to be called moral or immoral principles, and certain types of behaviour moral or immoral behaviour. But this same thesis explains—and it would be totally inadequate if it failed to do this—how it comes about that both communities and individuals differ, not only about what is morally justifiable or nonjustifiable, but about what is to be regarded as a moral issue at all.

There is a further point we must now consider briefly, since failure to take it into account has been responsible for much muddled thinking in ethics. We might call this the 'stipulative versus explanatory' approach to the problem of the moral and the non-moral. So far, I have been trying to determine what it is that makes some issue a specifically moral issue or some rule a specifically moral rule from the point of view of most communities. This may be termed the explanatory approach. But many moral philosophers are enamoured of what I call the stipulative approach, even if they would be chary of admitting this. The specific character of this approach is stipulation that a rule *must* possess such and such a property before, in their view, it may rank as a moral rule— and of course that such and such things *are* valuable in themselves and so forth.

Now let it be freely admitted for a start that a moral philosopher has as much right as, though no more right than, anyone else to lay down what *ought to be* regarded as a moral rule or a moral judgment. For just as a theologian can say that only rules issued by God are to count as moral (those originated by man being non-moral), so a Benthamite can declare that only those rules are moral which serve to promote the greatest happiness of the greatest number. Anyone, let me repeat, can do this sort of thing. But of philosophers at least we require reasons for stipulations of this kind. And although a Benthamite can give some superficially plausible reasons for asking us to accept his particular criterion, what he cannot do is to demonstrate that such a criterion is irrefutably valid (i.e. must be accepted by all intelligent and rational beings). If one is determined to lay down some criterion, it would perhaps be better to approach the matter in the following manner[7]:

It would be no use enquiring what sort of rules could be held to be moral rules, for the only answer would be that any sort at all can, there being no known limit to human stupidity. But it would be quite another matter to ask what sort of reason for assent to a rule would constitute it assent to a moral rule. Provisionally I suggest that we should say that a person assents to a rule as a moral rule only if he assents because he recognizes that the rule at least partly satisfies the following two criteria, which are obvious and familiar. (1) *Equity*. A moral rule cannot favour the interests of any particular people as against any others. (2) *Utility*. A moral rule must be such that its general observance over a period as long as it is possible to calculate will advance the interests of people generally more than it will impede these.

Now it may be the case that what has come to be morally prescribed has been influenced by consideration of the two criteria just quoted—or it may not be the case. (The first criterion is certainly not implicit in the moral rules of many primitive peoples; nor is it implicit in the moral rules of certain modern communities—i.e. the conception of 'equity' does not extend beyond the group.) So that to state that a rule, to rank as a moral rule, *must* satisfy or at least partly satisfy the criteria of equity and utility is to lay down a moral theory of a stipulative kind, even if, as in the present case, the theory is prefaced with the modest 'I suggest that we should say'. There is however no inherent necessity for what is regarded as a moral rule by some particular community to satisfy these particular criteria, even if it cannot be denied that, from the point of view of that mysteriously ubiquitous and convenient person 'the disinterested spectator,' these two criteria may well appear socially valuable.

For another view, we might turn to Professor Toulmin. According to him, 'What makes us call a judgment "ethical" is the fact that it is used to harmonize people's actions.'[8] It is not clear what Toulmin means by the phrase 'What makes us call.' If he means 'What *ought to* make us call', then he is making a stipulation and laying down a moral theory; but if he means 'What makes most people call', then he is offering an explanation. In the latter case, if we take 'harmonize people's actions' in a fully social sense, i.e. in a sense which would exclude merely harmonizing their actions in games or dressing for dinner, then the dictum seems to contain much truth; for no doubt the preservation of social harmony is just what is regarded by any community as of primary importance.

On the other hand, we do not get very far with the theory, once broadly favoured, that we may use the principle of reciprocity as a criterion of a moral rule. For the moment we apply this criterion to the system of rules and regulations operative in any society—primitive or modern—it breaks down. Not only do we prescribe the reciprocation of favours in mere matters of etiquette (i.e. in matters where we recognize no *moral* obligation to do this), but criminals often subscribe to rules enjoining reciprocity in their relations one with

---

[7] 'Competing Criteria' by F. S. McNeilly, *Mind*, July 1957, p. 302.
[8] *An Examination of the Place of Reason in Ethics*, p. 145.

another. So the criterion fails equally from the point of view of any 'normal' agent and from that of our friend the 'disinterested spectator'. It is worth noting that Toulmin's dictum, taken as a stipulation and interpreted narrowly, would also make it possible for a group of criminals to claim that the set of rules by which they abided (e.g. 'It is right to deceive, steal from and injure any non-members of the gang') were quite 'ethical': that is, expressly designed to harmonize people's (i.e. their own people's) actions.

There are many more theories which have been propounded regarding the properties a rule or judgment *must* have in order to rank as moral; but all such theories are doing is to *stipulate* that this or that property must be present and to hope that we will agree with the stipulation. My own view must also be classed as a theory, but a theory of a very different kind. For it is a theory about what has in fact *caused* various communities to label certain rules moral and other non-moral, or, more broadly, it is a theory devised to account for the notion of morality which all or most of us have.

Supplementary Paperback Reading

K. Baier, "The Point of View of Morality." (Bobbs-Merrill Reprint Series in Philosophy)

K. Baier, *The Moral Point of View*, abridged ed., Ch. 5 and 6. (Random House)

J. Dewey, *Theory of the Moral Life*, Ch. I. (Holt, Rinehart and Winston)

A. Duncan-Jones, *Butler's Moral Philosophy*, Ch. 8. (Penguin Books)

W. D. Falk, "Morality, Self, and Others," in H. N. Castaneda and G. Nakhnikian, *Morality and the Language of Conduct* (Wayne State University Press) Also published separately in the Bobbs-Merrill Reprint Series in Philosophy.

N. Fotion, *Moral Situations*. (Antioch Press)

W. K. Frankena, "Recent Conceptions of Morality," in H. N. Castaneda and G. Nakhnikian, *Morality and the Language of Conduct*. (Wayne State University Press) Also published separately in the Bobbs-Merrill Reprint Series in Philosophy.

W. K. Frankena, *Ethics*, Ch. 1. (Prentice-Hall)

A. Gewirth, "Positive 'Ethics' and Normative 'Science'," in J. J. Thomson and G. Dworkin, *Ethics*. (Harper and Row)

W. James, "The Moral Philosopher and the Moral Life." (Bobbs-Merrill Reprint Series in Philosophy)

M. Schlick, *Problems of Ethics*, Ch. I and IV. (Dover Publications)

S. E. Toulmin, *The Place of Reason in Ethics*, Ch. 10, 11, and 12. (Cambridge University Press)

G. J. Warnock, *Contemporary Moral Philosophy*, Ch. V. (St. Martin's Press)

2

ETHICAL

RELATIVISM

Introduction

Are moral values absolute, or are they relative? We may understand this question as asking: Are there any moral standards and rules of conduct that are universal (applicable to all mankind) or are they all culture-bound (applicable only to the members of a particular society or group)? Even when the question is interpreted in this way, however, it still remains unclear. For those who answer the question by claiming that all moral values are relative or culture-bound may be expressing any one of three different ideas. They may, first, be making an empirical or factual assertion. Or secondly, they may be making a normative claim. And thirdly, they may be understood to be uttering a meta-ethical principle. The term "ethical relativism" has been used to refer to any or all of these three positions. In order to keep clear the differences between them, we shall use the following terminology. We shall call the first position "descriptive relativism," the second "normative ethical relativism," and the third "meta-ethical relativism." Let us consider each in turn.

DESCRIPTIVE RELATIVISM

Certain facts about the moral values of different societies and about the way an individual's values are dependent on those of his society have been taken as empirical evidence in support of the claim that all moral values are relative to the particular culture in which they are accepted. These facts are cited by the relativist as reasons for holding a general theory about moral norms, namely, that no such norms are universal. This theory is what we shall designate "descriptive relativism." It is a factual or empirical theory because it holds that, as a matter of historical and sociological fact, no moral standard or rule of conduct has been universally recognized to be the basis of moral obligation. According to the descriptive relativist there are no moral norms common to all cultures. Each society has its own view of what is morally right and wrong and these views vary from society to society because of the differences in their moral codes. Thus it is a mistake to think there are common norms that bind all mankind in one moral community.

Those who accept the position of descriptive relativism point to certain facts as supporting evidence for their theory. These facts may be conveniently summed up under the following headings:

(1) The facts of cultural variability.
(2) Facts about the origin of moral beliefs and moral codes.

(3) The fact of ethnocentrism.

(1) The facts of cultural variability are now so familiar to everyone that they need hardly be enumerated in detail. We all know from reading anthropologists' studies of primitive cultures how extreme is the variation in the customs and taboos, the religions and moralities, the daily habits and the general outlook on life to be found in the cultures of different peoples. But we need not go beyond our own culture to recognize the facts of variability. Historians of Western civilization have long pointed out the great differences in the beliefs and values of people living in different periods. Great differences have also been discovered among the various socio-economic classes existing within the social structure at any one time. Finally, our own contemporary world reveals a tremendous variety of ways of living. No one who dwells in a modern city can escape the impact of this spectrum of different views on work and play, on family life and education, on what constitutes personal happiness, and on what is right and wrong.

(2) When we add to these facts of cultural and historical variability the recent psychological findings about how the individual's values reflect those of his own social group and his own time, we may begin to question the universal validity of our own values. For it is now a well-established fact that no moral values or beliefs are inborn. All our moral attitudes and judgments are learned from the social environment. Even our deepest convictions about justice and the rights of man are originally nothing but the "introjected" or "internalized" views of our culture, transmitted to us through our parents and teachers. Our very conscience itself is formed by the internalizing of the sanctions used by our society to support its moral norms. When we were told in childhood what we ought and ought not to do, and when our parents expressed their approval and disapproval of us for what we did, we were being taught the standards and rules of conduct accepted in our society. The result of this learning process (sometimes called "acculturation") was to ingrain in us a set of attitudes about our own conduct, so that even when our parents were no longer around to guide us or to blame us, we would guide or blame ourselves by thinking, "This is what I ought to do"; "That would be wrong to do"; and so on. If we then did something we believed was wrong we would feel guilty about it, whether or not anyone caught us at it or punished us for it.

It is this unconscious process of internalizing the norms of one's society through early childhood training that explains the origin of an individual's moral values. If we go beyond this and ask about the origin of society's values, we find a long and gradual development of traditions and customs which have given stability to the society's way of life and whose obscure beginnings lie in ritual magic, taboos, tribal ceremonies, and practices of religious worship. Whether we are dealing with the formation of an individual's conscience or the development of a society's moral code, then, the origin of a set of values seems to have little or nothing to do with rational, controlled thought. Neither individuals nor societies originally acquire their moral beliefs by means of logical reasoning or through the use of an objective method for gaining knowledge.

(3) Finally, the descriptive relativist points out another fact about men and their moralities that must be acknowledged. This is the fact that most men are ethnocentric (group centered). They think not only that there is but one true morality for all mankind, but that the one true morality is their own. They are convinced that the moral code under which they grew up and which formed their deepest feelings about right and wrong—namely, the moral code of their own society—is the only code for anyone to live by. Indeed, they often refuse even to entertain the possibility that their own values might be false or that another society's code might be more correct, more enlightened, or more advanced than their own. Thus ethnocentrism often leads to intolerance and dogmatism. It causes men to be extremely narrow-minded in their ethical outlook, afraid to admit any doubt about a moral issue, and unable to take a detached, objective stance regarding their own moral beliefs. Being absolutely certain that their beliefs are true, they can think only that those who disagree with them are in total error and ignorance on moral matters. Their attitude is: We are advanced, they are backward. We are civilized, they are savages.

It is but a short step from dogmatism to intolerance. Intolerance is simply dogmatism in action. Because the moral values of people directly affect their conduct, those who have divergent moral convictions will often come into active conflict with one another in the area of practical life. Each will believe he alone has the true morality and the other is living in the darkness of sin. Each will see the other as practising moral abominations. Each will then try to force the other to accept the truth, or at least will not allow the other to live by his own values. The self-righteous person will not tolerate the presence of "shocking" acts which he views with outraged indignation. Thus it comes about that no differences of opinion on moral matters will be permitted within a society. The ethnocentric society will tend to be a closed society, as far as moral belief and practice are concerned.

The argument for descriptive relativism, then, may be summarized as follows. Since every culture varies with respect to its moral rules and standards, and since each individual's moral beliefs—including his inner conviction of their absolute truth—have been learned within the framework of his own culture's moral code, it follows that there are no universal moral norms. If a person believes there are such norms, this is to be explained by his ethnocentrism, which leads him to project his own culture's norms upon everyone else and to consider those who disagree with him either as innocent but "morally blind" people or as sinners who do not want to face the truth about their own evil ways.

In order to assess the soundness of this argument it is necessary to make a distinction between (a) specific moral standards and rules, and (b) ultimate moral principles. Both (a) and (b) can be called "norms," and it is because the descriptive relativist often overlooks this distinction that his argument is open to doubt. A specific moral standard (such as personal courage or trustworthiness) functions as a criterion for judging whether and to what degree a person's character is morally good or bad. A specific rule of conduct (such as "Help others in time of need" or "Do not tell lies for one's own advantage") is a prescription of how people ought or ought not to act. It functions as a criterion for judging whether an action is right or wrong. In contrast with specific standards and rules, an ultimate moral principle is a universal proposition or statement about the conditions that must hold if a standard or rule is to be used as a criterion for judging *any* person or action. Such a principle will be of the form: Standard S or rule R applies to a person or action if and only if condition C is fulfilled. An example of an ultimate moral principle is that of utility, which we shall be examining in detail in Chapter 4. The principle of utility may be expressed thus: A standard or rule applies to a person or action if and only if the use of the standard or rule in the actual guidance of people's conduct will result in an increase in everyone's happiness or a decrease in everyone's unhappiness.

Now it is perfectly possible for an ultimate moral principle to be consistent with a variety of specific standards and rules as found in the moral codes of different societies. For if we take into account the traditions of a culture, the beliefs about reality and the attitudes toward life that are part of each culture's world-outlook, and if we also take into account the physical or geographical setting of each culture, we will find that a standard or rule which increases people's happiness in one culture will not increase, but rather decrease, people's happiness in another. In one society, for example, letting elderly people die when they can no longer contribute to economic production will be necessary for the survival of everyone else. But another society may have an abundant economy that can easily support people in their old age. Thus the principle of utility would require that in the first society the rule "Do not keep a person alive when he can no longer produce" be part of its moral code, and in the second society it would require a contrary rule. In this case the very same kind of action that is wrong in one society will be right in another. Yet there is a single principle that makes an action of that kind wrong (in one set of circumstances) and another action of that kind right (in a different set of circumstances). In other words, the reason why one action is wrong and the other right is based on one and the same principle, namely utility.

Having in mind this distinction between specific standards and rules on the one hand and ultimate moral principles on the other, what can we say about the argument for descriptive relativism given above? It will immediately be seen that the facts pointed out by the relativist as evidence in support of his theory do not show that ultimate moral principles are relative or culture-bound. They show only that specific standards and rules are relative or culture-bound. The fact that different societies accept different norms of good and bad, right and wrong, is a fact about the standards and rules that make up the various moral codes of those societies. Such a fact does not provide evidence that there is no single ultimate principle which, explicitly or implicitly, every society appeals to as the final justifying ground for its moral code. For if there were such a common ultimate principle, the actual variation in moral codes could be explained in terms of the different world-outlooks, traditions, and physical circumstances of the different societies.

Similarly, facts about ethnocentrism and the causal dependence of an individual's moral beliefs upon his society's moral code do not count as evidence against the view that there is a universal ultimate principle which everyone would refer to in giving a final justification for his society's standards and rules, if he were challenged to do so. Whether there is such a principle and if there is, what sort of conditions it specifies for the validity of specific standards and rules, are questions still to be explored. (In later chapters of this book we shall be considering some of the answers that philosophers have given to these questions.) But the facts cited by the descriptive relativist leave these questions open. We may accept those facts and still be consistent in affirming a single universal ultimate moral principle.

NORMATIVE ETHICAL RELATIVISM

The statement, "What is right in one society may be wrong in another," is a popular way of explaining what is meant by the "relativity of morals." It is usually contrasted with "ethical absolutism," taken as the view that "right and wrong do not vary from society to society." These statements are ambiguous, however, and it is important for us as moral philosophers to be mindful of their ambiguity. For they may be understood either as factual claims or as normative claims, and it makes a great deal of difference which way they are understood. (They may also be taken as meta-ethical claims, but we shall postpone this way of considering them until later.)

When it is said that what is right in one society may be wrong in another, this may be understood to mean that what is believed to be right in one society is believed to be wrong in another. And when it is said that moral right and wrong vary from society to society, this may be understood to mean that different moral norms are adopted by different societies, so that an act which fulfills the norms of one society may violate the norms of another. If this is what is meant, then we are here being told merely of the cultural variability of specific standards and rules, which we have already considered in connection with descriptive relativism.

But the statement, "What is right in one society may be wrong in another," may be interpreted in quite a different way. It may be taken as a normative claim rather than as a factual assertion. In that case it is understood to mean that moral norms are to be considered valid only within the society which has adopted them as part of its way of life. Such norms are not to be considered valid outside that society. The conclusion is then drawn that it is not legitimate to judge people in other societies by applying these norms to their conduct. This is the view we shall designate "normative ethical relativism." In order to be perfectly clear about what it claims, we shall examine two ways in which it can be stated, one focusing our attention upon moral judgments, the other on moral norms.

With regard to moral judgments, normative ethical relativism holds that two *apparently* contradictory statements can both be true. The argument runs as follows. Consider the two statements:

(1) It is wrong for unmarried women to have their faces unveiled in front of strangers.

(2) It is not wrong for . . . (as above).

Here it seems as if there is a flat contradiction between two moral judgments, so that if one is true the other must be false. But the normative ethical relativist holds that they are both true, because the statements as given in (1) and (2) are incomplete. They should read as follows:

(3) It is wrong for unmarried women *who are members of society S* to have their faces unveiled in front of strangers.

(4) It is not wrong for unmarried women *outside of society S* to have their faces unveiled in front of strangers.

Statements (3) and (4) are not contradictories. To assert one is not to deny the other. The normative ethical relativist simply translates all moral judgments of the form "Doing act X is right" into statements of the form "Doing X is right when the agent is a member of society S." The latter statement can then be seen to be consistent with statements of the form "Doing X is wrong when the agent is not a member of society S."

The normative ethical relativist's view of moral norms accounts for the foregoing theory of moral judgments. A moral norm, we have seen, is either a standard used in a judgment of good and bad character or a rule used in a judgment of right and wrong conduct. Thus a person is judged to be good in so far as he fulfills the standard and an action is judged to be right or wrong according to whether it conforms to or violates the rule. Now when a normative ethical relativist says that moral norms vary from society to society, he does not intend merely to assert the fact that different societies have adopted different norms. He is going beyond descriptive relativism and is making a normative claim. He is denying any universal validity to moral norms. He is saying that a moral standard or rule is applicable only to those who are members of the particular society which has adopted the standard or rule as part of its moral code. He therefore thinks it is illegitimate to judge the character or conduct of those outside the society by such a standard or rule. Anyone who uses the norms of one society as the basis for judging the character or conduct of persons in another society is consequently in error.

It is not that a normative ethical relativist necessarily believes in tolerance of other people's norms and their right to live by their norms. He would hold a relativist position even about tolerance itself. A society whose code included a rule of tolerance would be right in tolerating others, while a society that denied tolerance would be right (relatively to its own norm of intolerance) in prohibiting others from living by different norms. The normative ethical relativist would simply say that *we* should not judge the tolerant society to be any better than the intolerant one, for this would be applying our own norm of tolerance to those in other societies. Tolerance, like any other norm, is culturebound. Anyone who claimed that every society has a *right* to live by its own norms, provided that it respects a similar right on the part of other societies, is a normative ethical absolutist, since he holds at least one norm to apply validly to all societies, namely, the right to practice a way of life without interference from others.

If the normative ethical relativist is challenged to prove his position, he may do either of two things. On the one hand he may try to argue that his position follows from, or is based on, the very same facts that are cited by the descriptive relativist as evidence for *his* position. Or, on the other hand, he may turn for support to meta-ethical considerations. Putting aside the second move for the moment, let us look more closely at the first.

The logical relation between the *facts* cited by the descriptive relativist and the *theory* of normative ethical relativism is of central concern in all three of the readings of this chapter. In particular, each reading has something to say about whether the facts of descriptive relativism entail or support normative ethical relativism. In the first reading Professor W. T. Stace considers arguments both for and against normative ethical relativism. One of the arguments for it which he examines is that normative ethical relativism follows necessarily from the facts of cultural variability. This argument he rejects on the following ground: It is possible to accept those facts and to deny normative ethical relativism without contradicting oneself. The fact that societies differ about what is right and wrong does not mean that one society may not have more correct or enlightened moral beliefs than another. After all, just because two people disagree about whether a disease is caused by bacteria or by evil spirits does not lead us to conclude that there is no correct or enlightened view about the cause of the disease. So it does not follow from the fact that two societies differ about whether genocide is right that there is no correct or enlightened view about this moral matter.

It should be noted that a similar argument can be used with regard to the second and third facts asserted by the descriptive relativist. No contradiction is involved in asserting that all moral beliefs come from the social environment and denying normative ethical relativism. For the fact that a belief is learned from one's society does not mean it is neither true nor false, or that, if it is true, its truth is "relative" to the society in which it was learned. All of our beliefs, empirical ones no less than moral ones, are learned from our society. We are not born with any innate beliefs about chemistry or physics, which we learn only in our schools. Yet this does not make us sceptical about the universal validity of these sciences. So the fact that our moral beliefs come from our society and are learned in our homes and schools has no bearing on whether they have any universal validity. The origin or cause of a person's *acquiring* a belief does not determine whether the *content* of the belief is true or false, or even whether there are good grounds for his accepting that content to be true or false.

The same kind of argument holds for the third fact of descriptive relativism, the fact of ethnocentrism. People who are ethnocentric *believe* that the one true moral code is the code of their own society. But this leaves open the question: Is their belief true or false? Even when two people of different cultures have opposite moral beliefs and yet are both ethnocentric, so that one thinks his moral norms are valid for everyone and the other thinks *his* are, this has no bearing on the question of whether either one of them is correct, or whether neither is correct. We must inquire independently into the possibility of establishing the universal validity of a set of moral norms, regardless of who might or might not believe these norms to be universally valid.

According to Professor Stace, then, the theory of normative ethical relativism does not necessarily follow from the facts of descriptive relativism. In the last part of his essay he goes on to give an argument against normative ethical relativism, and it is left to the reader to decide how strong this argument is.

In the second reading of this chapter Professor P. W. Taylor examines the recent claim made by some social scientists that descriptive relativists have exaggerated the facts of cultural variability and have overlooked certain common elements shared by all societies. There are, they say, basic human needs, social structures, and psychological functions to be found in all cultures. They claim further that these "cultural universals" can be used as grounds for denying or doubting normative ethical relativism. Whether these elements common to all societies do indeed provide us with reasons for denying or doubting normative ethical relativism is the central question discussed in the second reading.

In the third reading Professor Carl Wellman draws our attention to a number of ways cultures do differ from one another, and then considers whether and to what extent such cultural variations lend support to normative ethical relativism. He takes up ten of these factors and studies them one by one in order to determine exactly what bearing each has on the claims of ethical relativists. The last two factors he discusses, variations in moral judgments and moral reasoning, are connected not only with normative ethical relativism but also with meta-ethical relativism. Let us now look more carefully at this latter type of relativism.

META-ETHICAL RELATIVISM

It will be convenient to discuss two forms of meta-ethical relativism separately. We shall call these two forms "semantical relativism" and "methodological relativism." According to semantical relativism, the meanings of moral terms like "good" and "right" vary from culture to culture. In one culture, saying that someone is a good man will be taken to mean that he is meek and humble and forgiving. In another culture the same statement will be taken to mean that the man is quick to avenge himself on others and is ruthless with his enemies. A similar variation exists in the meaning of the word "right." Thus in one society the statement "That act is right" might mean "That act must be done to uphold the honor of one's family." In another society it might mean "That act must be done if all the persons concerned are to be treated fairly and impartially." On the basis of considerations like these, semantical relativists argue that what a given word means in moral discourse depends on the culture in which the word is used. There is no one meaning of "good," "right," "duty," or "obligation." Whether this view can stand up to criticism depends on what analysis is given of the meaning of words and statements in moral language. This is a complex matter which will be fully dealt with in Chapter 7.

The second form of meta-ethical relativism, methodological relativism, maintains that different cultures use different methods of reasoning to justify moral judgments. The conclusion drawn is that the same judgment may be justified in one culture but not in another. Each method provides its own criteria for determining whether a reason given in a moral argument is a good or valid reason. If such criteria vary from culture to culture it may be possible to establish the truth of a moral belief in one culture and to show the same belief to be false in another culture. Moral knowledge, being based on different methods of verification, would then be culturally relative. Unless there were some uniform, cross-cultural method for gaining moral knowledge or a uniform, cross-cultural set of rules of reasoning that could tell us whether a person in *any* culture is reasoning correctly, no claim could be made for the universal validity of moral norms. And the methodological relativist argues that there is no such uniform, cross-cultural method or set of rules of reasoning. Whether his argument is to be accepted is a question that must be considered in the light of those methods that have been proposed by moral philosophers as ways of obtaining genuine moral knowledge. A number of such methods will be found in the essays contained in this book.

It has been claimed that one serious implication of methodological relativism is ethical scepticism, or the complete denial of moral knowledge. The reasoning behind this claim is as follows. When the methodological relativist asserts that all moral knowledge is "relative" to a given culture, he is ruling out the very conditions that make it possible for there to be such a thing as genuine moral knowledge at all. For he is saying that, if we investigate the assumptions underlying the alleged universal methods adopted by different cultures, we find that in every case one method will define "valid" or "good" reasons in one way and another method will define them in another way. It follows that the question of which, if any, of these given methods really does lead to moral knowledge is *logically undecidable*. For in order to choose between any two methods, a neutral third method must be used—a method that would enable us to give reasons for accepting one method and rejecting the other. But any such third method will itself merely postulate its own criteria of "valid" reasons, and we would then have to justify our choice of *these* criteria. Justifying our choice of these criteria, however, would in turn require our giving reasons for our choice, and such reasons would presuppose still another method. Since we cannot go to infinity in methods for justifying other methods, we are left at some point with an arbitrary decision. But no claim to genuine moral knowledge can rest on an arbitrary decision, since a different decision might lead to opposite conclusions regarding a moral issue and each decision would be completely without justification. This is precisely the kind of situation that the word "knowledge" precludes, if that word is to be understood in its ordinary sense. Therefore genuine moral knowledge is impossible.

Now the reply made to this argument by moral philosophers is simply to construct, clearly and systematically, a method of moral reasoning whose logical principles can be shown to be those which are in fact presupposed by anyone, in any culture, who wants to think rationally about moral matters. By considering how any reasonable being would carry on his thinking when he understood clearly the meaning of moral concepts and the function of moral judgments, the philosopher attempts to show that there is a valid way of determining whether any moral judgment is true or false and hence that there is a warranted method for obtaining genuine moral knowledge. In this book we shall become acquainted with some of the most important of these attempts.

ETHICAL ABSOLUTISM

Some consideration should here be given to the term "ethical absolutism," which is frequently used to refer to the opposite of ethical relativism, but which may also be used in other senses. Sometimes people will argue against ethical absolutism in one sense and think that they have thereby established the truth of ethical relativism, when in fact they have not. Let us see how this can happen.

When "ethical absolutism" is taken to mean the contradictory of ethical relativism it can be understood in three different ways, corresponding to the three kinds of relativism. Descriptive absolutism would be the view that there is one universal ultimate moral principle which, implicitly or explicitly, lies at the foundation of all the varying moral codes of different societies. We have seen how this position can be maintained in the face of the evidence of great variation among the specific standards and rules that constitute those moral codes. For different standards and rules can be derived from one ultimate principle when it is applied to the varying social and physical conditions under which the different ways of life of cultures are pursued.

Sometimes, however, when an ethical absolutist asserts that there is one true morality for all cultures, no matter how different may be their ways of life and their conditions of existence, he means something other than that all cultures do basically appeal to one ultimate principle. When the evidence of cultural variation is pointed out to this type of ethical absolutist, he will reply: "I was not asserting that there is one principle which all societies *consider to be* the ultimate foundation of morality. I was asserting that there is one principle that *is* the ultimate foundation of morality, whether all societies consider it to be so or not." As soon as his position is stated in this way, it is seen to be the denial of normative ethical relativism, not the denial of descriptive relativism. Let us therefore call this view "normative ethical absolutism." According to it there is an ultimate moral principle applicable to all mankind. This principle defines an ideal moral community of man based on a single "moral law" that applies to all men whether they recognize it or not. The people of a given culture might not acknowledge such an ultimate principle or law, but nevertheless it is binding upon them and is the source of their true rights and duties.

This view, of course, presupposes that there is a method of finding out what the ultimate "moral law" is and hence a method of finding out whether any given moral belief is true or false. The great task of the normative ethical absolutist is to tell us what this method is. But all he insists on, when confronted with the actual disagreements among people about what is right and wrong, is that these disagreements do not rule out the possibility of such a method. (This is parallel to the position we would all take concerning a scientific or empirical belief. The fact that different cultures might hold different beliefs about the causes of a disease, for instance, does not lead us to say that there are no true beliefs about the real causes of the disease. We simply say that the beliefs of some cultures are true and those of others are false. And we can say this even about a disease whose causes are still unknown, although in that case we cannot specify which of the disagreeing beliefs are true and which are false.)

The foregoing account of normative ethical absolutism shows that it presupposes that there is a cross-cultural method by which moral beliefs can be verified, even if no philosopher has yet succeeded in discovering that method or in establishing its universal validity. Now the view that such a method can be discovered and can be shown to be universally valid may be called "methodological absolutism." It is the exact opposite of methodological relativism. It should be noted that if methodological absolutism is true, then not only methodological relativism but also normative ethical relativism would be false. For if we know a way of verifying moral beliefs or justifying moral norms, we can claim that there is a set of norms valid for all mankind, and this is the denial of normative ethical relativism. Hence the logical foundation for normative ethical absolutism lies in methodological absolutism, and the meta-ethical task of showing that there is a cross-cultural method for acquiring moral knowledge becomes the first problem for the ethical absolutist.

In sharp contrast with the foregoing meanings of "ethical absolutism," the term may also be used to designate a certain view concerning the *nature* of moral norms. According to this view, if a rule of conduct is a moral rule, it must have no exceptions. The moral rule "It is wrong to break a promise" is taken by the ethical absolutist to mean that it is always wrong to break a promise, no matter what the circumstances might be. It would follow that it is our duty to keep a promise, even though we might do great harm to someone by keeping it. In other words an ethical absolutist (in the present sense of "ethical absolutism") believes that the application of a moral rule to varying circumstances does not allow us to make legitimate exceptions to it. Whether any moral philosopher has actually held such a position is questionable, although it is sometimes claimed that Immanuel Kant was an ethical absolutist in this sense. (See the reading by Kant in Chapter 5.)

What is important for us to understand at this point is that a normative ethical absolutist or a methodological absolutist, as defined earlier, may reject ethical absolutism in this latter sense. When the normative ethical absolutist says that there are moral norms applicable to all mankind, he does not mean that the application of these norms in varying circumstances must determine that one kind of act is always right (or that it is always wrong). One and the same norm can yield different results in the following way. Suppose the norm is expressed in the rule: Always do that act which will probably have better consequences than any alternative act open to your choice, where the standard of "better" is understood as "brings about more pleasure." Then in one situation a person might be following this rule by keeping his promise, while in a different situation he might be following this rule by breaking his promise. The latter case is illustrated by the person's failing to meet a friend at a time he had promised to because he has stopped on the way to help someone who had just been injured in an accident. Thus one and the same norm allows us to say either of two things regarding the keeping of promises: "Sometimes keeping one's promise is right and sometimes it is wrong" or "Although as a general rule it is right to keep one's promise, this rule does have legitimate exceptions."

Now this variation in the rightness and wrongness of keeping promises does not involve the giving up of normative ethical absolutism. For the basis for such variation lies in one moral norm that holds "absolutely" in all cultures, namely, the rule that we ought always to do what will bring about the best consequences in every situation. In so far as he considers it a valid rule for all mankind to follow, the absolutist would maintain that this rule does not vary from culture to culture. He would say that a culture which did not accept this rule was mistaken in its moral beliefs. Nevertheless, he would assert that when this one unchanging rule is applied to varying circumstances, the same kind of act that is right in one situation might be wrong in another. The normative ethical relativist, on the other hand, claims that what makes an act right is the society's believing it to be right (or the society's adopting norms according to which it is right) and that what makes the same kind of act wrong in another society is *that* society's believing it to be wrong (or adopting norms according to which it is wrong). Thus no society can be mistaken in its moral beliefs. It is this position which the absolutist emphatically rejects.

In a similar manner, the methodological absolutist might well accept a method of reasoning that justifies the varying judgments about keeping and breaking promises we have considered. But the variation in moral judgments is grounded on the one unvarying method by which the given rule was established. And it is this method that the absolutist claims to be cross-cultural, so that any society that did not use the method would, for that reason, be incapable of attaining genuine moral knowledge.

There is an important conclusion to be drawn from these considerations. It is that ethical absolutism (when understood as the denial of ethical relativism) may be true while ethical absolutism (when understood as the idea that no exceptions are to be made to moral rules) may be false. One need not be an ethical relativist in any of the three senses we have discussed to reject the latter type of absolutism. It is possible for relativism in any of these senses to be false and for the latter type of absolutism to be false at the same time. Whether either or both are false is a matter for each reader to try to decide by his own philosophical reflection as he engages in the study of ethics.

WALTER TERENCE STACE
Ethical Relativity

Any ethical position which denies that there is a single moral standard which is equally applicable to all men at all times may fairly be called a species of ethical relativity. There is not, the relativist asserts, merely one moral law, one code, one standard. There are many moral laws, codes, standards. What morality ordains in one place or age may be quite different from what morality ordains in another place or age. The moral code of Chinamen is quite different from that of Europeans, that of African savages quite different from both. Any morality, therefore, is relative to the age, the place, and the circumstances in which it is found. It is in no sense absolute.

This does not mean merely—as one might at first sight be inclined to suppose—that the very same kind of action which is *thought* right in one country and period may be *thought* wrong in another. This would be a mere platitude, the truth of which everyone would have to admit. Even the absolutist would admit this—would even wish to emphasize it—since he is well aware that different peoples have different sets of moral ideas, and his whole point is that some of these sets of ideas are false. What the relativist means to assert is, not this platitude, but that the very same kind of action which *is* right in one country and period may *be* wrong in another. And this, far from being a platitude, is a very startling assertion.

It is very important to grasp thoroughly the difference between the two ideas. For there is reason to think that many minds tend to find ethical relativity attractive because they fail to keep them clearly apart. It is so very obvious that moral ideas differ from country to country and from age to age. And it is so very easy, if you are mentally lazy, to suppose that to say this means the same as to say that no universal moral standard exists,—or in other words that it implies ethical relativity. We fail to see that the word "standard" is used in two different senses. It is perfectly true that, in one sense, there are many variable moral standards. We speak of judging a man by the standard of his time. And this implies that different times have different standards. And this, of course, is quite true. But when the word "standard" is used in this sense it means simply the set of moral ideas current during the period in question. It means what people *think* right, whether as a matter of fact it *is* right or not. On the other hand when the absolutist asserts that there exists a single universal moral "standard," he is not

From W. T. Stace, *The Concept of Morals* (1937). Reprinted by permission of the author.

using the word in this sense at all. He means by "standard" what *is* right as distinct from what people merely think right. His point is that although what people think right varies in different countries and periods, yet what actually is right is everywhere and always the same. And it follows that when the ethical relativist disputes the position of the absolutist and denies that any universal moral standard exists he too means by "standard" what actually is right. But it is exceedingly easy, if we are not careful, to slip loosely from using the word in the first sense to using it in the second sense; and to suppose that the variability of moral beliefs is the same thing as the variability of what really is moral. And unless we keep the two senses of the word "standard" distinct, we are likely to think the creed of ethical relativity much more plausible than it actually is.

The genuine relativist, then, does not merely mean that Chinamen may think right what Frenchmen think wrong. He means that what *is* wrong for the Frenchman may *be* right for the Chinaman. And if one enquires how, in those circumstances, one is to know what actually is right in China or in France, the answer comes quite glibly. What is right in China is the same as what people think right in China; and what is right in France is the same as what people think right in France. So that, if you want to know what is moral in any particular country or age all you have to do is to ascertain what are the moral ideas current in that age or country. Those ideas are, *for that age or country,* right. Thus what is morally right is identified with what is thought to be morally right, and the distinction which we made above between these two is simply denied. To put the same thing in another way, it is denied that there can be or ought to be any distinction between the two senses of the word "standard." There is only one kind of standard of right and wrong, namely, the moral ideas current in any particular age or country.

Moral right *means* what people think morally right. It has no other meaning. What Frenchmen think right is, therefore, right *for Frenchmen.* And evidently one must conclude—though I am not aware that relativists are anxious to draw one's attention to such unsavoury but yet absolutely necessary conclusions from their creed—that cannibalism is right for people who believe in it, that human sacrifice is right for those races which practice it, and that burning widows alive was right for Hindus until the British stepped in and compelled the Hindus to behave immorally by allowing their widows to remain alive.

When it is said that, according to the ethical relativist, what is thought right in any social group is right for that group, one must be careful not to misinterpret this. The relativist does not, of course, mean that there actually is an objective moral standard in France and a different objective standard in England, and that French and British opinions respectively give us correct information about these different standards. His point is rather that there are no objectively true moral standards at all. There is no single universal objective standard. Nor are there a variety of local objective standards. All standards are subjective. People's subjective feelings about morality are the only standards which exist.

To sum up. The ethical relativist consistently denies, it would seem, whatever the ethical absolutist asserts. For the absolutist there is a single universal moral standard. For the relativist there is no such standard. There are only local, ephemeral, and variable standards. For the absolutist there are two senses of the word "standard." Standards in the sense of sets of current moral ideas are relative and changeable. But the standard in the sense of what is actually morally right is absolute and unchanging. For the relativist no such distinction can be made. There is only one meaning of the word standard, namely, that which refers to local and variable sets of moral ideas. Or if it is insisted that the word must be allowed two meanings, then the relativist will say that there is at any rate no actual example of a standard in the absolute sense, and that the word as thus used is an empty name to which nothing in reality corresponds; so that the distinction between the two meanings becomes empty and useless. Finally—though this is merely saying the same thing in another way —the absolutist makes a distinction between what actually is right and what is thought right. The relativist rejects this distinction and identifies what is moral with what is thought moral by certain human beings or groups of human beings.

• • • • •

I shall now proceed to consider, first, the main arguments which can be urged in favour of ethical relativity; and secondly, the arguments which can be urged against it. . . .

There are, I think, [two] main arguments in favour of ethical relativity. The first is that which relies upon the actual varieties of moral "standards" found in the world. It was easy enough to believe in a single absolute morality in older times when there was no anthropology, when all humanity was divided clearly into two groups, Christian peoples and the "heathen." Christian peoples knew and possessed the one true morality. The rest were savages whose moral ideas could be ignored. But all this is changed. Greater knowledge has brought greater tolerance. We can no longer exalt our own morality as alone true, while dismissing all other moralities as false or inferior. The investigations of anthropologists have shown that there exist side by side in the world a bewildering variety of moral codes. On this topic endless volumes have been written, masses of evidence piled up. Anthropologists have ransacked the Melanesian Islands, the jungles of New Guinea, the steppes of Siberia, the deserts of Australia, the forests of central Africa, and have brought back with them countless examples of weird, extravagant, and fantastic "moral" customs with which to confound us. We learn that all kinds of horrible practices are, in this, that, or the other place, regarded as essential to virtue. We find that there is nothing, or next to nothing, which has always and everywhere been regarded as morally good by all men. Where then is our universal morality? Can we, in face of all this evidence, deny that it is nothing but an empty dream?

This argument, taken by itself, is a very weak one. It relies upon a single set of facts—the variable moral customs of the world. But this variability of moral ideas is admitted by both parties to the dispute, and is capable of ready explanation upon the hypothesis of either party. The relativist says that the facts are to be explained by the non-existence of any absolute moral standard. The absolutist says that they are to be explained by human ignorance of what the absolute moral standard is. And he can truly point out that men have differed widely in their opinions about all manner of topics including the subject-matters of the physical sciences—just as much as they differ about morals. And if the various different opinions which men have held about the shape of the earth do not prove that it has no one real shape, neither do the various opinions which they have held about morality prove that there is no one true morality.

Thus the facts can be explained equally plausibly on either hypothesis. There is nothing in the facts themselves which compels us to prefer the relativistic hypothesis to that of the absolutist. And therefore the argument fails to prove the relativist conclusion. If that conclusion is to be established, it must be by means of other considerations.

This is the essential point. But I will add some supplementary remarks. The work of the anthropologists, upon which ethical relativists seem to rely so heavily, has as a matter of fact added absolutely nothing *in principle* to what has always been known about the variability of moral ideas. Educated people have known all along that the Greeks tolerated sodomy, which in modern times has been regarded in some countries as an abominable crime; that the Hindus thought it a sacred duty to burn their widows; that trickery, now thought despicable, was once believed to be a virtue; that terrible torture was thought by our own ancestors only a few centuries ago to be a justifiable weapon of justice; that it was only yesterday that western peoples came to believe that slavery is immoral. Even the ancients knew very well that moral customs and ideas vary—witness the writings of Herodotus. Thus the principle of the variability of moral ideas was well understood long before modern anthropology was ever heard of. Anthropology has added nothing to the knowledge of this principle except a mass of new and extreme examples of it drawn from very remote sources. But to multiply examples of a principle already well known and universally admitted adds nothing to the argument which is built upon that principle. The discoveries of the anthropologists have no doubt been of the highest importance in their own sphere. But in my considered opinion they have thrown no new light upon the special problems of the moral philosopher.

Although the multiplication of examples has no logical bearing on the argument, it does have an immense *psychological* effect upon people's minds. These masses of anthropological learning are impressive. They are propounded in the sacred name of "science." If they are quoted in support of ethical relativity —as they often are—people *think* that they must prove something important. They bewilder and over-awe the simple-minded, batter down their resistance, make them ready to receive humbly the doctrine of ethical relativity from those who have acquired a reputation by their immense learning and their claims to be "scientific." Perhaps this is why so much ado is made by ethical relativists regarding the anthropological evidence. But we must refuse to be impressed. We must discount all this mass of evidence about the extraordinary moral customs of remote peoples. Once we have admitted—as everyone who is instructed must have admitted these last two thousand years without any anthropology at all— the principle that moral ideas vary, all this new evidence adds nothing to the argument. And the argument itself proves nothing for the reasons already given.

• • • • •

The [second] argument in favour of ethical relativity is a very strong one. . . . It consists in alleging that no one has ever been able to discover upon what foundation an absolute morality could rest, or from what source a universally binding moral code could derive its authority.

If, for example, it is an absolute and unalterable moral rule that all men ought to be unselfish, from whence does this *command* issue? For a command it certainly is, phrase it how you please. There is no difference in meaning between the sentence "You ought to be unselfish" and the sentence "Be unselfish." Now a command implies a commander. An obligation implies some authority which obliges. Who is this commander, what this authority? Thus the vastly difficult question is raised of *the basis of moral obligation*. Now the argument of the relativist would be that it is impossible to find any basis for a universally binding moral law; but that it is quite easy to discover a basis for morality if moral codes are admitted to be variable, emphemeral, and relative to time, place, and circumstance.

In this book I am assuming that it is no longer possible to solve this difficulty by saying naïvely that the universal moral law is based upon the uniform commands of God to all men. There will be many, no doubt, who will dispute this. But I am not writing for them. I am writing for those who feel the necessity of finding for morality a basis independent of particular religious dogmas. And I shall therefore make no attempt to argue the matter.

The problem which the absolutist has to face, then, is this. The religious basis of the one absolute morality having disappeared, can there be found for it any other, any secular, basis? If not, then it would seem that we cannot any longer believe in absolutism. We shall have to fall back upon belief in a variety of perhaps mutually inconsistent moral codes operating over restricted areas and limited periods. No one of these will be better, or more true, than any other. Each will be good and true for those living in those areas and periods. We shall have to fall back, in a word, on ethical relativity.

For there is no great difficulty in discovering the foundations of morality, or rather of moralities, if we adopt the relativistic hypothesis. Even if we cannot be quite certain *precisely* what these foundations are—and relativists themselves are not entirely agreed about them—we can at least see in a general way the *sort* of foundations they must have. We can see that the question on this basis is not in principle impossible of answer—although the details may be obscure; while, if we adopt the absolutist hypothesis—so the argument runs—no kind of answer is conceivable at all.

Relativists, speaking generally, offer two different solutions of the problem, either of which, or perhaps some compromise between the two, might be correct. According to some the basis of morality is in "emotion." According to others it is in "customs." I do not intend to examine these rival suggestions in detail. An understanding of the general principles involved in them will be quite sufficient for our purpose.

According to the first view emotions such as that of resentment give rise to the idea that the things or actions resented are immoral and bad. Westermarck, who is the chief exponent of this type of opinion, makes further distinctions. Not any resentment, but only impartial or "disinterested" resentment, is the source of moral disapproval. But with these refinements we need not concern ourselves. We can see, easily enough, that if in one community a particular type of act, say sodomy, comes for any reason—biological, historical, or merely accidental—to be resented by the majority of the members of the group, it will come to be regarded as "wrong" by that group. If in another community no such feeling of resentment or dislike arises, it will be thought to be morally unobjectionable. The sense of moral obligation and the commands of morality, then, have their source in *feelings*. And since the feelings of men, and of different groups of men, are variable, the moral codes which are based upon them will be variable too.

Moreover an emotion is not—at any rate according to the psychology implied by Westermarck's conceptions—anything rational. An emotion, as such, cannot be true or false, right or wrong. It simply *is*. If therefore one group of people feels resentment at murder, while another does not, it cannot be said that the moral ideas of the former are any better or more true or more right than those of the latter. They are simply different. What is right *means* simply what arouses certain kinds of feelings, say those of approval. What is wrong *means* simply what arouses resentment or disapproval. There is consequently no sense in asking whether a race of men is right in approving this or that kind of action. Their approving it is what makes it right. For them, therefore, it *is* right. And if another race disapproves it, then, for that race, it *is* wrong.

According to the other view it is custom which is the source of moral standards and ideas. That is "wrong" in any community which is contrary to the customs of that community. That is "right" which is in accordance with them. A moral standard, in fact, is simply identifiable with the set of customs which are in force in any particular region at any particular time. And as customs are variable, so are moral standards. Here too there can be no question of declaring that one set of customs is morally better than another. For the fact that something is the custom is what makes it morally good. And according to this view the sense of moral obligation is simply the force of social custom making itself felt in the individual consciousness.

These two views are not really incompatible. For customs surely have their roots in men's feelings. And to say that morality is based on customs is in the end the same as to say that it is based on feelings. One view emphasizes the outward behaviour which exhibits itself in customs; the other view emphasizes the inward feelings which give rise to this behaviour. The dispute is a professional one between rival schools of psychology. It does not affect the larger issues with which we are concerned.

No such easy solution of the problem of the basis of moral obligation is open to the absolutist. He believes in moral commands, obedience to which is obligatory on all men, whether they know it or not, whatever they feel, and whatever their customs may be. Such uniform obligation cannot be founded upon feelings, because feelings are—or are said to be—variable. And there is no set of customs which is more than local in its operation. The will of God as the source of a universal law is no longer a feasible suggestion. And there is obviously no mundane authority, king, or Pope, or super-state, to which all men admit allegiance, and which could have the recognized right to issue universally binding decrees. Where then is the absolutist to turn for an answer to the question? And if he cannot find one, he will have to admit the claims of the ethical relativist; or at least he will have to give up his own claims.

· · · · ·

This argument is undoubtedly very strong. It *is* absolutely essential to solve the problem of the basis of moral obligation if we are to believe in any kind of moral standards other than those provided by mere custom or by irrational emotions. It is idle to talk about a universal morality unless we can point to the source of its authority—or at least to do so is to indulge in a faith which is without rational ground. To cherish a blind faith in morality may be, for the average man whose business is primarily to live aright and not to theorize, sufficient. Perhaps it is his wisest course. But it will not do for the philosopher. His function, or at least one of his functions, is precisely to discover the rational grounds of our everyday beliefs—if they have any. Philosophically and intellectually, then, we cannot accept belief in a universally binding morality unless we can discover upon what foundation its obligatory character rests.

But in spite of the strength of the argument thus posed in favour of ethical relativity, it is not impregnable. For it leaves open one loop-hole. It is always possible that some theory, not yet examined, may provide a basis for a universal moral obligation. The argument rests upon the negative proposition that *there is no theory which can provide a basis for a universal morality*. But it is notoriously difficult to prove a negative. How can you prove that there are no green swans? All you can show is that none have been found so far. And then it is always possible that one will be found tomorrow. So it is here. The relativist shows that no theory of the basis of moral obligation has yet been discovered which could validate a universal morality. Perhaps. But it is just conceivable that one might be discovered in the course of this book.

It is time that we turned our attention from the case in favour of ethical relativity to the case against it. Now the case against it consists, to a very large extent, in urging that, if taken seriously and pressed to its logical conclusion, ethical relativity can only end in destroying the conception of morality altogether, in undermining its practical efficacy, in rendering meaningless many almost universally accepted truths about human affairs, in robbing human beings of any incentive to strive for a better world, in taking the life-blood out of every ideal and every aspiration which has ever ennobled the life of man.

• • • • •

First of all, then, ethical relativity, in asserting that the moral standards of particular social groups are the only standards which exist, renders meaningless all propositions which attempt to compare these standards with one another in respect of their moral worth. And this is a very serious matter indeed. We are accustomed to think that the moral ideas of one nation or social group may be "higher" or "lower" than those of another. We believe, for example, that Christian ethical ideals are nobler than those of the savage races of central Africa. Probably most of us would think that the Chinese moral standards are higher than those of the inhabitants of New Guinea. In short we habitually compare one civilization with another and judge the sets of ethical ideas to be found in them to be some better, some worse. The fact that such judgments are very difficult to make with any justice, and that they are frequently made on very superficial and prejudiced grounds, has no bearing on the question now at issue. The question is whether such judgments have any *meaning*. We habitually assume that they have.

But on the basis of ethical relativity they can have none whatever. For the relativist must hold that there is no *common* standard which can be applied to the various civilizations judged. Any such comparison of moral standards implies the existence of some superior standard which is applicable to both. And the existence of any such standard is precisely what the relativist denies. According to him the Christian standard is applicable only to Christians, the Chinese standard only to Chinese, the New Guinea standard only to the inhabitants of New Guinea.

What is true of comparisons between the moral standards of different races will also be true of comparisons between those of different ages. It is not unusual to ask such questions as whether the standard of our own day is superior to that which existed among our ancestors five hundred years ago. And when we remember that our ancestors employed slaves, practiced barbaric physical tortures, and burnt people alive, we may be inclined to think that it is. At any rate we assume that the question is one which has meaning and is capable of rational discussion. But if the ethical relativist is right, whatever we assert on this subject must be totally meaningless. For here again there is no common standard which could form the basis of any such judgments.

This in its turn implies that the whole notion of moral *progress* is a sheer delusion. Progress means an advance from lower to higher, from worse to better. But on the basis of ethical relativity it has no meaning to say that the standards of this age are better (or worse) than those of a previous age. For there is no common standard by which both can be measured. Thus it is nonsense to say that the morality of the New Testament is higher than that of the Old. And Jesus Christ, if he imagined that he was introducing into the world a higher ethical standard than existed before his time, was merely deluded.

There is indeed one way in which the ethical relativist can give some sort of meaning to judgments of higher or lower as applied to the moral ideas of different races or ages. What he will have to say is that we assume *our* standards to be the best simply because they are ours. And we judge other standards by our own. If we say that Chinese moral codes are better than those of African cannibals, what we *mean* by this is that they are better *according to our standards*. We mean, that is to say, that Chinese standards are *more like our own* than African standards are. "Better" accordingly *means* "more like us." "Worse" means "less like us." It thus becomes clear that judgments of better and worse in such cases do not express anything that is really true at all. They merely give expression to our perfectly groundless satisfaction with our own ideas. In short, they give expression to nothing but our egotism and self-conceit. Our moral ideals are not really better than those of the savage. We are simply deluded by our egotism into thinking they are. The African savage has just as good a right to think his morality the best as we have to think ours the best. His opinion is just as well grounded as ours, or rather both opinions are equally groundless.

• • • • •

Thus the ethical relativist must treat all judgments comparing different moralities as either entirely meaningless; or, if this course appears too drastic, he has the alternative of declaring that they have for their meaning-content nothing except the vanity and egotism of those who pass them. We are asked to believe that the highest moral ideals of humanity are not really any better than those of an Australian bushman. But if this is so, why strive for higher ideals? Thus the heart is taken out of all effort, and the meaning out of all human ideals and aspirations.

The ethical relativist may perhaps say that he is being misjudged. It is not true that, on the basis of his doctrine, all effort for moral improvement is vain. For if we take such a civilization as our own, and if we assume that the standard of morals theoretically accepted by it is that of Christian ethics, then there is surely plenty of room for improvement and "progress" in the way of making our practice accord with our theory. Effort may legimately be directed towards getting people to live up to whatever standards they profess to honour. Such effort will be, on the relativistic basis, perfectly meaningful; for it does not imply a comparison of standards by reference to a common standard, but only a comparison of actual achievements with an admitted and accepted standard within a social group.

Now I do not believe that even this plea can be accepted. For as soon as it comes to be effectively realized that our moral standard is no better than that of barbarians, why should anyone trouble to live up to it? It would be much easier to adopt some lower standard, to preach it assiduously until everyone believes it, when it would automatically become right. But even if we waive this point, and admit that the exhortation to practice what we preach may be meaningful, this does not touch the issue which was raised above. It will still be true that efforts to improve moral *beliefs,* as distinguished from moral *practice,* will be futile. It will still be true that Jesus Christ would have done better had he tried only to persuade humanity to live up to the old barbaric standards than he did in trying to propagate among them a new and more enlightened moral code. It will still be true that any reformer in the future who attempts to make men see even more noble ideals than those which we have inherited from the reformers of the past will be wasting his time.

I come now to a second point. Up to the present I have allowed it to be taken tacitly for granted that, though judgments comparing different races and ages in respect of the worth of their moral codes are impossible for the ethical relativist, yet judgments of comparison between individuals living within the same social group would be quite possible. For individuals living within the same social group would presumably be subject to the same moral code, that of their group, and this would therefore constitute, as between these individuals, a common standard by which they could both be measured. We have not here, as we had in the other case, the difficulty of the absence of any common standard of comparison. It should therefore be possible for the ethical relativist to say quite meaningfully that President Lincoln was a better man than some criminal or moral imbecile of his own time and country, or that Jesus was a better man than Judas Iscariot.

But is even this minimum of moral judgment really possible on relativist grounds? It seems to me that it is not. For when once the whole of humanity is abandoned as the area covered by a single moral standard, what smaller areas are to be adopted as the *loci* of different standards? Where are we to draw the lines of demarcation? We can split up humanity, perhaps,—though the procedure will be very arbitrary—into races, races into nations, nations into tribes, tribes into families, families into individuals. Where are we going to draw the *moral* boundaries? Does the *locus* of a particular moral standard reside in a race, a nation, a tribe, a family, or an individual? Perhaps the blessed phrase "social group" will be dragged in to save the situation. Each such group, we shall be told, has its own moral code which is, for it, right. But what *is* a "group"? Can anyone define it or give its boundaries? . . .

The difficulty is not, as might be thought, merely an academic difficulty of logical definition. If that were all, I should not press the point. But the ambiguity has practical consequences which are disastrous for morality. No one is likely to say that moral codes are confined within the arbitrary limits of the geographical divisions of countries. Nor are the notions of race, nation, or political state likely to help us. To bring out the essentially practical character of the difficulty let us put it in the form of concrete questions. Does the American nation constitute a "group" having a single moral standard? Or does the standard of what I ought to do change continuously as I cross the continent in a railway train? Do different States of the Union have different moral codes? Perhaps every town and village has its own peculiar standard. This may at first sight seem reasonable enough. "In Rome do as Rome does" may seem as good a rule in morals as it is in etiquette. But can we stop there? Within the village are numerous cliques each having its own set of ideas. Why should not each of these claim to be bound only by its own special and peculiar moral standards? And if it comes to that, why should not the gangsters of Chicago claim to constitute a group having its own morality, so that its murders and debaucheries must be viewed as "right" by the only standard which can legitimately be applied to it? And if it be answered that the nation will not tolerate this, that may be so. But this is to put the foundation of right simply in the superior force of the majority. In that case whoever is stronger will be right, however monstrous his ideas and actions. And if we cannot deny to any set of people the right to have its own morality, is it not clear that, in the end, we cannot even deny this right to the individual? Every individual man and woman can put up, on this view, an irrefutable claim to be judged by no standard except his or her own.

If these arguments are valid, the ethical relativist cannot really maintain that there is anywhere to be found a moral standard binding upon anybody against his will. And he cannot maintain that, even within the social group, there is a common standard as between individuals. And if that is so, then even judgments to the effect that one man is morally better than another become meaningless. All moral valuation thus vanishes. There is nothing to prevent each man from being a rule unto himself. The result will be moral chaos and the collapse of all effective standards.

Perhaps, in regard to the difficulty of defining the social group, the relativist may make the following suggestion. If we admit, he may say, that it is impossible or very difficult to define a group territorially or nationally or geographically, it is still possible to define it logically. We will simply define an ethical group as any set of persons (whether they live together in one place or are scattered about in many places over the earth) who recognizes one and the same moral standard. As a matter of fact such groups will as a rule be found occupying each something like a single locality. The people in one country, or at least in one village, tend to think much alike. But theoretically at least the members of an ethical group so defined might be scattered all over the face of the globe. However that may be, it will now be possible to make meaningful statements to the effect that one individual is morally better or worse than another, so long as we keep within the ethical group so defined. For the individuals of the ethical group will have as their common standard the ethical belief or beliefs the acknowledgment of which constitutes the defining characteristic of the group. By this common standard they can be judged and compared with one another. Therefore it is not true that ethical relativity necessarily makes all such judgments of moral comparison between individuals meaningless.

I admit the logic of this. Theoretically judgments of comparison can be given meaning in this way. Nevertheless there are fatal objections to the suggestion. . . .

•   •   •   •   •

. . . For how can I ever know whether two persons whom I wish to compare belong to the same ethical group or not? I wish to say that Jesus was a morally nobler man than Judas Iscariot. If the relativist cannot admit this, then surely his creed revolts our moral sense. But I cannot make this statement unless I have first made certain that Jesus and Judas had the same moral ideals. But had they? Personally I should think it almost certain that they had not. Judas may have paid homage, in some sort, to the moral teachings of his master. He may even have been quite sincere. But it seems to me incredible that he could ever really have made them parts of his mental and moral outlook, or even that he could have effectively understood them. Consequently the judgment that Jesus was better than Judas is meaningless after all. It is almost certain that the Chicago gangsters do not hold the same moral views (if it has any meaning to attribute moral views to them at all) as President Roosevelt. Therefore a judgment of moral comparison between the president and the gangster will be meaningless. I think it would be in general true to say that wherever there is between people a very wide discrepancy of moral practice, there is almost sure to be also a wide discrepancy of moral belief. And in no such case could we, on the relativistic basis suggested, make meaningful moral comparisons. It can hardly be said, therefore, that this suggestion at all helps the case of the ethical relativist.

But even if we assume that the difficulty about defining moral groups has been surmounted, a further difficulty presents itself. Suppose that we have now definitely decided what are the exact boundaries of the social group within which a moral standard is to be operative. And we will assume—as is invariably done by relativists themselves—that this group is to be some actually existing social community such as a tribe or nation. How are we to know, even then, what actually *is* the moral standard within that group? How is anyone to know? How is even a member of the group to know? For there are certain to be within the group—at least this will be true among advanced peoples—wide differences of opinion as to what is right, what wrong. Whose opinion, then, is to be taken as representing *the* moral standard of the group? Either we must take the opinion of the majority within the group, or the opinion of some minority. If we rely upon the ideas of the majority, the results will be disastrous. Wherever there is found among a people a small band of select spirits, or perhaps one man, working for the establishment of higher and nobler ideals than those commonly accepted by the group, we shall be compelled to hold that, for that people at that time, the majority are right, and that the reformers are wrong and are preaching what is immoral. We shall have to maintain, for example, that Jesus was preaching immoral doctrines to the Jews. Moral goodness will have to be equated always with the mediocre and sometimes with the definitely base and ignoble. If on the other hand we say that the moral standard of the group is to be identified with the moral opinions of some minority, then what minority is this to be? We cannot answer that it is to be the minority composed of the best and most enlightened individuals of the group. This would involve us in a palpably vicious circle. For by what standard are these individuals to be judged the best and the most enlightened? There is no principle by which we could select the right minority. And therefore we should have to consider every minority as good as every other. And this means that we should have no logical right whatever to resist the claim of the gangsters of Chicago—if such a claim were made—that their practices represent the highest standards of American morality. It means in the end that every individual is to be bound by no standard save his own.

The ethical relativists are great empiricists. *What* is the actual moral standard of any group can only be discovered, they tell us, by an examination on the ground of the moral opinions and customs of that group. But will they tell us how they propose to decide, when they get to the ground, which of the many moral opinions they are sure to find there is *the* right one in that group? To some extent they will be able to do this for the Melanesian Islanders—from whom apparently all lessons in the nature of morality are in future to be taken. But it is certain that they cannot do it for advanced peoples whose members have learnt to think for themselves and to entertain among themselves a wide variety of opinions. They cannot do it unless they accept the calamitous view that the ethical opinion of the majority is always right. We are left therefore once more with the conclusion that, even within a particular social group, anybody's moral opinion is as good as anybody else's, and that every man is entitled to be judged by his own standards.

Finally, not only is ethical relativity disastrous in its consequences for moral theory. It cannot be doubted that it must tend to be equally disastrous in its impact upon practical conduct. If men come really to believe that one moral standard is as good as another, they will conclude that their own moral standard has nothing special to recommend it. They might as well then slip down to some lower and easier standard. It is true that, for a time, it may be possible to hold one view in theory and to act practically upon another. But ideas, even philo-sophical ideas, are not so ineffectual that they can remain for ever idle in the upper chambers of the intellect. In the end they seep down to the level of practice. They get themselves acted on.

Speaking of the supposedly dangerous character of ethical relativity Wes-termarck says "Ethical subjectivism instead of being a danger is more likely to be an advantage to morality. Could it be brought home to people that there is no absolute standard in morality, they would perhaps be on the one hand more tolerant, and on the other hand more critical in their judgments." [1] Certainly, if we believe that any one moral standard is as good as any other, we *are* likely to be more tolerant. We shall tolerate widow-burning, human sacrifice, cannibal-ism, slavery, the infliction of physical torture, or any other of the thousand and one abominations which are, or have been, from time to time approved by one moral code or another. But this is not the kind of toleration that we want, and I do not think its cultivation will prove "an advantage to morality."

These, then, are the main arguments which the anti-relativist will urge against ethical relativity. And perhaps finally he will attempt a diagnosis of the social, intellectual, and psychological conditions of our time to which the emergence of ethical relativism is to be attributed. His diagnosis will be some-what as follows.

[1] *Ethical Relativity,* page 59.

We have abandoned, perhaps with good reason, the oracles of the past. Every age, of course, does this. But in our case it seems that none of us knows any more whither to turn. We do not know what to put in the place of that which has gone. What ought we, supposedly civilized peoples, to aim at? What are to be our ideals? What is right? What is wrong? What is beautiful? What is ugly? No man knows. We drift helplessly in this direction and that. We know not where we stand nor whither we are going.

There are, of course, thousands of voices frantically shouting directions. But they shout one another down, they contradict one another, and the upshot is mere uproar. And because of this confusion there creeps upon us an insidious scepticism and despair. Since no one knows what the truth is, we will deny that there is any truth. Since no one knows what right is, we will deny that there is any right. Since no one knows what the beautiful is, we will deny that there is any beauty. Or at least we will say—what comes to the same thing—that what people (the people of any particular age, region, society)—think to be true is true *for them;* that what people think morally right is morally right *for them;* that what people think beautiful is beautiful *for them.* There is no common and objective standard in any of these matters. Since all the voices contradict one another, they must be all equally right (or equally wrong, for it makes no difference which we say). It is from the practical confusion of our time that these doctrines issue. When all the despair and defeatism of our distracted age are expressed in abstract concepts, are erected into a philosophy, it is then called relativism—ethical relativism, esthetic relativism, relativity of truth. Ethical relativity is simply defeatism in morals.

And the diagnosis will proceed. Perhaps, it will say, the current pessimism as to our future is unjustified. But there is undoubtedly a widespread feeling that our civilization is rushing downwards to the abyss. If this should be true, and if nothing should check the headlong descent, then perhaps some historian of the future will seek to disentangle the causes. The causes will, of course, be found to be multitudinous and enormously complicated. And one must not exaggerate the relative importance of any of them. But it can hardly be doubted that our future historian will include somewhere in his list the failure of the men of our generation to hold steadfastly before themselves the notion of an (even comparatively) unchanging moral idea. He will cite that feebleness of intellectual and moral grasp which has led them weakly to harbour the belief that no one moral aim is really any better than any other, that each is good and true for those who entertain it. This meant, he will surely say, that men had given up in despair the struggle to attain moral truth. Civilization lives in and through its upward struggle. Whoever despairs and gives up the struggle, whether it be an individual or a whole civilization, is already inwardly dead.

And the philosophers of our age, where have they stood? They too, as is notorious, speak with many voices. But those who preach the various relativisms have taken upon themselves a heavy load of responsibility. By formulating abstractly the defeatism of the age they have made themselves the aiders and abettors of death. They are injecting poison into the veins of civilization. Their influence upon practical affairs may indeed be small. But it counts for something. And they cannot avoid their share of the general responsibility. They have failed to do what little they could to stem the tide. They have failed to do what Plato did for the men of his own age—find a way out of at least the intellectual confusions of the time.

PAUL W. TAYLOR
Social Science and Ethical Relativism

As a participant in the American Philosophical Association (Eastern Division) symposium on "Ethical Relativity in the Light of Recent Developments in Social Science," Professor Clyde Kluckhohn published a summary of recent studies in anthropology, sociology, and psychology concerning universal elements to be found in all human cultures.[1] "For at least a generation," he says, "American anthropology (and to a considerable degree, anthropology in the world in general) concentrated its attention upon the differences between peoples, neglecting the similarities. Recently, the balance has been righted somewhat."[2] He then goes on to give an account of these similarities as they have been set forth in recent published work by psychologists and sociologists as well as by anthropologists. Throughout this discussion Professor Kluckhohn appears to believe that such universal elements or similarities among different cultures are evidence against, or somehow provide the basis for an argument against, or at least justify a qualification of, ethical relativism. (By "ethical relativism" he means, and I shall mean, the assertion that two people or groups of people may hold contradictory ethical views without either being mistaken.[3]) I want to argue that these recent findings of the social scientists do not disprove or provide evidence against ethical relativism, and that they are not even relevant to the relativism-absolutism controversy in ethics.

It has long been the opinion of moral philosophers that the facts about the

From P. W. Taylor, "Social Science and Ethical Relativism," *Journal of Philosophy,* LV, No. 1 (1958), 32–44. Reprinted by permission of the editors of The Journal of Philosophy.

[1] Clyde Kluckhohn, "Ethical Relativity: Sic et Non," this JOURNAL, Vol. LII (Nov. 10, 1955), pp. 663–677.

[2] *Ibid.,* p. 664.

[3] If "holding contradictory ethical views" is interpreted as "disagreement in attitude" and not as a contradiction in the usual sense, then relativism is the view that there are no better reasons for taking one attitude rather than another, while absolutism is the view that such reasons can be given.

differences among the ethical judgments of different societies do not give support to ethical relativism. A person who denies relativism and claims that moral standards validly apply to all men everywhere and in every age may accept the scientific evidence of the contradictions among moral opinions of different cultures. He simply says some opinions are true (i.e., good reasons can be given for them) and some opinions are false (i.e., good reasons can be given against them). He might not know which are true and which are false. It might be *empirically* impossible for him at the time to give good reasons for or against certain opinions. But he believes that at least it makes sense to say that some are true and others are false, which is precisely what the ethical relativist denies. The ethical relativist claims it is *logically* impossible to give good reasons (reasons which are not culture-bound) for or against moral judgments.

Now just as the facts of cultural differences do not argue for ethical relativism, so the facts of cultural similarities do not argue against ethical relativism. Let us first examine the principle behind this statement and then consider the particular facts of cultural similarities pointed out by Professor Kluckhohn and see why they do not affect the argument for or against ethical relativism. Suppose that there were no differences in the ethical views of different societies. Indeed we can imagine without very much difficulty that a totalitarian power has conquered the world and has subjected everyone to a particular ethical code. By means of indoctrination, propaganda, censorship, brainwashing, and other techniques, the totalitarian power has made everyone in the world come to accept identical moral views. Would this make those moral views true? Of course not. Would this universal concurrence of moral opinion have any bearing on whether any moral view was true or false? I think we must again answer in the negative. Whether a given moral opinion is true or false depends not on who believes it or how many believe it, but on whether reasons can be given to justify it. And such reasons will not include counting the number of people who believe it. One can say that it is true if *rational* people believe it. But again what makes a person rational has nothing to do with how many people he agrees with in his moral opinions. Therefore, even if there were universal concurrence of moral opinion throughout the world, the ethical relativist would not be refuted and the ethical absolutist would not be vindicated. For the relativist would simply say: What is right in such a world is right because people believe it is right, or because they approve of it. If in another world, or in some future age, people (even one person) came to believe otherwise, then that which is right now, for everyone, would become wrong for those who disagreed. And neither person or group could be said to have a more valid opinion than the other. The absolutist would say: The fact that all people now agree about what is right and wrong does not make their beliefs true. They may be correct or they may be mistaken. To decide this we must examine their beliefs to see whether good reasons can be given for or against them.

But it may still be objected that the universal concurrence of moral opinion was imagined to be artificially forced on people, and this is what makes it irrelevant to the relativism-absolutism controversy. If everyone in the world came to have the same opinion naturally, without any interference from despots or thought controllers, then the relativist's position would be invalidated. The crux of this argument lies in the meaning of the word "naturally." If this means spontaneously and emotionally, without the discipline of rational thought, then relativism remains untouched. But if "naturally" means by the free exercise of reason and intelligence, then relativism would indeed be invalidated, but it would not be invalidated just because everyone agreed about morals.

If people came to agree about moral matters spontaneously and emotionally, the relativist would point out that a person's emotional life is conditioned in part by his social environment, and therefore whatever ethical opinions he arrived at through the spontaneous expression and development of his emotions would be relative to his social conditioning. And the fact that everyone had similar emotional reactions in ethical matters would merely imply that they had been subjected to similar environmental conditioning (though a conditioning which had not been deliberately controlled by human agents). Furthermore he would infer that *if* people had been subjected to *other* conditioning their moral opinions would be just as valid as the opinions of those who all agree under the same conditioning.

If, on the other hand, we accept the second meaning of "naturally," then relativism would be disproved and absolutism proved. For in this case rational beings would come to agree about what is right and wrong, and their opinions would be morally justifiable. But what would justify them is not their agreement but their rationality. (Being rational *means* being able to justify, to give good reasons for, one's opinions.) Even if rational beings did not agree, ethical relativism would not by that fact be shown to be true. For this would be a case of honest disagreement among enlightened and competent judges, whose disagreement must leave the correct moral judgment in doubt until further enlightenment brings about agreement. Ethical relativism would be proven only if two or more completely rational and enlightened judges disagreed. We cannot be sure that such a hypothetical eventuality would not happen, of course, and this is one of the reasons why we cannot be sure that ethical relativism is a mistaken view. But whether relativism or absolutism be true, it is sufficient for our argument that this question is not settled by pointing out either that everyone agrees or that no one agrees in their ethical judgments.

Let us now turn to Professor Kluckhohn's exposition of the specific findings of social scientists concerning the similarities among different societies, and let us see if anything can be inferred from them as to whether ethical relativism or ethical absolutism is true. Although Professor Kluckhohn does not classify the findings he discusses, I think they can be arranged into five major groups, according to the kind of factor whose universality is asserted: (1) the universality of morality in general, (2) the universality of certain human needs, (3) the universality of certain human capacities, (4) the universality of "basic field conditions," of social structures and psychological functions, and (5) the universality of certain sentiments, emotions, and attitudes.

(1) Professor Kluckhohn refers to "the universality of moral standards in

general," [4] and to the fact that even very different types of society "affirm the same moral value: allegiance to the norms of one's culture." [5] Examples given for universal moral standards in general are: a concept of murder as distinguished from "justifiable homicides," regulations upon sexual behavior, prohibitions upon untruth, and mutual obligations between parents and children. Variation occurs, however, "as to details of prescribed behavior, instrumentalities, and sanctions." [6] And at one point Professor Kluckhohn declares: "To be sure, there must be room left for relativity as regards specific moral rules." [7]

Now let us grant that in every culture there is a set of moral principles or rules of conduct to which the members of the society owe allegiance. If these principles or rules differ on such matters as what types of homicide are justified and what are to be considered murder, what types of sexual behavior are permissible, what circumstances exempt a person from the obligation to tell the truth, and what kinds of acts are obligatory with regard to one's parents or one's children, this variation will make almost all moral judgments culture-bound. What an ethical absolutist wants to know is not so much whether morality in general is good for society, but whether it is right to let a person die of neglect when he can no longer contribute to a society's economic production, whether it is right to kill unwanted infants, whether monogamy is the best sexual institution, whether a person ought to tell the truth under specified circumstances, and so on. No justification, however valid, of morality in general will be relevant to his problem. . . .

•   •   •   •   •

(2) After presenting certain recent findings in psychology, Professor Kluckhohn concludes that there is a "growing trend toward agreement" that "there are pan-human universals as regards needs and capacities that shape, or could rightly shape, at least the broad outlines of a morality that transcends cultural difference." [8] I wish to distinguish "needs" and "capacities," so I shall discuss only the former at this point. No doubt it is the case that human beings have certain fundamental needs which are present no matter what kind of society exists. But two ethical questions must be asked with reference to these needs: (1) Why ought these needs to be satisfied? (2) If some needs are not inborn (unlearned) and depend for their emergence and development on a certain type of physical and social environment, it is then at least theoretically within human capacity to control their emergence and development, and one must ask, What needs ought to be allowed to emerge and develop? Neither of these questions can be answered by indicating the universality of a certain number of needs in all existing cultures. One might say that at least the needs for survival of the individual ought to be satisfied. But this is to assume that

[4] Kluckhohn, loc. cit., p. 671.
[5] Ibid., p. 673.
[6] Ibid., p. 672.
[7] Ibid., p. 673.
[8] Ibid., p. 666.

survival is desirable, and there is not universal agreement on this, as the existence of people who want to commit suicide testifies. The relativist claims that no arguments can be given to show that committing suicide is wrong (or right), while the absolutist says there are such arguments. But their dispute clearly will not be resolved by pointing out universal or near-universal needs for the preservation of life, unless it is also shown why such needs ought to be fulfilled.

If reference is made to universal "drives," "motives," or "dynamic forces" among all men, the same reasoning applies, since the question to be answered is: *Ought* these drives or motives or dynamic forces to be satisfied, to be allowed to guide human behavior, whether in a pure or in a "sublimated" form? Professor Kluckhohn quotes Franz Boas: "The dynamic forces that mould social life are the same now as those that moulded life thousands of years ago." [9] But this common element cannot provide a basis for ethical absolutism unless reasons are given which justify the channeling of these dynamic forces in particular ways, rather than trying to repress, frustrate, or block them to whatever degree man is capable.

(3) The appeal to universal human capacities or potentialities in support of ethical absolutism is certainly not new with Professor Kluckhohn. It is becoming a very widespread idea among contemporary social scientists and psychologists who are interested in ethics. Perhaps the most prominent example is Erich Fromm, who in *Man for Himself* interprets human existence as "the unfolding of the specific powers of an organism." [10] He goes on to say that "all organisms have an inherent tendency to actualize their specific potentialities. *The aim of man's life,* therefore, is to be understood as *the unfolding of his powers according to the laws of his nature.*" [11] At another point he states, "There is no meaning to life except the meaning man gives his life by the unfolding of his powers, by living productively." [12] Now it has often been said that man is potentially anything he can become. He has the potentiality for sainthood or sadism, for benevolence or bigotry. The ethical question, of course, is concerned with *which* potentialities ought to be actualized. Fromm's answer to this is that those potentialities ought to be actualized which are peculiarly human. [13] But certainly there are many ways of behaving, thinking, and feeling which only man is capable of, yet which no psychologist or social scientist would want to judge as morally right. Fromm himself recognizes this difficulty and tries to get around it by making a distinction between "primary" and "secondary" potentialities. The former are actualized if "proper" or "normal" conditions are present, the latter are actualized under "abnormal, pathogenic" conditions which are "in contrast to existential needs." [14] It is clear that this distinction assumes

---

[9] *Ibid.*, p. 669.
[10] Erich Fromm, *Man for Himself* (New York, 1947), p. 19.
[11] *Ibid.*, p. 20. Italics are Fromm's.
[12] *Ibid.*, p. 45.
[13] *Ibid.*, p. 45.
[14] *Ibid.*, p. 218.

the moral criterion which, according to Fromm, the "science of man" is supposed to provide. Suppose someone wishes to actualize his "secondary" potentialities. To claim he is making a mistake or is doing what is morally wrong requires a justification on grounds other than the pointing out of other potentialities the person is capable of realizing, and other than asserting that his life is "abnormal" or "pathogenic." And clearly the fact that certain potentialities are common to all men, in all cultures, is not a good reason for the ethical judgment that they are the potentialities which ought to be actualized. For this is simply to say that a person or ght to do what other people can do, given the environmental conditions of their cultures. This rule is ambiguous, since part of man's potentiality is the ability to change his culture and this rule gives no guidance as to the morally proper or obligatory direction of change. Enough has been said, I think, to show that no reasonable or intelligent person would accept such a rule, and that the relativist and absolutist positions regarding moral standards are not affected by citing universal potentialities in man.

(4) The fourth category of universal elements which Professor Kluckhohn discusses includes a rather wide variety of "formal similarities" which may be suggested by the following very incomplete list: "basic field conditions" such as society, culture, and symbolic interaction (p. 666); "the experience of intimate association with the 'primary group' upon whom [the individual] was emotionally and otherwise dependent" (p. 667); having two parents of opposite sex and facing the emotional problems of being in competition with one's siblings (p. 668); possessing basically similar neurological mechanisms for dealing with problems (p. 668); the existence of music, graphic arts, dancing, parallels in linguistic structure, standards of personal excellence, kinship terminology, and age grading (p. 670); such "cultural constants" as family, religion, war, and communication (p. 670); "the notion of integration of individual to the group" (p. 671); and "the fundamental idea of reciprocity" (p. 671). These relationships, social structures, psychological functions, environmental conditions, etc., which are common to all human societies are no more relevant to the issue between relativism and absolutism in ethics than are the previous types of universals we have considered. To give evidence that everyone competes with his siblings or that everyone grows up in intimate association with two parents of opposite sex is not to give evidence that any particular set of family relations is better than any other. Nor is it to give evidence that one can or cannot make reasonable judgments about the proper way of living with one's siblings, parents, or children. Similarly, that there are such "cultural constants" as war and religion does not imply that wars are ethically right or that religion ought to continue to be a part of human culture. Of course if one has already given reasons for adopting a set of moral rules or for seeking a set of ideals in life, and if it is then demonstrated that wars violate these rules and prevent the realization of these ideals, and that religion gives dramatic symbolization of and emotional orientation toward the rules and ideals, then one may deduce the wrongness of war and the rightness of religion. But the relativist and absolutist are disputing over the first point: whether reasons can be given for adopting a set

of moral rules or for seeking certain ideals in life, and whether, if such reasons can be found, those reasons are not entirely culture-bound. And this dispute cannot be resolved by pointing out cultural universals of the sort mentioned above.

(5) The last group of universals are sentiments, emotions, and attitudes common to all human beings in all societies. Professor Kluckhohn speaks of the "universal sentiments" of "love, jealousy, respect, need for respect, and the like." Even if we expand this to include a wide range of emotions and attitudes, which I think Professor Kluckhohn and many other social scientists would be willing to do, the relativism-absolutism controversy is not logically involved. For the ethical issues concern such questions as, Whom ought we to love, and in what way? Under what circumstances, if any, is it proper or permissible to feel jealousy? Why should a person respect others? To acknowledge the universality of love, jealousy, and respect has nothing to do with answering these questions. It may be thought, however, that under the "emotive" theory of ethics, according to which ethical terms are expressive of attitudes (liking, disliking, approval, disapproval, etc.), these facts about the universality of certain attitudes would become relevant. But I do not think this is so, since the beliefs about which the relativist and absolutist disagree are concerned with what ought to be the objects of positive attitudes and what ought to be the objects of negative attitudes, as well as with what reasons, if any, can be cited to justify the taking of one attitude rather than another about a given object. It may be the case that in all human societies people have the experience of approving and disapproving of different things, but if they do not agree on what to approve of and what to disapprove of, the mere fact that they all have the experience of approving and disapproving is of no consequence for the truth or falsity, verifiability or unverifiability, reasonableness or unreasonableness, of moral utterances.

●　●　●　●　●

. . . What social scientists and psychologists can do in the attempt to work out a rationally justifiable decision or judgment concerning rules of conduct, objectives worth striving for, etc., is (1) to give us facts to help us to predict with greater probability the consequences of adopting various rules or objectives; (2) to widen our horizon of knowledge so that we can envisage alternatives we might not have thought of before; (3) to show us the origin of our attitudes and customs, their causes and effects in social history and in the individual psyche, so that we may understand how they influence our present judgments and how they might be changed; and (4) in general to make us well informed about all empirical knowledge that bears on the situation of choice or judgment. Now the pointing out of universal elements in all cultures will be relevant only so far as the knowledge of such universals contributes to these four tasks. But there would be nothing special about the fact that pan-human universals rather than peculiarities of societies were being pointed out. They would simply comprise further facts which, in the forming of a rational decision or judgment, would be helpful in varying degrees according to the situation.

CARL WELLMAN

The Ethical Implications of Cultural Relativity

It is often thought that the discoveries of anthropology have revolutionary implications for ethics. Readers of Sumner, Benedict, and Herskovits are apt to come away with the impression that the only moral obligation is to conform to one's society, that polygamy is as good as monogamy, or that no ethical judgment can be rationally justified. While these anthropologists might complain that they are being misinterpreted, they would not deny that their real intent is to challenge the traditional view of morals. Even the anthropologist whose scientific training has made him skeptical of sweeping generalities and wary of philosophical entanglements is inclined to believe that the scientific study of cultures has undermined the belief in ethical absolutes of any kind.

Just what has been discovered that forces us to revise our ethics? Science has shown that certain things that were once thought to be absolute are actually relative to culture. Something is relative to culture when it varies with and is causally determined by culture. Clearly, nothing can be both relative to culture and absolute, for to be absolute is to be fixed and invariable, independent of man and the same for all men.

Exactly which things are relative and in what degree is a question still being debated by cultural anthropologists. Important as this question is, I do not propose to discuss it. It is the empirical scientist who must tell us which things vary from culture to culture and to what extent each is causally determined by its culture. It is not for me to question the findings of the anthropologists in this area. Instead, let me turn to the philosophical problem of the implications of cultural relativity. Assuming for the moment that cultural relativity is a fact, what follows for ethics?

What follows depends in part upon just what turns out to be relative. Anthropologists are apt to use the word 'values' to refer indiscriminately to the things which have value, the characteristics which give these things their value, the attitudes of the persons who value these things, and the judgments of those people that these things have value. Similarly, one finds it hard to be sure whether 'morals' refers to the mores of a people, the set of principles an observer might formulate after observing their conduct, the practical beliefs the people themselves entertain, or the way they feel about certain kinds of conduct. Until such ambiguities are cleared up, one hardly knows what is being asserted when it is claimed that 'values' or 'morals' are relative.

From Carl Wellman, "The Ethical Implications of Cultural Relativity," *Journal of Philosophy*, LX, No. 7 (1963), 169–184. Reprinted by permission of the author and the editors of The Journal of Philosophy.

It seems to me there are at least ten quite different things of interest to the ethicist that the anthropologist might discover to be relative to culture: mores, social institutions, human nature, acts, goals, value experiences, moral emotions, moral concepts, moral judgments, and moral reasoning. Since I can hardly discuss all the ethical conclusions that various writers have tried to draw from these different facts of cultural relativity, what I propose to do is to examine critically the reasoning by which one ethical conclusion might be derived from each of them.

I

It has long been recognized that mores are relative to culture. Mores are those customs which are enforced by social pressure. They are established patterns of action to which the individual is expected to conform and from which he deviates only at the risk of disapproval and punishment. It seems clear that mores vary from society to society and that the mores of any given society depend upon its culture. What does this imply for ethics?

The conclusion most frequently drawn is that what is right in one society may be wrong in another. For example, although it would be wrong for one of us to kill his aged parents, this very act is right for an Eskimo. This is because our mores are different from those of Eskimo society, and it is the mores that make an act right or wrong.

Let us grant, for the sake of discussion, that different societies do have different mores. Why should we grant that the mores make an act right or wrong? It has been claimed that this is true by definition. 'Right' simply means according to the mores, and 'wrong' means in violation of the mores. There is something to be said for this analysis of our concepts of right and wrong. It seems to explain both the imperativeness and the impersonality of obligation. The 'ought' seems to tell one what to do and yet to be more than the command of any individual; perhaps its bindingness lies in the demands of society. Attractive as this interpretation appears at first glance, I cannot accept it. It can be shown that no naturalistic analysis of the meaning of ethical words is adequate. In addition, this particular analysis is objectionable in that it makes it self-contradictory to say that any customary way of acting is wrong. No doubt social reformers are often confused, but they are not always inconsistent.

If the view that the mores make an act right or wrong is not true by definition, it amounts to the moral principle that one ought always to conform to the mores of his society. None of the ways in which this principle is usually supported is adequate. (a) Any society unconsciously develops those mores which are conducive to survival and well-being under its special circumstances. Each individual ought to obey the mores of his society because this is the best way to promote the good life for the members of that society. I admit that there is a tendency for any society to develop those mores which fit its special circumstances, but I doubt that this is more than a tendency. There is room for reform in most societies, and this is particularly true when conditions are changing for one reason or another. (*b*) One ought to obey the mores of his society because disobedience would tend to destroy those mores. Without mores any society would lapse into a state of anarchy that would be intolerable for its members. It seems to me that this argument deserves to be taken seriously, but it does not prove that one ought always to obey the mores of his society. What it does show is that one ought generally to obey the mores of his society and that whenever he considers disobedience he should give due weight to the effects of his example upon social stability. (*c*) One ought to obey the mores of his society because disobedience tends to undermine their existence. It is important to preserve the mores, not simply to avoid anarchy, but because it is their mores which give shape and meaning to the life of any people. I grant that the individual does tend to think of his life in terms of the mores of his group and that anything which disrupts those mores tends to rob his life of significance. But once again, all this shows is that one should conform to the mores of his society on the whole. Although there is some obligation to conformity, this is not the only nor the most important obligation on the member of any society.

Therefore, it does not seem to me that one can properly say that the mores make an act right or wrong. One cannot define the meaning of these ethical words in terms of the mores, nor can one maintain the ethical principle that one ought always to obey the mores of his society. If the mores do not make acts right or wrong, the fact that different societies have different mores does not imply that the same kind of act can be right in one society and wrong in another.

II

Cultural relativity seems to apply to institutions as well as to mores. A social institution is a type of organization; it involves a pattern of activity in which two or more people play recognized roles. The family, the church, the government, the liberal arts college, the bridge club are all social institutions. Institutions can be classified more or less specifically. Thus monogamy, polygamy, and polyandry are specific institutions which fall under the generic institution of the family. Since the specific form an institution takes seems to vary from society to society depending upon the culture of that society, let us grant that social institutions are relative to culture. What does this imply for ethics?

A conclusion that is sometimes drawn is that we should never try to adopt an institution from another society or seek to impose one of our institutions upon another people. The main argument for this view is that each institution is an expression of the total culture of which it is a part. To try to take an institution out of its cultural environment is sure to maim or even kill it; to try to bring an institution into an alien culture is likely to disorganize and even destroy that cultural pattern. Thus the attempt to transport an institution from one society to another will fail to achieve its intended result and will produce many unintended and socially undesirable effects.

No doubt the attempt to import or export a social institution is often a dismal failure. The transported institution becomes a mere caricature of its former self, and the society into which it is introduced becomes demoralized or even destroyed. Extreme caution is certainly necessary. But is it not incautious to conclude that the attempt will always fail? The most glaring examples of cultural demoralization and destruction, such as the intervention of the white man in Africa, have involved much more than the imposition of one or two institutions. Moreover, some institutions may be less alien to a given culture than others. If so, there might be some institutions that the society could adopt with only minor modifications. In fact, societies seem to have been borrowing from one another for centuries. While the effects of this borrowing have often been bad, they have not always been totally destructive or even grossly demoralizing. Occasionally they may have been beneficial. It seems unnecessary to conclude that we should never import or export an institution from the fact that social institutions are culturally relative.

III

Another thing which may be relative to culture is human nature. As soon as one ponders the differences between the Chinese aristocrat and the Australian bushman, the American tycoon and the Indian yogi, one finds it hard to believe that there is anything basic to human nature which is shared by all men. And reflection upon the profound effects of enculturation easily leads one to the conclusion that what a man is depends upon the society in which he has been brought up. Therefore, let us assume that human nature is culturally relative and see what this implies.

This seems to imply that no kind of action, moral character, or social institution is made inevitable by human nature. This conclusion is important because it cuts the ground out from under one popular type of justification in ethics. For example, capitalism is sometimes defended as an ideal on the grounds that this is the only economic system that is possible in the light of man's greedy and competitive nature. Or it might be claimed that adultery is permissible because the ideal of marital fidelity runs counter to man's innate drives or instincts. If there is no fixed human nature, such arguments are left without any basis.

One may wonder, however, whether the only alternatives are an entirely fixed and an entirely plastic human nature. It might be that enculturation could mold a human being but only within certain limits. These limits might exist either because certain parts of human nature are not at all plastic or because all parts are only moderately plastic. For example, it might turn out that the need for food and the tendency to grow in a certain way cannot be modified at all by enculturation, or it might turn out that every element in human nature can be modified in some ways but not in others. In either case, what a man becomes would depend partly upon enculturation and partly upon the nature of the organism being enculturated.

Thus cultural relativity may be a matter of degree. Before we can decide just what follows from the fact that human nature is relative to culture we must know how far and in what ways it is relative. If there are certain limits to the plasticity of human nature, these do rule out some kinds of action, character, or institution. But anthropology indicates that within any such limits a great many alternatives remain. Human nature may make eating inevitable, but what we eat and when we eat and how we eat is up to us. At least we can say that to the degree that human nature is relative to culture no kind of action, moral character, or social institution is made impossible by human nature.

IV

It has been claimed that acts are also relative to culture. This is to say that the same general type of action may take on specific differences when performed in different societies because those societies have different cultures. For example, it is one thing for one of us to kill his aged parent; it is quite a different thing for an Eskimo to do such an act. One difference lies in the consequences of these two acts. In our society disposing of old and useless parents merely allows one to live in greater luxury; to an Eskimo this act may mean the difference between barely adequate subsistence and malnutrition for himself and his family. What are we to make of this fact that the nature of an act is culturally relative?

One possible conclusion is that the same kind of act may be right in one society and wrong in another. This presupposes that the rightness of an act depends upon its consequences and that its consequences may vary from society to society. Since I accept these presuppositions, I agree that the rightness or wrongness of an act is relative to its social context.

It is important, however, to distinguish this conclusion from two others with which it is often confused. To say that the rightness of an act is relative to the society in which it is performed is not to say that exactly the same sort of act can be both right and wrong. It is because the social context makes the acts different in kind that one can be right while the other is wrong. Compare an act of infanticide in our society with an act of infanticide in some South Seas society. Are these two acts the same or different? They are of the same kind inasmuch as both are acts of killing an infant. On the other hand, they are different in that such an act may be necessary to preserve the balance between family size and food resources in the South Seas while this is not the case in our society. These two acts are generically similar but specifically different; that is, they belong to different species of the same genus. Therefore, the conclusion that the same kind of act may be right in one society and wrong in another does not amount to saying that two acts which are precisely the same in every respect may differ in rightness or wrongness.

Neither is this conclusion to be confused with the view that acts are made right or wrong by the mores of society. No doubt our society disapproves of infanticide and some South Seas societies approve of it, but it is not *this* which makes infanticide wrong for us and right for them. If infanticide is wrong for us and right for them, it is because acts of infanticide have very different consequences in our society and in theirs, not because the practice is discouraged here and customary there.

The goals that individuals or groups aim for also seem relative to culture. What objects people select as goals varies from society to society depending upon the cultures of those societies. One group may strive for social prestige and the accumulation of great wealth, another may aim at easy comfort and the avoidance of any danger, a third may seek military glory and the conquest of other peoples. What follows from this fact of cultural relativity?

This fact is often taken as a basis for arguing that it is impossible to compare the value of acts, institutions, or total ways of life belonging to different societies. The argument rests on the assumptions that acts, institutions, and ways of life are means directed at certain ends, that means can be evaluated only in terms of their ends, and that ends are incommensurable with respect to value.

Granted these assumptions, the argument seems a good one, but I doubt that ends are really incommensurable. It seems to me that we can recognize that certain ends are more worth while than others, for example that pleasure is intrinsically better than pain. I may be mistaken, but until this has been shown, the conclusion that it is impossible to compare the value of acts, institutions, or ways of life belonging to different societies has not been established.

People from different societies apparently experience the same object or situation in quite different ways depending upon the cultural differences between their societies. The satisfying experience that a cultured Chinese might derive from eating bird's nest soup would be diametrically opposed to the experience I would undergo if I forced myself to gulp down my helping of that exotic dish out of politeness. Again, an experience which I would greatly value, sitting in the bleachers watching the Red Sox clinch the pennant, would be nothing but a boring observation of meaningless motions accompanied by the sensations of scorching sun, trickling sweat, and unyielding benches to a Hottentot visitor. In large measure the nature of any experience is determined by the process of enculturation that the experiencer has undergone. Thus, value experiences are also relative to culture.

It might seem to follow that the same experience could be good to one person and bad to another, but this is just what does *not* follow. The difference in value stems from the fact that, although confronted with similar objects or situations, the two people have very different experiences. The nature of a person's experience depends upon the kind of person he has become through the process of enculturation as much as upon the external stimulus. It would be a mistake to conclude that qualitatively identical experiences are good to me and bad to the Hottentot. Although he and I are in the same ballpark watching the same game, we are having very different experiences.

What one should conclude is that the same kind of object or situation can have different values to people from different societies. This follows from the fact that the nature of a person's experience depends in large measure upon the way in which he has been enculturated, together with the assumption that the value of any object or situation depends upon its effects on experience. Since my ethical view is that the value of objects and situations is derived from their impact upon experience, I accept the conclusion that the same kind of object or situation can have very different values to people who come from different cultures.

VII

It appears that moral emotions are also relative to culture. What a person desires, approves, or feels guilty about seems to vary from society to society depending upon the cultural differences between those societies. What does the fact that moral emotions are culturally relative imply for ethics?

One possible conclusion would be that the same kind of act or person can be morally good in one society and morally bad in another. This is supposed to follow from the fact that the same kind of act or person can be approved in one society and disapproved in another together with the view that to be morally good or bad is simply to be approved or disapproved.

That infanticide is approved in certain South Seas societies and disapproved in ours need not be doubted. That infanticide constitutes exactly the same kind of act in the two societies is, as we have seen, more dubious. But even if it did, I would not accept the conclusion in question; for I would not admit that the moral value of any act or person depends upon whether it is approved or disapproved. That the grounds for moral evaluation lie outside the moral emotions can be seen by the fact that it always makes sense to ask someone *why* he approves or disapproves of something. If approving or disapproving made its object morally good or bad, there would be no need of such justification. Thus, the fact that moral emotions are culturally relative does not prove that identical acts or persons can be morally good in one society and morally bad in another.

VIII

Both linguistic and psychological studies have suggested that people living in different societies conceptualize their experience in different ways. Probably moral concepts vary from society to society depending upon the cultural backgrounds from which they arise. The ancient Greek thought of virtue quite differently from the modern American; the Christian conception of obligation is probably absent from the mind of the African who has escaped the influence of any missionary. What are we to conclude from the fact that moral concepts are relative to culture?

The obvious implication appears to be that people of different cultural backgrounds are almost sure to disagree on any ethical question. Obvious as it may seem, this is not implied at all. In fact, people using different concepts could never disagree, for disagreement presupposes that both parties are thinking in the same terms. For one thing, on what question are they supposed to be disagreeing? If each person is using his own set of concepts, each person formulates his own question in his own terms. And if the two persons do not have any common set of ethical concepts, there is no way for formulating a single question that will be intelligible to both of them. Again, in what sense do their respective answers disagree? When an American says that Poland is undemocratic and a Russian insists that it is a fine example of democracy, it appears that they are disagreeing. No doubt they do disagree in many ways, but not in their utterances. Their statements are quite compatible, for they are using the word 'democracy' in different senses. Similarly, people of different cultures would only seem to disagree, if they attached different concepts to their ethical words.

The proper conclusion to draw is that any comparison between the ethical views of the members of different cultures can be only partial. As long as each view is stated only in its own terms there can be no comparison between them; comparison becomes possible only when they are stated in the same set of concepts. But if the sets of concepts are not identical, any translation of one view into the language of the other or of both into some neutral language will be approximate at best. Even where something approaching adequate translation is possible, some of the meaning will be lost or something will be added that was not in the original concept. For this reason, any claim that the ethical views of people in different societies are either identical or contradictory is likely to tell only part of the story. To some extent, at least, the ethics of different cultures are incommensurate.

IX

The aspect of cultural relativity most often emphasized is that pertaining to moral judgments. Objects that the members of one society think to be good are considered bad by another group; acts considered wrong in one society are thought of as right in another. Moreover, these differences in judgments of value and obligation seem to reflect cultural differences between the respective societies. There is a great deal of evidence to suggest that ethical judgments are relative to culture.

To many anthropologists and philosophers it is a corollary of this fact that one of a set of contrary ethical judgments is no more valid than another, or, put positively, that all ethical judgments are equally valid. Unfortunately, there is a crucial ambiguity lurking in this epistemological thicket. Ethical judgments might have equal validity either because all are valid or because none are: similarly one ethical judgment might be no more valid than another either because both are equally valid or because both are equally lacking in validity.

Since these two interpretations are quite different, let us consider them separately.

On the first interpretation, the conclusion to be drawn from the fact that ethical judgments are relative to culture is that every moral judgment is valid for the society in which it is made. Instead of denying the objective validity of ethical judgments, this view affirms it, but in a qualified form which will allow for the variations in ethical belief.

There seem to be three main ways of defending this position. (a) Ethical judgments have objective validity because it is possible to justify them rationally. However, this validity is limited to a given society because the premises used in such justification are those which are agreed upon in that society. Since there are no universally accepted premises, no universal validity is possible. I would wish to deny that justification is real if it is limited in this way. If all our reasoning really does rest on certain premises which can be rejected by others without error, then we must give up the claim to objective validity. When I claim validity for ethical judgments, I intend to claim more than that it is possible to support them with logical arguments; I also claim that it is incorrect to deny the premises of such arguments. (b) Any ethical judgment is an expression of a total pattern of culture. Hence it is possible to justify any single judgment in terms of its coherence with the total cultural configuration of the judger. But one cannot justify the culture as a whole, for it is not part of a more inclusive pattern. Therefore, ethical judgments have objective validity, but only in terms of a given cultural pattern. I would make the same objection to this view as to the preceding one. Since it allows justification to rest upon an arbitrary foundation, it is inadequate to support any significant claim to objective validity. (c) Any ethical judgment has objective validity because it is an expression of a moral code. The validity of a moral code rests on the fact that without conformity to a common code social cohesion breaks down, leading to disastrous results. Since any given moral code provides cohesion for one and only one society, each ethical judgment has validity for a single society. There are at least two difficulties with this defense of objectivity. Surely one could deny some ethical judgments without destroying the entire moral code they reflect; not every judgment could be shown to be essential to social stability. Moreover, the argument seems to rest on the ethical judgment that one ought not to contribute to the breakdown of social stability. How is this judgment to be shown to be valid? One must either appeal to some other basis of validity or argue in a circle. None of these arguments to show that every moral judgment is valid for the society in which it is made is adequate.

On the second interpretation, the conclusion to be drawn from the fact that moral judgments are relative to culture is that moral judgments have no objective validity. This amounts to saying that the distinction between true and false, correct and incorrect, does not apply to such judgments. This conclusion obviously does not follow simply from the fact that people disagree about ethical questions. We do not deny the objective validity of scientific judgments either on the grounds that different scientists propose alternative theories or on the grounds that the members of some societies hold fast to many unscientific beliefs.

Why, then, does the fact that moral judgments are relative to culture imply that they have no objective validity? (*a*) Individuals make different ethical judgments because they judge in terms of different frames of reference, and they adopt these frames of reference uncritically from their cultures. Since ethical judgments are the product of enculturation rather than reasoning, they cannot claim rational justification. I do not find this argument convincing, for it seems to confuse the origin of a judgment with its justification. The causes of a judgment are one thing; the reasons for or against it are another. It remains to be shown that any information about what causes us to judge as we do has any bearing on the question of whether or not our judgments are correct. (*b*) It is impossible to settle ethical questions by using the scientific method. Therefore, there is no objective way to show that one ethical judgment is any more correct than another, and, in the absence of any method of establishing the claim to objective validity, it makes no sense to continue to make the claim. I will concede that, if there is no rational method of establishing ethical judgments, then we might as well give up the claim to objective validity. And if the scientific method is restricted to the testing of hypotheses by checking the predictions they imply against the results of observation and experiment, it does seem to be inapplicable to ethical questions. What I will not concede is the tacit assumption that the scientific method is the only method of establishing the truth. Observation and experimentation do not figure prominently in the method used by mathematicians. I even wonder whether the person who concludes that ethical judgments have no objective validity can establish *this* conclusion by using the scientific method. The fact that ethical judgments cannot be established scientifically does not by itself prove that they cannot be established by any method of reasoning. (*c*) There might be some method of settling ethical disputes, but it could not be a method of reasoning. Any possible reasoning would have to rest upon certain premises. Since the members of different societies start from different premises, there is no basis for argument that does not beg the question. I suspect, however, that we have been looking for our premises in the wrong place. The model of deduction tempts us to search for very general premises from which all our more specific judgments can be deduced. Unfortunately, it is just in this area of universal moral principles that disagreement seems most frequent and irremedial. But suppose that these ethical generalizations are themselves inductions based upon particular moral judgments. Then we could argue for or against them in terms of relatively specific ethical judgments and the factual judgments that are in turn relevant to these. Until this possibility is explored further, we need not admit that there is no adequate basis for ethical reasoning. Thus it appears that none of these refutations of the objective validity of ethical judgments is really conclusive.

The fact that ethical judgments are relative to culture is often taken to prove that no ethical judgment can claim to be any more valid than any of its contraries. I have tried to show that, on neither of the two possible interpretations of this conclusion, does the conclusion necessarily follow from the fact of cultural relativity.

X

Finally, moral reasoning might turn out to be relative to culture. When some ethical statement is denied or even questioned, the person who made the statement is apt to leap to its defense. He attempts to justify his statement by producing reasons to support it. But speakers from different societies tend to justify their statements in different ways. The difference in their reasoning may be of two kinds. Either their reasoning may rest on different assumptions or they may draw inferences in a different manner. That is, the arguments they advance may either start from different premises or obey different logics. We can ignore the former case here; for it boils down to a difference in their judgments, and we have discussed that at length in the preceding section. Instead let us assume that people who belong to different societies tend to draw their moral conclusions according to different logics depending upon their respective cultures. What difference would it make if moral reasoning were thus culturally relative?

The most interesting conclusion that might be drawn from the fact that moral reasoning is relative to culture is that it has no objective validity. The claim to objective validity is empty where it cannot be substantiated. But how could one justify the claim that any given kind of moral reasoning is valid? To appeal to the same kind of reasoning would be circular. To appeal to some other kind of reasoning would not be sufficient to justify this kind; for each kind of reasoning involves principles of inference which go beyond, and therefore cannot be justified by appealing to, any other kind.

I find this line of argument inconclusive for several reasons. First, it is not clear that a given kind of reasoning cannot be justified by appealing to a different kind of reasoning. In fact, this seems to be a fairly common practice in logic. Various forms of syllogistic argument can be shown to be valid by reducing them to arguments of the form Barbara. Again, a logician will sometimes justify certain rules for natural deduction by an involved logical argument which does not itself use these same rules. Second, in what sense is it impossible to show another person that my moral arguments are valid? I can show him that the various moral arguments I advance conform to the principles of my logic. If he does not accept these principles, he will remain unconvinced. This may show that I cannot persuade him that my arguments are valid, but does it show that I have not proved that they are? It is not obvious that persuading a person and proving a point are identical. Third, is the claim to objective validity always empty in the absence of any justification for it? Perhaps some reasoning is ultimate in that it requires no further justification. To assume the opposite seems to lead to an infinite regress. If every valid justification stands in need of further justification, no amount of justification would ever be sufficient.

I do not claim to have established the objective validity of moral reasoning. I am not even sure how that validity might be established or even whether it needs to be established. All I have been trying to do is to suggest that such validity is not ruled out by the fact, if it is a fact, that moral reasoning is relative to culture.

• • • • •

No doubt the reader will wish to challenge my acceptance or rejection of this or that particular conclusion. Quite apart from such specific ethical questions, however, there are certain over-all logical conclusions which seem to me inevitable. (1) What conclusions one can legitimately draw from the facts of cultural relativity will depend upon *which* facts one starts from. It is worth distinguishing between the relativity of mores, social institutions, human nature, acts, goals, value experiences, moral emotions, moral concepts, moral judgments, and moral reasoning; for each of these has different implications for ethics. (2) By themselves the facts of cultural relativity do not imply anything for ethics. Any argument that is both interesting and valid requires additional premises. Thus it is only in conjunction with certain statements that go beyond anthropology that the findings of anthropology have any bearing at all on ethics. (3) What conclusions one should draw will obviously depend upon which of these additional premises one accepts. Therefore, one's ethical and epistemological theory will determine the significance one will attach to cultural relativity. (4) Before we can criticize or even understand the arguments by which ethical conclusions are derived from the facts of such relativity, we must make these additional premises explicit and see what can be said for or against them. My main purpose in this paper has been to make a start in this complicated yet crucial task.

Supplementary Paperback Reading

K. Baier, *The Moral Point of View*, abridged ed., Ch. 6. (Random House)
R. Benedict, *Patterns of Culture*. (Mentor)
A. Duncan-Jones, *Butler's Moral Philosophy*, Ch. 3. (Penguin Books)
A. Edel, *Ethical Judgment*, Ch. I, III, VII, and VIII. (Free Press)
M. Schlick, *Problems of Ethics*, Ch. V. (Dover Publications)
R. Taylor, *Good and Evil*, Ch. 1–3, 9–11 (Macmillan)
E. Westermarck, *Ethical Relativity*. (Littlefield, Adams and Co.)

3

PSYCHOLOGICAL

EGOISM

AND ETHICAL

EGOISM

Introduction

Among the normative ethical systems advanced by philosophers as valid for all mankind (ethical absolutism), there is one that must be examined at the beginning. It is claimed that this ethical system alone is consistent with human psychology and that therefore no other system can accomplish the task of guiding human conduct, which is the purpose any normative ethical system is designed to serve. This system is called "ethical egoism," and the psychological principle (with which it claims to be alone consistent) is called "psychological egoism." In order to assess the strength of this claim it is important to keep clear in our minds the differences between psychological and ethical egoism.

THE DISTINCTION BETWEEN PSYCHOLOGICAL EGOISM
AND ETHICAL EGOISM

Psychological egoism is a factual theory about human motivation and behavior; it is an explanation of why men act the way they do. Ethical egoism is a normative theory about human conduct; it sets forth a standard for determining how men *ought* to act. The psychological egoist tells us what ends all men in fact seek; the ethical egoist tells us what ends all men ought to seek.

The basic principle of psychological egoism may be stated in various ways, of which the following are typical:

(1) Every person acts always so as to promote his own self-interest.

(2) The sole end of every act is the agent's own good.

(3) All acts are really selfish, even if some of them appear to be unselfish.

(4) Everyone always does that which he most wants to do, or that which he least dislikes to do.

(5) Concern for one's own welfare always outweighs, in motivational strength, concern for anyone else's welfare.

Each of these statements says something slightly different from the others, but certain features are common to them all. First, they are factual claims about human beings; they make no value judgments. Second, they are universal claims about all human beings. And third, they are universal claims about all the actions (or all the motives) of every human being. Consequently, in order to falsify them it is sufficient to show that just one exception to what they state about human behavior has in fact occurred. We shall later consider what cases have been cited as exceptions, and how psychological egoists have replied to these alleged exceptions.

85

Ethical egoism is a normative theory. Its basic tenet is that self-interest is the sole valid standard of right conduct. This standard may be explained as follows. In order to know in any given case which of the alternatives open to a person's choice is the one he morally ought to do, we proceed thus. We calculate, first, the probable consequences that would result if the person were to do one alternative; next, the probable consequences that would result if he were to do a second alternative; and so on for every alternative open to him. We then ask ourselves, Which act will result in furthering the self-interest of the person to a greater extent than would result from his doing any other act? In other words, which of the alternatives will bring about more things that the person would like and fewer things that he would dislike than any other alternative would bring about? When we have answered this question, we know what the person ought to do. For we know which act is the best alternative, as judged by the standard of his self-interest.

It should be noted at this point, however, that there are three types of ethical egoism and that the foregoing account describes only one type. The three types may be called "universal ethical egoism," "individual ethical egoism," and "personal ethical egoism." Here is what differentiates them. Does the ethical egoist say, "*Every* person ought to do what will most further *his own* self-interest," or does he say, "*Every* person ought to do what will most further *my* self-interest," or does he say only, "*I* ought to do what will most further *my* self-interest"? In the first case we have universal egoism: the standard of right action is the agent's or doer's self-interest. This is the version of ethical egoism given in the preceding paragraph. For the individual ethical egoist, on the other hand, the standard of right action is not the agent's self-interest, but the self-interest of the ethical egoist himself. Thus if the population of the world consisted of four people, A, B, C, and D, then universal ethical egoism would hold that A ought to further A's self-interest, B ought to further B's, C ought to further C's, and D ought to further D's. According to individual ethical egoism, however, we would first have to know which of the four people was the individual ethical egoist before we could know what any of them ought to do. Suppose he were A. Then the theory states that A ought to further A's self-interest, B ought to further A's self-interest, and C and D likewise ought to further A's self-interest. Finally, the theory of personal ethical egoism is simply the view that the egoist alone ought to further his self-interest. It does not say anything about what other people ought to do. Thus if the personal egoist were A, then according to his theory A ought to further A's self-interest, but his theory would not tell B, C, and D what they ought or ought not to do. From now on we shall be concerned only with universal ethical egoism, since it is this form of the theory that has seriously been advocated by both ancient and modern philosophers. Its classic form is found in the ethical theory of Epicurus (a Greek philosopher of the fourth century, B.C.), according to whom the sole valid standard of right action is the avoidance of painful or unpleasant experiences to the agent. Its most important proponent in modern philosophy is Thomas Hobbes, whose views are set forth in the first reading of this chapter. (In so far as Hobbes appeals to a moral standard derived from God's commands, he is of course not to be considered an ethical egoist. It is with regard to the moral relations among men without reference to God that Hobbes may be thought of as a universal ethical egoist.)

Let us now examine the relation between psychological egoism and ethical egoism. It has been maintained by some philosophers that ethical egoism is the only normative ethical system compatible with psychological egoism, so that if the latter is true we have no choice but to accept ethical egoism. If all men always seek to promote their self-interest and can do nothing else, then it would be foolish or illogical to say that they *ought* to do something else. According to a traditional maxim of ethics, "ought" implies "can." To say that someone ought to do a certain act implies that he is able to do it. If he were unable to do it, there would be no point in telling him that he ought to do it. Now psychological egoism holds that it is impossible for anyone to do a genuinely altruistic or unselfish act. There is always the motive of self-interest behind any act that appears to be done from the desire to further the happiness or to lessen the unhappiness of another. Therefore we are never justified in telling a person that he ought to forget his own welfare and act out of concern for the welfare of others, since in fact he never will and never can do such a thing. It follows that ethical egoism is the only normative ethical system consistent with human motivation.

There are two ways in which this argument might be attacked. One is to deny the truth of the premise by rejecting psychological egoism. We shall consider below what reasons there might be for doing this. The other way is to challenge the claim that ethical egoism is the only normative system that is consistent with psychological egoism. Such a challenge might be stated as follows. The purpose of a normative ethical system is to have people do, or at least try to do, those actions that are judged by the system to be right and to have people refrain from doing those actions judged to be wrong. To accomplish this purpose the system must make known to people what it is they ought or ought not to do. Now there seems something strange in telling a person that he ought to do what he cannot help but do. If someone has no choice but to do a certain act, it is unavoidable. If it is unavoidable, why prescribe to him that he ought to do it? To say that he ought to do an act is to try to get him to do that act *rather than something else,* or at least it is to hope that he will do that act *instead of some alternative act.* But when we know he is going to do that act anyway and that he cannot choose to refrain from doing it, our "ought" statement is pointless. Now this seems to be what is happening if we accept both psychological egoism and ethical egoism. Psychological egoism tells us that everyone always acts so as to further his self-interest. There is no choice in the matter. A person simply cannot do otherwise; he *must* act from self-interest. Yet the ethical egoist prescribes that we *ought* to further our self-interest. Why say we ought to, when we already must? Why tell us that we ought to do something when we cannot avoid doing it? A further paradox now arises. If we cannot avoid doing what we ought to do, *then we are always doing what we ought.* So all of us are always good men. No one ever does, or can ever do, what is wrong. An ethical theory with such a consequence is simply absurd.

To this objection the ethical egoist can make the following reply. People may be intelligent or unintelligent in the pursuit of their self-interest. All men seek their own good, but do not always use the most effective means to realize it. This is partly due to their lack of knowledge about what the consequences of their acts will be. Thus, contrary to the conclusion drawn above, people *can* do wrong acts. These are acts that frustrate their long-range interests, or that do not promote their interests as much as some alternative act would have done if they had chosen it. But when people do wrong acts, they believe (mistakenly) that those acts will further their interests more than any alternative act. Notice that this view requires a slight change in our statement of psychological egoism. Instead of saying, "Everyone always does what will most further his self-interest," we must now say, "Everyone always does what he *thinks* will most further his self-interest." This allows for the possibility that what a person thinks will most further his self-interest may not in fact further it as much as some other act, or will not further it at all.

Another reply to the above objection to psychological and ethical egoism is this. People sometimes let themselves be swayed by immediate pleasures, or by the attractiveness of short-range goals, and so do acts which in the long run work against their own welfare and happiness. To see a doctor and undergo treatment for a chronic ailment is unpleasant and costly. We might want to avoid the inconvenience, discomfort, and expenses involved. Yet if we do not get medical treatment, our condition might become worse and eventually prove fatal. Thus our long-range self-interest sometimes requires us to face unpleasant facts, go through unpleasant experiences, and sacrifice some of our goals. (We might have been saving the thousand dollars which the treatment finally cost us for a vacation trip to Europe.) So there is an important function served by the ethical egoist's prescription. In telling us that we ought to promote our self-interest, he is advising us to withstand the temptation to enjoy immediate pleasures or to avoid immediate pains, if such discipline is necessary to achieve our more distant goals. And he is saying that, whenever we are faced with a choice between accomplishing a short-range purpose (such as going on a vacation trip) which involves the endangering of our long-range welfare or happiness, and on the other hand giving up the short-range goal in order to have a better chance to be happy in the long run, we ought to make the second choice. Thus the whole point of ethical egoism becomes clear. It is to advocate a certain ideal of moral character, which could be called "enlightened prudence." To become the kind of person we ought to be requires self-discipline and the development of inner strength of character. Many of us might fail to reach this ideal, or we might reject it as a false ideal. In either case ethical egoism does hold up a goal that we can choose to seek or not to seek. Its "ought" does imply a "can." Furthermore, we should notice that the egoist claims that this goal is the one true ideal of the moral life of man. Accordingly, ethical egoism is a form of normative ethical absolutism, since it proposes a moral norm to be valid for all mankind.

Let us now turn to some of the main arguments for and against psychological egoism and ethical egoism.

ARGUMENTS FOR AND AGAINST PSYCHOLOGICAL EGOISM

The arguments for psychological egoism are intended to point out certain facts of human life, these facts being claimed as evidence in support of the theory. The theory itself is taken to be an empirical generalization about the motives behind all human conduct. The first set of facts appealed to are simply the facts that show how selfish most people are most of the time. The second set are facts about the deceptive appearance of allegedly unselfish acts. Here the psychological egoist claims that there are always self-interested motives behind every altruistic-seeming act. Thus he tries to show that a person who gives a great deal of time, effort, and money to further a social welfare project, or who performs difficult and unpleasant tasks to alleviate human misery, or who risks his life to correct an injustice, or who even voluntarily gives up his life to avoid a disaster, is not really an unselfish person. A third set of facts given in support of psychological egoism are facts about unconscious motivation. Let us briefly look at each set of facts.

Concerning the first point—how widespread selfishness is in human life—we should notice that no *normative* ethical theory denies this. The purpose of normative ethics is to state how men ought to live, and all moral philosophers, no matter what their ethical system, have been quite aware that men do not live as they ought to. So even if it is true that most men are selfish most of the time, the facts which are cited to substantiate this claim are completely neutral between ethical egoism and those ethical theories that set up a norm other than self-interest as the supreme standard of morality. It is only if no one ever does or ever can act unselfishly that non-egoistic theories are confronted with a serious difficulty. For in that case it would be pointless to prescribe that men *ought* to be unselfish.

But is it true that *all* men are *always* selfish, that *all* the acts of *every* person are motivated by self-interest, as psychological egoism maintains? Such an absolutely universal generalization can be shown to be true only by showing that there never has been and never could be a single action with a disinterested or altruistic motive. All that is necessary to falsify this thesis once and for all is to point out one act not done to promote the agent's self-interest. This brings us to the second set of facts, since non-egoists usually cite what appear to be unselfish acts to refute the egoist's position. Here we must look carefully at what the egoist says about such cases.

First it is necessary to distinguish selfish and unselfish acts from selfish and unselfish motives. Let us define selfish and unselfish acts in terms of their foreseen consequences. When a person is about to do an act, he believes that certain consequences will result from his doing it. We shall call these foreseen consequences. Other consequences may occur which he at the time does not think will occur, and these may be called unforeseen consequences. Considering only their foreseen consequences, all acts fall into one or another of the following rough categories:

(1) They tend to promote the interests of others and involve some frustration of the agent's own interests.

(2) They tend to promote the interests of the agent and involve some frustration of the interests of others.

(3) They tend to promote the interests of both the agent and others and do not involve any frustration to anyone.

(4) They tend to frustrate the interests of both the agent and others and do not promote anyone's interests.

We may then label these various sorts of acts: (1) "unselfish"; (2) "selfish"; (3) "felicitous"; and (4) "irrational." Most psychological egoists admit that in fact there do occur acts of each of these types, but go on to say that they never meant to deny that "unselfish" acts, defined as acts of type (1), occur. People can and do choose to do acts which they foresee will bring happiness to others and will involve some unpleasantness, discomfort, or inconvenience to themselves. But, they hasten to add, all such acts are *motivated* by self-interest and hence ought not to be regarded as genuinely unselfish. Now in claiming this, the egoist wants to contrast self-interest with other kinds of motives—motives which, in his view, have been mistakenly believed sometimes to be the actual motives behind an act. So we must understand what it means to talk about these other kinds of motives (which the egoist denies ever do motivate human acts) if we are to understand what the egoist is saying about all actual human motives.

Let us then divide possible motives of human acts into the following categories, leaving open the question whether there actually occur instances of each possibility:

(a) The desire to promote the interests of the agent, combined with the willingness to frustrate others' interests only if this is foreseen as necessary to promoting the agent's interests. ("Self-interest without malice.")

(b) The desire to frustrate the interests of others as an end in itself. ("Pure malice.")

(c) The desire to promote the interests of others as a means to promoting the agent's interests. ("Self-interested use of others.")

(d) The desire to promote the interests of others as an end in itself. ("Pure benevolence or altruism.")

(e) Acting from the belief that one is under an obligation to do the act, or acting from a sense of duty, or doing an act as a matter of principle, disregarding its foreseen consequences to oneself and to others. ("Disinterestedness.")

The position of psychological egoism now under consideration may be formulated in terms of two statements: First, all acts of type (1) are motivated by motives of types (a) and (c). Second, no human acts in reality are ever motivated by motives of types (d) and (e). Suppose, then, the egoist is confronted with an act of type (1) and the person who does the act claims to be motivated by either a type (d) or type (e) motive. What will the egoist say about this? He will say that the person is either deceiving himself or deceiving others, or both. In the former case his self-deception is explained as a psychological rationalization. The person cannot admit to himself that his motive is self-interested, because this would weaken his ego-image and he cannot tolerate this. In the second case, the person is deliberately lying about something he is well aware of—namely, the results he consciously desires to bring about by doing the act. In neither case can we say that his act is genuinely unselfish or disinterested, since his self-interest lies not only behind the act itself, but also behind his rationalization (a defense mechanism of his ego) and behind his lying to others. When such explanations are given by the egoist for particular acts of apparent self-sacrifice, he usually claims that one of the following desired consequences (or a combination of them) is the agent's real motive:

(1) The agent believes in God and the act is done either out of fear of God's punishment or to obtain the rewards of Heaven.

(2) The act is done to avoid the disapproval of others or to achieve and keep up a good reputation among others.

(3) If the act is done without the knowledge of others (as in the case of giving a large sum *anonymously* to a charitable foundation), the agent acts from a sense of pride understood as ego-inflation. He wants to enjoy the feeling of self-congratulation at having done a good deed.

(4) From past experience the agent knows that if he does *not* do the act he will feel ashamed of himself and will suffer the pangs of a guilty conscience. His motive is to avoid these unpleasant feelings.

(5) If none of the above motives are at work, the agent is acting to satisfy unconscious desires and wishes. He is really "acting out" a wish fulfilment, or is trying to escape from anxieties, or is protecting his ego from threats, or is punishing himself in a masochistic act, and is unaware that he is doing any of these things.

Before we turn to the first four explanations of unselfish action, a special point must be made with regard to the fifth. The explanation in terms of unconscious motives can be objected to as simply irrelevant to both ethical and psychological egoism. Ethics deals only with men's voluntarily chosen conduct and only with their conscious aims and purposes. Whatever might be happening in their "unconscious" when they experience conscious desires and make deliberate choices is a matter for the psychologist to study and for the psychotherapist to treat. The whole point of psychiatric treatment is to help a person become sufficiently aware of his real emotions and his inner conflicts to be able to make free choices—choices based on his own values and on his own thinking. The task of ethics is to enlighten and guide the deliberation of the free agent as he makes his decisions in practical life. It can perform this task only on the level of conscious thought. If such thought has no influence over a person's motivation and conduct, the person is not a moral agent and no ethical system, not even ethical egoism, can guide his choices. As far as psychological egoism is concerned, unconscious motivation no more proves that all action is selfish or done from self-interest than that it is all unselfish or altruistic. The words "selfish," "self-interest," "unselfish," and "altruistic," in their ordinary meaning, are applied only to acts that are freely chosen and to motives that people are aware of. The real point of psychological egoism would be missed if all it turned out to mean was that human beings are motivated by desires and wishes of which they are unaware and that they do acts which fulfill certain psychological needs of their personalities.

Let us turn, then, to the other four kinds of explanation offered by the egoist for apparently unselfish action. Whatever conscious motive is given for such an act, the egoist will always insist that there is some element of desiring to further his own self-interest on the part of the agent, and that it is this desire that motivates him to do the act. The reader must decide for himself how objective and fair the egoist is in making this claim. In particular, he should try to think of acts that we would normally suppose were done out of simple kindness or affection toward others (for example, making a child happy on his birthday), or acts that we would ordinarily believe were done because the person felt obligated to do them (for example, telling the truth when that involves some disadvantage to oneself), and then see whether the egoist's view of the motivation behind such acts is an unbiased, undistorted, and true description of the facts.

There is one argument given by the psychological egoist, however, which rests on a semantic confusion and not on empirical claims about human motivation. Suppose an egoist is presented with a case in which a person is honest with himself and others and, as far as he is consciously aware of his own feelings and desires, he acts so as to help another person in need simply out of concern for that person at that time. He expects no praise or reward for his action, and gets none. He does not think about his action with any feelings of pride afterwards, since he forgets about it as soon as it is done. Nor would he feel guilty if he had not done it, since he did not believe he was obligated to do it. Finally, he did not do it with the conscious intention to further his own short-range or long-range interests, since he acted quite spontaneously and made no calculation of possible benefits to himself that might result from his doing the act. The egoist might then say the following about such a case: "Granted that in doing this act the person did not have what most people would call a selfish motive, or even a motive of self-interest. Still the act was a voluntary one, and all voluntary acts have some motive behind them. By doing the act the person was satisfying this motive. Hence he did gain satisfaction from doing the act. He would not have done it if no satisfaction of any of his motives would result from his doing it. Consequently the act served his self-interest after all, since it was done to satisfy whatever motive he did have in doing it."

Here the egoist has made a basic change in his position. For he is now claiming that the satisfaction of *any* motive is to be taken as self-interest, whereas what he had been saying before was that all action is motivated by a certain *kind* of motive, namely, the kind we would all classify under the general category of selfishness or self-interest. In ordinary life, we make a distinction between selfish and unselfish motives. By "unselfish motives" we mean motives of types (d) and (e) listed above. If the egoist now grants that *some* human acts, however few and far between, are motivated by motives of types (d) and (e), and yet are still to be considered as done from self-interest since these motives are being satisfied by the person when he does the act, then the egoist has changed completely the meaning of "self-interest." Indeed, his egoism is ethically harmless. For non-egoistic ethics demands that people do unselfish acts unselfishly (either out of genuine love for others or out of a sense of duty) and the egoist is now admitting that people sometimes do such acts from such motives. The psychological egoist who uses this argument, in other words, can have nothing to say against an altruist who prescribes that men ought to be unselfish in the ordinary meaning of "unselfish." It is merely an abuse of language on the part of the egoist to call all acts "selfish" or to say that they are all done from "self-interest" if his reason for using these terms is that all acts are motivated. If the egoist insists on using "selfish" and "self-interest" in this uncommon way, the altruist can simply say to him, "Call these acts what you please. What counts is that there are two different kinds of acts, one we ought to do and the other we ought to refrain from doing. That acts of the first kind are motivated takes nothing away from their moral goodness, since all acts, good and bad alike, are motivated. To call them 'selfish' simply because they are motivated is not to deny the real difference between what we ordinarily call selfish acts or motives and unselfish ones. The first are bad and the second are good. If both are to be classed as instances of self-interest, then self-interest is morally neutral. Only a certain kind of 'self-interest' would then be bad. It would be the kind which in ordinary life we call 'self-interest.' "

It should be noted that some of the confusions in the use of such terms as "selfish" and "self-interest" are brought to light and examined by Professor C. D. Broad in the second reading of this chapter. Professor Broad analyzes various forms of psychological egoism and then considers examples that raise doubts about the universality which the egoist claims for his theory of motivation.

Professor Broad also considers one argument for psychological egoism that we have not yet mentioned in this introduction. This is the argument that psychological egoism is true because it follows from the principle of psychological *hedonism*. Psychological hedonism states that the sole motive behind every action is the desire for pleasure, where it is understood that the pleasure desired is always the pleasure of the person who does the action, not the pleasure of someone else. The argument for this principle runs as follows. How can anyone desire anything but his own pleasure, since every action that satisfies a desire will bring pleasure to the person whose desire is satisfied? For satisfying a desire is nothing but the obtaining of a pleasure, just as displeasure is necessarily felt whenever a desire is frustrated. Professor Broad rejects this argument on the following ground. Suppose a man desires power, and suppose the experience of having power gives him pleasure. Then, Broad says, the man's pleasure *presupposes* his desire for power. Unless he wanted power, he would not experience pleasure upon obtaining it. But this means that what he desires is the power, not the pleasure he gets from having it. In other words, the fact that a person's satisfying his desire for something results in a pleasant experience does not mean that the something he desires is the pleasure experienced. Indeed, the pleasure itself *cannot* be what he desires, since it is experienced by him only as a result of his desiring something else.

This raises a final consideration for our reflection. It is a consideration about exactly what psychological egoism asserts. Is not the principle of psychological egoism actually an empty tautology, which tells us nothing about human conduct and motivation? This question arises from a certain kind of argument often propounded by the egoist. In support of his claim that everyone always does that which he most wants to do, or that which he least dislikes doing (see statement (4) at the beginning of this introduction), the egoist argues as follows. Suppose a person were confronted with two alternative acts, which we shall designate A and B. Let us further suppose that act A would ordinarily be called an unselfish act and B would ordinarily be called selfish. Now if the person chooses to do A rather than B, this shows:

(a) that his motives for doing A are stronger than his motives for doing B;

(b) that he prefers doing A to doing B;

(c) that he believes he would dislike doing B, or at least that he would not like doing B as much as he would like doing A;

(d) that he really wants to do A.

Therefore, the egoist concludes, everyone always does what he really wants to do. And since the person really wants to do the so-called "unselfish" act A, he is not really unselfish in doing it. He is doing what he prefers to do.

Two replies can be made to this argument. The first is similar to the reply to the argument considered in the preceding paragraphs. It is that the egoist is choosing to use the phrase "doing what one really wants to do" in a way that is entirely different from its ordinary meaning. For it can be seen from the egoist's argument that *every* act will be described by him in this way, since the evidence that the act is what the person really wants to do is simply the fact that he does it. Thus there can be no distinction between two kinds of acts, those that a person really wants to do and those that he feels he must do, or believes that he ought to do, but does not really want to do. In ordinary life, however, when we recognize our duties toward others and feel obligated to do something we do not enjoy doing (something we would not choose to do if we were not under such obligation), we say of the act that "we do not really want to do it." Usually such acts require us to go to some trouble or to spend time, effort, and money on something when we would clearly prefer not to be so inconvenienced and when we would very much prefer to spend the time, effort, and money on something we find enjoyable to do. Our moral obligations are sometimes burdensome (though not always so) and these are precisely the situations in which we say that we "must" or "have to" do something even though we would really like to do something else. It is with regard to such situations as these that we make the distinction between two kinds of acts, those we really want to do and those we are obliged to do, whether we want to or not. The psychological egoist, on the other hand, makes the phrase "doing what we really want to do" apply to every act. He thereby takes away its meaning, since the phrase is not being used to contrast one kind of act with another.

The second reply goes deeper into the confusions involved in the way the egoist uses language. We saw in the argument given above that when the egoist claims that a person always does what he really wants to do, the only evidence in support of this claim is the fact that the person does the act. In order to know what someone really wants to do, all we have to do is to wait until he chooses to do one act rather than another in a situation of choice. Then the fact that he chooses the act he does shows that that is the act he really wants to do. Now it follows from such an argument that to say "X really wants to do A" is simply to say "X chooses to do A in a situation of choice." But then the egoist's important-sounding statement "Everyone always does what he really wants to do" becomes nothing but the statement "Everyone always does what he does," which is a tautology. It says nothing; it gives us no information about human conduct. Yet the egoist intended to tell us something he considered important about human conduct, something empirically true. Therefore, if he still wishes to make an empirical claim, he cannot use the argument we have been examining.

ETHICAL EGOISM

We shall now briefly discuss some of the considerations brought forth by ethical egoists in support of their theory. When the ethical egoist states that everyone ought to act so as to promote his self-interest and he is asked why, there are two sorts of reply he might make. First, he might simply claim that this is an ultimate principle of normative ethics. Second, he might argue that this principle, if consistently followed by everyone, would have better results than those which would ensue if some other principle were consistently followed by everyone. Putting aside the first reply for the moment, let us look at the second. We see right away that this reply presupposes a standard of goodness by which some results are judged to be "better" than others. If this standard were anything but the fulfilment of everyone's self-interest to the greatest possible extent, it would seem that the position is not (universal) ethical egoism. Yet the fulfilment of everyone's self-interest in this argument constitutes an *end* to which the practice of each person following the rule "Do what will most promote my own interests" is taken as a *means*. Now suppose there were another, more effective means for bringing about this same end. For example, suppose that everyone's following the rule "Do what will most promote the interests of all people affected by my act" would actually tend to result in the fulfilment of everyone's self-interest to a greater extent than would result from everyone's following the rule "Do what will most promote my own interests." In that case, the egoist would have to admit that it is our moral duty to follow the former rule. But that rule, as we shall see in the next chapter, is a principle of utilitarianism, not of egoism. So in order to justify his own theory, the egoist would have to show that the universal practice of following the rule of self-interest will in fact be a more effective means to the promotion of everyone's self-interest than will the universal practice of utilitarianism.

However, most egoists have supported their theory in the first way mentioned above. They have held each person's promotion of his own self-interest to be the supreme norm or ultimate principle of ethics, not merely a means to some further end. This is the position called "categorical egoism" by Professor Brian Medlin in the third reading of this chapter, and it is this position he tries to refute. The reader should keep this in mind in following Professor Medlin's argument. A criticism of that argument is given by Professor John Hospers in the fourth reading. (Professor Hospers' term "impersonal ethical egoism" is equivalent to our term "universal ethical egoism.") The chapter ends with a critical assessment of Hospers' position by Professor William Baumer.

Some remarks must be added concerning the views of the English philosopher, Thomas Hobbes. He may be taken as an ethical egoist only with certain qualifications, which must now be examined. Hobbes distinguishes between two conditions of human life, which he calls "the state of nature" and "the Commonwealth." The state of nature is the human condition when there is no legal or political system governing the relations among men. People in the state of nature do not recognize anyone as having authority over them. Their conduct is not regulated by laws, and they are not organized into a civil community with an established government whose purpose is to make and enforce the law and to set social policies binding on everyone. In such a social condition it is impossible to break the law, since there are no laws to break. We might then inquire, What about moral laws? Even if a group of people have no legal system or form of government, they might still have a set of moral rules of conduct which they recognize as binding upon them and which they back up by sanctions. But Hobbes denies this. The state of nature, in his view, is neither a legal nor a moral community (disregarding the relation of man to God and considering only the relation of man to man). It is impossible in the state of nature to do anything morally wrong, since a "wrong" act means an act that violates a moral rule of conduct, and no such rules are binding upon men in that state.

Nevertheless, in the state of nature there is a standard of value. Meaning can be given to the words "good" and "bad," and the meaning Hobbes gives to them may be considered a form of ethical (or valuational) egoism. "*Good* and *evil*," Hobbes says, "are names that signify our appetites and aversions." That is, good is what we like or desire; evil is what we dislike or what we wish to avoid. "In the condition of mere nature," he asserts, "private appetite is the measure of good and evil." Thus a person's only directive for right conduct is what will bring about the things *he* wants and what will avoid the things *he* does not want. Furthermore, a person can do no wrong or injustice to others in the pursuit of his self-interest, because in the state of nature "the notions of right and wrong, justice and injustice, have there no place." Therefore Hobbes's position can be considered a form of ethical egoism.

It is true that Hobbes speaks of "laws of nature" as guiding men's conduct in the state of nature. But if we read him carefully, we notice that these "laws of nature" are simply maxims of prudence and carry with them no moral obligations toward others. That is, they are rules which an intelligent man will see he ought to follow if he is to be successful in the pursuit of his self-interest, but the interests of others make no claim on him. The only reason he has to consider the interests of others is to avoid their hostility, since this might lead them to try to frustrate his own interests. Thus the clever man in the state of nature will see that it is to his interest to protect himself from others. This might require that he join with someone else if that is a necessary means for mutual protection from the hostile action of a third person. But joining in with others and cooperating with them is never an end in itself. And there is no moral duty on one person's part to protect or further the interests of others.

Once a civil society is formed, however, moral obligation comes into existence. But even here the obligation is not altruistic. The obligation is simply to obey the law set up by the Sovereign, who is given the authority to punish any violator of the law. The purpose of the law is to maintain the security of each person by protecting him from the harm that others might do to him. Hence the obligation to obey the law is itself grounded on self-interest. It is binding only so long as the Sovereign makes sure that others will obey it, for unless he does so it will not be a means to the protection of one's own interests. Each man is motivated to obey the law by fear of punishment and not by a sense of duty toward others. Hobbes's view of man in civil society, then, is essentially as egoistic as his view of man in the state of nature. Indeed, an element of psychological egoism is introduced in this account of the basis of moral obligation. At one point Hobbes says, "Of the voluntary acts of every man, the object is some *good to himself*," which is a clear statement of the principle of psychological egoism. Hobbes makes this statement when he is explaining why a person would voluntarily renounce the condition of having no obligation to obey law and place himself under such an obligation (an act by which the social contract or covenant is brought into being). He thus gives the motive of self-interest as the reason for a person's deciding to become a member of a moral and legal community where his conduct can be judged as right or wrong.

One final point regarding ethical egoism should be mentioned. Sometimes the ethical egoist will claim that his view of the ultimate ground of morality is the only legitimate answer that can be given to the question "Why should I be moral?" When a person asks this question, he cannot be answered simply by saying, "Because it is your duty to be moral," since this amounts to saying, "It is morally right to be moral" or in other words it is giving a *moral* reason for being moral. But when the person asked the question he was demanding a reason why *any* moral reason ought to be considered in guiding his conduct. In asking the question he knows that an act which he acknowledges to be morally right ought to be done by him *if moral reasons are binding upon his conduct*. But he wants to know what reason can be given to justify this if-clause. He cannot be answered by the empty assertion that it is his moral duty to follow moral reasons. Now the egoist argues that, since no moral reason can be given in reply to this question, the only kind of reason must be a prudential one. The answer to "Why be moral?" can only be, "Because being moral is the best way to achieve your own long-range self-interest." So the ethical egoist concludes that it is to the standard of self-interest that the final appeal must be made if morality as a whole is to be justified to anyone.

An examination of the meaning and validity of the question "Why should I be moral?" will be one of the subjects considered in detail in the last chapter of this book, so we shall postpone discussion of this last argument for ethical egoism until then.

THOMAS HOBBES

The Ground of Moral and Legal Obligation

OF THE NATURAL CONDITION OF MANKIND AS CONCERNING THEIR FELICITY, AND MISERY

Nature hath made men so equal, in the faculties of the body, and mind; as that though there be found one man sometimes manifestly stronger in body, or of quicker mind than another; yet when all is reckoned together, the difference between man, and man, is not so considerable, as that one man can thereupon claim to himself any benefit, to which another may not pretend, as well as he. For as to the strength of body, the weakest has strength enough to kill the strongest, either by secret machination, or by confederacy with others, that are in the same danger with himself.

And as to the faculties of the mind, setting aside the arts grounded upon words, and especially that skill of proceeding upon general, and infallible rules, called science; which very few have, and but in few things; as being not a native faculty, born with us; nor attained, as prudence, while we look after somewhat else, I find yet a greater equality amongst men, than that of strength. For prudence, is but experience; which equal time, equally bestows on all men, in those things they equally apply themselves unto. That which may perhaps make such equality incredible, is but a vain conceit of one's own wisdom, which almost all men think they have in a greater degree, than the vulgar; that is, than all men but themselves, and a few others, whom by fame, or for concurring with themselves, they approve. For such is the nature of men, that howsoever they may acknowledge many others to be more witty, or more eloquent, or more

From Thomas Hobbes, *Leviathan, or the Matter, Form and Power of a Commonwealth, Ecclesiastical and Civil*; Parts I and II. (1651)

learned; yet they will hardly believe there be many so wise as themselves; for they see their own wit at hand, and other men's at a distance. But this proveth rather that men are in that point equal, than unequal. For there is not ordinarily a greater sign of the equal distribution of any thing, than that every man is contented with his share.

From this equality of ability, ariseth equality of hope in the attaining of our ends. And therefore if any two men desire the same thing, which nevertheless they cannot both enjoy, they become enemies; and in the way to their end, which is principally their own conservation, and sometimes their delectation only, endeavour to destroy, or subdue one another. And from hence it comes to pass, that where an invader hath no more to fear, than another man's single power; if one plant, sow, build, or possess a convenient seat, others may probably be expected to come prepared with forces united, to dispossess, and deprive him, not only of the fruit of his labour, but also of his life, or liberty. And the invader again is in the like danger of another.

And from this diffidence of one another, there is no way for any man to secure himself, so reasonable, as anticipation; that is, by force, or wiles, to master the persons of all men he can, so long, till he see no other power great enough to endanger him: and this is no more than his own conservation requireth, and is generally allowed. Also because there be some, that taking pleasure in contemplating their own power in the acts of conquest, which they pursue farther than their security requires; if others, that otherwise would be glad to be at ease within modest bounds, should not by invasion increase their power, they would not be able, long time, by standing only on their defence, to subsist. And by consequence, such augmentation of dominion over men being necessary to a man's conservation, it ought to be allowed him.

Again, men have no pleasure, but on the contrary a great deal of grief, in keeping company, where there is no power able to over-awe them all. For every man looketh that his companion should value him, at the same rate he sets upon himself: and upon all signs of contempt, or undervaluing, naturally endeavours, as far as he dares, (which amongst them that have no common power to keep them in quiet, is far enough to make them destroy each other), to extort a greater value from his contemners, by damage; and from others, by the example.

So that in the nature of man, we find three principal causes of quarrel. First, competition; secondly, diffidence; thirdly, glory.

The first, maketh men invade for gain; the second, for safety; and the third, for reputation. The first use violence, to make themselves masters of other men's persons, wives, children, and cattle; the second, to defend them; the third, for trifles, as a word, a smile, a different opinion, and any other sign of undervalue, either direct in their persons, or by reflection in their kindred, their friends, their nation, their profession, or their name.

Hereby it is manifest, that during the time men live without a common power to keep them all in awe, they are in that condition which is called war; and such a war, as is of every man, against every man. For WAR, consisteth not in battle only, or the act of fighting; but in a tract of time, wherein the will to contend by battle is sufficiently known: and therefore the notion of *time*, is to be considered in the nature of war; as it is in the nature of weather. For as the nature of foul weather, lieth not in a shower or two of rain; but in an inclination thereto of many days together: so the nature of war, consisteth not in actual fighting; but in the known disposition thereto, during all the time there is no assurance to the contrary. All other time is PEACE.

Whatsoever therefore is consequent to a time of war, where every man is enemy to every man; the same is consequent to the time, wherein men live without other security, than what their own strength, and their own invention shall furnish them withal. In such condition, there is no place for industry; because the fruit thereof is uncertain: and consequently no culture of the earth; no navigation, nor use of the commodities that may be imported by sea; no commodious building; no instruments of moving, and removing, such things as require much force; no knowledge of the face of the earth; no account of time; no arts; no letters; no society; and which is worst of all, continual fear, and danger of violent death; and the life of man, solitary, poor, nasty, brutish, and short.

It may seem strange to some man, that has not well weighed these things; that nature should thus dissociate, and render men apt to invade, and destroy one another: and he may therefore, not trusting to this inference, made from the passions, desire perhaps to have the same confirmed by experience. Let him therefore consider with himself, when taking a journey, he arms himself, and seeks to go well accompanied; when going to sleep, he locks his doors; when even in his house he locks his chests; and this when he knows there be laws, and public officers, armed, to revenge all injuries shall be done him; what opinion he has of his fellow-subjects, when he rides armed; of his fellow citizens, when he locks his doors; and of his children, and servants, when he locks his chests. Does he not there as much accuse mankind by his actions, as I do by my words? But neither of us accuse man's nature in it. The desires, and other passions of man, are in themselves no sin. No more are the actions, that proceed from those passions, till they know a law that forbids them: which till laws be made they cannot know: nor can any law be made, till they have agreed upon the person that shall make it.

It may peradventure be thought, there was never such a time, nor condition of war as this; and I believe it was never generally so, over all the world: but there are many places, where they live so now. For the savage people in many places of America, except the government of small families, the concord whereof dependeth on natural lust, have no government at all; and live at this day in that brutish manner, as I said before. Howsoever, it may be perceived what manner of life there would be, where there were no common power to fear, by the manner of life, which men that have formerly lived under a peaceful government, use to degenerate into, in a civil war.

But though there had never been any time, wherein particular men were in a condition of war one against another; yet in all times, kings, and persons of sovereign authority, because of their independency, are in continual jealousies, and in the state and posture of gladiators; having their weapons pointing, and their eyes fixed on one another; that is, their forts, garrisons, and guns upon the frontiers of their kingdoms; and continual spies upon their neighbours; which is a posture of war. But because they uphold thereby, the industry of their subjects; there does not follow from it, that misery, which accompanies the liberty of particular men.

To this war of every man, against every man, this also is consequent; that nothing can be unjust. The notions of right and wrong, justice and injustice have there no place. Where there is no common power, there is no law: where no law, no injustice. Force, and fraud, are in war the two cardinal virtues. Justice, and injustice are none of the faculties neither of the body, nor mind. If they were, they might be in a man that were alone in the world, as well as his senses, and passions. They are qualities, that relate to men in society, not in solitude. It is consequent also to the same condition, that there be no propriety, no dominion, no *mine* and *thine* distinct; but only that to be every man's, that he can get; and for so long, as he can keep it. And thus much for the ill condition, which man by mere nature is actually placed in; though with a possibility to come out of it, consisting partly in the passions, partly in his reason.

The passions that incline men to peace, are fear of death; desire of such things as are necessary to commodious living; and a hope by their industry to obtain them. And reason suggesteth convenient articles of peace, upon which men may be drawn to agreement. These articles, are they, which otherwise are called the Laws of Nature: whereof I shall speak more particularly, in the two following chapters.

OF THE FIRST AND SECOND NATURAL LAWS, AND OF CONTRACTS

The right of nature, which writers commonly call *jus naturale,* is the liberty each man hath, to use his own power, as he will himself, for the preservation of his own nature; that is to say, of his own life; and consequently, of doing any thing, which in his own judgment, and reason, he shall conceive to be the aptest means thereunto.

By LIBERTY, is understood, according to the proper signification of the word, the absence of external impediments: which impediments, may oft take away part of a man's power to do what he would; but cannot hinder him from using the power left him, according as his judgment, and reason shall dictate to him.

A LAW OF NATURE, *lex naturalis,* is a precept or general rule, found out by reason, by which a man is forbidden to do that, which is destructive of his life, or taketh away the means of preserving the same; and to omit that, by which he thinketh it may be best preserved. For though they that speak of this subject, use to confound *jus,* and *lex, right* and *law:* yet they ought to be distinguished; because RIGHT, consisteth in liberty to do, or to forbear; whereas LAW, determineth, and bindeth to one of them: so that law, and right, differ as much, as obligation, and liberty; which in one and the same matter are inconsistent.

And because the condition of man, as hath been declared in the precedent chapter, is a condition of war of every one against every one; in which case every one is governed by his own reason; and there is nothing he can make use of, that may not be a help unto him, in preserving his life against his enemies; it followeth, that in such a condition, every man has a right to every thing; even to one another's body. And therefore, as long as this natural right of every man to every thing endureth, there can be no security to any man, how strong or wise soever he be, of living out the time, which nature ordinarily alloweth men to live. And consequently it is a precept, or general rule of reason, *that every man, ought to endeavour peace, as far as he has hope of obtaining it; and when he cannot obtain it, that he may seek, and use, all helps, and advantages of war.* The first branch of which rule, containeth the first, and fundamental law of nature; which is, *to seek peace, and follow it.* The second, the sum of the right of nature; which is, *by all means we can, to defend ourselves.*

From this fundamental law of nature, by which men are commanded to endeavour peace, is derived this second law; *that a man be willing, when others are so too, as far-forth, as for peace, and defence of himself he shall think it necessary, to lay down this right to all things; and be contented with so much liberty against other men, as he would allow other men against himself.* For as long as every man holdeth this right, of doing any thing he liketh; so long are all men in the condition of war. But if other men will not lay down their right, as well as he; then there is no reason for any one, to divest himself of his: for that were to expose himself to prey, which no man is bound to, rather than to dispose himself to peace. This is that law of the Gospel; *whatsoever you require that others should do to you, that do ye to them.* And that law of all men, *quod tibi fieri non vis, alteri ne feceris.*[1]

To *lay down* a man's *right* to any thing, is to *divest* himself of the *liberty,* of hindering another of the benefit of his own right to the same. For he that renounceth, or passeth away his right, giveth not to any other man a right which he had not before; because there is nothing to which every man had not right by nature: but only standeth out of his way, that he may enjoy his own original right, without hindrance from him; not without hindrance from another. So that the effect which redoundeth to one man, by another man's defect of right, is but so much diminution of impediments to the use of his own right original.

Right is laid aside, either by simply renouncing it; or by transferring it to another. By *simply* RENOUNCING; when he cares not to whom the benefit thereof redoundeth. By TRANSFERRING; when he intendeth the benefit thereof to some certain person, or persons. And when a man hath in either manner abandoned, or granted away his right; then is he said to be OBLIGED, or BOUND, not to hinder those, to whom such right is granted, or abandoned, from the benefit of it: and that he *ought,* and it is his DUTY, not to make void that voluntary act of his own: and that such hindrance is INJUSTICE, and INJURY, as being *sine jure;*[2] the right being before renounced, or transferred. So that *injury,* or *injustice,* in the controversies of the world, is somewhat like to that, which in the disputations of

---

[1] ["What you do not want done to you, do not do to others."—Ed. note.]
[2] [i.e., without right.—Ed. note.]

scholars is called *absurdity*. For as it is there called an absurdity, to contradict what one maintained in the beginning: so in the world, it is called injustice, and injury, voluntarily to undo that, which from the beginning he had voluntarily done. The way by which a man either simply renounceth, or transferreth his right, is a declaration, or signification, by some voluntary and sufficient sign, or signs, that he doth so renounce, or transfer; or hath so renounced, or transferred the same, to him that accepteth it. And these signs are either words only, or actions only; or, as it happeneth most often, both words, and actions. And the same are the BONDS, by which men are bound, and obliged: bonds, that have their strength, not from their own nature, for nothing is more easily broken than a man's word, but from fear of some evil consequence upon the rupture.

Whensoever a man transferreth his right, or renounceth it; it is either in consideration of some right reciprocally transferred to himself; or for some other good he hopeth for thereby. For it is a voluntary act: and of the voluntary acts of every man, the object is some *good to himself*. And therefore there be some rights, which no man can be understood by any words, or other signs, to have abandoned, or transferred. As first a man cannot lay down the right of resisting them, that assault him by force, to take away his life; because he cannot be understood to aim thereby, at any good to himself. The same may be said of wounds, and chains, and imprisonment; both because there is no benefit consequent to such patience; as there is to the patience of suffering another to be wounded, or imprisoned: as also because a man cannot tell, when he seeth men proceed against him by violence, whether they intend his death or not. And lastly the motive, and end for which this renouncing, and transferring of right is introduced, is nothing else but the security of a man's person, in his life, and in the means of so preserving life, as not to be weary of it. And therefore if a man by words, or other signs, seem to despoil himself of the end, for which those signs were intended; he is not to be understood as if he meant it, or that it was his will; but that he was ignorant of how such words and actions were to be interpreted.

The mutual transferring of right, is that which men call CONTRACT.

There is difference between transferring of right to the thing; and transferring, or tradition, that is delivery of the thing itself. For the thing may be delivered together with the translation of the right; as in buying and selling with ready-money; or exchange of goods, or lands: and it may be delivered some time after.

Again, one of the contractors, may deliver the thing contracted for on his part, and leave the other to perform his part at some determinate time after, and in the mean time be trusted; and then the contract on his part, is called PACT, or COVENANT: or both parts may contract now, to perform hereafter: in which cases, he that is to perform in time to come, being trusted, his performance is called *keeping of promise*, or faith; and the failing of performance, if it be voluntary, *violation of faith*.

When the transferring of right, is not mutual: but one of the parties transferreth, in hope to gain thereby friendship, or service from another, or from his friends; or in hope to gain the reputation of charity, or magnanimity; or to deliver his mind from the pain of compassion; or in hope of reward in heaven; this is not contract, but GIFT, FREE-GIFT, GRACE: which words signify one and the same thing.

Signs of contract, are either *express*, or *by inference*. Express, are words spoken with understanding of what they signify: and such words are either of the time *present*, or *past*; as, *I give, I grant, I have given, I have granted, I will that this be yours*: or of the future; as, *I will give, I will grant*: which words of the future are called PROMISE.

•   •   •   •   •

If a covenant be made, wherein neither of the parties perform presently, but trust one another; in the condition of mere nature, which is a condition of war of every man against every man, upon any reasonable suspicion, it is void: but if there be a common power set over them both, with right and force sufficient to compel performance, it is not void. For he that performeth first, has no assurance the other will perform after; because the bonds of words are too weak to bridle men's ambition, avarice, anger, and other passions, without the fear of some coercive power; which in the condition of mere nature, where all men are equal, and judges of the justness of their own fears, cannot possibly be supposed. And therefore he which performeth first, does but betray himself to his enemy; contrary to the right, he can never abandon, of defending his life, and means of living.

But in a civil estate, where there is a power set up to constrain those that would otherwise violate their faith, that fear is no more reasonable: and for that cause, he which by the covenant is to perform first, is obliged so to do.

The cause of fear, which maketh such a covenant invalid, must be always something arising after the covenant made; as some new fact, or other sign of the will not to perform: else it cannot make the covenant void. For that which could not hinder a man from promising, ought not to be admitted as a hindrance of performing.

•   •   •   •   •

OF OTHER LAWS OF NATURE

From that law of nature, by which we are obliged to transfer to another, such rights, as being retained, hinder the peace of mankind, there followeth a third; which is this, *that men perform their covenants made*: without which, covenants are in vain, and but empty words; and the right of all men to all things remaining, we are still in the condition of war.

And in this law of nature, consisteth the fountain and original of JUSTICE. For where no covenant hath preceded, there hath no right been transferred, and every man has right to every thing; and consequently, no action can be unjust. But when a covenant is made, then to break it is *unjust*: and the definition of INJUSTICE, is no other than *the not performance of covenant*. And whatsoever is not unjust, is *just*.

But because covenants of mutual trust, where there is a fear of not performance on either part, as hath been said in the former chapter, are invalid; though the original of justice be the making of covenants; yet injustice actually there can be none, till the cause of such fear be taken away; which while men are in the natural condition of war, cannot be done. Therefore before the names of just, and unjust can have place, there must be some coercive power, to compel men equally to the performance of their covenants, by the terror of some punishment, greater than the benefit they expect by the breach of their covenant; and to make good that propriety, which by mutual contract men acquire, in recompense of the universal right they abandon: and such power there is none before the erection of a commonwealth. And this is also to be gathered out of the ordinary definition of justice in the Schools: for they say, that *justice is the constant will of giving to every man his own*. And therefore where there is no *own*, that is, no propriety, there is no injustice; and where there is no coercive power erected, that is, where there is no commonwealth, there is no propriety; all men having right to all things: therefore where there is no commonwealth, there nothing is unjust. So that the nature of justice, consisteth in keeping of valid covenants: but the validity of covenants begins not but with the constitution of a civil power, sufficient to compel men to keep them: and then it is also that propriety begins.

•　•　•　•　•

Whatsoever is done to a man, conformable to his own will signified to the doer, is no injury to him. For if he that doeth it, hath not passed away his original right to do what he please, by some antecedent covenant, there is no breach of covenant; and therefore no injury done him. And if he have; then his will to have it done being signified, is a release of that covenant: and so again there is no injury done him.

Justice of actions, is by writers divided into *commutative,* and *distributive*: and the former they say consisteth in proportion arithmetical; the latter in proportion geometrical. Commutative therefore, they place in the equality of value of the things contracted for; and distributive, in the distribution of equal benefit, to men of equal merit. As if it were injustice to sell dearer than we buy; or to give more to a man than he merits. The value of all things contracted for, is measured by the appetite of the contractors: and therefore the just value, is that which they be contented to give. And merit, besides that which is by covenant, where the performance on one part, meriteth the performance of the other part, and falls under justice commutative, not distributive, is not due by justice; but is rewarded of grace only. And therefore this distinction, in the sense wherein it useth to be expounded, is not right. To speak properly, commutative justice is the justice of a contractor: that is, a performance of covenant, in buying, and selling; hiring, and letting to hire; lending, and borrowing; exchanging, bartering, and other acts of contract.

And distributive justice, the justice of an arbitrator; that is to say, the act of defining what is just. Wherein, being trusted by them that make him arbitrator, if he perform his trust, he is said to distribute to every man his own: and this is indeed just distribution, and may be called, though improperly, distributive justice; but more properly equity; which also is a law of nature, as shall be shown in due place.

As justice dependeth on antecedent covenant; so does GRATITUDE depend on antecedent grace; that is to say, antecedent free gift: and is the fourth law of nature; which may be conceived in this form, *that a man which receiveth benefit from another of mere grace, endeavour that he which giveth it, have no reasonable cause to repent him of his good will.* For no man giveth, but with intention of good to himself; because gift is voluntary; and of all voluntary acts, the object is to every man his own good; of which if men see they shall be frustrated, there will be no beginning of benevolence, or trust; nor consequently of mutual help; nor of reconciliation of one man to another; and therefore they are to remain still in the condition of *war*; which is contrary to the first and fundamental law of nature, which commandeth men to *seek peace.* The breach of this law, is called *ingratitude*; and hath the same relation to grace, that injustice hath to obligation by covenant.

•   •   •   •   •

And because, though men be never so willing to observe these laws, there may nevertheless arise questions concerning a man's action; first, whether it were done, or not done; secondly, if done, whether against the law, or not against the law; the former whereof, is called a question *of fact*; the latter a question *of right*, therefore unless the parties to the question, covenant mutually to stand to the sentence of another, they are as far from peace as ever. This other to whose sentence they submit is called an ARBITRATOR. And therefore it is of the law of nature, *that they that are at controversy, submit their right to the judgment of an arbitrator.*

And seeing every man is presumed to do all things in order to his own benefit, no man is a fit arbitrator in his own cause; and if he were never so fit; yet equity allowing to each party equal benefit, if one be admitted to the judge, the other is to be admitted also; and so the controversy, that is, the cause of war, remains, against the law of nature.

For the same reason no man in any cause ought to be received for arbitrator, to whom greater profit, or honour, or pleasure apparently ariseth out of the victory of one party, than of the other: for he hath taken, though an unavoidable bribe, yet a bribe; and no man can be obliged to trust him. And thus also the controversy, and the condition of war remaineth, contrary to the law of nature.

And in a controversy of *fact*, the judge being to give no more credit to one, than to the other, if there be no other arguments, must give credit to a third; or to a third and fourth; or more: for else the question is undecided, and left to force, contrary to the law of nature.

These are the laws of nature, dictating peace, for a means of the conservation of men in multitudes; and which only concern the doctrine of civil society. There be other things tending to the destruction of particular men; as drunkenness, and all other parts of intemperance; which may therefore also be reckoned amongst those things which the law of nature hath forbidden; but are not necessary to be mentioned, nor are pertinent enough to this place.

And though this may seem too subtle a deduction of the laws of nature, to be taken notice of by all men; whereof the most part are too busy in getting food, and the rest too negligent to understand; yet to leave all men inexcusable, they have been contracted into one easy sum, intelligible even to the meanest capacity; and that is, *Do not that to another, which thou wouldest not have done to thyself;* which sheweth him, that he has no more to do in learning the laws of nature, but, when weighing the actions of other men with his own, they seem too heavy, to put them into the other part of the balance, and his own into their place, that his own passions, and self-love, may add nothing to the weight; and then there is none of these laws of nature that will not appear unto him very reasonable.

The laws of nature oblige *in foro interno;*[3] that is to say, they bind to a desire they should take place: but *in foro externo;*[4] that is, to the putting them in act, not always. For he that should be modest, and tractable, and perform all he promises, in such time, and place, where no man else should do so, should but make himself a prey to others, and procure his own certain ruin, contrary to the ground of all laws of nature, which tend to nature's preservation. And again, he that having sufficient security, that others shall observe the same laws towards him, observes them not himself, seeketh not peace, but war; and consequently the destruction of his nature by violence.

And whatsoever laws bind *in foro interno,* may be broken, not only by a fact contrary to the law, but also by a fact according to it, in case a man think it contrary. For though his action in this case, be according to the law; yet his purpose was against the law; which, where the obligation is *in foro interno,* is a breach.

The laws of nature are immutable and eternal; for injustice, ingratitude, arrogance, pride, iniquity, acception of persons, and the rest, can never be made lawful. For it can never be that war shall preserve life, and peace destroy it.

The same laws, because they oblige only to a desire, and endeavour, I mean an unfeigned and constant endeavour, are easy to be observed. For in that they require nothing but endeavour, he that endeavoureth their performance, fulfilleth them; and he that fulfilleth the law, is just.

And the science of them, is the true and only moral philosophy. For moral philosophy is nothing else but the science of what is *good,* and *evil,* in the conversation, and society of mankind. *Good,* and *evil,* are names that signify

---

[3] [literally, "in the internal forum"—that is, in a person's mind or conscience.—Ed. note.]

[4] [literally, "in the external forum"—that is, in the public world of action.—Ed. note.]

our appetites, and aversions; which in different tempers, customs, and doctrines of men, are different: and divers men, differ not only in their judgment, on the senses of what is pleasant, and unpleasant to the taste, smell, hearing, touch, and sight; but also of what is conformable, or disagreeable to reason, in the actions of common life. Nay, the same man, in divers times, differs from himself; and one time praiseth, that is, calleth good, what another time he dispraiseth, and calleth evil: from whence arise disputes, controversies, and at last war. And therefore so long as a man is in the condition of mere nature, which is a condition of war, as private appetite is the measure of good, and evil: and consequently all men agree on this, that peace is good, and therefore also the way, or means of peace, which, as I have shewed before, are *justice, gratitude, modesty, equity, mercy,* and the rest of the laws of nature, are good; that is to say; *moral virtues;* and their contrary *vices,* evil. Now the science of virtue and vice, is moral philosophy; and therefore the true doctrine of the laws of nature, is the true moral philosophy. But the writers of moral philosophy, though they acknowledge the same virtues and vices; yet not seeing wherein consisted their goodness; nor that they come to be praised, as the means of peaceable, sociable, and comfortable living, place them in a mediocrity of passions: as if not the cause, but the degree of daring, made fortitude; or not the cause, but the quantity of a gift, made liberality.

These dictates of reason, men used to call by the name of laws, but improperly: for they are but conclusions, or theorems concerning what conduceth to the conservation and defence of themselves; whereas law, properly, is the word of him, that by right hath command over others. But yet if we consider the same theorems, as delivered in the word of God, that by right commandeth all things; then are they properly called laws.

•   •   •   •   •

OF THE CAUSES, GENERATION, AND DEFINITION
OF A COMMONWEALTH

The final cause, end, or design of men, who naturally love liberty, and dominion over others, in the introduction of that restraint upon themselves, in which we see them live in commonwealths, is the foresight of their own preservation, and of a more contented life thereby; that is to say, of getting themselves out from that miserable condition of war, which is necessarily consequent, as hath been shown in chapter XIII, to the natural passions of men, when there is no visible power to keep them in awe, and tie them by fear of punishment to the performance of their covenants, and observation of those laws of nature set down in the fourteenth and fifteenth chapters.

For the laws of nature, as *justice, equity, modesty, mercy,* and, in sum, *doing to others, as we would be done to,* of themselves, without the terror of some power, to cause them to be observed, are contrary to our natural passions, that carry us to partiality, pride, revenge, and the like. And covenants, without the sword, are but words, and of no strength to secure a man at all. Therefore notwithstanding the laws of nature, which every one hath then kept, when he has the will to keep them, when he can do it safely, if there be no power erected, or not great enough for our security; every man will, and may lawfully rely on his own strength and art, for caution against all other men. And in all places, where men have lived by small families, to rob and spoil one another, has been a trade, and so far from being reputed against the law of nature, that the greater spoils they gained, the greater was their honour; and men observed no other laws therein, but the laws of honour; that is, to abstain from cruelty, leaving to men their lives, and instruments of husbandry. And as small families did then; so now do cities and kingdoms which are but greater families, for their own security, enlarge their dominions, upon all pretences of danger, and fear of invasion, or assistance that may be given to invaders, and endeavour as much as they can, to subdue, or weaken their neighbours, by open force, and secret arts, for want of other caution, justly; and are remembered for it in after ages with honour.

•　•　•　•　•

It is true, that certain living creatures, as bees, and ants, live sociably one with another, which are therefore by Aristotle numbered amongst political creatures; and yet have no other direction, than their particular judgments and appetites; nor speech, whereby one of them can signify to another, what he thinks expedient for the common benefit: and therefore some man may perhaps desire to know, why mankind cannot do the same. To which I answer,

First, that men are continually in competition for honour and dignity, which these creatures are not; and consequently amongst men there ariseth on that ground, envy and hatred, and finally war; but amongst these not so.

Secondly, that amongst these creatures, the common good differeth not from the private; and being by nature inclined to their private, they procure thereby the common benefit. But man, whose joy consisteth in comparing himself with other men, can relish nothing but what is eminent.

Thirdly, that these creatures, having not, as man, the use of reason, do not see, nor think they see any fault, in the administration of their common business; whereas amongst men, there are very many, that think themselves wiser, and abler to govern the public, better than the rest; and these strive to reform and innovate, one this way, another that way; and thereby bring it into distraction and civil war.

Fourthly, that these creatures, though they have some use of voice, in making known to one another their desires, and other affections; yet they want that art of words, by which some men can represent to others, that which is good, in the likeness of evil; and evil, in the likeness of good; and augment, or diminish the apparent greatness of good and evil; discontenting men, and troubling their peace at their pleasure.

Fifthly, irrational creatures cannot distinguish between *injury*, and *damage*; and therefore as long as they be at ease, they are not offended with their fellows: whereas man is then most troublesome, when he is most at ease: for then it is that he loves to shew his wisdom, and control the actions of them that govern the commonwealth.

Lastly, the agreement of these creatures is natural; that of men, is by covenant only, which is artificial: and therefore it is no wonder if there be somewhat else required, besides covenant, to make their agreement constant and lasting; which is a common power, to keep them in awe, and to direct their actions to the common benefit.

The only way to erect such a common power, as may be able to defend them from the invasion of foreigners, and the injuries of one another, and thereby to secure them in such sort, as that by their own industry, and by the fruits of the earth, they may nourish themselves and live contentedly; is, to confer all their power and strength upon one man, or upon one assembly of men, that may reduce all their wills, by plurality of voices, unto one will: which is as much as to say, to appoint one man, or assembly of men, to bear their person; and every one to own, and acknowledge himself to be author of whatsoever he that so beareth their person, shall act, or cause to be acted, in those things which concern the common peace and safety; and therein to submit their wills, every one to his will, and their judgments, to his judgment. This is more than consent, or concord; it is a real unity of them all, in one and the same person, made by covenant of every man with every man, in such manner, as if every man should say to every man, *I authorize and give up my right of governing myself, to this man, or to this assembly of men, on this condition, that thou give up thy right to him, and authorize all his actions in like manner.* This done, the multitude so united in one person, is called a COMMONWEALTH, in Latin CIVITAS. This is the generation of that great LEVIATHAN, or rather, to speak more reverently, of that *mortal god,* to which we owe under the *immortal God,* our peace and defence. For by this authority, given him by every particular man in the commonwealth, he hath the use of so much power and strength conferred on him, that by terror thereof, he is enabled to perform the wills of them all, to peace at home, and mutual aid against their enemies abroad. And in him consisteth the essence of the commonwealth; which, to define it, is *one person, of whose acts a great multitude, by mutual covenants one with another, have made themselves every one the author, to the end he may use the strength and means of them all, as he shall think expedient, for their peace and common defence.*

And he that carrieth this person, is called SOVEREIGN, and said to have *sovereign power;* and every one besides, his SUBJECT.

•   •   •   •   •

C. D. BROAD

Egoism as a Theory of Human Motives

There seem *prima facie* to be a number of different kinds of ultimate desire which all or most men have. Plausible examples would be the desire to get pleasant experiences and to avoid unpleasant ones, the desire to get and exercise power over others, and the desire to do what is right and to avoid doing what is wrong. Very naturally philosophers have tried to reduce this plurality. They have tried to show that there is one and only one kind of ultimate desire, and that all other desires which seem at first sight to be ultimate are really subordinate to this. I shall call the view that there really are several different kinds of ultimate desire *Pluralism of Ultimate Desires*; and I shall call the view that there is really only one kind of ultimate desire *Monism of Ultimate Desires*. Even if a person were a pluralist about ultimate desires, he might hold that there are certain important features common to all the different kinds of ultimate desire.

Now much the most important theory on this subject is that all kinds of ultimate desire are *egoistic*. This is not in itself necessarily a monistic theory. For there might be several irreducibly different kinds of ultimate desire, even if they were all egoistic. Moreover, there might be several irreducibly different, though not necessarily unrelated, senses of the word "egoistic"; and some desires might be egoistic in one sense and some in another, even if all were egoistic in some sense. But the theory often takes the special form that the only kind of ultimate desire is the desire to get or to prolong pleasant experiences, and to avoid or to cut short unpleasant experiences, for oneself. That *is* a monistic theory. I shall call the wider theory *Psychological Egoism,* and this special form of it *Psychological Hedonism*. Psychological Egoism might be true, even though psychological hedonism were false; but, if psychological egoism be false, psychological hedonism cannot be true.

I shall now discuss Psychological Egoism. I think it is best to begin by enumerating all the kinds of desire that I can think of which might reasonably be called "egoistic" in one sense or another.

(1) Everyone has a special desire for the continued existence of himself in his present bodily life, and a special dread of his own death. This may be called *Desire for Self-preservation.* (2) Everyone desires to get and to prolong

From C. D. Broad, "Egoism as a Theory of Human Motives," *The Hibbert Journal,* XLVIII (1949–50), 105–114. Reprinted in C. D. Broad, *Ethics and the History of Philosophy* (Routledge & Kegan Paul, Ltd., London, 1952). Reprinted here by permission of the author, the Hibbert Trust, and Routledge & Kegan Paul, Ltd.

experiences of certain kinds, and to avoid and to cut short experiences of certain other kinds, because the former are pleasant to him and the latter unpleasant. this may be called *Desire for one's own Happiness*. (3) Everyone desires to acquire, keep, and develop certain mental and bodily powers and dispositions, and to avoid, get rid of, or check certain others. In general he wants to be or to become a person of a certain kind, and wants not to be or to become a person of certain other kinds. This may be called *Desire to be a Self of a certain kind*. (4) Everyone desires to feel certain kinds of emotion towards himself and his own powers and dispositions, and not to feel certain other kinds of reflexive emotion. This may be called *Desire for Self-respect*. (5) Everyone desires to get and to keep for himself the exclusive possession of certain material objects or the means of buying and keeping such objects. This may be called *Desire to get and to keep Property*. (6) Everyone desires to get and to exercise power over certain other persons, so as to make them do what he wishes, regardless of whether they wish it or not. This may be called *Desire for Self-assertion*. (7) Everyone desires that other persons shall believe certain things about him and feel certain kinds of emotion towards him. He wants to be noticed, to be respected by some, to be loved by some, to be feared by some, and so on. Under this head come the *Desire for Self-display,* for *Affection,* and so on.

Lastly, it must be noted that some desires, which are concerned primarily with other things or persons, either would not exist at all or would be very much weaker or would take a different form if it were not for the fact that those things or persons already stand in certain relations to oneself. I shall call such relations *egoistic motive-stimulants*. The following are among the most important of these. (i) The relation of ownership. If a person owns a house or a wife, *e.g.,* he feels a much stronger desire to improve the house or to make the woman happy than if the house belongs to another or the woman is married to someone else. (ii) Blood-relationship. A person desires, *e.g.,* the well-being of his own children much more strongly than that of other children. (iii) Relations of love and friendship. A person desires strongly, *e.g.,* to be loved and respected by those whom he loves. He may desire only to be feared by those whom he hates. And he may desire only very mildly, if at all, to be loved and respected by those to whom he feels indifferent. (iv) The relationship of being fellow-members of an institution to which one feels loyalty and affection. Thus, *e.g.,* an Englishman will be inclined to do services to another Englishman which he would not do for a foreigner, and an Old Etonian will be inclined to do services to another Old Etonian which he would not do for an Old Harrovian.

I think that I have now given a reasonably adequate list of motives and motive-stimulants which could fairly be called "egoistic" in some sense or other. Our next business is to try to classify them and to consider their inter-relations.

(1) Let us begin by asking ourselves the following question. Which of these motives could act on a person if he had been the only person or thing that had ever existed? The answer is that he could still have had desires for *self-preservation,* for *his own happiness,* to be a *self of a certain kind,* and for *self-respect.* But he could not, unless he were under the delusion that there

were other persons or things, have desires for *property,* for *self-assertion,* or for *self-display.* Nor could he have any of those desires which are stimulated by family or other alio-relative relationships. I shall call those desires, and only those, which could be felt by a person who knew or believed himself to be the only existent in the universe, *Self-confined.*

(2) Any desire which is not self-confined may be described as *extra-verted;* for the person who has such a desire is necessarily considering, not only himself and his own qualities, dispositions, and states, but also some other thing or person. If the desire is egoistic, it will also be *intro-verted;* for the person who has such a desire will also be considering himself and his relations to that other person or thing, and this will be an essential factor conditioning his experience. Thus a self-confined desire is purely intro-verted, whilst a desire which is egoistic but not self-confined is both intro-verted and extra-verted. Now we may subdivide desires of the latter kind into two classes, according as the primary emphasis is on the former or the latter aspect. Suppose that the person is concerned primarily with himself and his own acts and experiences, and that he is concerned with the other thing or person only or mainly as an object of these acts or experiences or as the other term in a relationship to himself. Then I shall call the desire *Self-centred.* I shall use the term *Self-regarding* to include both desires which are self-centred and those which are self-confined. Under the head of self-centred desires come the desire for *property,* for *self-assertion,* for *self-display,* and for *affection.*

(3) Lastly, we come to desires which are both intro-verted and extra-verted, but where the primary emphasis is on the other person or thing and its states. Here the relationship of the other person or thing to oneself acts as a strong egoistic motive-stimulant, but one's primary desire is that the other person or thing shall be in a certain state. I will call such desires *Other-regarding.* A desire which is other-regarding, but involves an egoistic motive-stimulant, may be described as *Self-referential.* The desire of a mother to render services to her own children which she would not be willing to render to other children is an instance of a desire which is other-regarding but self-referential. So, too, is the desire of a man to inflict suffering on one who has injured him or one whom he envies.

Having thus classified the various kinds of egoistic desire, I will now say something about their inter-relations.

(1) It is obvious that self-preservation may be desired as a necessary condition of one's own happiness; since one cannot acquire or prolong pleasant experiences unless one continues to exist. So the desire for self-preservation *may* be subordinate to the desire for one's own happiness. But it seems pretty clear that a person often desires to go on living even when there is no prospect that the remainder of his life will contain a balance of pleasant over unpleasant experiences. . . .

(2) It is also obvious that property and power over others may be desired as a means to self-preservation or to happiness. So the desire to get and keep property, and the desire to get and exert power over others, *may* be subordinate

to the desire for self-preservation or for one's own happiness. But it seems fairly certain that the former desires are sometimes independent of the latter. Even if a person begins by desiring property or power only as a means—and it is very doubtful whether we always do begin in that way—it seems plain that he often comes to desire them for themselves, and to sacrifice happiness, security, and even life for them. Any miser, and almost any keen politician, provides an instance of this.

It is no answer to this to say that a person who desires power or property enjoys the experiences of getting and exercising power or of amassing and owning property, and then to argue that therefore his ultimate desire is to give himself those pleasant experiences. The premiss here is true, but the argument is self-stultifying. The experiences in question are pleasant to a person only in so far as he desires power or property. This kind of pleasant experience presupposes desires for something other than pleasant experiences, and therefore the latter desires cannot be derived from desire for that kind of pleasant experience.

Similar remarks apply to the desire for self-respect and the desire for self-display. If one already desires to feel certain emotions towards oneself, or to be the object of certain emotions in others, the experience of feeling those emotions or of knowing that others feel them towards one will be pleasant, because it will be the fulfilment of a pre-existing desire. But this kind of pleasure presupposes the existence of these desires, and therefore they cannot be derived from the desire for that kind of pleasure.

(3) Although the various kinds of egoistic desire cannot be reduced to a single ultimate egoistic desire, e.g., the desire for one's own happiness, they are often very much mixed up with each other. Take, e.g., the special desire which a mother feels for the health, happiness, and prosperity of her children. This is predominantly other-regarding, though it is self-referential. The mother is directly attracted by the thought of her child as surviving, as having good dispositions and pleasant experiences, and as being the object of love and respect to other persons. She is directly repelled by the thought of him dying, or having bad dispositions or unpleasant experiences, or being the object of hatred or contempt to other persons. The desire is therefore other-regarding. It is self-referential, because the fact that it is her child and not another's acts as a powerful motive-stimulant. She would not be prepared to make the same sacrifices for the survival or the welfare of a child which was not her own. But this self-referential other-regarding motive is almost always mingled with other motives which are self-regarding. One motive which a woman has for wanting her child to be happy, healthy and popular is the desire that other women shall envy her as the mother of a happy, healthy and popular child. This motive is subordinate to the self-centred desire for self-display. Another motive, which may be present, is the desire not to be burdened with an ailing, unhappy and unpopular child. This motive is subordinate to the self-contained desire for one's own happiness. But, although the self-referential other-regarding motive is

nearly always mixed with motives which are self-centred or self-confined, we cannot plausibly explain the behaviour of many mothers on many occasions towards their children without postulating the other-regarding motive.

We can now consider the various forms which Psychological Egoism might take. The most rigid form is that all human motives are ultimately egoistic, and that all egoistic motives are ultimately of one kind. That one kind has generally been supposed to be the desire for one's own happiness, and so this form of Psychological Egoism may in practice be identified with Psychological Hedonism. This theory amounts to saying that the only ultimate motives are *self-confined,* and that the only ultimate self-confined motive is *desire for one's own happiness.*

I have already tried to show by examples that this is false. Among self-confined motives, *e.g.,* is the desire for self-preservation, and this cannot be reduced to desire for one's own happiness. Then, again, there are self-regarding motives which are self-centred but not self-confined, such as the desire for affection, for gratitude, for power over others, and so on. And, finally, there are motives which are self-referential but predominantly other-regarding, such as a mother's desire for her children's welfare or a man's desire to injure one whom he hates.

It follows that the only form of Psychological Egoism that is worth discussing is the following. It might be alleged that all ultimate motives are *either* self-confined *or* self-centred *or* other-regarding but self-referential, some being of one kind and some of another. This is a much more modest theory than, *e.g.,* Psychological Hedonism. I think that it covers satisfactorily an immensely wide field of human motivation, but I am not sure that it is true without exception. I shall now discuss it in the light of some examples.

Case A. Take first the case of a man who does not expect to survive the death of his present body, and who makes a will, the contents of which will be known to no one during his lifetime.

(1) The motive of such a testator cannot possibly be the expectation of any experiences which he will enjoy after death through the provisions of his will being carried out; for he believes that he will have no more experiences after the death of his body. The only way in which this motive could be ascribed to such a man is by supposing that, although he is intellectually convinced of his future extinction, yet in practice he cannot help imagining himself as surviving and witnessing events which will happen after his death. I think that this kind of mental confusion is possible, and perhaps not uncommon; but I should doubt whether it is a plausible account of such a man's motives to say that they all involve this mistake.

(2) Can we say that his motive is the desire to enjoy during his life the pleasant experience of imagining the gratitude which the beneficiaries will feel towards him after his death? The answer is that this may well be *one* of his motives, but it cannot be primary, and therefore cannot be the only one. Unless he desired to be thought about in one way rather than another after his death,

the present experience of imagining himself as becoming the object of certain retrospective thoughts and emotions on the part of the beneficiaries would be neither attractive nor repulsive to him.

(3) I think it is plain, then, that the ultimate motive of such a man cannot be desire for his own happiness. But it might be desire for power over others. For he may be said to be exercising this power when he makes his will, even though the effects will not begin until after his death.

(4) Can we say that his motive in making the will is simply to ensure that certain persons will think about him and feel towards him in certain ways after his death? In that case his motive would come under the head of self-display. (This must, of course, be distinguished from the question, already discussed, whether his motive might be to give himself the pleasant experience of imagining their future feelings of gratitude towards him.) The answer is that self-display, in a wide sense, may be a motive, and a very strong one, in making a will; but it could hardly be the sole motive. A testator generally considers the relative needs of various possible beneficiaries, the question whether a certain person would appreciate and take care of a certain picture or house or book, the question whether a certain institution is doing work which he thinks important, and so on. In so far as he is influenced by these considerations, his motives are other-regarding. But they may all be self-referential. In making his will he may desire to benefit persons only in so far as they are *his* relatives or friends. He may desire to benefit institutions only in so far as *he* is or has been a member of them. And so on. I think that it would be quite plausible to hold that the motives of such a testator are all either self-regarding or self-referential, but that it would not be in the least plausible to say that they are all self-confined or that none of them are other-regarding.

Case B. Let us next consider the case of a man who subscribes anonymously to a certain charity. His motive cannot possibly be that of self-display. Can we say that his motive is to enjoy the pleasant experience of self-approval and of seeing an institution in which he is interested flourishing? The answer is, again, that these motives may exist and may be strong, but they cannot be primary and therefore cannot be his only motives. Unless he wants the institution to flourish, there will be nothing to attract him in the experience of seeing it flourish. And, unless he subscribes from some other motive than the desire to enjoy a feeling of self-approval, he will not obtain a feeling of self-approval. So here, again, it seems to me that some of his motives must be other-regarding. But it is quite possible that his other-regarding motives may all be self-referential. An essential factor in making him want to benefit this institution may be that it is *his* old college or that a great friend of *his* is at the head of it.

The question, then, that remains is this. Are there any cases in which it is reasonable to think that a person's motive is not egoistic in any of the senses mentioned? In practice, as we now see, this comes down to the question whether there are any cases in which an other-regarding motive is not stimulated by an egoistic motive-stimulus, *i.e.*, whether there is any other-regarding motive which is not also and essentially self-referential.

Case C. Let us consider the case of a person who deliberately chooses to devote his life to working among lepers, in the full knowledge that he will almost certainly contract leprosy and die in a particularly loathsome way. This is not an imaginary case. To give the Psychological Egoist the longest possible run for his money I will suppose that the person is a Roman Catholic priest, who believes that his action may secure for him a place in heaven in the next world and a reputation for sanctity and heroism in this, that it may be rewarded posthumously with canonisation, and that it will redound to the credit of the church of which he is an ordained member.

It is difficult to see what self-regarding or self-referential motives there could be *for* the action beside desire for happiness in heaven, desire to gain a reputation for sanctity and heroism and perhaps to be canonised after death, and desire to glorify the church of which one is a priest. Obviously there are extremely strong self-confined and self-centred motives *against* choosing this kind of life. And in many cases there must have been very strong self-referential other-regarding motives *against* it. For the person who made such a choice must sometimes have been a young man of good family and brilliant prospects, whose parents were heart-broken at his decision, and whose friends thought him an obstinate fool for making it.

Now there is no doubt at all that there was an other-regarding motive, viz., a direct desire to alleviate the sufferings of the lepers. No one who was not dying in the last ditch for an over-simple theory of human nature would deny this. The only questions that are worth raising about it are these. (1) Is this other-regarding motive stimulated by an egoistic motive-stimulus and thus rendered self-referential? (2) Suppose that this motive had not been supported by the various self-regarding and self-referential motives *for* deciding to go and work among the lepers, would it have sufficed, in presence of the motives *against* doing so, to ensure the choice that was actually made?

As regards the first question, I cannot see that there was any special pre-existing relationship between a young priest in Europe and a number of unknown lepers in Asia which might plausibly be held to act as an egoistic motive-stimulus. The lepers are neither his relatives nor his friends nor his benefactors nor members of any community or institution to which he belongs.

As regards the sufficiency of the other-regarding motive, whether stimulated egoistically or not, in the absence of all self-regarding motives tending in the same direction, no conclusive answer can be given. I cannot prove that a single person in the whole course of history *would* have decided to work among lepers, if all the motives against doing so had been present, whilst the hope of heaven, the desire to gain a reputation for sanctity and heroism, and the desire to glorify and extend one's church had been wholly absent. Nor can the Psychological Egoist prove that *no* single person would have so decided under these hypothetical conditions. Factors which cannot be eliminated cannot be shown to be necessary and cannot be shown to be superfluous: and there we must leave the matter.

I suspect that a Psychological Egoist might be tempted to say that the intending medical missionary found the experience of imagining the sufferings of the lepers intensely unpleasant, and that his primary motive for deciding to spend his life working among them was to get rid of this unpleasant experience. This, I think, is what Locke, *e.g.,* would have had to say in accordance with his theory of motivation. About this suggestion there are two remarks to be made.

(1) This motive cannot have been primary, and therefore cannot have been the only motive. Unless this person desired that the lepers should have their sufferings alleviated, there is no reason why the thought of their sufferings should be an unpleasant experience to him. A malicious man, *e.g.,* finds the thought of the sufferings of an enemy a very pleasant experience. This kind of pleasure presupposes a desire for the well-being or the ill-being of others.

(2) If his primary motive were to rid himself of the unpleasant experience of imagining the sufferings of the lepers, he could hardly choose a less effective means than to go and work among them. For the imagination would then be replaced by actual sense-perception; whilst, if he stayed at home and devoted himself to other activities, he would have a reasonably good chance of diverting his attention from the sufferings of the lepers. In point of fact one knows that such a person would reproach himself in so far as he managed to forget about the lepers. He would *wish* to keep them and their sufferings constantly in mind, as an additional stimulus to doing what he believes he ought to do, viz., to take active steps to help and relieve them. . . .

I will now summarise the results of this discussion.

(1) If Psychological Egoism asserts that all ultimate motives are self-confined; or that they are all either self-confined or self-centred, some being of one kind and some of the other; or that all self-confined motives can be reduced to the desire for one's own happiness; it is certainly false. It is not even a close approximation to the truth.

(2) If it asserts that all ultimate motives are either self-regarding or self-referential, some being of one kind and some of the other; and that all other-regarding motives require a self-referential stimulus, it is a close approximation to the truth. It is true, I think, that in most people and at most times other-regarding motives are very weak unless stimulated by a self-referential stimulus. . . .

(3) Nevertheless, Psychological Egoism, even in its most diluted form, is very doubtful if taken as a universal proposition. Some persons at some times are strongly influenced by other-regarding motives which cannot plausibly be held to be stimulated by a self-referential stimulus. It seems reasonable to hold that the presence of these other-regarding motives is *necessary* to account for their choice of the alternatives which they do choose, and for their persistence in the course which they have adopted, though this can never be conclusively established in any particular case. Whether it is also *sufficient* cannot be decided with certainty, for self-regarding and self-referential components are always present in one's total motive for choosing such an action.

•   •   •   •   •

BRIAN MEDLIN

Ultimate Principles and Ethical Egoism

I believe that it is now pretty generally accepted by professional philosophers that ultimate ethical principles must be arbitrary. One cannot derive conclusions about what should be merely from accounts of what is the case; one cannot decide how people ought to behave merely from one's knowledge of how they do behave. To arrive at a conclusion in ethics one must have at least one ethical premiss. This premiss, if it be in turn a conclusion, must be the conclusion of an argument containing at least one ethical premiss. And so we can go back, indefinitely but not for ever. Sooner or later, we must come to at least one ethical premiss which is not deduced but baldly asserted. Here we must be arational; neither rational nor irrational, for here there is no room for reason even to go wrong.

But the triumph of Hume in ethics has been a limited one. What appears quite natural to a handful of specialists appears quite monstrous to the majority of decent intelligent men. At any rate, it has been my experience that people who are normally rational resist the above account of the logic of moral language, not by argument—for that can't be done—but by tooth and nail. And they resist from the best motives. They see the philosopher wantonly unravelling the whole fabric of morality. If our ultimate principles are arbitrary, they say, if those principles came out of thin air, then anyone can hold any principle he pleases. Unless moral assertions are statements of fact about the world and either true or false, we can't claim that any man is wrong, whatever his principles may be, whatever his behaviour. We have to surrender the luxury of calling one another scoundrels. That this anxiety flourishes because its roots are in confusion is evident when we consider that we don't call people scoundrels, anyhow, for being mistaken about their facts. Fools, perhaps, but that's another matter. Nevertheless, it doesn't become us to be high-up. The layman's uneasiness, however irrational it may be, is very natural and he must be reassured.

People cling to objectivist theories of morality from moral motives. It's a very queer thing that by doing so they often thwart their own purposes. There are evil opinions abroad, as anyone who walks abroad knows. The one we meet with most often, whether in pub or parlour, is the doctrine that everyone should look after himself. However refreshing he may find it after the high-minded pomposities of this morning's editorial, the good fellow knows this doctrine is

From Brian Medlin, "Ultimate Principles and Ethical Egoism," *Australasian Journal of Philosophy*, XXXV, No. 2 (1957), 111–118. Reprinted by permission of the author and the editor of the *Australasian Journal of Philosophy*.

wrong and he wants to knock it down. But while he believes that moral language is used to make statements either true or false, the best he can do is to claim that what the egoist says is false. Unfortunately, the egoist can claim that it's true. And since the supposed fact in question between them is not a publicly ascertainable one, their disagreement can never be resolved. And it is here that even good fellows waver, when they find they have no refutation available. The egoist's word seems as reliable as their own. Some begin half to believe that perhaps it is possible to supply an egoistic basis for conventional morality, some that it may be impossible to supply any other basis. I'm not going to try to prop up our conventional morality, which I fear to be a task beyond my strength, but in what follows I do want to refute the doctrine of ethical egoism. I want to resolve this disagreement by showing that what the egoist says is inconsistent. It is true that there are moral disagreements which can never be resolved, but this isn't one of them. The proper objection to the man who says 'Everyone should look after his own interests regardless of the interests of others' is not that he isn't speaking the truth, but simply that he isn't speaking.

We should first make two distinctions. This done, ethical egoism will lose much of its plausibility.

I. UNIVERSAL AND INDIVIDUAL EGOISM

Universal egoism maintains that everyone (including the speaker) ought to look after his own interests and to disregard those of other people except in so far as their interests contribute towards his own.

Individual egoism is the attitude that the egoist is going to look after himself and no one else. The egoist cannot promulgate that he is going to look after himself. He can't even preach that he *should* look after himself and preach this alone. When he tries to convince me that he should look after himself, he is attempting so to dispose me that I shall approve when he drinks my beer and steals Tom's wife. I cannot approve of his looking after himself and himself alone without so far approving of his achieving his happiness, regardless of the happiness of myself and others. So that when he sets out to persuade me that he should look after himself regardless of others, he must also set out to persuade me that I should look after him regardless of myself and others. Very small chance he has! And if the individual egoist cannot promulgate his doctrine without enlarging it, what he has is no doctrine at all.

A person enjoying such an attitude may believe that other people are fools not to look after themselves. Yet he himself would be a fool to tell them so. If he did tell them, though, he wouldn't consider that he was giving them *moral* advice. Persuasion to the effect that one should ignore the claims of morality because morality doesn't pay, to the effect that one has insufficient selfish motive and, therefore, insufficient motive for moral behaviour is not moral persuasion. For this reason I doubt that we should call the individual egoist's attitude an ethical one. And I don't doubt this in the way someone may doubt whether to call the ethical standards of Satan 'ethical' standards. A malign morality is none the less a morality for being malign. But the attitude we're considering is one of mere contempt for all moral considerations whatsoever. An indifference to morals may be wicked, but it is not a perverse morality. So far as I am aware, most egoists imagine that they are putting forward a doctrine in ethics, though there may be a few who are prepared to proclaim themselves individual egoists. If the good fellow wants to know how he should justify conventional morality to an individual egoist, the answer is that he shouldn't and can't. Buy your car elsewhere, blackguard him whenever you meet, and let it go at that.

2. CATEGORICAL AND HYPOTHETICAL EGOISM

Categorical egoism is the doctrine that we all ought to observe our own interests, *because that is what we ought to do*. For the categorical egoist the egoistic dogma is the ultimate principle in ethics.

The hypothetical egoist, on the other hand, maintains that we all ought to observe our own interests, because . . . If we want such and such an end, we must do so and so (look after ourselves). The hypothetical egoist is not a real egoist at all. He is very likely an unwitting utilitarian who believes mistakenly that the general happiness will be increased if each man looks wisely to his own. Of course, a man may believe that egoism is enjoined on us by God and he may therefore promulgate the doctrine and observe it in his conduct, not in the hope of achieving thereby a remote end, but simply in order to obey God. But neither is *he* a real egoist. He believes, ultimately, that we should obey God, even should God command us to altruism.

An ethical egoist will have to maintain the doctrine in both its universal and categorical forms. Should he retreat to hypothetical egoism he is no longer an egoist. Should he retreat to individual egoism his doctrine, while logically impregnable, is no longer ethical, no longer even a doctrine. He may wish to quarrel with this and if so, I submit peacefully. Let him call himself what he will, it makes no difference. I'm a philosopher, not a rat-catcher, and I don't see it as my job to dig vermin out of such burrows as individual egoism.

Obviously something strange goes on as soon as the ethical egoist tries to promulgate his doctrine. What is he doing when he urges upon his audience that they should each observe his own interests and those interests alone? Is he not acting contrary to the egoistic principle? It cannot be to his advantage to convince them, for seizing always their own advantage they will impair his. Surely if he does believe what he says, he should try to persuade them otherwise. Not perhaps that they should devote themselves to his interests, for they'd hardly swallow that; but that everyone should devote himself to the service of others. But is not to believe that someone should act in a certain way to try to persuade him to do so? Of course, we don't always try to persuade people to act as we think they should act. We may be lazy, for instance. But in so far as we believe that Tom should do so and so, we have a tendency to induce him to do so and so. Does it makes sense to say: 'Of course you should do this, but for goodness' sake don't'? Only where we mean: 'You should do this for certain reasons, but here are even more persuasive reasons for not doing it.' If the egoist believes ultimately that others should mind themselves alone, then, he must persuade them accordingly. If he doesn't persuade them, he is no universal egoist. It certainly makes sense to say: 'I know very well that Tom should act in such and such a way. But I know also that it's not to my advantage that he should so act. So I'd better dissuade him from it.' And this is just what the egoist must say, if he is to consider his own advantage and disregard everyone else's. That is, he must behave as an individual egoist, if he is to be an egoist at all.

He may want to make two kinds of objection here:

1. That it will not be to his disadvantage to promulgate the doctrine, provided that his audience fully understand what is to their ultimate advantage. This objection can be developed in a number of ways, but I think that it will always be possible to push the egoist into either individual or hypothetical egoism.

2. That it is to the egoist's advantage to preach the doctrine if the pleasure he gets out of doing this more than pays for the injuries he must endure at the hands of his converts. It is hard to believe that many people would be satisfied with a doctrine which they could only consistently promulgate in very special circumstances. Besides, this looks suspiciously like individual egoism in disguise.

I shall say no more on these two points because I want to advance a further criticism which seems to me at once fatal and irrefutable.

Now it is time to show the anxious layman that we have means of dealing with ethical egoism which are denied him; and denied him by just that objectivism which he thinks essential to morality. For the very fact that our ultimate principles must be arbitrary means they can't be anything we please. Just because they come out of thin air they can't come out of hot air. Because these principles are not propositions about matters of fact and cannot be deduced from propositions about matters of fact, they must be the fruit of our own attitudes. We assert them largely to modify the attitudes of our fellows but by asserting them we express our own desires and purposes. This means that we cannot use moral language cavalierly. Evidently we cannot say something like 'All human desires and purposes are bad'. This would be to express our own desires and purposes, thereby committing a kind of absurdity. Nor, I shall argue, can we say 'Everyone should observe his own interests regardless of the interests of others'.

Remembering that the principle is meant to be both universal and categorical, let us ask what kind of attitude the egoist is expressing. Wouldn't that attitude be equally well expressed by the conjunction of an infinite number of avowals thus?—

I want myself to come out on top	and	I don't care about Tom, Dick, Harry . . .
and		and
I want Tom to come out on top	and	I don't care about myself, Dick, Harry . . .

	and	
and		and
I want Dick to come out on top	and	I don't care about myself, Tom, Harry . . .
and		and
I want Harry to come out on top	and	I don't care about myself, Dick, Tom . . .
etc.		etc.

From this analysis it is obvious that the principle expressing such an attitude must be inconsistent.

But now the egoist may claim that he hasn't been properly understood. When he says 'Everyone should look after himself and himself alone', he means 'Let each man do what he wants regardless of what anyone else wants'. The egoist may claim that what he values is merely that he and Tom and Dick and Harry should each do what he wants and not care about what anyone else may want and that this doesn't involve his principle in any inconsistency. Nor need it. But even if it doesn't, he's no better off. Just what does he value? Is it the well-being of himself, Tom, Dick and Harry or merely their going on in a certain way regardless of whether or not this is going to promote their well-being? When he urges Tom, say, to do what he wants, is he appealing to Tom's self-interest? If so, his attitude can be expressed thus:

I want myself to be happy		I want myself not to care about Tom, Dick, Harry . . .
and	and	
I want Tom to be happy		

We need go no further to see that the principle expressing such an attitude must be inconsistent. I have made this kind of move already. What concerns me now is the alternative position the egoist must take up to be safe from it. If the egoist values merely that people should go on in a certain way, regardless of whether or not this is going to promote their well-being, then he is not appealing to the self-interest of his audience when he urges them to regard their own interests. If Tom has any regard for himself at all, the egoist's blandishments will leave him cold. Further, the egoist doesn't even have his own interest in mind when he says that, like everyone else, he should look after himself. A funny kind of egoism this turns out to be.

Perhaps now, claiming that he is indeed appealing to the self-interest of his audience, the egoist may attempt to counter the objection of the previous paragraph. He may move into 'Let each man do what he wants and let each man disregard what others want when their desires clash with his own'. Now his attitude may be expressed thus:

I want everyone to be happy	and	I want everyone to disregard the happiness of others when their happiness clashes with his own.

The egoist may claim justly that a man can have such an attitude and also that in a certain kind of world such a man could get what he wanted. Our objection to the egoist has been that his desires are incompatible. And this is still so. If he and Tom and Dick and Harry did go on as he recommends by saying 'Let each man disregard the happiness of others, when their happiness conflicts with his own', then assuredly they'd all be completely miserable. Yet he wants them to be happy. He is attempting to counter this by saying that it is merely a fact about the world that they'd make one another miserable by going on as he recommends. The world could conceivably have been different. For this reason, he says, this principle is not inconsistent. This argument may not seem very compelling, but I advance it on the egoist's behalf because I'm interested in the reply to it. For now we don't even need to tell him that the world isn't in fact like that. (What it's like makes no difference.) Now we can point out to him that he is arguing not as an egoist but as a utilitarian. He has slipped into hypothetical egoism to save his principle from inconsistency. If the world were such that we always made ourselves and others happy by doing one another down, then we could find good utilitarian reasons for urging that we should do one another down.

If, then, he is to save his principle, the egoist must do one of two things. He must give up the claim that he is appealing to the self-interest of his audience, that he has even his own interest in mind. Or he must admit that, in the conjunction above, although 'I want everyone to be happy' refers to ends, nevertheless 'I want everyone to disregard the happiness of others when their happiness conflicts with his own' can refer only to means. That is, his so-called ultimate principle is really compounded of a principle and a moral rule subordinate to that principle. That is, he is really a utilitarian who is urging everyone to go on in a certain way so that everyone may be happy. A utilitarian, what's more, who is ludicrously mistaken about the nature of the world. Things being as they are, his moral rule is a very bad one. Things being as they are, it can only be deduced from his principle by means of an empirical premiss which is manifestly false. Good fellows don't need to fear him. They may rest easy that the world is and must be on their side and the best thing they can do is be good.

It may be worth pointing out that objections similar to those I have brought against the egoist can be made to the altruist. The man who holds that the principle 'Let everyone observe the interests of others' is both universal and categorical can be compelled to choose between two alternatives, equally repugnant. He must give up the claim that he is concerned for the well-being of himself and others. Or he must admit that, though 'I want everyone to be happy' refers to ends, nevertheless 'I want everyone to disregard his own happiness when it conflicts with the happiness of others' can refer only to means.

I have said from time to time that the egoistic principle is inconsistent. I have not said it is contradictory. This for the reason that we can, without contradiction, express inconsistent desires and purposes. To do so is not to say anything like 'Goliath was ten feet tall and not ten feet tall'. Don't we all want to eat our cake and have it too? And when we say we do we aren't asserting a contradiction. We are not asserting a contradiction whether we be making an avowal of our attitudes or stating a fact about them. We all have conflicting motives. As a utilitarian exuding benevolence I want the man who mows my landlord's grass to be happy, but as a slug-a-bed I should like to see him scourged. None of this, however, can do the egoist any good. For we assert our ultimate principles not only to express our own attitudes but also to induce similar attitudes in others, to dispose them to conduct themselves as we wish. In so far as their desires conflict, people don't know what to do. And, therefore, no expression of incompatible desires can ever serve for an ultimate principle of human conduct.

JOHN HOSPERS
Baier and Medlin on Ethical Egoism

In his excellent book *The Moral Point of View*, Professor Kurt Baier attempts to refute ethical egoism—the doctrine that my sole duty is to promote my own interests exclusively—in the following way:

"Let B and K be candidates for the presidency of a certain country and let it be granted that it is in the interest of either to be elected, but that only one can succeed. It would then be in the interest of B but against the interest of K if B were elected, and vice versa, and therefore in the interest of B but against the interest of K if K were liquidated, and vice versa. But from this it would follow that B ought to liquidate K, that it is wrong for B not to do so, that B has not 'done his duty' until he has liquidated K; and vice versa. Similarly K, knowing that his own liquidation is in the interest of B and therefore anticipating B's attempts to secure it, ought to take steps to foil B's endeavors. It would be wrong for him not to do so. He would 'not have done his duty' until he had made sure of stopping B. It follows that if K prevents B from liquidating him, his act must be said to be both wrong and not wrong—wrong because it is the prevention of what B ought to do, his duty, and wrong for B not to do it; not wrong because it is what K ought to do, his duty, and wrong for K not to do it. But one and the same act (logically) cannot be both morally wrong and not morally wrong. . . .

"This is obviously absurd. For morality is designed to apply in just such cases,

From John Hospers, "Baier and Medlin on Ethical Egoism," *Philosophical Studies*, XII, Nos. 1–2(1961), 10–16. Reprinted by permission of the author.

namely, those where interests conflict. But if the point of view of morality were that of self-interest, then there could *never* be moral solutions of conflicts of interest." [1]

We are to assume at the outset that killing K not only seems to be, but really *is* to B's interest and that killing B really is to K's interest. (If it were to the interest of each to work out a compromise, then no problem would arise.) Operating on this assumption, what can be said of Professor Baier's one-shot refutation of egoism? His argument can be schematized in the following way:

1. Every adequate ethical theory must be able to provide solutions for conflicts of interest.
2. Ethical egoism is unable to provide solutions for conflicts of interest.
3. Therefore, ethical egoism is not an adequate ethical theory.

So much for the argument for the inadequacy of ethical egoism. But his criticism goes even further:

4. Any view which is guilty of self-contradiction is thereby refuted.
5. Ethical egoism is guilty of self-contradiction.
6. Therefore, ethical egoism is refuted.

We may examine the second argument first, since if a theory is guilty of self-contradiction no further refutation of it is necessary.

Let it be admitted that to say that one and the same act is both right and wrong is to be guilty of a self-contradiction, since the proposition that it is wrong entails that it is not right, and an act cannot be both right and not right. (I shall waive any discussion of a point whose truth is presupposed in Baier's argument, namely that rightness and wrongness are properties. I shall also waive discussion of the possibility that even if they are properties they are to-you and to-me properties, e.g., something can be interesting to you and not interesting to me, and rightness might be like interestingness.)

We may admit, then, at least for purposes of the argument, that to say that Brutus killing Caesar was both right and wrong involves a contradiction. But the case presented by Professor Baier is not that of one and the same act being both right and wrong. It is a case of *two* acts, one by B and the other by K. They are two acts of the same *kind,* namely attempted murder (or the attempt to foil the murder-attempt of the other), but there is no contradiction in two such acts being attempted or in both being right. It might well be B's duty to try to dispose of K, and K's duty to try to dispose of B. Since there are two acts here, one by B and one by K, the situation of one and the same act being both right and wrong does not arise, and no contradiction arises either.

So much for the argument concerning contradiction. But the inadequacy argument remains, and it seems much more plausible. It is true that we usually expect an ethical theory to be able to settle conflicts of interest; for example, if husband and wife both want custody of the children, we expect the ethical theory to tell us (in conjunction, of course, with empirical premises) which one's wish

---

[1] *The Moral Point of View.* (Ithaca, N.Y.: Cornell University Press, 1958), pp. 189–90.

should be granted; every judge in a courtroom must make such decisions. The judge in arbitrating such a case could not use ethical egoism as a way of settling it, for if it is the interest of both husband and wife to have the same thing and they can't both have it, he will *have* to decide against the interest of one of them; and egoism, which tells each person to follow his own interest exclusively, can provide no basis for settling the dispute. This does seem to be a very serious criticism.

What would the egoist reply to such a charge? I must first distinguish the *personal* egoist from the *impersonal* egoist. The personal egoist is one who says that *his* sole duty is to promote his own interest exclusively, but makes no pronouncement about what other people should do. (Some would not consider this an ethical theory at all, since it does not fulfill the criterion of generality. And if the theory is restated so as not to talk about duties at all—not "It is my duty to promote my own interest exclusively" but "*I'm going* to promote my own interest exclusively," which is the kind of thing that most practicing egoists say—then of course there is no ethical theory at all, but only a prediction or expression of determination with regard to one's future behavior.) The impersonal egoist is one who says that the duty of *each and every person* (including himself) is to pursue his own interest exclusively.

How will the egoist react to Baier's inadequacy argument? The *personal* egoist will not be disturbed at all. According to him, his one duty is to pursue exclusively his own interest; so if he happens to be B he will try to kill K, and if he is K he will try to kill B (and foil K's attempts to kill him); and if he is neither B nor K he will not concern himself with the conflict of interest one way or the other. Of course if there is something in it for him, he will: if he stands to gain a fortune if K wins, then he will do what he can to assist K's victory in order to gain the fortune. But otherwise he will ignore the matter. "But doesn't an ethical theory have to have a means of deciding what to do or say in cases of conflict of interest? If you had to advise B or K, what would you say?" The answer is, of course, that if there is nothing in it for him the personal egoist will not bother to advise either party or to aid either cause. If asked for advice on the matter, he would probably say, "Get lost, you bother me." (Nor would the personal egoist be likely to engage in philosophical discussion. It would hardly be to his interest to allow other people to plant in his mind the seeds of skepticism concerning his egoistic doctrine.)

So far, then, egoism has not been refuted. It has been shown to be inadequate *only if* you expect an ethical theory to arbitrate conflicts of interest. Thus, it *would* be insufficient for the judge in a divorce court. The judge has nothing to gain either way, but he has to decide on a matter of conflict of interest between husband and wife. If the judge were a personal egoist, his principle would simply be to follow *his own* interest; but this principle wouldn't help him at all in dealing with the case at hand. Here he needs instructions, not for promoting his own interest, but for settling cases of conflict of interest between *other* people.

And this, of course, the theory cannot provide; but the personal egoist doesn't mind this at all. He has no wish to arbitrate other people's conflicts of interest. He will gladly leave such activities to the "suckers."

What of the *impersonal* egoist? His view is that he should pursue his own interest exclusively, that B should pursue B's, that K should pursue K's, and so on for everyone else. What will he say in the case of B and K? He will advise K to try to win out over B by whatever means he can, and will advise B to try to win out over K by whatever means he can: in other words, to settle the thing by force or craft, and may the strongest or cleverest man win. Does his advice to B contradict his advice to K? Not at all; he is urging each one to try to gain victory over the other; this is not very different from telling each of the two competing teams to try and win the game. His view does not, of course, provide a *rational* means of settling the conflict of interest, but it does provide a means: it tells each party to try to emerge victorious, though of course only one of them *can* emerge victorious.

So far, there seems to be no difficulty for the impersonal egoist. But, as an impersonal egoist, he does have a stake in the general acceptance of his doctrine; for he does say of other people, not just himself, that each should pursue his own interest exclusively. If he sees B, he will urge B to try to win over K (even if he has nothing to gain personally by B's victory), and if he sees K, he will urge K to try to win over B. But there is, while no outright contradiction, a curious *tactical incongruity* in his view. For if the impersonal egoist advises others to pursue their own interest, might not this interfere with the promotion of *his own* interest, and yet is he not committed by his own doctrine to pursuing his own interest exclusively? If he advises B and K, but neither B nor K is a threat to him, there is no problem; but if I advise my business competitor to pursue his own interest with a vengeance, may he not follow my advice and pursue his interest so wholeheartedly that he forces me out of business? For the sake of *my own* interest, then, I may be well advised to keep my egoistic doctrine to myself, lest others use it against me.

An impersonal egoist, therefore, may simply prefer to keep his own counsel and not advise others at all. In this case, he escapes the difficulty just as the personal egoist did. He will pursue his own interest regardless of who else opposes it; and while he does, as an impersonal egoist, advise others to pursue *their* own interests, he will do this only when doing it does not imperil *his* interest.

Thus, *if* you are an impersonal egoist, and *if* as an impersonal egoist you have a stake in advising others—and only then—you will feel a conflict between the promotion of your egoistic doctrine and the promotion of your own interests, which will be damaged if others pursue their interests at the expense of yours. But this hardly *refutes* the impersonal egoist's doctrine; it concerns only a tactical matter of when to publicize it.

But now another objection to ethical egoism presents itself. Suppose you are an impersonal egoist, and are suggesting courses of action to your acquaintances. Acquantance A asks you what to do, and you say to him, "Pursue your own interest exclusively, and if B tries to get the better of you, cut him down.

Even if you could save B's life by lifting a finger, there is no reason for you to do so as long as it doesn't promote your interest." Later on, B asks you what you think *he* should do. So you say to him, "Pursue your own interest exclusively, and if A tries to get the better of you, cut him down. Even if you could save A's life by lifting a finger, there is no reason for you to do so as long as it doesn't promote your interest." And you say similar things to your other acquaintances.

Suppose, now, that an onlooker heard you say all these things. He might wonder (with good reason) exactly what you were advising—what the general drift of your advice was. You tell A to do what is to his interest and ignore B, so our onlooker thinks you are a friend of A's and an enemy of B's. But then you tell B to do what is to his interest and ignore A, and our onlooker now concludes that you are a friend of B and an enemy of A. And in fact what are you anyway? It sounds to the onlooker as if you are pathologically addicted to changing your mind. Perhaps, like some people, you are so impressed by whoever you are with at the moment that you forget all about the interests of those who aren't right there before you. This might explain the sudden shift in attitude.

But the curious thing is that the egoist doesn't consider this a shift in attitude at all, but a consistent expression of *one* attitude, the "impersonal egoistic" attitude. But that is just the point of the objection. *Is* it a single consistent attitude? When you are in the presence of A, it is only A's interest that counts; but a moment later, when you are in the presence of B, it is only B's interest that counts. Isn't this very strange? Can the question of whose interests count really depend on whom you happen to be addressing or confronting at the moment?

The charge, in short, is that the impersonal egoist is guilty of issuing *inconsistent directives*. This charge is made, for example, by Dr. Brian Medlin.[2] According to Medlin, when the (impersonal) egoist is talking to himself he says "I want myself to come out on top, and I don't care about Tom, Dick, Harry . . ."; when he is talking to Tom he says (in effect), "I want Tom to come out on top and I don't care about myself, Dick, Harry . . ."; when he is talking to Dick he says, "I want Dick to come out on top, and I don't care about myself, Tom, Harry . . ."; and so on in a conjunction of an infinite number of avowals. "From this analysis," he concludes, "it is obvious that the principle expressing such an attitude must be inconsistent." (The same conclusion follows if the egoist says to Tom, "You alone count," and to Dick, "You alone count," and so on.)

Now, if this is what the impersonal egoist really means to say, then of course what he says *is* inconsistent. But perhaps that is not what he means to say; at any rate, it is not what he *needs* to say. What else might he mean?

It might be suggested, first, that all that the egoist wants to say is that if you tend to your interests (happiness, or welfare, or whatever) and I to my interests and Tom to Tom's interests, and so on, everyone will be happier (or have more welfare, etc.) than they would if they did not adopt such a completely

[2] "Ultimate Principles and Ethical Egoism," *Australasian Journal of Philosophy*, 35(No. 2):111–18 (August 1957).

laissez-faire policy with regard to one another's interests. But two things should be noted about this: (1) If the egoist says this, he is making an *empirical* claim —a claim that human beings will be happier pursuing a policy of splendid isolation with regard to each other than by behaving cooperatively, helping one another in time of need, and so on—and this empirical claim is very dubious indeed; it seems rather to be the case that the welfare of human beings is not independent but *inter*dependent, and that "no man is an island." If each person pursued his own interest to the exclusion of others, there would be less happiness in the world, not more. But whatever may be said of this empirical claim, (2) when the egoist makes this claim he is no longer an egoist but a utilitarian; he is arguing that the general welfare (or the maximum total fulfillment of human interests) is what should be striven for, and that the best means of achieving it is by a policy of isolation. But in admitting that the general welfare is the end to be aimed at he is already forsaking his egoism.

Is there anything else, then, that the impersonal egoist can be alleged to mean? The charge against him is that his directives to different people are inconsistent with one another. He, Tom, Dick, and Harry cannot each be the *only* person who counts, or the only person he hopes will come out on top. Is not the egoist, if he abandons the utilitarian argument (above) and retreats back to his egoism, caught in this web of inconsistency? Is he not saying to Tom that he hopes Tom will come out on top (and by implication that Dick won't), and then the next moment saying to Dick that he hopes Dick will come out on top (and by implication that Tom won't), and so on, thereby patting each one on the back before his face and poking him in the nose behind his back?

The egoist *need* not, I think, be guilty of such duplicity. What if he assembled Tom, Dick, Harry, and everyone else into his presence at the same moment? What would he say to them all together? He might say, "I *hope* that each of you comes out on top." But in that case, he *is* saying something self-contradictory, since of course each of them cannot come out on top—only one of them can. But he need not say this; suppose that instead he says, "I hope each of you *tries* to come out on top," or "Each of you should *try* to come out the victor." There is surely no inconsistency here. The hope he is expressing here is the kind of hope that the interested but impartial spectator expresses at a game. Perhaps the egoist likes to live life in a dangerous cutthroat manner, unwilling to help others in need but not desiring others to help him either. He wants life to be spicy and dangerous; to him the whole world is one vast egoistic game, and living life accordingly is the way to make it interesting and exciting. It may be that, if our egoist says this, his egoism is somewhat diluted from the stronger and earlier form of "I hope that you all win" or "Each of you alone counts"— but at least, in this latest formulation, he is not caught in an inconsistency.

Whether or not the egoist, then, is caught in an inconsistency depends on what, exactly, we take him to be saying. It should not be assumed that because the egoist in some formulations of his doctrine is guilty of inconsistency, he is therefore inconsistent in all of them.

WILLIAM H. BAUMER
Indefensible Impersonal Egoism

It is sometimes argued, *e.g.*, by John Hospers, that impersonal egoism is at least not an impossible ethical view, and is not accompanied by such odd self-referring characteristics as would make it tantamount to impossible.[1] This essay is a three-part argument to show that such a view of impersonal egoism is mistaken. The first part is a formulation of the basic principle of impersonal egoism. The second is devoted to establishing that Hospers' analogy with trying to win a game both fails and is unnecessary. The third segment of the argument is to show that, *pace* Hospers and Brian Medlin, impersonal ethical egoism is absurd even given a non-emotive analysis of ethical language.[2]

Impersonal egoism is supposed to be a view which involves the determination of all questions of right and wrong, if not also good and bad, in terms of the satisfactions of the interests of each particular agent. No appeal to any sort of general happiness principle is admissible. The satisfactions, however, may well be long-term ones; it is not to be supposed that impersonal egoism is nonprudential. Its principle is formulable as follows:

> *Each person ought to do those acts, and only those acts, which lead to the most efficient satisfaction of the most interests he himself has.*

It may be objected that this principle introduces an appeal to ends to be achieved, and does not take into account the possibility of impersonal egoism formulated as prescriptions and proscriptions of various actions.[3] But the principle as here formulated is categorical; there are no conditions which might—and again might not—be satisfied attached to it. Thus it does not depend on those ethical positions which have appealed to ends to be achieved, such as utilitarianism or Deweyan pragmatism, as the ultimate justification of moral judgements. Unlike Medlin's, this formulation is not offered with an emotive analysis of ethical language in the background. To press for a formulation of the basic principle of impersonal

---

Professor Baumer has written this essay especially for the second edition of *Problems of Moral Philosophy*. It is a slightly revised version of his article, "Indefensible Impersonal Egoism," *Philosophical Studies*, XVIII, No. 5 (1967), 72–75.

[1] John Hospers "Baier and Medlin on Ethical Egoism," *Philosophical Studies*, 12:10–16 (1961); cf. his *Human Conduct* (New York: Harcourt, Brace, and World, 1961), pp. 157–72. See also: Peter Hare, "In Defense of Impersonal Egoism," *Philosophical Studies*, 17:94–95 (1966).

[2] Brian Medlin, "Ultimate Principles and Ethical Egoism," *Australasian Journal of Philosophy*, 35:111–18 (1957).

[3] Cf. Daniel Kading and Martin Kramer, "Mr. Hospers' Defense of Impersonal Egoism," *Philosophical Studies*, 15:44–46 (1964).

egoism here which would be stated simply in terms of prescriptions or proscriptions of various actions would be to seek the impossible, since it would mean seeking a principle governing one's pursuit of his interests which makes no mention of any interests to be pursued in any way. Finally, it is impossible to do without such a principle here, impossible to follow the pattern of simply having a set of moral rules specifying what ought and ought not be done. Such an approach would not involve the general prohibition of anything not in one's own interests which is the defining characteristic of impersonal egoism.

Positions such as that advocated by Hospers attempt to make impersonal egoism plausible by presenting it as a view which urges that everyone should try to win, claiming that this is analogous to the spectator at a sports contest impartially cheering on both sides. This is supposed to remove the embarrassment of a view which cannot be preached if it is to be practiced, since it is hardly apparent that the promotion of the doctrine of impersonal egoism is in the interests of any particular agent. Unfortunately, one element overlooked in such arguments is that everyone is both spectator and player in this "game," and thus must be urging on everyone, including himself. A far more serious difficulty, and one which invalidates the analogy, is this: We think of sports contests as going on according to certain rules and conventions. One does not, for example, turn a pea shooter on one's opponent in a golf match at the moment he is attempting to blast out of a sand trap. But impersonal egoism does not apply within such a larger context, and is not to be applied within the customary limitations of a non-egoistic moral scheme. If an analogy with a contest is to be introduced, the appropriate one is warfare conducted with no consideration of any humanitarian concerns. After all, the obligation one has on the basis of impersonal egoism is not to try to fulfill one's interests in a competitively balanced or fair situation, as a game analogy might suggest. Rather, this obligation is to fulfill, or try to fulfill, one's interests simpliciter.[4] On the view of impersonal egoism it is not merely odd but downright "immoral" for someone not to take every possible advantage which promotes his own interests most efficiently. In only this sense is anything "against the rules" of the "game." The proposed analogy, in short, assimilates a peripheral aspect of impersonal egoism to a peripheral aspect of a sports contest while neglecting the dissimilarities between the central aspects of these. Thus it fails.

The impersonal egoist, though, need not be disturbed by the collapse of this analogy, for he did not need it in the first place. It is only on the assumption of an emotive analysis of ethical language[5] that the egoist must preach his view to others. If this is rejected, as it certainly can be, all the impersonal egoist has to be able to do is to express his view consistently should this be required. Views such as that advanced by Hospers suppose he can, and thus suppose that this is a possible ethical position. But he cannot, and it is not. Consider the following sort of situation where Mr. Alpha and Mr. Bravo have conflicting

---

[4] [That is, with no conditions restricting the fulfillment of interests.—Ed. note.]

[5] [According to an emotive analysis of ethical language, to state what kinds of acts ought to be done is to try to get others to do them.—Ed. note.]

interests. These are not merely conflicting interests prima facie but on balance; they are also precisely the interests each ought to fulfill on the basis of the impersonal egoism principle. To say these interests conflict is to say that Alpha's fulfillment of his interests will prevent Bravo's fulfilling his and conversely. Such a situation, it might be remarked, is hardly unlikely; it arises whenever each of two (or more) agents can best fulfill his own interests by gaining one goal which only one of all those involved can gain, e.g., a particular socio-economic position. In such a situation it follows from impersonal egoism that Alpha ought to do those acts which will bring about the fulfillment of his interests while Bravo ought to do certain acts which will prevent Alpha's fulfilling his interests, and conversely. Unfortunately for impersonal egoism, this is absurd. The following makes this clear.

If someone ought, on balance, to do a certain act, it cannot on pain of contradiction be, on balance, wrong for him to do that. But to say it is not wrong for him to do that act is to say that he has the right to do it, i.e., that the act is permissively right for him. It follows that if an act is one which someone ought to do, then it is an act which it is permissively right for him to do. Furthermore, if it is permissively right for someone to do a given act, then no one has the right to prevent him from doing that. This is so since to say that someone has such a right of prevention is to say that the act to be prevented is in some sense wrong, and the same act cannot be both in some sense wrong and also permissively right, at least on balance. It is, in this connection, important to differentiate preventing an act from urging its non-performance or some such. At least so far as acts which are only permissively right are concerned, it is perfectly appropriate to suggest that the agent do something else, and so forth. To prevent an act, though, is not merely to urge it not be done, advise against it, and so on; it is to *stop* its being done. But note what this yields: if someone ought, on balance, to do a certain act, then it is wrong for anyone to prevent his doing that act.

The foregoing development of the interrelations of the meanings of the terms involved applies to the conflicting interests of Alpha and Bravo with interesting results. Alpha, while he ought to prevent Bravo's fulfilling his own interests, is at the same time wrong in doing so, for Bravo ought to fulfill his own interests. Bravo, while he ought to prevent Alpha's fulfilling his own interests, is wrong in doing so since Alpha ought to fulfill his own interests. In short, given impersonal egoism and the interrelations of the meanings of "ought to do," "wrong," and "prevent," it follows that each one, Alpha and Bravo, is doing what he ought and ought not do. Further absurdities involved in impersonal egoism could be generated, but two are twice enough.[6] It cannot, incidentally, be supposed that these can successfully be removed by insisting upon an emotive analysis of the terms here. Though such an appeal might be supposed to destroy the above introduction of interrelations of meanings of ethical terms, it does not prevent inconsistency. Medlin has shown that.

[6] For a somewhat similar argument, see Kurt Baier, *The Moral Point of View* (Ithaca, N.Y.: Cornell University Press, 1958), pp. 189–90.

Impersonal egoism, then, can be formulated as something other than unintentional utilitarianism, and can be formulated on the basis of some alternative to an emotive analysis of ethical language. It cannot, however, be helpfully assimilated to cheering on participants in a sporting contest. It also cannot be taken as a possible ethical position, for absurd positions are not possible ones, ethical or otherwise.

Supplementary Paperback Reading

B. H. Baumrin, *Hobbes's* Leviathan: *Interpretation and Criticism.* (Wadsworth)

J. A. Brunton, "Egoism and Morality," in J. Margolis, *Contemporary Ethical Theory.* (Random House)

J. Dewey, *Theory of the Moral Life,* Ch. VI. (Holt, Rinehart and Winston)

A. Duncan-Jones, *Butler's Moral Philosophy,* Ch. 3–5. (Penguin Books)

A. C. Ewing, *Ethics,* Ch. II. (Free Press)

W. D. Falk, "Morality, Self, and Others," in H. N. Castaneda and G. Nakhnikian, *Morality and the Language of Conduct.* (Wayne State University Press) Also in J. J. Thomson and G. Dworkin, *Ethics.* (Harper and Row) and in Bobbs-Merrill Reprint Series in Philosophy.

D. P. Gauthier, *Morality and Rational Self-Interest.* (Prentice-Hall)

W. James, *Principles of Psychology,* Vol. II, Ch. 26. (Dover Publications)

P. H. Nowell-Smith, *Ethics,* Ch. 10. (Penguin Books)

R. G. Olson, *The Morality of Self-Interest.* (Harcourt, Brace and World)

R. Peters, *Hobbes,* Ch. 6–9. (Penguin Books)

M. Schlick, *Problems of Ethics,* Ch. II and III. (Dover Publications)

H. Sidgwick, *The Methods of Ethics,* Book I, Ch. 7, and Book II. (Dover Publications)

Note: The classic criticism of psychological egoism was made by Joseph Butler in his *Sermons Preached at the Rolls Chapel* (1726). It is available in an inexpensive paperback: J. Butler, *Five Sermons,* edited by S. M. Brown, Jr. (Bobbs-Merrill)

4

CLASSICAL

UTILITARIAN

ETHICS

Introduction

A normative ethical system is a set of moral principles by reference to which anyone can determine, in any situation of choice, what he ought or ought not to do. One such system is utilitarianism, and in this chapter we study its classical formulation in the writings of two British philosophers, Jeremy Bentham (1748–1832) and John Stuart Mill (1806–1873). In the following chapter we shall consider a normative ethical system that is diametrically opposed to utilitarianism, and there we shall meet with some of the major objections philosophers have raised against utilitarianism.

UTILITY AS THE TEST OF RIGHT AND WRONG

The basic concept of utilitarian ethics is, as its name indicates, the idea of utility: an act is right if it is useful. As soon as this is said the question arises, Useful for what end? For unless we know the end to which something is to be judged as a means, we do not know how to decide whether it is useful or not.

The answer given by utilitarianism is that an act is right when it is useful in bringing about a *desirable* or *good* end, an end that has *intrinsic value*. The concept of intrinsic value will be studied in detail in Chapter 8. A preliminary account, however, must be given here if we are to understand utilitarian ethics. By "intrinsic value" is meant the value something has as an end in itself, and not as a means to some further end. This may be explained as follows. There are certain things we value because of their consequences or effects, but we do not value them in themselves. Thus we think it is a good thing to go to the dentist because we want healthy teeth and we have reason to believe that the dentist is a person who can help bring about this end. But few people find visiting the dentist good in itself. In other words, the act of visiting the dentist is done not for its own sake but for the sake of something else. This something else may in turn be valued not as an end in itself but as a means to other ends. Eventually, however, we arrive at certain experiences or conditions of life that we want to have and enjoy just for their own sake. These are ends that we judge to be intrinsically good; they have for us intrinsic value. The experience of undergoing dental treatment, on the other hand, has only instrumental value for us. We consider it good only because we think it is a means to some further end. If we did not value the end, the means would lose its value. Thus suppose we did not mind losing our teeth or having toothaches. We would not then think going to the dentist was worthwhile. So the value of some things is entirely *derivative*.

They derive all their value from the value of something else. Other things—things that are sought for their own sake—have *non-derivative* value. Their value is not derived from the value of something else and hence is intrinsic to them. Derivative value, in short, is instrumental value; non-derivative value is intrinsic value. Of course it is possible for one and the same thing to have both kinds of value. For example, if a person enjoys playing tennis and also does it for the exercise, the game of tennis has both intrinsic and instrumental value for him. In this case playing tennis is both intrinsically good and instrumentally good. In contrast to this, going to the dentist is intrinsically bad but instrumentally good. Two other combinations are also possible. Something can be intrinsically good but instrumentally bad (for example, eating too much of our favorite dessert), and something can be both intrinsically and instrumentally bad (for example, having a painful illness involving heavy medical expenses).

Now the basic principle of utilitarian ethics is that *the right depends on the good.* This means that we can know whether an act is morally right only by finding out what its consequences are and then determining the intrinsic goodness (or badness) of those consequences. The moral rightness of an act is not itself an intrinsic value. On the contrary, an act is right only when it is instrumentally good and its rightness consists in its instrumental goodness. Our next question is, What is the standard of intrinsic value by which utilitarians judge the goodness of the consequences of a right act? Classical utilitarians have proposed two different answers to this. Some, like Jeremy Bentham, have said "pleasure"; others, like John Stuart Mill, have said "happiness," and have added that happiness is not merely a sum total of pleasures. A third answer has been suggested by a twentieth-century philosopher, G. E. Moore, who has claimed that intrinsic goodness cannot be defined in terms of either pleasure or happiness, but is a unique and indefinable property of things. Thus we have three types of utilitarianism, according to these three views of the end to which morally right conduct is a means. They are called "hedonistic utilitarianism" (from the Greek word *hedone,* meaning pleasure); "eudaemonistic utilitarianism" (from the Greek word *eudaemonia,* meaning happiness or welfare); and "agathistic utilitarianism" (from the Greek word *agathos,* meaning good). In this chapter we consider only the first two types of utilitarian ethics. The third will be studied in Chapters 7 and 8, where we shall be reading from the works of G. E. Moore.

The fundamental norm of hedonistic utilitarianism may be stated thus: An act is right if it brings about pleasure (or prevents the bringing about of pain); an act is wrong if it brings about pain (or prevents the bringing about of pleasure). The fundamental norm of eudaemonistic utilitarianism may be stated in a similar way, merely by substituting "happiness" for "pleasure" and "unhappiness" for "pain." As soon as we state the norm of utilitarian ethics in either of these ways, we see that another question immediately arises: Pleasure or happiness *for whom,* pain or unhappiness *for whom?*

Three alternative answers have been given by utilitarians: (a) Pleasure or happiness for the agent himself; that is, for the person who is doing the act.

(This is one form of ethical egoism, which we have studied in the preceding chapter.) (b) Pleasure or happiness for all others but the agent. (c) Pleasure or happiness for everyone, including the agent. These answers define three kinds of utilitarian ethical systems, which are called (a) egoistic utilitarianism, (b) altruistic utilitarianism, and (c) universalistic utilitarianism. They vary independently with the three types already mentioned (namely, hedonistic, eudaemonistic, and agathistic utilitarianism). By working out all the possible combinations of these two classifications, we could arrive at nine distinct types of utilitarianism (egoistic hedonistic, altruistic hedonistic, universalistic hedonistic, egoistic eudaemonistic, etc.). In this chapter we shall be dealing with only two of these: universalistic hedonistic (the theory of Jeremy Bentham) and universalistic eudaemonistic (the theory of John Stuart Mill).

Let us now examine the principle of utility as it is applied in universalistic hedonistic and eudaemonistic systems. In order to know what we ought to do in any situation of choice, we proceed as follows. We specify all the alternative courses of action open to our choice. We then calculate to the best of our ability the probable consequences that would ensue if we were to choose each alternative. In this calculation we ask ourselves, How much pleasure (or happiness) and how much pain (or unhappiness) will result in my own life and in the lives of all people who will be affected by my doing this act? When we have done this for all the alternatives open to us, we then compare those consequences in order to find out which one leads to a greater amount of pleasure (or happiness) and a smaller amount of pain (or unhappiness) than any other alternative. The act that in this way is found to *maximize intrinsic value and minimize intrinsic disvalue* is the act we morally ought to do. To do any other act in the given situation would be morally wrong.

In the practical affairs of everyday life, of course, we cannot stop and make such detailed calculations every time we have alternative courses of action open to us. Indeed, if we were to do this we might cause more unhappiness or less happiness to be brought about in the world than if we were to make choices on the basis of habits we had developed from our past experience. Thus it would be wrong for us, according to the principle of utility, to try to make an accurate calculation each time. What we must do is to use our common sense and choose on the basis of similar situations in the past. After all, it does not take much thought to predict that murdering someone is going to produce more unhappiness in the world than respecting that person's life. We need not have committed a murder in the past to know this. We need only use our imagination to be able to make a reasonable prediction about what would happen if we were to do such an act.

It is important to realize that for the utilitarian no act is morally wrong in itself. Its wrongness depends entirely on its consequences. Take the act of murder, for instance. If the consequences of murdering a particular man in a particular set of circumstances (say, assassinating Hitler in 1935) were to bring about less unhappiness in the world than would be caused by the man himself were he to remain alive, it is not wrong to murder him. Indeed, it is our duty to do so, since the circumstances are such that our refraining from doing the act will result in more unhappiness (intrinsic disvalue) and less happiness (intrinsic value) than our doing it. This might at first appear to be a shocking and outrageous teaching. But the utilitarian would argue, What, after all, is wrong with the act of murder? Is it not that it causes so much pain and unhappiness both to the victim and to his kin, and prevents the victim from having the chance to enjoy his right to the pursuit of happiness? Suppose the nature of man and the world were very different from what they in fact are, so that everyone at the age of thirty suddenly deteriorated physically and mentally and became incapable of having any pleasant experiences thereafter in his life. Suppose, further, that there was a way of killing people at that age which gave them great pleasure up to the final moment of death. Finally, suppose that their death at this time in their lives was celebrated by others as a happy event, in the way births are often celebrated in our own culture. In such a world why should the murder of people at thirty be condemned? Since there would be more unhappiness in the world as a result of respecting their lives, what would be wrong in ending their lives? Indeed, it is just such considerations as these that have led some people in our actual world to advocate the painless killing of human beings under certain specified circumstances. Thus it has been suggested that a doctor be permitted to administer a drug that will painlessly cause the death of a person who has an incurable disease when, first, there is no likelihood that a cure will be discovered in the period the person will remain alive; second, when his suffering is intense and cannot be alleviated by medical means; and third, when both the person himself and his relatives have asked that such a drug be administered to him.

This example brings to light another aspect of utilitarian ethics. It shows that, from the utilitarian point of view, it is sometimes right to do an act which is known to bring about unhappiness. But this is true only when the act in question will bring about *less unhappiness than any possible alternative.* In that sort of situation to do anything else—even to "do nothing," that is, to let events take their course without trying to change them—would be deliberately to cause more unhappiness to people than is necessary. Situations of this unfortunate kind may occur in time of war or when there are natural disasters such as floods and earthquakes, as well as in cases of people suffering from incurable diseases.

We must now point out an important difference between hedonistic and eudaemonistic types of utilitarianism, a difference originally recognized by Mill as separating his own ethical theory from that of Bentham. Mill argues that in calculating the good and bad consequences of an act in order to determine whether it is right or wrong, we must consider not only the *quantity* of pleasure that will result from doing it but also the *quality* of such pleasure. Bentham, on the other hand, claims that good and bad consequences are to be measured purely in terms of the quantity of pleasure and pain involved. What is the difference between the quantity and quality of a pleasant experience? Bentham defines quantity in terms of seven variables: intensity, duration, certainty, propinquity, fecundity, purity, and extent. This is his famous "hedonic calculus," and the reader is advised to study carefully Bentham's explanation of these seven factors in the first reading of this chapter. Eudaemonistic utilitarians like Mill criticize Bentham on this point because they think the "hedonic calculus" has the following implications. If each person in the world were to do his duty and live a morally upright life, he would be making it possible in the future for everyone to have the most intense and pure pleasures throughout his life, regardless of the source of those pleasures. Thus in a perfect world everyone might be living like an animal, enjoying food and sex and other bodily pleasures, but not in the least caring to have the less intense and less pure pleasures of the intellect and the aesthetic sensibility. But how can the ultimate purpose of morality, the end and aim of the whole struggle for brotherhood and freedom in human history, consist of a social condition (not unlike that "Brave New World" envisioned by the novelist Aldous Huxley) in which people live like contented pigs? "Better to be a man dissatisfied than a pig satisfied. Better to be Socrates dissatisfied than a fool satisfied," Mill declares. Surely the ultimate goal of morality must be a life of dignity, nobility, and cultivated taste—a humane and civilized life fit for the best qualities in man. The reader should notice how Mill determines the superior or inferior quality of a pleasure in this argument, and then should try to decide for himself whether this is a sound objection to hedonisic utilitarianism.

ACT-UTILITARIANISM AND RULE-UTILITARIANISM

What is the function of moral rules of conduct, according to utilitarianism? Two different answers are given to this question by utilitarians, and this has been used as a basis for distinguishing two types of utilitarianism, one called "act" or "unrestricted" utilitarianism, the other called "rule" or "restricted" utilitarianism. The distinction may be put this way. For all utilitarians, the principle of utility is the *ultimate* test of the rightness or wrongness of human conduct. But in applying this test, do we apply it directly to particular acts, or do we restrict its application to rules of conduct, and let those rules determine whether a particular act is right or wrong? In the first case, which is unrestricted or act-utilitarianism, we must find out what are the consequences of a *particular act* in order to know whether it is right or wrong. It is this type of utilitarianism that has been presented in the foregoing section of this introduction. The principle of utility is applied directly to each alternative act in a situation of choice. The right act is then defined as the one which has greater utility than any other alternative. It would be wrong for a person to do any of these other alternatives, because if he were to do any of them he would *not* thereby maximize intrinsic value and minimize intrinsic disvalue in the world, and a person's duty is always to do that act among all those open to his choice which has such consequences.

According to restricted or rule-utilitarianism, on the other hand, an act is right if it conforms to a valid rule of conduct and wrong if it violates such a rule. And it is the test of utility that determines the validity of rules of conduct. Thus the one true normative ethical system binding upon all mankind is a set of rules such that, if people regulated their conduct by these rules, greater intrinsic value and less intrinsic disvalue would result for everyone than if they regulated their conduct by a different set of rules. To "regulate one's conduct by a rule" is explained by reference to the two kinds of rules: positive rules or requirements, and negative rules or prohibitions. A positive rule prescribes to everyone that he is obligated to do a certain kind of act in a certain set of circumstances. Thus the rule "Keep your promises" tells us that, in the circumstances where we have promised someone to do something and we now have the choice to keep or to break our promise, we must keep it. The right act is to do what the rule prescribes, the wrong act is not to do what it prescribes. A negative rule forbids everyone to do a certain kind of act in a certain set of circumstances. It prescribes that a person refrain from doing an act when he has the choice of doing or not doing it. Thus the rule "Thou shalt not steal" tells us what we must not do, rather than what we must do. Just as acting in accordance with a positive rule means doing what the rule prescribes, so acting in accordance with a negative rule means refraining from doing what the rule prohibits. And just as it is wrong to refrain from doing what is required by a positive rule, so it is wrong to do what is forbidden by a negative rule. "Right" and "wrong," in this way, can be defined as action that conforms to or that violates a rule of conduct which is binding upon us. But how do we know, among all the possible rules that could regulate our conduct, which ones do really bind us? The rule-utilitarian's answer is: those rules which, when people conform to them, bring about more happiness or pleasure for everyone and less unhappiness or pain for everyone, than would be brought about by their conforming to any other set of rules.

Is it ever the case that an act which was right according to act-utilitarianism would be wrong according to rule-utilitarianism, or vice versa? That there seem to be such cases is shown by the following examples. We would all agree that the rule "Never lie to a person who asks you a direct question" has much greater utility than the rule "Always lie to a person who asks you a direct question," since many of the advantages of civilized society would not come about if people were constantly trying to deceive one another. Yet we can easily imagine a set of circumstances in which following the first rule will produce much more pain and unhappiness than following the second rule. For example, suppose the Gestapo in Nazi Germany questioned someone who was hiding a group of Jews in his home. When the Nazis asked him, "Do you know where there are any Jews?" the person's act of telling the truth would result in the Jews he had been protecting being sent to a concentration camp. Given this situation, the ethical system of act-utilitarianism would clearly indicate that it would be right to lie and wrong to tell the truth. But it would seem that the opposite moral judgment is implied by rule-utilitarianism, since the rule "Tell the truth," has greater utility when everyone follows it than the rule "Do not tell the truth."

Consider another case. Suppose a person sees a wallet lying on the ground. The wallet contains two hundred dollars and its owner's name and address are clearly written on a card in it. Suppose further that no one is around, so that it would be easy for the person to remove the money, leave the wallet where he had found it, and walk away without anyone's knowing what he had done. Finally, let us suppose the wallet belongs to a millionaire, whereas the man who finds it is poor and needs the money to keep his family from starving. Here is a set of circumstances where act-utilitarianism would appear to imply that it was right for the man to take the money even though it did not belong to him. Rule-utilitarianism, it would seem, has the opposite consequence, since taking the money would be doing what is forbidden by the rule "Thou shalt not steal" and hence would be wrong. This rule is of greater general utility than the rule "Steal whenever it is probable you will not be caught."

Examples like these have been given by philosophers to show that an act may be right (or wrong) according to act-utilitarianism and wrong (or right) according to rule-utilitarianism. Thus the usefulness of a person's doing a *particular* action is quite different from the usefulness of a society's having a set of general rules requiring everyone to do or refrain from doing certain *kinds* of action. Although it may cause more unhappiness to have a poor man pay his debts to a wealthy man than not to have him pay them, the general social practice of having debts paid yields less unhappiness in the long run for everyone than to have no debts paid. And if the usefulness of the rule "One must pay one's debts" determines the rightness or wrongness of every action that falls under the rule, it will be wrong for the poor man not to pay his debts to the wealthy man. The conclusion that is often drawn is that act-utilitarianism and rule-utilitarianism cannot both be true, since they entail contradictory moral judgments of the same action. Whether this is indeed the case will be a matter for further consideration in the next chapter.

THE "PROOF" OF THE PRINCIPLE OF UTILITY

Why should either of these two kinds of utilitarianism be accepted as a normative ethical system for all men to follow? The utilitarian's general answer would be that no limitation on human freedom is justified unless it serves a good purpose. If a society is to have rules that require people to refrain from doing what they might want to do, or if a society is to prescribe that a person must do something which, independently of that prescription, he would not choose to do, there must be some consequence thereby brought about whose goodness outweighs the intrinsic badness of these restrictions themselves. The next step is to imagine what would be missing were no such limitations placed on people's freedom of action. Here the utilitarian argues that in such a situation the amenities of social existence would be impossible. All the benefits obtained from the advancement of the arts and sciences as well as from the production and maintenance of a high economic standard of living could not be achieved without some restrictions on human freedom. Thus moral rules and particular prescriptions are devices invented by men as necessary means for the carrying on of civilized life. Their reason-for-being lies in their social function, and as long as they benefit everyone when they are generally followed, they are justified.

This argument appeals to the principle of utility as the rational ground of morality. If someone were to challenge this appeal, the utilitarian would reply: "How else can we justify rules of conduct and particular prescriptions other than by showing the *purpose* for which rational beings would decide to use them as guides to their actions? Furthermore, if this purpose were anything other than the promotion of happiness or pleasure, could we consider such beings rational? The principle of utility, in short, is built into the very conception of a rational ground for rules and prescriptions of conduct."

Jeremy Bentham's defense of utilitarianism (as distinct from his systematic construction of a utilitarian ethical system) is not so much an argument in support of it as it is an attack on anyone who would reject it. In a series of ten questions, Bentham challenges the person who doubts the principle of utility to state an alternative ethical system that is equally rational. He asks the doubter whether he believes his moral judgments are justifiable and, if so, whether it is not the principle of utility which he himself uses in justifying them. And if the answer to the latter query is "no," Bentham asks him to consider whether the word "right" can have any other meaning than "maximizing pleasure and minimizing pain." Bentham states explicitly that the words "right" and "wrong" can have no other meaning than what is, and is not, conformable to the principle of utility. (We shall have occasion critically to examine this last point when we study the meaning of value words in Chapter 7.)

The most famous "proof" of utilitarianism is that offered by John Stuart Mill in his book *Utilitarianism*. In the fourth chapter of that book, titled "Of What Sort of Proof the Principle of Utility Is Susceptible," Mill sets forth the following three-step argument. The first step consists in drawing an analogy between, "The only proof that a sound is audible is that people hear it; the only proof that an object is visible is that people see it," and, "The sole evidence that anything is desirable is that people do actually desire it."

The second step of the argument may be formulated in the following deduction:

(1) Happiness is a good.
   (Because: Happiness is desired by people; if something is desired it is desirable, according to the argument from analogy already given; and "desirable" means the same as "good.")
(2) Each person's happiness is a good to that person.
   (Because: Each person desires his own happiness; and his own happiness is therefore a good to him, by premise (1).)

(3) *Therefore*, the general happiness is a good to the aggregate of all persons.

The third step of Mill's argument is an attempt to prove that happiness is not only one of the criteria of morality, but is the sole criterion. His proof of this consists in a detailed account of human motivation which is intended to show: (1) that people never desire anything as an end in itself except happiness, and (2) that it is a psychological and metaphysical impossibility for anyone to desire anything "except in proportion as the idea of it is pleasant."

Whether this three-step argument will stand up to critical scrutiny must be decided by each reader as he examines Mill's reasoning. As Mill himself puts it, "If this doctrine be true, the principle of utility is proved. Whether it is so or not must now be left to the consideration of the thoughtful reader."

SOME DIFFICULTIES

There are a number of problems involved in the logical development of a utilitarian system of ethics and in the application of such a system to cases in practical life. One problem concerns the difficulty of knowing what is right and wrong, especially in act-utilitarianism. If we must find out which of all the alternatives open to us will lead to the best consequences in each situation of choice, we can never know what we ought to do with certainty, and in many cases the obtaining of such knowledge will take so much time and effort that we shall not be able to discover what we ought to do within the limits set by the decision-situation. If someone has been hurt in an automobile accident and we are confronted with the choice between stopping our car and helping him or continuing on our way to the airport where we have to take a plane on a business trip, we must first predict what will probably happen if we were to do each of the alternatives before we can know what we ought to do. But by the time we carry out such a calculation we might either miss the plane or, if we finally decide to turn back and help the person, his condition might have become so bad in the meantime that he is now beyond the point of benefiting from our help. And whichever alternative we finally choose, we can never know that what we did was right or wrong. For suppose we stopped in time to help the person and by so doing we saved his life. We would not even then know that we had done the right thing unless we knew what kind of a person he was. If he were a vicious and sadistic man who constantly made others unhappy, it might have been better for the world not to have saved his life, or at least the choice of helping him might have been worse than the choice of catching the plane and successfully accomplishing the purpose of the business trip. Or, even if the person himself was not vicious and sadistic, his future children might be. So we cannot know whether we ought to have saved his life unless we can predict the character of his future children!

The act-utilitarian's reply to arguments of this type is as follows. With regard to our never knowing what is right and wrong because the consequences of human actions are never certain, his answer is that we usually can make a reasonable prediction of the probable consequences, and that is all that we can morally be held responsible for. In the given example, unless we had some special evidence about the viciousness of the man's character, the probable consequences of saving his life would be better than letting him die. And we must simply assume that his future children will not cause more suffering in the world than if they had never been born. For we can be held responsible only for what any reasonable person would be expected to know in the given situation, and we have no reason to predict one way or another about what the man's children are going to be like.

With regard to the time element in coming to a decision, the act-utilitarian would say that we must consider the right and wrong of the act of calculation itself, as well as the right and wrong of the alternatives whose consequences are being calculated. In the given situation of our example, there are three alternatives open to our choice, not just two:

(a) Stopping immediately to help the injured person.

(b) Driving on to catch the plane.

(c) Hesitating while calculating the probable consequences of doing (a) and of doing (b) before deciding to do either (a) or (b).

If the consequences of doing (c) were worse than the consequences of doing (a) or (b)—as would be the case if the injured person were to die while we were calculating and our hesitation made us miss the plane—then it is our duty *not* to make a careful calculation in that kind of situation. We must decide quickly. If it then turns out that we decided in the wrong way, we cannot be blamed for what we did because any reasonable person in such a situation would have predicted that to hesitate in order to make a careful calculation would probably result in worse consequences than not to hesitate.

Another difficulty involved in the systematic development of act-utilitarianism concerns the wrongness of acts done without the knowledge of others. Suppose a man were to perform the "perfect" crime by murdering someone without leaving any clues. As a result, the murderer is never caught and punished. Now compare this case with an exactly similar act of murder, except that the killer leaves some clues, is eventually caught, and is sentenced to life imprisonment. Ordinarily we would say that the two acts of murder were equally wrong, and that whether a murderer is caught has nothing to do with the wrongness of his act. Yet according to act-utilitarianism it would seem that the first act is not as bad as the second. For the consequences of the first act do not involve as much unhappiness as is involved in the consequences of the second, since the murderer gets away with his act and does not suffer imprisonment. The fact that his act is a "perfect" crime makes it better than the same crime done by someone who is careless about leaving evidence. This seems the very opposite of our ordinary moral judgments of the two cases. If there is any moral difference between them, we would say the first is worse than the second precisely because the criminal escapes punishment.

The act-utilitarian might reply that in fact the first case is worse than the second because, although the criminal does not suffer punishment by law, he will suffer the pangs of a bad conscience and will forever live in fear of the police. Furthermore, his not getting caught may encourage him and others to commit more crimes, and so bring about worse consequences than would have happened if he had been caught and imprisoned. Still, the argument against act-utilitarianism can be revised to take at least some of these points into account. Suppose the man who commits the "perfect" crime is a hardened, amoral kind of man without a conscience, is fully confident that he will never be caught or even suspected by the police, and has no desire to commit another murder because the motive for his one crime was revenge directed at the particular person who was his victim. Again we would say that none of these facts makes the crime any the less wrong; indeed, we should say they are all completely *irrelevant* to the wrongness of his action. Yet by the theory of act-utilitarianism all of these factors *are* relevant, since they make a difference to the consequences of the action.

It should be observed that the foregoing type of argument cannot be used against the rule-utilitarian. According to his theory both acts of murder are equally wrong, since both are violations of the same rule of conduct—namely, that we ought to respect the lives of others. The consequences that follow the performance of each particular act do not determine the rightness or wrongness of the act, and therefore the crime can be judged to be wrong regardless of whether the criminal is caught, feels guilty, or will be encouraged to commit another crime. The rule that all murderers be punished by law is itself a valid rule for rule-utilitarians because the consequences of having such a rule regulating people's conduct are better than the consequences of not having it regulate their conduct. Hence, by the same reasoning that shows the act of murder to be wrong, the rule-utilitarian shows the act of apprehending and punishing a murderer to be right.

We shall now examine a final difficulty that has been considered by some philosophers to be a sufficient reason for rejecting both act- and rule-utilitarianism. According to both of these ethical systems utility is the ultimate moral norm. But exactly what is utility? We have analyzed it as "the maximizing of intrinsic value and the minimizing of intrinsic disvalue." Let us now look more closely at what this means. It will be helpful for the purposes of the present argument to think of measurable units of intrinsic value and disvalue. We shall accordingly speak of units of happiness and unhappiness, giving plus and minus signs to happiness and unhappiness, respectively. This will enable us to see the difficulty more clearly, although no particular view of what is to be taken as the measurement of a unit of happiness or unhappiness will be presupposed. We all know in general what it means to be very happy, quite happy, not especially happy, rather unhappy, and extremely unhappy. Thus the idea of degrees of happiness corresponds to something in our experience. We also know what it means to be happy for a brief moment, or for a few hours, or for a day, and we use such phrases as "It was a happy two-week vacation," "I was not very happy during my early teens," and "He has led an unhappy life." There is some basis, therefore, in our everyday concept of happiness (and also of pleasure) that gives meaning to the idea of quantities or amounts of happiness, even though we do not ordinarily measure these quantities in arithmetical terms. It should be noted that Jeremy Bentham's "hedonic calculus" is an attempt to set out a quantitative analysis of intrinsic value, where the sole standard of such value is taken to be pleasure. The seven aspects of pleasure (intensity, duration, certainty, propinquity, fecundity, purity, and extent) could perhaps be used as measurable dimensions, although Bentham himself does not tell us how to assign units to them.

What, then, does the utilitarian mean by maximizing intrinsic value and minimizing intrinsic disvalue? There are five variables or factors that must be introduced in order to make this idea clear. First, it means to bring about, in the case of *one* person, the greatest balance of value over disvalue. Thus if one act or rule yields +1000 units of happiness and −500 units of unhappiness for a given person, while another act or rule yields +700 units and −100 units for that person, then, all other factors being equal, the second alternative is better than the first, since the balance of the second (+600) is greater than the balance of the first (+500). Similarly, to "minimize disvalue" would mean that an act or rule which yielded +100 and −300 for a given person would be better than one that yielded +500 and −1000 for the same person, other things being equal (even though more happiness is produced by the second than by the first).

The second factor is that the happiness and unhappiness of *all persons* affected must be considered. (This is Bentham's dimension of "extent.") Thus if four persons, A, B, C, and D, each experience some difference of happiness or unhappiness in their lives as a consequence of the act or rule but no difference occurs in the lives of anyone else, then the calculation of maximum value and minimum disvalue must include the balance of pluses and minuses occurring in the experience of every one of the four persons. Suppose in one case the balance is +300 for A, +200 for B, −300 for C, and −400 for D. And suppose the alternative yields +200 for A, +100 for B, −400 for C, and +500 for D. Then if someone were to claim that the first is better than the second because D's happiness or unhappiness does not count (D, for example, might be a slave while A, B, and C are free men), this conclusion would not be acceptable to utilitarians. For them, the second alternative is better than the first because the second yields a higher total balance than the first when *all* persons are considered.

The third factor in the utilitarian calculus has been tacitly assumed in the foregoing discussion of the second factor. This is the principle that, in calculating the units of happiness or unhappiness for different persons, the same criteria for measuring quantity are used. If totals of +500 and −200 represent sums of happiness and unhappiness in the experience of A and +300 and −400 represent sums of happiness and unhappiness in the experience of B, then one unit of plus (or minus) for A must be equal to one unit of plus (or minus) for B. No differences between A and B are to be considered as grounds for assigning a different weight to one or the other's happiness or unhappiness. When utilitarians assert that everyone's happiness is to count *equally,* they mean that, in calculating consequences, it is irrelevant *whose* happiness or unhappiness is affected by the act or rule. This may be called the principle of the equality of worth of every person as a person. (It does not mean, of course, that everyone is just as morally good or bad as everyone else!)

A fourth factor must now be brought in. Some utilitarians believe (although Bentham and Mill were not clear about this) that, other things being equal, the intrinsic value and disvalue resulting from an act or rule should be distributed *as widely as possible* among all those who are affected. This, presumably, is one way to interpret the utilitarian motto, "The greatest happiness of the greatest number." Suppose, as we have done above, that only four individuals are affected by an act (or rule) and its alternative. Suppose further that the calculus of consequences for one alternative comes out: $+100$ for A, $+200$ for B, $+50$ for C, and $+150$ for D, while that of the second alternative comes out: $+800$ for A, $+500$ for B, -100 for C, and -200 for D. Now, although the sum total for the second is $+1000$ whereas it is only $+500$ for the first, the first is better than the second because it distributes happiness among all four persons while the second distributes happiness among only two, allowing the other two to suffer. At least, this is the conclusion that would follow if we were to distribute happiness as widely as possible. A similar conclusion would be drawn if the total consequences for both alternatives added up to more unhappiness than happiness. For example, suppose the first alternative yields -200 for A, -50 for B, -150 for C, and -100 for D; and suppose the second yields -700 for A, $+250$ for B, $+800$ for C, and -600 for D. Here both totals come out negative: -500 in the first case and -250 in the second. Yet, if we distribute unhappiness as widely as possible (on the principle that, when one person or a few have to suffer very much when everyone does not share in the suffering, then everyone should share in it if that will lessen the amount of suffering for the one or the few), we must conclude that the first alternative is better than the second.

However, many utilitarians have balked at these implications of the "widest distribution" idea. It seems to them wrong deliberately to increase the total amount of suffering in the world when an alternative is available which will produce less suffering (in our last example, to cut it in half). And it would seem to them equally wrong deliberately to lessen the total amount of happiness we are able to produce, especially when we are given the choice of an alternative which would bring about twice as much happiness as another. Some utilitarians have attempted to escape this dilemma by introducing a fifth factor in their calculus. (It should be noted that John Stuart Mill makes this attempt in the last section of his book *Utilitarianism,* parts of which are included in the second reading of this chapter.)

This last factor is *justice.* In deciding which of two alternative acts we ought to do, or which of two rules we ought to adopt as a guide to everyone's conduct, we must ask, Do the consequences of the act or rule distribute happiness and unhappiness *justly* or *fairly* among all who are affected by it? The concept of justice can be understood most clearly by considering what it means to treat people differently. Thus the principle of justice has been stated in the following way by Henry Sidgwick, who was one of the great moral philosophers of the nineteenth century:

It cannot be right for A to treat B in a manner in which it would be wrong for B to treat A, merely on the ground that they are two different individuals, and without there being any difference between the natures or circumstances of the two which can be stated as a reasonable ground for difference of treatment. (H. Sidgwick, *The Methods of Ethics,* 7th ed., London: Macmillan and Co., Ltd., 1907, p. 380.)

If we accept this principle, as utilitarians do, we must always be able to show a *relevant difference* between any two people who are being treated differently, so far as their happiness is concerned. Suppose, for example, that the consequences of an act or rule are such that one person, A, experiences more happiness or less unhappiness than another person, B. In such a situation A and B are being treated differently. This happened in all our examples above, where we assigned different amounts of happiness and unhappiness to the different people affected by an act or rule. In calculating these amounts we did not exclude anyone and we did not allow one person's happiness to count more than another's. (This was in accordance with the second and third factors on our list.) But we saw that, even so, people will be affected in different ways by an act or rule. Thus we were confronted with the problem: How should the varying amounts of happiness and unhappiness be distributed among all those affected? We have seen the difficulties involved in trying to make the distribution as *wide* as possible. We must now consider what is involved in making the distribution as *fair* as possible.

What will or will not be accepted as a just or fair distribution will depend on what we believe to be "reasonable grounds" for difference of treatment among persons. To give such grounds is to point out *relevant* differences among those who are to be treated differently, and the task of defining justice then becomes the problem of determining *valid criteria of relevance*. What differences among people make it just for them to be treated differently, as far as their happiness is concerned?

It has been suggested that a utilitarian could easily answer this question within the framework of his own ethical theory. He could say, Let us apply the test of utility to any proposed criterion of a relevant difference. That is, let us simply predict the probable consequences of a society's using one criterion, then of its using another, and so on, and see which criterion results in maximum intrinsic value and minimum intrinsic disvalue for everyone in the society, when compared with the results of using any other criterion. By this test, for example it could be shown that difference of treatment based on a person's race or religion results in much less intrinsic value and much more intrinsic disvalue for everyone than results from basing difference of treatment on such factors as people's differing needs and abilities. According to the principle of utility itself, therefore, race and religion cannot be accepted as valid criteria of relevant differences while need and ability can.

This reply, however, will not do, since it begs the very question at issue. This can be seen when we realize that a person does not know how to *apply* the principle of utility unless he knows what it means to "maximize intrinsic value and minimize intrinsic disvalue," and this is precisely what one is trying to determine in discussing what is a just distribution of happiness and unhappiness or a just difference of treatment. As we saw above, in order to decide what it means to maximize intrinsic value and minimize intrinsic disvalue we must take into account five factors, the fifth of which is justice. So unless we already know what justice (principles of just distribution or just difference of treatment) is, we do not know what it means to maximize intrinsic value and minimize intrinsic disvalue. Now the proposal we are considering is that a just distribution or a just difference of treatment is one that will maximize intrinsic value and minimize intrinsic disvalue. This is to reason in a circle. We are assuming what we are trying to prove, since a person must know beforehand what a just distribution or a just difference of treatment is in order to know what will maximize intrinsic value and minimize intrinsic disvalue.

Utilitarianism, then, is left with a fundamental problem, and it is because of this that some contemporary philosophers have rejected it. They do not believe that principles of justice can be derived from a utilitarian ethical system. Yet they hold that justice is one of the basic concepts of morality. Since, in their view, it cannot be validated by appeal to the principle of utility itself, utilitarianism must be considered inadequate as a normative ethical system.

In order to appreciate the full implications of this criticism and in order to see how utilitarians might reply to it, we shall take up the matter again in the next chapter. And in the last chapter of this book we shall consider a non-utilitarian theory of justice.

JEREMY BENTHAM
Utility and Pleasure

CHAPTER I:
OF THE PRINCIPLE OF UTILITY

I. Nature has placed mankind under the governance of two sovereign masters, *pain* and *pleasure*. It is for them alone to point out what we ought to do, as well as to determine what we shall do. On the one hand the standard of right and wrong, on the other the chain of causes and effects, are fastened to their throne. They govern us in all we do, in all we say, in all we think: every effort we can make to throw off our subjection, will serve but to demonstrate and confirm it. In words a man may pretend to abjure their empire: but in reality he will remain subject to it all the while. The *principle of utility* recognizes this subjection, and assumes it for the foundation of that system, the object of which

From Jeremy Bentham, *An Introduction to the Principles of Morals and Legislation;* Chapters I, III, and IV. (1789)

is to rear the fabric of felicity by the hands of reason and of law. Systems which attempt to question it, deal in sounds instead of sense, in caprice instead of reason, in darkness instead of light.

But enough of metaphor and declamation: it is not by such means that moral science is to be improved.

II. The principle of utility is the foundation of the present work: it will be proper therefore at the outset to give an explicit and determinate account of what is meant by it. By the principle of utility is meant that principle which approves or disapproves of every action whatsoever, according to the tendency which it appears to have to augment or diminish the happiness of the party whose interest is in question: or, what is the same thing in other words, to promote or to oppose that happiness. I say of every action whatsoever; and therefore not only of every action of a private individual, but of every measure of government.

III. By utility is meant that property in any object, whereby it tends to produce benefit, advantage, pleasure, good, or happiness, (all this in the present case comes to the same thing) or (what comes again to the same thing) to prevent the happening of mischief, pain, evil, or unhappiness to the party whose interest is considered: if that party be the community in general, then the happiness of the community: if a particular individual, then the happiness of that individual.

IV. The interest of the community is one of the most general expressions that can occur in the phraseology of morals: no wonder that the meaning of it is often lost. When it has a meaning, it is this. The community is a fictitious *body*, composed of the individual persons who are considered as constituting as it were its *members*. The interest of the community then is, what?—the sum of the interests of the several members who compose it.

V. It is in vain to talk of the interest of the community, without understanding what is the interest of the individual. A thing is said to promote the interest, or to be *for* the interest, of an individual, when it tends to add to the sum total of his pleasures: or, what comes to the same thing, to diminish the sum total of his pains.

VI. An action then may be said to be conformable to the principle of utility, or, for shortness sake, to utility, (meaning with respect to the community at large) when the tendency it has to augment the happiness of the community is greater than any it has to diminish it.

VII. A measure of government (which is but a particular kind of action, performed by a particular person or persons) may be said to be conformable to or dictated by the principle of utility, when in like manner the tendency which it has to augment the happiness of the community is greater than any which it has to diminish it.

VIII. When an action, or in particular a measure of government, is supposed by a man to be conformable to the principle of utility, it may be convenient, for the purposes of discourse to imagine a kind of law or dictate, called a law or dictate of utility: and to speak of the action in question, as being conformable to such law or dictate.

IX. A man may be said to be a partizan of the principle of utility, when the approbation or disapprobation he annexes to any action, or to any measure, is determined by and proportioned to the tendency which he conceives it to have to augment or to diminish the happiness of the community: or in other words, to its conformity or unconformity to the laws or dictates of utility.

X. Of an action that is conformable to the principle of utility one may always say either that it is one that ought to be done, or at least that it is not one that ought not to be done. One may say also, that it is right it should be done; at least that it is not wrong it should be done: that it is a right action; at least that it is not a wrong action. When thus interpreted, the words *ought*, and *right* and *wrong*, and others of that stamp, have a meaning: when otherwise, they have none.

XI. Has the rectitude of this principle been ever formally contested? It should seem that it had, by those who have not known what they have been meaning. Is it susceptible of any direct proof? It should seem not: for that which is used to prove every thing else, cannot itself be proved: a chain of proofs must have their commencement somewhere. To give such proof is as impossible as it is needless.

XII. Not that there is or ever has been that human creature breathing, however stupid or perverse, who has not on many, perhaps on most occasions of his life, deferred to it. By the natural constitution of the human frame, on most occasions of their lives men in general embrace this principle, without thinking of it: if not for the ordering of their own actions, yet for the trying of their own actions, as well as of those of other men. There have been, at the same time, not many, perhaps, even of the most intelligent, who have been disposed to embrace it purely and without reserve. There are even few who have not taken some occasion or other to quarrel with it, either on account of their not understanding always how to apply it, or on account of some prejudice or other which they were afraid to examine into, or could not bear to part with. For such is the stuff that man is made of: in principle and in practice, in a right track and in a wrong one, the rarest of all human qualities is consistency.

XIII. When a man attempts to combat the principle of utility, it is with reasons drawn, without his being aware of it, from that very principle itself. His arguments, if they prove any thing, prove not that the principle is *wrong*, but that, according to the applications he supposes to be made of it, it is *misapplied*. Is it possible for a man to move the earth? Yes; but he must first find out another earth to stand upon.

XIV. To disprove the propriety of it by arguments is impossible; but, from the causes that have been mentioned, or from some confused or partial view of it, a man may happen to be disposed not to relish it. Where this is the case, if he thinks the settling of his opinions on such a subject worth the trouble, let him take the following steps, and at length, perhaps, he may come to reconcile himself to it.

1. Let him settle with himself, whether he would wish to discard this principle altogether; if so, let him consider what it is that all his reasonings (in matters of politics especially) can amount to?

2. If he would, let him settle with himself, whether he would judge and act without any principle, or whether there is any other he would judge and act by?

3. If there be, let him examine and satisfy himself whether the principle he thinks he has found is really any separate intelligible principle; or whether it be not a mere principle in words, a kind of phrase, which at bottom expresses neither more nor less than the mere averment of his own unfounded sentiments; that is, what in another person he might be apt to call caprice?

4. If he is inclined to think that his own approbation or disapprobation, annexed to the idea of an act, without any regard to its consequences, is a sufficient foundation for him to judge and act upon, let him ask himself whether his sentiment is to be a standard of right and wrong, with respect to every other man, or whether every man's sentiment has the same privilege of being a standard to itself?

5. In the first case, let him ask himself whether his principle is not despotical, and hostile to all the rest of human race?

6. In the second case, whether it is not anarchial, and whether at this rate there are not as many different standards of right and wrong as there are men? and whether even to the same man, the same thing, which is right to-day, may not (without the least change in its nature) be wrong to-morrow? and whether the same thing is not right and wrong in the same place at the same time? and in either case, whether all argument is not at an end? and whether, when two men have said, 'I like this,' and 'I don't like it,' they can (upon such a principle) have any thing more to say?

7. If he should have said to himself, No: for that the sentiment which he proposes as a standard must be grounded on reflection, let him say on what particulars the reflection is to turn? if on particulars having relation to the utility of the act, then let him say whether this is not deserting his own principle and borrowing assistance from that very one in opposition to which he sets it up: or if not on those particulars, on what other particulars?

8. If he should be for compounding the matter, and adopting his own principle in part, and the principle of utility in part, let him say how far he will adopt it?

9. When he has settled with himself where he will stop, then let him ask himself how he justifies to himself the adopting it so far? and why he will not adopt it any farther?

10. Admitting any other principle than the principle of utility to be a right principle, a principle that is right for a man to pursue; admitting (what is not true) that the word *right* can have a meaning without reference to utility, let him say whether there is any such thing as a *motive* that a man can have to pursue the dictates of it: if there is, let him say what that motive is, and how it is

to be distinguished from those which enforce the dictates of utility: if not, then lastly let him say what it is this other principle can be good for?

CHAPTER III:

OF THE FOUR SANCTIONS OR SOURCES OF PAIN AND PLEASURE

I. It has been shown that the happiness of the individuals, of whom a community is composed, that is, their pleasures and their security, is the end and the sole end which the legislator ought to have in view: the sole standard, in conformity to which each individual ought, as far as depends upon the legislator, to be *made* to fashion his behaviour. But whether it be this or any thing else that is to be *done*, there is nothing by which a man can ultimately be *made* to do it, but either pain or pleasure. Having taken a general view of these two grand objects (*viz.* pleasure, and what comes to the same thing, immunity from pain) in the character of *final* causes; it will be necessary to take a view of pleasure and pain itself, in the character of *efficient* causes or means.

II. There are four distinguishable sources from which pleasure and pain are in use to flow: considered separately, they may be termed the *physical*, the *political*, the *moral*, and the *religious:* and inasmuch as the pleasures and pains belonging to each of them are capable of giving a binding force to any law or rule of conduct, they may all of them be termed *sanctions*.

III. If it be in the present life, and from the ordinary course of nature, not purposely modified by the interposition of the will of any human being, nor by any extraordinary interposition of any superior invisible being, that the pleasure or the pain takes place or is expected, it may be said to issue from or to belong to the *physical sanction*.

IV. If at the hands of a *particular* person or set of persons in the community, who under names correspondent to that of *judge*, are chosen for the particular purpose of dispensing it, according to the will of the sovereign or supreme ruling power in the state, it may be said to issue from the *political sanction*.

V. If at the hands of such *chance* persons in the community, as the party in question may happen in the course of his life to have concerns with, according to each man's spontaneous disposition, and not according to any settled or concerted rule, it may be said to issue from the *moral* or *popular sanction*.

VI. If from the immediate hand of a superior invisible being, either in the present life, or in a future, it may be said to issue from the *religious sanction*.

VII. Pleasures or pains which may be expected to issue from the *physical*, *political*, or *moral* sanctions, must all of them be expected to be experienced, if ever, in the *present* life: those which may be expected to issue from the *religious* sanction, may be expected to be experienced either in the *present* life or in a *future*.

VIII. Those which can be experienced in the present life, can of course be no others than such as human nature in the course of the present life is susceptible of: and from each of these sources may flow all the pleasures or pains of which, in the course of the present life, human nature is susceptible. With regard to these then (with which alone we have in this place any concern) those of them which belong to any one of those sanctions, differ not ultimately in kind from those which belong to any one of the other three: the only difference there is among them lies in the circumstances that accompany their production. A suffering which befalls a man in the natural and spontaneous course of things, shall be styled, for instance, a *calamity*; in which case, if it be supposed to befall him through any imprudence of his, it may be styled a punishment issuing from the physical sanction. Now this same suffering, if inflicted by the law, will be what is commonly called a *punishment*; if incurred for want of any friendly assistance, which the misconduct, or supposed misconduct, of the sufferer has occasioned to be withholden, a punishment issuing from the *moral* sanction; if through the immediate interposition of a particular providence, a punishment issuing from the religious sanction.

IX. A man's goods, or his person, are consumed by fire. If this happened to him by what is called an accident, it was a calamity: if by reason of his own imprudence (for instance, from his neglecting to put his candle out) it may be styled a punishment of the physical sanction: if it happened to him by the sentence of the political magistrate, a punishment belonging to the political sanction; that is, what is commonly called a punishment: if for want of any assistance which his *neighbour* withheld from him out of some dislike to his *moral* character, a punishment of the *moral* sanction: if by an immediate act of *God's* displeasure, manifested on account of some *sin* committed by him, or through any distraction of mind, occasioned by the dread of such displeasure, a punishment of the *religious* sanction.

X. As to such of the pleasures and pains belonging to the religious sanction, as regard a future life, of what kind these may be we cannot know. These lie not open to our observation. During the present life they are matter only of expectation: and, whether that expectation be derived from natural or revealed religion, the particular kind of pleasure or pain, if it be different from all those which lie open to our observation, is what we can have no idea of. The best ideas we can obtain of such pains and pleasures are altogether unliquidated in point of quality. In what other respects our ideas of them *may* be liquidated will be considered in another place.

XI. Of these four sanctions the physical is altogether, we may observe, the ground-work of the political and the moral: so is it also of the religious, in as far as the latter bears relation to the present life. It is included in each of those other three. This may operate in any case, (that is, any of the pains or pleasures belonging to it may operate) independently of *them*: none of *them* can operate but by means of this. In a word, the powers of nature may operate of themselves; but neither the magistrate, nor men at large, *can* operate, nor is God in the case in question *supposed* to operate, but through the powers of nature.

XII. For these four objects, which in their nature have so much in common, it seemed of use to find a common name. It seemed of use, in the first place, for the convenience of giving a name to certain pleasures and pains, for which a name equally characteristic could hardly otherwise have been found: in the second place, for the sake of holding up the efficacy of certain moral forces, the influence of which is apt not to be sufficiently attended to. Does the political sanction exert an influence over the conduct of mankind? The moral, the religious sanctions do so too. In every inch of his career are the operations of the political magistrate liable to be aided or impeded by these two foreign powers: who, one or other of them, or both, are sure to be either his rivals or his allies. Does it happen to him to leave them out in his calculations? he will be sure almost to find himself mistaken in the result. Of all this we shall find abundant proofs in the sequel of this work. It behoves him, therefore, to have them continually before his eyes; and that under such a name as exhibits the relation they bear to his own purposes and designs.

CHAPTER IV:
VALUE OF A LOT OF PLEASURE OR PAIN, HOW TO BE MEASURED

I. Pleasures then, and the avoidance of pains, are the *ends* which the legislator has in view: it behoves him therefore to understand their *value*. Pleasures and pains are the *instruments* he has to work with: it behoves him therefore to understand their force, which is again, in other words, their value.

II. To a person considered *by himself,* the value of a pleasure or pain considered *by itself,* will be greater or less, according to the four following circumstances:[1]

1. Its *intensity.*
2. Its *duration.*
3. Its *certainty* or *uncertainty.*
4. Its *propinquity* or *remoteness.*

III. These are the circumstances which are to be considered in estimating a pleasure or a pain considered each of them by itself. But when the value of any pleasure or pain is considered for the purpose of estimating the tendency of any *act* by which it is produced, there are two other circumstances to be taken into the account; these are,

5. Its *fecundity,* or the chance is has of being followed by sensations of the *same* kind: that is, pleasures, if it be a pleasure: pains, if it be a pain.

[1] These circumstances have since been denominated *elements* or *dimensions* of *value* in a pleasure or a pain.

Not long after the publication of the first edition, the following memoriter verses were framed, in the view of lodging more effectually, in the memory, these points, on which the whole fabric of morals and legislation may be seen to rest.

Intense, long, certain, speedy, fruitful, pure—
Such marks in *pleasures* and in *pains* endure.
Such pleasures seek if *private* be thy end:
If it be *public,* wide let them *extend.*
Such *pains* avoid, whichever be thy view:
If pains *must* come, let them *extend* to few.

6. Its *purity,* or the chance it has of *not* being followed by sensations of the *opposite* kind: that is, pains, if it be a pleasure: pleasures, if it be a pain.

These two last, however, are in strictness scarcely to be deemed properties of the pleasure or the pain itself; they are not, therefore, in strictness to be taken into the account of the value of that pleasure or that pain. They are in strictness to be deemed properties only of the act, or other event, by which such pleasure or pain has been produced; and accordingly are only to be taken into the account of the tendency of such act or such event.

IV. To a *number* of persons, with reference to each of whom the value of a pleasure or a pain is considered, it will be greater or less, according to seven circumstances: to wit, the six preceding ones; *viz.*

1. Its *intensity.*
2. Its *duration.*
3. Its *certainty* or *uncertainty.*
4. Its *propinquity* or *remoteness.*
5. Its *fecundity.*
6. Its *purity.*

And one other; to wit:

7. Its *extent;* that is, the number of persons to whom it *extends;* or (in other words) who are affected by it.

V. To take an exact account then of the general tendency of any act, by which the interests of a community are affected, proceed as follows. Begin with any one person of those whose interests seem most immediately to be affected by it: and take an account,

1. Of the value of each distinguishable *pleasure* which appears to be produced by it in the *first* instance.

2. Of the value of each *pain* which appears to be produced by it in the *first* instance.

3. Of the value of each pleasure which appears to be produced by it *after* the first. This constitutes the *fecundity* of the first *pleasure* and the *impurity* of the first *pain.*

4. Of the value of each *pain* which appears to be produced by it after the first. This constitutes the *fecundity* of the first *pain,* and the *impurity* of the first pleasure.

5. Sum up all the values of all the *pleasures* on the one side, and those of all the pains on the other. The balance, if it be on the side of pleasure, will give the *good* tendency of the act upon the whole, with respect to the interests of that *individual* person; if on the side of pain, the *bad* tendency of it upon the whole.

6. Take an account of the *number* of persons whose interests appear to be concerned; and repeat the above process with respect to each. *Sum up* the numbers expressive of the degrees of *good* tendency, which the act has, with respect to each individual, in regard to whom the tendency of it is *good* upon the whole: do this again with respect to each individual, in regard to whom the tendency of it is *good* upon the whole: do this again with respect to each

individual, in regard to whom the tendency of it is *bad* upon the whole. Take the *balance;* which, if on the side of *pleasure,* will give the general *good tendency* of the act, with respect to the total number or community of individuals concerned; if on the side of pain, the general *evil tendency,* with respect to the same community.

VI. It is not to be expceted that this process should be strictly pursued previously to every moral judgment, or to every legislative or judicial operation. It may, however, be always kept in view: and as near as the process actually pursued on these occasions approaches to it, so near will such process approach to the character of an exact one.

VII. The same process is alike applicable to pleasure and pain, in whatever shape they appear: and by whatever denomination they are distinguished: to pleasure, whether it be called *good* (which is properly the cause or instrument of pleasure) or *profit* (which is distant pleasure, or the cause or instrument of distant pleasure,) or *convenience,* or *advantage, benefit, emolument, happiness,* and so forth: to pain, whether it be called *evil,* (which corresponds to *good*) or *mischief,* or *inconvenience,* or *disadvantage,* or *loss,* or *unhappiness,* and so forth.

VIII. Nor is this a novel and unwarranted, any more than it is a useless theory. In all this there is nothing but what the practice of mankind, wheresoever they have a clear view of their own interest, is perfectly conformable to. An article of property, an estate in land, for instance, is valuable, on what account? On account of the pleasures of all kinds which it enables a man to produce, and what comes to the same thing the pains of all kinds which it enables him to avert. But the value of such an article of property is universally understood to rise or fall according to the length or shortness of the time which a man had in it: the certainty or uncertainty of its coming into possession: and the nearness or remoteness of the time at which, if at all, it is to come into possession. As to the *intensity* of the pleasures which a man may derive from it, this is never thought of, because it depends upon the use which each particular person may come to make of it; which cannot be estimated till the particular pleasures he may come to derive from it, or the particular pains he may come to exclude by means of it, are brought to view. For the same reason, neither does he think of the *fecundity* or *purity* of those pleasures.

Thus much for pleasure and pain, happiness and unhappiness, in *general.*

JOHN STUART MILL
Utilitarianism

CHAPTER I

GENERAL REMARKS

There are few circumstances among those which make up the present condition of human knowledge, more unlike what might have been expected, or more significant of the backward state in which speculation on the most important subjects still lingers, than the little progress which has been made in the decision of the controversy respecting the criterion of right and wrong. From the dawn of philosophy, the question concerning the *summum bonum,* or, what is the same thing, concerning the foundation of morality, has been accounted the main problem in speculative thought, has occupied the most gifted intellects, and divided them into sects and schools, carrying on a vigorous warfare against one another. And after more than two thousand years the same discussions continue, philosophers are still ranged under the same contending banners, and neither thinkers nor mankind at large seem nearer to being unanimous on the subject, than when the youth Socrates listened to the old Protagoras, and asserted (if Plato's dialogue be grounded on a real conversation) the theory of utilitarianism against the popular morality of the so-called sophist.

It is true that similar confusion and uncertainty, and in some cases similar discordance, exist respecting the first principles of all the sciences, not excepting that which is deemed the most certain of them, mathematics; without much impairing, generally indeed without impairing at all, the trustworthiness of the conclusions of those sciences. An apparent anomaly, the explanation of which is, that the detailed doctrines of a science are not usually deduced from, nor depend for their evidence upon, what are called its first principles. Were it not so, there would be no science more precarious, or whose conclusions were more insufficiently made out, than algebra; which derives none of its certainty from what are commonly taught to learners as its elements, since these, as laid down by some of its most eminent teachers, are as full of fictions as English law, and of mysteries as theology. The truths which are ultimately accepted as the first principles of a science, are really the last results of metaphysical analysis, practised on the elementary notions with which the science is conversant; and their relation to the science is not that of foundations to an edifice, but of roots to a tree, which may perform their office equally well though they be never dug down to and exposed to light. But though in science the particular truths precede the general theory, the contrary might be expected to be the case with a

From John Stuart Mill, *Utilitarianism;* Chapters I–V. (1863)

practical art, such as morals or legislation. All action is for the sake of some end, and rules of action, it seems natural to suppose, must take their whole character and colour from the end to which they are subservient. When we engage in a pursuit, a clear and precise conception of what we are pursuing would seem to be the first thing we need, instead of the last we are to look forward to. A test of right and wrong must be the means, one would think, of ascertaining what is right or wrong, and not a consequence of having already ascertained it.

The difficulty is not avoided by having recourse to the popular theory of a natural faculty, a sense or instinct, informing us of right and wrong. For—besides that the existence of such a moral instinct is itself one of the matters in dispute—those believers in it who have any pretensions to philosophy, have been obliged to abandon the idea that it discerns what is right or wrong in the particular case in hand, as our other senses discern the sight or sound actually present. Our moral faculty, according to all those of its interpreters who are entitled to the name of thinkers, supplies us only with the general principles of moral judgments; it is a branch of our reason, not of our sensitive faculty; and must be looked to for the abstract doctrines of morality, not for perception of it in the concrete. The intuitive, no less than what may be termed the inductive, school of ethics, insists on the necessity of general laws. They both agree that the morality of an individual action is not a question of direct perception, but of the application of a law to an individual case. They recognise also, to a great extent, the same moral laws; but differ as to their evidence, and the source from which they derive their authority. According to the one opinion, the principles of morals are evident à priori, requiring nothing to command assent, except that the meaning of the terms be understood. According to the other doctrine, right and wrong, as well as truth and falsehood, are questions of observation and experience. But both hold equally that morality must be deduced from principles; and the intuitive school affirm as strongly as the inductive, that there is a science of morals. Yet they seldom attempt to make out a list of the à priori principles which are to serve as the premises of the science; still more rarely do they make any effort to reduce those various principles to one first principle, or common ground of obligation. They either assume the ordinary precepts of morals as of à priori authority, or they lay down as the common groundwork of those maxims, some generality much less obviously authoritative than the maxims themselves, and which has never succeeded in gaining popular acceptance. Yet to support their pretensions there ought either to be some one fundamental principle or law, at the root of all morality, or if there be several, there should be a determinate order of precedence among them; and the one principle, or the rule for deciding between the various principles when they conflict, ought to be self-evident.

To inquire how far the bad effects of this deficiency have been mitigated in practice, or to what extent the moral beliefs of mankind have been vitiated or made uncertain by the absence of any distinct recognition of an ultimate standard, would imply a complete survey and criticism of past and present ethical doctrine. It would, however, be easy to show that whatever steadiness or consistency these moral beliefs have attained, has been mainly due to the tacit influence of a standard not recognised. Although the non-existence of an acknowledged first principle has made ethics not so much a guide as a consecration of men's actual sentiments, still, as men's sentiments, both of favour and of aversion, are greatly influenced by what they suppose to be the effects of things upon their happiness, the principle of utility, or as Bentham latterly called it, the greatest happiness principle, has had a large share in forming the moral doctrines even of those who most scornfully reject its authority. Nor is there any school of thought which refuses to admit that the influence of actions on happiness is a most material and even predominant consideration in many of the details of morals, however unwilling to acknowledge it as the fundamental principle of morality, and the source of moral obligation. I might go much further, and say that to all those à *priori* moralists who deem it necessary to argue at all, utilitarian arguments are indispensable. It is not my present purpose to criticize these thinkers; but I cannot help referring, for illustration, to a systematic treatise by one of the most illustrious of them, the *Metaphysics of Ethics,* by Kant. This remarkable man, whose system of thought will long remain one of the landmarks in the history of philosophical speculation, does, in the treatise in question, lay down an universal first principle as the origin and ground of moral obligation; it is this:—'So act, that the rule on which thou actest would admit of being adopted as a law by all rational beings.' But when he begins to deduce from this precept any of the actual duties of morality, he fails, almost grotesquely, to show that there would be any contradiction, any logical (not to say physical) impossibility, in the adoption by all rational beings of the most outrageously immoral rules of conduct. All he shows is that the *consequences* of their universal adoption would be such as no one would choose to incur.

On the present occasion, I shall, without further discussion of the other theories, attempt to contribute something towards the understanding and appreciation of the Utilitarian or Happiness theory, and towards such proof as it is susceptible of. It is evident that this cannot be proof in the ordinary and popular meaning of the term. Questions of ultimate ends are not amenable to direct proof. Whatever can be proved to be good, must be so by being shown to be a means to something admitted to be good without proof. The medical art is proved to be good, by its conducing to health; but how is it possible to prove that health is good? The art of music is good, for the reason, among others, that it produces pleasure; but what proof is it possible to give that pleasure is good? If, then, it is asserted that there is a comprehensive formula, including all things which are in themselves good, and that whatever else is good, is not so as an end, but as a mean, the formula may be accepted or rejected, but it is not a subject of what is commonly understood by proof. We are not, however, to infer that its acceptance or rejection must depend on blind impulse, or arbitrary choice. There is a larger meaning of the word proof, in which this question is as amenable to it as any other of the disputed questions of philosophy. The subject is within the cognizance of the rational faculty; and neither does that faculty deal with

JOHN STUART MILL 163

it solely in the way of intuition. Considerations may be presented capable of determining the intellect either to give or withhold its assent to the doctrine; and this is equivalent to proof.

We shall examine presently of what nature are these considerations; in what manner they apply to the case, and what rational grounds, therefore, can be given for accepting or rejecting the utilitarian formula. But it is a preliminary condition of rational acceptance or rejection, that the formula should be correctly understood. I believe that the very imperfect notion ordinarily formed of its meaning, is the chief obstacle which impedes its reception; and that could it be cleared, even from only the grosser misconceptions, the question would be greatly simplified, and a large proportion of its difficulties removed. Before, therefore, I attempt to enter into the philosophical grounds which can be given for assenting to the utilitarian standard, I shall offer some illustrations of the doctrine itself, with the view of showing more clearly what it is, distinguishing it from what it is not, and disposing of such of the practical objections to it as either originate in, or are closely connected with, mistaken interpretations of its meaning. Having thus prepared the ground, I shall afterwards endeavour to throw such light as I can upon the question, considered as one of philosophical theory.

CHAPTER II
WHAT UTILITARIANISM IS

A passing remark is all that needs be given to the ignorant blunder of supposing that those who stand up for utility as the test of right and wrong, used the term in that restricted and merely colloquial sense in which utility is opposed to pleasure. An apology is due to the philosophical opponents of utilitarianism, for even the momentary appearance of confounding them with any one capable of so absurd a misconception; which is the more extraordinary, inasmuch as the contrary accusation, of referring everything to pleasure, and that too in its grossest form, is another of the common charges against utilitarianism: and, as has been pointedly remarked by an able writer, the same sort of persons, and often the very same persons, denounce the theory 'as impracticably dry when the word utility precedes the word pleasure, and as too practicably voluptuous when the word pleasure precedes the word utility.' Those who know anything about the matter are aware that every writer, from Epicurus to Bentham, who maintained the theory of utility, meant by it, not something to be contradistinguished from pleasure, but pleasure itself, together with exemption from pain; and instead of opposing the useful to the agreeable or the ornamental, have always declared that the useful means these, among other things. Yet the common herd, including the herd of writers, not only in newspapers and periodicals, but in books of weight and pretension, are perpetually falling into this shallow mistake. Having caught up the word utilitarian, while knowing nothing whatever about it but its sound, they habitually express by it the rejection, or the neglect, of pleasure in some of its forms; of beauty, of ornament, or of amusement. Nor is the term thus ignorantly misapplied solely in disparagement, but occasionally in compliment; as though it implied superiority to frivolity and the mere pleasures of the moment. And this perverted use is the only one in which the word is popularly known, and the one from which the new generation are acquiring their sole notion of its meaning. Those who introduced the word, but who had for many years discontinued it as a distinctive appellation, may well feel themselves called upon to resume it, if by doing so they can hope to contribute anything towards rescuing it from this utter degradation.

The creed which accepts as the foundation of morals, Utility, or the Greatest Happiness Principle, holds that actions are right in proportion as they tend to promote happiness, wrong as they tend to produce the reverse of happiness. By happiness is intended pleasure, and the absence of pain; by unhappiness, pain, and the privation of pleasure. To give a clear view of the moral standard set up by the theory, much more requires to be said; in particular, what things it includes in the ideas of pain and pleasure; and to what extent this is left an open question. But these supplementary explanations do not affect the theory of life on which this theory of morality is grounded—namely, that pleasure, and freedom from pain, are the only things desirable as ends; and that all desirable things (which are as numerous in the utilitarian as in any other scheme) are desirable either for the pleasure inherent in themselves, or as means to the promotion of pleasure and the prevention of pain.

Now, such a theory of life excites in many minds, and among them in some of the most estimable in feeling and purpose, inveterate dislike. To suppose that life has (as they express it) no higher end than pleasure—no better and nobler object of desire and pursuit—they designate as utterly mean and grovelling; as a doctrine worthy only of swine, to whom the followers of Epicurus were, at a very early period, contemptuously likened; and modern holders of the doctrine are occasionally made the subject of equally polite comparisons by its German, French, and English assailants.

When thus attacked, the Epicureans have always answered, that it is not they, but their accusers, who represent human nature in a degrading light; since the accusation supposes human beings to be capable of no pleasures except those of which swine are capable. If this supposition were true, the charge could not be gainsaid, but would then be no longer an imputation; for if the sources of pleasure were precisely the same to human beings and to swine, the rule of life which is good enough for the one would be good enough for the other. The comparison of the Epicurean life to that of beasts is felt as degrading, precisely because a beast's pleasures do not satisfy a human being's conceptions of happiness. Human beings have faculties more elevated than the animal appetites, and when once made conscious of them, do not regard anything as happiness which does not include their gratification. I do not, indeed, consider the Epicureans to have been by any means faultless in drawing out their scheme of consequences from the utilitarian principle. To do this in any sufficient manner, many Stoic, as well as Christian elements require to be included. But there is no known Epicurean theory of life which does not assign to the pleasures of the intellect, of the feelings and imagination, and of the moral sentiments, a much higher value as pleasures than to those of mere sensation. It must be admitted, however, that utilitarian writers in general have placed the superiority of mental over bodily pleasures chiefly in the greater permanency, safety, uncostliness, &c., of the former—that is, in their circumstantial advantages rather than in their intrinsic nature. And on all these points utilitarians have fully proved their case; but they might have taken the other, and, as it may be called, higher ground, with entire consistency. It is quite compatible with the principle of utility to recognise the fact, that some *kinds* of pleasure are more desirable and more valuable than others. It would be absurd that while, in estimating all other things, quality is considered as well as quantity, the estimation of pleasures should be supposed to depend on quantity alone.

If I am asked, what I mean by difference of quality in pleasures, or what makes one pleasure more valuable than another, merely as a pleasure, except its being greater in amount, there is but one possible answer. Of two pleasures, if there be one to which all or almost all who have experience of both give a decided preference, irrespective of any feeling of moral obligation to prefer it, that is the more desirable pleasure. If one of the two is, by those who are competently acquainted with both, placed so far above the other that they prefer it, even though knowing it to be attended with a greater amount of discontent, and would not resign it for any quantity of the other pleasure which their nature is capable of, we are justified in ascribing to the preferred enjoyment a superiority in quality, so far outweighing quantity as to render it, in comparison, of small account.

Now it is an unquestionable fact that those who are equally acquainted with, and equally capable of appreciating and enjoying, both, do give a most marked preference to the manner of existence which employs their higher faculties. Few human creatures would consent to be changed into any of the lower animals, for a promise of the fullest allowance of a beast's pleasures; no intelligent human being would consent to be a fool, no instructed person would be an ignoramus, no person of feeling and conscience would be selfish and base, even though they should be persuaded that the fool, the dunce, or the rascal is better satisfied with his lot than they are with theirs. They would not resign what they possess more than he, for the most complete satisfaction of all the desires which they have in common with him. If they ever fancy they would, it is only in cases of unhappiness so extreme, that to escape from it they would exchange their lot for almost any other, however undesirable in their own eyes. A being of higher faculties requires more to make him happy, is capable probably of more acute suffering, and is certainly accessible to it at more points, than one of an inferior type; but in spite of these liabilities, he can never really wish to sink into what he feels to be a lower grade of existence. We may give what explanation we please of this unwillingness; we may attribute it to pride, a name which is given indiscriminately to some of the most and to some of the least estimable feelings of which mankind are capable; we may refer it to the love of liberty and personal independence, an appeal to which was with the Stoics one of the most effective means for the inculcation of it; to the love of power, or to the love of excitement, both of which do really enter into and contribute to it: but its most appropriate appellation is a sense of dignity, which all human beings possess in one form or other, and in some, though by no means in exact, proportion to their higher faculties, and which is so essential a part of the happiness of those in whom it is strong, that nothing which conflicts with it could be, otherwise than momentarily, an object of desire to them. Whoever supposes that this preference takes place at a sacrifice of happiness—that the superior being, in anything like the equal circumstances, is not happier than the inferior—confounds the two very different ideas, of happiness, and content. It is indisputable that the being whose capacities of enjoyment are low, has the greatest chance of having them fully satisfied; and a highly-endowed being will always feel that any happiness which he can look for, as the world is constituted, is imperfect. But he can learn to bear its imperfections, if they are at all bearable; and they will not make him envy the being who is indeed unconscious of the imperfections, but only because he feels not at all the good which those imperfections qualify. It is better to be a human being dissatisfied than a pig satisfied; better to be Socrates dissatisfied than a fool satisfied. And if the fool, or the pig, is of a different opinion, it is because they only know their own side of the question. The other party to the comparison knows both sides.

It may be objected, that many who are capable of the higher pleasures, occasionally, under the influence of temptation, postpone them to the lower. But this is quite compatible with a full appreciation of the intrinsic superiority of the higher. Men often, from infirmity of character, make their election for the nearer good, though they know it to be the less valuable; and this no less when the choice is between two bodily pleasures, than when it is between bodily and mental. They pursue sensual indulgences to the injury of health, though perfectly aware that health is the greater good. It may be further objected, that many who begin with youthful enthusiasm for everything noble, as they advance in years sink into indolence and selfishness. But I do not believe that those who undergo this very common change, voluntarily choose the lower description of pleasures in preference to the higher. I believe that before they devote themselves exclusively to the one, they have already become incapable of the other. Capacity for the nobler feelings is in most natures a very tender plant, easily killed, not only by hostile influences, but by mere want of sustenance; and in the majority of young persons it speedily dies away if the occupations to which their position in life has devoted them, and the society into which it has thrown them, are not favourable to keeping that higher capacity in exercise. Men lose their high aspirations as they lose their intellectual tastes, because they have not time or opportunity for indulging them; and they addict themselves to inferior pleasures, not because they deliberately prefer them, but because they are either the only ones to which they have access, or the only ones which they are any longer capable of enjoying. It may be questioned whether any one who has remained equally susceptible to both classes of pleasures, ever knowingly and calmly preferred the lower; though many, in all ages, have broken down in an ineffectual attempt to combine both.

From this verdict of the only competent judges, I apprehend there can be no appeal. On a question which is the best worth having of two pleasures, or which of two modes of existence is the most grateful to the feelings, apart from its moral attributes and from its consequences, the judgment of those who are qualified by knowledge of both, or, if they differ, that of the majority among them, must be admitted as final. And there needs be the less hesitation to accept this judgment respecting the quality of pleasures, since there is no other tribunal to be referred to even on the question of quantity. What means are there of determining which is the acutest of two pains, or the intensest of two pleasurable sensations, except the general suffrage of those who are familar with both? Neither pains nor pleasures are homogeneous, and pain is always heterogeneous with pleasure. What is there to decide whether a particular pleasure is worth purchasing at the cost of a particular pain, except the feelings and judgment of the experienced? When, therefore, those feelings and judgment declare the pleasures derived from the higher faculties to be preferable *in kind*, apart from the question of intensity, to those of which the animal nature, disjoined from the higher faculties, is susceptible, they are entitled on this subject to the same regard.

I have dwelt on this point, as being a necessary part of a perfectly just conception of Utility or Happiness, considered as the directive rule of human conduct. But it is by no means an indispensable condition to the acceptance of the utilitarian standard; for that standard is not the agent's own greatest happiness, but the greatest amount of happiness altogether; and if it may possibly be doubted whether a noble character is always the happier for its nobleness, there can be no doubt that it makes other people happier, and that the world in general is immensely a gainer by it. Utilitarianism, therefore, could only attain its end by the general cultivation of nobleness of character, even if each individual were only benefited by the nobleness of others, and his own, so far as happiness is concerned, were a sheer deduction from the benefit. But the bare enunciation of such an absurdity as this last, renders refutation superfluous.

According to the Greatest Happiness Principle, as above explained, the ultimate end, with reference to and for the sake of which all other things are desirable (whether we are considering our own good or that of other people), is an existence exempt as far as possible from pain, and as rich as possible in enjoyments, both in point of quantity and quality; the test of quality, and the rule for measuring it against quantity, being the preference felt by those who, in their opportunities of experience, to which must be added their habits of self-consciousness and self-observation, are best furnished with the means of comparison. This, being, according to the utilitarian opinion, the end of human action, is necessarily also the standard of morality; which may accordingly be defined, the rules and precepts for human conduct, by the observance of which an existence such as has been described might be, to the greatest extent possible, secured to all mankind; and not to them only, but, so far as the nature of things admits, to the whole sentient creation.

Against this doctrine, however, arises another class of objectors, who say that happiness, in any form, cannot be the rational purpose of human life and action; because, in the first place, it is unattainable: and they contemptuously ask, What right hast thou to be happy? a question which Mr. Carlyle clenches by the addition, What right, a short time ago, hadst thou even *to be*? Next, they say, that men can do *without* happiness; that all noble human beings have felt this, and could not have become noble but by learning the lesson of Entsagen, or renunciation; which lesson, thoroughly learnt and submitted to, they affirm to be the beginning and necessary condition of all virtue.

The first of these objections would go to the root of the matter were it well founded; for if no happiness is to be had at all by human beings, the attainment of it cannot be the end of morality, or of any rational conduct. Though, even in that case, something might still be said for the utilitarian theory; since utility includes not solely the pursuit of happiness, but the prevention of mitigation of unhappiness; and if the former aim be chimerical, there will be all the greater scope and more imperative need for the latter, so long at least as mankind think fit to live, and do not take refuge in the simultaneous act of suicide recommended under certain conditions by Novalis. When, however, it is thus positively asserted to be impossible that human life should be happy, the assertion, if not something like a verbal quibble, is at least an exaggeration. If by happiness be meant a continuity of highly pleasurable excitement, it is evident enough that this is impossible. A state of exalted pleasure lasts only moments, or in some cases, and with some intermissions, hours or days, and is the occasional brilliant flash of enjoyment, not its permanent and steady flame. Of this the philosophers who have taught that happiness is the end of life were as fully aware as those who taunt them. The happiness which they meant was not a life of rapture; but moments of such, in an existence made up of few and transitory pains, many and various pleasures, with a decided predominance of the active over the passive, and having as the foundation of the whole, not to expect more from life than it is capable of bestowing. A life thus composed, to those who have been fortunate enough to obtain it, has always appeared worthy of the name of happiness. And such an existence is even now the lot of many, during some considerable portion of their lives. The present wretched education, and wretched social arrangements, are the only real hindrance to its being attainable by almost all.

·   ·   ·   ·   ·

. . . All the grand sources, in short, of human suffering are in a great degree, many of them almost entirely, conquerable by human care and effort; and though their removal is grievously slow—though a long succession of generations will perish in the breach before the conquest is completed, and this world becomes all that if will and knowledge were not wanting, it might easily be made—yet every mind sufficiently intelligent and generous to bear a part, however small and unconspicuous, in the endeavour, will draw a noble enjoyment from the contest itself, which he would not for any bribe in the form of selfish indulgence consent to be without.

And this leads to the true estimation of what is said by the objectors concerning the possibility, and the obligation, of learning to do without happiness. Unquestionably it is possible to do without happiness; it is done involuntarily by nineteen-twentieths of mankind, even in those parts of our present world which are least deep in barbarism; and it often has to be done voluntarily by the hero or the martyr, for the sake of something which he prizes more than his individual happiness. But this something, what is it, unless the happiness of others, or some of the requisites of happiness? It is noble to be capable of resigning entirely one's own portion of happiness, or chances of it: but, after all, this self-sacrifice must be for some end; it is not its own end; and if we are told that its end is not happiness, but virtue, which is better than happiness, I ask, would the sacrifice be made if the hero or martyr did not believe that it would earn for others immunity from similar sacrifices? Would it be made, if he thought that his renunciation of happiness for himself would produce no fruit for any of his fellow creatures, but to make their lot like his, and place them also in the condition of persons who have renounced happiness? All honour to those who can abnegate for themselves the personal enjoyment of life, when by such renunciation they contribute worthily to increase the amount of happiness in the world; but he who does it, or professes to do it, for any other purpose, is no more deserving of admiration than the ascetic mounted on his pillar. He may be an inspiriting proof of what men *can* do, but assuredly not an example of what they *should*.

Though it is only in a very imperfect state of the world's arrangements that any one can best serve the happiness of others by the absolute sacrifice of his own, yet so long as the world is in that imperfect state, I fully acknowledge that the readiness to make such a sacrifice is the highest virtue which can be found in man. I will add, that in this condition of the world, paradoxical as the assertion may be, the conscious ability to do without happiness gives the best prospect of realizing such happiness as is attainable. For nothing except that consciousness can raise a person above the chances of life, by making him feel that, let fate and fortune do their worst, they have not power to subdue him: which, once felt, frees him from excess of anxiety concerning the evils of life, and enables him, like many a Stoic in the worst times of the Roman Empire, to cultivate in tranquillity the sources of satisfaction accessible to him, without concerning himself about the uncertainty of their duration, any more than about their inevitable end.

Meanwhile, let utilitarians never cease to claim the morality of self-devotion as a possession which belongs by as good a right to them, as either to the Stoic or to the Transcendentalist. The utilitarian morality does recognise in human beings the power of sacrificing their own greatest good for the good of others. It only refuses to admit that the sacrifice is itself a good. A sacrifice which does not increase, or tend to increase, the sum total of happiness, it considers as wasted. The only self-renunciation which it applauds, is devotion to the happiness, or to some of the means of happiness, of others; either of mankind collectively, or of individuals within the limits imposed by the collective interests of mankind.

I must again repeat, what the assailants of utilitarianism seldom have the justice to acknowledge, that the happiness which forms the utilitarian standard of what is right in conduct, is not the agent's own happiness, but that of all concerned. As between his own happiness and that of others, utilitarianism requires him to be as strictly impartial as a disinterested and benevolent spectator. In the golden rule of Jesus of Nazareth, we read the complete spirit of the ethics of utility. To do as one would be done by, and to love one's neighbour as oneself, constitute the ideal perfection of utilitarian morality. As the means of making the nearest approach to this ideal, utility would enjoin, first, that laws and social arrangements should place the happiness, or (as speaking practically it may be called) the interest, of every individual, as nearly as possible in harmony with the interest of the whole; and secondly, that education and opinion, which have so vast a power over human character, should so use that power as to establish in the mind of every individual an indissoluble association between his own happiness and the good of the whole; especially between his own happiness and the practice of such modes of conduct, negative and positive, as regard for the universal happiness prescribes: so that not only he may be unable to conceive the possibility of happiness to himself, consistently with conduct opposed to the general good, but also that a direct impulse to promote the general good may be in every individual one of the habitual motives of action, and the sentiments connected therewith may fill a large and prominent place in every human being's sentient existence. If the impugners of the utilitarian morality represented it to their own minds in this its true character, I know not what recommendation possessed by any other morality they could possibly affirm to be wanting to it: what more beautiful or more exalted developments of human nature any other ethical system can be supposed to foster, or what springs of action, not accessible to the utilitarian, such systems rely on for giving effect to their mandates.

The objectors to utilitarianism cannot always be charged with representing it in a discreditable light. On the contrary, those among them who entertain anything like a just idea of its disinterested character, sometimes find fault with its standard as being too high for humanity. They say it is exacting too much to require that people shall always act from the inducement of promoting the general interests of society. But this is to mistake the very meaning of a standard of morals, and to confound the rule of action with the motive of it. It is the business of ethics to tell us what are our duties, or by what test we may know them; but no system of ethics requires that the sole motive of all we do shall be a feeling of duty; on the contrary, ninety-nine hundredths of all our actions are done from other motives, and rightly so done, if the rule of duty does not condemn them. It is the more unjust to utilitarianism that this particular misapprehension should be made a ground of objection to it, inasmuch as utilitarian moralists have gone beyond almost all others in affirming that the motive has nothing to do with the morality of the action, though much with the worth of the agent. He who saves a fellow creature from drowning does what is morally right, whether his motive be duty, or the hope of being paid for his trouble: he who betrays the friend that trusts him, is guilty of a crime, even if his object be to serve another friend to whom he is under greater obligations.[1] But to speak only of actions done from the motive of duty, and in direct obedience to principle: it is a misapprehension of the utilitarian mode of thought, to conceive it as implying that people should fix their minds upon so wide a generality as the world, or society at large. The great majority of good actions are intended, not for the benefit of the world, but for that of individuals, of which the good of the world is made up; and the thoughts of the most virtuous man need not on these occasions travel beyond the particular persons concerned, except so far as is necessary to assure himself that in benefiting them he is not violating the rights—that is, the legitimate and authorized expectations—of any one else. The multiplication of happiness is, according to the utilitarian ethics, the object of virtue: the occasions on which any person (except one in a thousand) has it in his power to do this on an extended scale, in other words, to be a public benefactor, are but exceptional; and on these occasions alone is he called on to consider public utility; in every other case, private utility, the interest or happiness of some few persons, is all he has to attend to. Those alone the influence of whose actions extends to society in general, need concern themselves habitually about so large an object. In the case of abstinences indeed —of things which people forbear to do, from moral considerations, though the

---

[1] An opponent, whose intellectual and moral fairness it is a pleasure to acknowledge (the Rev. J. Llewellyn Davies), has objected to this passage, saying, "Surely the rightness or wrongness of saving a man from drowning does depend very much upon the motive with which it is done. Suppose that a tyrant, when his enemy jumped into the sea to escape from him, saved him from drowning simply in order that he might inflict upon him more exquisite tortures, would it tend to clearness to speak of that rescue as 'a morally right action?' Or suppose again, according to one of the stock illustrations of ethical inquiries, that a man betrayed a trust received from a friend, because the discharge of it would fatally injure that friend himself or some one belonging to him, would utilitarianism compel one to call the betrayal 'a crime' as much as if it had been done from the meanest motive?"

I submit, that he who saves another from drowning in order to kill him by torture afterwards, does not differ only in motive from him who does the same thing from duty or benevolence; the act itself is different. The rescue of the man is, in the case supposed, only the necessary first step of an act far more atrocious than leaving him to drown would have been. Had Mr. Davies said, "The rightness or wrongness of saving a man from drowning does depend very much"—not upon the motive, but—"upon the *intention*," no utilitarian would have differed from him. Mr. Davies, by an oversight too common not to be quite venial, has in this case confounded the very different ideas of Motive and Intention. There is no point which utilitarian thinkers (and Bentham pre-eminently) have taken more pains to illustrate than this. The morality of the action depends entirely upon the intention—that is, upon what the agent *wills to do*. But the motive, that is, the feeling which makes him will so to do, when it makes no difference in the act, makes none in the morality: though it makes a great difference in our moral estimation of the agent, especially if it indicates a good or a bad habitual *disposition*—a bent of character from which useful, or from which hurtful actions are likely to arise.

consequences in the particular case might be beneficial—it would be unworthy of an intelligent agent not to be consciously aware that the action is of a class which, if practised generally, would be generally injurious, and that this is the ground of the obligation to abstain from it. The amount of regard for the public interest implied in this recognition, is no greater than is demanded by every system of morals; for they all enjoin to abstain from whatever is manifestly pernicious to society.

·   ·   ·   ·   ·

Again, Utility is often summarily stigmatized as an immoral doctrine by giving it the name of Expediency, and taking advantage of the popular use of that term to contrast it with Principle. But the Expedient, in the sense in which it is opposed to the Right, generally means that which is expedient for the particular interest of the agent himself; as when a minister sacrifices the interest of his country to keep himself in place. When it means anything better than this, it means that which is expedient for some immediate object, some temporary purpose, but which violates a rule whose observance is expedient in a much higher degree. The Expedient, in this sense, instead of being the same thing with the useful, is a branch of the hurtful. Thus, it would often be expedient for the purpose of getting over some momentary embarrassment, or attaining some object immediately useful to ourselves or others, to tell a lie. But inasmuch as the cultivation in ourselves of a sensitive feeling on the subject of veracity, is one of the most useful, and the enfeeblement of that feeling one of the most hurtful, things to which our conduct can be instrumental; and inasmuch as any, even unintentional, deviation from truth, does that much towards weakening the trustworthiness of human assertion, which is not only the principal support of all present social well-being, but the insufficiency of which does more than any one thing that can be named to keep back civilization, virtue, everything on which human happiness on the largest scale depends; we feel that the violation, for a present advantage, of a rule of such transcendant expediency, is not expedient, and that he who, for the sake of a convenience to himself or to some other individual, does what depends on him to deprive mankind of the good, and inflict upon them the evil, involved in the greater or less reliance which they can place in each other's word, acts the part of one of their worst enemies. Yet that even this rule, sacred as it is, admits of possible exceptions, is acknowledged by all moralists; the chief of which is when the withholding of some fact (as of information from a malefactor, or of bad news from a person dangerously ill) would preserve some one (especially a person other than oneself) from great and unmerited evil, and when the withholding can only be effected by denial. But in order that the exception may not extend itself beyond the need, and may have the least possible effect in weakening reliance on veracity, it ought to be recognised, and, if possible, its limits defined; and if the principle of utility is good for anything, it must be good for weighing these conflicting utilities against one another, and marking out the region within which one or the other preponderates.

Again, defenders of utility often find themselves called upon to reply to such objections as this—that there is not time, previous to action, for calculating and weighing the effects of any line of conduct on the general happiness. This is exactly as if any one were to say that it is impossible to guide our conduct by Christianity, because there is not time, on every occasion on which anything has to be done, to read through the Old and New Testaments. The answer to the objection is, that there has been ample time, namely, the whole past duration of the human species. During all that time mankind have been learning by experience the tendencies of actions; on which experience all the prudence, as well as all the morality of life, is dependent. People talk as if the commencement of this course of experience had hitherto been put off, and as if, at the moment when some man feels tempted to meddle with the property or life of another, he had to begin considering for the first time whether murder and theft are injurious to human happiness. Even then I do not think that he would find the question very puzzling; but, at all events, the matter is now done to his hand. It is truly a whimsical supposition that if mankind were agreed in considering utility to be the test of morality, they would remain without any agreement as to what *is* useful, and would take no measures for having their notions on the subject taught to the young, and enforced by law and opinion. There is no difficulty in proving any ethical standard whatever to work ill, if we suppose universal idiocy to be conjoined with it, but on any hypothesis short of that, mankind must by this time have acquired positive beliefs as to the effects of some actions on their happiness; and the beliefs which have thus come down are the rules of morality for the multitude, and for the philosopher until he has succeeded in finding better. That philosophers might easily do this, even now, on many subjects; that the received code of ethics is by no means of divine right; and that mankind have still much to learn as to the effects of actions on the general happiness, I admit, or rather, earnestly maintain. The corollaries from the principle of utility, like the precepts of every practical art, admit of indefinite improvement, and, in a progressive state of the human mind, their improvement is perpetually going on. But to consider the rules of morality as improvable, is one thing; to pass over the intermediate generalizations entirely, and endeavour to test each individual action directly by the first principle, is another. It is a strange notion that the acknowledgment of a first principle is inconsistent with the admission of secondary ones. To inform a traveller respecting the place of his ultimate destination, is not to forbid the use of landmarks and direction-posts on the way. The proposition that happiness is the end and aim of morality, does not mean that no road ought to be laid down to that goal, or that persons going thither should not be advised to take one direction rather than another. Men really ought to leave off talking a kind of nonsense on this subject, which they would neither talk nor listen to in other matters of practical concernment. Nobody argues that the art of navigation is not founded on astronomy, because sailors cannot wait to calculate the Nautical Almanack. Being rational creatures, they go to sea with it ready calculated; and all rational creatures go out upon the sea of life with their minds made up on the common questions of right and wrong, as well as on many of the far more difficult questions of wise and foolish. And this, as long as foresight is a human quality, it is to be presumed they will continue to do. Whatever we adopt as the fundamental principle of morality, we require subordinate principles to apply it by: the impossibility of doing without them, being common to all systems, can afford no argument against any one in particular: but gravely to argue as if no such secondary principles could be had, and as if mankind had remained till now, and always must remain, without drawing any general conclusions from the experience of human life, is as high a pitch, I think, as absurdity has ever reached in philosophical controversy.

The remainder of the stock arguments against utilitarianism mostly consist in laying to its charge the common infirmities of human nature, and the general difficulties which embarrass conscientious persons in shaping their course through life. We are told that an utilitarian will be apt to make his own particular case an exception to moral rules, and, when under temptation, will see an utility in the breach of a rule, greater than he will see in its observance. But is utility the only creed which is able to furnish us with excuses for evil doing, and means of cheating our own conscience? They are afforded in abundance by all doctrines which recognise as a fact in morals the existence of conflicting considerations; which all doctrines do, that have been believed by sane persons. It is not the fault of any creed, but of the complicated nature of human affairs, that rules of conduct cannot be so framed as to require no exceptions, and that hardly any kind of action can safely be laid down as either always obligatory or always condemnable. There is no ethical creed which does not temper the rigidity of its laws, by giving a certain latitude, under the moral responsibility of the agent, for accommodation to peculiarities of circumstances; and under every creed, at the opening thus made, self-deception and dishonest casuistry get in. There exists no moral system under which there do not arise unequivocal cases of conflicting obligation. These are the real difficulties, the knotty points both in the theory of ethics, and in the conscientious guidance of personal conduct. They are overcome practically with greater or with less success according to the intellect and virtue of the individual; but it can hardly be pretended that any one will be the less qualified for dealing with them, from possessing an ultimate standard to which conflicting rights and duties can be referred. If utility is the ultimate source of moral obligations, utility may be invoked to decide between them when their demands are incompatible. Though the application of the standard may be difficult, it is better than none at all: while in other systems, the moral laws all claiming independent authority, there is no common umpire entitled to interfere between them; their claims to precedence one over another rest on litttle better than sophistry, and unless determined, as they generally are, by the unacknowledged influence of considerations of utility, afford a free scope for the action of personal desires and partialities. We must remember that only in these cases of conflict between secondary principles is it requisite that first principles should be appealed to. There is no case of moral obligation in which some secondary principle is not involved; and if only one, there can seldom be any real doubt which one it is, in the mind of any person by whom the principle itself is recognised.

CHAPTER III
OF THE ULTIMATE SANCTION OF THE PRINCIPLE OF UTILITY

The question is often asked, and properly so, in regard to any supposed moral standard—What is its sanction? what are the motives to obey it? or more specifically, what is the source of its obligation? whence does it derive its binding force? It is a necessary part of moral philosophy to provide the answer to this question; which, though frequently assuming the shape of an objection to the utilitarian morality, as if it had some special applicability to that above others, really arises in regard to all standards. It arises, in fact, whenever a person is called on to *adopt* a standard or refer morality to any basis on which he has not been accustomed to rest it. For the customary morality, that which education and opinion have consecrated, is the only one which presents itself to the mind with the feeling of being *in itself* obligatory; and when a person is asked to believe that this morality *derives* its obligation from some general principle round which custom has not thrown the same halo, the assertion is to him a paradox; the supposed corollaries seem to have a more binding force than the original theorem; the superstructure seems to stand better without, than with, what is represented as its foundation. He says to himself, I feel that I am bound not to rob or murder, betray or deceive; but why am I bound to promote the general happiness? If my own happiness lies in something else, why may I not give that the preference?

If the view adopted by the utilitarian philosophy of the nature of the moral sense be correct, this difficulty will always present itself, until the influences which form moral character have taken the same hold of the principle which they have taken of some of the consequences—until, by the improvement of education, the feeling of unity with our fellow creatures shall be (what it cannot be doubted that Christ intended it to be) as deeply rooted in our character, and to our own consciousness as completely a part of our nature, as the horror of crime is in an ordinarily well-brought up young person. In the mean time, however, the difficulty has no peculiar application to the doctrine of utility, but is inherent in every attempt to analyse morality and reduce it to principles; which, unless the principle is already in men's minds invested with as much sacredness as any of its applications, always seems to divest them of a part of their sanctity.

The principle of utility either has, or there is no reason why it might not have, all the sanctions which belong to any other system of morals. Those sanctions are either external or internal. Of the external sanctions it is not necessary to speak at any length. They are, the hope of favour and the fear of displeasure from our fellow creatures or from the Ruler of the Universe, along with whatever we may have of sympathy or affection for them or of love and awe of Him, inclining us to do his will independently of selfish consequences. There is evidently no reason why all these motives for observance should not attach themselves to the utilitarian morality, as completely and as powerfully as to any other. Indeed, those of them which refer to our fellow creatures are sure to do so, in proportion to the amount of general intelligence; for whether there be any other ground of moral obligation than the general happiness or not, men do desire happiness; and however imperfect may be their own practice, they desire and commend all conduct in others towards themselves, by which they think their happiness is promoted. With regard to the religious motive, if men believe, as most profess to do, in the goodness of God, those who think that conduciveness to the general happiness is the essence, or even only the criterion, of good, must necessarily believe that it is also that which God approves. The whole force therefore of external reward and punishment, whether physical or moral, and whether proceeding from God or from our fellow men, together with all that the capacities of human nature admit, of disinterested devotion to either, become available to enforce the utilitarian morality, in proportion as that morality is recognised; and the more powerfully, the more the appliances of education and general cultivation are bent to the purpose.

So far as to external sanctions. The internal sanction of duty, whatever our standard of duty may be, is one and the same—a feeling in our own mind; a pain, more or less intense, attendant on violation of duty, which in properly-cultivated moral natures rises, in the more serious cases, into shrinking from it as an impossibility. This feeling, when disinterested, and connecting itself with the pure idea of duty, and not with some particular form of it, or with any of the merely accessory circumstances, is the essence of Conscience; though in that complex phenomenon as it actually exists, the simple fact is in general all encrusted over with collateral associations, derived from sympathy, from love, and still more from fear; from all the forms of religious feeling; from the recollections of childhood and of all our past life; from self-esteem, desire of the esteem of others, and occasionally even self-abasement. This extreme complication is, I apprehend, the origin of the sort of mystical character which, by a tendency of the human mind of which there are many other examples, is apt to be attributed to the idea of moral obligation, and which leads people to believe that the idea cannot possibly attach itself to any other objects than those which, by a supposed mysterious law, are found in our present experience to excite it. Its binding force, however, consists in the existence of a mass of feeling which must be broken through in order to do what violates our standard of right, and which, if we do nevertheless violate that standard, will probably have to be encountered afterwards in the form of remorse. Whatever theory we have of the nature or origin of conscience, this is what essentially constitutes it.

The ultimate sanction, therefore, of all morality (external motives apart) being a subjective feeling in our own minds, I see nothing embarrassing to those whose standard is utility, in the question, what is the sanction of that particular standard? We may answer, the same as of all other moral standards—the conscientious feelings of mankind. Undoubtedly this sanction has no binding efficacy on those who do not possess the feelings it appeals to; but neither will these persons be more obedient to any other moral principle than to the utilitarian one. On them morality of any kind has no hold but through the external sanctions. Meanwhile the feelings exist, a fact in human nature, the reality of which, and the great power with which they are capable of acting on those in whom they have been duly cultivated, are proved by experience. No reason has ever been shown why they may not be cultivated to as great intensity in connexion with the utilitarian, as with any other rule of morals.

There is, I am aware, a disposition to believe that a person who sees in moral obligation a transcendental fact, an objective reality belonging to the province of 'Things in themselves,' is likely to be more obedient to it than one who believes it to be entirely subjective, having its seat in human consciousness only. But whatever a person's opinion may be on this point of Ontology, the force he is really urged by is his own subjective feeling, and is exactly measured by its strength. No one's belief that Duty is an objective reality is stronger than the belief that God is so; yet the belief in God, apart from the expectation of actual reward and punishment, only operates on conduct through, and in proportion to, the subjective religious feeling. The sanction, so far as it is disinterested, is always in the mind itself; and the notion therefore of the transcendental moralists must be, that this sanction will not exist *in* the mind unless it is believed to have its root out of the mind; and that if a person is able to say to himself, That which is restraining me, and which is called my conscience, is only a feeling in my own mind, he may possibly draw the conclusion that when the feeling ceases the obligation ceases, and that if he find the feeling inconvenient, he may disregard it, and endeavour to get rid of it. But is this danger confined to the utilitarian morality? Does the belief that moral obligation has its seat outside the mind make the feeling of it too strong to be got rid of? The fact is so far otherwise, that all moralists admit and lament the ease with which, in the generality of minds, conscience can be silenced or stifled. The question, Need I obey my conscience? is quite as often put to themselves by persons who never heard of the principle of utility, as by its adherents. Those whose conscientious feelings are so weak as to allow of their asking this question, if they answer it affirmatively, will not do so because they believe in the transcendental theory, but because of the external sanctions.

•　•　•　•　•

CHAPTER IV
OF WHAT SORT OF PROOF THE PRINCIPLE OF UTILITY
IS SUSCEPTIBLE

It has already been remarked, that questions of ultimate ends do not admit of proof, in the ordinary acceptation of the term. To be incapable of proof by reasoning is common to all first principles; to the first premises of our knowledge, as well as to those of our conduct. But the former, being matters of fact, may be the subject of a direct appeal to the faculties which judge of fact—namely, our senses, and our internal consciousness. Can an appeal be made to the same faculties on questions of practical ends? Or by what other faculty is cognizance taken of them?

Questions about ends are, in other words, questions what things are desirable. The utilitarian doctrine is, that happiness is desirable, and the only thing desirable, as an end; all other things being only desirable as means to that end. What ought to be required of this doctrine—what conditions is it requisite that the doctrine should fulfil—to make good its claim to be believed?

The only proof capable of being given that an object is visible, is that people actually see it. The only proof that a sound is audible, is that people hear it: and so of the other sources of our experience. In like manner, I apprehend, the sole evidence it is possible to produce that anything is desirable, is that people do actually desire it. If the end which the utilitarian doctrine proposes to itself were not, in theory and in practice, acknowledged to be an end, nothing could ever convince any person that it was so. No reason can be given why the general happiness is desirable, except that each person, so far as he believes it to be attainable, desires his own happiness. This, however, being a fact, we have not only all the proof which the case admits of, but all which it is possible to require, that happiness is a good: that each person's happiness is a good to that person, and the general happiness, therefore, a good to the aggregate of all persons. Happiness has made out its title as *one* of the ends of conduct, and consequently one of the criteria of morality.

But it has not, by this alone, proved itself to be the sole criterion. To do that, it would seem, by the same rule, necessary to show, not only that people desire happiness, but that they never desire anything else. Now it is palpable that they do desire things which, in common language, are decidedly distinguished from happiness. They desire, for example, virtue, and the absence of vice, no less really than pleasure and the absence of pain. The desire of virtue is not as universal, but it is as authentic a fact, as the desire of happiness. And hence the opponents of the utilitarian standard deem that they have a right to infer that there are other ends of human action besides happiness, and that happiness is not the standard of approbation and disapprobation.

But does the utilitarian doctrine deny that people desire virtue, or maintain that virtue is not a thing to be desired? The very reverse. It maintains not only that virtue is to be desired, but that it is to be desired disinterestedly, for itself. Whatever may be the opinion of utilitarian moralists as to the original conditions by which virtue is made virtue; however they may believe (as they do) that actions and dispositions are only virtuous because they promote another end than virtue; yet this being granted, and it having been decided, from considerations of this description, what *is* virtuous, they not only place virtue at the very head of the things which are good as means to the ultimate end, but they also recognise as a psychological fact the possibility of its being, to the individual, a good in itself, without looking to any end beyond it; and hold, that the mind is not in a right state, not in a state conformable to Utility, not in the state most conducive to the general happiness, unless it does love virtue in this manner—as a thing desirable in itself, even although, in the individual instance, it should not produce those other desirable consequences which it tends to produce, and on account of which it is held to be virtue. This opinion is not, in the smallest degree, a departure from the Happiness principle. The ingredients of happiness are very various, and each of them is desirable in itself, and not merely when considered as swelling an aggregate. The principle of utility does not mean that any given pleasure, as music, for instance, or any given exemption from pain, as for example health, are to be looked upon as a means to a collective something termed happiness, and to be desired on that account. They are desired and desirable in and for themselves; besides being means, they are a part of the end. Virtue, according to the utilitarian doctrine, is not naturally and originally part of the end, but it is capable of becoming so; and in those who love it disinterestedly it has become so, and is desired and cherished, not as a means to happiness, but as a part of their happiness.

To illustrate this farther, we may remember that virtue is not the only thing, originally a means, and which if it were not a means to anything else, would be and remain indifferent, but which by association with what it is a means to, comes to be desired for itself, and that too with the utmost intensity. What, for example, shall we say of the love of money? There is nothing originally more desirable about money than about any heap of glittering pebbles. Its worth is solely that of the things which it will buy; the desires for other things than itself, which it is a means of gratifying. Yet the love of money is not only one of the strongest moving forces of human life, but money is, in many cases, desired in and for itself; the desire to possess it is often stronger than the desire to use it, and goes on increasing when all the desires which point to ends beyond it, to be encompassed by it, are falling off. It may be then said truly, that money is desired not for the sake of an end, but as part of the end. From being a means to happiness, it has come to be itself a principal ingredient of the individual's conception of happiness. The same may be said of the majority of the great objects of human life—power, for example, or fame; except that to each of these there is a certain amount of immediate pleasure annexed, which has at least the semblance of being naturally inherent in them; a thing which cannot be said of money. Still, however, the strongest natural attraction, both of power and of fame, is the immense aid they give to the attainment of our other wishes; and it is the strong association thus generated between them and all our objects of desire, which gives to the direct desire of them the intensity it often assumes, so as in some characters to surpass in strength all other desires. In these cases the means have become a part of the end, and a more important part of it than any of the things which they are means to. What was once desired as an instrument for the attainment of happiness, has come to be desired for its own sake. In being desired for its own sake it is, however, desired as *part* of happiness. The person is made, or thinks he would be made, happy by its mere possession; and is made unhappy by failure to obtain it. The desire of it is not a different thing from the desire of happiness, any more than the love of music, or the desire of health. They are included in happiness. They are some of the elements of which the desire of happiness is made up. Happiness is not an abstract idea, but a concrete whole; and these are some of its parts. And the utilitarian standard sanctions and approves their being so. Life would be a poor thing, very ill provided with sources of happiness, if there were not this provision of nature, by which things originally indifferent, but conducive to, or otherwise associated with, the satisfaction of our primitive desires, become in themselves sources of pleasure more valuable than the primitive pleasures, both in permanency, in the space of human existence that they are capable of covering, and even in intensity.

Virtue, according to the utilitarian conception, is a good of this description. There was no original desire of it, or motive to it, save its conduciveness to pleasure, and especially to protection from pain. But through the association thus formed, it may be felt a good in itself, and desired as such with as great intensity as any other good; and with this difference between it and the love of money, of power, or of fame, that all of these may, and often do, render the individual noxious to the other members of the society to which he belongs, whereas there is nothing which makes him so much a blessing to them as the cultivation of the disinterested love of virtue. And consequently, the utilitarian standard, while it tolerates and approves those other acquired desires, up to the point beyond which they would be more injurious to the general happiness than promotive of it, enjoins and requires the cultivation of the love of virtue up to the greatest strength possible, as being above all things important to the general happiness.

It results from the preceding considerations, that there is in reality nothing desired except happiness. Whatever is desired otherwise than as a means to some end beyond itself, and ultimately to happiness, is desired as itself a part of happiness, and is not desired for itself until it has become so. Those who desire virtue for its own sake, desire it either because the consciousness of it is a pleasure, or because the consciousness of being without it is a pain, or for both reasons united; as in truth the pleasure and pain seldom exist separately, but almost always together, the same person feeling pleasure in the degree of virtue attained, and pain in not having attained more. If one of these gave him no pleasure, and the other no pain, he would not love or desire virtue, or would desire it only for the other benefits which it might produce to himself or to persons whom he cared for.

We have now, then, an answer to the question, of what sort of proof the principle of utility is susceptible. If the opinion which I have now stated is psychologically true—if human nature is so constituted as to desire nothing which is not either a part of happiness or a means of happiness, we can have no other proof, and we require no other, that these are the only things desirable. If so, happiness is the sole end of human action, and the promotion of it the test by which to judge of all human conduct; from whence it necessarily follows that it must be the criterion of morality, since a part is included in the whole.

And now to decide whether this is really so; whether mankind do desire nothing for itself but that which is a pleasure to them, or of which the absence is a pain; we have evidently arrived at a question of fact and experience, dependent, like all similar questions, upon evidence. It can only be determined by practised self-consciousness and self-observation, assisted by observation of others. I believe that these sources of evidence, impartially consulted, will declare that desiring a thing and finding it pleasant, aversion to it and thinking of it as painful, are phenomena entirely inseparable, or rather two parts of the same phenomenon; in strictness of language, two different modes of naming the same psychological fact: that to think of an object as desirable (unless for the sake of its consequences), and to think of it as pleasant, are one and the same thing; and that to desire anything, except in proportion as the idea of it is pleasant, is a physical and metaphysical impossibility.

So obvious does this appear to me, that I expect it will hardly be disputed: and the objection made will be, not that desire can possibly be directed to anything ultimately except pleasure and exemption from pain, but that the will is a different thing from desire; that a person of confirmed virtue, or any other person whose purposes are fixed, carries out his purposes without any thought of the pleasure he has in contemplating them, or expects to derive from their fulfilment; and persists in acting on them, even though these pleasures are much diminished, by changes in his character or decay of his passive sensibilities, or are outweighed by the pains which the pursuit of the purposes may bring upon him. All this I fully admit, and have stated it elsewhere, as positively and emphatically as any one. Will, the active phenomenon, is a different thing from desire, the state of passive sensibility, and though originally an offshoot from it, may in time take root and detach itself from the parent stock; so much so, that in the case of an habitual purpose, instead of willing the thing because we desire it, we often desire it only because we will it. This, however, is but an instance of that familiar fact, the power of habit, and is nowise confined to the case of virtuous actions. Many indifferent things, which men originally did from a motive of some sort, they continue to do from habit. Sometimes this is done unconsciously, the consciousness coming only after the action: at other times with conscious volition, but volition which has become habitual, and is put into operation by the force of habit, in opposition perhaps to the deliberate preference, as often happens with those who have contracted habits of vicious or hurtful indulgence. Third and last comes the case in which the habitual act of will in the individual instance is not in contradiction to the general intention prevailing at other times, but in fulfilment of it; as in the case of the person of confirmed virtue, and of all who pursue deliberately and consistently any determinate end. The distinction between will and desire thus understood, is an authentic and highly important psychological fact; but the fact consists solely in this—that will, like all other parts of our constitution, is amenable to habit, and that we may will from habit what we no longer desire for itself, or desire only because we will it. It is not the less true that will, in the beginning, is entirely produced by desire; including in that term the repelling influence of pain as well as the attractive one of pleasure. Let us take into consideration, no longer the person who has a confirmed will to do right, but him in whom that virtuous will is still feeble, conquerable by temptation, and not to be fully relied on; by what means can it be strengthened? How can the will to be virtuous, where it does not exist in sufficient force, be implanted or awakened? Only by making the person *desire* virtue—by making him think of it in a pleasurable light, or of its absence in a painful one. It is by associating the doing right with pleasure, or the doing wrong with pain, or by eliciting and impressing and bringing home to the person's experience the pleasure naturally involved in the one or the pain in the other, that it is possible to call forth that will to be virtuous, which, when confirmed, acts without any thought of either pleasure or pain. Will is the child of desire, and passes out of the dominion of its parent only to come under that of habit. That which is the result of habit affords no presumption of being intrinsically good; and there would be no reason for wishing that the purpose of virtue should become independent of pleasure and pain, were it not that the influence of the pleasurable and painful associations which prompt to virtue is not sufficiently to be depended on for unerring constancy of action until it has acquired the support of habit. Both in feeling and in conduct, habit is the only thing which imparts certainty; and it is because of the importance to others of being able to rely absolutely on one's feelings and conduct, and to oneself of being able to rely on one's own, that the will to do right ought to be cultivated into this habitual independence. In other words, this state of the will is a means to good, not intrinsically a good; and does not contradict the doctrine that nothing is a good to human beings but in so far as it is either itself pleasurable, or a means of attaining pleasure or averting pain.

But if this doctrine be true, the principle of utility is proved. Whether it is so or not, must now be left to the consideration of the thoughtful reader.

CHAPTER V
ON THE CONNEXION BETWEEN JUSTICE AND UTILITY

In all ages of speculation, one of the strongest obstacles to the reception of the doctrine that Utility or Happiness is the criterion of right and wrong, has been drawn from the idea of Justice. The powerful sentiment, and apparently clear perception, which that word recalls with a rapidity and certainty resembling an instinct, have seemed to the majority of thinkers to point to an inherent quality in things; to show that the Just must have an existence in Nature as something absolute—generically distinct from every variety of the Expedient, and, in idea, opposed to it, though (as is commonly acknowledged) never, in the long run, disjoined from it in fact.

In the case of this, as of our other moral sentiments, there is no necessary connexion between the question of its origin, and that of its binding force. That a feeling is bestowed on us by Nature, does not necessarily legitimate all its promptings. The feeling of justice might be a peculiar instinct, and might yet require, like our other instincts, to be controlled and enlightened by a higher reason. If we have intellectual instincts, leading us to judge in a particular way, as well as animal instincts that prompt us to act in a particular way, there is no necessity that the former should be more infallible in their sphere than the latter in theirs: it may as well happen that wrong judgments are occasionally suggested by those, as wrong actions by these. But though it is one thing to believe that we have natural feelings of justice, and another to acknowledge them as an ultimate criterion of conduct, these two opinions are very closely connected in point of fact. Mankind are always predisposed to believe that any subjective feeling, not otherwise accounted for, is a revelation of some objective reality. Our present object is to determine whether the reality, to which the feeling of justice corresponds, is one which needs any such special revelation; whether the justice or injustice of an action is a thing intrinsically peculiar, and distinct from all its other qualities, or only a combination of certain of those qualities, presented under a peculiar aspect. For the purpose of this inquiry, it is practically important to consider whether the feeling itself, of justice and injustice, is *sui generis* like our sensations of colour and taste, or a derivative feeling, formed by a combination of others. And this it is the more essential to examine, as people are in general willing enough to allow, that objectively the dictates of justice coincide with a part of the field of General Expediency; but inasmuch as the subjective mental feeling of Justice is different from that which commonly attaches to simple expediency, and, except in extreme cases of the latter, is far more imperative in its demands, people find it difficult to see, in Justice, only a particular kind or branch of general utility, and think that its superior binding force requires a totally different origin.

To throw light upon this question, it is necessary to attempt to ascertain what is the distinguishing character of justice, or of injustice: what is the quality, or whether there is any quality, attributed in common to all modes of conduct designated as unjust (for justice, like many other moral attributes, is best defined by its opposite), and distinguishing them from such modes of conduct as are disapproved, but without having that particular epithet of disapprobation applied to them. If, in everything which men are accustomed to characterize as just or unjust, some one common attribute or collection of attributes is always present, we may judge whether this particular attribute or combination of attributes would be capable of gathering round it a sentiment of that peculiar character and intensity by virtue of the general laws of our emotional constitution, or whether the sentiment is inexplicable, and requires to be regarded as a special provision of Nature. If we find the former to be the case, we shall, in resolving this question, have resolved also the main problem: if the latter, we shall have to seek for some other mode of investigating it.

To find the common attributes of a variety of objects, it is necessary to begin by surveying the objects themselves in the concrete. Let us therefore advert successively to the various modes of action, and arrangements of human affairs, which are classed, by universal or widely spread opinion, as Just or as Unjust. The things well known to excite the sentiments associated with those names, are of a very multifarious character. I shall pass them rapidly in review, without studying any particular arrangement.

In the first place, it is mostly considered unjust to deprive any one of his personal liberty, his property, or any other thing which belongs to him by law. Here, therefore, is one instance of the application of the terms just and unjust in a perfectly definite sense, namely, that it is just to respect, unjust to violate, the *legal rights* of any one. But this judgment admits of several exceptions, arising from the other forms in which the notions of justice and injustice present themselves. For example, the person who suffers the deprivation may (as the phrase is) have *forfeited* the rights which he is so deprived of: a case to which we shall return presently. But also,

Secondly; the legal rights of which he is deprived, may be rights which *ought* not to have belonged to him; in other words, the law which confers on him these rights, may be a bad law. When it is so, or when (which is the same thing for our purpose) it is supposed to be so, opinions will differ as to the justice or injustice of infringing it. Some maintain that no law, however bad, ought to be disobeyed by an individual citizen; that his opposition to it, if shown at all, should only be shown in endeavouring to get it altered by competent authority. This opinion (which condemns many of the most illustrious benefactors of mankind, and would often protect pernicious institutions against the only weapons which, in the state of things existing at the time, have any chance of succeeding against them) is defended, by those who hold it, on grounds of expediency; principally on that of the importance, to the common interest of mankind, of maintaining inviolate the sentiment of submission to law. Other persons, again, hold the directly contrary opinion, that any law, judged to be bad, may blamelessly be disobeyed, even though it be not judged to be unjust, but only inexpedient; while others would confine the licence of disobedience to the case of unjust laws: but again, some say, that all laws which are inexpedient are unjust; since every law imposes some restriction on the natural liberty of mankind, which restriction is an injustice, unless legitimated by tending to their good. Among these diversities of opinion, it seems to be universally admitted that there may be unjust laws, and that law, consequently, is not the ultimate criterion of justice, but may give to one person a benefit, or impose on another an evil, which justice condemns. When, however, a law is thought to be unjust, it seems always to be regarded as being so in the same way in which a breach of law is unjust, namely, by infringing somebody's right; which, as it cannot in this case be a legal right, receives a different appellation, and is called a moral right. We may say, therefore, that a second case of injustice consists in taking or withholding from any person that to which he has a *moral right*.

Thirdly, it is universally considered just that each person should obtain that (whether good or evil) which he *deserves;* and unjust that he should obtain a good, or be made to undergo an evil, which he does not deserve. This is, perhaps, the clearest and most emphatic form in which the idea of justice is conceived by the general mind. As it involves the notion of desert, the question arises what constitutes desert? Speaking in a general way, a person is understood to deserve good if he does right, evil if he does wrong; and in a more particular sense, to deserve good from those to whom he does or has done good, and evil from those to whom he does or has done evil. The precept of returning good for evil has never been regarded as a case of the fulfilment of justice, but as one in which the claims of justice are waived, in obedience to other considerations.

Fourthly, it is confessedly unjust to *break faith* with any one: to violate an engagement, either express or implied, or disappoint expectations raised by our own conduct, at least if we have raised those expectations knowingly and voluntarily. Like the other obligations of justice already spoken of, this one is not regarded as absolute, but as capable of being overruled by a stronger obligation of justice on the other side; or by such conduct on the part of the person concerned as is deemed to absolve us from our obligation to him, and to constitute a *forfeiture* of the benefit which he has been led to expect.

Fifthly, it is, by universal admission, inconsistent with justice to be *partial*; to show favour or preference to one person over another, in matters to which favour and preference do not properly apply. Impartiality, however, does not seem to be regarded as a duty in itself, but rather as instrumental to some other duty; for it is admitted that favour and preference are not always censurable, and indeed the cases in which they are condemned are rather the exception than the rule. A person would be more likely to be blamed than applauded for giving his family or friends no superiority in good offices over strangers, when he could do so without violating any other duty; and no one thinks it unjust to seek one person in preference to another as a friend, connexion, or companion. Impartiality where rights are concerned is of course obligatory, but this is involved in the more general obligation of giving to every one his right. A tribunal, for example, must be impartial, because it is bound to award, without regard to any other consideration, a disputed object to the one of two parties who has the right to it. There are other cases in which impartiality means, being solely influenced by desert; as with those who, in the capacity of judges, preceptors, or parents, administer reward and punishment as such. There are cases, again, in which it means, being solely influenced by consideration for the public interest; as in making a selection among candidates for a government employment. Impartiality, in short, as an obligation of justice, may be said to mean, being exclusively influenced by the considerations which it is supposed ought to influence the particular case in hand; and resisting the solicitation of any motives which prompt to conduct different from what those considerations would dictate.

Nearly allied to the idea of impartiality, is that of *equality*; which often enters as a component part both into the conception of justice and into the practice of it, and, in the eyes of many persons, constitutes its essence. But in this, still more than in any other case, the notion of justice varies in different persons, and always conforms in its variations to their notion of utility. Each person maintains that equality is the dictate of justice, except where he thinks that expediency requires inequality. The justice of giving equal protection to the rights of all, is maintained by those who support the most outrageous inequality in the rights themselves. Even in slave countries it is theoretically admitted that the rights of the slave, such as they are, ought to be as sacred as those of the master; and that a tribunal which fails to enforce them with equal strictness is wanting in justice; while, at the same time, institutions which leave to the slave scarcely any rights to enforce, are not deemed unjust, because they are not deemed inexpedient. Those who think that utility requires distinctions of rank, do not consider it unjust that riches and social privileges should be unequally dispensed; but those who think this inequality inexpedient, think it unjust also. Whoever thinks that government is necessary, sees no injustice in as much inequality as is constituted by giving to the magistrate powers not granted to other people. Even among those who hold levelling doctrines, there are as many questions of justice as there are differences of opinion about expediency. Some Communists consider it unjust that the produce of the labour of the community should be shared on any other principle than that of exact equality; others think it just that those should receive most whose needs are greatest; while others hold that those who work harder, or who produce more, or whose services are more valuable to the community, may justly claim a larger quota in the division of the produce. And the sense of natural justice may be plausibly appealed to in behalf of every one of these opinions.

Among so many diverse applications of the term Justice, which yet is not regarded as ambiguous, it is a matter of some difficulty to seize the mental link which holds them together, and on which the moral sentiment adhering to the term essentially depends.

● ● ● ● ●

. . . We do not call anything wrong, unless we mean to imply that a person ought to be punished in some way or other for doing it; if not by law, by the opinion of his fellow creatures; if not by opinion, by the reproaches of his own conscience. This seems the real turning point of the distinction between morality and simple expediency. It is a part of the notion of Duty in every one of its forms, that a person may rightfully be compelled to fulfil it. Duty is a thing which may be *exacted* from a person, as one exacts a debt. Unless we think that it might be exacted from him, we do not call it his duty. Reasons of prudence, or the interest of other people, may militate against actually exacting it; but the person himself, it is clearly understood, would not be entitled to complain. There are other things, on the contrary, which we wish that people should do, which we like or admire them for doing, perhaps dislike or despise them for not doing, but yet admit that they are not bound to do; it is not a case of moral obligation; we do not blame them, that is, we do not think that they are proper objects of punishment. How we come by these ideas of deserving and not deserving punishment, will appear, perhaps, in the sequel; but I think there is no doubt that this distinction lies at the bottom of the notions of right and wrong; that we call any conduct wrong, or employ instead, some other term of dislike or disparagement, according as we think that the person ought, or ought not, to be punished for it; and we say that it would be right to do so and so, or merely that it would be desirable or laudable, according as we would wish to see the person whom it concerns, compelled or only persuaded and exhorted, to act in that manner.

This, therefore, being the characteristic difference which marks off, not justice, but morality in general, from the remaining provinces of Expediency and Worthiness; the character is still to be sought which distinguishes justice from other branches of morality. Now it is known that ethical writers divide moral duties into two classes, denoted by the ill-chosen expressions, duties of perfect and of imperfect obligation; the latter being those in which, though the act is obligatory, the particular occasions of performing it are left to our choice; as in the case of charity or beneficence, which we are indeed bound to practise, but not towards any definite person, nor at any prescribed time. In the more precise language of philosophic jurists, duties of perfect obligation are those duties in virtue of which a correlative *right* resides in some person or persons; duties of imperfect obligation are those moral obligations which do not give birth to any right. I think it will be found that this distinction exactly coincides with that which exists between justice and the other obligations of morality. In our survey of the various popular acceptations of justice, the term appeared generally to involve the idea of a personal right—a claim on the part of one or more individuals, like that which the law gives when it confers a proprietary or other legal right. Whether the injustice consists in depriving a person of a possession, or in breaking faith with him, or in treating him worse than he deserves, or worse than other people who have no greater claims, in each case the supposition implies two things—a wrong done, and some assignable person who is wronged. Injustice may also be done by treating a person better than others; but the wrong in this case is to his competitors, who are also assignable persons. It seems to me that this feature in the case—a right in some person, correlative to the moral obligation—constitutes the specific difference between justice, and generosity or beneficence. Justice implies something which it is not only right to do, and wrong not to do, but which some individual person can claim from us as his moral right. No one has a moral right to our generosity or beneficence, because we are not morally bound to practise those virtues towards any given individual. And it will be found with respect to this as with respect to every correct definition, that the instances which seem to conflict with it are those which most confirm it. For if a moralist attempts, as some have done, to make out that mankind generally, though not any given individual, have a right to all the good we can do them, he at once, by that thesis, includes generosity and beneficence within the category of justice. He is obliged to say, that our utmost exertions are *due* to our fellow creatures, thus assimilating them to a debt; or that nothing less can be a sufficient *return* for what society does for us, thus classing the case as one of gratitude; both of which are acknowledged cases of justice. Wherever there is a right, the case is one of justice, and not of the virtue of beneficence: and whoever does not place the distinction between justice and morality in general where we have now placed it, will be found to make no distinction between them at all, but to merge all morality in justice.

•   •   •   •   •

The sentiment of justice, in that one of its elements which consist of the desire to punish, is . . . , I conceive, the natural feeling of retaliation or vengeance, rendered by intellect and sympathy applicable to those injuries, that is, to those hurts, which wound us through, or in common with, society at large. This sentiment, in itself, has nothing moral in it; what is moral is, the exclusive subordination of it to the social sympathies, so as to wait on and obey their call. For the natural feeling tends to make us resent indiscriminately whatever any one does that is disagreeable to us; but when moralized by the social feeling, it only acts in the directions conformable to the general good: just persons resenting a hurt to society, though not otherwise a hurt to themselves, and not resenting a hurt to themselves, however painful, unless it be of the kind which society has a common interest with them in the repression of.

It is no objection against this doctrine to say, that when we feel our sentiment of justice outraged, we are not thinking of society at large, or of any collective interest, but only of the individual case. It is common enough certainly, though the reverse of commendable, to feel resentment merely because we have suffered pain; but a person whose resentment is really a moral feeling, that is, who considers whether an act is blameable before he allows himself to resent it—such a person, though he may not say expressly to himself that he is standing up for the interest of society, certainly does feel that he is asserting a rule which is for the benefit of others as well as for his own. If he is not feeling this—if he is regarding the act solely as it affects him individually—he is not consciously just; he is not concerning himself about the justice of his actions. This is admitted even by anti-utilitarian moralists. When Kant (as before remarked) propounds as the fundamental principle of morals, 'So act, that thy rule of conduct might be adopted as a law by all rational beings,' he virtually acknowledges that the interest of mankind collectively, or at least of mankind indiscriminately, must be in the mind of the agent when conscientiously deciding on the morality of the act. Otherwise he uses words without a meaning: for, that a rule even of utter selfishness could not *possibly* be adopted by all rational beings—that there is any insuperable obstacle in the nature of things to its adoption—cannot be even plausibly maintained. To give any meaning to Kant's principle, the sense put upon it must be, that we ought to shape our conduct by a rule which all rational beings might adopt *with benefit to their collective interest*.

To recapitulate: the idea of justice supposes two things; a rule of conduct, and a sentiment which sanctions the rule. The first must be supposed common to all mankind, and intended for their good. The other (the sentiment) is a desire that punishment may be suffered by those who infringe the rule. There is involved, in addition, the conception of some definite person who suffers by the infringement; whose rights (to use the expression appropriated to the case) are violated by it. And the sentiment of justice appears to me to be, the animal desire to repel or retaliate a hurt or damage to oneself, or to those with whom one sympathizes, widened so as to include all persons, by the human capacity of enlarged sympathy, and the human conception of intelligent self-interest. From the latter elements, the feeling derives its morality; from the former, its peculiar impressiveness, and energy of self-assertion.

I have, throughout, treated the idea of a *right* residing in the injured person, and violated by the injury, not as a separate element in the composition of the idea and sentiment, but as one of the forms in which the other two elements clothe themselves. These elements are, a hurt to some assignable person or persons on the one hand, and a demand for punishment on the other. An examination of our own minds, I think, will show, that these two things include all that we mean when we speak of violation of a right. When we call anything a person's right, we mean that he has a valid claim on society to protect him in the possession of it, either by the force of law, or by that of education and opinion. If he has what we consider a sufficient claim, on whatever account, to have something guaranteed to him by society, we say that he has a right to it. If we desire to prove that anything does not belong to him by right, we think this done as soon as it is admitted that society ought not to take measures for securing it to him, but should leave it to chance, or to his own exertions. Thus, a person is said to have a right to what he can earn in fair professional competition; because society ought not to allow any other person to hinder him from endeavouring to earn in that manner as much as he can. But he has not a right to three hundred a year, though he may happen to be earning it; because society is not called on to provide that he shall earn that sum. On the contrary, if he owns ten thousand pounds three per cent. stock he *has* a right to three hundred a year; because society has come under an obligation to provide him with an income of that amount.

To have a right, then, is, I conceive, to have something which society ought to defend me in the possession of. If the objector goes on to ask why it ought, I can give him no other reason than general utility. If that expression does not seem to convey a sufficient feeling of the strength of the obligation, nor to account for the peculiar energy of the feeling, it is because there goes to the composition of the sentiment, not a rational only but also an animal element, the thirst for retaliation; and this thirst derives its intensity, as well as its moral justification, from the extraordinarily important and impressive kind of utility which is concerned. The interest involved is that of security, to every one's feelings the most vital of all interests. Nearly all other earthly benefits are needed by one person, not needed by another; and many of them can, if necessary, be cheerfully foregone, or replaced by something else; but security no human being can possibly do without; on it we depend for all our immunity from evil, and for the whole value of all and every good, beyond the passing moment; since nothing but the gratification of the instant could be of any worth to us, if we could be deprived of everything the next instant by whoever was momentarily stronger than ourselves. Now this most indispensable of all necessaries, after physical nutriment, cannot be had, unless the machinery for providing it is kept unintermittedly in active play. Our notion, therefore, of the claim we have on our fellow creatures to join in making safe for us the very groundwork of our existence, gathers feelings round it so much more intense than those concerned in any of the more common cases of utility, that the difference in degree (as is often the case in psychology) becomes a real difference in kind. The claim assumes that character of absoluteness, that apparent infinity, and incommensurability with all other considerations, which constitute the distinction between the feeling of right and wrong and that of ordinary expediency and inexpediency. The feelings concerned are so powerful, and we count so positively on finding a responsive feeling in others (all being alike interested), that *ought* and *should* grow into *must,* and recognised indispensability becomes a moral necessity, analogous to physical, and often not inferior to it in binding force.

•   •   •   •   •

. . . Justice is a name for certain classes of moral rules, which concern the essentials of human well-being more nearly, and are therefore of more absolute obligation, than any other rules for the guidance of life; and the notion which we have found to be of the essence of the idea of justice, that of a right residing in an individual, implies and testifies to this more binding obligation.

The moral rules which forbid mankind to hurt one another (in which we must never forget to include wrongful interference with each other's freedom) are more vital to human well-being than any maxims, however important, which only point out the best mode of managing some department of human affairs. They have also the peculiarity, that they are the main element in determining the whole of the social feelings of mankind. It is their observance which alone preserves peace among human beings: if obedience to them were not the rule, and disobedience the exception, every one would see in every one else a probable enemy, against whom he must be perpetually guarding himself. What is hardly less important, these are the precepts which mankind have the strongest and the most direct inducements for impressing upon one another. By merely giving to each other prudential instruction or exhortation, they may gain, or think they gain, nothing: in inculcating on each other the duty of positive beneficence they have an unmistakeable interest, but far less in degree: a person may possibly not need the benefits of others; but he always needs that they should not do him hurt. Thus the moralities which protect every individual from being harmed by others, either directly or by being hindered in his freedom of pursuing his own good, are at once those which he himself has most at heart, and those which he has the strongest interest in publishing and enforcing by word and deed. It is by a person's observance of these, that his fitness to exist as one of the fellowship of human beings, is tested and decided; for on that depends his being a nuisance or not to those with whom he is in contact. Now it is these moralities primarily, which compose the obligations of justice. The most marked cases of injustice, and those which give the tone to the feeling of repugnance which characterizes the sentiment, are acts of wrongful aggression, or wrongful exercise of power over some one; the next are those which consist in wrongfully withholding from him something which is his due; in both cases, inflicting on him a positive hurt, either in the form of direct suffering, or of the privation of some good which he had reasonable ground either of a physical or of a social kind, for counting upon.

The same powerful motives which command the observance of these primary moralities, enjoin the punishment of those who violate them; and as the impulses of self-defence, of defence of others, and of vengeance, are all called forth against such persons, retribution, or evil for evil, becomes closely connected with the sentiment of justice, and is universally included in the idea. Good for good is also one of the dictates of justice; and this, though its social utility is evident, and though it carries with it a natural human feeling, has not at first sight that obvious connexion with hurt or injury, which, existing in the most elementary cases of just and unjust, is the source of the characteristic intensity of the sentiment. But the connexion, though less obvious, is not less real. He who accepts benefits, and denies a return of them when needed, inflicts a real hurt, by disappointing one of the most natural and reasonable of expectations, and one which he must at least tacitly have encouraged, otherwise the benefits would seldom have been conferred. The important rank, among human evils and wrongs, of the disappointment of expectation, is shown in the fact that it constitutes the principal criminality of two such highly immoral acts as a breach of friendship and a breach of promise. Few hurts which human beings can sustain are greater, and none wound more, than when that on which they habitually and with full assurance relied, fails them in the hour of need; and few wrongs are greater than this mere withholding of good; none excite more resentment, either in the person suffering, or in a sympathizing spectator. The principle, therefore, of giving to each what they deserve, that is, good for good as well as evil for evil, is not only included within the idea of Justice as we have defined it, but is a proper object of that intensity of sentiment, which places the Just, in human estimation, above the simply Expedient.

Most of the maxims of justice current in the world, and commonly appealed to in its transactions, are simply instrumental to carrying into effect the principles of justice which we have now spoken of. That a person is only responsible for what he has done voluntarily, or could voluntarily have avoided; that it is unjust to condemn any person unheard; that the punishment ought to be proportioned to the offence, and the like, are maxims intended to prevent the just principle of evil for evil from being perverted to the infliction of evil without justification. The greater part of these common maxims have come into use from the practice of courts of justice, which have been naturally led to a more complete recognition and elaboration than was likely to suggest itself to others, of the rules necessary to enable them to fulfil their double function, of inflicting punishment when due, and of awarding to each person his right.

That first of judicial virtues, impartiality, is an obligation of justice, partly for the reason last mentioned; as being a necessary condition of the fulfilment of the other obligations of justice. But this is not the only source of the exalted rank, among human obligations, of those maxims of equality and impartiality, which, both in popular estimation and in that of the most enlightened, are included among the precepts of justice. In one point of view, they may be considered as corollaries from the principles already laid down. If it is a duty to do to each according to his deserts, returning good for good as well as repressing evil by evil, it necessarily follows that we should treat all equally well (when no higher duty forbids) who have deserved equally well of us, and that society should treat all equally well who have deserved equally well of it, that is, who have deserved equally well absolutely. This is the highest abstract standard of social and distributive justice; towards which all institutions, and the efforts of all virtuous citizens, should be made in the utmost possible degree to converge. But this great moral duty rests upon a still deeper foundation, being a direct emanation from the first principle of morals, and not a mere logical corollary from secondary or derivative doctrines. It is involved in the very meaning of Utility, or the Greatest-Happiness Principle. That principle is a mere form of words without rational signification, unless one person's happiness, supposed equal in degree (with the proper allowance made for kind), is counted for exactly as much as another's. Those conditions being supplied, Bentham's dictum, 'everybody to count for one, nobody for more than one,' might be written under the principle of utility as an explanatory commentary.[2] The equal claim of everybody to happiness in the estimation of the moralist and the legislator, involves an equal claim to all the means of happiness, except in so far as the inevitable conditions of human life, and the general interest, in which that of every individual is included, set limits to the maxim; and those limits ought to be strictly construed. As every other maxim of justice, so this, is by no means applied or held applicable universally; on the contrary, as I have already remarked, it bends to every person's ideas of social expediency. But in whatever case it is deemed applicable at all, it is held to be the dictate of justice. All persons are deemed to have a *right* to equality of treatment, except when some recognised social expediency requires the reverse. And hence all social inequalities which have ceased to be considered expedient, assume the character not of simple inexpediency, but of injustice, and appear so tyrannical, that people are apt to wonder how they ever could have been tolerated; forgetful that they themselves perhaps tolerate other inequalities under an equally mistaken notion of expediency, the correction of which would make that which they approve seem quite as monstrous as what they have at last learnt to condemn. The entire

[2] This implication, in the first principle of the utilitarian scheme, of perfect impartiality between persons, is regarded by Mr. Herbert Spencer (in his 'Social Statics') as a disproof of the pretentions of utility to be a sufficient guide to right; since (he says) the principle of utility presupposes the anterior principle, that everybody has an equal right to happiness. It may be more correctly described as supposing that equal amounts of happiness are equally desirable, whether felt by the same or by different persons. This, however, is not a presupposition; not a premise needful to support the principle of utility, but the very principle itself; for what is the principle of utility, if it be not that 'happiness' and 'desirable' are synonymous terms? If there is any anterior principle implied, it can be no other than this, that the truths of arithmetic are applicable to the valuation of happiness, as of all other measurable quantities.

history of social improvement has been a series of transitions, by which one custom or institution after another, from being a supposed primary necessity of social existence, has passed into the rank of an universally stigmatized injustice and tyranny. So it has been with the distinctions of slaves and freemen, nobles and serfs, patricians and plebians; and so it will be, and in part already is, with the aristocracies of colour, race, and sex. . . .

Supplementary Paperback Reading

M. D. Bayles, *Contemporary Utilitarianism*. (Anchor Books)

R. B. Brandt, "Toward a Credible Form of Utilitarianism," in H. N. Castaneda and G. Nakhnikian, *Morality and the Language of Conduct*. (Wayne State University Press) Also in M. D. Bayles, *Contemporary Utilitarianism*. (Anchor Books), and in B. Brody, *Moral Rules and Particular Circumstances*. (Prentice-Hall)

R. B. Brandt, "Some Merits of One Form of Rule-Utilitarianism." (Bobbs-Merrill Reprint Series in Philosophy)

K. Britton, *John Stuart Mill*, Ch. 2. (Penguin Books)

J. Dewey, *Theory of the Moral Life*, Ch. II. (Holt, Rinehart and Winston)

B. J. Diggs, "Rules and Utilitarianism," in M. D. Bayles, *Contemporary Utilitarianism*. (Anchor Books)

A. Donagan, "Is There a Credible Form of Utilitarianism?" in M. D. Bayles, *Contemporary Utilitarianism*. (Anchor Books)

A. C. Ewing, *Ethics*, Ch. III and V. (Free Press)

W. K. Frankena, *Ethics*, Ch. 3. (Prentice-Hall)

R. M. Hare, *Freedom and Reason*, Ch. 7. (Oxford University Press)

J. Harrison, "Utilitarianism, Universalisation, and Our Duty to Be Just," in M. D. Bayles, *Contemporary Utilitarianism*. (Anchor Books) Also in Bobbs-Merrill Reprint Series in Philosophy, and in J. J. Thomson and G. Dworkin, *Ethics* (Harper and Row), and in B. Brody, *Moral Rules and Particular Circumstances*. (Prentice-Hall)

N. Kretzmann, "Desire as a Proof of Desirability," in J. M. Smith and E. Sosa, *Mill's Utilitarianism: Text and Criticism*. (Wadsworth)

J. D. Mabbott, "Interpretations of Mill's 'Utilitarianism'," in P. Foot, *Theories of Ethics*. (Oxford University Press) Also in J. M. Smith and E. Sosa, *Mill's Utilitarianism: Text and Criticism*. (Wadsworth)

H. J. McCloskey, "An Examination of Restricted Utilitarianism," in M. D. Bayles, *Contemporary Utilitarianism*. (Anchor Books) Also in Bobbs-Merrill Reprint Series in Philosophy.

H. J. McCloskey, "A Non-Utilitarian Approach to Punishment," in M. D. Bayles, *Contemporary Utilitarianism*. (Anchor Books)

G. E. Moore, *Principia Ethica,* Ch. V. (Cambridge University Press)

G. E. Moore, *Ethics,* Ch. I–V. (Oxford University Press)

H. Sidgwick, *The Methods of Ethics,* Book IV. (Dover Publications)

J. J. C. Smart, "Extreme and Restricted Utilitarianism," in M. D. Bayles, *Contemporary Utilitarianism*. (Anchor Books) Also in P. Foot, *Theories of Ethics* (Oxford University Press) and in J. J. Thomson and G. Dworkin, *Ethics* (Harper and Row)

J. J. C. Smart, "An Outline of a System of Utilitarian Ethics," in R. Ekman, *Readings in the Problems of Ethics.* (Scribner's)

J. M. Smith and E. Sosa, *Mill's Utilitarianism: Text and Criticism.* (Wadsworth)

E. Sosa, "Mill's *Utilitarianism,*" in J. M. Smith and E. Sosa, *Mill's* Utilitarianism: *Text and Criticism.* (Wadsworth)

T. L. S. Sprigge, "A Utilitarian Reply to Dr. McCloskey," in M. D. Bayles, *Contemporary Utilitarianism*. (Anchor Books)

C. Strang, "What If Everyone Did That?" in B. Brody, *Moral Rules and Particular Circumstances* (Prentice-Hall), and in J. J. Thomson and G. Dworkin, *Ethics.* (Harper and Row)

J. O. Urmson, "The Interpretation of the Moral Philosophy of J. S. Mill," in M. D. Bayles, *Contemporary Utilitarianism*. (Anchor Books) Also in P. Foot, *Theories of Ethics* (Oxford University Press) and in J. M. Smith and E. Sosa, *Mill's* Utilitarianism: *Text and Criticism* (Wadsworth).

Note: A full bibliography on utilitarianism is given in the following paperback book, which is a contemporary study of the relation between justice and utility: N. Rescher, *Distributive Justice: A Constructive Critique of the Utilitarian Theory of Distribution.* (Bobbs-Merrill)

5

DEONTOLOGICAL

ETHICS AND

CRITICISMS OF

UTILITARIANISM

Introduction

All normative ethical systems can be divided into two groups, depending on how they define the relation between right action and intrinsic value. If the rightness of an act is entirely determined by the intrinsic value of its consequences (act-utilitarianism) or of the rule which it falls under (rule-utilitarianism), the ethical system is called "teleological." The basic norm in such a system is a standard of intrinsic goodness, while right, duty, and obligation are all subordinate norms. Unless we know whether the results brought about are good or bad, we cannot know whether the conduct in question is right or wrong.

The other type of ethical system holds that the rightness of an act (and our duty to perform it) is either *not entirely* determined by the intrinsic value of its consequences or is *not at all* determined by such value. Ethical systems of this kind are called "deontological," from the Greek word meaning "ought." The basic principle of deontological ethics is that the right (what we ought to do) does not entirely depend on the good (what we judge to be intrinsically valuable), and this is the exact contradictory of the basic principle of teleological ethics. In this chapter we are presented with two of the most famous deontological theories in Western philosophy: that of Immanuel Kant and that of Sir David Ross. According to Kant's theory, the rightness of an act does not depend *at all* on the value of its consequences. In order to know whether an act is right or wrong we need only see whether it is in accordance with a valid moral rule, and the test for a valid moral rule is a purely formal one, as Kant conceives it. For this reason his ethical system has been called "formalistic." The theory of Sir David Ross is that the rightness of an act may in part be determined by the goodness of its consequences, but it is never *wholly* determined by such goodness.

Each of these philosophers not only defends his own deontological ethical system but also attacks utilitarianism. Since their views are contradicted by utilitarian ethics, one of their tasks is to show that utilitarianism is false. In addition to these criticisms of utilitarianism made by deontologists, we have also included in this chapter an article by Professor John Rawls, in which he constructs an argument that utilitarians might use in reply to these criticisms.

THE FORMALISTIC ETHICS OF IMMANUEL KANT

In the short book titled *Fundamental Principles of the Metaphysic of Morals*, the major part of which is reprinted in this chapter, Immanuel Kant sets forth the foundations of a formalistic type of deontological ethics. The work is divided into a Preface and three main Sections. In the Preface Kant states his over-all purpose. This is to show that, in his own words, "the basis of obligation must not be sought in the nature of man, or in the circumstances in the world in which he is placed, but *a priori* simply in the conceptions of pure reason." Kant believes that moral philosophy, whose task is to establish an ultimate criterion for the validity of moral rules, must be what he calls "pure." By this he means it must show how an ultimate criterion can be established a priori, entirely free of empirical considerations. Once this criterion is shown to be grounded on pure reason, its application to particular rules and acts may require the use of empirical knowledge.

In the First Section Kant analyzes what he takes to be the key concept of morality, which he calls "the good will." This is the key concept because without it Kant does not think we can even understand what the terms "right conduct" and "moral duty" mean, to say nothing of knowing what specific conduct is right or what our moral duty is. Kant's analysis of the concept of the good will is to be found in his "three propositions of morality." The first proposition describes what kind of motive a person must have to be properly called a morally good man, or as Kant puts it, a man of good will. The main point here is that the motive must be entirely separate from (though not necessarily antagonistic to) the person's inclinations and his self-interest. The man of good will not only acts in accordance with duty, he acts for the sake of duty. This means that his sole motive for doing what is right is his recognition of the fact that it is the right thing to do. He does what is right just because it is right, and for no other reason. If a man did what was right simply because he liked doing that kind of act (that is, if his inclinations led him in that direction) or because doing it served his self-interest, there would be nothing morally admirable about him. Having a good will, therefore, is a necessary condition for being a good man. Kant also argues that it is a sufficient condition. Even if a person were unable to carry out what duty required of him, he must be judged, from the moral point of view, to be a good man as long as he "summoned all the means in his power" to do his duty. This is not to say that having good intentions is enough to be a good man. One must not only have good intentions (which for Kant means that one seeks to do one's duty for duty's sake), but must also strive with all one's will-power and self-determination to perform the act which is one's duty.

The second proposition of morality concerns the moral worth or value of the good will. Here Kant is asking, What must be the basis of its value if its presence alone is sufficient for judging a person to be morally good? His answer is that because the good will has such unconditional worth, its value cannot depend on the bringing about of any ends or purposes. For in that case it would be judged merely as a means, and its value would be conditional upon the achievement of ends as well as upon the value of such ends. But since its value is unconditional, it must derive its value solely from the *principle* which it exemplifies. At this point Kant does not tell us what this principle is.

The third proposition of morality describes the kind of emotion or inner attitude that dominates a person's state of mind when he is motivated by a good will. The emotion or attitude is not that of kindliness, benevolence, or love. For these have to do with a person's inclinations, not with the pure will to do one's duty. The latter is the motive to do an act as a matter of principle, regardless of one's inclinations (that is, regardless of whether one wants to do the act or not). The predominant attitude of the man of good will must be appropriate to the desire to do his duty just because it is his duty. Such an attitude, Kant believes, can only be a deep sense of the binding obligation to obey the moral law, which he calls "respect for the moral law."

Throughout this discussion of the good will and the morally good man, Kant has not told us what our duty is. He has not yet answered the question How do we know what acts are right? This will be the main subject of the Second Section of his book. However, at the end of the First Section he makes a transition from the concept of the good will to the concept of right action, and this passage paves the way for the argument of the Second Section. It is clear from Kant's idea of the good will that, whatever may be the standard of right action, that standard cannot be the utility of the action in producing certain results (as an act-utilitarian would claim). The only other possibility is to make the standard a matter of the conformity of an action to a rule or principle. Our next question is, What conditions must be satisfied by a rule if it is to be a valid moral rule, that is, if it is to be binding upon all mankind as a moral duty? Again, we cannot appeal to the consequences of following the rule (as a rule-utilitarian would do), since this would make the ground of duty empirical, which it cannot be if duty is to be recognized as binding upon one's will regardless of ends, consequences, and inclinations. So we are left with the claim that, to be valid, a rule must pass the test of the supreme principle or ultimate criterion of morality, which Kant calls "the categorical imperative." It is this principle which a person consciously or unconsciously recognizes when he acknowledges an act to be his moral duty. Kant now argues that if the moral law or supreme principle of morality operates in this way, binding the will of a good man independently of his inclinations and purposes, it must be of a certain sort. It cannot demand that any *particular* ends be brought about, so all that remains for it to demand is that the person act on a "maxim" or principle which he, as a rational being, could prescribe as a rule for every other person to act on. Kant puts this in a highly abstract way:

As I have deprived the will of every impulse which could arise to it from obedience to any law, there remains nothing but the universal conformity of its actions to law in general, which alone is to serve the will as a principle.

He sums this up in the following statement, the full meaning of which he intends to explain in the Second Section: "I am never to act otherwise than so *that I could also will that my maxim should become a universal law.*"

The Second Section opens with a reiteration of the idea that the ultimate principle of morality must be grounded a priori if it is to have that necessity and universality which it must have for the man of good will to recognize it as the ground of his duty and so be motivated by pure respect for the moral law. In Kant's terms, the moral law must be "apodictic," that is, universal (applying to everyone without exception) and necessary (not contingent upon the nature of the world).

He then begins a careful analysis of the conditions that any rule of conduct must satisfy if it is to be considered a moral rule—a rule validly binding upon all mankind and binding upon them in the way he has described in the First Section. These conditions are as follows:

For a rule to be a moral rule, it must prescribe to us categorically, not hypothetically. Reason: A moral rule prescribes what we ought to do without reference to any purposes or consequences, as was shown in the First Section. Now a hypothetical prescription (or "imperative") only tells us what we ought to do if we want to bring about certain ends. If we did not seek those ends, it would lose its prescriptive force. But a moral rule never depends for its prescriptive force upon what ends a person seeks. Therefore it must prescribe to us independently of our ends, that is, categorically.

In this way Kant has explained what a categorical imperative is; he has given a definition of the term "categorical imperative." But he must now tell us how this ultimate test of a moral rule is to be applied, so that we can know whether a rule does or does not satisfy its conditions. Otherwise we would be left in the dark about what the categorical imperative commands us to do. So Kant proceeds to give us three formulations of the categorical imperative, which he believes are simply different ways of saying the same thing. Each formulation, however, throws a new light on morality and brings out a new aspect of its supreme principle. Although the fundamental nature of moral duty remains the same, each formulation in its own way sets forth the conditions that must be fulfilled by a rule of conduct if it is to be a moral rule.

FIRST FORMULATION: *For a rule to be a moral rule, it must be consistently universalizable.* Reason: The ground of moral duty rests on no empirical conditions, for if it did, it could not be the object of respect by the good man and could not motivate him independently of all his inclinations and purposes. Now if the reason for acting in accordance with a rule or "maxim" was anything but the fact that the rule could become a universal law, empirical conditions would be placed upon the ultimate test for a moral rule and the rule would thereby lose its a priori necessity and universality. Therefore, only the one condition, that the rule can become a universal law, is sufficient as the ground of its moral validity. And this condition simply means that the rule can be prescribed as a guide to everyone's conduct (that is, it is universalizable) without involving a self-contradiction. It should be noted that Kant gives four cases that are intended to be examples of consistent universalizability. The careful reader will question whether these cases do exemplify what Kant intends them to.

SECOND FORMULATION: *For a rule to be a moral rule, it must be such that, if all men were to follow it, they would treat each other as ends in themselves, never as means only.* Reason: A moral rule is binding upon a person as a rational being. A rational being would always treat every other rational being the same way he would treat himself, for if he did not he would be inconsistent and this is contrary to the nature of a rational being. But each rational being recognizes himself as having an absolute worth as an end, and not merely a relative worth depending on some end for which he can be used as a means. Therefore, no rule of conduct universally prescribing to all persons *as* rational beings can prescribe action by which one treats another merely as a means.

THIRD FORMULATION: *For a rule to be a moral rule, it must be capable of being self-imposed by the will of each person when he is universally legislating* (that is, when he is deciding to adopt rules for the guidance of his own and others' conduct). Reason: If a rule of conduct were imposed upon a person by someone else's will (for example, by the will of the State, by one's parents' will, or by God's will), it could not be a moral rule unless it was recognized by the person himself as validly binding upon him. Absence of such recognition would mean that he sees himself as being coerced or forced to obey the rule, not as being under an obligation to act in accordance with it. Now to see himself as being under an obligation to act in accordance with the rule, when he is *not* coerced to obey it, is to recognize the rule as validly binding upon him. He thus sees that it is his own will—not anyone else's—which is the source of his obligation to follow it. In other words, he sees that he is prescribing the rule to himself. Now this rule binds him as a rational being, not as an individual with a unique personality. But if it binds him as a rational being, it binds everyone else as a rational being (again disregarding their individual personalities). Thus in prescribing the rule to himself, he is prescribing it to everyone. By imposing upon himself an obligation to follow it, he imposes the same obligation upon all others. A moral rule, then, is a rule that is self-imposed by a universally legislating will.

The concept of a will that is a universal legislator and is the source of the very rules of conduct that bind a person regardless of his inclinations and ends is given the name "the autonomy of the will" by Kant. This concept becomes of central importance in the Third Section of the book, but Kant also uses it in the Second Section as the basis for his view of the moral community of mankind. This moral community, which he calls "the kingdom of ends," may be briefly explained as follows.

If all men were to prescribe rules binding upon themselves, each would be a sovereign because he would be the creator of the rules, and each would be a subject because he would be under an obligation to obey the rules. Furthermore, what would be a duty for one member of such a rule-governed community would be a duty for everyone else, since the same rules would prescribe to everyone equally. No one would be exempt from the obligation to obey, and no one would have rules imposed upon him against his (rational) will. Each would therefore have the same worth as a person. There would be no inferiors or superiors. No individual and no group would have special privileges, that is, privileges not granted to everyone alike. No one would be permitted to use another merely as a means to his own ends, since no one would be willing to set up a rule allowing others to use *him* merely as a means to *their* ends. In such a community of rational beings the autonomy of the will is the ground of individual worth. This is Kant's vision of what society would be like if everyone were fully moral; that is, if all men were men of good will.

Let us now turn to the Third Section of the book. Here Kant is giving his proof that there is a moral law, whose nature he has been analyzing in the First and Second Sections. Up to this point he has explained what kinds of rules must be binding upon men, and in what manner they must be binding, if there is such a thing as morality at all. He now sets himself the task of showing that morality is a fact, that the categorical imperative does impose a valid obligation upon all rational beings, including all men. There are three basic steps in his argument. The first is given in the opening subsection, titled "The Concept of Freedom Is the Key That Explains the Autonomy of the Will." Here Kant argues that *if* men have freedom of the will, *then* they must be obligated to obey the categorical imperative. The argument consists in showing that freedom of the will is nothing but the autonomy of the will ("the property of the will to be a law to itself"), and that the autonomy of the will, as has been shown in the Second Section, is another way of expressing the principle of the categorical imperative. Therefore, Kant concludes, "a free will and a will subject to moral laws are one and the same." So, *if* men are free, they are bound by moral rules. He must next show that men are in fact free.

In the second step of the argument, contained in the subsection titled "Freedom Must Be Presupposed as a Property of the Will of all Rational Beings," he argues that anyone is really free who can act only under "the idea of freedom," that is, who must *conceive of himself* as being free when he is using his practical reason in deliberating about what he ought to do. Now all rational beings are like this, because in reasoning about what they ought to do they identify whatever reasons or "judgments" they have for or against doing one thing rather than another as *reasons of their own,* not as coming from others. This is what Kant means by saying that the practical reason "must regard itself as the author of its principles independent on foreign influences." Consequently, all rational beings, and hence all men, must think of themselves as being free when they deliberate about actions open to their choice, and if they must think of themselves as free, they are free (as far as moral choice is concerned).

This two-step argument may be summed up as follows, placing the second step first:

(1) All rational beings must conceive of themselves as free.
(2) If any being must conceive of himself as free, he is free, from the practical point of view.

(3) Therefore, all rational beings (and hence all men) are free, from the practical point of view.

(4) To be free is to have autonomy of the will.
(5) The autonomy of the will is one way of expressing the principle of the categorical imperative.

(6) Therefore, to be free is to be subject to the categorical imperative.

(7) All men are free, from the practical point of view. (By (3).)

(8) Therefore, all men are, from the practical point of view, subject to the categorical imperative. (By (6).)

It should be noted that Kant always qualifies his assertion that men are free by the phrase "from the practical point of view." He does this for the following reasons. Although men *may* be mistaken in conceiving of themselves as free, nevertheless they must think of themselves in this way in their practical life. Moreover, our reason cannot *show* that we are mistaken in believing ourselves to be free. It is true that we are unable to give either an empirical or an a priori argument to guarantee our freedom, but neither can it be established by argument that we are not free. We are therefore justified in regarding ourselves as free agents because in the conduct of our lives we cannot help conceiving of ourselves this way and we have no reason to deny our freedom.

Kant then proceeds to show how the nature of man must be understood if he is to be seen as free "from the practical point of view." This is the third step of the argument. It is Kant's attempt to account for the freedom of the will in a world which can be known in terms of cause and effect. (In the next chapter we shall consider this problem in greater detail.) The solution Kant offers is that we can take two standpoints in viewing human conduct and human reasoning. We can take the scientific or psychological point of view, or we can take the moral or practical point of view. From the first standpoint, we try to understand the causes of behavior and of thought. We are interested in explaining why a man does what he does and thinks as he thinks. We see how his action and thought fit into the order of the empirical world of nature. In Kant's terms, we understand man as a member of the phenomenal world, the world we come to know through our senses. From the other standpoint, however, we see human conduct and thought in a different light. When we take this standpoint we are not interested in causal explanation. Instead, we are asking, What ought a person to do, and why? We shift from facts to values, from "is" to "ought." We adopt this second point of view whenever we carry on moral discourse by making moral judgments, justifying them, and prescribing conduct to ourselves and others. It is within this framework that man is conceived to be a free moral agent. As such, he can deliberate about alternatives open to his choice and can act according to his deliberation. When we take this point of view toward a person, whether it is ourself or another, we think of the person as being subject to obligations and duties. In Kant's terms, we understand man as a member of the intelligible world, that is, as a rational being confronted with choices and at the same time bound by moral rules. Only in this double light can we fully comprehend the nature of man and his place in the universe. And it is just because we take these two standpoints that the categorical imperative can apply to us when we have the freedom to decide to conform to it or to violate it. Not being perfect, we do not always do what we ought. The man of good will is not forced to do his duty, and that is why he can be admired as a good man when he does his duty for its own sake.

Prima facie DUTIES

In the twentieth century a new kind of deontological ethics has been developed. It arose out of a dissatisfaction with utilitarian ethics, especially the "agathistic" or "ideal" utilitarianism set forth by G. E. Moore in his books *Principia Ethica* (1903) and *Ethics* (1912). (We shall be reading parts of these books in Chapters 7 and 8.) In 1930 the Oxford philosopher Sir David Ross published a book called *The Right and the Good*, in which he attacks utilitarianism and at the same time propounds a deontological theory of his own. He begins with the question "What makes right acts right?" and tries to show that the utility of an action ("productivity of the maximum good") cannot be the correct answer to this question. His argument appeals to cases in which the utilitarian himself would admit that we have a moral obligation to do a certain act (say, to keep a promise), yet his theory would imply the contrary.

In a situation of choice among alternatives open to us, Ross's view is that we will often have moral reasons for, and moral reasons against, doing each alternative. We must then weigh these reasons and compare them with each other in order to determine, first, whether we have a duty to do or to refrain from doing an alternative and, second, to determine which, among all the alternatives we have a duty to do, is the one that imposes the heaviest or most important duty upon us. Only then do we know what we ought to do. This is the process of moral reasoning by which a person either deliberates *before* making a decision about what he ought to do, or by which he justifies a moral judgment about a certain action *after* he or another has made such a decision. In either case the logic of the reasoning process is the same. Let us examine this logic.

Any given alternative act may fall under a number of moral rules, some of which it conforms to and some of which it violates. For example, it may be an act that the agent has promised to do and also an act someone will benefit from. On the other hand, it may be an unjust act and also involve the deceiving of others. Such a case would be a prison warden's secretly allowing a prisoner to escape, which the warden had promised a wealthy friend of the prisoner he would do in return for a large bribe. The warden's act fulfills a promise and benefits both the prisoner and his wealthy friend. But the act is one of injustice (assuming that the prisoner had in fact committed a crime and had been fairly tried), and it is also an act of deception of society. We all believe that the warden has done what he ought not to have done; he has violated his moral duty. Yet we arrive at this conclusion only because we consider the reasons against his act to weigh more heavily than the reasons for doing it.

Each reason consists in the appeal to a moral rule which imposes a duty: to keep one's promise; to benefit others when one can help them; to be just; and to be honest. Each of these duties determines a reason for (or against) doing the act even though each, by itself, does not tell us whether we finally ought or ought not to do the act. Thus each of these duties is termed a *prima facie* duty. When we acknowledge a *prima facie* duty to do something, we recognize that, *if all other things were equal,* we ought to do it. That is, it is a duty "at first glance," but not an "actual duty" or duty *sans phrase* (without qualification). Since there may be another duty to refrain from doing the act, we cannot assume, just because we have a *prima facie* duty to do it, that therefore we ought to do it. This is because the contrary duty might outweigh the first duty. In such a case the contrary duty is also merely a *prima facie* duty. We cannot assume that we ought not to do something just because we have a duty to refrain from doing it. We must also weigh this duty against any duties that might obligate us to do the act in question. Only then will we know what we actually ought to do in the given situation of choice, that is, what our *actual* duty is.

Ross then argues that there are many types of *prima facie* duties (he lists six of them), any of which may be cited as valid reasons for or against doing an act. What makes right acts right, in his view, is the outcome of weighing these *prima facie* duties against each other in any given case where more than one applies. He concludes that the utilitarians are therefore mistaken in thinking that there is only one standard that makes a right act right; namely, the fact that it produces more good than any alternative act. Ross points out a number of cases where the utilitarian norm would conflict with the outcome of weighing *prima facie* duties. He also shows how at least some of the *prima facie* duties themselves are inconsistent with the principle of utility, although he grants that utility sometimes does determine a *prima facie*, though not an actual, duty.

Two questions may be raised in connection with Ross's form of deontological ethics: (1) How do we determine the proper weight to be assigned to various *prima facie* duties when they conflict? (2) How do we know what are our *prima facie* duties in the first place?

Ross's answer to both questions is the same. We must simply consult our deepest moral convictions. When an act has a certain characteristic in virtue of which we find ourselves convinced that we ought, or ought not, to do it, then we *know* that this characteristic is a morally relevant one. It determines a *prima facie* duty. For example, the proposition that an act, *qua* fulfilling a promise, is *prima facie* right, Ross claims to be self-evident. By this he means that if a person with "sufficient mental maturity" were to give "sufficient attention" to what the proposition states, he would be convinced of its truth without the need of any proof. "We are dealing," Ross declares, "with propositions that cannot be proved, but that just as certainly need no proof." Here the question must be raised: Suppose a person were to disagree with Ross's list of *prima facie* duties, or with Ross's way of weighing them against one another. One suspects that if Ross found such a person denying or even doubting, for example, the proposition that an act, in so far as it is the fulfilling of a promise, is *prima facie* right, he would claim that the person either lacked "sufficient mental maturity" or did not give "sufficient attention" to the proposition, so that his inner convictions are not to be considered as knowledge of self-evident truths. Thus it is incumbent upon Ross to specify some *method* by which we can tell when a person has "sufficient mental maturity" to obtain moral knowledge without the need of proof, or a *method* by which we can decide whether someone has or has not given "sufficient attention" to a statement about *prima facie* duties, if we are to consider his views about such duties to be true.

Ross appears to recognize this difficulty at the end of the reading, for he there tries to argue that our deepest moral convictions are "apprehensions" or "instances of knowledge," and not merely beliefs we happen to be certain of. His argument rests upon the idea that the data of ethics, that is, the set of facts which any ethical theory must accord with if it is to be accepted as a true theory, are not the moral convictions of anyone, but only of "thoughtful and well-educated" people. Even *their* convictions, however, might be false, so we can accept only those of their convictions "which stand better the test of reflection." But although Ross claims that such reflection results from the development over many generations of "an extremely delicate power of appreciation of moral distinctions," he does not explain exactly how such a power of appreciation operates, or just how we are to go about "reflecting" on moral propositions. He simply relies upon "the verdicts of the moral consciousness of the best people" as the ultimate court of appeal.

It should be remarked here that, by introducing the concept of "the best people," Ross is in danger of arguing in a vicious circle. If he means the *morally* best, then presumably the best people are those who correctly recognize their *prima facie* duties and balance them correctly in concluding what is their actual duty in any given situation. But this presupposes what we are trying to find out, since it assumes there is a way of knowing what our *prima facie* duties are and how they are to be weighed in arriving at our actual duties. It is *this* way of knowing that we are in search of. Without this way of knowing, we do not know what people to pick out as our examples of "the best people," whose "verdicts" are to be taken as the ultimate data of ethics.

FURTHER CONSIDERATIONS OF RULE-UTILITARIANISM

In the Introduction to Chapter 4 the distinction was made between two forms of utilitarian ethics, act-utilitarianism and rule-utilitarianism. According to act-utilitarianism an act is right if doing it in a certain set of circumstances will bring about more intrinsic value and less intrinsic disvalue than would result from doing any alternative act in the given circumstances. According to rule-utilitarianism an act is right if it conforms to a valid rule of conduct, wrong if it violates such a rule. And what makes a rule of conduct valid is its utility. If more intrinsic value and less intrinsic disvalue would result from everyone's following a certain rule than would result from everyone's following an alternative rule, then the rule in question is valid. The whole system of rules that makes up the moral code of a society is thus seen as a vast instrument for regulating the conduct of everyone in such a way that the happiness of the entire community will be maximized and its unhappiness minimized.

Rule-utilitarianism has been developed in the twentieth century as a reply to some of the objections made against earlier forms of utilitarianism. Contemporary rule-utilitarians argue that their theory can account for the obligations and *prima facie* duties which philosophers like Ross have claimed to be incompatible with utilitarianism. An example of how such a defense of utilitarianism can be made is presented in Professor John Rawls's article "Two Concepts of Rules." (Professor Rawls's own views, which involve a criticism of ultilitarianism on grounds of justice, are given in another article by him titled "Justice as Fairness," to be found in the last chapter of this book.)

Rawls makes a distinction between a social practice and the particular acts that fall under it, and then points out how the justification of a social practice as a whole, which is based on its utility, differs from the justification of particular acts, which is based on conformity to the rules defining the social practice. Although Rawls does not claim that this distinction is sufficient to establish rule-utilitarianism as an adequate ethical theory, he does show how the distinction can be used to defend utilitarianism against those critics who appeal to the obligation to keep a promise and the obligation not to punish an innocent man as cases which cannot be accounted for by utilitarians.

Connected with the distinction between a social practice as a whole and the particular acts falling under it is another distinction: that between two ways of conceiving of rules of conduct. Rawls distinguishes the "summary" concept of rules from the "practice" concept. A rule is a universal prescription; it tells us what *anyone* ought or ought not to do in a certain set of circumstances. Thus all rules are generalized guides to the conduct of everyone, not particular commands to this or that individual. How is this generalized or universal aspect of a rule to be conceived? There are two possible answers. The first, which is the summary concept, is that a rule is a summary of a large number of particular cases of acts done and of acts not done whenever a given set of circumstances occurred in the past. If in each case a person's doing the act tended to bring about greater happiness than his not doing it, the rule emerges that, in circumstances of the kind in question, that kind of act ought to be done. If in each case a person's refraining from doing the act resulted in more happiness (or less unhappiness) than his doing it, the rule becomes: In circumstances of this kind, an act of this kind ought not to be done. Thus both positive rules and negative rules are understood as summaries of particular acts. The acts come first, the rules follow.

The practice concept of rules looks at rules in a very different way. Rules are seen as defining social practices, so that we cannot even *describe* an act as being of a cetrain kind (say, as an act of promising or as an act of punishing) without referring to a set of rules. Here the rules must first be given in order for the particular act to be done, in the sense that a person must conform to the rules if his act is to be described in a certain way. For example, we cannot describe the action of a man who is running from one point to another in an open field as "stealing base" unless we know the rules of baseball and conceive of his action as part of that game. The same would apply to a person's act of uttering the words "I promise," or to a judge's sentencing someone to a prison term. In neither case can we describe these acts as promising or punishing unless we know the rules that govern the moral and legal "games" of promising and punishing.

The practice concept of rules, combined with the distinction between justifying a social practice as a whole and justifying a particular act falling under it, enables the rule-utilitarian to deny act-utilitarianism and at the same time make a reply to the objections raised by deontologists and other critics of utilitarianism. He denies act-utilitarianism because the nature of certain acts is such that the person who performs them must *not* calculate the utility of the consequences of his performing them, and must *not* weigh this utility with the utility of the rules that define such acts. As Rawls points out, a person does not understand what a promise is if he thinks that he is obligated to keep his promise only if the consequences of doing so are better than the consequences of his breaking it. Similarly, a judge who asks himself whether his sending a duly tried and convicted criminal to jail would have better or worse consequences than letting him go would neither be functioning in the role of a judge nor be understanding what the practice of legal punishment means. On the other hand, the justification of the whole social practices of promising and legal punishment would seem to be utilitarian, since the amenities of civilized life in society would not be possible without such practices and hence no one's interests would be served by their abolition.

Whether this constitutes an adequate defense of rule-utilitarianism against act-utilitarianism on the one hand and against deontological ethics on the other is a question of serious concern on the part of contemporary moral philosophers. Some important considerations relevant to this question are the following:

(1) Although it is true that we cannot understand the nature of certain acts without knowing the rules defining the practice in terms of which the acts are described, these rules are not the same as the *moral* rules that impose the obligation to do the acts. In order to make a promise, for instance, we must understand the rules defining the practice of promising. We must, indeed, follow those rules in order to make a promise at all. But having made a promise in accordance with such rules, it is possible for us either to keep it or to break it. And in order to know whether we *ought* to keep it or break it we must know (in addition to the practice-defining rules) that there is a valid moral rule that obligates us to keep our promises. We must also know whether that moral rule binds us in every case to keep our promises, no matter what might be the consequences of our doing so. For we might be in circumstances where the consequences are such that there is a legitimate exception to the rule, and it would be necessary for us to know this if we were to know whether we should keep or break the promise in the given circumstances.

(2) This last point raises a further problem for rule-utilitarianism. It may be the case that the moral rule that imposes the obligation to keep promises is justified on grounds of utility, but this leaves open the question whether the obligation to keep a promise *in every particular case* always outweighs the utility of

breaking a promise *in every particular case*. Suppose, for example, that A has borrowed some money from B and has promised to pay it back by a certain date. Suppose further that A's child has meanwhile come down with a grave illness that requires many months of hospital care, so that if A repays his debt to B he will not be able to afford this hospital care. Does the obligation to keep his promise outweigh all consideration of the consequences of his doing so? Rawls himself admits that legitimate exceptions can be made to the rule of promise-keeping. "Various defenses for not keeping one's promise are allowed," he says, "but among them there isn't the one that, on general utilitarian grounds, the promisor (truly) thought his action best on the whole, even though there may be the defense that the consequences of keeping one's promise would have been *extremely* severe." Now if we can make a legitimate exception to the rule in those cases where our keeping a promise would have *extremely* bad consequences, it would seem that act-utilitarians could reply: Why do the consequences have to be *extremely* bad for there to be a legitimate exception? If consequences are relevant in justifying the breaking of a promise, why shouldn't we be doing what is morally right when we (truly) think that the consequences of breaking our promise will be better, *however slightly better*, than the consequences of our keeping it? And if this is granted, rule-utilitarianism collapses into act-utilitarianism. An act is right when its consequences are better than those of any alternative, and we need not consider whether the act conforms to or violates a rule.

(3) It may further be the case that, although practice-defining rules should be conceived in the "practice" way and not in the "summary" way, moral rules that prescribe what we ought to do (and thereby determine our moral obligations) should be conceived in the "summary" way. After all, the moral rules binding us to do certain acts described by practice-defining rules might well be justified because, in the past, the vast majority of acts conforming to the moral rule in question had better consequences than would have occurred if the vast majority of acts were done contrary to the moral rule. The general utility of the rule is thus identified with the statistical probability, based on past experience of particular cases, that future conformity with the rule will, in the vast majority of cases, have better consequences than would result from a general violation of the rule. This "summary" view would then allow for a utilitarian justification of breaking the rule in any given case, as well as a utilitarian justification of having the rule as a general guide to everyone's conduct in normal circumstances.

(4) There is a question whether any genuine distinction between act- and rule-utilitarianism can finally be made, in spite of the apparent differences between them. Consider the examples by which the two theories were originally distinguished in the Introduction to Chapter 4. The first example was that of lying to the Gestapo to protect innocent people; the second was taking the money out of a wallet belonging to someone else to keep ones' family from starving. These examples were given as cases where the breaking of valid moral rules (telling the truth and not stealing, respectively) would have better consequences than conforming to the rules. Are the acts in question right or wrong? It would seem that rule-utilitarians would say they are wrong while act-utilitarians would

say they are right. Yet there is a way of looking at these acts which would allow a rule-utilitarian to argue that they are right, and thus agree with the act-utilitarian's view. Let us see how this can be done.

Each act may be considered not as a violation of a moral rule but as a legitimate exception to a moral rule. What makes an exception legitimate? The answer might be either that the exception is required by a higher moral rule or that its consequences are better than those of not making an exception in the given circumstances. According to the first answer, whenever there is a conflict of rules (that is, a situation where following one rule involves breaking the other, and vice versa) we must make an exception to one of the conflicting rules. Our exception is legitimate when the rule we follow in making the exception imposes a heavier obligation or a higher duty on us than does the rule to which we make the exception. Thus in the first example given, the duty to obey the rule "Prevent harm from being done to innocent people" outweighs the rule "Tell the truth." In this case it is right to lie. According to the second test of a legitimate exception, we must balance the duty of following the rule with the badness of the consequences of following it in the given circumstances. If the badness of the consequences outweighs the duty, an exception to the rule is legitimate. Thus in the second example, if the badness of having one's family starve is judged to be worse than stealing, it is right to steal.

Whichever of these two methods for determining legitimate exceptions to rules is used, a rule-utilitarian could fit it into his ethical system. With regard to the first method, he would say that there must be some *principle* by which the two conflicting rules are weighed against each other. This principle will be a *second-order moral rule,* according to which one first-order rule (say, to prevent harm) imposes a heavier obligation than another first-order rule (say, to tell the truth). *And the test for the validity of any second-order rule is the same as the test for the validity of first-order rules, namely, its utility.* If the consequences of everyone's following a certain second-order rule, whenever two first-order rules conflict, are better than everyone's following the opposite second-order rule in the same circumstances, then the former second-order rule is valid. With regard to the second method, the rule-utilitarian would say that reference to some principle is necessary to decide whether the badness of the consequences in a given case is to count more heavily than the breaking of a rule. Here again the test for the validity of any such principle is taken to be the utility of the general practice of everyone's following it whenever it is applicable. If the consequences of everyone's following it are better than the consequences of everyone's following some alternative principle, then it is a valid moral principle.

Since a rule-utilitarian in this manner could account for every case in which his position was apparently contradicted by act-utilitarianism, it would seem that no genuine distinction can be drawn between the two theories.

(5) Nevertheless, there remain the "hard core" cases where rule-utilitarians want to deny what seem to them to be the implications of act-utilitarianism. For example, the driver of a car bribes a policeman not to give him a ticket for speeding. If this act is done in secret rather than openly, the policeman would not

lose his job and the driver would not be brought into court (things which would happen if the act became known to the public). The rule-utilitarian would argue that this difference in the consequences of doing the act secretly and doing it openly makes no difference to the wrongness of the act, whereas an act-utilitarian would have to admit such a difference to be relevant. To take another case, if a teacher knowingly allows a student to cheat and does nothing about it, the rule-utilitarian would say that the student and the teacher are both doing wrong acts, and that it makes no difference whether anyone else finds out about it. The act-utilitarian, on the other hand, would have to admit that the consequences of people's finding out about the acts in comparison with the consequences of their not finding out about them would be relevant to judging the moral wrongness of the acts. Now our question is this: In such cases as these, where the breaking of rules involves an *injustice,* are the views of act-utilitarianism and rule-utilitarianism ultimately irreconcilable?

In order to answer this question, we should notice that the wrongness of these acts is of a special sort. For these are cases where *an exception is made in someone's favor.* This is quite different from cases where *an exception is made to a moral rule in a certain set of circumstances.* We have seen how the latter can sometimes be considered legitimate, either because the consequences of making an exception in the given circumstances are good while the consequences of following the rule in those same circumstances are bad (act-utilitarianism) or because the general rule of making such exceptions in the given circumstances, if followed by everyone, would have better consequences than everyone's following an alternative general rule (rule-utilitarianism). When legitimate exceptions to rules are determined in either of these ways, it is always the case that, if it is legitimate for one person to make an exception to a certain rule in certain circumstances, it is legitimate for anyone else to make the same exception in the same circumstances. Thus what has been called "the principle of universalizability" is preserved: What is right (or wrong) for one person is right (or wrong) for everyone.

When an exception is made in someone's favor, however, this principle of universalizability is violated. For then one person is permitted to do something which others are forbidden to do in the *same* circumstances. The exception itself is not made into a general rule whereby it becomes permissible for *anyone* to do an act when *anyone* is in a certain set of circumstances. On the contrary, one person is given a special privilege or advantage which is denied to others. Whenever someone asks that an exception be made in his own favor, he contradicts Kant's categorical imperative, for he is not willing to make the maxim of his own act a universal law. The rules of conduct that bind others are not accepted as binding upon him. He grants that his own case is similar to that of others, and yet he thinks he should be treated in a way different from them. This position, however, is not only contrary to Kant's deontological ethics; it is also contrary to both act-utilitarianism and rule-utilitarianism. For neither of these theories allows us to judge an act done by one person to be right and another exactly similar act done by someone else to be wrong. If the circumstances are exactly similar, then both acts will have the same consequences and therefore, according to act-utilitarianism, will *both* be either right or wrong, depending on whether the consequences are better or worse than those of some other act done in the same circumstances. Similarly, if one act is right because it conforms to a rule which is valid according to rule-utilitarianism, then every other act, no matter who does it, is also right if it conforms to the same rule. Both types of utilitarianism, then, accept the principle of universalizability and reject any exception being made in favor of some particular person. Thus we are again unable to find any ultimate conflict between the two theories, despite their apparent disagreement about what makes right acts right and wrong acts wrong. Whether they can be found to contradict each other on any other point in ethics is still an open question, but these considerations are sufficient to make us wonder just how different the two theories are.

IMMANUEL KANT

Fundamental Principles of the Metaphysic of Morals

PREFACE

As my concern here is with moral philosophy, I limit the question suggested to this: Whether it is not of the utmost necessity to construct a pure moral philosophy, perfectly cleared of everything which is only empirical, and which belongs to anthropology? for that such a philosophy must be possible is evident from the common idea of duty and of the moral laws. Everyone must admit that if a law is to have moral force, *i.e.* to be the basis of an obligation, it must carry with it absolute necessity; that, for example, the precept, "Thou shalt not lie," is not valid for men alone, as if other rational beings had no need to observe it; and so with all the other moral laws properly so called; that, therefore, the basis of obligation must not be sought in the nature of man, or in the circumstances in the world in which he is placed, but *à priori* simply in the conceptions of pure reason; and although any other precept which is founded on principles of mere experience may be in certain respects universal, yet in as far as it rests

From Immanuel Kant, *Fundamental Principles of the Metaphysic of Morals*, translated by T. K. Abbott; Preface and Sections I, II, and III. (Originally published under the title, *Grundlegung zur Metaphysik der Sitten*, 1785; this translation first published in 1873.)

even in the least degree on an empirical basis, perhaps only as to a motive, such a precept, while it may be a practical rule, can never be called a moral law.

Thus not only are moral laws with their principles essentially distinguished from every other kind of practical knowledge in which there is anything empirical, but all moral philosophy rests wholly on its pure part. When applied to man, it does not borrow the least thing from the knowledge of man himself (anthropology), but gives laws *à priori* to him as a rational being. No doubt these laws require a judgment sharpened by experience, in order on the one hand to distinguish in what cases they are applicable, and on the other to procure for them access to the will of the man, and effectual influence on conduct; since man is acted on by so many inclinations that, though capable of the idea of a practical pure reason, he is not so easily able to make it effective *in concreto* in his life.

A metaphysic of morals is therefore indispensably necessary, not merely for speculative reasons, in order to investigate the sources of the practical principles which are to be found *à priori* in our reason, but also because morals themselves are liable to all sorts of corruption, as long as we are without that clue and supreme canon by which to estimate them correctly. For in order that an action should be morally good, it is not enough that it *conform* to the moral law, but it must also be done *for the sake of the law,* otherwise that conformity is only very contingent and uncertain; since a principle which is not moral, although it may now and then produce actions conformable to the law, will also often produce actions which contradict it. Now it is only in a pure philosophy that we can look for the moral law in its purity and genuineness (and, in a practical matter, this is of the utmost consequence): we must, therefore, begin with pure philosophy (metaphysic), and without it there cannot be any moral philosophy at all. That which mingles these pure principles with the empirical does not deserve the name of philosophy (for what distinguishes philosophy from common rational knowledge is, that it treats in separate sciences what the latter only comprehends confusedly); much less does it deserve that of moral philosophy, since by this confusion it even spoils the purity of morals themselves, and counteracts its own end.

* * * * *

FIRST SECTION:

TRANSITION FROM THE COMMON RATIONAL KNOWLEDGE
OF MORALITY TO THE PHILOSOPHICAL

[The Good Will]

Nothing can possibly be conceived in the world, or even out of it, which can be called good, without qualification, except a Good Will. Intelligence, wit, judgment, and the other *talents* of the mind, however they may be named, or courage, resolution, perseverance, as qualities of temperament, are undoubtedly good and desirable in many respects; but these gifts of nature may also become extremely bad and mischievous if the will which is to make use of them, and which, therefore, constitutes what is called *character,* is not good. It is the same with the *gifts of fortune.* Power, riches, honour, even health, and the general well-being and contentment with one's condition which is called *happiness,* inspire pride, and often presumption, if there is not a good will to correct the influence of these on the mind, and with this also to rectify the whole principle of acting, and adapt it to its end. The sight of a being who is not adorned with a single feature of a pure and good will, enjoying unbroken prosperity, can never give pleasure to an impartial rational spectator. Thus a good will appears to constitute the indispensable condition even of being worthy of happiness.

There are even some qualities which are of service to this good will itself, and may facilitate its action, yet which have no intrinsic unconditional value, but always presuppose a good will, and this qualifies the esteem that we justly have for them, and does not permit us to regard them as absolutely good. Moderation in the affections and passions, self-control, and calm deliberation are not only good in many respects, but even seem to constitute part of the intrinsic worth of the person; but they are far from deserving to be called good without qualification, although they have been so unconditionally praised by the ancients. For without the principles of a good will, they may become extremely bad; and the coolness of a villain not only makes him far more dangerous, but also directly makes him more abominable in our eyes than he would have been without it.

A good will is good not because of what it performs or effects, not by its aptness for the attainment of some proposed end, but simply by virtue of the volition, that is, it is good in itself, and considered by itself is to be esteemed much higher than all that can be brought about by it in favour of any inclination, nay, even of the sum-total of all inclinations. Even if it should happen that, owing to special disfavour of fortune, or the niggardly provision of a step-motherly nature, this will should wholly lack power to accomplish its purpose, if with its greatest efforts it should yet achieve nothing, and there should remain only the good will (not, to be sure, a mere wish, but the summoning of all means in our power), then, like a jewel, it would still shine by its own light, as a thing which has its whole value in itself. Its usefulness or fruitlessness can neither add to nor take away anything from this value. It would be, as it were, only the setting to enable us to handle it the more conveniently in common commerce, or to attract to it the attention of those who are not yet connoisseurs, but not to recommend it to true connoisseurs, or to determine its value.

[Why Reason Was Made to Guide the Will]

There is, however, something so strange in this idea of the absolute value of the mere will, in which no account is taken of its utility, that notwithstanding the thorough assent of even common reason to the idea, yet a suspicion must arise that it may perhaps really be the product of mere high-blown fancy, and that we may have misunderstood the purpose of nature in assigning reason as the governor of our will. Therefore we will examine this idea from this point of view.

In the physical constitution of an organized being, that is, a being adapted suitably to the purposes of life, we assume it as a fundamental principle that no organ for any purpose will be found but what is also the fittest and best adapted for that purpose. Now in a being which has reason and a will, if the proper object of nature were its *conservation,* its *welfare,* in a word, its *happiness,* then nature would have hit upon a very bad arrangement in selecting the reason of the creature to carry out this purpose. For all the actions which the creature has to perform with a view to this purpose, and the whole rule of its conduct, would be far more surely prescribed to it by instinct, and that end would have been attained thereby much more certainly than it ever can be by reason. Should reason have been communicated to this favoured creature over and above, it must only have served it to contemplate the happy constitution of its nature, to admire it, to congratulate itself thereon, and to feel thankful for it to the beneficent cause, but not that it should subject its desires to that weak and delusive guidance, and meddle bunglingly with the purpose of nature. In a word, nature would have taken care that reason should not break forth into *practical exercise,* nor have the presumption, with its weak insight, to think out for itself the plan of happiness, and of the means of attaining it. Nature would not only have taken on herself the choice of the ends, but also of the means, and with wise foresight would have entrusted both to instinct.

And, in fact, we find that the more a cultivated reason applies itself with deliberate purpose to the enjoyment of life and happiness, so much the more does the man fail of true satisfaction. And from this circumstance there arises in many, if they are candid enough to confess it, a certain degree of *misology,* that is, hatred of reason, especially in the case of those who are most experienced in the use of it, because after calculating all the advantages they derive, I do not say from the invention of all the arts of common luxury, but even from the sciences (which seem to them to be after all only a luxury of the under-standing), they find that they have, in fact, only brought more trouble on their shoulders, rather than gained in happiness; and they end by envying, rather than depising, the more common stamp of men who keep closer to the guidance of mere instinct, and do not allow their reason much influence on their con-duct. And this we must admit, that the judgment of those who would very much lower the lofty eulogies of the advantages which reason gives us in regard to the happiness and satisfaction of life, or who would even reduce them below zero, is by no means morose or ungrateful to the goodness with which the world is governed, but that there lies at the root of these judgments the idea that our existence has a different and far nobler end, for which, and not for happiness, reason is properly intended, and which must, therefore, be regarded as the supreme condition to which the private ends of man must, for the most part, be postponed.

For as reason is not competent to guide the will with certainty in regard to its objects and the satisfaction of all our wants (which it to some extent even multiplies), this being an end to which an implanted instinct would have led with much greater certainty; and since, nevertheless, reason is imparted to us as a practical faculty, *i.e.* as one which is to have influence on the *will*, therefore, admitting that nature generally in the distribution of her capacities has adapted the means to the end, its true destination must be to produce a *will*, not merely good as a *means* to something else, but *good in itself*, for which reason was absolutely necessary. This will then, though not indeed the sole and complete good, must be the supreme good and the condition of every other, even of the desire of happiness. Under these circumstances, there is nothing inconsistent with the wisdom of nature in the fact that the cultivation of the reason, which is requisite for the first and unconditional purpose, does in many ways interfere, at least in this life, with the attainment of the second, which is always conditional, namely, happiness. Nay, it may even reduce it to nothing, without nature thereby failing of her purpose. For reason recognizes the establishment of a good will as its highest practical destination, and in attaining this purpose is capable only of a satisfaction of its own proper kind, namely, that from the attainment of an end, which end again is determined by reason only, notwithstanding that this may involve many a disappointment to the ends of inclination.

[The First Proposition of Morality]

We have then to develop the notion of a will which deserves to be highly esteemed for itself, and is good without a view to anything further, a notion which exists already in the sound natural understanding, requiring rather to be cleared up than to be taught, and which in estimating the value of our actions always takes the first place, and constitutes the condition of all the rest. In order to do this, we will take the notion of duty, which includes that of a good will, although implying certain subjective restrictions and hindrances. These, however, far from concealing it, or rendering it unrecognizable, rather bring it out by contrast, and make it shine forth so much the brighter.

I omit here all actions which are already recognized as inconsistent with duty although they may be useful for this or that purpose, for with these the question whether they are done *from duty* cannot arise at all, since they even conflict with it. I also set aside those actions which really conform to duty, but to which men have *no* direct *inclination*, performing them because they are impelled thereto by some other inclination. For in this case we can readily distinguish whether the action which agrees with duty is done *from duty,* or from a selfish view. It is much harder to make this distinction when the action accords with duty, and the subject has besides a *direct* inclination to it. For example, it is always a matter of duty that a dealer should not overcharge an inexperienced purchaser; and wherever there is much commerce the prudent tradesman does not overcharge, but keeps a fixed price for everyone, so that a child buys of him as well as any other. Men are thus *honestly* served; but this is not enough to make us believe that the tradesman has so acted from duty and from principles of honesty: his own advantage required it; it is out of the question in this case to suppose that he might besides have a direct inclination in favour of the buyers, so that, as it were, from love he should give no advantage to one over another. Accordingly the action was done neither from duty nor from direct inclination, but merely with a selfish view.

On the other hand, it is a duty to maintain one's life; and, in addition, everyone has also a direct inclination to do so. But on this account the often anxious care which most men take for it has no intrinsic worth, and their maxim has no moral import. They preserve their life *as duty requires,* no doubt, but not *because duty requires.* On the other hand, if adversity and hopeless sorrow have completely taken away the relish for life; if the unfortunate one, strong in mind, indignant at his fate rather than desponding or dejected, wishes for death, and yet preserves his life without loving it—not from inclination or fear, but from duty—then his maxim has a moral worth.

To be beneficent when we can is a duty; and besides this, there are many minds so sympathetically constituted that, without any other motive of vanity or self-interest, they find a pleasure in spreading joy around them, and can take delight in the satisfaction of others so far as it is their own work. But I maintain that in such a case an action of this kind, however proper, however amiable it may be, has nevertheless no true moral worth, but is on a level with other inclinations, *e.g.* the inclination to honour, which, if it is happily directed to that which is in fact of public utility and accordant with duty, and consequently honourable, deserves praise and encouragement, but not esteem. For the maxim lacks the moral import, namely, that such actions be done *from duty,* not from inclination. Put the case that the mind of that philanthropist was clouded by sorrow of his own, extinguishing all sympathy with the lot of others, and that while he still has the power to benefit others in distress, he is not touched by their trouble because he is absorbed with his own; and now suppose that he tears himself out of this dead insensibility, and performs the action without any inclination to it, but simply from duty, then first has his action its genuine moral worth. Further still; if nature has put little sympathy in the heart of this or that man; if he, supposed to be an upright man, is by temperament cold and indifferent to the sufferings of others, perhaps because in respect of his own he is provided with the special gift of patience and fortitude, and supposes, or even requires, that others should have the same—and such a man would certainly not be the meanest product of nature—but if nature had not specially framed him for a philanthropist, would he not still find in himself a source from whence to give himself a far higher worth than that of a good-natured temperament could be? Unquestionably. It is just in this that the moral worth of the character is brought out which is incomparably the highest of all, namely, that he is beneficent, not from inclination, but from duty.

To secure one's own happiness is a duty, at least indirectly; for discontent with one's condition, under a pressure of many anxieties and amidst unsatisfied wants, might easily become a great *temptation to transgression of duty.* But here again, without looking to duty, all men have already the strongest and most intimate inclination to happiness, because it is just in this idea that all inclinations are combined in one total. But the precept of happiness is often of such a sort that it greatly interferes with some inclinations, and yet a man cannot form any definite and certain conception of the sum of satisfaction of all of them which is called happiness. It is not then to be wondered at that a single inclination, definite both as to what it promises and as to the time within which it can be gratified, is often able to overcome such a fluctuating idea, and that a gouty patient, for instance, can choose to enjoy what he likes, and to suffer what he may, since, according to his calculation, on this occasion at least, he has [only] not sacrificed the enjoyment of the present moment to a possibly mistaken expectation of a happiness which is supposed to be found in health. But even in this case, if the general desire for happiness did not influence his will, and supposing that in his particular case health was not a necessary element in this calculation, there yet remains in this, as in all other cases, this law, namely, that he should promote his happiness not from inclination but from duty, and by this would his conduct first acquire true moral worth.

It is in this manner, undoubtedly, that we are to understand those passages of Scripture also in which we are commanded to love our neighbour, even our enemy. For love, as an affection, cannot be commanded, but beneficence for duty's sake may; even though we are not impelled to it by any inclination—nay, are even repelled by a natural and unconquerable aversion. This is *practical* love, and not *pathological*—a love which is seated in the will, and not in the propensions of sense—in principles of action and not of tender sympathy; and it is this love alone which can be commanded.

[The Second Proposition of Morality]

The second proposition is: That an action done from duty derives its moral worth, *not from the purpose* which is to be attained by it, but from the maxim by which it is determined, and therefore does not depend on the realization of the object of the action, but merely on the *principle of volition* by which the action has taken place, without regard to any object of desire. It is clear from what precedes that the purposes which we may have in view in our actions, or their effects regarded as ends and springs of the will, cannot give to actions any unconditional or moral worth. In what, then, can their worth lie, if it is not to consist in the will and in reference to its expected effect? It cannot lie anywhere but in the *principle of the will* without regard to the ends which can be attained by the action. For the will stands between its *à priori principle,* which is formal, and its *à posteriori* spring, which is material, as between two roads, and as it must be determined by something, it follows that it must be determined by the formal principle of volition when an action is done from duty, in which case every material principle has been withdrawn from it.

[The Third Proposition of Morality]

The third proposition, which is a consequence of the two preceding, I would express thus: *Duty is the necessity of acting from respect for the law.* I may have *inclination* for an object as the effect of my proposed action, but I cannot have *respect* for it, just for this reason, that it is an effect and not an energy of will. Similarly, I cannot have respect for inclination, whether my own or another's; I can at most, if my own, approve it; if another's, sometimes even love it; *i.e.* look on it as favourable to my own interest. It is only what is connected with my will as a principle, by no means as an effect—what does not subserve my inclination, but overpowers it, or at least in case of choice excludes it from its calculation—in other words, simply the law of itself, which can be an object of respect, and hence a command. Now an action done from duty must wholly exclude the influence of inclination, and with it every object of the will, so that nothing remains which can determine the will except objectively the *law*, and subjectively *pure respect* for this practical law, and consequently the maxim[1] that I should follow this law even to the thwarting of all my inclinations.

Thus the moral worth of an action does not lie in the effect expected from it, nor in any principle of action which requires to borrow its motive from this expected effect. For all these effects—agreeableness of one's condition, and even the promotion of the happiness of others—could have been also brought about by other causes, so that for this there would have been no need of the will of a rational being; whereas it is in this alone that the supreme and unconditional good can be found. The pre-eminent good which we call moral can therefore consist in nothing else than *the conception of law* in itself, *which certainly is only possible in a rational being*, in so far as this conception, and not the expected effect, determines the will. This is a good which is already present in the person who acts accordingly, and we have not to wait for it to appear first in the result.

[The Supreme Principle of Morality: The Categorical Imperative]

But what sort of law can that be, the conception of which must determine the will, even without paying any regard to the effect expected from it, in order that this will may be called good absolutely and without qualification? As I have deprived the will of every impulse which could arise to it from obedience to any law, there remains nothing but the universal conformity of its actions to law in general, which alone is to serve the will as a principle, *i.e.* I am never to act otherwise than so *that I could also will that my maxim should become a universal law*. Here, now, it is the simple conformity to law in general, without assuming any particular law applicable to certain actions, that serves the will as its principle, and must so serve it, if duty is not to be a vain delusion and a chimerical notion. The common reason of men in its practical judgments perfectly coincides with this, and always has in view the principle here suggested. Let the question be, for example: May I when in distress make a promise with the intention not to keep it? I readily distinguish here between the two significations which the question may have: Whether it is prudent, or whether it is right, to make a false promise? The former may undoubtedly often be the

---

[1] A *maxim* is the subjective principle of volition. The objective principle (*i.e.* that which would also serve subjectively as a practical principle to all rational beings if reason had full power over the faculty of desire) is the practical *law*.

case. I see clearly indeed that it is not enough to extricate myself from a present difficulty by means of this subterfuge, but it must be well considered whether there may not hereafter spring from this lie much greater inconvenience than that from which I now free myself, and as, with all my supposed *cunning*, the consequences cannot be so easily foreseen but that credit once lost may be much more injurious to me than any mischief which I seek to avoid at present, it should be considered whether it would not be more *prudent* to act herein according to a universal maxim, and to make it a habit to promise nothing except with the intention of keeping it. But it is soon clear to me that such a maxim will still only be based on the fear of consequences. Now it is a wholly different thing to be truthful from duty, and to be so from apprehension of injurious consequences. In the first case, the very notion of the action already implies a law for me; in the second case, I must first look about elsewhere to see what results may be combined with it which would affect myself. For to deviate from the principle of duty is beyond all doubt wicked; but to be unfaithful to my maxim of prudence may often be very advantageous to me, although to abide by it is certainly safer. The shortest way, however, and an unerring one, to discover the answer to this question whether a lying promise is consistent with duty, is to ask myself, Should I be content that my maxim (to extricate myself from difficulty by a false promise) should hold good as a universal law, for myself as well as for others? and should I be able to say to myself, "Every one may make a deceitful promise when he finds himself in a difficulty from which he cannot otherwise extricate himself"? Then I presently become aware that while I can will the lie, I can by no means will that lying should be a universal law. For with such a law there would be no promises at all, since it would be in vain to allege my intention in regard to my future actions to those who would not believe this allegation, or if they over-hastily did so, would pay me back in my own coin. Hence my maxim, as soon as it should be made a universal law, would necessarily destroy itself.

I do not, therefore, need any far-reaching penetration to discern what I have to do in order that my will may be morally good. Inexperienced in the course of the world, incapable of being prepared for all its contingencies, I only ask myself: Canst thou also will that thy maxim should be a universal law? If not, then it must be rejected, and that not because of a disadvantage accruing from it to myself or even to others, but because it cannot enter as a principle into a possible universal legislation, and reason extorts from me immediate respect for such legislation. I do not indeed as yet *discern* on what this respect is based (this the philosopher may inquire), but at least I understand this, that it is an estimation of the worth which far outweighs all worth of what is recommended by inclination, and that the necessity of acting from *pure* respect for the practical law is what constitutes duty, to which every other motive must give place, because it is the condition of a will being good *in itself*, and the worth of such a will is above everything.

Thus, then, without quitting the moral knowledge of common human reason, we have arrived at its principle. And although, no doubt, common men do not conceive it in such an abstract and universal form, yet they always have it really before their eyes, and use it as the standard of their decision.

• • • • •

SECOND SECTION:
TRANSITION FROM POPULAR MORAL PHILOSOPHY
TO THE METAPHYSIC OF MORALS

[The Impossibility of an Empirical Moral Philosophy]

If we have hitherto drawn our notion of duty from the common use of our practical reason, it is by no means to be inferred that we have treated it as an empirical notion. On the contrary, if we attend to the experience of men's conduct, we meet frequent and, as we ourselves allow, just complaints that one cannot find a single certain example of the disposition to act from pure duty. Although many things are done in *conformity* with what *duty* prescribes, it is nevertheless always doubtful whether they are done strictly *from duty*, so as to have a moral worth. Hence there have at all times been philosophers who have altogether denied that this disposition actually exists at all in human actions, and have ascribed everything to a more or less refined self-love. Not that they have on that account questioned the soundness of the conception of morality; on the contrary, they spoke with sincere regret of the frailty and corruption of human nature, which though noble enough to take as its rule an idea so worthy of respect, is yet too weak to follow it, and employs reason, which ought to give it the law, only for the purpose of providing for the interest of the inclinations, whether singly or at the best in the greatest possible harmony with one another.

In fact, it is absolutely impossible to make out by experience with complete certainty a single case in which the maxim of an action, however right in itself, rested simply on moral grounds and on the conception of duty. Sometimes it happens that with the sharpest self-examination we can find nothing beside the moral principle of duty which could have been powerful enough to move us to this or that action and to so great a sacrifice; yet we cannot from this infer with certainty that it was not really some secret impulse of self-love, under the false appearance of duty, that was the actual determining cause of the will. We like then to flatter ourselves by falsely taking credit for a more noble motive; whereas in fact we can never, even by the strictest examination, get completely behind the secret springs of action; since, when the question is of moral worth, it is not with the actions which we see that we are concerned, but with those inward principles of them which we do not see.

Moreover, we cannot better serve the wishes of those who ridicule all morality as a mere chimera of human imagination overstepping itself from vanity, than by conceding to them that notions of duty must be drawn only from experience (as from indolence, people are ready to think is also the case with all other notions); for this is to prepare for them a certain triumph. I am willing to admit out of love of humanity that even most of our actions are correct, but if we look closer at them we everywhere come upon the dear self which is always prominent, and it is this they have in view, and not the strict command of duty which would often require self-denial. Without being an enemy of virtue, a cool observer, one that does not mistake the wish for good, however lively, for its reality, may sometimes doubt whether true virtue is actually found anywhere in the world, and this especially as years increase and the judgment is partly made wiser by experience, and partly also more acute in observation. This being so, nothing can secure us from falling away altogether from our ideas of duty, or maintain in the soul a well-grounded respect for its law, but the clear conviction that although there should never have been actions which really sprang from such pure sources, yet whether this or that takes place is not at all the question; but that reason of itself, independent on all experience, ordains what ought to take place, that accordingly actions of which perhaps the world has hitherto never given an example, the feasibility even of which might be very much doubted by one who founds everything on experience, are nevertheless inflexibly commanded by reason; that, [for example], even though there might never yet have been a sincere friend, yet not a whit the less is pure sincerity in friendship required of every man, because, prior to all experience, this duty is involved as duty in the idea of a reason determining the will by *à priori* principles.

When we add further that, unless we deny that the notion of morality has any truth or reference to any possible object, we must admit that its law must be valid, not merely for men, but for all *rational creatures generally*, not merely under certain contingent conditions or with exceptions, but *with absolute necessity*, then it is clear that no experience could enable us to infer even the possibility of such apodictic laws. For with what right could we bring into unbounded respect as a universal precept for every rational nature that which perhaps holds only under the contingent conditions of humanity? Or how could laws of the determination of *our* will be regarded as laws of the determination of the will of rational beings generally, and for us only as such, if they were merely empirical, and did not take their origin wholly *à priori* from pure but practical reason?

Nor could anything be more fatal to morality than that we should wish to derive it from examples. For every example of it that is set before me must be first itself tested by principles of morality, whether it is worthy to serve as an original example, *i.e.* as a pattern, but by no means can it authoritatively furnish the conception of morality. Even the Holy One of the Gospels must first be compared with our ideal of moral perfection before we can recognize Him as such; and so He says of Himself, "Why call ye Me [whom you see] good; none is good [the model of good] but God only [whom ye do not see]." But whence have we the conception of God as the supreme good? Simply from the *idea* of moral perfection, which reason frames *à priori*, and connects inseparably with the notion of a free will. Imitation finds no place at all in morality, and examples serve only for encouragement, *i.e.* they put beyond doubt the feasibility of what the law commands, they make visible that which the practical rule expresses more generally, but they can never authorize us to set aside the true original which lies in reason, and to guide ourselves by examples.

.   •   •   •   •   •

From what has been said, it is clear that all moral conceptions have their seat and origin completely *à priori* in the reason, and that, moreover, in the commonest reason just as truly as in that which is in the highest degree speculative; that they cannot be obtained by abstraction from any empirical, and therefore merely contingent knowledge; that it is just this purity of their origin that makes them worthy to serve as our supreme practical principle, and that just in proportion as we add anything empirical, we detract from their genuine influence, and from the absolute value of actions; that it is not only of the greatest necessity, in a purely speculative point of view, but is also of the greatest practical importance, to derive these notions and laws from pure reason, to present them pure and unmixed, and even to determine the compass of this practical or pure rational knowledge, *i.e.* to determine the whole faculty of pure practical reason; and, in doing so, we must not make its principles dependent on the particular nature of human reason, though in speculative philosophy this may be permitted, or may even at times be necessary; but since moral laws ought to hold good for every rational creature, we must derive them from the general concept of a rational being. In this way, although for its *application* to man morality has need of anthropology, yet, in the first instance, we must treat it independently as pure philosophy, *i.e.* as metaphysic, complete in itself (a thing which in such distinct branches of science is easily done); knowing well that unless we are in possession of this, it would not only be vain to determine the moral element of duty in right actions for purposes of speculative criticism, but it would be impossible to base morals on their genuine principles, even for common practical purposes, especially of moral instruction, so as to produce pure moral dispositions, and to engraft them on men's minds to the promotion of the greatest possible good in the world.

But in order that in this study we may not merely advance by the natural steps from the common moral judgment (in this case very worthy of respect) to the philosophical, as has been already done, but also from a popular philosophy, which goes no further than it can reach by groping with the help of examples, to metaphysic (which does not allow itself to be checked by anything empirical, and as it must measure the whole extent of this kind of rational knowledge, goes as far as ideal conceptions, where even examples fail us), we must follow and clearly describe the practical faculty of reason, from the general rules of its determination to the point where the notion of duty springs from it.

[Imperatives: Hypothetical and Categorical]

Everything in nature works according to laws. Rational beings alone have the faculty of acting according *to the conception* of laws, that is according to principles, *i.e.* have a *will*. Since the deduction of actions from principles requires *reason*, the will is nothing but practical reason. If reason infallibly determines the will, then the actions of such a being which are recognized as objectively necessary are subjectively necessary also, *i.e.* the will is a faculty to choose *that only* which reason independent on inclination recognizes as practically necessary, *i.e.* as good. But if reason of itself does not sufficiently determine the will, if the latter is subject also to subjective conditions (particular impulses) which do not always coincide with the objective conditions; in a word, if the will does not *in itself* completely accord with reason (which is actually the case with men), then the actions which objectively are recognized as necessary are subjectively contingent, and the determination of such a will according to objective laws is *obligation*, that is to say, the relation of the objective laws to a will that is not thoroughly good is conceived as the determination of the will of a rational being by principles of reason, but which the will from its nature does not of necessity follow.

The conception of an objective principle, in so far as it is obligatory for a will, is called a command (of reason), and the formula of the command is called an Imperative.

All imperatives are expressed by the word *ought* [or *shall*], and thereby indicate the relation of an objective law of reason to a will, which from its subjective constitution is not necessarily determined by it (an obligation). They say that something would be good to do or to forbear, but they say it to a will which does not always do a thing because it is conceived to be good to do it. That is practically *good*, however, which determines the will by means of the conceptions of reason, and consequently not from subjective causes, but objectively, that is on principles which are valid for every rational being as such. It is distinguished from the *pleasant*, as that which influences the will only by means of sensation from merely subjective causes, valid only for the sense of this or that one, and not as a principle of reason, which holds for every one.

A perfectly good will would therefore be equally subject to objective laws (viz. laws of good), but could not be conceived as *obliged* thereby to act lawfully, because of itself from its subjective constitution it can only be determined by the conception of good. Therefore no imperatives hold for the Divine will, or in general for a *holy* will; *ought* is here out of place, because the volition is already of itself necessarily in unison with the law. Therefore imperatives are only formulæ to express the relation of objective laws of all volition to the subjective imperfection of the will of this or that rational being, *e.g.* the human will.

Now all *imperatives* command either *hypothetically* or *categorically*. The former represent the practical necessity of a possible action as means to something else that is willed (or at least which one might possibly will). The categorical imperative would be that which represented an action as necessary of itself without reference to another end, *i.e.*, as objectively necessary.

Since every practical law represents a possible action as good, and on this account, for a subject who is practically determinable by reason, necessary, all imperatives are formulæ determining an action which is necessary according to the principle of a will good in some respects. If now the action is good only as a means *to something else,* then the imperative is *hypothetical;* if it is conceived as good *in itself* and consequently as being necessarily the principle of a will which of itself conforms to reason, then it is *categorical.*

Thus the imperative declares what action possible by me would be good, and presents the practical rule in relation to a will which does not forthwith perform an action simply because it is good, whether because the subject does not always know that it is good, or because, even if it know this, yet its maxims might be opposed to the objective principles of practical reason.

Accordingly the hypothetical imperative only says that the action is good for some purpose, *possible* or *actual.* In the first case it is a Problematical, in the second an Assertorial practical principle. The categorical imperative which declares an action to be objectively necessary in itself without reference to any purpose, *i.e.* without any other end, is valid as an Apodictic (practical) principle.

Whatever is possible only by the power of some rational being may also be conceived as a possible purpose of some will; and therefore the principles of action as regards the means necessary to attain some possible purpose are in fact infinitely numerous. All sciences have a practical part, consisting of problems expressing that some end is possible for us, and of imperatives directing how it may be attained. These may, therefore, be called in general imperatives of Skill. Here there is no question whether the end is rational and good, but only what one must do in order to attain it. The precepts for the physician to make his patient thoroughly healthy, and for a poisoner to ensure certain death, are of equal value in this respect, that each serves to effect its purpose perfectly. Since in early youth it cannot be known what ends are likely to occur to us in the course of life, parents seek to have their children taught a *great many things,* and provide for their *skill* in the use of means for all sorts of arbitrary ends, of none of which can they determine whether it may not perhaps hereafter be an object to their pupil, but which it is at all events *possible* that he might aim at; and this anxiety is so great that they commonly neglect to form and correct their judgment on the value of the things which may be chosen as ends.

There is *one* end, however, which may be assumed to be actually such to all rational beings (so far as imperatives apply to them, viz. as dependent beings), and, therefore, one purpose which they not merely *may* have, but which we may with certainty assume that they all actually *have* by a natural necessity, and this is *happiness.* The hypothetical imperative which expresses the practical necessity of an action as means to the advancement of happiness is Assertorial. We are not to present it as necessary for an uncertain and merely possible purpose, but for a purpose which we may presuppose with certainty and *à priori* in every man, because it belongs to his being. Now skill in the choice of means to his own greatest well-being may be called *prudence,* in the narrowest sense. And thus the imperative which refers to the choice of means to one's own happiness, *i.e.* the precept of prudence, is still always *hypothetical;* the action is not commanded absolutely, but only as means to another purpose.

Finally, there is an imperative which commands a certain conduct imme-diately, without having as its condition any other purpose to be attained by it. This imperative is Categorical. It concerns not the matter of the action, or its intended result, but its form and the principle of which it is itself a result; and what is essentially good in it consists in the mental disposition, let the conse-quence be what it may. This imperative may be called that of Morality.

There is a marked distinction also between the volitions on these three sorts of principles in the *dissimilarity* of the obligation of the will. In order to mark this difference more clearly, I think they would be most suitably named in their order if we said they are either *rules* of skill, or *counsels* of prudence, or com-*mands* (*laws*) of morality. For it is *law* only that involves the conception of an *unconditional* and objective necessity, which is consequently universally valid; and commands are laws which must be obeyed, that is, must be followed, even in opposition to inclination. *Counsels,* indeed, involve necessity, but one which can only hold under a contingent subjective condition, *viz.* they depend on whether this or that man reckons this or that as part of his happiness; the categorical imperative, on the contrary, is not limited by any condition, and as being absolutely, although practically, necessary, may be quite properly called a command. We might also call the first kind of imperative *technical* (belonging to art), the second *pragmatic* (to welfare), the third *moral* (belonging to free conduct generally, that is, to morals).

[The Rational Ground
of Hypothetical Imperatives]

Now arises the question, how are all these imperatives possible? This question does not seek to know how we can conceive the accomplishment of the action which the imperative ordains, but merely how we can conceive the obligation of the will which the imperative expresses. No special explanation is needed to show how an imperative of skill is possible. Whoever wills the end, wills also (so far as reason decides his conduct) the means in his power which are indispensably necessary thereto. This proposition is, as regards the volition, analytical; for, in willing an object as my effect, there is already thought the causality of myself as an acting cause, that is to say, the use of the means; and the imperative educes from the conception of volition of an end the conception of actions necessary to this end. Synthetical propositions must no doubt be employed in defining the means to a proposed end; but they do not concern the principle, the act of the will, but the object and its realization. [For example], that in order to bisect a line on an unerring principle I must draw from its ex-tremities two intersecting arcs; this no doubt is taught by mathematics only in synthetical propositions; but if I know that it is only by this process that the in-tended operation can be performed, then to say that if I fully will the operation, I also will the action required for it, is an analytical proposition; for it is one and the same thing to conceive something as an effect which I can produce in a cer-tain way, and to conceive myself as acting in this way.

If it were only equally easy to give a definite conception of happiness, the imperatives of prudence would correspond exactly with those of skill, and would likewise be analytical. For in this case as in that, it could be said, whoever wills the end, wills also (according to the dictate of reason necessarily) the indispensable means thereto which are in his power. But, unfortunately, the notion of happiness is so indefinite that although every man wishes to attain it, yet he never can say definitely and consistently what it is that he really wishes and wills. The reason of this is that all the elements which belong to the notion of happiness are altogether empirical, *i.e.* they must be borrowed from experience, and nevertheless the idea of happiness requires an absolute whole, a maximum of welfare in my present and all future circumstances. Now it is impossible that the most clear-sighted and at the same time most powerful being (supposed finite) should frame to himself a definite conception of what he really wills in this. Does he will riches, how much anxiety, envy, and snares might he not thereby draw upon his shoulders? Does he will knowledge and discernment, perhaps it might prove to be only an eye so much the sharper to show him so much the more fearfully the evils that are now concealed from him, and that cannot be avoided, or to impose more wants or his desires, which already give him concern enough. Would he have long life? who guarantees to him that it would not be a long misery? would he at least have health? how often has uneasiness of the body restrained from excesses into which perfect health would have allowed one to fall? and so on. In short, he is unable, on any principle, to determine with certainty what would make him truly happy; because to do so he would need to be omniscient. We cannot therefore act on any definite principles to secure happiness, but only on empirical counsels, [for example] of regimen, frugality, courtesy, reserve, &c., which experience teaches do, on the average, most promote well-being. Hence it follows that the imperatives of prudence do not, strictly speaking, command at all, that is, they cannot present actions objectively as practically *necessary*; that they are rather to be regarded as counsels (*consilia*) than precepts (*præcepta*) of reason, that the problem to determine certainly and universally what action would promote the happiness of a rational being is completely insoluble, and consequently no imperative respecting it is possible which should, in the strict sense, command to do what makes happy; because happiness is not an ideal of reason but of imagination, resting solely on empirical grounds, and it is vain to expect that these should define an action by which one could attain the totality of a series of consequences which is really endless. This imperative of prudence would, however, be an analytical proposition if we assume that the means to happiness could be certainly assigned; for it is distinguished from the imperative of skill only by this, that in the latter the end is merely possible, in the former it is given; as, however, both only ordain the means to that which we suppose to be willed as an end, it follows that the imperative which ordains the willing of the means to him who wills the end is in both cases analytical. Thus there is no difficulty in regard to the possibility of an imperative of this kind either.

[The Rational Ground
of the Categorical Imperative]

On the other hand, the question, how the imperative of *morality* is possible, is undoubtedly one, the only one, demanding a solution, as this is not at all hypothetical, and the objective necessity which it presents cannot rest on any hypothesis, as is the case with the hypothetical imperatives. Only here we must never leave out of consideration that we *cannot* make out *by any example,* in other words empirically, whether there is such an imperative at all; but it is rather to be feared that all those which seem to be categorical may yet be at bottom hypothetical. For instance, when the precept is: Thou shalt not promise deceitfully; and it is assumed that the necessity of this is not a mere counsel to avoid some other evil, so that it should mean: Thou shalt not make a lying promise, lest if it become known thou shouldst destroy thy credit, but that an action of this kind must be regarded as evil in itself, so that the imperative of the prohibition is categorical; then we cannot show with certainty in any example that the will was determined merely by the law, without any other spring of action, although it may appear to be so. For it is always possible that fear of disgrace, perhaps also obscure dread of other dangers, may have a secret influence on the will. Who can prove by experience the non-existence of a cause when all that experience tells us is that we do not perceive it? But in such a case the so-called moral imperative, which as such appears to be categorical and unconditional, would in reality be only a pragmatic precept, drawing our attention to our own interests, and merely teaching us to take these into consideration.

We shall therefore have to investigate *à priori* the possibility of a categorical imperative, as we have not in this case the advantage of its reality being given in experience, so that [the elucidation of] its possibility should be requisite only for its explanation, not for its establishment. In the meantime it may be discerned beforehand that the categorical imperative alone has the purport of a practical law: all the rest may indeed be called *principles* of the will but not laws, since whatever is only necessary for the attainment of some arbitrary purpose may be considered as in itself contingent, and we can at any time be free from the precept if we give up the purpose: on the contrary, the unconditional command leaves the will no liberty to choose the opposite; consequently it alone carries with it that necessity which we require in a law.

Secondly, in the case of this categorical imperative or law of morality, the difficulty (of discerning its possibility) is a very profound one. It is an *à priori* synthetical practical proposition;[2] and as there is so much difficulty in discern-

---

[2] I connect the act with the will without presupposing any condition resulting from any inclination, but *à priori,* and therefore necessarily (though only objectively, *i.e.* assuming the idea of a reason possessing full power over all subjective motives). This is accordingly a practical proposition which does not deduce the willing of an action by mere analysis from another already presupposed (for we have not such a perfect will), but connects it immediately with the conception of the will of a rational being, as something not contained in it.

ing the possibility of speculative propositions of this kind, it may readily be supposed that the difficulty will be no less with the practical.

[First Formulation of the Categorical Imperative: Universal Law]

In this problem we will first inquire whether the mere conception of a categorical imperative may not perhaps supply us also with the formula of it, containing the proposition which alone can be a categorical imperative; for even if we know the tenor of such an absolute command, yet how it is possible will require further special and laborious study, which we postpone to the last section.

When I conceive a hypothetical imperative, in general I do not know beforehand what it will contain until I am given the condition. But when I conceive a categorical imperative, I know at once what it contains. For as the imperative contains besides the law only the necessity that the maxims[3] shall conform to this law, while the law contain no conditions restricting it, there remains nothing but the general statement that the maxim of the action should conform to a universal law, and it is this conformity alone that the imperative properly represents as necessary.

There is therefore but one categorical imperative, namely, this: *Act only on that maxim whereby thou canst at the same time will that it should become a universal law.*

Now if all imperatives of duty can be deduced from this one imperative as from their principle, then, although it should remain undecided whether what is called duty is not merely a vain notion, yet at least we shall be able to show what we understand by it and what this notion means.

Since the universality of the law according to which effects are produced constitutes what is properly called *nature* in the most general sense (as to form), that is the existence of things so far as it is determined by general laws, the imperative of duty may be expressed thus: *Act as if the maxim of thy action were to become by thy will a universal law of nature.*

[Four Illustrations]

We will now enumerate a few duties, adopting the usual division of them into duties to ourselves and to others, and into perfect and imperfect duties.

1. A man reduced to despair by a series of misfortunes feels wearied of life, but is still so far in possession of his reason that he can ask himself whether it would not be contrary to his duty to himself to take his own life. Now he inquires whether the maxim of his action could become a universal law of nature. His maxim is: From self-love I adopt it as a principle to shorten my life

---

[3] A Maxim is a subjective principle of action, and must be distinguished from the *objective principle*, namely, practical law. The former contains the practical rule set by reason according to the conditions of the subject (often its ignorance or its inclinations), so that it is the principle on which the subject *acts;* but the law is the objective principle valid for every rational being, and is the principle on which it *ought to act* that is an imperative.

when its longer duration is likely to bring more evil than satisfaction. It is asked then simply whether this principle founded on self-love can become a universal law of nature. Now we see at once that a system of nature of which it should be a law to destroy life by means of the very feeling whose special nature it is to impel to the improvement of life would contradict itself, and therefore could not exist as a system of nature; hence that maxim cannot possibly exist as a universal law of nature, and consequently would be wholly inconsistent with the supreme principle of all duty.

2. Another finds himself forced by necessity to borrow money. He knows that he will not be able to repay it, but sees also that nothing will be lent to him, unless he promises stoutly to repay it in a definite time. He desires to make this promise, but he has still so much conscience as to ask himself: Is it not un-lawful and inconsistent with duty to get out of a difficulty in this way? Suppose, however, that he resolves to do so, then the maxim of his action would be ex-pressed thus: When I think myself in want of money, I will borrow money and promise to repay it, although I know that I never can do so. Now this principle of self-love or of one's own advantage may perhaps be consistent with my whole future welfare; but the question now is, Is it right? I change then the suggestion of self-love into a universal law, and state the question thus: How would it be if my maxim were a universal law? Then I see at once that it could never hold as a universal law of nature, but would necessarily contradict itself. For supposing it to be a universal law that everyone when he thinks himself in a difficulty should be able to promise whatever he pleases, with the purpose of not keeping his promise, the promise itself would become impossible, as well as the end that one might have in view in it, since no one would consider that anything was promised to him, but would ridicule all such statements as vain pretences.

3. A third finds in himself a talent which with the help of some culture might make him a useful man in many respects. But he finds himself in com-fortable circumstances, and prefers to indulge in pleasure rather than to take pains in enlarging and improving his happy natural capacities. He asks, how-ever, whether his maxim of neglect of his natural gifts, besides agreeing with his inclination to indulgence, agrees also with what is called duty. He sees then that a system of nature could indeed subsist with such a universal law although men (like the South Sea islanders) should let their talents rest, and resolve to devote their lives merely to idleness, amusement, and propagation of their species—in a word, to enjoyment; but he cannot possibly *will* that this should be a universal law of nature, or be implanted in us as such by a natural in-stinct. For, as a rational being, he necessarily wills that his faculties be devel-oped, since they serve him, and have been given him, for all sorts of possible purposes.

4. A fourth, who is in prosperity, while he sees that others have to contend with great wretchedness and that he could help them, thinks: What concern is it of mine? Let everyone be as happy as Heaven pleases, or as he can make himself; I will take nothing from him nor even envy him, only I do not wish to

contribute anything to his welfare or to his assistance in distress! Now no doubt if such a mode of thinking were a universal law, the human race might very well subsist, and doubtless even better than in a state in which everyone talks of sympathy and good-will, or even takes care occasionally to put it into practice, but, on the other side, also cheats when he can, betrays the rights of men, or otherwise violates them. But although it is possible that a universal law of nature might exist in accordance with that maxim, it is impossible to *will* that such a principle should have the universal validity of a law of nature. For a will which resolved this would contradict itself, inasmuch as many cases might occur in which one would have need of the love and sympathy of others, and in which, by such a law of nature, sprung from his own will, he would deprive himself of all hope of the aid he desires.

These are a few of the many actual duties, or at least what we regard as such, which obviously fall into two classes on the one principle that we have laid down. We must be *able to will* that a maxim of our action should be a universal law. This is the canon of the moral appreciation of the action generally. Some actions are of such a character that their maxim cannot without contradiction be even *conceived* as a universal law of nature, far from it being possible that we should *will* that it *should* be so. In others this intrinsic impossibility is not found, but still it is impossible to *will* that their maxim should be raised to the universality of a law of nature, since such a will would contradict itself. It is easily seen that the former violate strict or rigorous (inflexible) duty; the latter only laxer (meritorious) duty. Thus it has been completely shown by these examples how all duties depend as regards the nature of the obligation (not the object of the action) on the same principle.

[Transgressions of the Moral Law]

If now we attend to ourselves on occasion of any transgression of duty, we shall find that we in fact do not will that our maxim should be a universal law, for that is impossible for us; on the contrary, we will that the opposite should remain a universal law, only we assume the liberty of making an *exception* in our own favour or (just for this time only) in favour of our inclination. Consequently if we considered all cases from one and the same point of view, namely, that of reason, we should find a contradiction in our own will, namely, that a certain principle should be objectively necessary as a universal law, and yet subjectively should not be universal, but admit of exceptions. As, however, we at one moment regard our action from the point of view of a will wholly conformed to reason, and then again look at the same action from the point of view of a will affected by inclination, there is not really any contradiction, but an antagonism of inclination to the precept of reason, whereby the universality of the principle is changed into a mere generality, so that the practical principle of reason shall meet the maxim half way. Now, although this cannot be justified in our own impartial judgment, yet it proves that we do really recognize the validity of the categorical imperative and (with all respect for it) only allow ourselves a few exceptions, which we think unimportant and forced from us.

[The Need for an *A Priori* Proof of the Categorical Imperative]

We have thus established at least this much, that if duty is a conception which is to have any import and real legislative authority for our actions, it can only be expressed in categorical, and not at all in hypothetical imperatives. We have also, which is of great importance, exhibited clearly and definitely for every practical application the content of the categorical imperative, which must contain the principle of all duty if there is such a thing at all. We have not yet, however, advanced so far as to prove *à priori* that there actually is such an imperative, that there is a practical law which commands absolutely of itself, and without any other impulse, and that the following of this law is duty.

With the view of attaining to this it is of extreme importance to remember that we must not allow ourselves to think of deducing the reality of this principle from the *particular attributes of human nature*. For duty is to be a practical, unconditional necessity of action; it must therefore hold for all rational beings (to whom an imperative can apply at all), and *for this reason only* be also a law for all human wills. On the contrary, whatever is deduced from the particular natural characteristics of humanity, from certain feelings and propensions, nay, even, if possible, from any particular tendency proper to human reason, and which need not necessarily hold for the will of every rational being; this may indeed supply us with a maxim, but not with a law; with a subjective principle on which we may have a propension and inclination to act, but not with an objective principle on which we should be *enjoined* to act, even though all our propensions, inclinations, and natural dispositions were opposed to it. In fact, the sublimity and intrinsic dignity of the command in duty are so much the more evident, the less subjective impulses favour it and the more they oppose it, without being able in the slightest degree to weaken the obligation of the law or to diminish its validity.

Here then we see philosophy brought to a critical position, since it has to be firmly fixed, notwithstanding that it has nothing to support it in heaven or earth. Here it must show its purity as absolute director of its own laws, not the herald of those which are whispered to it by an implanted sense or who knows what tutelary nature. Although these may be better than nothing, yet they can never afford principles dictated by reason, which must have their source wholly *à priori* and thence their commanding authority, expecting everything from the supremacy of the law and the due respect for it, nothing from inclination, or else condemning the man to self-contempt and inward abhorrence.

Thus every empirical element is not only quite incapable of being an aid to the principle of morality, but is even highly prejudicial to the purity of morals; for the proper and inestimable worth of an absolutely good will consists just in this, that the principle of action is free from all influence of contingent grounds, which alone experience can furnish. We cannot too much or too often repeat our warning against this lax and even mean habit of thought which seeks for its principle amongst empirical motives and laws; for human reason in its weariness is glad to rest on this pillow, and in a dream of sweet illusions (in which, instead of Juno, it embraces a cloud) it substitutes for morality a bastard patched up from limbs of various derivation, which looks like anything one chooses to see in it; only not like virtue to one who has once beheld her in her true form.[4]

The question then is this: Is it a necessary law *for all rational beings* that they should always judge of their actions by maxims of which they can themselves will that they should serve as universal laws? If it is so, then it must be connected (altogether *à priori*) with the very conception of the will of a rational being generally. But in order to discover this connexion we must, however reluctantly, take a step into metaphysic, although into a domain of it which is distinct from speculative philosophy, namely, the metaphysic of morals. In a practical philosophy, where it is not the reasons of what *happens* that we have to ascertain, but the laws of what *ought to happen,* even although it never does, *i.e.* objective practical laws, there it is not necessary to inquire into the reason why anything pleases or displeases, how the pleasure of mere sensation differs from taste, and whether the latter is distinct from a general satisfaction of reason; on what the feeling of pleasure or pain rests, and how from it desires and inclinations arise, and from these again maxims by the co-operation of reason: for all this belongs to an empirical psychology, which would constitute the second part of physics, if we regard physics as the *philosophy* of nature, so far as it is based on *empirical laws.* But here we are concerned with objective practical laws, and consequently with the relation of the will to itself so far as it is determined by reason alone, in which case whatever has reference to anything empirical is necessarily excluded; since if *reason of itself alone* determines the conduct (and it is the possibility of this that we are now investigating), it must necessarily do so *à priori.*

[Second Formulation of the Categorical Imperative: Humanity as an End in Itself]

The will is conceived as a faculty of determining oneself to action *in accordance with the conception of certain laws.* And such a faculty can be found only in rational beings. Now that which serves the will as the objective ground of its self-determination is the *end,* and if this is assigned by reason alone, it must hold for all rational beings. On the other hand, that which merely contains the ground of possibility of the action of which the effect is the end, this is called the *means.* The subjective ground of the desire is the *spring,* the objective ground of the volition is the *motive;* hence the distinction between subjective ends which rest on springs, and objective ends which depend on motives valid for every rational being. Practical principles are *formal* when they abstract from all subjective ends; they are *material* when they assume these, and therefore particular springs of action. The ends which a rational being proposes to himself

---

[4] To behold virtue in her proper form is nothing else but to contemplate morality stripped of all admixture of sensible things and of every spurious ornament of reward or self-love. How much she then eclipses everything else that appears charming to the affections, every one may readily perceive with the least exertion of his reason, if it be not wholly spoiled for abstraction.

at pleasure as *effects* of his actions (material ends) are all only relative, for it is only their relation to the particular desires of the subject that gives them their worth, which therefore cannot furnish principles universal and necessary for all rational beings and for every volition, that is to say practical laws. Hence all these relative ends can give rise only to hypothetical imperatives.

Supposing, however, that there were something *whose existence* has *in itself* an absolute worth, something which, being *an end in itself,* could be a source of definite laws, then in this and and this alone would lie the source of a possible categorical imperative, *i.e.* a practical law.

Now I say: man and generally any rational being *exists* as an end in himself, *not merely as a means* to be arbitrarily used by this or that will, but in all his actions, whether they concern himself or other rational beings, must be always regarded at the same time as an end. All objects of the inclinations have only a conditional worth; for if the inclinations and the wants founded on them did not exist, then their object would be without value. But the inclinations themselves being sources of want are so far from having an absolute worth for which they should be desired, that, on the contrary, it must be the universal wish of every rational being to be wholly free from them. Thus the worth of any object which is *to be acquired* by our action is always conditional. Beings whose existence depends not on our will but on nature's, have nevertheless, if they are nonrational beings, only a relative value as means, and are therefore called *things;* rational beings, on the contrary, are called *persons,* because their very nature points them out as ends in themselves, that is as something which must not be used merely as means, and so far therefore restricts freedom of action (and is an object of respect). These, therefore, are not merely subjective ends whose existence has a worth *for us* as an effect of our action, but *objective ends,* that is things whose existence is an end in itself: an end moreover for which no other can be substituted, which they should subserve *merely* as means, for otherwise nothing whatever would possess *absolute worth;* but if all worth were conditioned and therefore contingent, then there would be no supreme practical principle of reason whatever.

If then there is a supreme practical principle or, in respect of the human will, a categorical imperative, it must be one which, being drawn from the conception of that which is necessarily an end for everyone because it is *an end in itself,* constitutes an *objective* principle of will, and can therefore serve as a universal practical law. The foundation of this principle is: *rational nature exists as an end in itself.* Man necessarily conceives his own existence as being so: so far then this is a *subjective* principle of human actions. But every other rational being regards its existence similarly, just on the same rational principle that holds for me[5]: so that it is at the same time an objective principle, from which as a supreme practical law all laws of the will must be capable of being deduced. Accordingly the practical imperative will be as follows: *So act as to treat humanity, whether in thine own person or in that of any other, in every*

---

[5] This proposition is here stated as a postulate. The ground of it will be found in the concluding section.

case as an end withal, never as means only. We will now inquire whether this can be practically carried out.

[Four Illustrations]

To abide by the previous examples:

Firstly, under the head of necessary duty to oneself: He who contemplates suicide should ask himself whether his action can be consistent with the idea of humanity *as an end in itself.* If he destroys himself in order to escape from painful circumstances, he uses a person merely as *a means* to maintain a tolerable condition up to the end of life. But a man is not a thing, that is to say, something which can be used merely as means, but must in all his actions be always considered as an end in himself. I cannot, therefore, dispose in any way of a man in my own person so as to mutilate him, to damage or kill him. (It belongs to ethics proper to define this principle more precisely, so as to avoid all misunderstanding, *e.g.* as to the amputation of the limbs in order to preserve myself; as to exposing my life to danger with a view to preserve it, &c. This question is therefore omitted here.)

Secondly, as regards necessary duties, or those of strict obligation, towards others; he who is thinking of making a lying promise to others will see at once that he would be using another man *merely as a mean,* without the latter containing at the same time the end in himself. For he whom I propose by such a promise to use for my own purposes cannot possibly assent to my mode of acting towards him, and therefore cannot himself contain the end of this action. This violation of the principle of humanity in other men is more obvious if we take in examples of attacks on the freedom and property of others. For then it is clear that he who transgresses the rights of men intends to use the person of others merely as means, without considering that as rational beings they ought always to be esteemed also as ends, that is, as beings who must be capable of containing in themselves the end of the very same action.[6]

Thirdly, as regards contingent (meritorious) duties to oneself; it is not enough that the action does not violate humanity in our own person as an end in itself, it must also *harmonize with* it. Now there are in humanity capacities of greater perfection which belong to the end that nature has in view in regard to humanity in ourselves as the subject: to neglect these might perhaps be consistent with the *maintenance* of humanity as an end in itself, but not with the *advancement* of this end.

Fourthly, as regards meritorious duties towards others: the natural end which all men have is their own happiness. Now humanity might indeed

---

[6] Let it not be thought that the common: *quod tibi non vis fieri, &c.,* [that which you do not wish to be done to you, do not do to others] could serve here as the rule or principle. For it is only a deduction from the former, though with several limitations; it cannot be a universal law, for it does not contain the principle of duties to oneself, nor of the duties of benevolence to others (for many a one would gladly consent that others should not benefit him, provided only that he might be excused from showing benevolence to them), nor finally that of duties of strict obligation to one another, for on this principle the criminal might argue against the judge who punishes him, and so on.

subsist, although no one should contribute anything to the happiness of others, provided he did not intentionally withdraw anything from it; but after all, this would only harmonize negatively, not positively, with *humanity as an end in itself*, if everyone does not also endeavour, as far as in him lies, to forward the ends of others. For the ends of any subject which is an end in himself, ought as far as possible to be *my* ends also, if that conception is to have its *full* effect with me.

[Third Formulation of the Categorical Imperative: The Autonomy of the Will as Universal Legislator]

This principle, that humanity and generally every rational nature is *an end in itself* (which is the supreme limiting condition of every man's freedom of action), is not borrowed from experience, *firstly*, because it is universal, applying as it does to all rational beings whatever, and experience is not capable of determining anything about them; *secondly*, because it does not present humanity as an end to men (subjectively), that is as an object which men do of themselves actually adopt as an end; but as an objective end, which must as a law constitute the supreme limiting condition of all our subjective ends, let them be what we will; it must therefore spring from pure reason. In fact the objective principle of all practical legislation lies (according to the first principle) in *the rule* and its form of universality which makes it capable of being a law (say, *e.g.*, a law of nature); but the *subjective* principle is in the *end*; now by the second principle the subject of all ends is each rational being inasmuch as it is an end in itself. Hence follows the third practical principle of the will, which is the ultimate condition of its harmony with the universal practical reason, viz.: the idea of *the will of every rational being as a universally legislative will*.

On this principle all maxims are rejected which are inconsistent with the will being itself universal legislator. Thus the will is not subject simply to the law, but so subject that it must be regarded *as itself giving the law*, and on this ground only, subject to the law (of which it can regard itself as the author).

In the previous imperatives, namely, that based on the conception of the conformity of actions to general laws, as in a *physical system of nature*, and that based on the universal *prerogative* of rational beings as *ends* in themselves— these imperatives just because they were conceived as categorical, excluded from any share in their authority all admixture of any interest as a spring of action; they were, however, only *assumed* to be categorical, because such an assumption was necessary to explain the conception of duty. But we could not prove independently that there are practical propositions which command categorically, nor can it be proved in this section; one thing, however, could be done, namely, to indicate in the imperative itself by some determinate expression, that in the case of volition from duty all interest is renounced, which is the specific criterion of categorical as distinguished from hypothetical imperatives. This is done in the present (third) formula of the principle, namely, in the idea of the will of every rational being as a *universally legislating will*.

For although a will *which is subject to laws* may be attached to this law by means of an interest, yet a will which is itself a supreme lawgiver so far as it is such cannot possibly depend on any interest, since a will so dependent would itself still need another law restricting the interest of its self-love by the condition that it should be valid as universal law.

Thus the *principle* that every human will is *a will which in all its maxims gives universal laws,*[7] provided it be otherwise justified, would be very *well adapted* to be the categorical imperative, in this respect, namely, that just because of the idea of universal legislation it is *not based on any interest,* and therefore it alone among all possible imperatives can be *unconditional.* Or still better, converting the proposition, if there is a categorical imperative (*i.e.,* a law for the will of every rational being), it can only command that everything be done from maxims of one's will regarded as a will which could at the same time will that it should itself give universal laws, for in that case only the practical principle and the imperative which it obeys are unconditional, since they cannot be based on any interest.

Looking back now on all previous attempts to discover the principle of morality, we need not wonder why they all failed. It was seen that man was bound to laws by duty, but it was not observed that the laws to which he is subject are *only those of his own giving,* though at the same time they are *universal,* and that he is only bound to act in conformity with his own will; a will, however, which is designed by nature to give universal laws. For when one has conceived man only as subject to a law (no matter what), then this law required some interest, either by way of attraction or constraint, since it did not originate as a law from *his own* will, but this will was according to a law obliged by *something else* to act in a certain manner. Now by this necessary consequence all the labour spent in finding a supreme principle of *duty* was irrevocably lost. For men never elicited duty, but only a necessity of acting from a certain interest. Whether this interest was private or otherwise, in any case the imperative must be conditional, and could not by any means be capable of being a moral command. I will therefore call this the principle of *Autonomy* of the will, in contrast with every other which I accordingly reckon as *Heteronomy.*

[The Kingdom of Ends]

The conception of every rational being as one which must consider itself as giving in all the maxims of its will universal laws, so as to judge itself and its actions from this point of view—this conception leads to another which depends on it and is very fruitful, namely, that of a *kingdom of ends.*

By a *kingdom* I understand the union of different rational beings in a system by common laws. Now since it is by laws that ends are determined as regards their universal validity, hence, if we abstract from the personal differences of rational beings, and likewise from all the content of their private ends, we shall be able to conceive all ends combined in a systematic whole (including

---

[7] I may be excused from adducing examples to elucidate this principle, as those which have already been used to elucidate the categorical imperative and its formula would all serve for the like purpose here.

both rational beings as ends in themselves, and also the special ends which each may propose to himself), that is to say, we can conceive a kingdom of ends, which on the preceding principles is possible.

For all rational beings come under the *law* that each of them must treat itself and all others *never merely as means,* but in every case *at the same time as ends in themselves.* Hence results a systematic union of rational beings by common objective laws, *i.e.,* a kingdom which may be called a kingdom of ends, since what these laws have in view is just the relation of these beings to one another as ends and means. It is certainly only an ideal.

A rational being belongs as a *member* to the kingdom of ends when, although giving universal laws in it, he is also himself subject to these laws. He belongs to it *as sovereign* when, while giving laws, he is not subject to the will of any other.

A rational being must always regard himself as giving laws either as member or as sovereign in a kingdom of ends which is rendered possible by the freedom of will. He cannot, however, maintain the latter position merely by the maxims of his will, but only in case he is a completely independent being without wants and with unrestricted power adequate to his will.

Morality consists then in the reference of all action to the legislation which alone can render a kingdom of ends possible. This legislation must be capable of existing in every rational being, and of emanating from his will, so that the principle of this will is, never to act on any maxim which could not without contradiction be also a universal law, and accordingly always so to act *that the will could at the same time regard itself as giving in its maxims universal laws.* If now the maxims of rational beings are not by their own nature coincident with this objective principle, then the necessity of acting on it is called practical necessitation, i.e. *duty.* Duty does not apply to the sovereign in the kingdom of ends, but it does to every member of it and to all in the same degree.

The practical necessity of acting on this principle, *i.e.* duty, does not rest at all on feelings, impulses, or inclinations, but solely on the relation of rational beings to one another, a relation in which the will of a rational being must always be regarded as *legislative,* since otherwise it could not be conceived as *an end in itself.* Reason then refers every maxim of the will, regarding it as legislating universally, to every other will and also to every action towards oneself; and this not on account of any other practical motive or any future advantage, but from the idea of the *dignity* of a rational being, obeying no law but that which he himself also gives.

In the kingdom of ends everything has either Value or Dignity. Whatever has a value can be replaced by something else which is *equivalent;* whatever, on the other hand, is above all value, and therefore admits of no equivalent, has a dignity.

Whatever has reference to the general inclinations and wants of mankind has a *market value;* whatever, without presupposing a want, corresponds to a certain taste, that is to a satisfaction in the mere purposeless play of our faculties, has a *fancy value;* but that which constitutes the condition under which alone anything can be an end in itself, this has not merely a relative worth, *i.e.* value, but an intrinsic worth, that is *dignity*.

Now morality is the condition under which alone a rational being can be an end in himself, since by this alone it is possible that he should be a legislating member in the kingdom of ends. Thus morality, and humanity as capable of it, is that which alone has dignity. Skill and diligence in labour have a market value; wit, lively imagination, and humour, have fancy value; on the other hand, fidelity to promises, benevolence from principle (not from instinct), have an intrinsic worth. Neither nature nor art contains anything which in default of these it could put in their place, for their worth consists not in the effects which spring from them, not in the use and advantage which they secure, but in the disposition of mind, that is, the maxims of the will which are ready to manifest themselves in such actions, even though they should not have the desired effect. These actions also need no recommendation from any subjective taste or sentiment, that they may be looked on with immediate favour and satisfaction: they need no immediate propension or feeling for them; they exhibit the will that performs them as an object of an immediate respect, and nothing but reason is required to *impose* them on the will; not to *flatter* it into them, which, in the case of duties, would be a contradiction. This estimation therefore shows that the worth of such a disposition is dignity, and places it infinitely above all value, with which it cannot for a moment be brought into comparison or competition without as it were violating its sanctity.

What then is it which justifies virtue or the morally good disposition, in making such lofty claims? It is nothing less than the privilege it secures to the rational being of participating in the giving of universal laws, by which it qualifies him to be a member of a possible kingdom of ends, a privilege to which he was already destined by his own nature as being an end in himself, and on that account legislating in the kingdom of ends; free as regards all laws of physical nature, and obeying those only which he himself gives, and by which his maxims can belong to a system of universal law, to which at the same time he submits himself. For nothing has any worth except what the law assigns it. Now the legislation itself which assigns the worth of everything must for that very reason possess dignity, that is an unconditional incomparable worth; and the word *respect* alone supplies a becoming expression for the esteem which a rational being must have for it. *Autonomy* then is the basis of the dignity of human and of every rational nature.

●　　●　　●　　●　　●

The Autonomy of the Will as the Supreme Principle of Morality

Autonomy of the will is that property of it by which it is a law to itself (independently on any property of the objects of volition). The principle of autonomy then is: Always so to choose that the same volition shall comprehend the maxims of our choice as a universal law. We cannot prove that this practical rule is an imperative, *i.e.*, that the will of every rational being is necessarily bound to it as a condition, by a mere analysis of the conceptions which occur in it, since it is a synthetical proposition; we must advance beyond the cognition of the objects to a critical examination of the subject, that is of the pure practical reason, for this synthetic proposition which commands apodictically must be capable of being cognized wholly *à priori*. This matter, however, does not belong to the present section. But that the principle of autonomy in question is the sole principle of morals can be readily shown by mere analysis of the conceptions of morality. For by this analysis we find that its principle must be a categorical imperative, and that what this commands is neither more nor less than this very autonomy.

Heteronomy of the Will as the Source of all Spurious Principles of Morality
If the will seeks the law which is to determine it *anywhere else* than in the fitness of its maxims to be universal laws of its own dictation, consequently if it goes out of itself and seeks this law in the character of any of its objects, there always results *heteronomy*. The will in that case does not give itself the law, but it is given by the object through its relation to the will. This relation, whether it rests on inclination or on conceptions of reason, only admits of hypothetical imperatives: I ought to do something *because I wish for something else*. On the contrary, the moral, and therefore categorical, imperative says: I ought to do so and so, even though I should not wish for anything else. [For example], the former says: I ought not to lie if I would retain my reputation; the latter says: I ought not to lie although it should not bring me the least discredit. The latter therefore must so far abstract from all objects that they shall have no *influence* on the will, in order that practical reason (will) may not be restricted to administering an interest not belonging to it, but may simply show its own commanding authority as the supreme legislation. Thus, [for example], I ought to endeavour to promote the happiness of others, not as if its realization involved any concern of mine (whether by immediate inclination or by any satisfaction indirectly gained through reason), but simply because a maxim which excludes it cannot be comprehended as a universal law in one and the same volition.

● ● ● ● ●

THIRD SECTION:
TRANSITION FROM THE METAPHYSIC OF MORALS
TO THE CRITIQUE OF PURE PRACTICAL REASON

The Concept of Freedom Is the Key that Explains the Autonomy of the Will
The will is a kind of causality belonging to living beings in so far as they are rational, and *freedom* would be this property of such causality that it can be efficient, independently on foreign causes *determining* it; just as *physical necessity* is the property that the causality of all irrational beings has of being determined to activity by the influence of foreign causes.

The preceding definition of freedom is *negative,* and therefore unfruitful for the discovery of its essence; but it leads to a *positive* conception which is so much the more full and fruitful. Since the conception of causality involves that of laws, according to which, by something that we call cause, something else, namely, the effect, must be produced [laid down]; hence, although freedom is not a property of the will depending on physical laws, yet it is not for that reason lawless; on the contrary, it must be a causality acting according to immutable laws, but a peculiar kind; otherwise a free will would be an absurdity. Physical necessity is a heteronomy of the efficient causes, for every effect is possible only according to this law, that something else determines the efficient cause to exert its causality. What else then can freedom of the will be but autonomy, that is the property of the will to be a law to itself? But the proposition: The will is in every action a law to itself, only expresses the principle, to act on no other maxim than that which can also have as an object itself as a universal law. Now this is precisely the formula of the categorical imperative and is the principle of morality, so that a free will and a will subject to moral laws are one and the same.

On the hypothesis, then, of freedom of the will, morality together with its principle follows from it by mere analysis of the conception. However, the latter is a synthetic proposition; viz., an absolutely good will is that whose maxim can always include itself regarded as a universal law; for this property of its maxim can never be discovered by analysing the conception of an absolutely good will. Now such synthetic propositions are only possible in this way: that the two cognitions are connected together by their union with a third in which they are both to be found. The *positive* concept of freedom furnishes this third cognition, which cannot, as with physical causes, be the nature of the sensible world (in the concept of which we find conjoined the concept of something in relation as cause to *something else* as effect). We cannot now at once show what this third is to which freedom points us, and of which we have an idea *à priori,* nor can we make intelligible how the concept of freedom is shown to be legitimate from principles of pure practical reason, and with it the possibility of a categorical imperative; but some further preparation is required.

Freedom Must Be Presupposed as a Property of the Will of All Rational Beings
It is not enough to predicate freedom of our own will, from whatever reason, if we have not sufficient grounds for predicating the same of all rational beings. For as morality serves as a law for us only because we are *rational beings,* it must also hold for all rational beings; and as it must be deduced simply from the property of freedom, it must be shown that freedom also is a property of all rational beings. It is not enough, then, to prove it from certain supposed experiences of human nature (which indeed is quite impossible, and it can only be shown *à priori*), but we must show that it belongs to the activity of all rational beings endowed with a will. Now I say every being that cannot act except *under the idea of freedom* is just for that reason in a practical point of view really free, that is to say, all laws which are inseparably connected with freedom have the same force for him as if his will had been shown to be free in

itself by a proof theoretically conclusive.[8] Now I affirm that we must attribute to every rational being which has a will that it has also the idea of freedom and acts entirely under this idea. For in such a being we conceive a reason that is practical, that is, has causality in reference to its objects. Now we cannot possibly conceive a reason consciously receiving a bias from any other quarter with respect to its judgments, for then the subject would ascribe the determination of its judgment not to its own reason, but to an impulse. It must regard itself as the author of its principles independent on foreign influences. Consequently as practical reason or as the will of a rational being it must regard itself as free, that is to say, the will of such a being cannot be a will of its own except under the idea of freedom. This idea must therefore in a practical point of view be ascribed to every rational being.

Of the Interest Attaching to the Ideas of Morality

We have finally reduced the definite conception of morality to the idea of freedom. This latter, however, we could not prove to be actually a property of ourselves or of human nature; only we saw that it must be presupposed if we would conceive a being as rational and conscious of its causality in respect of its actions, i.e., as endowed with a will; and so we find that on just the same grounds we must ascribe to every being endowed with reason and will this attribute of determining itself to action under the idea of its freedom.

Now it resulted also from the presupposition of this idea that we became aware of a law that the subjective principles of action, i.e. maxims, must also be so assumed that they can also hold as objective, that is, universal principles, and so serve as universal laws of our own dictation. But why, then, should I subject myself to this principle and that simply as a rational being, thus also subjecting to it all other beings endowed with reason? I will allow that no interest urges me to this, for that would not give a categorical imperative, but I must take an interest in it and discern how this comes to pass; for this "I ought" is properly an "I would," valid for every rational being, provided only that reason determined his actions without any hindrance. But for beings that are in addition affected as we are by springs of a different kind, namely sensibility, and in whose case that is not always done which reason alone would do, for these that necessity is expressed only as an "ought," and the subjective necessity is different from the objective.

It seems, then, as if the moral law, that is, the principle of autonomy of the will, were properly speaking only presupposed in the idea of freedom, and as if we could not prove its reality and objective necessity independently. In that case we should still have gained something considerable by at least determining the

---

[8] I adopt this method of assuming freedom merely as an idea which rational beings suppose in their actions, in order to avoid the necessity of proving it in its theoretical aspect also. The former is sufficient for my purpose; for even though the speculative proof should not be made out, yet a being that cannot act except with the idea of freedom is bound by the same laws that would oblige a being who was actually free. Thus we can escape here from the onus which presses on the theory.

true principle more exactly than had previously been done; but as regards its validity and the practical necessity of subjecting oneself to it, we should not have advanced a step. For if we were asked why the universal validity of our maxim as a law must be the condition restricting our actions, and on what we ground the worth which we assign to this matter of acting—a worth so great that there cannot be any higher interest; and if we were asked further how it happens that it is by this alone a man believes he feels his own personal worth, in comparison with which that of an agreeable or disagreeable condition is to be regarded as nothing, to these questions we could give no satisfactory answer.

We find indeed sometimes that we can take an interest in a personal quality which does not involve any interest of external condition, provided this quality makes us capable of participating in the condition in case reason were to effect the allotment; that is to say, the mere being worthy of happiness can interest of itself even without the motive of participating in this happiness. This judgment, however, is in fact only the effect of the importance of the moral law which we before presupposed (when by the idea of freedom we detach ourselves from every empirical interest); but that we ought to detach ourselves from these interests, *i.e.,* to consider ourselves as free in action and yet as subject to certain laws, so as to find a worth simply in our own person which can compensate us for the loss of everything that gives worth to our condition; this we are not yet able to discern in this way, nor do we see how it is possible so to act—in other words, *whence the moral law derives its obligation.*

It must be freely admitted that there is a sort of circle here from which it seems impossible to escape. In the order of efficient causes we assume ourselves free, in order that in the order of ends we may conceive ourselves as subject to moral laws: and we afterwards conceive ourselves as subject to these laws, because we have attributed to ourselves freedom of will: for freedom and self-legislation of will are both autonomy, and therefore are reciprocal conceptions, and for this very reason one must not be used to explain the other or give the reason of it, but at most only for logical purposes to reduce apparently different notions of the same object to one single concept (as we reduce different fractions of the same value to the lowest terms).

[The Two Points of View]

One resource remains to us, namely, to inquire whether we do not occupy different points of view when by means of freedom we think ourselves as causes efficient *à priori,* and when we form our conception of ourselves from our actions as effects which we see before our eyes.

It is a remark which needs no subtle reflection to make, but which we may assume that even the commonest understanding can make, although it be after its fashion by an obscure discernment of judgment which it calls feeling, that all the "ideas" that come to us involuntarily (as those of the senses) do not enable us to know objects otherwise than as they affect us; so that what they may be in themselves remains unknown to us, and consequently that as regards "ideas" of this kind even with the closest attention and clearness that the understanding can apply to them, we can by them only attain to the knowledge of *appearances,* never to that of *things in themselves.* As soon as this distinction has once been made (perhaps merely in consequence of the difference observed between the ideas given us from without, and in which we are passive, and those that we produce simply from ourselves, and in which we show our own activity), then it follows of itself that we must admit and assume behind the appearance something else that is not an appearance, namely, the things in themselves; although we must admit that as they can never be known to us except as they affect us, we can come no nearer to them, nor can we ever know what they are in themselves. This must furnish a distinction, however crude, between a *world of sense* and the *world of understanding,* of which the former may be different according to the difference of the sensuous impressions in various observers, while the second which is its basis always remains the same. Even as to himself, a man cannot pretend to know what he is in himself from the knowledge he has by internal sensation. For as he does not as it were create himself, and does not come by the conception of himself *à priori* but empirically, it naturally follows that he can obtain his knowledge even of himself only by the inner sense, and consequently only through the appearances of his nature and the way in which his consciousness is affected. At the same time beyond these characteristics of his own subject, made up of mere appearances, he must necessarily suppose something else as their basis, namely, his *ego,* whatever its characteristics in itself may be. Thus in respect to mere perception and receptivity of sensations he must reckon himself as belonging to the *world of sense;* but in respect of whatever there may be of pure activity in him (that which reaches consciousness immediately and not through affecting the senses) he must reckon himself as belonging to the *intellectual world,* of which, however, he has no further knowledge. To such a conclusion the reflecting man must come with respect to all the things which can be presented to him: it is probably to be met with even in persons of the commonest understanding, who, as is well known, are very much inclined to suppose behind the objects of the senses something else invisible and acting of itself. They spoil it, however, by presently sensualizing this invisible again; that is to say, wanting to make it an object of intuition, so that they do not become a whit the wiser.

Now man really finds in himself a faculty by which he distinguishes himself from everything else, even from himself as affected by objects, and that is *Reason.* This being pure spontaneity is even elevated above the *understanding.* For although the latter is a spontaneity and does not, like sense, merely contain intuitions that arise when we are affected by things (and are therefore passive), yet it cannot produce from its activity any other conceptions than those which merely serve *to bring the intuitions of sense under rules,* and thereby to unite them in one consciousness, and without this use of the sensibility it could not think at all; whereas, on the contrary, Reason shows so pure a spontaneity in the case of what I call Ideas [Ideal Conceptions] that it thereby far transcends everything that the sensibility can give it, and exhibits its most important function in distinguishing the world of sense from that of understanding, and thereby prescribing the limits of the understanding itself.

For this reason a rational being must regard himself *qua* intelligence (not from the side of his lower faculties) as belonging not to the world of sense, but to that of understanding; hence he has two points of view from which he can regard himself, and recognize laws of the exercise of his faculties, and consequently of all his actions: *first,* so far as he belongs to the world of sense, he finds himself subject to laws of nature (heteronomy); *secondly,* as belonging to the intelligible world, under laws which, being independent on nature, have their foundation not in experience but in reason alone.

As a reasonable being, and consequently belonging to the intelligible world, man can never conceive the causality of his own will otherwise than on condition of the idea of freedom, for independence on the determining causes of the sensible world (an independence which Reason must always ascribe to itself) is freedom. Now the idea of freedom is inseparably connected with the conception of *autonomy,* and this again with the universal principle of morality which is ideally the foundation of all actions of *rational* beings, just as the law of nature is of all phenomena.

Now the suspicion is removed which we raised above, that there was a latent circle involved in our reasoning from freedom to autonomy, and from this to the moral law, [namely]: that we laid down the idea of freedom because of the moral law only that we might afterwards in turn infer the latter from freedom, and that consequently we could assign no reason at all for this law, but could only [present] it as a *petitio principii*[9] which well-disposed minds would gladly concede to us, but which we could never put forward as a provable proposition. For now we see that when we conceive ourselves as free we transfer ourselves into the world of understanding as members of it, and recognize the autonomy of the will with its consequence, morality; whereas, if we conceive ourselves as under obligation, we consider ourselves as belonging to the world of sense, and at the same time to the world of understanding.

How Is a Categorical Imperative Possible?

Every rational being reckons himself *qua* intelligence as belonging to the world of understanding, and it is simply as an efficient cause belonging to that world that he calls his causality a *will.* On the other side he is also conscious of himself as a part of the world of sense in which his actions, which are mere appearances [phenomena] of that causality, are displayed; we cannot, however, discern how they are possible from this causality which we do not know; but instead of that, these actions as belonging to the sensible world must be viewed as determined by other phenomena, namely, desires and inclinations. If therefore I were only a member of the world of understanding, then all my actions would perfectly conform to the principle of autonomy of the pure will; if I were only a part of the world of sense, they would necessarily be assumed to conform wholly to the

---

[9] [a begging of the question—Ed. note.]

natural laws of desires and inclinations, in other words, to the heteronomy of nature. (The former would rest on morality as the supreme principle, the latter on happiness.) Since, however, *the world of understanding contains the foundation of the world of sense, and consequently of its laws also,* and accordingly gives the law to my will (which belongs wholly to the world of understanding) directly, and must be conceived as doing so, it follows that, although on the one side I must regard myself as a being belonging to the world of sense, yet on the other side I must recognize myself as subject as an intelligence to the law of the world of understanding, *i.e.* to reason, which contains this law in the idea of freedom, and therefore as subject to the autonomy of the will: consequently I must regard the laws of the world of understanding as imperatives for me, and the actions which conform to them as duties.

And thus what makes categorical imperatives possible is this, that the idea of freedom makes me a member of an intelligible world, in consequence of which, if I were nothing else, all my actions *would* always conform to the autonomy of the will; but as I at the same time intuite myself as a member of the world of sense, they *ought* so to conform, and this *categorical* "ought" implies a synthetic *à priori* proposition, inasmuch as besides my will as affected by sensible desires there is added further the idea of the same will, but as belonging to the world of the understanding, pure and practical of itself, which contains the supreme condition according to Reason of the former will; precisely as to the intuitions of sense there are added concep.s of the understanding which of themselves signify nothing but regular form in general, and in this way synthetic *à priori* propositions become possible, on which all knowledge of physical nature rests.

The practical use of common human reason confirms this reasoning. There is no one, not even the most consummate villain, provided only that he is otherwise accustomed to the use of reason, who, when we set before him examples of honesty of purpose, of steadfastness in following good maxims, of sympathy and general benevolence (even combined with great sacrifices of advantages and comfort), does not wish that he might also possess these qualities. Only on account of his inclinations and impulses he cannot attain this in himself, but at the same time he wishes to be free from such inclinations which are burdensome to himself. He proves by this that he transfers himself in thought with a will free from the impulses of the sensibility into an order of things wholly different from that of his desires in the field of the sensibility; since he cannot expect to obtain by that wish any gratification of his desires nor any position which would satisfy any of his actual or supposable inclinations (for this would destroy the pre-eminence of the very idea which wrests that wish from him): he can only expect a greater intrinsic worth of his own person. This better person, however, he imagines himself to be when he transfers himself to the point of view of a member of the world of the understanding, to which he is involuntarily forced by the idea of freedom, *i.e.,* of independence on *determining* causes of the world of sense; and from this point of view he is conscious of a good will, which by his own confession constitutes the law for the bad will that he possesses as a member of the world of sense—a law whose authority he recognizes while transgressing it. What he morally "ought" is then what he necessarily "would" as a member of the world of the understanding, and is conceived by him as an "ought" only inasmuch as he likewise considers himself as a member of the world of sense.

On the Extreme Limits of all Practical Philosophy

• • • • •

The claims to freedom of will made even by common reason are founded on the consciousness and the admitted supposition that reason is independent on merely subjectively determined causes which together constitute what belongs to sensation only and which consequently come under the general designation of sensibility. Man considering himself in this way as an intelligence places himself thereby in a different order of things and in a relation to determining grounds of a wholly different kind when on the one hand he thinks of himself as an intelligence endowed with a will, and consequently with causality, and when on the other he perceives himself as a phenomenon in the world of sense (as he really is also), and affirms that his causality is subject to external determination according to laws of nature. Now he soon becomes aware that both can hold good, nay, must hold good at the same time. For there is not the smallest contradiction in saying that a *thing in appearance* (belonging to the world of sense) is subject to certain laws, on which the very same *as a thing* or being *in itself* is independent; and that he must conceive and think of himself in this two-fold way, rests as to the first on the consciousness of himself as an object affected through the senses, and as to the second on the consciousness of himself as an intelligence, *i.e.*, as independent on sensible impressions in the employ-ment of his reason (in other words as belonging to the world of understanding).

Hence it comes to pass that man claims the possession of a will which takes no account of anything that comes under the head of desires and inclinations, and on the contrary conceives actions as possible to him, nay, even as necessary, which can only be done by disregarding all desires and sensible inclinations. The causality of such actions lies in him as an intelligence and in the laws of effects and actions [which depend] on the principles of an intelligible world, of which indeed he knows nothing more than that in it pure reason alone inde-pendent on sensibility gives the law; moreover since it is only in that world, as an intelligence, that he is his proper self (being as man only the appearance of himself) those laws apply to him directly and categorically, so that the incitements of inclinations and appetites (in other words the whole nature of the world of sense) cannot impair the laws of his volition as an intelligence. Nay, he does not even hold himself responsible for the former or ascribe them to his proper self, *i.e.*, his will: he only ascribes to his will any indulgence which he might yield them if he allowed them to influence his maxims to the prejudice of the rational laws of the will.

When practical Reason *thinks* itself into a world of understanding, it does not thereby transcend its own limits, as it would if it tried to enter it by *intuition* or *sensation*. The former is only a negative thought in respect of the world of sense, which does not give any laws to reason in determining the will, and is positive only in this single point that this freedom as a negative characteristic is at the same time conjoined with a (positive) faculty and even with a causality of reason, which we designate a will, namely, a faculty of so acting that the principle of the actions shall conform to the essential character of a rational motive, *i.e.*, the condition that the maxim have universal validity as a law. But were it to borrow an *object of will,* that is, a motive, from the world of understanding, then it would overstep its bounds and pretend to be acquainted with something of which it knows nothing. The conception of a world of the understanding is then only a *point of view* which Reason finds itself compelled to take outside the appearances in order to *conceive itself as practical,* which would not be possible if the influences of the sensibility had a determining power on man, but which is necessary unless he is to be denied the consciousness of himself as an intelligence, and consequently as a rational cause, energizing by reason, that is, operating freely. This thought certainly involves the idea of an order and a system of laws different from that of the mechanism of nature which belongs to the sensible world; and it makes the conception of an intelligible world necessary (that is to say, the whole system of rational beings as things in themselves). But it does not in the least authorize us to think of it further than as to its *formal* condition only, that is, the universality of the maxims of the will as laws, and consequently the autonomy of the latter, which alone is consistent with its freedom; whereas, on the contrary, all laws that refer to a definite object give heteronomy, which only belongs to laws of nature, and can only apply to the sensible world.

But Reason would overstep all its bounds if it undertook to *explain how* pure reason can be practical, which would be exactly the same problem as to explain *how freedom is possible.*

For we can explain nothing but that which we can reduce to laws, the object of which can be given in some possible experience. But freedom is a mere Idea [Ideal Conception], the objective reality of which can in no wise be shown according to laws of nature, and consequently not in any possible experience; and for this reason it can never be comprehended or understood, because we cannot support it by any sort of example or analogy. It holds good only as a necessary hypothesis of reason in a being that believes itself conscious of a will, that is, of a faculty distinct from mere desire (namely, a faculty of determining itself to action as an intelligence, in other words, by laws of reason independently on natural instincts). Now where determination according to laws of nature ceases, there all *explanation* ceases also, and nothing remains but *defence,* i.e., the removal of the objections of those who pretend to have seen deeper into the nature of things, and thereupon boldly declare freedom impossible. We can only point out to them that the supposed contradiction that they have discovered in it arises only from this, that in order to be able to apply the law of nature to human actions, they must necessarily consider man as an appearance: then when we demand of them that they should also think of him *qua* intelligence as a thing in itself, they still persist in considering him in this respect also as an appearance. In this view it would no doubt be a contradiction to suppose the causality of the same subject (that is, his will) to be withdrawn from all the natural laws of the sensible world. But this contradiction disappears, if they would only bethink themselves and admit, as is reasonable, that behind the appearances there must also lie at their root (although hidden) the things in themselves, and that we cannot expect the laws of these to be the same as those that govern their appearances.

• • • • •

The question then: How a categorical imperative is possible can be answered to this extent that we can assign the only hypothesis on which it is possible, namely, the idea of freedom; and we can also discern the necessity of this hypothesis, and this is sufficient for the *practical exercise* of reason, that is, for the conviction of the *validity of this imperative,* and hence of the moral law; but how this hypothesis itself is possible can never be discerned by any human reason. On the hypothesis, however, that the will of an intelligence is free, its *autonomy,* as the essential formal condition of its determination, is a necessary consequence.

WILLIAM DAVID ROSS
Prima Facie Duties

. . . A . . . theory has been put forward by Professor Moore: that what makes actions right is that they are productive of more *good* than could have been produced by any other action open to the agent.

This theory is in fact the culmination of all the attempts to base rightness on productivity of some sort of result. The first form this attempt takes is the attempt to base rightness on conduciveness to the advantage or pleasure of the agent. This theory comes to grief over the fact, which stares us in the face, that a great part of duty consists in an observance of the rights and a furtherance of the interests of others, whatever the cost to ourselves may be. Plato and others may be right in holding that a regard for the rights of others never in the long run involves a loss of happiness for the agent, that 'the just life profits a man'. But

From W. D. Ross, *The Right and the Good* (1930). Reprinted by permission of The Clarendon Press, Oxford.

this, even if true, is irrelevant to the rightness of the act. As soon as a man does an action *because* he thinks he will promote his own interests thereby, he is acting not from a sense of its rightness but from self-interest.

To the egoistic theory hedonistic utilitarianism supplies a much-needed amendment. It points out correctly that the fact that a certain pleasure will be enjoyed by the agent is no reason why he *ought* to bring it into being rather than an equal or greater pleasure to be enjoyed by another, though, human nature being what it is, it makes it not unlikely that he *will* try to bring it into being. But hedonistic utilitarianism in its turn needs a correction. On reflection it seems clear that pleasure is not the only thing in life that we think good in itself, that for instance we think the possession of a good character, or an intelligent understanding of the world, as good or better. A great advance is made by the substitution of 'productive of the greatest good' for 'productive of the greatest pleasure'.

Not only is this theory more attractive than hedonistic utilitarianism, but its logical relation to that theory is such that the latter could not be true unless *it* were true, while it might be true though hedonistic utilitarianism were not. It is in fact one of the logical bases of hedonistic utilitarianism. For the view that what produces the maximum pleasure is right has for its bases the views (1) that what produces the maximum good is right, and (2) that pleasure is the only thing good in itself. If they were not assuming that what produces the maximum *good* is right, the utilitarians' attempt to show that pleasure is the only thing good in itself, which is in fact the point they take most pains to establish, would have been quite irrelevant to their attempt to prove that only what produces the maximum *pleasure* is right. If, therefore, it can be shown that productivity of the maximum good is not what makes all right actions right, we shall *a fortiori* have refuted hedonistic utilitarianism.

When a plain man fulfils a promise because he thinks he ought to do so, it seems clear that he does so with no thought of its total consequences, still less with any opinion that these are likely to be the best possible. He thinks in fact much more of the past than of the future. What makes him think it right to act in a certain way is the fact that he has promised to do so—that and, usually, nothing more. That his act will produce the best possible consequences is not his reason for calling it right. What lends colour to the theory we are examining, then, is not the actions (which form probably a great majority of our actions) in which some such reflection as 'I have promised' is the only reason we give ourselves for thinking a certain action right, but the exceptional cases in which the consequences of fulfilling a promise (for instance) would be so disastrous to others that we judge it right not to do so. It must of course be admitted that such cases exist. If I have promised to meet a friend at a particular time for some trivial purpose, I should certainly think myself justified in breaking my engagement if by doing so I could prevent a serious accident or bring relief to the victims of one. And the supporters of the view we are examining hold that my thinking so is due to my thinking that I shall bring more good into existence by the one action than by the other. A different account may, however, be given of the matter, an account which will, I believe, show itself to be the true one. It may be said that besides the duty of fulfilling promises I have and recognize a duty of relieving distress,[1] and that when I think it right to do the latter at the cost of not doing the former, it is not because I think I shall produce more good thereby but because I think it the duty which is in the circumstances more of a duty. This account surely corresponds much more closely with what we really think in such a situation. If, so far as I can see, I could bring equal amounts of good into being by fulfilling my promise and by helping some one to whom I had made no promise, I should not hesitate to regard the former as my duty. Yet on the view that what is right is right because it is productive of the most good I should not so regard it.

There are two theories, each in its way simple, that offer a solution of such cases of conscience. One is the view of Kant, that there are certain duties of perfect obligation, such as those of fulfilling promises, of paying debts, of telling the truth, which admit of no exception whatever in favour of duties of imperfect obligation, such as that of relieving distress. The other is the view of, for instance, Professor Moore and Dr. Rashdall, that there is only the duty of producing good, and that all 'conflicts of duties' should be resolved by asking 'by which action will most good be produced?' But it is more important that our theory fit the facts than that it be simple, and the account we have given above corresponds (it seems to me) better than either of the simpler theories with what we really think, viz. that normally promise-keeping, for example, should come before benevolence, but that when and only when the good to be produced by the benevolent act is very great and the promise comparatively trivial, the act of benevolence becomes our duty.

In fact the theory of 'ideal utilitarianism', if I may for brevity refer so to the theory of Professor Moore, seems to simplify unduly our relations to our fellows. It says, in effect, that the only morally significant relation in which my neighbours stand to me is that of being possible beneficiaries by my action.[2] They do stand in this relation to me, and this relation is morally significant. But they may also stand to me in the relation of promisee to promiser, of creditor to debtor, of wife to husband, of child to parent, of friend to friend, of fellow countryman to fellow countryman, and the like; and each of these relations is the foundation of a *prima facie* duty, which is more or less incumbent on me according to the circumstances of the case. When I am in a situation, as perhaps I always am, in which more than one of these *prima facie* duties is incumbent on me, what I have to do is to study the situation as fully as I can until I form the considered opinion (it is never more) that in the circumstances one of them is more incumbent than any other; then I am bound to think that to do this *prima facie* duty is my duty *sans phrase* in the situation.

[1] These are not strictly speaking duties, but things that tend to be our duty, or *prima facie* duties. Cf. below.
[2] Some will think it, apart from other considerations, a sufficient refutation of this view to point out that I also stand in that relation to myself, so that for this view the distinction of oneself from others is morally insignificant.

252 DEONTOLOGICAL ETHICS AND CRITICISMS OF UTILITARIANISM

I suggest '*prima facie* duty' or 'conditional duty' as a brief way of referring to the characteristic (quite distinct from that of being a duty proper) which an act has, in virtue of being of a certain kind (e.g. the keeping of a promise), of being an act which would be a duty proper if it were not at the same time of another kind which is morally significant. Whether an act is a duty proper or actual duty depends on *all* the morally significant kinds it is an instance of. The phrase '*prima facie* duty' must be apologized for, since (1) it suggests that what we are speaking of is a certain kind of duty, whereas it is in fact not a duty, but something related in a special way to duty. Strictly speaking, we want not a phrase in which duty is qualified by an adjective, but a separate noun. (2) '*Prima*' *facie* suggests that one is speaking only of an appearance which a moral situation presents at first sight, and which may turn out to be illusory; whereas what I am speaking of is an objective fact involved in the nature of the situation, or more strictly in an element of its nature, though not, as duty proper does, arising from its *whole* nature. I can, however, think of no term which fully meets the case. 'Claim' has been suggested by Professor Prichard. The word 'claim' has the advantage of being quite a familiar one in this connexion, and it seems to cover much of the ground. It would be quite natural to say, 'a person to whom I have made a promise has a claim on me', and also, 'a person whose distress I could relieve (at the cost of breaking the promise) has a claim on me'. But (1) while 'claim' is appropriate from *their* point of view, we want a word to express the corresponding fact from the agent's point of view—the fact of his being subject to claims that can be made against him; and ordinary language provides us with no such correlative to 'claim'. And (2) (what is more important) 'claim' seems inevitably to suggest two persons, one of whom might make a claim on the other; and while this covers the ground of social duty, it is inappropriate in the case of that important part of duty which is the duty of cultivating a certain kind of character in oneself. It would be artificial, I think, and at any rate metaphorical, to say that one's character has a claim on oneself.

There is nothing arbitrary about these *prima facie* duties. Each rests on a definite circumstance which cannot seriously be held to be without moral significance. Of *prima facie* duties I suggest, without claiming completeness or finality for it, the following division.[3]

(1) Some duties rest on previous acts of my own. These duties seem to include two kinds, (*a*) those resting on a promise or what may fairly be called

---

[3] I should make it plain at this stage that I am *assuming* the correctness of some of our main convictions as to *prima facie* duties, or, more strictly, am claiming that we *know* them to be true. To me it seems as self-evident as anything could be, that to make a promise, for instance, is to create a moral claim on us in someone else. Many readers will perhaps say that they do *not* know this to be true. If so, I certainly cannot prove it to them; I can only ask them to reflect again, in the hope that they will ultimately agree that they also know it to be true. The main moral convictions of the plain man seem to me to be, not opinions which it is for philosophy to prove or disprove, but knowledge from the start; and in my own case I seem to find little difficulty in distinguishing these essential convictions from other moral convictions which I also have, which are merely fallible opinions based on an imperfect study of the working for good or evil of certain institutions or types of action.

an implicit promise, such as the implicit undertaking not to tell lies which seems to be implied in the act of entering into conversation (at any rate by civilized men), or of writing books that purport to be history and not fiction. These may be called the duties of fidelity. (*b*) Those resting on a previous wrongful act. These may be called the duties of reparation. (2) Some rest on previous acts of other men, i.e. services done by them to me. These may be loosely described as the duties of gratitude. (3) Some rest on the fact or possibility of a distribution of pleasure or happiness (or of the means thereto) which is not in accordance with the merit of the persons concerned; in such cases there arises a duty to upset or prevent such a distribution. These are the duties of justice. (4) Some rest on the mere fact that there are other beings in the world whose condition we can make better in respect of virtue, or of intelligence, or of pleasure. These are the duties of beneficence. (5) Some rest on the fact that we can improve our own condition in respect of virtue or of intelligence. These are the duties of self-improvement. (6) I think that we should distinguish from (4) the duties that may be summed up under the title of 'not injuring others'. No doubt to injure others is incidentally to fail to do them good; but it seems to me clear that non-maleficence is apprehended as a duty distinct from that of beneficence, and as a duty of a more stringent character. It will be noticed that this alone among the types of duty has been stated in a negative way. An attempt might no doubt be made to state this duty, like the others, in a positive way. It might be said that it is really the duty to prevent ourselves from acting either from an inclination to harm others or from an inclination to seek our own pleasure, in doing which we should incidentally harm them. But on reflection it seems clear that the primary duty here is the duty not to harm others, this being a duty whether or not we have an inclination that if followed would lead to our harming them; and that when we have such an inclination the primary duty not to harm others gives rise to a consequential duty to resist the inclination. The recognition of this duty of non-maleficence is the first step on the way to the recognition of the duty of beneficence; and that accounts for the prominence of the commands 'thou shalt not kill', 'thou shalt not commit adultery', 'thou shalt not steal', 'thou shalt not bear false witness', in so early a code as the Decalogue. But even when we have come to recognize the duty of beneficence, it appears to me that the duty of non-maleficence is recognized as a distinct one, and as *prima facie* more binding. We should not in general consider it justifiable to kill one person in order to keep another alive, or to steal from one in order to give alms to another.

The essential defect of the 'ideal utilitarian' theory is that it ignores, or at least does not do full justice to, the highly personal character of duty. If the only duty is to produce the maximum of good, the question who is to have the good—whether it is myself, or my benefactor, or a person to whom I have made a promise to confer that good on him, or a mere fellow man to whom I stand in no such special relation—should make no difference to my having a duty to produce that good. But we are all in fact sure that it makes a vast difference.

One or two other comments must be made on this provisional list of the divisions of duty. (1) The nomenclature is not strictly correct. For by 'fidelity' or 'gratitude' we mean, strictly, certain states of motivation; and, as I have urged, it is not our duty to have certain motives, but to do certain acts. By 'fidelity', for instance, is meant, strictly, the disposition to fulfil promises and implicit promises *because we have made them.* We have no general word to cover the actual fulfilment of promises and implicit promises *irrespective of motive;* and I use 'fidelity', loosely but perhaps conveniently, to fill this gap. So too I use 'gratitude' for the returning of services, irrespective of motive. The term 'justice' is not so much confined, in ordinary usage, to a certain state of motivation, for we should often talk of a man as acting justly even when we did not think his motive was the wish to do what was just simply for the sake of doing so. Less apology is therefore needed for our use of 'justice' in this sense. And I have used the word 'beneficence' rather than 'benevolence', in order to emphasize the fact that it is our duty to do certain things, and not to do them from certain motives.

(2) If the objection be made, that this catalogue of the main types of duty is an unsystematic one resting on no logical principle, it may be replied, first, that it makes no claim to being ultimate. It is a *prima facie* classification of the duties which reflection on our moral convictions seems actually to reveal. And if these convictions are, as I would claim that they are, of the nature of knowledge, and if I have not misstated them, the list will be a list of authentic conditional duties, correct as far as it goes though not necessarily complete. The list of *goods* put forward by the rival theory is reached by exactly the same method—the only sound one in the circumstances—viz. that of direct reflection on what we really think. Loyalty to the facts is worth more than a symmetrical architectonic or a hastily reached simplicity. If further reflection discovers a perfect logical basis for this or for a better classification, so much the better.

(3) It may, again, be objected that our theory that there are these various and often conflicting types of *prima facie* duty leaves us with no principle upon which to discern what is our actual duty in particular circumstances. But this objection is not one which the rival theory is in a position to bring forward. For when we have to choose between the production of two heterogeneous goods, say knowledge and pleasure, the 'ideal utilitarian' theory can only fall back on an opinion, for which no logical basis can be offered, that one of the goods is the greater; and this is no better than a similar opinion that one of two duties is the more urgent. And again, when we consider the infinite variety of the effects of our actions in the way of pleasure, it must surely be admitted that the claim which *hedonism* sometimes makes, that it offers a readily applicable criterion of right conduct, is quite illusory.

I am unwilling, however, to content myself with an *argumentum ad hominem,* and I would contend that in principle there is no reason to anticipate that every act that is our duty is so for one and the same reason. Why should two sets of circumstances, or one set of circumstances, *not* possess different characteristics, any one of which makes a certain act our *prima facie* duty? When I ask what it is that makes me in certain cases sure that I have a *prima facie* duty to do so and so, I find that it lies in the fact that I have made a promise;

when I ask the same question in another case, I find the answer lies in the fact that I have done a wrong. And if on reflection I find (as I think I do) that neither of these reasons is reducible to the other, I must not on any *a priori* ground assume that such a reduction is possible.

•   •   •   •   •

It is necessary to say something by way of clearing up the relation between *prima facie* duties and the actual or absolute duty to do one particular act in particular circumstances. If, as almost all moralists except Kant are agreed, and as most plain men think, it is sometimes right to tell a lie or to break a promise, it must be maintained that there is a difference between *prima facie* duty and actual or absolute duty. When we think ourselves justified in breaking, and indeed morally obliged to break, a promise in order to relieve some one's distress, we do not for a moment cease to recognize a *prima facie* duty to keep our promise, and this leads us to feel, not indeed shame or repentance, but certainly compunction, for behaving as we do; we recognize, further, that it is our duty to make up somehow to the promisee for the breaking of the promise. We have to distinguish from the characteristic of being our duty that of tending to be our duty. Any act that we do contains various elements in virtue of which it falls under various categories. In virtue of being the breaking of a promise, for instance, it tends to be wrong; in virtue of being an instance of relieving distress it tends to be right. Tendency to be one's duty may be called a parti-resultant attribute, i.e. one which belongs to an act in virtue of some one component in its nature. *Being* one's duty is a toti-resultant attribute, one which belongs to an act in virtue of its whole nature and of nothing less than this.

•   •   •   •   •

Something should be said of the relation between our apprehension of the *prima facie* rightness of certain types of act and our mental attitude towards particular acts. It is proper to use the word 'apprehension' in the former case and not in the latter. That an act, *qua* fulfilling a promise, or *qua* effecting a just distribution of good, or *qua* returning services rendered, or *qua* promoting the good of others, or *qua* promoting the virtue or insight of the agent, is *prima facie* right, is self-evident; not in the sense that it is evident from the beginning of our lives, or as soon as we attend to the proposition for the first time, but in the sense that when we have reached sufficient mental maturity and have given sufficient attention to the proposition it is evident without any need of proof, or of evidence beyond itself. It is self-evident just as a mathematical axiom, or the validity of a form of inference, is evident. The moral order expressed in these propositions is just as much part of the fundamental nature of the universe (and, we may add, of any possible universe in which there were moral agents at all) as is the spatial or numerical structure expressed in the axioms of geometry or arithmetic. In our confidence that these propositions are true there is involved the same trust in our reason that is involved in our confidence in mathematics; and we should have no justification for trusting it in the latter sphere and distrusting it in the former. In both cases we are dealing with propositions that cannot be proved, but that just as certainly need no proof.

· · · · ·

Supposing it to be agreed, as I think on reflection it must, that· no one *means* by 'right' just 'productive of the best possible consequences', or 'optimific', the attributes 'right' and 'optimific' might stand in either of two kinds of relation to each other. (1) They might be so related that we could apprehend *a priori,* either immediately or deductively, that any act that is optimific is right and any act that is right is optimific, as we can apprehend that any triangle that is equilateral is equiangular and *vice versa.* Professor Moore's view is, I think, that the coextensiveness of 'right' and 'optimific' is apprehended immediately.[4] He rejects the possibility of any proof of it. Or (2) the two attributes might be such that the question whether they are invariably connected had to be answered by means of an inductive inquiry. Now at first sight it might seem as if the constant connexion of the two attributes could be immediately apprehended. It might seem absurd to suggest that it could be right for any one to do an act which would produce consequences less good than those which would be produced by some other act in his power. Yet a little thought will convince us that this is not absurd. The type of case in which it is easiest to see that this is so is, perhaps, that in which one has made a promise. In such a case we all think that *prima facie* it is our duty to fulfil the promise irrespective of the precise goodness of the total consequences. And though we do not think it is necessarily our actual or absolute duty to do so, we are far from thinking that any, even the slightest, gain in the value of the total consequences will necessarily justify us in doing something else instead. Suppose, to simplify the case by abstraction, that the fulfilment of a promise to A would produce 1,000 units of good[5] for him, but that by doing some other act I could produce 1,001 units of good for B, to whom I have made no promise, the other consequences of the two acts being of equal value; should we really think it self-evident that it was our duty to do the second act and not the first? I think not. We should, I fancy, hold that only a much greater disparity of value between the total consequences would justify us in failing to discharge our *prima facie* duty to A. After all, a promise is a promise, and is not to be treated so lightly as the theory we are examining would imply. What, exactly, a promise is, is not so easy to determine, but we are surely agreed that it constitutes a serious moral limitation to our freedom of action. To produce the 1,001 units of good for B rather than fulfil our promise to A would be to take, not perhaps our duty as philanthropists too seriously, but certainly our duty as makers of promises too lightly.

---

[4] *Ethics,* 181.
[5] I am assuming that good is objectively quantitative, but not that we can accurately assign an exact quantitative measure to it. Since it is of a definite amount, we can make the *supposition* that its amount is so-and-so, though we cannot with any confidence *assert* that it is.

Or consider another phase of the same problem. If I have promised to confer on A a particular benefit containing 1,000 units of good, is it self-evident that if by doing some different act I could produce 1,001 units of good for A himself (the other consequences of the two acts being supposed equal in value), it would be right for me to do so? Again, I think not. Apart from my general *prima facie* duty to do A what good I can, I have another *prima facie* duty to do him the particular service I have promised to do him, and this is not to be set aside in consequence of a disparity of good of the order of 1,001 to 1,000, though a much greater disparity might justify me in so doing.

Or again, suppose that A is a very good and B a very bad man, should I then, even when I have made no promise, think it self-evidently right to produce 1,001 units of good for B rather than 1,000 for A? Surely not. I should be sensible of a *prima facie* duty of justice, i.e. of producing a distribution of goods in proportion to merit, which is not outweighed by such a slight disparity in the total goods to be produced.

Such instances—and they might easily be added to—make it clear that there is no self-evident connexion between the attributes 'right' and 'optimific'. The theory we are examining has a certain attractiveness when applied to our decision that a particular act is our duty (though I have tried to show that it does not agree with our actual moral judgments even here). But it is not even plausible when applied to our recognition of *prima facie* duty. For if it were self-evident that the right coincides with the optimific, it should be self-evident that what is *prima facie* right is *prima facie* optimific. But whereas we are certain that keeping a promise is *prima facie* right, we are not certain that it is *prima facie* optimific (though we are perhaps certain that it is *prima facie* bonific). Our certainty that it is *prima facie* right depends not on its consequences but on its being the fulfilment of a promise. The theory we are examining involves too much difference between the evident ground of our conviction about *prima facie* duty and the alleged ground of our conviction about actual duty.

The coextensiveness of the right and the optimific is, then, not self-evident. And I can see no way of proving it deductively; nor, so far as I know, has any one tried to do so. There remains the question whether it can be established inductively. Such an inquiry, to be conclusive, would have to be very thorough and extensive. We should have to take a large variety of the acts which we, to the best of our ability, judge to be right. We should have to trace as far as possible their consequences, not only for the persons directly affected but also for those indirectly affected, and to these no limit can be set. To make our inquiry thoroughly conclusive, we should have to do what we cannot do, viz. trace these consequences into an unending future. And even to make it reasonably conclusive, we should have to trace them far into the future. It is clear that the most we could possibly say is that a large variety of typical acts that are judged right appear, so far as we can trace their consequences, to produce more good than any other acts possible to the agents in the circumstances. And such a result falls far short of proving the constant connexion of the two attributes. But it is surely clear that no inductive inquiry justifying even this result has ever been carried through. The advocates of utilitarian systems have been so much persuaded either of the identity or of the self-evident connexion of the attributes 'right' and 'optimific' (or 'felicific') that they have not attempted even such an inductive inquiry as is possible. And in view of the enormous complexity of the task and the inevitable inconclusiveness of the result, it is worth no one's while to make the attempt. What, after all, would be gained by it? If, as I have tried to show, for an act to be right and to be optimific are not the same thing, and an act's being optimific is not even the ground of its being right, then if we could ask ourselves (though the question is really unmeaning) which we ought to do, right acts because they are right or optimific acts because they are optimific, our answer must be 'the former'. If they are optimific as well as right, that is interesting but not morally important; if not, we still ought to do them (which is only another way of saying that they *are* the right acts), and the question whether they are optimific has no importance for moral theory.

There is one direction in which a fairly serious attempt has been made to show the connexion of the attributes 'right' and 'optimific'. One of the most evident facts of our moral consciousness is the sense which we have of the sanctity of promises, a sense which does not, on the face of it, involve the thought that one will be bringing more good into existence by fulfilling the promise than by breaking it. It is plain, I think, that in our normal thought we consider that the fact that we have made a promise is in itself sufficient to create a duty of keeping it, the sense of duty resting on remembrance of the past promise and not on thoughts of the future consequences of its fulfilment. Utilitarianism tries to show that this is not so, that the sanctity of promises rests on the good consequences of the fulfilment of them and the bad consequences of their non-fulfilment. It does so in this way: it points out that when you break a promise you not only fail to confer a certain advantage on your promisee but you diminish his confidence, and indirectly the confidence of others, in the fulfilment of promises. You thus strike a blow at one of the devices that have been found most useful in the relations between man and man—the device on which, for example, the whole system of commercial credit rests—and you tend to bring about a state of things wherein each man, being entirely unable to rely on the keeping of promises by others, will have to do everything for himself, to the enormous impoverishment of human well-being.

To put the matter otherwise, utilitarians say that when a promise ought to be kept it is because the total good to be produced by keeping it is greater than the total good to be produced by breaking it, the former including as its main element the maintenance and strengthening of general mutual confidence, and the latter being greatly diminished by a weakening of this confidence. They say, in fact, that the case I put some pages back never arises—the case in which by fulfilling a promise I shall bring into being 1,000 units of good for my promisee, and by breaking it 1,001 units of good for some one else, the other effects of the two acts being of equal value. The other effects, they say, never are of equal value. By keeping my promise I am helping to strengthen the system of mutual confidence; by breaking it I am helping to weaken this; so that really the first act produces $1,000 + x$ units of good, and the second $1,001 - y$ units, and the difference between $+x$ and $-y$ is enough to outweigh the slight superiority in the *immediate* effects of the second act. In answer to this it may be pointed out that there must be *some* amount of good that exceeds the difference between $+x$ and $-y$ (i.e. exceeds $x + y$); say, $x + y + z$. Let us suppose the *immediate* good effects of the second act to be assessed not at $1,001$ but at $1,000 + x + y + z$. Then its *net* good effects are $1,000 + x + z$, i.e. greater than those of the fulfilment of the promise; and the utilitarian is bound to say forthwith that the promise should be broken. Now, we may ask whether that is really the way we think about promises? Do we really think that the production of the slightest balance of good, no matter who will enjoy it, by the breach of a promise frees us from the obligation to keep our promise? We need not doubt that a system by which promises are made and kept is one that has great advantages for the general well-being. But that is not the whole truth. To make a promise is not merely to adapt an ingenious device for promoting the general well-being; it is to put oneself in a new relation to one person in particular, a relation which creates a specifically new *prima facie* duty to him, not reducible to the duty of promoting the general well-being of society. By all means let us try to foresee the net good effects of keeping one's promise and the net good effects of breaking it, but even if we assess the first at $1,000 + x$ and the second at $1,000 + x + z$, the question still remains whether it is not our duty to fulfil the promise. It may be suspected, too, that the effect of a single keeping or breaking of a promise in strengthening or weakening the fabric of mutual confidence is greatly exaggerated by the theory we are examining. And if we suppose two men dying together alone, do we think that the duty of one to fulfil before he dies a promise he has made to the other would be extinguished by the fact that neither act would have any effect on the general confidence? Any one who holds this may be suspected of not having reflected on what a promise is.

I conclude that the attributes 'right' and 'optimific' are not identical, and that we do not know either by intuition, by deduction, or by induction that they coincide in their application, still less that the latter is the foundation of the former. It must be added, however, that if we are ever under no special obligation such as that of fidelity to a promisee or of gratitude to a benefactor, we ought to do what will produce most good; and that even when we are under a special obligation the tendency of acts to promote general good is one of the main factors in determining whether they are right.

In what has preceded, a good deal of use has been made of 'what we really think' about moral questions; a certain theory has been rejected because it does not agree with what we really think. It might be said that this is in principle wrong; that we should not be content to expound what our present moral consciousness tells us but should aim at a criticism of our existing moral consciousness in the light of theory. Now I do not doubt that the moral consciousness of men has in detail undergone a good deal of modification as regards the things we think right, at the hands of moral theory. But if we are told, for instance, that we should give up our view that there is a special obligatoriness attaching to the keeping of promises because it is self-evident that the only duty is to produce as much good as possible, we have to ask ourselves whether we really, when we reflect, *are* convinced that this is self-evident, and whether we really *can* get rid of our view that promise-keeping has a bindingness independent of productiveness of maximum good. In my own experience I find that I cannot, in spite of a very genuine attempt to do so; and I venture to think that most people will find the same, and that just because they cannot lose the sense of special obligation, they cannot accept as self-evident, or even as true, the theory which would require them to do so. In fact it seems, on reflection, self-evident that a promise, simply as such, is something that *prima facie* ought to be kept, and it does *not,* on reflection, seem self-evident that production of maximum good is the only thing that makes an act obligatory. And to ask us to give up at the bidding of a theory our actual apprehension of what is right and what is wrong seems like asking people to repudiate their actual experience of beauty, at the bidding of a theory which says 'only that which satisfies such and such conditions can be beautiful'. If what I have called our actual apprehension is (as I would maintain that it is) truly an apprehension, i.e. an instance of knowledge, the request is nothing less than absurd.

I would maintain, in fact, that what we are apt to describe as 'what we think' about moral questions contains a considerable amount that we do not think but know, and that this forms the standard by reference to which the truth of any moral theory has to be tested, instead of having itself to be tested by reference to any theory. I hope that I have in what precedes indicated what in my view these elements of knowledge are that are involved in our ordinary moral consciousness.

It would be a mistake to found a natural science on 'what we really think', i.e. on what reasonably thoughtful and well-educated people think about the subjects of the science before they have studied them scientifically. For such opinions are interpretations, and often misinterpretations, of sense-experience; and the man of science must appeal from these to sense-experience itself, which furnishes his real data. In ethics no such appeal is possible. We have no more direct way of access to the facts about rightness and goodness and about what things are right or good, than by thinking about them; the moral convictions of thoughtful and well-educated people are the data of ethics just as sense-perceptions are the data of a natural science. Just as some of the latter have to be rejected as illusory, so have some of the former; but as the latter are rejected only when they are in conflict with other more accurate sense-perceptions, the former are rejected only when they are in conflict with other convictions which stand better the test of reflection. The existing body of moral convictions of the best people is the cumulative product of the moral reflection of many generations, which has developed an extremely delicate power of appreciation of moral distinctions; and this the theorist cannot afford to treat with anything other than the greatest respect. The verdicts of the moral consciousness of the best people are the foundation on which he must build; though he must first compare them with one another and eliminate any contradictions they may contain.

JOHN RAWLS
Two Concepts of Rules

In this paper I want to show the importance of the distinction between justifying a practice and justifying a particular action falling under it, and I want to explain the logical basis of this distinction and how it is possible to miss its significance. While the distinction has frequently been made, and is now becoming commonplace, there remains the task of explaining the tendency either to overlook it altogether, or to fail to appreciate its importance.

To show the importance of the distinction I am going to defend utilitarianism against those objections which have traditionally been made against it in connection with punishment and the obligation to keep promises. I hope to show that if one uses the distinction in question then one can state utilitarianism in a way which makes it a much better explication of our considered moral judgments than these traditional objections would seem to admit. Thus the importance of the distinction is shown by the way it strengthens the utilitarian view regardless of whether that view is completely defensible or not.

To explain how the significance of the distinction may be overlooked, I am going to discuss two conceptions of rules. One of these conceptions conceals the importance of distinguishing between the justification of a rule or practice and the justification of a particular action falling under it. The other conception makes it clear why this distinction must be made and what is its logical basis.

I

The subject of punishment, in the sense of attaching legal penalties to the violation of legal rules, has always been a troubling moral question. The trouble about it has not been that people disagree as to whether or not punishment is justifiable. Most people have held that, freed from certain abuses, it is an

From John Rawls, "Two Concepts of Rules," *Philosophical Review*, LXIV, No. 1 (1955), 3–32. Reprinted by permission of the author and the editors of the *Philosophical Review*.

acceptable institution. Only a few have rejected punishment entirely, which is rather surprising when one considers all that can be said against it. The difficulty is with the justification of punishment: various arguments for it have been given by moral philosophers, but so far none of them has won any sort of general acceptance; no justification is without those who detest it. I hope to show that the use of the aforementioned distinction enables one to state the utilitarian view in a way which allows for the sound points of its critics.

For our purposes we may say that there are two justifications of punishment. What we may call the retributive view is that punishment is justified on the grounds that wrongdoing merits punishment. It is morally fitting that a person who does wrong should suffer in proportion to his wrongdoing. That a criminal should be punished follows from his guilt, and the severity of the appropriate punishment depends on the depravity of his act. The state of affairs where a wrongdoer suffers punishment is morally better than the state of affairs where he does not; and it is better irrespective of any of the consequences of punishing him.

What we may call the utilitarian view holds that on the principle that bygones are bygones and that only future consequences are material to present decisions, punishment is justifiable only by reference to the probable consequences of maintaining it as one of the devices of the social order. Wrongs committed in the past are, as such, not relevant considerations for deciding what to do. If punishment can be shown to promote effectively the interest of society it is justifiable, otherwise it is not.

I have stated these two competing views very roughly to make one feel the conflict between them: one feels the force of *both* arguments and one wonders how they can be reconciled. From my introductory remarks it is obvious that the resolution which I am going to propose is that in this case one must distinguish between justifying a practice as a system of rules to be applied and enforced, and justifying a particular action which falls under these rules; utilitarian arguments are appropriate with regard to questions about practices, while retributive arguments fit the application of particular rules to particular cases.

We might try to get clear about this distinction by imagining how a father might answer the question of his son. Suppose the son asks, "Why was *J* put in jail yesterday?" The father answers, "Because he robbed the bank at B. He was duly tried and found guilty. That's why he was put in jail yesterday." But suppose the son had asked a different question, namely, "Why do people put other people in jail?" Then the father might answer, "To protect good people from bad people" or "To stop people from doing things that would make it uneasy for all of us; for otherwise we wouldn't be able to go to bed at night and sleep in peace." There are two very different questions here. One question emphasizes the proper name: it asks why *J* was punished rather than someone else, or it asks what he was punished for. The other question asks why we have the institution of punishment: why do people punish one another rather than, say, always forgiving one another?

Thus the father says in effect that a particular man is punished, rather than some other man, because he is guilty, and he is guilty because he broke the law (past tense). In his case the law looks back, the judge looks back, the jury looks back, and a penalty is visited upon him for something he did. That a man is to be punished, and what his punishment is to be, is settled by its being shown that he broke the law and that the law assigns that penalty for the violation of it.

On the other hand we have the institution of punishment itself, and recommend and accept various changes in it, because it is thought by the (ideal) legislator and by those to whom the law applies that, as a part of a system of law impartially applied from case to case arising under it, it will have the consequence, in the long run, of furthering the interests of society.

One can say, then, that the judge and the legislator stand in different positions and look in different directions: one to the past, the other to the future. The justification of what the judge does, *qua* judge, sounds like the retributive view; the justification of what the (ideal) legislator does, *qua* legislator, sounds like the utilitarian view. Thus both views have a point (this is as it should be since intelligent and sensitive persons have been on both sides of the argument); and one's initial confusion disappears once one sees that these views apply to persons holding different offices with different duties, and situated differently with respect to the system of rules that make up the criminal law.

One might say, however, that the utilitarian view is more fundamental since it applies to a more fundamental office, for the judge carries out the legislator's will so far as he can determine it. Once the legislator decides to have laws and to assign penalties for their violation (as things are there must be both the law and the penalty) an institution is set up which involves a retributive conception of particular cases. It is part of the concept of the criminal law as a system of rules that the application and enforcement of these rules in particular cases should be justifiable by arguments of a retributive character. The decision whether or not to use law rather than some other mechanism of social control, and the decision as to what laws to have and what penalties to assign, may be settled by utilitarian arguments; but if one decides to have laws then one has decided on something whose working in particular cases is retributive in form.

The answer, then, to the confusion engendered by the two views of punishment is quite simple: one distinguishes two offices, that of the judge and that of the legislator, and one distinguishes their different stations with respect to the system of rules which make up the law; and then one notes that the different sorts of considerations which would usually be offered as reasons for what is done under the cover of these offices can be paired off with the competing justifications of punishment. One reconciles the two views by the time-honored device of making them apply to different situations.

•   •   •   •   •

. . . The real question, however, is whether the utilitarian, in justifying punishment, hasn't used arguments which commit him to accepting the infliction of suffering on innocent persons if it is for the good of society (whether or not one calls this punishment). More generally, isn't the utilitarian committed in principle to accepting many practices which he, as a morally sensitive person, wouldn't want to accept? Retributionists are inclined to hold that there is no way to stop the utilitarian principle from justifying too much except by adding to it a principle which distributes certain rights to individuals. Then the amended criterion is not the greatest benefit of society *simpliciter,* but the greatest benefit of society subject to the constraint that no one's rights may be violated. Now while I think that the classical utilitarians proposed a criterion of this more complicated sort, I do not want to argue that point here. What I want to show is that there is *another* way of preventing the utilitarian principle from justifying too much, or at least of making it much less likely to do so: namely, by stating utilitarianism in a way which accounts for the distinction between the justification of an institution and the justification of a particular action falling under it.

I begin by defining the institution of punishment as follows: a person is said to suffer punishment whenever he is legally deprived of some of the normal rights of a citizen on the ground that he has violated a rule of law, the violation having been established by trial according to the due process of law, provided that the deprivation is carried out by the recognized legal authorities of the state, that the rule of law clearly specifies both the offense and the attached penalty, that the courts construe statutes strictly, and that the statute was on the books prior to the time of the offense. This definition specifies what I shall understand by punishment. The question is whether utilitarian arguments may be found to justify institutions widely different from this and such as one would find cruel and arbitrary.

This question is best answered, I think, by taking up a particular accusation. Consider the following from Carritt:

> . . . the utilitarian must hold that we are justified in inflicting pain always and only to prevent worse pain or bring about greater happiness. This, then, is all we need to consider in so-called punishment, which must be purely preventive. But if some kind of very cruel crime becomes common, and none of the criminals can be caught, it might be highly expedient, as an example, to hang an innocent man, if a charge against him could be so framed that he were universally thought guilty; indeed this would only fail to be an ideal instance of utilitarian 'punishment' because the victim himself would not have been so likely as a real felon to commit such a crime in the future; in all other respects it would be perfectly deterrent and therefore felicific.[1]

Carritt is trying to show that there are occasions when a utilitarian argument would justify taking an action which would be generally condemned; and thus that utilitarianism justifies too much. But the failure of Carritt's argument lies in the fact that he makes no distinction between the justification of the general system of rules which constitutes penal institutions and the justification of particular applications of these rules to particular cases by the various officials whose job it is to administer them. This becomes perfectly clear when one asks who the "we" are of whom Carritt speaks. Who is this who has a sort of absolute authority on particular occasions to decide that an innocent man shall be "pun-

---

[1] *Ethical and Political Thinking* (Oxford, 1947), p. 65.

ished" if everyone can be convinced that he is guilty? Is this person the legislator, or the judge, or the body of private citizens, or what? It is utterly crucial to know who is to decide such matters, and by what authority, for all of this must be written into the rules of the institution. Until one knows these things one doesn't know what the institution is whose justification is being challenged; and as the utilitarian principle applies to the institution one doesn't know whether it is justifiable on utilitarian grounds or not.

Once this is understood it is clear what the countermove to Carritt's argument is. One must describe more carefully what the *institution* is which his example suggests, and then ask oneself whether or not it is likely that having this institution would be for the benefit of society in the long run. One must not content oneself with the vague thought that, when it's a question of *this* case, it would be a good thing if *somebody* did something even if an innocent person were to suffer.

Try to imagine, then, an institution (which we may call "telishment") which is such that the officials set up by it have authority to arrange a trial for the condemnation of an innocent man whenever they are of the opinion that doing so would be in the best interests of society. The discretion of officials is limited, however, by the rule that they may not condemn an innocent man to undergo such an ordeal unless there is, at the time, a wave of offenses similar to that with which they charge him and telish him for. We may imagine that the officials having the discretionary authority are the judges of the higher courts in consultation with the chief of police, the minister of justice, and a committee of the legislature.

Once one realizes that one is involved in setting up an *institution,* one sees that the hazards are very great. For example, what check is there on the officials? How is one to tell whether or not their actions are authorized? How is one to limit the risks involved in allowing such systematic deception? How is one to avoid giving anything short of complete discretion to the authorities to telish anyone they like? In addition to these considerations, it is obvious that people will come to have a very different attitude towards their penal system when telishment is adjoined to it. They will be uncertain as to whether a convicted man has been punished or telished. They will wonder whether or not they should feel sorry for him. They will wonder whether the same fate won't at any time fall on them. If one pictures how such an institution would actually work, and the enormous risks involved in it, it seems clear that it would serve no useful purpose. A utilitarian justification for this institution is most unlikely.

•   •   •   •   •

II

I shall now consider the question of promises. The objection to utilitarianism in connection with promises seems to be this: it is believed that on the utilitarian view when a person makes a promise the only ground upon which he should keep it, if he should keep it, is that by keeping it he will realize the most good on the whole. So that if one asks the question "Why should I keep *my* promise?" the utilitarian answer is understood to be that doing so in *this* case will have the best consequences. And this answer is said, quite rightly, to conflict with the way in which the obligation to keep promises is regarded.

Now of course critics of utilitarianism are not unaware that one defense sometimes attributed to utilitarians is the consideration involving the practice of promise-keeping. In this connection they are supposed to argue something like this: it must be admitted that we feel strictly about keeping promises, more strictly than it might seem our view can account for. But when we consider the matter carefully it is always necessary to take into account the effect which our action will have on the practice of making promises. The promisor must weigh, not only the effects of breaking his promise on the particular case, but also the effect which his breaking his promise will have on the practice itself. Since the practice is of great utilitarian value, and since breaking one's promise always seriously damages it, one will seldom be justified in breaking one's promise. If we view our individual promises in the wider context of the practice of promising itself we can account for the strictness of the obligation to keep promises. There is always one very strong utilitarian consideration in favor of keeping them, and this will insure that when the question arises as to whether or not to keep a promise it will usually turn out that one should, even where the facts of the particular case taken by itself would seem to justify one's breaking it. In this way the strictness with which we view the obligation to keep promises is accounted for.

Ross has criticized this defense as follows: however great the value of the practice of promising, on utilitarian grounds, there must be some value which is greater, and one can imagine it to be obtainable by breaking a promise. Therefore there might be a case where the promisor could argue that breaking his promise was justified as leading to a better state of affairs on the whole. And the promisor could argue in this way no matter how slight the advantage won by breaking the promise. If one were to challenge the promisor his defense would be that what he did was best on the whole in view of all the utilitarian considerations, which in this case *include* the importance of the practice. Ross feels that such a defense would be unacceptable. I think he is right insofar as he is protesting against the appeal to consequences in general and without further explanation. Yet it is extremely difficult to weigh the force of Ross's argument. The kind of case imagined seems unrealistic and one feels that it needs to be described. One is inclined to think that it would either turn out that such a case came under an exception defined by the practice itself, in which case there would not be an appeal to consequences in general on the particular case, or it would happen that the circumstances were so peculiar that the conditions which the practice presupposes no longer obtained. But certainly Ross is right in thinking that it strikes us as wrong for a person to defend breaking a promise by a general appeal to consequences. For a general utilitarian defense is not open to the promisor: it is not one of the defenses allowed by the practice of making promises.

Ross gives two further counterarguments: First, he holds that it overesti-mates the damage done to the practice of promising by a failure to keep a promise. One who breaks a promise harms his own name certainly, but it isn't clear that a broken promise always damages the practice itself sufficiently to account for the strictness of the obligation. Second, and more important, I think, he raises the question of what one is to say of a promise which isn't known to have been made except to the promisor and the promisee, as in the case of a promise a son makes to his dying father concerning the handling of the estate. In this sort of case the consideration relating to the practice doesn't weigh on the promisor at all, and yet one feels that this sort of promise is as binding as other promises. The question of the effect which breaking it has on the practice seems irrelevant. The only consequence seems to be that one can break the promise without running any risk of being censured; but the obligation itself seems not the least weakened. Hence it is doubtful whether the effect on the practice ever weighs in the particular case; certainly it cannot account for the strictness of the obligation where it fails to obtain. It seems to follow that a utilitarian account of the obligation to keep promises cannot be successfully carried out.

From what I have said in connection with punishment, one can foresee what I am going to say about these arguments and counterarguments. They fail to make the distinction between the justification of a practice and the justification of a particular action falling under it, and therefore they fall into the mistake of taking it for granted that the promisor, like Carritt's official, is entitled with-out restriction to bring utilitarian considerations to bear in deciding whether to keep *his* promise. But if one considers what the practice of promising is one will see, I think, that it is such as not to allow this sort of general discretion to the promisor. Indeed, the point of the practice is to abdicate one's title to act in accordance with utilitarian and prudential considerations in order that the future may be tied down and plans coordinated in advance. There are obvious utilitarian advantages in having a practice which denies to the promisor, as a defense, any general appeal to the utilitarian principle in accordance with which the practice itself may be justified. There is nothing contradictory, or surprising, in this: utilitarian (or aesthetic) reasons might properly be given in arguing that the game of chess, or baseball, is satisfactory just as it is, or in arguing that it should be changed in various respects, but a player in a game cannot properly appeal to such considerations as reasons for his making one move rather than another. It is a mistake to think that if the practice is justified on utilitarian grounds then the promisor must have complete liberty to use utilitarian argu-ments to decide whether or not to keep his promise. The practice forbids this general defense; and it is a purpose of the practice to do this. Therefore what the above arguments presuppose—the idea that if the utilitarian view is accepted then the promisor is bound if, and only if, the application of the utilitarian principle to his own case shows that keeping it is best on the whole—is false. The promisor is bound because he promised: weighing the case on its merits is not open to him.

Is this to say that in particular cases one cannot deliberate whether or not to keep one's promise? Of course not. But to do so is to deliberate whether the various excuses, exceptions and defenses, which are understood by, and which constitute an important part of, the practice, apply to one's own case. Various defenses for not keeping one's promise are allowed, but among them there isn't the one that, on general utilitarian grounds, the promisor (truly) thought his action best on the whole, even though there may be the defense that the consequences of keeping one's promise would have been *extremely* severe. While there are too many complexities here to consider all the necessary details, one can see that the general defense isn't allowed if one asks the following question: what would one say of someone who, when asked why he broke his promise, replied simply that breaking it was best on the whole? Assuming that his reply is sincere, and that his belief was reasonable (i.e., one need not consider the possibility that he was mistaken), I think that one would question whether or not he knows what it means to say "I promise" (in the appropriate circumstances). It would be said of someone who used this excuse without further explanation that he didn't understand what defenses the practice, which defines a promise, allows to him. If a child were to use this excuse one would correct him; for it is part of the way one is taught the concept of a promise to be corrected if one uses this excuse. The point of having the practice would be lost if the practice did allow this excuse.

•   •   •   •   •

III

So far I have tried to show the importance of the distinction between the justification of a practice and the justification of a particular action falling under it by indicating how this distinction might be used to defend utilitarianism against two longstanding objections. One might be tempted to close the discussion at this point by saying that utilitarian considerations should be understood as applying to practices in the first instance and not to particular actions falling under them except insofar as the practices admit of it. One might say that in this modified form it is a better account of our considered moral opinions and let it go at that. But to stop here would be to neglect the interesting question as to how one can fail to appreciate the significance of this rather obvious distinction and can take it for granted that utilitarianism has the consequence that particular cases may always be decided on general utilitarian grounds. I want to argue that this mistake may be connected with misconceiving the logical status of the rules of practices; and to show this I am going to examine two conceptions of rules, two ways of placing them within the utilitarian theory.

The conception which conceals from us the significance of the distinction I am going to call the summary view. It regards rules in the following way: one supposes that each person decides what he shall do in particular cases by applying the utilitarian principle; one supposes further that different people will decide the same particular case in the same way and that there will be recurrences of cases similar to those previously decided. Thus it will happen that in cases of certain kinds the same decision will be made either by the same person at different times or by different persons at the same time. If a case occurs frequently enough one supposes that a rule is formulated to cover that sort of case. I have called this conception the summary view because rules are pictured as summaries of past decisions arrived at by the *direct* application of the utilitarian principle to particular cases. Rules are regarded as reports that cases of a certain sort have been found on *other* grounds to be properly decided in a certain way (although, of course, they do not *say* this).

There are several things to notice about this way of placing rules within the utilitarian theory.

1. The point of having rules derives from the fact that similar cases tend to recur and that one can decide cases more quickly if one records past decisions in the form of rules. If similar cases didn't recur, one would be required to apply the utilitarian principle directly, case by case, and rules reporting past decisions would be of no use.

2. The decisions made on particular cases are logically prior to rules. Since rules gain their point from the need to apply the utilitarian principle to many similar cases, it follows that a particular case (or several cases similar to it) may exist whether or not there is a rule covering that case. We are pictured as recognizing particular cases prior to there being a rule which covers them, for it is only if we meet with a number of cases of a certain sort that we formulate a rule. . . .

3. Each person is in principle always entitled to reconsider the correctness of a rule and to question whether or not it is proper to follow it in a particular case. As rules are guides and aids, one may ask whether in past decisions there might not have been a mistake in applying the utilitarian principle to get the rule in question, and wonder whether or not it is best in this case. The reason for rules is that people are not able to apply the utilitarian principle effortlessly and flawlessly; there is need to save time and to post a guide. On this view a society of rational utilitarians would be a society without rules in which each person applied the utilitarian principle directly and smoothly, and without error, case by case. On the other hand, ours is a society in which rules are formulated to serve as aids in reaching these ideally rational decisions on particular cases, guides which have been built up and tested by the experience of generations. If one applies this view to rules, one is interpreting them as maxims, as "rules of thumb"; and it is doubtful that anything to which the summary conception did apply would be called a *rule*. Arguing as if one regarded rules in this way is a mistake one makes while doing philosophy.

4. The concept of a *general* rule takes the following form. One is pictured as estimating on what percentage of the cases likely to arise a given rule may be relied upon to express the correct decision, that is, the decision that would be arrived at if one were to correctly apply the utilitarian principle case by case. If one estimates that by and large the rule will give the correct decision, or if one estimates that the likelihood of making a mistake by applying the utilitarian principle directly on one's own is greater than the likelihood of making a mis-

take by following the rule, and if these considerations held of persons generally, then one would be justified in urging its adoption as a general rule. In this way *general* rules might be accounted for on the summary view. . . .

The other conception of rules I will call the practice conception. On this view rules are pictured as defining a practice. Practices are set up for various reasons, but one of them is that in many areas of conduct each person's deciding what to do on utilitarian grounds case by case leads to confusion, and that the attempt to coordinate behavior by trying to foresee how others will act is bound to fail. As an alternative one realizes that what is required is the establishment of a practice, the specification of a new form of activity; and from this one sees that a practice necessarily involves the abdication of full liberty to act on utilitarian and prudential grounds. It is the mark of a practice that being taught how to engage in it involves being instructed in the rules which define it, and that appeal is made to those rules to correct the behavior of those engaged in it. Those engaged in a practice recognize the rules as defining it. The rules cannot be taken as simply describing how those engaged in the practice in fact behave: it is not simply that they act as if they were obeying the rules. Thus it is essential to the notion of a practice that the rules are publicly known and understood as definitive; and it is essential also that the rules of a practice can be taught and can be acted upon to yield a coherent practice. On this conception, then, rules are not generalizations from the decisions of individuals applying the utilitarian principle directly and independently to recurrent particular cases. On the contrary, rules define a practice and are themselves the subject of the utilitarian principle.

To show the important differences between this way of fitting rules into the utilitarian theory and the previous way, I shall consider the differences between the two conceptions on the points previously discussed.

1. In contrast with the summary view, the rules of practices are logically prior to particular cases. This is so because there cannot be a particular case of an action falling under a rule of a practice unless there is the practice. This can be made clearer as follows: in a practice there are rules setting up offices, specifying certain forms of action appropriate to various offices, establishing penalties for the breach of rules, and so on. We may think of the rules of a practice as defining offices, moves, and offenses. Now what is meant by saying that the practice is logically prior to particular cases is this: given any rule which specifies a form of action (a move), a particular action which would be taken as falling under this rule given that there is the practice would not be *described as* that sort of action unless there was the practice. In the case of actions specified by practices it is logically impossible to perform them outside the stage-setting provided by those practices, for unless there is the practice, and unless the requisite proprieties are fulfilled, whatever one does, whatever movements one makes, will fail to count as a form of action which the practice specifies. What one does will be described in some *other* way.

One may illustrate this point from the game of baseball. Many of the actions one performs in a game of baseball one can do by oneself or with others whether there is the game or not. For example, one can throw a ball, run, or swing a peculiarly shaped piece of wood. But one cannot steal base, or strike out, or draw a walk, or make an error, or balk; although one can do certain things which appear to resemble these actions such as sliding into a bag, missing a grounder and so on. Striking out, stealing a base, balking, etc., are all actions which can only happen in a game. No matter what a person did, what he did would not be described as stealing a base or striking out or drawing a walk unless he could also be described as playing baseball, and for him to be doing this presupposes the rule-like practice which constitutes the game. The practice is logically prior to particular cases: unless there is the practice the terms referring to actions specified by it lack a sense.

2. The practice view leads to an entirely different conception of the authority which each person has to decide on the propriety of following a rule in particular cases. To engage in a practice, to perform those actions specified by a practice, means to follow the appropriate rules. If one wants to do an action which a certain practice specifies then there is no way to do it except to follow the rules which define it. Therefore, it doesn't make sense for a person to raise the question whether or not a rule of a practice correctly applies to *his* case where the action he contemplates is a form of action defined by a practice. If someone were to raise such a question, he would simply show that he didn't understand the situation in which he was acting. If one wants to perform an action specified by a practice, the only legitimate question concerns the nature of the practice itself ("How do I go about making a will?").

This point is illustrated by the behavior expected of a player in games. If one wants to play a game, one doesn't treat the rules of the game as guides as to what is best in particular cases. In a game of baseball if a batter were to ask "Can I have four strikes?" it would be assumed that he was asking what the rule was; and if, when told what the rule was, he were to say that he meant that on this occasion he thought it would be best on the whole for him to have four strikes rather than three, this would be most kindly taken as a joke. One might contend that baseball would be a better game if four strikes were allowed instead of three; but one cannot picture the rules as guides to what is best on the whole in particular cases, and question their applicability to particular cases as particular cases.

3 and 4. To complete the four points of comparison with the summary conception, it is clear from what has been said that rules of practices are not guides to help one decide particular cases correctly as judged by some higher ethical principle. And neither the quasi-statistical notion of generality, nor the notion of a particular exception, can apply to the rules of practices. A more or less general rule of a practice must be a rule which according to the structure of the practice applies to more or fewer of the kinds of cases arising under it; or it must be a rule which is more or less basic to the understanding of the practice. Again, a particular case cannot be an exception to a rule of a practice. An exception is rather a qualification or a further specification of the rule.

•   •   •   •   •

If one compares the two conceptions of rules I have discussed, one can see how the summary conception misses the significance of the distinction between justifying a practice and justifying actions falling under it. On this view rules are regarded as guides whose purpose it is to indicate the ideally rational decision on the given particular case which the flawless application of the utilitarian principle would yield. One has, in principle, full option to use the guides or to discard them as the situation warrants without one's moral office being altered in any way: whether one discards the rules or not, one always holds the office of a rational person seeking case by case to realize the best on the whole. But on the practice conception, if one holds an office defined by a practice then questions regarding one's actions in this office are settled by reference to the rules which define the practice. If one seeks to question these rules, then one's office undergoes a fundamental change: one then assumes the office of one empowered to change and criticize the rules, or the office of a reformer, and so on. The summary conception does away with the distinction of offices and the various forms of argument appropriate to each. On that conception there is one office and so no offices at all. It therefore obscures the fact that the utilitarian principle must, in the case of actions and offices defined by a practice, apply to the practice, so that general utilitarian arguments are not available to those who act in offices so defined.

·   ·   ·   ·   ·

IV

What I have tried to show by distinguishing between two conceptions of rules is that there is a way of regarding rules which allows the option to consider particular cases on general utilitarian grounds; whereas there is another conception which does not admit of such discretion except insofar as the rules themselves authorize it. I want to suggest that the tendency while doing philosophy to picture rules in accordance with the summary conception is what may have blinded moral philosophers to the significance of the distinction between justifying a practice and justifying a particular action falling under it; and it does so by misrepresenting the logical force of the reference to the rules in the case of a challenge to a particular action falling under a practice, and by obscuring the fact that where there is a practice, it is the practice itself that must be the subject of the utilitarian principle.

It is surely no accident that two of the traditional test cases of utilitarianism, punishment and promises, are clear cases of practices. Under the influence of the summary conception it is natural to suppose that the officials of a penal system, and one who has made a promise, may decide what to do in particular cases on utilitarian grounds. One fails to see that a general discretion to decide particular cases on utilitarian grounds is incompatible with the concept of a practice; and that what discretion one does have is itself defined by the practice (e.g., a judge may have discretion to determine the penalty within certain limits). The traditional objections to utilitarianism which I have discussed presuppose the attribution to judges, and to those who have made promises, of a plenitude of moral authority to decide particular cases on utilitarian grounds. But once one fits utilitarianism together with the notion of a practice, and notes that punishment and promising are practices, then one sees that this attribution is logically precluded.

That punishment and promising are practices is beyond question. In the case of promising this is shown by the fact that the form of words "I promise" is a performative utterance which presupposes the stage-setting of the practice and the proprieties defined by it. Saying the words "I promise" will only be promising given the existence of the practice. It would be absurd to interpret the rules about promising in accordance with the summary conception. It is absurd to say, for example, that the rule that promises should be kept could have arisen from its being found in past cases to be best on the whole to keep one's promise; for unless there were already the understanding that one keeps one's promises as part of the practice itself there couldn't have been any cases of promising.

It must, of course, be granted that the rules defining promising are not codified, and that one's conception of what they are necessarily depends on one's moral training. Therefore it is likely that there is considerable variation in the way people understand the practice, and room for argument as to how it is best set up. For example, differences as to how strictly various defenses are to be taken, or just what defenses are available, are likely to arise amongst persons with different backgrounds. But irrespective of these variations it belongs to the concept of the practice of promising that the general utilitarian defense is not available to the promisor. That this is so accounts for the force of the traditional objection which I have discussed. And the point I wish to make is that when one fits the utilitarian view together with the practice conception of rules, as one must in the appropriate cases, then there is nothing in that view which entails that there must be such a defense, either in the practice of promising, or in any other practice.

Punishment is also a clear case. There are many actions in the sequence of events which constitute someone's being punished which presuppose a practice. One can see this by considering the definition of punishment which I gave when discussing Carritt's criticism of utilitarianism. The definition there stated refers to such things as the normal rights of a citizen, rules of law, due process of law, trials and courts of law, statutes, etc., none of which can exist outside the elaborate stage-setting of a legal system. It is also the case that many of the actions for which people are punished presuppose practices. For example, one is punished for stealing, for trespassing, and the like, which presuppose the institution of property. It is impossible to say what punishment is, or to describe a particular instance of it, without referring to offices, actions, and offenses specified by practices. Punishment is a move in an elaborate legal game and presupposes the complex of practices which make up the legal order. The same thing is true of the less formal sorts of punishment: a parent or guardian or someone in proper authority may punish a child, but no one else can.

There is one mistaken interpretation of what I have been saying which it is worthwhile to warn against. One might think that the use I am making of the distinction between justifying a practice and justifying the particular actions falling under it involves one in a definite social and political attitude in that it leads to a kind of conservatism. It might seem that I am saying that for each person the social practices of his society provide the standard of justification for his actions; therefore let each person abide by them and his conduct will be justified.

This interpretation is entirely wrong. The point I have been making is rather a logical point. To be sure, it has consequences in matters of ethical theory; but in itself it leads to no particular social or political attitude. It is simply that where a form of action is specified by a practice there is no justification possible of the particular action of a particular person save by reference to the practice. In such cases the action is what it is in virtue of the practice and to explain it is to refer to the practice. There is no inference whatsoever to be drawn with respect to whether or not one should accept the practices of one's society. One can be as radical as one likes but in the case of actions specified by practices the objects of one's radicalism must be the social practices and people's acceptance of them.

Supplementary Paperback Reading

For further criticisms of utilitarianism see Supplementary Paperback Reading listed at the end of Chapter 4.

Two superb studies of Kant's *Fundamental Principles of the Metaphysic of Morals* are now available in paperback:

R. P. Wolff, *Kant: Foundations of the Metaphysics of Morals, Text and Critical Essays.* (Bobbs-Merrill) This volume contains the Lewis White Beck translation of the *Grundlegung zur Metaphysik der Sitten* along with nine critical essays on Kant's work, by contemporary philosophers.

H. J. Paton, *The Categorical Imperative: A Study in Kant's Moral Philosophy.* (Harper Torchbooks) Originally published in 1947, this has become a contemporary classic of Kantian scholarship. Paton's own translation of the *Grundlegung zur Metaphysik der Sitten* along with his analysis of Kant's argument is published in: I. Kant, *Groundwork of the Metaphysic of Morals.* (Harper Torchbooks)

Other paperback reading on deontological ethics:

K. Baier, "Moral Obligation." (Bobbs-Merrill Reprint Series in Philosophy)

J. Bennett, "Whatever the Consequences," in J. J. Thomson and G. Dworkin, *Ethics.* (Harper and Row)

R. M. Blake, "The Ground of Moral Obligation." (Bobbs-Merrill Reprint Series in Philosophy)

C. D. Broad, "Conscience and Conscientious Action," in J. Feinberg, *Moral Concepts* (Oxford University Press), and in J. J. Thomson and G. Dworkin, *Ethics.* (Harper and Row)

E. F. Carritt, "Duty for Duty's Sake," in R. Ekman, *Readings in the Problems of Ethics.* (Scribner's)

R. M. Chisholm, "Supererogation and Offence: A Conceptual Scheme for Ethics," in J. J. Thomson and G. Dworkin, *Ethics.* (Harper and Row)

J. Dewey, *Theory of the Moral Life,* Ch. III. (Holt, Rinehart and Winston)

A. C. Ewing, *Ethics,* Ch. IV and VII. (Free Press)

J. Feinberg, "Supererogation and Rules," in J. J. Thomson and G. Dworkin, *Ethics.* (Harper and Row)

W. K. Frankena, *Ethics,* Ch. 2. (Prentice-Hall)

A. C. Garnett, "Conscience and Conscientiousness," in J. Feinberg, *Moral Concepts.* (Oxford University Press)

E. A. Gellner, "Ethics and Logic," in J. Margolis, *Contemporary Ethical Theory.* (Random House)

R. M. Hare, "Universalisability." (Bobbs-Merrill Reprint Series in Philosophy)

H. L. A. Hart, "Legal and Moral Obligation." (Bobbs-Merrill Reprint Series in Philosophy)

W. D. Hudson, *Ethical Intuitionism.* (St. Martin's Press)

A. Isenberg, "Deontology and the Ethics of Lying," in J. J. Thomson and G. Dworkin, *Ethics.* (Harper and Row)

S. Körner, *Kant,* Ch. 6 and 7. (Penguin Books)

J. Ladd, "The Desire to Do One's Duty for Its Own Sake," in H. N. Castaneda and G. Nakhnikian, *Morality and the Language of Conduct.* (Wayne State University Press)

P. H. Nowell-Smith, *Ethics,* Ch. 17, 18. (Penguin Books)

J. Rawls, "The Sense of Justice," in J. Feinberg, *Moral Concepts.* (Oxford University Press)

C. Strang, "What If Everyone Did That?" in J. J. Thomson and G. Dworkin, *Ethics.* (Harper and Row), and in B. Brody, *Moral Rules and Particular Circumstances.* (Prentice-Hall)

J. O. Urmson, "Saints and Heroes," in J. Feinberg, *Moral Concepts* (Oxford University Press) and in Bobbs-Merrill Reprint Series in Philosophy.

C. H. Whiteley, "On Duties," in J. Feinberg, *Moral Concepts.* (Oxford University Press)

6

MORAL

RESPONSIBILITY

AND

FREE WILL

Introduction

In this chapter we are concerned with one of the most difficult and important problems in the whole field of moral philosophy. It is a problem that has been the preoccupation of thinkers since the beginning of philosophy, and it remains to this day a source of great perplexity. Within the limits of this chapter we cannot expect to find complete and final answers to the many questions raised in it, but we may hope to make some progress in sorting out different questions that are frequently confused with one another. In this way the main issues will be clarified and we shall have made an orderly start on our own reflection about the problem.

PRELIMINARY STATEMENT OF THE PROBLEM

The problem of moral responsibility and freedom of the will may be approached in the following way. Suppose we have accepted a normative ethical system according to which certain acts are right and others are wrong. (It does not matter for our present purposes what specific norms make up the system, or whether the system is deontological, utilitarian, or of some other kind.) If we then judge that a particular act done by someone was not the right thing for him to do in the given situation, we can always ask the further questions: Should he or should he not be held responsible for doing it? Was the act excusable or inexcusable? Is the person at fault for having done it?

The conditions under which we normally excuse a person and do not believe he should be held morally responsible for an act he has done are of four kinds: (a) excusable ignorance of the consequences or circumstances of an act; (b) the presence of a constraint which forced the person to do the act and which was of a degree of strength no ordinary amount of will power could overcome; (c) the circumstances in which the act was done were beyond the person's control; (d) the absence of either the ability or the opportunity, or both, to do an alternative act that would be the right thing to do in the given situation.

(a) In the first case we excuse a person because, in our estimation, he could not reasonably be expected to have foreseen that the bad consequences of what he did would happen, or because he could not reasonably be expected to have known how to prevent the consequences from happening. For example, a man meets an old acquaintance whom he has not seen for some time and asks him how his wife and children are, not knowing that his friend's entire family has recently been killed in an automobile accident. Here we do not blame him for the hurt he causes because it would be unreasonable to expect him to know the unusual circumstances in his friend's recent life. Contrast this with a case where we do hold someone responsible for the harmful consequences of his act because we think he should have known that they might occur. Thus we do not excuse an engineer who miscalculates the stresses in a bridge he is building, with the result that it collapses a year after it is built. Not knowing how to prevent bad consequences which *are* foreseen by someone may also be a case of excusable ignorance. We do not hold the passengers in an airplane at fault for not knowing how to fly it if something goes wrong with the motors and it crashes, but we might blame the pilots.

(b) The second condition of excusability occurs in a situation in which we say of a person, "he did not do the act of his own free will," or "he could not help it," or "it was not a matter of his own choice." Here there is either some *external* constraint being exerted upon the person or he feels an *inner* compulsion which makes him do something and he finds it is beyond his power to control this drive. In the first kind of case we say that the act was done against the person's will. He did not want to do it but was forced to. An example would be a man's being compelled to participate in a bank robbery because the robber threatens to kill him if he does not do as he is told. We withdraw our condemnation of the man and consider him innocent when we discover that his act was done under coercion. In this way we contrast his case with that of someone who helps the robber "of his own free will," desiring to get a share of the cash.

In the second form of constraint, the compelling element comes from "inside" rather than from someone else. The person cannot help doing what he does because he feels driven by an uncontrollable impulse or craving. An example is the overwhelming desire for a drug which the addict experiences if he has not been able to get his usual amount at the usual time. It should be noted that we do not morally excuse an addict who commits a crime in order to obtain his drug, because the formation of the habit was in the beginning a matter of his own free choice, and ordinarily it would be reasonable to expect him to know the probable consequences of forming such a habit. It may happen, however, that a neurotic or psychotic person will do wrong acts under the influence of an inner compulsion, and this compulsion did not develop from choices he had freely made in the past. The shoplifting of a kleptomaniac is an example. He won't be able to keep himself from stealing even when he knows he will be caught. Such a person feels an inner drive to take something; he cannot avoid doing it because it is beyond his will power to control this impulse. In this kind of situation we tend to think of the man as mentally or emotionally ill, in need of special therapy to get rid of his compulsion. Although he knowingly breaks the law, he does not do so voluntarily. Thus we distinguish between his case and that of a bank robber who has carefully and coolly planned his crime over many weeks and feels no inner drive to carry out his plan. The kleptomaniac, we think, cannot stop himself from stealing, no matter how hard he tries. But the bank robber can give up his plan, as is shown by the fact that he does so when something unforeseen occurs, such as a reinforcement of police protection for the bank. This is how, in ordinary life, we make the distinction between a person who is not to be held responsible (accountable) for his action and one who is. We base our distinction on the presence or absence of internal compulsion.

(c) A third condition of excusability occurs when the circumstances of an act, as distinct from the inner drive to do it, are beyond a person's control. There are many such clearly recognized excuses which we accept as legitimate reasons for failure to fulfill an obligation or carry out a duty. Illness, accidents, unexpected call of higher obligations are typical instances. In each case, however, the circumstances that prevent the person from fulfilling his obligation must be beyond his control at the time and must not be due to his own voluntary acts in the past. Thus we do not excuse a person who misses an appointment because he got into a traffic accident as a result of his own reckless driving, nor do we excuse him if the accident was the result of a breakdown in his car which could have been avoided had he taken proper care of his car beforehand.

(d) Finally, there are situations in which a wrong act is done or a right act is not done because the person lacked either the ability or the opportunity to do the right act. If someone cannot swim, we do not blame him for not jumping in to try to save a drowning man (though we would hold him responsible if he did not call for help or throw the man a life preserver when one was available). On the other hand, a person might be able to swim but fail to save a drowning man because he sees him only when it is too late. In cases like these we say that the consequences were unavoidable, since it was not within the power of the person to prevent their happening.

There are two important points to realize about all four of these conditions of excusability. The first is that, in so far as any actual situation satisfies one or more of these conditions, it can be significantly contrasted with a situation of the opposite kind, where these conditions are not satisfied. The second is that situations of both kinds do occur in everyday life. Thus, just as there are cases where a person could not have foreseen the harmful consequences of his acts, there are other cases where a person does foresee such consequences and still chooses to do the act. (A man who intends to murder someone not only foresees that his victim will die but wants this to happen.) Just as there are acts done under the coercion of another person, so there are acts done when no such external constraint is present. A man who fires a shotgun at the house of a civil-rights worker in the South may have decided to do it entirely by himself and may have acted under no external compulsion. It is possible, indeed, to act in opposition to a considerable amount of external constraint. Whenever a person commits a crime he does so in spite of, rather than because of, such external constraints as threat of punishment, fear of the police, and general social disapproval. Again, consider the case in which an internal urge or drive compels a person to act against his own will. This kind of case is to be contrasted with that of a person freely choosing to do something after carefully deliberating about it. A man might be in full control of himself as he works out a plan to embezzle funds, and feel under no compulsion as he calmly carries out his plan. In connection with the third kind of situation, just as we are sometimes prevented from doing what we ought to do by circumstances beyond our control, there are other cases where we don't do what we ought simply because we don't want to. We sometimes try to avoid our obligations when we find them onerous. Finally, although in a given situation we may lack the ability or the opportunity to do what would be right, just as often we have the capacity and the opportunity to do any number of alternatives open to our choice and yet we knowingly choose to do what is wrong. For example, the man who does not report accurately his income in order to avoid paying a tax certainly has the ability and opportunity to make out an accurate report, and knows that this would be the right thing for him to do.

In everyday life, then, there are occasions when we excuse a person and occasions when we hold someone responsible for what he does. Now the problem of free will arises when the theory of determinism, or universal causation, is applied to human choice and conduct. Determinism is the principle that every event has a cause. This principle is used by the sciences of psychology, sociology, and anthropology in explaining man's behavior. Although these sciences have developed only recently, they have already made impressive achievements in our understanding of why men act, feel, and choose as they do. As these sciences progress, our ability to account for human feelings, motives, and beliefs will greatly increase, and along with such knowledge will develop our ability to give causal explanations for human decisions and conduct. Accordingly, many people are beginning to think about man the way they think about animals and machines. They take the same scientific point of view toward all of them, and in doing so see their activities not as chance events occurring in a haphazard or unpredictable manner, but as events that happen in an orderly way. This order is discovered when scientists are able to explain the events in terms of causal laws. It is true that the laws by which human behavior is to be explained may be far more complex and far more difficult to discover than the laws of the inanimate world and of the plant and (lower) animal world. But this does not mean that the human world is any the less explainable by causal laws. Man is a part of nature, and nature is an order of causes and effects which the sciences are gradually revealing to us. Everything in nature happens in accordance with this order, and the choices of individual men must be understood in this light.

The principle of determinism, that every event has a cause, is accepted by all scientists with regard to the subject matter of their particular science, since the aim of their science is to find a causal explanation for anything that happens within the domain of that science, and to look for such an explanation is to assume that the happening is caused. What is a causal explanation? This is a difficult question to answer; it gives rise to many subtle disputes in the philosophy of science. Here we can only suggest an answer sufficient to bring out the relevance of determinism to free will and moral responsibility. To give a causal explanation of an event is to show how the event is related to other events by a causal law. Every causal law is of the following form: Given certain conditions in space and time and a set of changes occurring at a certain time, a new set of changes will take place under the given conditions. For example, when a gas is heated it will expand (certain conditions remaining constant). A chemist may thus explain the expansion of a gas as the effect of an increase in its temperature, along with the law that relates, in a functional equation, the temperature, pressure, and volume of a gas. Causal laws are always universal statements; they apply to all events of a certain kind *whenever* they occur, not just to a particular set of events that occurred at a particular time in the past. If we know the causal law according to which events of a certain kind are followed by events of another kind under certain conditions, then we are able to predict, when the first set of events occur under the stated conditions, that the second set of events will follow. In this way predictions of future events are based on the very same laws by which we explain present and past events. The definition of "cause" and "effect" may then be given as follows: If any law holds true of two sets of changes in the world such that, whenever changes of the first set occur under certain conditions, changes of the second set will follow, the events making up the first set are the *causes* of the events making up the second set, and the latter are the *effects* of the former. Thus the set of events that are the causes of an effect constitute a *sufficient condition* for the occurrence of the effect. If at a certain time the sufficient condition for an event occurs, the event must then occur. It will be causally or physically impossible for the sufficient condition to occur without the event following it. Hence given the causes, the effect must follow.

A *causal explanation* of any event consists in specifying the causal law which states a universal connection between events of the kind to be explained and a set of events which they invariably follow when certain conditions remain constant. Thus the principle of determinism may be taken to mean: There is a causal explanation for every event occurring in the universe. To say this, however, is not to say that anyone *knows* the causal explanation for any given event. It only says that such an explanation is theoretically possible. The ideal goal of the empirical sciences would be to find a system of causal laws in terms of which every event in the universe could be explained. Such an ideal, of course, can only be approached gradually as scientists obtain more and more knowledge of the world; it may never be reached. But the determinist is not bothered by this fact. He merely claims that, however ignorant of causal laws mankind may remain, those laws are nevertheless in constant operation and no exception to them ever occurs.

What has determinism got to do with conditions of excusability and moral responsibility? The true answer to this question may be, "Nothing whatever," but many people have thought otherwise. They have believed that there is a contradiction between determinism and moral responsibility, so that if it is legitimate to hold people morally responsible for at least some of their acts, we must reject the principle of determinism. The kind of freedom which is necessary for moral responsibility, they argue, is the freedom of *indeterminism*. A man's "will" must be undetermined at the time of choice if he is to be held responsible for what he does. And this means that no causal explanation will

282 MORAL RESPONSIBILITY AND FREE WILL

account for his choice. Thus the question: When is a man morally responsible? has come to be hinged upon the question: Is determinism true?

The usual argument that moral responsibility is incompatible with determinism runs as follows. Let us consider only cases where the four types of conditions of excusability discussed above do *not* hold, since it is only in these situations that we ordinarily believe it is justified to hold people responsible for their acts. Now in such situations, although a person may not appear to be under external or internal constraint, and may appear to have the ability and opportunity to do a number of alternatives open to his choice, these appearances are mere illusions if his choice and subsequent action are causally determined. For suppose they are determined. Then, given the causal laws operating in his situation of choice, only one "alternative" course of action can possibly occur, namely, the one which will be the effect of the previous causes that are occurring in the situation. The act that the person finally chooses to do is inevitable, since there was some set of events which was a sufficient condition for his choosing to do that particular act and, given the occurrence of the sufficient condition, the choice of that act must take place. No other act could occur in the world as it was at that time, for the world at that time included the events which were sufficient for the occurrence of the given act. And that is just another way of saying that the act the person finally chose to do was *caused*.

The argument then continues in the following way. In a deterministic universe (that is, a universe in which every event is caused) the future is not really open. When someone thinks he has a number of alternative courses of action open to him, any one of which can be brought about as a result of his decision to do it, he is under an illusion. Actually only one of these imagined alternatives is going to be realized. It will be the one which must occur as the effect of the causes that are operating in the situation at that time. It does no good to argue that among these causes must be the person's own choice to do the act. For even though it is quite true (when conditions of excusability are absent) that a person's own choice is the cause of one act being done by him rather than another, his choice itself is the effect of previous causes, and these in turn are the effects of still earlier causes, and so on until we get back to the formation of the individual's personality and character in his childhood. In other words, if there is a causal explanation for the person's act in terms of his deliberation and choice, there is equally a causal explanation of why he deliberated and chose the way he did. This causal explanation may be very complex, but however difficult it may be to discover it (given the present state of the science of psychology), the causes are operating so as to bring about every thought and every feeling that goes into the deliberative process and emerges in the specific choice.

The conclusion drawn by the determinist is this. Since there was in fact only one possibility for action, given the past causes and surrounding conditions of the person's choice, he was not really able to choose any other alternative. His ability to *do* other alternatives and his opportunity to choose them *if he wished* are not to the point, since he, being the kind of person he was, could in fact only choose one of the acts. Similarly, the absence of external and internal constraints only gives him the false belief that he is free to choose among the alternatives. He *feels* free when he chooses because he does not feel any inner compulsion or external constraint upon him, and it is perfectly true that there is no such compulsion or constraint. Still, only one of the alternatives can in fact be chosen by him, and this one alone is the single possibility open to him, regardless of what he might feel or think at the time of choice. Now suppose the act he finally chooses to do is something he and others believe to be morally wrong. Then, the determinist goes on, he cannot be held responsible for it, since he could not have done otherwise. It was the only thing he could have done in the situation, given the kind of person he was and the circumstances of his life at that moment of choice.

Some philosophers have been convinced by this argument and have thought that, in order to preserve moral responsibility in human life, it is necessary to deny determinism. Confronted with the choice between determinism and no responsibility or responsibility but not determinism, they have opted for the latter. They have held that a human being is not merely a *personality* entirely explainable in empirical terms. He is also a *moral agent.* When he is confronted with the choice between right and wrong, he considers himself to be a free agent with a moral self. It is his own moral self that makes the choice and that can accordingly be held responsible (answerable) for what he does. The moral self, in this view, is not to be identified with the personality or formed character of a person. A position of this sort is called *libertarianism,* and Professor C. A. Campbell gives an argument in support of it in the second reading of this chapter. Professor Campbell tries to show how the actions we do as moral agents are not merely the effect of our formed character at the time of doing them. If we carefully introspect what is occurring in our experience at the time we make a choice between doing our duty and letting ourselves give in to our desires, we shall find, he argues, that we exercise a kind of freedom that is "contra-causal." Consequently we can be held responsible for the choice that we make, as moral agents, in such circumstances.

How is the moral self, when so understood, related to the formed character or personality, in the light of the findings of contemporary psychology concerning the causes of people's actions and choices? Those who believe in a moral self argue that these factors operating on one's personality set certain directions or tendencies for choice, but do not completely determine it. At a given stage in one's personality development there is a *probability* that one will choose to do certain kinds of acts and not others. But this is a probability only, not a certainty. An individual's motives, desires, beliefs, and attitudes will set limits to the possibilities of choice open to his moral self. For an individual with a certain kind of personality, it will be psychologically improbable (if not impossible) for him to commit murder; for someone with another kind of personality, such an act will be quite possible, and at certain times in his life might even become probable. But this does not mean that he *must* choose to commit murder. It only means that he has a tendency to do so, and if he is aware of the moral aspects of the act, his moral self can counteract this tendency and so enable him to refrain from doing the act. Indeed, this is exactly what happens to anyone who is faced with a choice between doing what he believes is right and doing what he wants to do. "The conflict between duty and interest," as such a choice is often called in ethics, is just the area where our moral self comes into play as a determining factor in our deliberation and conduct. No matter what direction the tendencies of our personality might pull (or push) us in, it is our moral self that finally makes the choice between doing our duty and yielding to our interest. As long as we have a sense of duty or a sense of responsibility, we can use self-control and will power to overcome the tendencies of our personality that pull (or push) us in the wrong direction. A moral agent, in fact, is defined as one who can recognize the moral aspects of the choice open to him and can exert the power of self-determination in making his choice, within the limits set by the tendencies of his personality. It is this which distinguishes men, who are moral agents, from animals, which are not. Therefore, unless a person totally lacks any sense of what is morally right and wrong, he has a moral self and can accordingly be held responsible if he fails to do what he ought to do. He cannot cite his personality tendencies as an excuse. Having a personality, in short, is not one of the conditions of excusability.

Sometimes the moral self is understood to be the "soul" of a person, conceived in terms of the traditional metaphysics of Christian theology. The soul is an immaterial substance, created by God and endowed with freedom of the will. It resides in the body until death, after which it continues its existence in some supernatural condition. The freedom of the will is thought of as a God-given capacity or faculty of the soul, which operates at the moment of choice between good and evil. When a person knowingly chooses to do evil, he (that is, his soul) is held accountable for his action and is subject to God's punishment. In this chapter we shall not consider the arguments for and against the existence of a soul. This would take us into the realms of metaphysics and theology, and the problem of free will is difficult enough to handle even when we do not introduce these theological considerations.

We have seen how some philosophers, like Professor Campbell, have conceived of the moral agent as a moral self, not entirely subject to causal laws and thus able to make a free choice among alternatives. This view, as was noted above, is called *libertarianism*. It is also sometimes called *incompatibilism* because it assumes that free will and determinism are incompatible. Now many philosophers deny this assumption. They believe it is possible to accept the principle of determinism and still hold oneself and others morally responsible. They do not think it is necessary to speak of an undetermined "moral self" in order to account for the freedom of choice necessary for moral responsibility. In their view, which has been called *compatibilism* or *soft determinism*, free choice and free action are empirical concepts, exemplified in everyday life, and perfectly consistent with universal causation. Let us now examine some of the main points made by these philosophers in arguing that free will and determinism are compatible.

THE CONCEPT OF FREEDOM

What does it mean to say that someone freely chooses to do an act, or acts of his own free will? The first thing to notice is that freedom and the absence of freedom are matters of degree. A free act is one that is *comparatively* free. There is a continuum or gradation of acts, ranging all the way from clear-cut cases with regard to which we would ordinarily say there is no freedom at all, to clear-cut cases of what we ordinarily call free acts. Thus a man who is in jail is not free to get out; a person whose life is threatened if he disobeys someone with power over him is not free; and so on for other cases concerning which, in everyday life, we say there is no (or very little) freedom. Similarly, we say that a person did something of his own free will when he was not forced or compelled to do it and when he could just as easily have done something else instead. But this does not require us to claim that there are "absolutely" free acts that have nothing in common with unfree acts or with acts which we would describe as being partly or somewhat free.

If freedom is a matter of degree, then the question whether a given act is or is not free cannot be the same as the question whether the act is or is not determined. For determinism and indeterminism are not matters of degree. Here it is all or nothing: either there is a sufficient condition for the act to occur or there is not; either the act is determined or it is not. Even if someone argues that there is a "tendency" in a person to do a certain act, as long as this tendency is not sufficient to cause the person to do the act the question remains, Is the act determined or not? And this means, Would any causal explanation completely account for the person's doing the act in the given circumstances? If the answer is yes, then the act is absolutely determined, and there is no point in saying that a "high degree" of causal determination is operating in this instance, or that the act is "mostly" determined. If the act is not completely determined, then it is simply not determined. In that case there is no sufficient condition for the occurrence of the act and no causal explanation will be able to account for the person's doing the act.

In reply to this it might be argued that causal explanations are always only probable, never certain, and that probability is a matter of degree. But this argument confuses the two very different statements: (1) All human acts are determined. (2) Act X is determined by such-and-such causes. Statement (1) is the claim that *some* causal explanation can provide a completely adequate account of why any human act has occurred. Statement (2) is the entirely different claim to have knowledge of the specific causal explanation for the occurrence of a particular act, X. Now it is true that our knowledge of specific causal explanations is never more than probable, since it involves reference to causal laws or empirical generalizations, and these can never be established with certainty. So no one can know with certainty the true causal explanation of any particular act.

But this in no way throws doubt upon the issue of whether every act is determined. The causal explanation of a given act might be totally unknown to us, yet such an explanation, if known, could provide a complete and true account of why the act was done. For it would specify the events that constituted at that time a sufficient condition for the act's being done. Indeterminism (which is entailed by libertarianism) is the denial that there is any such sufficient condition for the act. Hence with regard to an undetermined act, the indeterminist and the libertarian must hold that there is no causal explanation, *known or unknown,* for that act.

Degrees of freedom, then, are not to be thought of as being in inverse proportion to degrees of determinism. There are no degrees of determinism. What, then, are the conditions whose fulfilment in varying degrees is the criterion for varying degrees of freedom? This is the question we must answer if we are to define the terms "free" and "unfree" as applied to human choices and acts. The way to discover such conditions is as follows. First, consider clear-cut cases or paradigms of what are ordinarily called free choices and acts. Next, consider paradigms of what are commonly recognized as unfree choices and acts—cases we would all agree (before knowing anything about determinism or indeterminism) to place at the other end of the continuum. Then notice the properties or characteristics which these two groups of cases do *not* have in common, and especially those properties we ourselves point out when we are asked about a member of the first group, "What *makes* that a case of freedom of choice or action?" and which we point out when asked about a member of the other group, "*Why* do you call that an unfree choice or action?" Finally, after specifying these properties, turn to the unclear and problematic cases, those which tend to fall near the center of the continuum. Regarding these cases, ask yourself, "What is it about them that makes it difficult for me to decide whether they are free or unfree?" We shall then find that all these problematic cases exemplify some of the properties which we noticed in the clear-cut cases of freedom and at the same time have other properties in common with our paradigms of unfree choices and acts. By bringing out these properties, we make clear to ourselves the conditions which define degrees of freedom. That is, we come to understand what criteria or tests must be satisfied in varying degrees by human choices and acts if we are to say that they are free or unfree in varying degrees. (In the readings of this chapter several suggestions are made by philosophers as to what these criteria of freedom are.)

The problem of free will can then be formulated in a precise way. It consists of two questions: (1) Are these defining properties of free choices and acts consistent with the principle of determinism? (2) Are these properties such that we are morally justified in holding people responsible for their choices and acts *to the extent that they are free?* Now a number of contemporary philosophers answer both of these questions in the affirmative, and so maintain the position that the kind of freedom necessary for moral responsibility is perfectly compatible with determinism. This position, we have seen, is called "compatibilism" or "soft determinism." It is to be contrasted with a position that combines determinism with incompatibilism, a view which is sometimes called simply "deter-minism" and sometimes "hard determinism" to distinguish it from soft determin-ism. Hard determinism consists in the following three propositions. First, what-ever may be the properties by which we distinguish between free and unfree acts, they are not such as to make it morally justifiable for us to hold people responsible. Second, determinism is true. Third, even if the defining properties of freedom are compatible with determinism, the kinds of causes that operate upon free choices and acts (including the causes involved in personality devel-opment) require us to change our concept of moral responsibility, or at least to reject the traditional concept.

SOFT DETERMINISM AND HARD DETERMINISM

The readings in this chapter begin and end with two presentations of soft de-terminism or compatibilism. In the first reading Professor Moritz Schlick argues that the alleged problem of free will is what he describes as a "pseudo-problem." He means by this that if we eliminate all the semantic confusions involved in our talk about freedom, causation, and responsibility, we will see that there is really no problem. Having clarified our terms, we will come to recognize that all three of the following assertions are true: (1) Some acts are free. (2) All acts are determined. (3) People can be rightly held responsible for their free acts. Since all of these assertions are held to be mutually consistent, this theory is a compatibilist or soft determinist one.

A direct attack on Schlick's arguments is made by Professor Campbell in the second reading. As was noted earlier, Campbell ends up by claiming (on grounds of introspection) that moral responsibility requires a "contra-causal" type of freedom and that people do in fact exercise such freedom at certain moments of choice between duty and desire. Thus Campbell not only takes a libertarian view, but also attempts to show that the problem of free will is a real problem, not a pseudo-problem.

In the last reading of the chapter, Professor Francis V. Raab gives reasons that support a form of soft determinism somewhat similar to Schlick's. Raab's arguments are of special interest, however, because they rest on a detailed analy-sis of the meaning of the word "could." Why is this word of importance in the free will controversy? The answer lies in the fact that when we say in everyday life that someone acted of his own free will or acted freely, we mean that he could have done otherwise than he did. Thus if a person has done act X in a certain situation and if we say he did X freely, we mean that he did not have to do X in that situation but could have done something else instead. The meaning of "free" as applied to human acts, therefore, depends on the meaning of "could" as used in sentences of the form "He could have done otherwise." Professor Raab then analyzes the meaning of "could" in such contexts and comes to the conclu-sion that it does *not* mean that the act which the person did was *uncaused*. What it does mean, according to him, is that the person had the ability to do other acts than the one he did and that he was not under coercion or duress to

MORAL RESPONSIBILITY AND FREE WILL

do what he did, both of which claims are compatible with determinism. Professor Raab goes on to argue that a person is morally responsible for his acts whenever the usual grounds for excusing behavior do not hold, and these situations often occur in everyday life. Thus both freedom and responsibility are consistent with determinism, which is the thesis of soft determinism.

The opposite thesis is defended by Professors Paul Edwards and John Hospers in the third and fourth readings of this chapter. In his essay called "Hard and Soft Determinism," Professor Edwards first outlines the position of soft determinism and then claims that it overlooks an important fact. The soft determinist shows that we can and sometimes do act as we choose to act, but he does not go on to ask, What causes us to *choose* to do one act rather than another? If a determinist were asked this question, he would reply, It is our personality and character that cause us to choose one way rather than another, since they are what determine the specific volitions and desires which we bring to the situation of choice and which we carry out when we act "freely." We must then, as determinists, inquire into the causes that explain our personality and character. Now if we do this, Professor Edwards argues, we find that "a person's character is ultimately the product of factors over which he had no control," namely, factors that occurred in infancy and early childhood. A person is not, after all, in control of the way his parents and teachers treated him as a child, and these are among the main determinants in the formation of his personality and character. But how can a person be held responsible for something that is beyond his control? Here the position of hard determinism emerges. For this argument leads to the conclusion that moral responsibility is not compatible with determinism, if we take into account *all* of the causal factors behind a person's behavior. At least, this is the conclusion Professor Edwards draws in this essay, thus defending a position of hard determinism.

It should be noted that Professor Edwards does not deny that there is a difference between free and unfree acts. He argues only that the difference between them is not a sufficient ground for holding people morally responsible for their free acts and for excusing them for their unfree acts.

The case for hard determinism presented by Professor Hospers in his essay "The Range of Human Freedom" is based on three points. The first point is an analysis of unconscious motivation and the neurotic personality which is intended to show that, in many cases where we ordinarily hold people responsible for what they do, we ought not so to hold them because they cannot help what they do. The second point is the drawing of a parallel between neurotic and normal persons which is intended to show that neither is to be held responsible because neither "has caused his own character, which makes him what he is." (This second point is a more detailed argument in support of the view set forth by Professor Edwards.) The third point is an analysis of the word "could" which is intended to show that holding a person responsible for his own character is meaningless. This third argument requires some preliminary remarks.

Suppose a person is in a situation of choice and decides to do act X rather than act Y. The statement "He did X of his own free will" is equivalent to the statement "Although he did X, he could have done Y instead," and "He could have done Y" is equivalent to, "He *would* have done Y if he had *chosen* to do Y." But, Professor Hospers continues, even though the person would have been able to do Y if he had chosen to, we cannot say that his act (doing X) was free unless we know that he could have *chosen* to do Y instead. In order for his act to be free, he must not only have the ability to do an alternative act, but his choice between the two alternatives must be a free choice. Now just as "He was free to do X" was analyzed as, "He could have done otherwise," which in turn was analyzed as "He would have done otherwise if he had chosen," so let us analyze "He was free to choose" as "He could have chosen otherwise," which in turn becomes "He would have chosen otherwise if he had *wanted* or *desired* to choose otherwise." But here again it would seem that his choice was not really free, even though we acknowledge that he would have chosen otherwise if he had wanted to, unless we also know that *he could have wanted* to choose otherwise.

It is at this point that Professor Hospers raises the question: Does it make sense to talk about a person's being able to have different wants and desires from the ones he does have? He then answers this question in the negative by making a distinction between two levels of moral discourse. On the first level we speak of being responsible for our actions, and on this level the phrase "could have done otherwise" makes sense. On the second level we speak of motives, desires, wants, character, and personality traits. On this level the concept of moral responsibility does not apply, since "could have had a different character," "could have wanted to choose otherwise," and other "could" statements about motives and personality traits make no sense. Thus we do not know what it would mean for a person to be held responsible for his wants, desires, or character. Professor Hospers concludes, "Instead of saying it is *false* that we are responsible for our own characters, I should prefer to say that the utterance is meaningless."

In the next reading Professor Sidney Hook makes a number of criticisms of these arguments for hard determinism. He first distinguishes between an *empty but meaningful* concept and a *vacuous and meaningless* one. A concept of the first kind would be, for example, the concept of a dog who grows to the size of an elephant. This is meaningful because we can specify the conditions which must be fulfilled for a dog to be described in this way, but it is empty because there is no such dog. An example of a concept that is vacuous and meaningless is the concept of a dog who is completely invisible, inaudible, intangible, and unperceivable in any other way. Here we cannot say that there is no such dog, for we don't even know what it would mean for there to be one. We cannot specify the conditions that must be satisfied for such a dog to exist or not to exist. Now the question is, Are hard determinists claiming that the concept of moral responsibility is empty but meaningful, or are they saying it is vacuous and meaningless? If the first claim is being made, then it makes sense to say that people ought not to be held morally responsible. We would know what it *means* to hold someone responsible even if, as hard determinists claim, we are never justified in doing so. But if the concept is meaningless, then it doesn't make sense to claim that we are never justified in holding anyone responsible, since we do not understand what it means to do so. The hard determinist cannot have it both ways. Professor Hospers, for example, begins with an account of neurotic criminals who do things they cannot avoid doing, given their anxieties, inner conflicts, compulsive obsessions, unconscious motives, and the like. So he argues persuasively that it is cruel and unfair to blame them or hold them morally responsible for their crimes. And when he shifts from neurotic to normal persons, he argues that it is wrong to hold anyone responsible under any conditions, since no one has control over the original formation of his own character. These arguments both presuppose that it *makes sense* to talk about responsibility for character as well as for conduct. Yet in the last section of his essay, as we have noted, Professor Hospers claims it is meaningless to talk about being responsible for one's own character. He thus lays himself open to the following criticism by Professor Hook: If moral responsibility is a vacuous concept, then moral innocence is, too, since the morally innocent are those who are not to be held responsible for an act. Hence it cannot make sense to plead for the innocent, to defend them against those who unjustly blame them. But this is precisely what Professor Hospers does, and therefore he is inconsistent.

There is a further inconsistency involved here, according to Professor Hook. In holding that others are unjustified in blaming the innocent, Professors Edwards and Hospers are blaming people for blaming the innocent, when no one is to be blamed for anything! If a murderer cannot be held responsible (because he did not entirely shape his own character), neither can the members of a jury who decide he is guilty, nor the judge who sentences him, nor the warden who imprisons him, nor the family of the murdered person who blame him.

Professor Hook then goes on to raise further doubts about hard determinism. He questions the hard determinists' view of holding a person responsible, and so punishing or blaming him, only when doing so tends to influence the future conduct and character of the person. He argues that this is not the whole story, since at least one additional condition of moral responsibility seems to be presupposed, namely, that the person has "a tendency to respond to valid reasons, to behave rationally, to respond to human emotions in a human way." (Professor Campbell makes a similar point in his criticism of the soft determinist, Schlick.) Thus we might punish or even "blame" a dog in order to change his future behavior, but we do not hold dogs morally responsible for what they do. And if we reflect about the situations in which we hold ourselves responsible (answerable, accountable) for having done something we believe to be wrong, it seems quite clear that we don't blame ourselves only if we know that doing so will tend to make us refrain from doing a similar act in the future. We seem to hold ourselves responsible for the past act, quite regardless of the future consequences of our taking such an attitude toward ourselves. We think we are justified in taking such an attitude whenever we acknowledge that we had no legitimate excuse for doing the act. We would continue to think this even if we knew we were about to die and would thus be prevented from changing our character so as to refrain from similar conduct in the future. At any rate, if our only reason to hold ourselves responsible were in order to make ourselves better persons in the future, we would be treating ourselves the way we treat children and animals. In blaming or punishing them, we are *training* them; we are not dealing with them as responsible moral agents. Indeed, we might excuse them because they are children or animals and still punish or verbally reprimand them in order to "condition" them not to do similar acts in the future.

Now, as Professor Hook points out, not only does this differ from what we do when we hold ourselves morally responsible, it also makes us feel "lessened as a human being," if all our actions are excused or explained away as not being our fault. "Our dignity as rational human beings," he states, "sometimes leads us to protest . . . that we really *are* responsible and that we are prepared to take the consequences of our responsibility." Finally, it might well be the case that, if we did *not* hold ourselves as being accountable for our acts, we might weaken whatever will power, determination, and self-control we are now able to exert to do the right and abstain from doing the wrong. Thus the theory of hard determinism might itself become a factor in weakening or corrupting us, and might end by destroying our sense of human dignity. Would the hard determinist then hold himself responsible for these possible effects of teaching his own theory?

One additional consideration should be raised regarding Professor Hook's remarks on moral responsibility. This is the fact that much of what he says applies to the utilitarian view of blame and punishment often advocated by *soft* determinists. Professor Schlick, for example, holds that blame and punishment are applied to a person in order to motivate him and others to refrain from doing certain acts. This view of moral responsibility, which is accepted by many soft determinists because it is consistent with the principle of determinism, is open to the same criticisms raised by Professor Hook against the hard determinist view of responsibility. Whether these criticisms can be met by any determinist, hard or soft, is a problem for the reader to try to work out for himself. It may be that here is the point where determinism and moral responsibility are most evidently in conflict. And so we come back to the question with which we began: Must determinism be denied if moral responsibility is to be a meaningful and justifiable concept in human life?

MORITZ SCHLICK
When Is a Man Responsible?

I. THE PSEUDO-PROBLEM OF FREEDOM OF THE WILL

With hesitation and reluctance I prepare to add this chapter to the discussion of ethical problems. For in it I must speak of a matter which, even at present, is thought to be a fundamental ethical question, but which got into ethics and has become a much discussed problem only because of a misunderstanding. This is the so-called problem of the freedom of the will. Moreover, this pseudo-problem has long since been settled by the efforts of certain sensible persons; and, above all, the state of affairs just described has been often disclosed—with exceptional clarity—by Hume. Hence it is really one of the greatest scandals of philosophy that again and again so much paper and printer's ink is devoted to this matter, to say nothing of the expenditure of thought, which could have been applied to more important problems (assuming that it would have sufficed for these). Thus I should truly be ashamed to write a chapter on "freedom." In the chapter heading, the word "responsible" indicates what concerns ethics, and designates the point at which misunderstanding arises. Therefore the concept of responsibility constitutes our theme, and if in the process of its clarification I also must speak of the concept of freedom I shall, of course, say only what others have already said better; consoling myself with the thought that in this way alone can anything be done to put an end at last to that scandal.

The main task of ethics . . . is to explain moral behavior. To explain means to refer back to laws: every science, including psychology, is possible only in so far as there are such laws to which the events can be referred. Since the assumption that *all* events are subject to universal laws is called the principle of causality, one can also say, "Every science presupposes the principle of causality." Therefore every explanation of human behavior must also assume the validity of casual laws; in this case the existence of psychological laws. . . . All of our experience strengthens us in the belief that this presupposition is realized, at least to the extent required for all purposes of practical life in intercourse with nature and human beings, and also for the most precise demands of technique. Whether, indeed, the principle of causality holds universally, whether, that is, *determinism* is true, we do not know; no one knows. But we do know that it is impossible to settle the dispute between determinism and indetermin-

From *Problems of Ethics* by Moritz Schlick, Dover Publications, Inc., New York. Reprinted through the permission of the publisher. Translated from the German by David Rynin (1939).

ism by mere reflection and speculation, by the consideration of so many reasons for and so many reasons against (which collectively and individually are but pseudo-reasons). Such an attempt becomes especially ridiculous when one considers with what enormous expenditure of experimental and logical skill contemporary physics carefully approaches the question of whether causality can be maintained for the most minute intra-atomic events. . . .

Fortunately, it is not necessary to lay claim to a final solution of the causal problem in order to say what is necessary in ethics concerning responsibility; there is required only an analysis of the concept, the careful determination of the meaning which is in fact joined to the words "responsibility" and "freedom" as these are actually used. If men had made clear to themselves the sense of those propositions, which we use in everyday life, that pseudo-argument which lies at the root of the pseudo-problem, and which recurs thousands of times within and outside of philosophical books, would never have arisen.

The argument runs as follows: "If determinism is true, if, that is, all events obey immutable laws, then my will too is always determined, by my innate character and my motives. Hence my decisions are necessary, not free. But if so, then I am not responsible for my acts, for I would be accountable for them only if I could do something about the way my decisions went; but I can do nothing about it, since they proceed with necessity from my character and the motives. And I have made neither, and have no power over them: the motives come from without, and my character is the necessary product of the innate tendencies and the external influences which have been effective during my lifetime. Thus determinism and moral responsibility are incompatible. Moral responsibility presupposes freedom, that is, exemption from causality."

This process of reasoning rests upon a whole series of confusions, just as the links of a chain hang together. We must show these confusions to be such, and thus destroy them.

2. TWO MEANINGS OF THE WORD "LAW"

It all begins with an erroneous interpretation of the meaning of "law." In practice this is understood as a rule by which the state prescribes certain behavior to its citizens. These rules often contradict the natural desires of the citizens (for if they did not do so, there would be no reason for making them), and are in fact not followed by many of them; while others obey, but under *compulsion*. The state does in fact compel its citizens by imposing certain sanctions (punishments) which serve to bring their desires into harmony with the prescribed laws.

In natural science, on the other hand, the word "law" means something quite different. The natural law is not a *pre*scription as to how something should behave, but a formula, a *de*scription of how something does in fact behave. The two forms of "laws" have only this in common: both tend to be expressed in *formulae*. Otherwise they have absolutely nothing to do with one another, and it is very blameworthy that the same word has been used for two such different things; but even more so that philosophers have allowed themselves to be led into serious errors by this usage. Since natural laws are only descriptions of what happens, there can be in regard to them no talk of "compulsion." The laws of celestial mechanics do not prescribe to the planets how they have to move, as though the planets would actually like to move quite otherwise, and are only forced by these burdensome laws of Kepler to move in orderly paths; no, these laws do not in any way "compel" the planets, but express only what in fact planets actually do.

If we apply this to volition, we are enlightened at once; even before the other confusions are discovered. When we say that a man's will "obeys psychological laws," these are not civic laws, which compel him to make certain decisions, or dictate desires to him, which he would in fact prefer not to have. They are laws of nature, merely expressing which desires he *actually has* under given conditions; they describe the nature of the will in the same manner as the astronomical laws describe the nature of planets. "Compulsion" occurs where man is prevented from realizing his natural desires. How could the rule according to which these natural desires arise itself be considered as "compulsion"?

3. COMPULSION AND NECESSITY

But this is the second confusion to which the first leads almost inevitably: after conceiving the laws of nature, anthropomorphically, as order imposed *nolens volens* upon the events, one adds to them the concept of "necessity." This word, derived from "need," also comes to us from practice, and is used there in the sense of inescapable compulsion. To apply the word with this meaning to natural laws is of course senseless, for the presupposition of an opposing desire is lacking; and it is then confused with something altogether different, which is actually an attribute of natural laws. That is, universality. It is of the essence of natural laws to be universally valid, for only when we have found a rule which holds of events without exception do we *call* the rule a law of nature. Thus when we say "a natural law holds necessarily" this has but one legitimate meaning: "It holds in *all* cases where it is applicable." It is again very deplorable that the word "necessary" has been applied to natural laws (or, what amounts to the same thing, with reference to causality), for it is quite superfluous, since the expression "universally valid" is available. Universal validity is something altogether different from "compulsion"; these concepts belong to spheres so remote from each other that once insight into the error has been gained one can no longer conceive the possibility of a confusion.

The confusion of two concepts always carries with it the confusion of their contradictory opposites. The opposite of the universal validity of a formula, of the existence of a law, is the nonexistence of a law, indeterminism, acausality; while the opposite of compulsion is what in practice everyone calls "freedom." Here emerges the nonsense, trailing through centuries, that freedom means "exemption from the causal principle," or "not subject to the laws of nature."

Hence it is believed necessary to vindicate indeterminism in order to save human freedom.

4. FREEDOM AND INDETERMINISM

This is quite mistaken. Ethics has, so to speak, no moral interest in the purely theoretical question of "determinism or indeterminism?," but only a theoretical interest, namely: in so far as it seeks the laws of conduct, and can find them only to the extent that causality holds. But the question of whether man is morally free (that is, has that freedom which, as we shall show, is the presupposition of moral responsibility) is altogether different from the problem of determinism. Hume was especially clear on this point. He indicated the inadmissible confusion of the concepts of "indeterminism" and "freedom"; but he retained, inappropriately, the word "freedom" for both, calling the one freedom of "the will," the other, genuine kind, "freedom of conduct." He showed that morality is interested only in the latter, and that such freedom, in general, is unquestionably to be attributed to mankind. And this is quite correct. Freedom means the opposite of compulsion; a man is *free* if he does not act under *compulsion*, and he is compelled or unfree when he is hindered from without in the realization of his natural desires. Hence he is unfree when he is locked up, or chained, or when someone forces him at the point of a gun to do what otherwise he would not do. This is quite clear, and everyone will admit that the everyday or legal notion of the lack of freedom is thus correctly interpreted, and that a man will be considered quite free and responsible if no such external compulsion is exerted upon him. There are certain cases which lie between these clearly described ones, as, say, when someone acts under the influence of alcohol or a narcotic. In such cases we consider the man to be more or less unfree, and hold him less accountable, because we rightly view the influence of the drug as "external," even though it is found within the body; it prevents him from making decisions in the manner peculiar to his nature. If he takes the narcotic of his own will, we make him completely responsible for *this* act and transfer a part of the responsibility to the consequences, making, as it were, an average or mean condemnation of the whole. In the case also of a person who is mentally ill we do not consider him free with respect to those acts in which the disease expresses itself, because we view the illness as a disturbing factor which hinders the normal functioning of his natural tendencies. We make not him but his disease responsible.

5. THE NATURE OF RESPONSIBILITY

But what does this really signify? What do we mean by this concept of responsibility which goes along with that of "freedom," and which plays such an important role in morality? It is easy to attain complete clarity in this matter; we need only carefully determine the manner in which the concept is used. What is the case in practice when we impute "responsibility" to a person? What is our aim in doing this? The judge has to discover who is responsible for a given act in order that he may *punish* him. We are inclined to be less concerned with the inquiry as to who deserves *reward* for an act, and we have no special officials for this; but of course the principle would be the same. But let us stick to punishment in order to make the idea clear. What is punishment, actually? The view still often expressed, that it is a natural *retaliation* for past wrong, ought no longer to be defended in cultivated society; for the opinion that an increase in sorrow can be "made good again" by further sorrow is altogether barbarous. Certainly the origin of punishment may lie in an impulse of retaliation or vengeance; but what is such an impulse except the instinctive desire to destroy the *cause* of the deed to be avenged, by the destruction of or injury to the malefactor? Punishment is concerned only with the institution of causes, of *motives* of conduct, and this alone is its meaning. Punishment is an educative measure, and as such is a means to the formation of motives, which are in part to prevent the wrongdoer from repeating the act (reformation) and in part to prevent others from committing a similar act (intimidation). Analogously, in the case of reward we are concerned with an incentive.

Hence the question regarding responsibility is the question: Who, in a given case, is to be punished? Who is to be considered the true wrongdoer? This problem is not identical with that regarding the original instigator of the act; for the great-grandparents of the man, from whom he inherited his character, might in the end be the cause, or the statesmen who are responsible for his social milieu, and so forth. But the "doer" is the one *upon whom the motive must have acted* in order, with certainty, to have prevented the act (or called it forth, as the case may be). Consideration of remote causes is of no help here, for in the first place their actual contribution cannot be determined, and in the second place they are generally out of reach. Rather, we must find the person in whom the decisive junction of causes lies. The question of who is responsible is the question concerning the *correct point of application of the motive*. And the important thing is that in this its meaning is completely exhausted; behind it there lurks no mysterious connection between transgression and requital, which is merely *indicated* by the described state of affairs. It is a matter only of knowing who is to be punished or rewarded, in order that punishment and reward function as such—be able to achieve their goal.

Thus, all the facts connected with the concepts of responsibility and imputation are at once made intelligible. We do not charge an insane person with responsibility, for the very reason that he offers no unified point for the application of a motive. It would be pointless to try to affect him by means of promises or threats, when his confused soul fails to respond to such influence because its normal mechanism is out of order. We do not try to give him motives, but try to heal him (metaphorically, we make his sickness responsible, and try to remove its causes). When a man is forced by threats to commit certain acts we do not blame him, but the one who held the pistol at his breast. The reason is clear: the act would have been prevented had we been able to restrain the person who threatened him; and this person is the one whom we must influence in order to prevent similar acts in the future.

6. THE CONSCIOUSNESS OF RESPONSIBILITY

But much more important than the question of when a man is said to be responsible is that of when he *himself* feels responsible. Our whole treatment would be untenable if it gave no explanation of this. It is, then, a welcome confirmation of the view here developed that the subjective feeling of responsibility coincides with the objective judgment. It is a fact of experience that, in general, the person blamed or condemned is conscious of the fact that he was "rightly" taken to account—of course, under the supposition that no error has been made, that the assumed state of affairs actually occurred. What is this consciousness of having been the true doer of the act, the actual instigator? Evidently not merely that it was he who took the steps required for its performance; but there must be added the awareness that he did it "independently," "of his own initiative," or however it be expressed. This feeling is simply the consciousness of *freedom*, which is merely the knowledge of having acted of one's *own* desires. And "one's own desires" are those which have their origin in the regularity of one's character in the given situation, and are not imposed by an external power, as explained above. The absence of the external power expresses itself in the well-known feeling (usually considered characteristic of the consciousness of freedom) *that one could also have acted otherwise.* How this indubitable experience ever came to be an argument in favor of indeterminism is incomprehensible to me. It is of course obvious that I should have acted differently had I *willed* something else; but the feeling never says that I could also have willed something else, even though this is true, if, that is, other motives had been present. And it says even less that under *exactly the same* inner and outer conditions I could also have willed something else. How could such a feeling inform me of anything regarding the purely theoretical question of whether the principle of causality holds or not? Of course, after what has been said on the subject, I do not undertake to demonstrate the principle, but I do deny that from any such fact of consciousness the least follows regarding the principle's validity. This feeling is not the consciousness of the absence of a cause, but of something altogether different, namely, of *freedom*, which consists in the fact that I can act as I desire.

Thus the feeling of responsibility assumes that I acted freely, that my own desires impelled me; and if because of this feeling I willingly suffer blame for my behavior or reproach myself, and thereby admit that I might have acted otherwise, this means that other behavior was compatible with the laws of volition—of course, granted other motives. And I myself desire the existence of such motives and bear the pain (regret and sorrow) caused me by my behavior so that its repetition will be prevented. To blame oneself means just to apply motives of improvement to oneself, which is usually the task of the educator. But if, for example, one does something under the influence of torture, feelings

of guilt and regret are absent, for one knows that according to the laws of volition no other behavior was possible—no matter what ideas, because of their feeling tones, might have functioned as motives. The important thing, always, is
that the feeling of responsibility means the realization that one's self, one's own
psychic processes constitute the point at which motives must be applied in order
to govern the acts of one's body.

•   •   •   •   •

C. A. CAMPBELL
Is "Freewill" a Pseudo-Problem?

•   •   •   •

III

Here then, in substance is Schlick's theory. Let us now examine it.

In the first place, it is surely quite unplausible to suggest that the common
assumption that moral freedom postulates some breach of causal continuity
arises from a confusion of two different types of law. Schlick's distinction between descriptive and prescriptive law is, of course, sound. It was no doubt
worth pointing out, too, that descriptive laws cannot be said to compel human
behaviour in the same way as prescriptive laws do. But it seems to me evident
that the usual reason why it is held that moral freedom implies some breach of
causal continuity, is not a belief that causal laws 'compel' as civil laws 'compel,'
but simply the belief that the admission of unbroken causal continuity entails
a *further* admission which is directly incompatible with moral responsibility;
viz. the admission that no man could have acted otherwise than he in fact did.
Now it may, of course, be an error thus to assume that a man is not morally
responsible for an act, a fit subject for moral praise and blame in respect of it,
unless he could have acted otherwise than he did. Or, if *this* is not an error, it
may still be an error to assume that a man could not have acted otherwise than
he did, in the sense of the phrase that is crucial for moral responsibility, without
there occurring some breach of causal continuity. Into these matters we shall
have to enter very fully at a later stage. But the relevant point at the moment is

From C. A. Campbell, "Is 'Freewill' a Pseudo-Problem?" *Mind*, LX, No. 240 (1951),
441–465. Reprinted by permission of the author and the editor of *Mind*. [The first two
sections of the article, in which Professor Campbell summarizes the theory of Moritz
Schlick contained in the preceding reading, have been omitted.—Ed. note.]

that these (not *prima facie* absurd) assumptions about the conditions of moral responsibility have very commonly, indeed normally, been made, and that they are entirely adequate to explain why the problem of Free Will finds its usual formulation in terms of partial exemption from causal law. Schlick's distinction between prescriptive and descriptive laws has no bearing at all upon the truth or falsity of these assumptions. Yet if these assumptions are accepted, it is (I suggest) really inevitable that the Free Will problem should be formulated in the way to which Schlick takes exception. Recognition of the distinction upon which Schlick and his followers lay so much stress can make not a jot of difference.

As we have seen, however, Schlick does later proceed to the much more important business of disputing these common assumptions about the conditions of moral responsibility. He offers us an analysis of moral responsibility which flatly contradicts these assumptions; an analysis according to which the only freedom demanded by morality is a freedom which is compatible with Determinism. If this analysis can be sustained, there is certainly no problem of 'Free Will' in the traditional sense.

But it seems a simple matter to show that Schlick's analysis is untenable. Let us test it by Schlick's own claim that it gives us what we mean by 'moral responsibility' in ordinary linguistic usage.

We do not ordinarily consider the lower animals to be morally responsible. But *ought* we not to do so if Schlick is right about what we mean by moral responsibility? It is quite possible, by punishing the dog who absconds with the succulent chops designed for its master's luncheon, favourably to influence its motives in respect of its future behaviour in like circumstances. If moral responsibility is to be linked with punishment as Schlick links it, and punishment conceived as a form of education, we should surely hold the dog morally responsible? The plain fact, of course, is that we don't. We don't, because we suppose that the dog 'couldn't help it': that its action (unlike what we usually believe to be true of human beings) was simply a link in a continuous chain of causes and effects. In other words, we do commonly demand the contra-causal sort of freedom as a condition of moral responsibility.

Again, we do ordinarily consider it proper, in certain circumstances, to speak of a person no longer living as morally responsible for some present situation. But *ought* we to do so if we accept Schlick's essentially 'forward-looking' interpretation of punishment and responsibility? Clearly we cannot now favourably affect the dead man's motives. No doubt they could *at one time* have been favourably affected. But that cannot be relevant to our judgment of responsibility if, as Schlick insists, the question of who is responsible 'is a matter only of knowing who is to be punished or rewarded.' Indeed he expressly tells us, as we saw earlier, that in asking this question we are not concerned with a 'great-grand-parent' who may have been the 'original instigator,' because, for one reason, this 'remote cause' is 'out of reach.' We cannot bring the appropriate educative influence to bear upon it. But the plain fact, of course, is that we do frequently assign moral responsibility for present situations to persons who have long been inacessible to any punitive action on our part. And Schlick's position is still more paradoxical in respect of our apportionment of responsibility for occurrences in the distant past. Since in these cases there is no agent whatsoever whom we can favourably influence by punishment, the question of moral responsibility here should have no meaning for us. But of course it has. Historical writings are studded with examples.

Possibly the criticism just made may seem to some to result from taking Schlick's analysis too much *au pied de la lettre*.[1] The absurd consequences deduced, it may be said, would not follow if we interpreted Schlick as meaning that a man is morally responsible where his motive is such as can *in principle* be favourably affected by reward or punishment—whether or not we who pass the judgment are in a position to take such action. But with every desire to be fair to Schlick, I cannot see how he could accept this modification and still retain the essence of his theory. For the essence of his theory seems to be that moral responsibility has its whole meaning and importance for us in relation to our potential control of future conduct in the interests of society. (I agree that it is hard to believe that anybody *really* thinks this. But it is perhaps less hard to believe to-day than it has ever been before in the history of modern ethics.)

Again, we ordinarily consider that, in certain circumstances, the *degree* of a man's moral responsibility for an act is affected by considerations of his inherited nature, or of his environment, or of both. It is our normal habit to 'make allowances' (as we say) when we have reason to believe that a malefactor had a vicious heredity, or was nurtured in his formative years in a harmful environment. We say in such cases 'Poor chap, he is more to be pitied than blamed. We could scarcely expect him to behave like a decent citizen with *his* parentage or upbringing.' But this extremely common sort of judgment has no point at all if we mean by normal responsibility what Schlick says that we mean. On *that* meaning the degree of a man's moral responsibility must presumably be dependent upon the degree to which we can favourably affect his future motives, which is quite another matter. Now there is no reason to believe that the motives of a man with a bad heredity or a bad upbringing are either less or more subject to educative influence than those of his more fortunate fellows. Yet it is plain matter of fact that we do commonly consider the degree of a man's moral responsibility to be affected by these two factors.

A final point. The extremity of paradox in Schlick's identification of the question 'Who is morally blameworthy?' with the question 'Who is to be punished?' is apt to be partially concealed from us just because it is our normal habit to include in the meaning of 'punishment' an element of 'requital for moral transgression' which Schlick expressly denies to it. On that account we commonly think of 'punishment,' in its strict sense, as implying moral blameworthiness in the person punished. But if we remember to mean by punishment what Schlick means by it, a purely 'educative measure,' with no retributive ingredi-

---

[1] [That is, to take it too literally.—Ed. note.]

ents, his identification of the two questions loses such plausibility as it might otherwise have. For clearly we often think it proper to 'punish' a person, in *Schlick's* sense, where we are not at all prepared to say that the person is morally blameworthy. We may even think him morally commendable. A case in point would be the unmistakably sincere but muddle-headed person who at the cost of great suffering to himself steadfastly pursues as his 'duty' a course which, in our judgment is fraught with danger to the common weal. We should most of us feel entitled, in the public interest, to bring such action to bear upon the man's motives as might induce him to refrain in future from his socially injurious behavior: in other words, to inflict upon him what Schlick would call 'punishment.' But we should most of us feel perfectly clear that in so 'punishing' this misguided citizen we are not proclaiming his moral blameworthiness or moral wickedness.

Adopting Schlick's own criterion, then, looking simply 'to the manner in which the concept is used,' we seem bound to admit that constantly people do assign moral responsibility where Schlick's theory says they shouldn't, don't assign moral responsibility where Schlick's theory says they should, and assign degrees of moral responsibility where on Schlick's theory there should be no difference in degree. I think we may reasonably conclude that Schlick's account of what we mean by moral responsibility breaks down.

The rebuttal of Schlick's arguments, however, will not suffice of itself to refute the pseudo-problem theory. The indebtedness to Schlick of most later advocates of the theory may be conceded, but certainly it does not comprehend all of significance that they have to say on the problem. There are recent analyses of the conditions of moral responsibility containing sufficient new matter, or sufficient old matter in a more precise and telling form, to require of us now something of a fresh start. In the section which follows I propose to consider some representative samples of these analyses—all of which, of course, are designed to show that the freedom which moral responsibility implies is not in fact a contra-causal type of freedom.

But before reopening the general question of the nature and conditions of moral responsibility there is a *caveat* which it seems to me worth while to enter. The difficulties in the way of a clear answer are not slight; but they are apt to seem a good deal more formidable than they really are because of a common tendency to consider in unduly close association two distinct questions: the question 'Is a contra-causal type of freedom implied by moral responsibility?' and the question 'Does a contra-causal type of freedom anywhere exist?' It seems to me that many philosophers (and I suspect that Moritz Schlick is among them) begin their enquiry with so firm a conviction that the contra-causal sort of freedom nowhere exists, that they find it hard to take very seriously the possibility that it is *this* sort of freedom that moral responsibility implies. For they are loath to abandon the commonsense belief that moral responsibility itself is something real. The implicit reasoning I take to be this. Moral responsibility is real. If moral responsibility is real, the freedom implied in it must be a fact. But contra-causal freedom is not a fact. Therefore contra-causal freedom is not the freedom implied in moral responsibility. I think we should be on our guard against allowing this or some similar train of reasoning (whose premises, after all, are far from indubitable) to seduce us into distorting what we actually find when we set about a direct analysis of moral responsibility and its conditions.

IV

The pseudo-problem theorists usually, and naturally, develop their analysis of moral responsibility by way of contrast with a view which, while it has enjoyed a good deal of philosophic support, I can perhaps best describe as the common view. It will be well to remind ourselves, therefore, of the main features of this view.

So far as the *meaning,* as distinct from the *conditions,* of moral responsibility is concerned, the common view is very simple. If we ask ourselves whether a certain person is morally responsible for a given act (or it may be just 'in general'), what we are considering, it would be said, is whether or not that person is a fit subject upon whom to pass moral judgment; whether he can fittingly be deemed morally good or bad, morally praiseworthy or blameworthy. This does not take us any great way: but (*pace* Schlick) so far as it goes it does not seem to me seriously disputable. The really interesting and controversial question is about the *conditions* of moral responsibility, and in particular the question whether freedom of a contra-causal kind is among these conditions.

The answer of the common man to the latter question is that it most certainly *is* among the conditions. Why does he feel so sure about this? Not, I argued earlier, because the common man supposes that causal law exercises 'compulsion' in the sense that prescriptive laws do, but simply because he does not see how a person can be deemed morally praiseworthy or blameworthy in respect of an act which he could not help performing. From the stand-point of moral praise and blame, he would say—though not necessarily from other stand-points—it is a matter of indifference whether it is by reason of some external constraint or by reason of his own given nature that the man could not help doing what he did. It is quite enough to make moral praise and blame futile that in either case there were no genuine alternatives, no open possibilities, before the man when he acted. He could not have acted otherwise than he did. And the common man might not unreasonably go on to stress the fact that we all, even if we are linguistic philosophers, do in our actual practice of moral judgment appear to accept the common view. He might insist upon the point alluded to earlier in this paper, that we do all, in passing moral censure, 'make allowances' for influences in a man's hereditary nature or environmental circumstances which we regard as having made it more than ordinarily difficult for him to act otherwise than he did: the implication being that if we supposed that the man's heredity and environment made it not merely very *difficult* but actually *impossible* for him to act otherwise than he did, we could not properly assign moral blame to him at all.

Let us put the argument implicit in the common view a little more sharply. The moral 'ought' implies 'can.' If we say that A morally ought to have done X, we imply that in our opinion, he could have done X. But we assign moral blame to a man only for failing to do what we think he morally ought to have done. Hence if we morally blame A for not having done X, we imply that he could have done X even though in fact he did not. In other words, we imply that A could have acted otherwise than he did. And that means that we imply, as a necessary condition of a man's being morally blameworthy, that he enjoyed a freedom of a kind not compatible with unbroken causal continuity.

V

Now what is it that is supposed to be wrong with this simple piece of argument? —For, of course, it must be rejected by all these philosophers who tell us that the traditional problem of Free Will is a mere pseudo-problem. The argument looks as though it were doing little more than reading off necessary implications of the fundamental categories of our moral thinking. One's inclination is to ask 'If one is to think morally at all, how else than this *can* we think?'

In point of fact, there is pretty general agreement among the contemporary critics as to what is wrong with the argument. Their answer in general terms is as follows. No doubt A's moral responsibility does imply that he could have acted otherwise. But this expression 'could have acted otherwise' stands in dire need of analysis. When we analyse it, we find that it is not, as is so often supposed, simple and unambiguous, and we find that in *some* at least of its possible meanings it implies *no* breach of causal continuity between character and conduct. Having got this clear, we can further discern that only in one of these *latter* meanings is there any compulsion upon our moral thinking to assert that if A is morally blameworthy for an act, A 'could have acted otherwise than he did.' It follows that, contrary to common belief, our moral thinking does *not* require us to posit a contra-causal freedom as a condition of moral responsibility.

So much of importance obviously turns upon the validity or otherwise of this line of criticism that we must examine it in some detail and with express regard to the *ipsissima verba*[2] of the critics.

In the course of a recent article in *Mind*, entitled 'Free Will and Moral Responsibility,' Mr. Nowell Smith (having earlier affirmed his belief that 'the traditional problem has been solved') explains very concisely the nature of the confusion which, as he thinks, has led to the demand for a contra-causal freedom. He begins by frankly recognising that "It is evident that one of the necessary conditions of moral action is that the agent 'could have acted otherwise'" and he adds "it is to this fact that the Libertarian is drawing attention." Then, after showing (unexceptionably, I think) how the relationship of 'ought' to 'can' warrants the proposition which he has accepted as evident, and how it induces

[2] [i.e., the very words themselves.—Ed. note.]

the Libertarian to assert the existence of action that is 'uncaused,' he proceeds to point out, in a crucial passage, the nature of the Libertarian's error:

The fallacy in the argument (he contends) lies in supposing that when we say 'A could have acted otherwise' we mean that A, *being what he was and being placed in the circumstances in which he was placed,* could have done something other than what he did. But in fact we never do mean this.

What then *do* we mean here by 'A could have acted otherwise'? Mr. Nowell Smith does not tell us in so many words, but the passage I have quoted leaves little doubt how he would answer. What we really mean by the expression, he implies, is not a *categorical* but a *hypothetical* proposition. We mean 'A could have acted otherwise, *if he did not happen to be what he in fact was,* or *if he were placed in circumstances other than those in which he was in fact placed.*' Now, *these* propositions, it is easy to see, are in no way incompatible with acceptance of the causal principle in its full rigour. Accordingly the claim that our fundamental moral thinking obliges us to assert a contra-causal freedom as a condition of moral responsibility is disproved.

Such is the 'analytical solution' of our problem offered (with obvious confidence) by one able philosopher of to-day, and entirely representative of the views of many other able philosophers. Yet I make bold to say that its falsity stares one in the face. It seems perfectly plain that the hypothetical propositions which Mr. Nowell Smith proposes to substitute for the categorical proposition cannot express 'what we really mean' in this context by 'A could have acted otherwise,' for the simple reason that these hypothetical propositions have no bearing whatsoever upon the question of the moral responsibility of A. And it is A whose moral responsibility we are talking about—a definite person A with a definitive character and in a definitive set of circumstances. What conceivable significance could it have for our attitude to A's responsibility to know that someone with a *different* character (or A with a different character, if that collocation of words has any meaning), or A in a different set of circumstances from those in which A as we are concerned with him was in fact placed, 'could have acted otherwise'? No doubt this supposititious being *could* have acted otherwise than the definitive person A acted. But the point is that where we are reflecting, as we are supposed in this context to be reflecting, upon the question of A's moral responsibility, our interest in this supposititious being is precisely *nil*.

The two hypothetical propositions suggested in Mr. Nowell Smith's account of the matter do not, however, exhaust the speculations that have been made along these lines. Another very common suggestion by the analysts is that what we really mean by 'A could have acted otherwise' is 'A could have acted otherwise *if he had willed, or chosen, otherwise.*' This was among the suggestions offered by G. E. Moore in the well-known chapter on Free Will in his *Ethics*. It is, I think, the suggestion he most strongly favoured: though it is fair to add that neither about this nor about any other of his suggestions is Moore in the least dogmatic. He does claim, for, I think, convincing reasons, that "we *very often* mean by 'could' merely 'would, *if* so-and-so had chosen.' " And he concludes "I must confess that I cannot feel certain that this may not be all that we usually mean and understand by the assertion that we have Free Will."

This third hypothetical proposition appears to enjoy also the support of Mr. C. L. Stevenson. Mr. Stevenson begins the chapter of *Ethics and Language* entitled 'Avoidability-Indeterminism' with the now familar pronouncement of his School that 'controversy about freedom and determinism of the will . . . presents no permanent difficulty to ethics, being largely a product of confusions.' A major confusion (if I understand him rightly) he takes to lie in the meaning of the term 'avoidable,' when we say '*A*'s action was avoidable'—or, I presume, '*A* could have acted otherwise.' He himself offers the following definition of 'avoidable'—" '*A*'s action was avoidable' has the meaning of 'If *A* had made a certain choice, which in fact he did not make, his action would not have occurred.' " This I think we may regard as in substance identical with the suggestion that what we really mean by '*A* could have acted otherwise' is '*A* could have acted otherwise *if* he had chosen (or willed) otherwise.' For clarity's sake we shall here keep to this earlier formulation. In either formulation the special significance of the third hypothetical proposition, as of the two hypothetical propositions already considered, is that it is compatible with strict determinism. If this be indeed all that we mean by the 'freedom' that conditions moral responsibility, then those philosophers are certainly wrong who hold that moral freedom is of the contra-causal type.

Now this third hypothetical proposition does at least possess the merit, not shared by its predecessors, of having a real relevance to the question of moral responsibility. If, *e.g.*, *A* had promised to meet us at 2 P.M., and he chanced to break his leg at 1 P.M., we should not blame him for his failure to discharge his promise. For we should be satisfied that he *could not* have acted otherwise, even if he had so chosen; or *could not*, at any rate, in a way which would have enabled him to meet us at 2 P.M. The freedom to translate one's choice into action, which we saw earlier is for Schlick the *only* freedom required for moral responsibility, is without doubt *one* of the conditions of moral responsibility.

But it seems easy to show that this third hypothetical proposition does not exhaust what we mean, and *sometimes* is not even *part* of what we mean, by the expression 'could have acted otherwise' in its moral context. Thus it can hardly be even part of what we mean in the case of that class of wrong actions (and it is a large class) concerning which there is really no question whether the agent could have acted otherwise, *if* he had chosen otherwise. Take lying, for example. Only in some very abnormal situation could it occur to one to doubt whether *A*, whose power of speech was evinced by his telling a lie, was in a position to tell what he took to be the truth *if* he had so chosen. Of course he was. Yet it still makes good sense for one's moral thinking to ask whether *A*, when lying, 'could have acted otherwise': and we still require an affirmative answer to this question if *A*'s moral blameworthiness is to be established. It seems apparent, therefore, that in this class of cases at any rate one does *not* mean by '*A* could have acted otherwise.' 'A could have acted otherwise *if* he had so chosen.'

What then *does* one mean in this class of cases by 'A could have acted otherwise'? I submit that the expression is taken in its simple, categorical meaning, without any suppressed 'if' clause to qualify it. Or perhaps, in order to keep before us the important truth that it is only as expressions of *will* or *choice* that acts are of moral import, it might be better to say that a condition of A's moral responsibility is that he could have *chosen* otherwise. We saw that there is no real question whether A who told a lie could have acted otherwise *if* he had chosen otherwise. But there is a very real question, at least for any person who approaches the question of moral responsibility at a tolerably advanced level of reflexion, about whether A could have *chosen* otherwise. Such a person will doubtless be acquainted with the claims advanced in some quarters that causal law operates universally: or/and with the theories of some philosophies that the universe is throughout the expression of a single supreme principle; or/and with the doctrines of some theologians that the world is created, sustained and governed by an Omniscient and Omnipotent Being. Very understandably such world-views awaken in him doubts about the validity of his first, easy, instinctive assumption that there are genuinely open possibilities before a man at the moment of moral choice. It thus becomes for him a real question whether a man could have chosen otherwise than he actually did, and, in consequence, whether man's moral responsibility is really defensible. For how can a man be morally responsible, he asks himself, if his choices, like all other events in the universe, could not have been otherwise than they in fact were? It is precisely against the background of world-views such as these that for reflective people the problem of moral responsibility normally arises.

Furthermore, to the man who has attained this level of reflexion, it will in *no* class of cases be a sufficient condition of moral responsibility for an act that one could have acted otherwise *if* one had chosen otherwise—not even in these cases where there *was* some possibility of the operation of 'external constraint.' In these cases he will, indeed, expressly recognise freedom from external constraint as a *necessary condition,* but not as a *sufficient* condition. For he will be aware that, even granted *this* freedom, it is still conceivable that the agent had no freedom to choose otherwise than he did, and he will therefore require that the latter sort of freedom be added if moral responsibility for the act is to be established.

I have been contending that, for persons at a *tolerably advanced level of reflexion,* 'A could have acted otherwise,' as a condition of A's moral responsibility, means 'A could have chosen otherwise.' The qualification italicised is of some importance. The unreflective or unsophisticated person, the ordinary 'man in the street,' who does not know or much care what scientists and theologians and philosophers have said about the world, sees well enough that A is morally responsible only if he could have acted otherwise, but in his intellectual innocence he will, very probably, envisage nothing capable of preventing A from having acted otherwise except some material impediment—like the broken leg in the example above. Accordingly, for the unreflective person, 'A could have acted otherwise,' as a condition of moral responsibility, *is* apt to mean no more than '*A* could have acted otherwise *if* he had so chosen.'

It would appear, then, that the view now favoured by many philosophers, that the freedom required for moral responsibility is merely freedom from external constraint, is a view which they share only with the less reflective type of layman. Yet it should be plain that on a matter of this sort the view of the unreflective person is of little value by comparison with the view of the reflective person. There are some contexts, no doubt, in which lack of sophistication is an asset. But this is not one of them. The question at issue here is as to the kind of impediments which might have prevented a man from acting otherwise than he in fact did: and on this question knowledge and reflexion are surely prerequisites of any answer that is worth listening to. It is simply on account of the limitations of his mental vision that the unreflective man interprets the expression 'could have acted otherwise,' in its context as a condition of moral responsibility, solely in terms of external constraint. He has failed (as yet) to reach the intellectual level at which one takes into account the implications for moral choices of the world-views of science, religion, and philosophy. If on a matter of this complexity the philosopher finds that his analysis accords with the utterances of the uneducated he has, I suggest, better cause for uneasiness than for self-congratulation.

This concludes the main part of what it seems to me necessary to say in answer to the pseudo-problem theorists. My object so far has been to expose the falsity of those innovations (chiefly Positivist) in the way of argument and analysis which are supposed by many to have made it impossible any longer to formulate the problem of Free Will in the traditional manner. My contention is that, at least so far as these innovations are concerned, the simple time-honoured argument still holds from the nature of the moral ought to the conclusion that moral responsibility implies a contra-causal type of freedom. The attempts to avoid that conclusion by analysing the proposition '*A* could have acted otherwise' (acknowledged to be implied in *some* sense in *A*'s moral responsibility) into one or other of certain hypothetical propositions which are compatible with unbroken causal continuity, break down hopelessly when tested against the touchstone of actual moral thinking. . . .

•   •   •   •   •

VI

[It is sometimes argued that a] contra-causal freedom, . . . such as is implied in the 'categorical' interpretation of the proposition '*A* could have chosen otherwise than he did,' posits a breach of causal continuity betwen a man's character and his conduct. Now apart from the general presumption in favour of the universality of causal law, there are special reasons for disallowing the breach that is here alleged. It is the common assumption of social intercourse that our acquaintances will act 'in character'; that their choices will exhibit the 'natural' response of their characters to the given situation. And this assumption seems to be amply substantiated, over a wide range of conduct, by the actual success which attends predictions made on this basis. Where there should be, on the contra-causal hypothesis, chaotic variability, there is found in fact a large measure of intelligible continuity. Moreover, what is the alternative to admitting that a person's choices flow from his character? Surely just that the so-called 'choice' is not *that person's* choice at all: that, relatively to the person concerned, it is a mere 'accident.' Now we cannot really believe this. But if it *were* the case, it would certainly not help to establish *moral* freedom, the freedom required for *moral* responsibility. For clearly a man cannot be morally responsible for an act which does not express his own choice but is, on the contrary, attributable simply to chance.

These are clearly considerations worthy of all respect. It is not surprising if they have played a big part in persuading people to respond sympathetically to the view that 'Free Will,' in its usual contra-causal formulation, is a pseudo-problem. A full answer to them is obviously not practicable in what is little more than an appendix to the body of this paper; but I am hopeful that something can be said, even in a little space, to show that they are very far from being as conclusive against a contra-causal freedom as they are often supposed to be.

To begin with the less troublesome of the two main objections indicated —the objection that the break in causal continuity which free will involves is inconsistent with the predictability of conduct on the basis of the agent's known character. All that is necessary to meet this objection, I suggest, is the frank recognition, which is perfectly open to the Libertarian, that there is a wide area of human conduct, determinable on clear general principles, within which free will does not effectively operate. The most important of these general principles (I have no space to deal here with the others) has often enough been stated by Libertarians. Free will does not operate in these practical situations in which no conflict arises in the agent's mind between what he conceives to be his 'duty' and what he feels to be his 'strongest desire.' It does not operate here because there just is no occasion for it to operate. There is no reason whatever why the agent should here even contemplate choosing any course other than that prescribed by his strongest desire. In all such situations, therefore, he naturally wills in accordance with strongest desire. But his 'strongest desire' is simply the specific *ad hoc* expression of that system of conative and emotive dispositions which we call his 'character.' In all such situations, therefore, whatever may be the case elsewhere, his will is in effect determined by his character as so far formed. Now when we bear in mind that there are an almost immeasurably greater number of situations in a man's life that conform to *this* pattern than there are situations in which an agent is aware of a conflict between strongest desire and duty, it is apparent that a Libertarianism which accepts the limitation of free will to the *latter* type of situation is not open to the stock objection on the score of 'predictability.' For there still remains a vast area of human behaviour in which prediction on the basis of known character may be expected to succeed: an area which will accommodate without difficulty, I think, all these empirical facts about successful prediction which the critic is apt to suppose fatal to Free Will.

So far as I can see, such a delimitation of the field of effective free will denies to the Libertarian absolutely nothing which matters to him. For it is precisely that small sector of the field of choices which our principle of delimitation still leaves open to free will—the sector in which strongest desire clashes with duty—that is crucial for moral responsibility. It is, I believe, with respect to such situations, and in the last resort to such situations alone, that the agent himself recognises that moral praise and blame are appropriate. They are appropriate, according as he does or does not 'rise to duty' in the face of opposing desires; always granted, that is, that he is free to choose between these courses as genuinely open possibilities. If the reality of freedom be conceded *here*, everything is conceded that the Libertarian has any real interest in securing.

But, of course, the most vital question is, can the reality of freedom be conceded even here? In particular, can the standard objection be met which we stated, that if the person's choice does not, in these situations as elsewhere, flow from his *character*, then it is not *that person's* choice at all.

This is, perhaps, of all the objections to a contra-causal freedom, the one which is generally felt to be the most conclusive. For the assumption upon which it is based, *viz.*, that no intelligible meaning can attach to the claim that an act which is not an expression of the self's *character* may nevertheless be the *self's* act, is apt to be regarded as self-evident. The Libertarian is accordingly charged with being in effect an *In*determinist, whose 'free will,' in so far as it does not flow from the agent's character, can only be a matter of 'chance.' Has the Libertarian—who invariably repudiates this charge and claims to be a *Self*-determinist—any way of showing that, contrary to the assumption of his critics, we *can* meaningfully talk of an act as the self's act even though, in an important sense, it is not an expression of the self's 'character'?

I think that he has. I want to suggest that what prevents the critics from finding a meaning in this way of talking is that they are looking for it in the wrong way; or better, perhaps, with the wrong orientation. They are looking for it from the standpoint of the *external observer;* the standpoint proper to, because alone possible for, apprehension of the physical world. Now from the external standpoint we may observe processes of change. But one thing which, by common consent, *cannot* be observed from without is *creative activity.* Yet —and here lies the crux of the whole matter—it is precisely creative activity which we are trying to understand when we are trying to understand what is traditionally designated by 'free will.' For if there should be an act which is genuinely the self's act and is nevertheless not an expression of its character, such an act, in which the self 'transcends' its character as so far formed, would seem to be essentially of the nature of creative activity. It follows that to look for a meaning in 'free will' from the external standpoint is absurd. It is to look for it in a way that ensures that it will not be found. Granted that a creative activity of any kind is at least *possible* (and I know of no ground for its *a priori* rejection), there is one way, and one way only, in which we can hope to apprehend it, and that is from the *inner* standpoint of direct participation.

It seems to me therefore, that if the Libertarian's claim to find a meaning in a 'free' will which is genuinely the self's will, though not an expression of the self's character, is to be subjected to any test that is worth applying, that test must be undertaken from the inner standpoint. We ought to place ourselves imaginatively at the standpoint of the agent engaged in the typical moral situation in which free will is claimed, and ask ourselves whether from *this* standpoint the claim in question does or does not have meaning for us. That the appeal must be to introspection is no doubt unfortunate. But he would be a very doctrinaire critic of introspection who declined to make use of it when in the nature of the case no other means of apprehension is available. Everyone must make the introspective experiment for himself: but I may perhaps venture to report, though at this late stage with extreme brevity, what I at least seem to find when I make the experiment myself.

In the situation of moral conflict, then, I (as agent) have before my mind a course of action X, which I believe to be my duty; and also a course of action Y, incompatible with X, which I feel to be that which I most strongly desire. Y is, as it is sometimes expressed, 'in the line of least resistance' for me—the course which I am aware I should take if I let my purely desiring nature operate without hindrance. It is the course towards which I am aware that my *character*, as so far formed, naturally inclines me. Now, as actually engaged in this situation, I find that I cannot help believing that I *can* rise to duty and choose X; the 'rising to duty' being effected by what is commonly called 'effort of will.' And I further find, if I ask myself just what it is I am believing when I believe that I 'can' rise to duty, that I cannot help believing that it lies with me here and now, quite absolutely, which of two genuinely open possibilities I adopt; whether, that is, I make the effort of will and choose X, or, on the other hand, let my desiring nature, my character as so far formed, 'have its way,' and choose Y, the course 'in the line of least resistance.' These beliefs may, of course, be illusory, but that is not at present in point. For the present argument all that matters is whether beliefs of this sort are in fact discoverable in the moral agent in the situation of 'moral temptation.' For my own part, I cannot doubt the introspective evidence that they are.

Now here is the vital point. No matter which course, X or Y, I choose in this situation, I cannot doubt, *qua* practical being engaged in it, that my choice is *not* just the expression of my formed character, and yet *is* a choice made by my *self*. For suppose I make the effort and choose X (my 'duty'). Since my very purpose in making the 'effort' is to enable me to act against the existing 'set' of desire, which is the expression of my character as so far formed, I cannot possibly regard the act itself as the expression of my *character*. On the other hand, introspection makes it equally clear that I am certain that it is *I* who choose; that the act is not an 'accident,' but is genuinely *my* act. Or suppose that I choose Y (the end of 'strongest desire'). The course chosen here is, it is true, in conformity with my 'character.' But since I find myself unable to doubt that I *could* have made the effort and chosen X, I cannot possibly regard the choice of Y as *just* the expression of my character. Yet here again I find that I cannot doubt that the choice is *my* choice, a choice for which *I* am justly to be blamed.

What this amounts to is that I *can* and *do* attach meaning, *qua* moral agent, to an act which is not the self's character and yet is genuinely the self's act. And having no good reason to suppose that other persons have a fundamentally different mental constitution, it seems to me probable that anyone else who undertakes a similar experiment will be obliged to submit a similar report. I conclude, therefore, that the argument against 'free will' on the score of its 'meaninglessness' must be held to fail. 'Free Will' does have meaning; though, because it is of the nature of a creative activity, its meaning is discoverable only in an intuition of the practical consciousness of the participating agent. To the agent making a moral choice in the situation where duty clashes with desire, his 'self' is known to him as a creatively active self, a self which declines to be identified with his 'character' as so formed. Not, of course, that the self's character—let it be added to obviate misunderstanding—either is, or is supposed by the agent to be, devoid of bearing upon his choices, even in the 'sector' in which free will is held to operate. On the contrary, such a bearing is manifest in the empirically verifiable fact that we find it 'harder' (as we say) to make the effort of will required to 'rise to duty' in proportion to the extent that the 'dutiful' course conflicts with the course to which our character as so far formed inclines us. It is only in the polemics of the critics that a 'free' will is supposed to be incompatible with recognising the bearing of 'character' upon choice.

"But what" (it may be asked) "of the all-important question of the *value* of this 'subjective certainty,'? Even if what you say is sound as 'phenomenology,' is there any reason to suppose that the conviction on which you lay so much stress is in fact *true*?" I agree that the question is important; far more important, indeed, than is always realised, for it is not always realised that the only direct evidence there *could* be for a creative activity like 'free will' is an intuition of the practical consciousness. But this question falls outside the purview of the present paper. The aim of the paper has not been to offer a constructive defence of free will. It has been to show that the problem as traditionally posed is a real, and not a pseudo, problem. A serious threat to that thesis, it was acknowledged, arises from the apparent difficulty of attaching meaning to an act which is not the expression of the self's character and yet *is* the self's own act. The object of my brief phenomenological analysis was to provide evidence that such an act *does* have meaning for us in the one context in which there is any sense in *expecting* it to have meaning.

PAUL EDWARDS
Hard and Soft Determinism

In his essay "The Dilemma of Determinism," William James makes a distinction that will serve as a point of departure for my remarks. He there distinguishes between the philosophers he calls "hard" determinists and those he labels "soft" determinists. . . .

The theory James calls soft determinism, especially the Hume-Mill-Schlick variety of it, has been extremely fashionable during the last twenty-five years, while hardly anybody can be found today who has anything good to say for hard determinism. In opposition to this contemporary trend, I should like to strike a blow on behalf of hard determinism in my talk today. I shall also try to bring out exactly what is really at issue between hard and soft determinism. I think the nature of this dispute has frequently been misconceived chiefly because many writers, including James, have a very inaccurate notion of what is maintained by actual hard determinists, as distinct from the bogey men they set up in order to score an easy victory.

To begin with, it is necessary to spell more fully the main contentions of the soft determinists. Since it is the dominant form of soft determinism at the present time, I shall confine myself to the Hume-Mill-Schlick theory. According to this theory there is in the first place no contradiction whatsoever between determinism and the proposition that human beings are sometimes free agents. When we call an action "free" we never in any ordinary situation mean that it was uncaused; and this emphatically includes the kind of action about which we pass moral judgments. By calling an action "free" we mean that the agent was not compelled or constrained to perform it. Sometimes people act in a certain way because of threats or because they have been drugged or because of a posthypnotic suggestion or because of an irrational overpowering urge such as the one that makes a kleptomaniac steal something he does not really need. On such occasions human beings are not free agents. But on other occasions they act in certain ways because of their own rational desires, because of their own unimpeded efforts, because they have chosen to act in these ways. On these occasions they are free agents although their actions are just as much caused as actions that are not deemed free. In distinguishing between free and unfree actions we do not try to mark the presence and absence of causes but attempt to indicate the *kind* of causes that are present.

From Paul Edwards, "Hard and Soft Determinism," in Sidney Hook, ed., *Determinism and Freedom in the Age of Modern Science* (1958). Reprinted by permission of the author, the editor, and New York University Press (New York).
[NOTE: Mr. Edwards would like it to be known that he no longer accepts the position advocated in this paper.]

Secondly there is no antithesis between determinism and moral responsibility. When we judge a person morally responsible for a certain action, we do indeed presuppose that he was a free agent at the time of the action. But the freedom presupposed is not the contracausal freedom about which indeterminists go into such ecstatic raptures. It is nothing more than the freedom already mentioned—the ability to act according to one's choices or desires. Since determinism is compatible with freedom in this sense, it is also compatible with moral responsibility. In other words, the world is after all wonderful: we can be determinists and yet go on punishing our enemies and our children, and we can go on blaming ourselves, all without a bad intellectual conscience.

Mill, who was probably the greatest moralizer among the soft determinists, recognized with particular satisfaction the influence or alleged influence of one class of human desires. Not only, for example, does such lowly desire as my desire to get a new car influence my conduct. It is equally true, or so at least Mill believed, that my desire to become a more virtuous person does on occasion influence my actions. By suitable training and efforts my desire to change my character may in fact bring about the desired changes. If Mill were alive today he might point to contemporary psychiatry as an illustration of his point. Let us suppose that I have an intense desire to become famous, but that I also have an intense desire to become a happier and more lovable person who, among other things, does not greatly care about fame. Let us suppose, furthermore, that I know of a therapy that can transform fame-seeking and unlovable into lovable and fame-indifferent character structures. If, now, I have enough money, energy, and courage, and if a few other conditions are fulfilled, my desire may actually lead to a major change in my character. Since we can, therefore, at least to some extent, form our own character, determinism according to Mill is compatible not only with judgments of moral responsibility about this or that particular *action* flowing from an unimpeded desire, but also, within limits, with moral judgments about the *character* of human beings.

I think that several of Mill's observations were well worth making and that James's verdict on his theory as a "quagmire of evasion" is far too derogatory. I think hard determinists have occasionally written in such a way as to suggest that they deny the casual efficacy of human desires and efforts. Thus Holbach wrote:

> You will say that I feel free. This is an illusion, which may be compared to that of the fly in the fable, who, lighting upon the pole of a heavy carriage, applauded himself for directing its course. Man, who thinks himself free, is a fly who imagines he has power to move the universe, while he is himself unknowingly carried along by it.

There is also the following passage in Schopenhauer:

> Every man, being what he is and placed in the circumstances which for the moment obtain, but which on their part also arise by strict necessity, can absolutely never do anything else than just what at that moment he does do. Accordingly, the

whole course of a man's life, in all its incidents great and small, is as necessarily predetermined as the course of a clock.

Voltaire expresses himself in much the same way in the article on "Destiny" in the *Philosophical Dictionary*.

> Everything happens through immutable laws, . . . everything is necessary. . . . "There are," some persons say, "some events which are necessary and others which are not." It would be very comic that one part of the world was arranged, and the other were not; that one part of what happens had to happen and that another part of what happens did not have to happen. If one looks closely at it, one sees that the doctrine contrary to that of destiny is absurd; but there are many people destined to reason badly; others not to reason at all, others to persecute those who reason. . . .
>   . . . I necessarily have the passion for writing this, and you have the passion for condemning me; both of us are equally fools, equally the toy of destiny. Your nature is to do harm, mine is to love truth, and to make it public in spite of you.

Furthermore there can be little doubt that Hume and Mill and Schlick were a great deal clearer about the relation between motives and actions than the hard determinists, who either conceived it, like Collins, as one of logical necessity or, like Priestley and Voltaire and Schopenhauer, as necessarily involving coercion or constraint.

But when all is said and done, there remains a good deal of truth in James's charge that soft determinism is an evasion. For a careful reading of their works shows that none of the hard determinists really denied that human desires, efforts, and choices make a difference in the course of events. Any remarks to the contrary are at most temporary lapses. This, then, is hardly the point at issue. If it is not the point at issue, what is? Let me at this stage imagine a hard determinist replying to a champion of the Hume-Mill theory. "You are right," he would say, "in maintaining that some of our actions are caused by our desires and choices. But you do not pursue the subject far enough. You arbitrarily stop at the desires and volitions. We must not stop there. We must go on to ask where *they* come from; and if determinism is true there can be no doubt about the answer to this question. Ultimately our desires and our whole character are derived from our inherited equipment and the environmental influences to which we were subjected at the beginning of our lives. It is clear that we had no hand in shaping either of these." A hard determinist could quote a number of eminent supporters. "Our volitions and our desires," wrote Holbach in his little book *Good Sense*, "are never in our power. You think yourself free, because you do what you will; but are you free to will or not to will; to desire or not to desire?" And Schopenhauer expressed the same thought in the following epigram: "A man can surely do what he wills to do, but he cannot determine what he wills."

Let me turn once more to the topic of character transformation by means of psychiatry to bring out this point with full force. Let us suppose that both *A* and *B* are compulsive and suffer intensely from their neuroses. Let us assume that there is a therapy that could help them, which could materially change their character structure, but that it takes a great deal of energy and courage to undertake the treatment. Let us suppose that A has the necessary energy and courage while B lacks it. A undergoes the therapy and changes in the desired way. B just gets more and more compulsive and more and more miserable. Now, it is true that A helped form his own later character. But his starting point, his desire to change, his energy and courage, were already there. They may or may not have been the result of previous efforts on his own part. But there must have been a first effort, and the effort at that time was the result of factors that were not of his making.

The fact that a person's character is ultimately the product of factors over which he had no control is not denied by the soft determinists, though many of them don't like to be reminded of it when they are in a moralizing mood. Since the hard determinists admit that our desires and choices do on occasion influence the course of our lives, there is thus no disagreement between the soft and the hard determinists about the empirical facts. However, some hard determinists infer from some of these facts that human beings are never morally responsible for their actions. The soft determinists, as already stated, do not draw any such inference. In the remainder of my paper I shall try to show just what it is that hard determinists are inferring and why, in my opinion, they are justified in their conclusion.

I shall begin by adopting for my purposes a distinction introduced by C. A. Campbell in his extremely valuable article "Is Free Will a Pseudo-Problem?" [1] in which he distinguishes between two conceptions of moral responsibility. Different persons, he says, require different conditions to be fulfilled before holding human beings morally responsible for what they do. First, there is what Campbell calls the ordinary unreflective person, who is rather ignorant and who is not greatly concerned with the theories of science, philosophy, and religion. If the unreflective person is sure that the agent to be judged was acting under coercion or constraint, he will not hold him responsible. If, however, he is sure that the action was performed in accordance with the agent's unimpeded rational desire, if he is sure that the action would not have taken place but for the agent's decision, then the unreflective person will consider ascription of moral responsibility justified. The fact that the agent did not ultimately make his own character will either not occur to him, or else it will not be considered a sufficient ground for withholding a judgment of moral responsibility.

In addition to such unreflective persons, continues Campbell, there are others who have reached "a tolerably advanced level of reflection."

Such a person will doubtless be acquainted with the claims advanced in some quarters that causal law operates universally; or/and with the theories of some philosophies that the universe is throughout the expression of a single supreme principle; or/and with the doctrines of some theologians that the world is created, sustained and governed by an Omniscient and Omnipotent Being.

[1] *Mind*, 1951. [See the second reading of this chapter.—Ed. note.]

Such a person will tend to require the fulfillment of a further condition before holding anybody morally responsible. He will require not only that the agent was not coerced or constrained but also—and this is taken to be an additional condition—that he "could have chosen otherwise than he actually did." I should prefer to put this somewhat differently, but it will not affect the main conclusion drawn by Campbell, with which I agree. The reflective person, I should prefer to express it, requires not only that the agent was not coerced; he also requires that the agent *originally chose his own character*—the character that now displays itself in his choices and desires and efforts. Campbell concludes that determinism is indeed compatible with judgments of moral responsibility in the unreflective sense, but that it is incompatible with judgments of moral responsibility in the reflective sense.

Although I do not follow Campbell in rejecting determinism, I agree basically with his analysis, with one other qualification. I do not think it is a question of the different senses in which the term is used by ignorant and unreflective people, on the one hand, and by those who are interested in science, religion, and philosophy, on the other. The very same persons, whether educated or uneducated, use it in certain contexts in the one sense and in other contexts in the other. Practically all human beings, no matter how much interested they are in science, religion, and philosophy, employ what Campbell calls the unreflective conception when they are dominated by violent emotions like anger, indignation, or hate, and especially when the conduct they are judging has been personally injurious to them. On the other hand, a great many people, whether they are educated or not, will employ what Campbell calls the reflective conception when they are not consumed with hate or anger—when they are judging a situation calmly and reflectively and when the fact that the agent did not ultimately shape his own character has been vividly brought to their attention. Clarence Darrow in his celebrated pleas repeatedly appealed to the jury on precisely this ground. If any of you, he would say, had been reared in an environment like that of the accused or had to suffer from his defective heredity, *you* would now be standing in the dock. . . .

•   •   •   •   •

Darrow nearly always convinced the jury that the accused could not be held morally responsible for his acts; and certainly the majority of the jurors were relatively uneducated.

I have so far merely distinguished between two concepts of moral responsibility. I now wish to go a step farther and claim that only one of them can be considered, properly speaking, a moral concept. This is not an easy point to make clear, but I can at least indicate what I mean. We do not normally consider just any positive or negative feeling a "moral" emotion. Nor do we consider just any sentence containing the words "good" or "bad" expressions of "moral" judgment. For example, if a man hates a woman because she rejected him, this would not be counted as a moral emotion. If, however, he disapproves, say, of Senator McCarthy's libelous speech against Adlai Stevenson before the

1952 election because he disapproves of slander in general and not merely because he likes Stevenson and dislikes McCarthy, his feeling would be counted as moral. A feeling or judgment must in a certain sense be "impersonal" before we consider it moral. To this I would add that it must also be independent of violent emotions. Confining myself to judgments, I would say that a judgment was "moral" only if it was formulated in a calm and reflective mood, or at least if it is supported in a calm and reflective state of mind. If this is so, it follows that what Campbell calls the reflective sense of "moral responsibility" is the only one that qualifies as a properly moral use of the term.

Before I conclude I wish to avoid a certain misunderstanding of my remarks. From the fact that human beings do not ultimately shape their own character, I said, it *follows* that they are never morally responsible. I do not mean that by reminding people of the ultimate causes of their character one makes them more charitable and less vengeful. Maybe one does, but that is not what I mean. I mean "follow" or "imply" in the same sense as, or in a sense closely akin to, that in which the conclusion of a valid syllogism follows from the premises. The effectiveness of Darrow's pleas does not merely show, I am arguing, how powerfully he could sway the emotions of the jurors. His pleas also brought into the open one of the conditions the jurors, like others, consider necessary on reflection before they hold an agent morally responsible. Or perhaps I should say that Darrow *committed* the jurors in their reflective nature to a certain ground for the ascription of moral responsibility.

JOHN HOSPERS
The Range of Human Freedom

I am in agreement to a very large extent with the conclusions of Professor Edwards' paper, and am happy in these days of "soft determinism" to hear the other view so forcefully and fearlessly stated. As a preparation for developing my own views on the subject, I want to mention a factor that I think is of enormous importance and relevance: namely, unconscious motivation. There are many actions—not those of an insane person (however the term "insane" be defined), nor of a person ignorant of the effects of his action, nor ignorant of some relevant fact about the situation, nor in any obvious way mentally deranged—for which human beings in general and the courts in particular are

From John Hospers, "What Means This Freedom?" in Sidney Hook, ed., *Determinism and Freedom in the Age of Modern Science* (1958). Reprinted by permission of the author, the editor, and New York University Press (New York).

inclined to hold the doer responsible, and for which, I would say, he should not be held responsible. The deed may be planned, it may be carried out in cold calculation, it may spring from the agent's character and be continuous with the rest of his behavior, and it may be perfectly true that he could have done differently *if* he had wanted to; nonetheless his behavior was brought about by unconscious conflicts developed in infancy, over which he had no control and of which (without training in psychiatry) he does not even have knowledge. He may even *think* he knows why he acted as he did, he may *think* he has conscious control over his actions, he may even *think* he is fully responsible for them; but he is not. Psychiatric casebooks provide hundreds of examples. The law and common sense, though puzzled sometimes by such cases, are gradually becoming aware that they exist; but at this early stage countless tragic blunders still occur because neither the law nor the public in general is aware of the genesis of criminal actions. The mother blames her daughter for choosing the wrong men as candidates for husbands; but though the daughter thinks she is choosing freely and spends a considerable amount of time "deciding" among them, the identification with her sick father, resulting from Oedipal fantasies in early childhood, prevents her from caring for any but sick men, twenty or thirty years older than herself. Blaming her is beside the point; she cannot help it, and she cannot change it. Countless criminal acts are thought out in great detail; yet the participants are (without their own knowledge) acting out fantasies, fears, and defenses from early childhood, over whose coming and going they have no conscious control.

Now, I am not saying that none of these persons should be in jails or asylums. Often society must be protected against them. Nor am I saying that people should cease the practices of blaming and praising, punishing and rewarding; in general these devices are justified by the results—although very often they have practically no effect; the deeds are done from inner compulsion, which is not lessened when the threat of punishment is great. I am only saying that frequently persons we think responsible are not properly to be called so; we mistakenly think them responsible because we assume they are like those in whom no unconscious drive (toward this type of behavior) is present, and that their behavior can be changed by reasoning, exhorting, or threatening.

I

I have said that these persons are not responsible. But what is the criterion for responsibility? Under precisely what conditions is a person to be held morally responsible for an action? Disregarding here those conditions that have to do with a person's *ignorance* of the situation or the effects of his action, let us concentrate on those having to do with his "inner state." There are several criteria that might be suggested:

1. The first idea that comes to mind is that responsibility is determined by the presence or absence of *premeditation*—the opposite of "premeditated" being, presumably, "unthinking" or "impulsive." But this will not do—both because

some acts are not premeditated but responsible, and because some are premeditated and not responsible.

Many acts we call responsible can be as unthinking or impulsive as you please. If you rush across the street to help the victim of an automobile collision, you are (at least so we would ordinarily say) acting responsibly, but you did not do so out of premeditation; you saw the accident, you didn't think, you rushed to the scene without hesitation. It was like a reflex action. But you acted responsibly: unlike the knee jerk, the act was the result of past training and past thought about situations of this kind; that is why you ran to help instead of ignoring the incident or running away. When something done originally from conviction or training becomes habitual, it becomes *like* a reflex action. As Aristotle said, virtue should become second nature through habit: a virtuous act should be performed *as if* by instinct; this, far from detracting from its moral worth, testifies to one's mastery of the desired type of behavior; one does not have to make a moral effort each time it is repeated.

There are also premeditated acts for which, I would say, the person is not responsible. Premeditation, especially when it is so exaggerated as to issue in no action at all, can be the result of neurotic disturbance or what we sometimes call an emotional "block," which the person inherits from long-past situations. In Hamlet's revenge on his uncle (I use this example because it is familiar to all of us), there was no lack, but rather a surfeit, of premeditation; his actions were so exquisitely premeditated as to make Freud and Dr. Ernest Jones look more closely to find out what lay behind them. The very premeditation camouflaged unconscious motives of which Hamlet himself was not aware. I think this is an important point, since it seems that the courts often assume that premeditation is a criterion of responsibility. If failure to kill his uncle had been considered a crime, every court in the land would have convicted Hamlet. Again: a woman's decision to stay with her husband in spite of endless "mental cruelty" is, if she is the victim of an unconscious masochistic "will to punishment," one for which she is not responsible; she is the victim and not the agent, no matter how profound her conviction that she is the agent; she is caught in a masochistic web (of complicated genesis) dating back to babyhood, perhaps a repetition of a comparable situation involving her own parents, a repetition-compulsion that, as Freud said, goes "beyond the pleasure principle." Again: a criminal whose crime was carefully planned step by step is usually considered responsible, but as we shall see in later examples, the overwhelming impulse toward it, stemming from an unusually humiliating ego defeat in early childhood, was as compulsive as any can be.

2. Shall we say, then, that a person is not responsible for his act unless he can *defend it with reasons*? I am afraid that this criterion is no better than the previous one. First, intellectuals are usually better at giving reasons than non-intellectuals, and according to this criterion would be more responsible than persons acting from moral conviction not implemented by reasoning; yet it is very doubtful whether we should want to say that the latter are the more responsible. Second, the giving of reasons itself may be suspect. The reasons

may be rationalizations camouflaging unconscious motives of which the agent knows nothing. Hamlet gave many reasons for not doing what he felt it was his duty to do: the time was not right, his uncle's soul might go to heaven, etc. His various "reasons" contradicted one another, and if an overpowering compulsion had not been present, the highly intellectual Hamlet would not have been taken in for a moment by these rationalizations. The real reason, the Oedipal conflict that made his uncle's crime the accomplishment of his own deepest desire, binding their fates into one and paralyzing him into inaction, was unconscious and of course unknown to him. One's intelligence and reasoning power do not enable one to escape from unconsciously motivated behavior; it only gives one greater facility in rationalizing that behavior; one's intelligence is simply used in the interests of the neurosis—it is pressed into service to justify with reasons what one does quite independently of the reasons.

If these two criteria are inadequate, let us seek others.

3. Shall we say that a person is responsible for his action unless it is the *result of unconscious forces* of which he knows nothing? Many psychoanalysts would probably accept this criterion. If it is not largely reflected in the language of responsibility as ordinarily used, this may be due to ignorance of fact: most people do not know that there are such things as unconscious motives and unconscious conflicts causing human beings to act. But it may be that if they did, perhaps they would refrain from holding persons responsible for certain actions.

I do not wish here to quarrel with this criterion of responsibility. I only want to point out the fact that if this criterion is employed a far greater number of actions will be excluded from the domain of responsibility than we might at first suppose. Whether we are neat or untidy, whether we are selfish or unselfish, whether we provoke scenes or avoid them, even whether we can exert our powers of will to change our behavior—all these may, and often do, have their source in our unconscious life.

4. Shall we say that a person is responsible for his act unless it is *compelled?* Here we are reminded of Aristotle's assertion (*Nicomachean Ethics*, Book III) that a person is responsible for his act except for reasons of either ignorance or compulsion. Ignorance is not part of our problem here (unless it is unconsciously induced ignorance of facts previously remembered and selectively forgotten—in which case the forgetting is again compulsive), but compulsion is. How will compulsion do as a criterion? The difficulty is to state just what it means. When we say an act is compelled in a psychological sense, our language is metaphorical—which is not to say that there is no point in it or that, properly interpreted, it is not true. Our actions are compelled in a literal sense if someone has us in chains or is controlling our bodily movements. When we say that the storm compelled us to jettison the cargo of the ship (Aristotle's example), we have a less literal sense of compulsion, for at least it is open to us to go down with the ship. When psychoanalysts say that a man was compelled by unconscious conflicts to wash his hands constantly, this is also not a literal use of "compel"; for nobody forced his hands under the tap. Still, it is a typical example

of what psychologists call *compulsive* behavior: it has unconscious causes inaccessible to introspection, and moreover nothing can change it—it is as inevitable for him to do it as it would be if someone were forcing his hands under the tap. In this it is exactly like the action of a powerful external force; it is just as little within one's conscious control.

In its area of application this interpretation of responsibility comes to much the same as the previous one. And this area is very great indeed. For if we cannot be held responsible for the infantile situations (in which we were after all passive victims), then neither, it would seem, can we be held responsible for compulsive actions occurring in adulthood that are inevitable consequences of those infantile situations. And, psychiatrists and psychoanalysts tell us, actions fulfilling this description are characteristic of all people some of the time and some people most of the time. Their occurrence, once the infantile events have taken place, is inevitable, just as the explosion is inevitable once the fuse has been lighted; there is simply more "delayed action" in the psychological explosions than there is in the physical ones.

(I have not used the word "inevitable" here to mean "causally determined," for according to such a definition every event would be inevitable if one accepted the causal principle in some form or other; and probably nobody except certain philosophers uses "inevitable" in this sense. Rather, I use "inevitable" in its ordinary sense of "cannot be avoided." To the extent, therefore, that adult neurotic manifestations *can* be avoided, once the infantile patterns have become set, the assertion that they are inevitable is not true.)

5. There is still another criterion, which I prefer to the previous ones, by which a man's responsibility for an act can be measured: the degree to which that act can be (or could have been) *changed by the use of reasons.* Suppose that the man who washes his hands constantly does so, he says, for hygienic reasons, believing that if he doesn't do so he will be poisoned by germs. We now convince him, on the best medical authority, that his belief is groundless. Now, the test of his responsibility is whether the changed belief will result in changed behavior. If it does not, as with the compulsive hand washer, he is not acting responsibly, but if it does, he is. It is not the *use* of reasons, but their *efficacy in changing behavior,* that is being made the criterion of responsibility. And clearly in neurotic cases no such change occurs; in fact, this is often made the defining characteristic of neurotic behavior: it is unchangeable by any rational considerations.

II

I have suggested these criteria to distinguish actions for which we can call the agent responsible from those for which we cannot. Even persons with extensive knowledge of psychiatry do not, I think, use any one of these criteria to the exclusion of the others; a conjunction of two or more may be used at once. But however they may be combined or selected in actual application, I believe we can make the distinction along some such lines as we have suggested.

But is there not still another possible meaning of "responsibility" that we have not yet mentioned? Even after we have made all the above distinctions, there remains a question in our minds whether we are, in the final analysis, *responsible for any of our actions at all.* The issue may be put this way: How can anyone be responsible for his actions, since they grow out of his character, which is shaped and molded and made what it is by influences—some hereditary, but most of them stemming from early parental environment—that were not of his own making or choosing? This question, I believe, still troubles many people who would agree to all the distinctions we have just made but still have the feeling that "this isn't all." They have the uneasy suspicion that there is a more ultimate sense, a "deeper" sense, in which we are *not* responsible for our actions, since we are not responsible for the character out of which those actions spring. This, of course, is the sense Professor Edwards was describing.

Let us take as an example a criminal who, let us say, strangled several persons and is himself now condemned to die in the electric chair. Jury and public alike hold him fully responsible (at least they utter the words "he is responsible"), for the murders were planned down to the minutest detail, and the defendant tells the jury exactly how he planned them. But now we find out how it all came about; we learn of parents who rejected him from babyhood, of the childhood spent in one foster home after another, where it was always plain to him that he was not wanted; of the constantly frustrated early desire for affection, the hard shell of nonchalance and bitterness that he assumed to cover the painful and humiliating fact of being unwanted, and his subsequent attempts to heal these wounds to his shattered ego through defensive aggression.

The criminal is the most passive person in this world, helpless as a baby in his motorically inexpressible fury. Not only does he try to wreak revenge on the mother of the earliest period of his babyhood; his criminality is based on the inner feeling of being incapable of making the mother even feel that the child seeks revenge on her. The situation is that of a dwarf trying to annoy a giant who superciliously refuses to see these attempts . . . Because of his inner feeling of being a dwarf, the criminotic uses, so to speak, dynamite. Of that the giant must take cognizance. True, the "revenge" harms the avenger. He may be legally executed. However, the primary inner aim of forcing the giant to acknowledge the dwarf's fury is fulfilled.[1]

The poor victim is not conscious of the inner forces that exact from him this ghastly toll; he battles, he schemes, he revels in pseudo-aggression, he is miserable, but he does not know what works within him to produce these catastrophic acts of crime. His aggressive actions are the wriggling of a worm on a fisherman's hook. And if this is so, it seems difficult to say any longer, "He is responsible." Rather, we shall put him behind bars for the protection of society, but we shall no longer flatter our feeling of moral superiority by calling him personally responsible for what he did.

Let us suppose it were established that a man commits murder only if,

---

[1] Edmund Bergler, *The Basic Neurosis* (New York: Grune and Stratton, 1949), p. 305.

sometime during the previous week, he has eaten a certain combination of foods —say, tuna fish salad at a meal also including peas, mushroom soup, and blue- berry pie. What if we were to track down the factors common to all murders committed in this country during the last twenty years and found this factor present in all of them, and only in them? The example is of course empirically absurd; but may it not be that there is *some* combination of factors that regularly leads to homicide, factors such as are described in general terms in the above quotation? (Indeed the situation in the quotation is less fortunate than in our hypothetical example, for it is easy to avoid certain foods once we have been warned about them, but the situation of the infant is thrust on him; something has already happened to him once and for all, before he knows it has hap- pened.) When such specific factors are discovered, won't they make it clear that it is foolish and pointless, as well as immoral, to hold human beings respon- sible for crimes? Or, if one prefers biological to psychological factors, suppose a neurologist is called in to testify at a murder trial and produces X-ray pictures of the brain of the criminal; anyone can see, he argues, that the *cella turcica* was already calcified at the age of nineteen; it should be a flexible bone, growing, enabling the gland to grow.[2] All the defendant's disorders might have resulted from this early calcification. Now, this particular explanation may be empirically false; but who can say that no such factors, far more complex, to be sure, exist?

When we know such things as these, we no longer feel so much tempted to say that the criminal is responsible for his crime; and we tend also (do we not?) to excuse him—not legally (we still confine him to prison) but morally; we no longer call him a monster or hold him personally responsible for what he did. Moreover, we do this in general, not merely in the case of crime: "You must excuse Grandmother for being irritable; she's really quite ill and is suffering some pain all the time." Or: "The dog always bites children after she's had a litter of pups; you can't blame her for it: she's not feeling well, and besides she naturally wants to defend them." Or: "She's nervous and jumpy, but do excuse her: she has a severe glandular disturbance."

Let us note that the more *thoroughly* and *in detail* we know the causal factors leading a person to behave as he does, the more we tend to exempt him from responsibility. When we know nothing of the man except what we see him do, we say he is an ungrateful cad who expects much of other people and does nothing in return, and we are usually indignant. When we learn that his parents were the same way and, having no guilt feelings about this mode of behavior themselves, brought him up to be greedy and avaricious, we see that we could hardly expect him to have developed moral feelings in this direction. When we learn, in addition, that he is not aware of being ungrateful or selfish, but unconsciously represses the memory of events unfavorable to himself, we feel that the situation is unfortunate but "not really his fault." When we know that this behavior of his, which makes others angry, occurs more constantly when he feels tense or insecure, and that he now feels tense and insecure, and

---

[2] Meyer Levin, *Compulsion* (New York: Simon and Schuster, 1956), p. 403.

that relief from pressure will diminish it, then we tend to "feel sorry for the poor guy" and say he's more to be pitied than censured. We no longer want to say that he is personally responsible; we might rather blame nature or his parents for having given him an unfortunate constitution or temperament.

In recent years a new form of punishment has been imposed on middle-aged and elderly parents. Their children, now in their twenties, thirties or even forties, present them with a modern grievance: "My analysis proves that *you* are responsible for my neurosis." Overawed by these authoritative statements, the poor tired parents fall easy victims to the newest variations on the scapegoat theory.

In my opinion, this senseless cruelty—which disinters educational sins which had been buried for decades, and uses them as the basis for accusations which the victims cannot answer—is unjustified. Yes, "the truth loves to be centrally located" (Melville), and few parents—since they are human—have been perfect. But granting their mistakes, they acted as *their* neurotic difficulties forced them to act. To turn the tables and declare the children not guilty because of the *impersonal* nature of their own neuroses, while at the same time the parents are *personally* blamed, is worse than illogical; it is profoundly unjust.[3]

And so, it would now appear, neither of the parties is responsible: "they acted as their neurotic difficulties forced them to act." The patients are not responsible for their neurotic manifestations, but then neither are the parents responsible for theirs; and so, of course, for their parents in turn, and theirs before them. It is the twentieth-century version of the family curse, the curse on the House of Atreus.

"But," a critic complains, "it's immoral to exonerate people indiscriminately in this way. I might have thought it fit to excuse somebody because he was born on the other side of the tracks, if I didn't know so many bank presidents who were also born on the other side of the tracks." Now, I submit that the most immoral thing in this situation is the critic's caricature of the conditions of the excuse. Nobody is excused merely because he was born on the other side of the tracks. But if he was born on the other side of the tracks *and* was a highly narcissistic infant to begin with *and* was repudiated or neglected by his parents *and* . . . (here we list a finite number of conditions), and if this complex of factors is *regularly* followed by certain behavior traits in adulthood, and moreover *unavoidably* so—that is, they occur no matter what he or anyone else tries to do—then we excuse him morally and say he is not responsible for his deed. If he is not responsible for *A,* a series of events occurring in his babyhood, then neither is he responsible for *B,* a series of things he does in adulthood, provided that *B* inevitably—that is, unavoidably—follows upon the occurrence of *A.* And according to psychiatrists and psychoanalysts, this often happens.

But one may still object that so far we have talked only about neurotic behavior. Isn't nonneurotic or normal or not unconsciously motivated (or whatever you want to call it) behavior still within the area of responsibility? There are reasons for answering "No" even here, for the normal person no more than

[3] Edmund Bergler, *The Superego* (New York: Grune and Stratton, 1952), p. 320.

the neurotic one has caused his own character, which makes him what he is. Granted that neurotics are not responsible for their behavior (that part of it which we call neurotic) because it stems from undigested infantile conflicts that they had no part in bringing about, and that are external to them just as surely as if their behavior had been forced on them by a malevolent deity (which is indeed one theory on the subject); but the so-called normal person is equally the product of causes in which his volition took no part. And if, unlike the neurotic's, his behavior is changeable by rational considerations, and if he has the will power to overcome the effects of an unfortunate early environment, this again is no credit to him; he is just lucky. If energy is available to him in a form in which it can be mobilized for constructive purposes, this is no credit to him, for this too is part of his psychic legacy. Those of us who can discipline ourselves and develop habits of concentration of purpose tend to blame those who cannot, and call them lazy and weak-willed; but what we fail to see is that they literally *cannot* do what we expect; if their psyches were structured like ours, they could, but as they are burdened with a tyrannical superego (to use psychoanalytic jargon for the moment), and a weak defenseless ego whose energies are constantly consumed in fighting endless charges of the superego, they simply cannot do it, and it is irrational to expect it of them. We cannot with justification blame them for their inability, any more than we can congratulate ourselves for our ability. This lesson is hard to learn, for we constantly and naïvely assume that other people are constructed as we ourselves are.

For example: A child raised under slum conditions, whose parents are socially ambitious and envy families with money, but who nevertheless squander the little they have on drink, may simply be unable in later life to mobilize a drive sufficient to overcome these early conditions. Common sense would expect that he would develop the virtue of thrift; he would make quite sure that he would never again endure the grinding poverty he had experienced as a child. But in fact it is not so: the exact conditions are too complex to be specified in detail here, but when certain conditions are fulfilled (concerning the subject's early life), he will always thereafter be a spendthrift, and no rational considerations will be able to change this. He will listen to the rational considerations and see the force of these, but they will not be able to change him, even if he tries; he cannot change his wasteful habits any more than he can lift the Empire State Building with his bare hands. We moralize and plead with him to be thrifty, but we do not see how strong, how utterly overpowering, and how constantly with him, is the opposite drive, which is so easily manageable with us. But he is possessed by the all-consuming, all-encompassing urge to make the world see that he belongs, that he has arrived, that he is just as well off as anyone else, that the awful humiliations were not real, that they never actually occurred, for isn't he now able to spend and spend? The humiliation must be blotted out; and conspicuous, flashy, expensive, and wasteful buying will do this; it shows the world what the world must know! True, it is only for the moment; true, it is in the end self-defeating, for wasteful consumption is the best way to bring poverty back again; but the person with an overpowering drive to mend a lesion to his narcissism cannot resist the avalanche of that drive with his puny rational consideration. A man with his back against the wall and a gun at his throat doesn't think of what may happen ten years hence. (Consciously, of course, he knows nothing of this drive; all that appears to consciousness is its shattering effects; he knows only that he must keep on spending—not why—and that he is unable to resist.) He hasn't in him the psychic capacity, the energy to stem the tide of a drive that at that moment is all-powerful. We, seated comfortably away from this flood, sit in judgment on him and blame him and exhort him and criticize him; but he, carried along by the flood, cannot do otherwise than he does. He may fight with all the strength of which he is capable, but it is not enough. And we, who are rational enough at least to exonerate a man in a situation of "overpowering impulse" when we recognize it to be one, do not even recognize this as an example of it; and so, in addition to being swept away in the flood that childhood conditions rendered inevitable, he must also endure our lectures, our criticisms, and our moral excoriation.

But, one will say, he could have overcome his spendthrift tendencies; some people do. Quite true: some people do. They are lucky. They have it in them to overcome early deficiencies by exerting great effort, and they are capable of exerting the effort. Some of us, luckier still, can overcome them with but little effort; and a few, the luckiest, haven't the deficiencies to overcome. It's all a matter of luck. The least lucky are those who can't overcome them, even with great effort, and those who haven't the ability to exert the effort.

But, one persists, it isn't a matter simply of luck; it *is* a matter of effort. Very well then, it's a matter of effort; without exerting the effort you may not overcome the deficiency. But whether or not you are the kind of person who has it in him to exert the effort is a matter of luck.

All this is well known to psychoanalysts. They can predict from minimal cues that most of us don't notice, whether a person is going to turn out to be lucky or not. "The analyst," they say, "must be able to use the residue of the patient's unconscious guilt so as to remove the symptom or character trait that creates the guilt. The guilt must not only be present, but *available* for use, *mobilizable*. If it is used up (absorbed) in criminal activity, or in an excessive amount of self-damaging tendencies, then it cannot be used for therapeutic purposes, and the prognosis is negative." Not all philosophers will relish the analyst's way of putting the matter, but at least as a physician he can soon detect whether the patient is lucky or unlucky—and he knows that whichever it is, it *isn't the patient's fault*. The patient's conscious volition cannot remedy the deficiency. Even whether he will co-operate with the analyst is really out of the patient's hands: if he continually projects the denying-mother fantasy on the analyst and unconsciously identifies him always with the cruel, harsh forbidder of the nursery, thus frustrating any attempt at impersonal observation, the sessions are useless; yet if it happens that way, he can't help that either. That fatal projection is not under his control; whether it occurs or not depends on how his unconscious identifications have developed since his infancy. He can try, yes—but the ability to try enough for the therapy to have effect is also beyond his control; the capacity to try more than just so much is either there or it isn't—and either way "it's in the lap of the gods."

The position, then, is this: if we *can* overcome the effects of early environment, the ability to do so is itself a product of the early environment. We did not give ourselves this ability; and if we lack it we cannot be blamed for not having it. Sometimes, to be sure, moral exhortation brings out an ability that is there but not being used, and in this lies its *occasional* utility; but very often its use is pointless, because the ability is not there. The only thing that can overcome a desire, as Spinoza said, is a stronger contrary desire; and many times there simply is no wherewithal for producing a stronger contrary desire. Those of us who do have the wherewithal are lucky.

There is one possible practical advantage in remembering this. It may prevent us (unless we are compulsive blamers) from indulging in righteous indignation and committing the sin of spiritual pride, thanking God that we are not as this publican here. And it will protect from our useless moralizings those who are least equipped by nature for enduring them. As with responsibility, so with deserts. Someone commits a crime and is punished by the state; "he deserved it," we say self-righteously—as if we were moral and he immoral, when in fact we are lucky and he is unlucky—forgetting that there, but for the grace of God and a fortunate early environment, go we. Or, as Clarence Darrow said in his speech for the defense in the Loeb-Leopold case:

> I do not believe that people are in jail because they deserve to be. . . . I know what causes the emotional life. . . . I know it is practically left out of some. Without it they cannot act with the rest. They cannot feel the moral shocks which safeguard others. Is [this man] to blame that his machine is imperfect? Who is to blame? I do not know. I have never in my life been interested so much in fixing blame as I have in relieving people from blame. I am not wise enough to fix it.[4]

III

I want to make it quite clear that I have not been arguing for determinism. Though I find it difficult to give any sense to the term "indeterminism," because I do not know what it would be like to come across an uncaused event, let us grant indeterminists everything they want, at least in words—influences that suggest but do not constrain, a measure of acausality in an otherwise rigidly causal order, and so on—whatever these phrases may mean. With all this granted, exactly the same situation faces the indeterminist and the determinist; all we have been saying would still hold true. "Are our powers innate or acquired?"

Suppose the powers are declared innate; then the villain may sensibly ask whether he is responsible for what he was born with. A negative reply is inevitable.

[4] Levin, *op. cit.*, pp. 439–40, 469.

Are they then acquired? Then the ability to acquire them—was *that* innate? or acquired? It is innate? Very well then. . . .[5]

The same fact remains—that we did not cause our characters, that the influences that made us what we are are influences over which we had no control and of whose very existence we had no knowledge at the time. This fact remains for "determinism" and "indeterminism" alike. And it is this fact to which I would appeal, not the specific tenets of traditional forms of "determinism," which seem to me, when analyzed, empirically empty.

"But," it may be asked, "isn't it your view that nothing ultimately *could* be other than it is? And isn't this deterministic? And isn't it deterministic if you say that human beings could never act otherwise than they do, and that their desires and temperaments could not, when you consider their antecedent conditions, be other than they are?"

I reply that all these charges rest on confusions.

1. To say that nothing *could* be other than it is, is, taken literally, nonsense; and if taken as a way of saying something else, misleading and confusing. If you say, "I can't do it," this invites the question, "No? Not even if you want to?" "Can" and "could" are power words, used in the context of human action; when applied to nature they are merely anthropomorphic. "Could" has no application to nature—unless, of course, it is uttered in a theological context: one might say that God *could* have made things different. But with regard to inanimate nature "could" has no meaning. Or perhaps it is intended to mean that the order of nature is in some sense *necessary*. But in that case the sense of "necessary" must be specified. I know what "necessary" means when we are talking about propositions, but not when we are talking about the sequence of events in nature.

2. What of the charge that we could never have acted otherwise than we did? This, I submit, is simply not true. Here the exponents of Hume-Mill-Schlick-Ayer "soft determinism" are quite right. I could have gone to the opera today instead of coming here; that is, if certain conditions had been different, I should have gone. I could have done many other things instead of what I did, if some condition or other had been different, specifically if my desire had been different. I repeat that "could" is a power word, and "I could have done this" means approximately "I *should* have done this *if* I had wanted to." In this sense, all of us could often have done otherwise than we did. I would not want to say that I should have done differently even if *all* the conditions leading up to my action had been the same (this is generally not what we mean by "could" anyway); but to assert that I could have is empty, for if I *did* act different from the time before, we would automatically say that one or more of the conditions were different, whether we had independent evidence for this or not, thus rendering the assertion immune to empirical refutation. (Once again, the vacuousness of "determinism.")

[5] W. I. Matson, "The Irrelevance of Free-will to Moral Responsibility," *Mind*, LXV (October 1956), p. 495.

3. Well, then, could we ever have, not acted, but *desired* otherwise than we did desire? This gets us once again to the heart of the matter we were discussing in the previous section. Russell said, "We can do as we please but we can't please as we please." But I am persuaded that even this statement conceals a fatal mistake. Let us follow the same analysis through. "I could have done X" means "I should have done X if I had wanted to." "I could have wanted X" by the same analysis would mean "I should have wanted X if I had wanted to"—which seems to make no sense at all. (What does Russell want? To please as he doesn't please?)

What does this show? It shows, I think, that the only meaningful context of "can" and "could have" is that of *action*. "Could have acted differently" makes sense; "could have desired differently," as we have just seen, does not. Because a word or phrase makes good sense in one context, let us not assume that it does so in another.

I conclude, then, with the following suggestion; that we operate on two levels of moral discourse, which we shouldn't confuse; one (let's call it the upper level) is that of actions; the other (the lower, or deeper, level) is that of the springs of action. Most moral talk occurs on the upper level. It is on this level that the Hume-Mill-Schlick-Ayer analysis of freedom fully applies. As we have just seen, "can" and "could" acquire their meaning on this level; so, I suspect, does "freedom." So does the distinction between compulsive and noncompulsive behavior, and among the senses of "responsibility," discussed in the first section of this paper, according to which we are responsible for some things and not for others. All these distinctions are perfectly valid on this level (or in this dimension) of moral discourse; and it is, after all, the usual one—we are practical beings interested in changing the course of human behavior, so it is natural enough that 99 per cent of our moral talk occurs here.

But when we descend to what I have called the lower level of moral discourse, as we occasionally do in thoughtful moments when there is no immediate need for action, then we must admit that we are ultimately the kind of persons we are because of conditions occurring outside us, over which we had no control. But while this is true, we should beware of extending the moral terminology we used on the other level to this one also. "Could" and "can," as we have seen, no longer have meaning here. "Right" and "wrong," which apply only to actions, have no meaning here either. I suspect that the same is true of "responsibility," for now that we have recalled often forgotten facts about our being the product of outside forces, we must ask in all seriousness what would be added by saying that we are not *responsible* for our own characters and temperaments. What would it mean even? Has it a significant opposite? What would it be like to be responsible for one's own character? What possible situation is describable by this phrase? Instead of saying that it is *false* that we are responsible for our own characters, I should prefer to say that the utterance is meaningless—meaningless in the sense that it describes no possible situation, though it seems to because the word "responsible" is the same one we used on the upper level, where it marks a real distinction. If this is so, the result is that *moral* terms—at least the terms "could have" and "responsible"—simply drop out on the lower level. What remains, shorn now of moral terminology, is the point we tried to bring out in Part II: whether or not we have personality disturbances, whether or not we have the ability to overcome deficiencies of early environment, is like the answer to the question whether or not we shall be struck down by a dread disease: "it's all a matter of luck." It is important to keep this in mind, for people almost always forget it, with consequences in human intolerance and unnecessary suffering that are incalculable.

SIDNEY HOOK
Criticism of Hard Determinism

The fatal error in the papers of Professors Hospers and Edwards, as read, is that they alternate between two conceptions of "moral responsibility"—one, a conception of moral responsibility as *empty* but meaningful, and the other as *vacuous* and meaningless. On the first conception, although it may be true *in fact* that no one is morally responsible, we can state the conditions under which one might be. We can differentiate between the two states. On the second, there are no possible conditions under which anyone can be declared "morally responsible." The expression has no intelligible opposite and thus makes no sense.

The force of most of their arguments, which gives them an air of high moral concern, is based on the assumption that under certain circumstances individuals are being *improperly* considered responsible. Hospers actually says that "frequently persons we think responsible are not properly to be called so," and Edwards implies the same thing. They explicitly appeal against the injustice of improperly blaming the morally innocent who, because their desires are determined, are the victims, not the agents, of misfortune. We eagerly await the description of the set of conditions under which an individual is properly held responsible, under which he is not a victim of circumstances. It then turns out that even if his desires were undetermined, even if circumstances were completely different, he would still not be responsible, would still be a morally innocent victim. The *empty* conception of moral responsibility becomes completely *vacuous*. This makes the whole procedure of Professors Hospers and Edwards methodologically self-defeating, and particularly their expressions of concern about the injustice of blaming the morally innocent. For to be morally

From Sidney Hook, "Necessity, Indeterminism, and Sentimentalism," in Sidney Hook, ed., *Determinism and Freedom in the Age of Modern Science* (1958). Reprinted by permission of the author and New York University Press (New York).

innocent of having committed an evil deed entails that one is not responsible for its commission, and to be morally guilty entails that one is. *If moral responsibility is a vacuous expression, then moral innocence and guilt are too.* Were Hospers and Edwards consistent they could not plead for the innocent or condemn the guilty. Edwards in places suggests that a person would be responsible if he could *ultimately and completely shape or choose* his own character. But this is explaining an obscure notion by a still obscurer one. Since every decision to shape or choose one's character, to be responsible, must be one's own, and therefore already an indication of the kind of person one is, the notion that one can ultimately and completely shape or choose one's character is unintelligible. C. A. Campbell, to be sure, tries to distinguish between a choice that is the expression of a *formed character,* and therefore determined, and a choice of a *self.* But on Hospers' and Edwards' argument what is true of character must be true of self. Either the self has the power to mold character or it has not. In either case it cannot be held responsible for having or not having such a native power. And the same is true if we bring in a Self to explain the powers of the self and a Great Self to explain the powers of the Self, etc.

It is true that the notion of moral responsibility is often ambiguous and not clearly defined in ordinary experience. But . . . we can recognize certain actions in which we clearly admit the presence of excusing conditions—infancy, insanity, paralysis, duress, coercion, etc.—and actions in which we do not. We then try to formulate the principle we recognize in this distinction and apply it to more complicated and borderline cases. We find that we tend to hold individuals responsible for their voluntary or uncoerced actions, for knowingly doing or not doing what it was in their power to do or leave undone. All these terms are vague and need further specification. There are difficulties in ascertaining in particular instances what it was in one's power to do or leave undone. Nonetheless, no one can live in human society without learning to recognize the distinction between the actions he holds others and himself responsible for and the actions he does not.

For all its vagueness there is more agreement about how the distinction is to be applied than about the grounds of the distinction. No one blames a crawling infant who overturns a kerosene stove that starts a fire. Almost everybody would blame a man who, normal in every other way and by all known tests, insures a house beyond its value and then sets fire to it without giving its occupants a chance to escape. If we make a list of the circumstances behind actions for which we hold individuals responsible and those for which we do not, we shall find that as a rule the first class consists of those in which evidence exists that praise and reward, blame and punishment, tend to influence the future conduct of those involved and/or those tempted. This is not the whole story. Campbell objects[1] that animals are not held responsible for their actions even though we can re-educate their desires and impulses by punishment. This is true, but it is also true that the higher the animal in the scale of intelligence, the more

---

[1] *Mind,* 1951. [See the second reading of this chapter.—Ed. note.]

likely we are to blame it. If we believed that an animal could think like a man we would blame it like a man. The behavior of infants, too, is modifiable by appropriate reward and punishment even though we do not hold them morally responsible. But as the age of rationality approaches we gradually do. This suggests that in addition to susceptibility to reward and punishment, we attribute responsibility where there is a tendency to respond to valid reasons, to behave rationally, to respond to human emotions in a human way. Perhaps a third element involved in the attribution of moral responsibility to voluntary action is the assumption that voluntary action is *approved* action. A man is morally responsible for an action he commits to the extent that he *approves* of it. If he sincerely disapproves of his action, regards it as wrong and condemns it as wrong, but still commits it we tend to regard him as ill, as acting under "compulsion." It is some such consideration as this that lies behind our extenuation of certain kinds of apparently voluntary action (as when we say: "He didn't mean to do it"), especially where ignorance is present.

There may be other elements involved in the complex notion of moral responsibility, but the foregoing explains an interesting phenomenological fact. Sickness, accident, or incapacity aside, one feels lessened as a human being if one's actions are always excused or explained away on the ground that despite appearances one is really not responsible for them. It means being treated like an object, an infant, or someone out of his mind. Our dignity as rational human beings sometimes leads us to protest, when a zealous friend seeks to extenuate our conduct on the ground that we were not responsible (we didn't know or intend what we were doing, etc.), that we really *are* responsible and that we are prepared to take the consequences of our responsibility. As bad as the priggishness of the self-righteous is the whine of the self-pitying.

The so-called "hard" determinism professed by Professors Hospers and Edwards, especially in the popular form defended by Darrow, whom Edwards so extravagantly praised, often leads to sentimentality, to so much pity for the criminal as a victim not of a special set of particular circumstances but of any circumstances in general (referred to as heredity and environment, the sway of the law of causality) that there is not sufficient pity or concern left for the criminal's victims—not only for his past victims but his future ones and the victims of others his actions may inspire. To blame and to punish, of course, are two distinct things logically (except where blame is considered a form of punishment), but psychologically there is a great reluctance to punish if one believes there is no blame. Darrow as a "hard" determinist argued on a priori grounds that everyone was blameless and often won acquittals not on the evidence but despite it. If needless pain and cruelty are evils, then punishment that prevents or deters human beings from committing actions likely to result in much greater pain and cruelty than it imposes is sometimes the lesser evil.

It is argued by Professor Edwards that "hard" determinism, which, according to him, entails the belief that no one is morally responsible because no one ultimately shapes his own character, leads to the abandonment of retributive punishment. Even if this were so, it would not make the doctrine of "hard" determinism any more intelligible. But historically it is not so. From Augustine to Calvin to Barth the torment of eternal damnation is assigned and approved independently of moral responsibility. It is not related of the oft-quoted Puritan who piously observed to his son when they saw a man being led to the gallows, "There but for the grace of God go I," that he opposed retributive punishment. Nor can Edwards consistently with his own theory assert that "hard" determinists *should* repudiate retributive punishment, or morally blame them or anyone else, as he freely does, for approving of retributive punishment. For has he not told us that a man can't help having the character he has, no matter what kind of a character it is? Further, if retributive punishment is the enemy, there seems to me to be no necessary logical connection between a belief in moral responsibility and approval of retributive punishment. Certainly, "soft" determinists who assign responsibility to actions only when there is reason to believe that blame or punishment will modify future conduct are hardly likely to defend retributive punishment.

Why, after all, is retributive punishment evil? Not because the wrongdoer "ultimately did not shape his own character"—whatever that may mean—but simply because the pain inflicted on him gratuitously adds to the sum total of suffering in the world without any compensating alleviation of anybody else's sufferings. Even if an individual were considered able "ultimately to shape his own character" and were held morally responsible for an evil act, punishment that would be purely retributive and that did not contribute to deterring him or others from evil doing, or did nothing toward rehabilitating him, would still be morally wrong. This is quite evident in situations in which the "hard" determinist who is not a fatalist, if there be any such, admits that a man is to some extent, not ultimately but proximately, responsible for some change in his character—for example, when his desire to gamble leads him to steal a beggar's portion. In such situations retributive punishment as such would be regarded as morally wrong. Directed only to the past, it would not give the beggar back his portion or wipe out his pain, and therefore the new sufferings it inflicts are futile and needlessly cruel. If one can oppose retributive punishment when one believes a person is proximately responsible for his action, one can oppose it even when one believes a person is ultimately responsible, whatever the cognitive content of that belief turns out to be. If retributive punishment is the target of their criticism, Hospers and Edwards are training their guns in the wrong direction.

Far from diminishing the amount of needless cruelty and suffering in the world, I am firmly convinced that the belief that nobody is ever morally responsible, in addition to being false, is quite certain to have a mischievous effect and to increase the amount of needless cruelty and suffering. For it justifies Smerdyakov's formula in *The Brothers Karamazov*: "All things are permissible." One of the commonest experiences is to meet someone whose belief that he can't help doing what he is doing (or failing to do) is often an excuse for not doing as well as he can or at least better than he is at present doing. What often passes as irremediable evil in this world, or inevitable suffering, is a consequence of our failure to act in time. We are responsible, whether we admit it or not, for what it is in our power to do; and most of the time we can't be sure what it is in our power to do until we attempt it. In spite of the alleged inevitabilities in personal life and history human effort can redetermine the direction of events, even though it cannot determine the conditions that make human effort possible. It is time enough to reconcile oneself to a secret shame or a public tyranny after one has done one's best to overcome it, and even then it isn't necessary.

To say, as Professor Hospers does, that "It's all a matter of luck" is no more sensible than saying: "Nothing is a matter of luck"—assuming "luck" has a meaning in a world of hard determinism. It is true that we did not choose to be born. It is also true that we choose, most of us, to keep on living. It is not true that everything that happens to us is like "being struck down by a dread disease." The treatment and cure of disease—to use an illustration that can serve as a moral paradigm for the whole human situation—would never have begun unless we believed that some things that were did not have to be, that they could be different, and that *we* could make them different. And what we can make different we are responsible for.

FRANCIS V. RAAB
Free Will and the Ambiguity of "Could"

I

To paraphrase Moore—whether Free Will is or is not consistent with the causal principle depends upon the meaning of the word "could." I shall try to show that this is correct, and that in the usual and important sense of "could," there is no inconsistency between "so and so could have done (or chosen) otherwise" sentences (Free Will sentences) and the causal principle.

I shall not try to defend the causal principle. Its role in our thinking is far too subtle for easy talk of its "truth" and "proofs of its truth." I realize that it has often been argued that since free will is a fact, and since free will is incompatible with the causal principle, the causal principle is therefore false. However, if the following analysis is correct, the second premise is false, and thus one powerful argument against the causal principle will have been removed. Only in

From F. V. Raab, "Free Will and the Ambiguity of 'Could,'" *Philosophical Review*, LXIV, No. 1 (1955), 60–77. Reprinted by permission of the author and the editors of the *Philosophical Review*.

this sense could my argument be regarded as a defense of the causal principle, but I still do not intend it to be so.

There are customary uses of "could" sentences which refer either to the presence of an ability to do or to choose to do something, or to the conjunction of an ability with the absence of duress, or merely to the absence of duress when the presence of an ability is already taken for granted. Sentences which refer to such states of affairs are confirmable or refutable in well-known and commonly accepted ways. There is another possible use of a "could" sentence which is equivalent to a sentence asserting the absence of causality in a specific situation. A "could" sentence so used cannot be tested by any of the methods required to test "could" sentences in their customary use. I know of no way of testing "could" sentences in this atypical use.

However, the indeterminist, starting with the acceptable premise that we occasionally have an experience or inward perception of having acted or chosen freely, concludes that this experience is capable of verifying a "could" sentence in its atypical use. He holds either that the experience of having acted or chosen freely *is* the experience of the absence of causality with respect to that choice or action, or that the experience of having acted or chosen freely would be entirely illusory unless it be granted that nothing caused that action or choice. Now while I do think that on many occasions we experience freedom of choice or action, I seriously question whether we ever experience the absence of causality even in our choice. Not having an experience of the presence of causality is not the same as having the experience of the absence of the causal relation. I think that the experience of acting or choosing freely is just the experience of the absence of constraint upon our will. But the experience of the absence of constraint is not the experience of the absence of causality, for even though causality might involve a kind of necessity, this kind of necessity does not involve constraint or compulsion as these terms are ordinarily used. The "logic" of these terms is connected with that of blameworthiness and excusability, and thus they are not purely descriptive terms, but normative as well. Crudely put, whenever we say that a person's actions are blameworthy or excusable, compelled or uncompelled, we are involved in value discourse.

Suppose, however, that we momentarily grant that I do experience the absence of causality in having chosen or performed action Y; and, that it is just this experience which verifies the assertion: "I could have chosen (or done) X instead of Y," or "I chose (or did) Y freely." But how would I verify the assertion: "Jones could have chosen (or done) X instead of Y"? Surely I cannot have an experience of the absence of causality with respect to Jones's choice or performance of Y. I have to take note of whether he had ever chosen to do (or had done) X before, whether he was in acute pain, etc. Only by doing this can I test: "Jones could have done (or chosen to do) X instead of Y." We know that a person may experience a pain so acute that he becomes irrational, and when we want to settle whether at a given time in a given situation, Jones could have done otherwise than he did do, we would among other things ask him if he had been in intense pain. But we would not ask him if he had experienced the absence of causality in his performance or choice. If we did experience the absence of causality, nothing would more quickly prove the truth of a "could" sentence, in its atypical use, than an appeal to such an experience. Yet if we were convinced that people did experience such a thing when they experienced freedom of the will, why is it that we would not ask Jones whether he experienced the absence of causality? Instead, we rely on inquiries about pain, threats to one's life, abilities, and past performances.

To show some of the various uses of a "could" sentence we can imagine the following situation. Jones, a track star, a high-jumper, is discussing the track meet of the previous day with Smith, who was one of the spectators. Jones won the high-jump contest and Smith is congratulating him on his performance. However, Jones says that he *could* have jumped even higher than he did. Smith doubts this, so Jones leads him over to the high-jump pit where yesterday's meet was held. He proceeds to warm up on a few trial jumps and then sets the pole six inches higher than he had jumped on the previous day. He clears this new level three or four times. Would we not say that he has proved that he *could* have jumped higher yesterday? And would we not say this despite the fact that we would also want to say that Jones's performance of yesterday was caused—and thus in another sense of "could," Jones *could* not have jumped higher yesterday?

Still, Smith is a person difficult to convince. He admits that Jones has proved that *now* he can jump higher than he did yesterday, but he wants Jones to prove that he *could* have jumped higher *yesterday*. He thinks it possible that Jones mastered, overnight, some technique for his improved performance. So Jones takes Smith to the track coach who has kept records on Jones's previous performances. The records show that Jones, on each of the five days preceding the track meet, had consistently jumped higher than he did on the day of the meet. Smith now admits that Jones has proved that he had this ability on the day of the meet, yet he says he is not convinced that Jones *could* have jumped higher than he did. This puzzles Jones, but he finally sees through Smith's doubt. Perhaps Smith is thinking that he, Jones, may have had an acute pain on the day of the meet or that he was handicapped by a muscular cramp, or even that a gambler who had bet much money on Jones's not jumping higher than he did, threatened Jones to keep under wraps. So Jones now proceeds to remove these doubts about his having been under duress. He provides Smith with the testimony of a physician who examined him just before the meet, and also with the testimony of the coach and his teammates, who heard no complaints from Jones, and who noticed nothing that would indicate that he was in pain. The police captain of the small college town says that there were no gamblers in the community, etc. Jones has proved that he had the ability and that he was under no duress. Would we not say that Jones has proved that he *could* have jumped higher than he did—even though we believe that his actual performance was caused and thus that in another sense of "could" he could not have jumped higher?

But even though Smith accepts the fact that Jones had the ability and was not under duress, he persists in asking Jones to prove that yesterday he *could* have jumped higher than he did. Jones is momentarily at a loss to attach any meaning to this new request, for he can think of nothing that he or anyone else could do to remove Smith's doubt. In the usual senses of the word "could," Jones has verified his assertion that he could have jumped higher yesterday. Finally, Smith thinks that he sees what it is he wants to know from Jones, and he says, "What I mean is, *could* you have jumped higher than you did if everything were exactly the same as it was when you jumped below the level of your ability?" Jones thinks he sees the point of this question and answers, "Sure I *could,* if I had chosen to." But this won't do for Smith, and he now says, "No, I mean *could* you have jumped higher if *everything,* even your choice or decision to jump no higher than you did yesterday, was exactly what it was yesterday?" To this Jones replies, "Are you asking the silly question whether I *could* have jumped higher than I did even though I had chosen to jump below the level of my ability? Well, I suppose I *could* have or rather that I might have (notice the shift from "could" to "might" because in what follows it is uncertain whether Jones is any longer the *author* of his performance—an ambiguity in the "I" can arise). It sometimes happens that people who have the ability to jump a certain height jump that high even though they chose or intended to jump below the level of their ability. When an athlete is straining himself to his near limit, he sometimes overreaches himself and jumps higher than he set himself to do. It's hard to have exact control over what one does in such situations." But still this isn't what Smith was driving at, and he now sees even more clearly what he wants to say, "What I really mean is: Could you have jumped higher than you did yesterday, even if everything were *exactly* the same as it was when you made your jumps yesterday, and by 'everything' I mean your state of mind, i.e., your desire to jump just as high as you did, your feeling of competitiveness, your choice to jump below the level of your abilities, and exactly the same control over your muscles, and the very same condition of your muscles—so that they don't make you go higher than you want or decide to go—as well as the conditions of the track and the wind velocity, etc.?"

Now in this sense of "could," would we not be inclined to say that it is false that Jones could have jumped higher? But then why bother to ask anyone such a question as if he were in a privileged position to answer it? Jones was in a rather privileged position to answer the other "could" questions; but to this, his answer would be no different and no more informed than that of Smith or someone who never knew Jones or anything about high-jumping. The reason for their common answer reflects nothing more than their commitment to the causal principle. None of them has access to any special facts in the high-jump situation which leads him to say that such a "could" sentence is false. This then can hardly be called a normal use of "could" since no facts of the kind considered in the verification of the other "could" sentences are pertinent. Surely it is a strange use of "could" in which such sentences are never challengeable by any facts specific to the situation under consideration, and the falsity of such sentences is quite universally assumed (except by those who have been persuaded by a philosophical type of argument such as the indeterminists resort to) merely by a deduction from the causal principle.

When we have our wits about us we never, in this untestable sense of "could," ask people whether they could have done otherwise than they did, for we assume the answer in advance of any evidence. There is just no point in asking such a question because there are no special facts known to anyone which would help them to answer it. None of the usual evidence-moves for confirming or refuting the typical "could" sentences is relevant to settling assertions involving this use of "could."

It does seem then that when these "could" sentences are used, we can distinguish their different meanings by noting what is said or done by way of confirming or refuting them. When the verification is different in kind, we must assume that the meaning is different. The same is true, for example, of how we come to see the difference between other types of moral sentences, such as the difference between the logical "cannot" and the law-of-nature "cannot," or between the logically necessary and the nomologically necessary. We recognize that a "cannot" sentence belongs to the modality of logic by appealing to the presence of self-contradiction or perhaps some related criterion. We recognize that a sentence asserts a purely nomological "cannot" by the appeal to the absence of exceptions, the confidence we have in issuing counterfactuals, the coherence of the sentence within a deductive theory, etc.

It might be thought that the analogy of the high-jump situation with situations involving moral choice or just plain choice is too inexact to sustain any workable theory with regard to the latter situations. But this difference is only apparent. Obviously, from what we have already said about the situation, Jones did exercise choice in jumping as high as he did. For we have shown that he had the ability to jump higher, and he was under no duress. Would it not be queer to admit that Jones had the ability to jump higher and that he was under no duress and yet that even though he could have jumped higher, he did not choose to jump as high as he did? Certainly he did choose or decide to jump just as he did, otherwise his careful and controlled behavior could not be accounted for. He was under a self-imposed restraint which can only be attributed to the fact that he was acting out a choice. If we had asked Jones why he didn't jump as high as he could have, the kind of answer we would have expected is that he wanted to see if he could exercise that kind of control, or that he didn't want to try too hard lest he strain some muscles which would hamper him in a more important track meet a few days later. In other words he gives a reason for his under-performance. When people give purpose-type reasons for their actions, we attribute choice to those very actions. Would it not be paradoxical to say: The reason he gave for doing what he did was the true reason for doing what he did, but he did not exercise choice, i.e., he did not choose to do what he did? So I would conclude that Jones exercised choice in jumping as he did jump, and that we verify this choice just as we verified that he could have jumped higher than he did. In verifying the latter we verify the former. Now does the fact that Jones actually chose to jump just as he did make us say that the true sentence "He could have jumped higher than he did" is equivalent to the sentence "Jones's jumping as high as he did was uncaused?" If so, how could *we* verify the latter? But don't we usually think we *can* verify the former kind of sentence?

Now what about the added complication of a moral choice? Suppose Jones had jumped just as he did after having promised his coach to go all out and perform up to his usual standards. Would we not say that Jones, since he could by his own admission have jumped higher than he did, was morally blame-worthy for not having kept his promise? When we know the facts of Jones's ability and that he was under no duress, we say he could have jumped higher than he did. But is this to say that the jump he actually made was uncaused? I think we would all want to say that his action was caused but that that fact is irrelevant as an excuse for his under-performance. Further, we want to be able to prove that he could have jumped higher than he did and we would do so by pointing to his previous record and to the absence of duress. If we had to prove that his action was uncaused before we could truthfully say that he could have done otherwise, we would never be able to condemn anyone, for he could always hold out and say, "I know it looks as if I could have done otherwise but unless you can actually experience (or otherwise prove) the absence of causality in my doing what I did, then you cannot say that I could have done or chosen otherwise." But don't we believe that we can prove that Jones could have done or chosen otherwise just by showing that he had done and chosen such things before and that he had been under no duress?

A second feature of the verification of "could" sentences is that a certain person may be in a privileged position to verify them—just as Jones would be in a position to verify the sentence "Jones could not have jumped higher than he in fact did," while someone who knew nothing about him could not verify it. But if the "could" in the above sentence is being used in its atypical sense, then anyone a thousand miles away knows the answer just as well as Jones does.

A third point is that when "could" sentences are being used in their normal, verifiable sense, they are sometimes true of but one person. For example, if Jones were the world's best high-jumper, it might be said that he alone could have jumped higher than he did on the day of the track meet, while the others could not have. If "could" were intended in the unverifiable sense, the above distinction could not be made, the first part of the assertion would be false.

To summarize: "Could have done otherwise" sentences are ambiguous. In one of their uses they may be either confirmable or refutable, and more easily so by some than by others, and can be uniquely true of a given individual. In their other use they are unverifiable, are thought always to be false, are such that no one is better situated than anyone else in claiming them to be false, and do not permit the above distinction to be made with respect to a unique individual.

It would be helpful if we gave names to these different uses of "could," such as "the possession-of-an-ability 'could,'" or "the absence-of-duress 'could,'" or "the possession-of-an-ability plus the absence-of-duress 'could,'" or the "no-one-could-ever-have-done-otherwise-than-he-did 'could.'" Thus if the names were attached, when one used "could" sentences there would be no ambiguity to present difficulties. Had Smith so named the sense of "could" which he had in mind, he would easily have seen that Jones had decisively answered his questions step by step. We can now see that there is no inconsistency between the sentence "Jones could have jumped higher than he did" (where "could" is being used in one of its verifiable senses) and the sentence "Jones could not have jumped higher than he did" (where the "could" is being used in its unverifiable sense).

The bearing of this conclusion on the problem of free will is as follows: Since the normal, verifiable, "could" sentences have the same uses as sentences asserting that so and so was free to do X, or free to do X instead of Y (which he did do), there is then no inconsistency between the sentence "Jones was free to jump higher than he did" and the sentence "Jones could not have jumped higher than he did" (where the "could" is being used in the unverifiable, no-one-could-have-done-otherwise-than-he-did sense).

Verifiable "could" sentences are used in the same way as sentences ascribing free will to a person. We never say that Jones was free to do X instead of Y when we know that Jones lacks the ability to do X: i.e., when we know that Jones could not have done X. Also, we never say that Jones was free to do X instead of Y when we know that he was under duress, i.e., that he could not have done otherwise. Nor do we ever say that Jones was not free to do X instead of Y when we know that he was not under duress and that he had the ability to do X: i.e., when we know that he could have done X instead of Y. Thus just as we recognize a verifiable sense of "could," there is a verifiable sense of "free," and in both cases these verifiable uses are the customary and significant uses when it is said that so and so acted freely or of his own free will. Indeed, if it is held that "free" sentences are used as equivalents to sentences asserting the absence of causality, then they are never verifiable in the usual ways. Furthermore, how does one verify that nothing caused a person to do what he did? What special facts can one cite? And cite them one must, for there is no general principle from which to deduce a specific instance of the absence of causality. If the sentence "Jones was free to do X instead of Y" means that "nothing caused Jones to do Y," or "Jones's action (Y) was uncaused," then since its manner of verification is entirely unclear it could never be rationally contested. Further, if "free" sentences are thought to assert the absence of causes, then in order to show any one of them to be true we must show, at the very least, the absence of uniformity in a specific situation. But nothing of this sort is ever even attempted. How can a sentence about an action be importantly descriptive when it is never confirmable or refutable by any evidence-moves? And yet do we not want to say that sentences ascribing freedom are quite often true and demonstrably so?

In fact, when we hear someone say that so and so was free to do X instead of Y (when we had thought that he wasn't), we are willing to consider evidence in favor of this assertion, and we shall believe it just in so far as we are satisfied with the evidence. But if such a sentence were thought to assert the absence of a cause for doing Y, on what grounds would we believe it to be true of a person?

If a sentence of the kind "I could not have been polite to him" is being used in the sense that no one could have done otherwise than he did, then there is never any point in asking a person for the reason why he could not, for in this unverifiable sense we assume in advance of special evidence that a person could not have acted otherwise than as he did. And when someone gives us a reason such as "Because I was feeling quite nauseated," we should reply, "Look, you don't have to give me reasons, for no one could ever have behaved otherwise than he in fact did." In the unverifiable sense of a "could not have done otherwise" sentence, they are always true and can be asserted by the most ignorant as well as the most learned, by those who haven't given a moment's thought to the situation about which they made this assertion, as well as by those who have thought intensively about it. Such sentences will always be true no matter what the circumstances are, or the nature and abilities of the people involved. Surely this shows that this type of "could not have done otherwise" sentence is not what we have in mind when we are commenting on our own or others' past behavior. When a person who is being tried for a crime and pleads not guilty on the grounds of duress says, "I couldn't have done otherwise" or "I wasn't free to do anything else," we listen attentively to what he says in his defense. But if we all thought that he was using the "couldn't" in the unverifiable sense, we would pay no attention to his plea, for in that sense of "couldn't" we already accept that he could not have done otherwise. He proves duress not by citing the causal principle, but by making well known and accepted evidence-moves. This shows that the "could" or "couldn't" sentences of ordinary speech cannot be construed as making assertions about the absence of, or mere presence of causes, respectively, for doing what we did in fact do. We never use "could" or "couldn't" sentences without thinking of special facts about ourselves or about the situation; and when we hear them we often contradict them, demand evidence, and reflect upon the situation about which they are made. This activity becomes superfluous if these sentences are assertions about the absence or presence of causes.

The preceding analysis holds equally for sentences of the kind: "I could have chosen X instead of Y," or "I couldn't have chosen X instead of Y." The point of using such sentences is either to show that I was not under duress in choosing Y; or, as in some cases, that I had the ability to choose X; or that I was forced to choose Y (meaning perhaps that I had no choice at all); or, less frequently, that I didn't have the ability to choose X. If the "couldn't" is being used in the unverifiable sense, then there is no point in challenging the assertion by asking for the reason why I couldn't have chosen X instead of Y. But in fact we do ask for reasons, and in reply we do not expect someone to say, "Don't you know that what a person did choose is the only thing he could have chosen?" Instead we expect to hear something like, "I was being tortured." The sentence "I could have chosen X instead of Y" functions in the same way as the sentence "I was free to choose X instead of Y," or even "I chose Y freely" or "I was free to choose Y." And of course this is the typical use of "free" sentences, and they are verifiable.

It has been said that we are free when our choice alone would have made or enabled us to act otherwise than we did. But it is often asked whether we *could* have chosen differently. Well, if "could" is meant in the unverifiable sense, the answer is negative. However, if we are using "could" in the customary, verifiable sense, there are many occasions on which we could have chosen otherwise because we were not under duress and had the ability to choose what we in fact did not choose. Thus we are very often free to have chosen otherwise than we did.

It is sometimes thought that the problem of the freedom of the will, or choice, is separate from that of freedom of action, apparently because it seems that choice and decision are prior to action. But we must not overlook the fact that we very frequently regard choice (and decision) as part of the action chosen. For example, if a detective were trying to get a detailed narrative of someone's past behavior, he might come to a place where he asks the question, "What did you decide to do then?" and the answer he is given is, "I decided to call my lawyer." Would not the detective have a right to assume that the person *did* call his lawyer? Or again, notice the absurdity of "He *chose* the better paying job, but he *took* the lower paying one." (There are situations in which one might say this but not without an explanation such as: "The better paying job fell through at the last moment.") Choosing and deciding are "success-verbs," and thus if the actions which were chosen or decided upon are not performed through some fault of the agent, we take back the claim that he chose or decided to do them. Because choices are so often considered as parts of an action, it seems incorrect to speak of choosing our choices. To choose to choose to take a higher paying job is to do nothing more than to choose to take the higher paying job. Usually we reserve the expression "morally right" for actions, but occasionally we speak of morally right choices. This is understandable if choices are already parts of actions. Furthermore, do we not often confirm or refute sentences of the kind "I could have *chosen* otherwise" or "I was free to *choose* otherwise" by making the very same evidence-moves that we make to confirm or refute "I could have *done* otherwise" or "I was free to *do* otherwise"?

II

There are a number of kinds of influences upon behavior which are commonly recognized as grounds for excusing behavior. Some of these influences come under the heading of "duress." Whenever assertions like "I couldn't have done otherwise" (where the "couldn't" is being used to point to the presence of duress) are challenged, there is a class of evidence-moves made either to support or refute the assertion. Typically these evidence-moves point to the presence of pain in varying degree, like a heart attack or torture, or to the presence of a threat to one's life or the life or well-being of one's family, or to physical, motoric, restraint. There are other types of influence upon behavior which frequently serve to excuse it, but not all excuses are duress-type excuses. For example, we excuse a man for being unfriendly to us or for failing to help us in some small way when he is known to have a bad headache, but we would not so excuse a druggist's failure to fill a prescription properly when it leads to someone's death. When the stakes are low, we are more ready to accept such an excuse. But when human life is at stake there are very few types of acceptable excuses. Such excuses refer to what may be called a duress-situation. That the situations described above are considered as duress or excuse-situations is connected with our conception of the extent of human abilities, especially "second order" abilities or success-dispositions.

Suppose we justified our signing a false confession by saying that we were tortured into doing it. Now what if our listener said belligerently, "So what?" as if to challenge the putative connection between being tortured and signing the confession? When a person does not accept any one of these usual evidence-moves as an excuse for behavior, what are we to say to him? We might say, "Perhaps you'd understand if you were tortured awhile," and feel that that was the end of the matter. We would feel that we were within our rights in making this evidence-move and that his failure to accept it is due to some deficiency in his understanding. Yet this need not be so. He might very well understand the connection between being tortured and confessing, but not regard it as a necessary one. He might point to cases where persons withstood the torture without confessing, or died rather than confess, or committed suicide. About all we can do then is to say that most people could not have endured such torture. Thus the reason for our general acceptance of torture as grounds for excusing behavior is that the majority of us have not been trained to resist torture, and therefore cannot successfully withstand it. But the conditions of life in a community can become so threatening that such commonly accepted excuses will no longer serve as excuses. What happens then is that we refuse to accept these excuses because we believe that people have the ability of a higher order, if you will, to steel themselves against confessing under torture, or an ability to know that they could not so steel themselves, and thus commit suicide when they are caught, etc. We might well admit that the person who confessed under torture did not have a first-order ability to withstand the torture, but that he had either a second-order ability to train himself to withstand it—by Yoga, etc.—or that he had another ability to elude his torturers or captors in some way—by suicide, etc. Thus when the life of the community is threatened there is some reason for no longer accepting the once accepted excuses. We then blame people who have given away important information to the enemy for not making use of a higher or different ability to counteract a first-order liability or disability or weakness. We may not blame the drunken driver, qua drunk, for running over a pedestrian, but we do blame him for driving while drunk or for drinking at all. We have learned that people have the ability to keep themselves from getting into situations where they will act foolishly or recklessly. If alcohol was an unknown beverage, and someone became drunk from it, we would probably excuse his running over a pedestrian on the grounds that he couldn't have reasonably foreseen the effects of his driving after he had drunk it. But then again, we might blame him for not following the obvious rule that one shouldn't imbibe unknown substances. Of course, the total circumstances of his action are bound to be more complicated, and they would have to be taken into account before excuse or blame could be established.

However, we cannot indiscriminately refuse to accept the commonly accepted duress-type excuses. When individuals are not reared under Spartan conditions, they cannot be expected to suddenly have within themselves the power to withstand torture or to have firmly before their minds the welfare of the community while they are being tortured. They cannot be blamed for their confessions, because they haven't been prepared for their ordeal and thus their higher order capacities haven't had a chance to be exercised. People who joined the French resistance movement during the Nazi occupation certainly knew what they were getting into (and carried this consciousness into their daily lives) and could reasonably have more demanded of them than of the average Parisian.

There are of course supreme limits to human abilities. Thus no person has the ability, of any order, to jump over the Empire State Building. Excuses offered for unsatisfactory behavior which appeal to such factors are absolute excuses, or else the concept of an excuse no longer applies.

III

It is easy to see the bearing of the preceding discussion upon the notions that "ought" implies "can," and "ought to have done otherwise" implies "could have done otherwise." The responsible use of an "ought to have done otherwise" sentence requires that a specific "could have done otherwise" sentence be true, and verifiably true. If we were unable to verify sentences of this type, we would have no grounds for saying of anyone that he ought to have done otherwise—providing, of course, that the latter sentence is being used as a blame-sentence, a sentence affixing responsibility. (Some uses of such a sentence are merely instructional in their intent, e.g., saying this to a small child when we are aware that he did not know he was doing wrong.)

The mere fact that we say of a person that he ought to have done otherwise, does not imply that he could have done otherwise. Instead, the legitimate use of an "ought to have done otherwise" sentence depends upon the truth of a specific "could have done otherwise" sentence. We are justified in affixing blame only when we have ascertained that a person could have done otherwise. If we are challenged to prove that a person could have done otherwise, or that he was free to have done otherwise, we make some well-known and accepted evidence-moves to show that the person had the ability to do otherwise, and that he was not under duress. To prove that he had the ability, we show that on previous and subsequent occasions he had done or chosen otherwise, i.e., that he knew how to do this other thing which we believe that he should have done. To prove that he was under no duress, we show that he was not in pain, had not been threatened, or even that he was not suffering from a grave personality disturbance. When we have done all this, we have done all that can be done to prove that he could have done otherwise. There is no further evidence that can or need be given to establish blame. We do not need to show that the action in question was uncaused, for this can never be shown unless it is thought that when one has shown that the action was not done under duress one has shown that it was uncaused. But this is unreasonable, for then we would have to say that the vast majority of our actions, since they are not done under duress, are uncaused.

"Could have done otherwise" or "was free to do otherwise" sentences are challengeable in well-known ways, and thus "ought to have done otherwise" sentences are challengeable. If "was free to do otherwise" means that "what was done was uncaused," then it is never challengeable, for we have no way to show that something was uncaused. Thus we could never be the least bit certain that we were justified in blaming someone, and the concept of blame would accordingly become worthless, if not meaningless. However we do blame or excuse, and we do so on the basis of readily available evidence—except for the borderline cases mentioned in the preceding section, where the kind and amount of evidence we need would require exhaustive investigations.

IV

Duress is not the only generally accepted ground for excusing behavior. We also accept psychosis or a psychotic episode as an excuse. Thus the class of excusable behavior includes that done because of an internal pain, torture, threats to the life or well being of the agent or his family, as well as that done because of mental deterioration or grave personality disturbances. In the former class of excusable behavior the agent acts against his will, while in the latter he acts in accord with his will; or perhaps we might want to say that the agent had no will or that he was incapable of acting from intent. In the former class the agent can give, because he is conscious of, the reason why he acted as he did. In the latter, the agent acts without himself having a reason, or if he offers one—as the paranoid killer would—it is unacceptable because delusional.

In recent times, with the development of analytic psychiatry, the question is being raised whether we should recognize a much larger class of behavior as excusable behavior, namely neurotic behavior. Every day we learn of parents who criminally neglect the welfare of their children because of some compulsivity, or of a person who commits patricide because of an unconscious father-hatred originating in that person's infancy. But if all criminal behavior is unconsciously motivated, does it follow that we should not begin to recognize a much larger class of excuses than we do? There is also the speculation that as the doctrines of analytic psychiatry penetrate to the level of general public thinking we shall come to accept new grounds for excusing behavior.

But there are several contrary factors to be reckoned with. First, the community, for its own protection, may not accept neurotic excuses. It will have to "punish" violent and destructive behavior. It might be said that this is just being inhumane because the neurotic could not have acted otherwise. But I think the community might say that he *could* have acted otherwise—that he had the ability to seek psychiatric counsel, and that he should have done so. Undoubtedly as psychiatric knowledge becomes common knowledge, everyone will be equipped with cues by which to recognize his own neurotic hostility, etc., and will be expected to seek treatment. If his neurosis issues in criminal behavior, we shall blame him for not correcting a dangerous tendency, just as we now blame the drunken driver who injures another, not for driving carelessly, but for driving (or drinking) at all. But this is speculation. The question whether we should accept such neurotic excuses depends upon the effect of doing so on the community, and what that community will conceive a neurotic person's ability to avoid criminal behavior to be. However, if it should happen that with the increase of psychiatric knowledge on the part of the general public we came to excuse a much larger class of behavior than we now do, we would just decrease the range of our concept of free behavior, and thereby decrease the range of the legitimate use of the expression "could have done otherwise" where the "could" is used in its verifiable sense.

Supplementary Paperback Reading

A classic study of the problem of moral responsibility and free will:
Jonathan Edwards, *Freedom of the Will* (1754). Edited, with an introduction, by A. S. Kaufman and W. K. Frankena. (Bobbs-Merrill)

Paperback collections of essays pertaining to the problem of moral responsibility and free will:

H. B. Acton, *The Philosophy of Punishment*. (St. Martin's Press, Papermac)

B. Berofsky, *Free Will and Determinism*. (Harper and Row)

P. E. Davis, *Moral Duty and Legal Responsibility: A Philosophical-Legal Casebook.* (Appleton-Century-Crofts)

W. F. Enteman, *The Problem of Free Will*. (Scribner's)

H. L. A. Hart, *Punishment and Responsibility: Essays in the Philosophy of Law.* (Oxford University Press)

S. Hook, *Determinism and Freedom in the Age of Modern Science*. (Collier Books)

K. Lehrer, *Freedom and Determinism*. (Random House)

S. Morgenbesser and J. Walsh, *Free Will*. (Prentice-Hall)

Essays contained in paperback books, or reprinted separately, other than those to be found in the collections listed above:

K. Baier, "Responsibility and Action," in M. Brand, *The Nature of Human Action.* (Scott, Foresman)

K. Baier, "Responsibility and Freedom," in R. T. DeGeorge, *Ethics and Society.* (Anchor Books)

S. I. Benn and R. S. Peters, "Punishment," in J. Margolis, *Contemporary Ethical Theory*. (Random House)

R. M. Chisholm, "He Could Have Done Otherwise," in M. Brand, *The Nature of Human Action*. (Scott, Foresman)

J. W. R. Cox, "Can I Know Beforehand What I Am Going To Decide?" (Bobbs-Merrill Reprint Series in Philosophy)

T. Duggan and B. Gert, "Voluntary Abilities," in M. Brand, *The Nature of Human Action*. (Scott, Foresman)

A. C. Ewing, *Ethics*, Ch. VIII. (Free Press)

J. Feinberg, "Action and Responsibility," in A. R. White, *The Philosophy of Action*. (Oxford University Press)

P. J. Fitzgerald, "Voluntary and Involuntary Acts," in A. R. White, *The Philosophy of Action*. (Oxford University Press)

W. K. Frankena, "Obligation and Ability," in J. Margolis, *Contemporary Ethical Theory*. (Random House)

C. Ginet, "Can the Will Be Caused?" (Bobbs-Merrill Reprint Series in Philosophy)

B. Goldberg and H. Heidelberger, "Mr. Lehrer on the Constitution of Cans," in M. Brand, *The Nature of Human Action*. (Scott, Foresman)

A. S. Kaufman, "Ability," in M. Brand, *The Nature of Human Action*. (Scott, Foresman)

K. Lehrer, "Ifs, Cans, and Causes," in M. Brand, *The Nature of Human Action*. (Scott, Foresman)

K. Lehrer, "Cans and Conditionals: A Rejoinder," in M. Brand, *The Nature of Human Action*. (Scott, Foresman)

K. Lehrer, "Decisions and Causes." (Bobbs-Merrill Reprint Series in Philosophy)

G. E. Moore, *Ethics*, Ch. VI. (Oxford University Press)

C. W. K. Mundle, "Punishment and Desert," in J. J. Thomson and G. Dworkin, *Ethics*. (Harper and Row)

P. H. Nowell-Smith, *Ethics*, Ch. 19 and 20. (Penguin Books)

D. Pears, "Predicting and Deciding," in P. F. Strawson, *Studies in the Philosophy of Thought and Action*. (Oxford University Press)

A. M. Quinton, "On Punishment," in J. Margolis, *Contemporary Ethical Theory*. (Random House)

F. V. Raab, "The Relevance of Morals to Our Denials of Responsibility," in H. N. Castaneda and G. Nakhnikian, *Morality and the Language of Conduct*. (Wayne State University Press)

C. L. Stevenson, *Ethics and Language*, Ch. XIV. (Yale University Press)

C. L. Stevenson, *Facts and Values*, Essay VIII. (Yale University Press)

R. Taylor, "I Can." (Bobbs-Merrill Reprint Series in Philosophy)

7

VALUES

AND

FACTS

Introduction

Normative ethics is concerned with what ought to be, not with what is. Its task is to tell us how men ought and ought not to act, not to tell us how men do in fact act. It holds up ideals for us to strive for, ideals that are not shown to be false merely because we fail to live up to them. Furthermore, to describe how men do act is not to show us how they ought to act. The fact that most men do a certain thing does not make it right. Even the moral code actually accepted by a given society only tells us what some men believe to be right; it does not tell us what is right. In other words, it tells us about morality as it is, not about morality as it ought to be. Thus the difference between the "is" and the "ought," between facts and values, underlies the whole domain of normative ethics. Indeed, it is just this difference that separates ethics from sociology, psychology, and anthropology. Ethics is not a social science; yet it is not entirely unrelated to the social sciences. Ethics is not psychology; yet it can make use of the findings of psychology (for example, in predicting the probable consequences of acts or rules with regard to people's happiness), and in the last chapter we saw how the findings of psychology have a direct bearing on the ethical problem of free will and moral responsibility. Although facts are not values they are nevertheless related, and no discussion of the problems of ethics can omit a consideration of their relation.

In this chapter we shall be concerned with three fundamental questions: (1) What is the difference between facts and values? (2) How are they related to each other? (3) What is a value judgment? Each reading in this chapter will set forth a theory that provides answers to all three of these questions, and each reading will be found to be at variance with the other readings with regard to these questions. The disputes arising among these theories are still unsettled in contemporary moral philosophy.

NATURALISM AND NONNATURALISM

We shall begin by considering two opposite theories regarding the relation between facts and values: naturalism and nonnaturalism. According to naturalism, values are one kind of fact; according to nonnaturalism, values and facts are separate kinds of things, absolutely irreducible to one another. We can best understand what is meant by these claims if we take a "fact" to be an empirically verifiable statement about events and objects in the real world, and if we let the word "value" designate a value judgment about what is right or good. When we state a fact we assert that some object exists or some event occurs, or else we describe the properties of an object or event. When we utter a value judgment, we are evaluating, appraising, or judging the value of something. Consider the difference between the statement "Mohandas Gandhi was assassinated in 1948," and the statement "Mohandas Gandhi was a good man." The first statement expresses a fact about Gandhi but does not evaluate him, positively or negatively. The second statement expresses an evaluation of Gandhi by commending him and placing him high in an order of merit. Facts are empirical assertions; they tell us about the nature of an object or event, and we can determine whether they are true or false by appeal to experience. Values are normative assertions; they tell us whether something is good or bad, right or wrong, desirable or undesirable. How can we determine their truth or falsity? The basic contradiction between naturalism and nonnaturalism lies in the different answers they give to this question.

Naturalism holds that value judgments are empirically verifiable, just as facts are. Thus one way the statement "Gandhi was a good man" is verified (or falsified) is by finding out whether Gandhi was benevolent or cruel, honest or dishonest, courageous or cowardly. Another way to verify the statement is to see what were the consequences of Gandhi's acts. If his acts generally led to a decrease in human suffering, then the statement is confirmed as true. If his acts tended to have the contrary effect, the statement is disconfirmed as false. The value judgment that Gandhi was a good man is, therefore, one type of factual statement. It is equivalent either to, Gandhi was benevolent, honest, and courageous; or to, Gandhi acted in such a way as to lessen the amount of suffering in the world. Both of these assertions are empirically verifiable, and hence these values are reducible to facts.[1]

The nonnaturalist takes the opposite position. In his view a value judgment is not one type of factual statement, but is a unique kind of statement. Value judgments are true or false, but their truth or falsity cannot be known by appeal to sense experience. How then can we determine whether they are true or false? The nonnaturalist's answer is that we directly apprehend their truth or falsity by having a moral intuition. A moral intuition is the immediate awareness of the presence of a value-property (such as rightness or goodness) in an act, object, or person. Suppose someone makes the value judgment "Breaking your promise is wrong." We can know that this assertion is true by directly apprehending or intuiting the wrongness of breaking one's promise. We are simply aware that it is our duty not to break our promises; if a person were not aware of this, he would be morally blind. He would be lacking in the knowledge most of us gained in our moral upbringing. Although we do not see, hear, touch, taste, or smell the quality of wrongness in the act of promise-breaking, we nevertheless

[1] Two naturalistic theories of value judgments have been presented in this book. One is by R. B. Perry in the first reading of Chapter 1, according to which "X is good" is equivalent to "X is the object of a positive interest." The other is by Jeremy Bentham in the first reading of Chapter 4, according to which "Act X is right" is equivalent to "Act X will bring about more pleasure than any alternative act."

immediately grasp the truth of the statement that it is wrong to break a promise, for we are directly aware of the wrongness of that kind of act. (It will be noticed that this is a brief summary of the position developed by Sir David Ross, as presented in Chapter 5. Ross's theory is one kind of nonnaturalism or, as it is sometimes called, intuitionism.)

Let us now consider the value judgment given above, "Gandhi was a good man." According to the nonnaturalist or intuitionist, this statement is not empirically verifiable, and yet it is either true or false. It is true if the value-property of moral goodness did belong to the character of the man named Gandhi, false if it did not. And we know whether it did or did not by having a moral intuition of his character. Indeed, merely by knowing that he was a benevolent, honest, and courageous man we would know that he was good, since the property of goodness belongs to anyone having that kind of moral character. But the property of goodness is not *reducible to* the properties of benevolence, honesty, and courage. The reason why it is not is given in the first reading of this chapter, which we now discuss.

In 1903 Professor G. E. Moore of Cambridge University published one of the most important books ever written in moral philosophy, *Principia Ethica*. In that book, parts of which comprise our first reading, Moore does two things. He sets forth a nonnaturalist or intuitionist theory of value judgments, and he constructs an argument against naturalism. Moore believed that these two things were logically connected. If we accept his argument against naturalism, he thought, we must accept his own nonnaturalistic position about values. However, when we come to the second and third readings of this chapter we shall see that it is possible to accept Moore's criticism of naturalism and at the same time *not* accept a nonnaturalistic theory of value.

Let us first look at Moore's nonnaturalism. Moore is a nonnaturalist only about judgments of intrinsic value, not about judgments of instrumental or extrinsic value. (This distinction will be examined at length in the following chapter.) Thus the judgment that something is a good means to a given end is, for Moore, empirically verifiable. That my wristwatch is a good wristwatch is shown to be true if it keeps accurate time, does not require frequent repairs, is easy to read, is shockproof, and so on. All of these empirical properties of the watch are those which make it an efficient instrument for telling the time. Similarly, judgments about the moral rightness or wrongness of an act, in Moore's view, are judgments of instrumental value, since he is an act-utilitarian. An act is judged to be right if it tends to bring about better consequences than would be brought about by any alternative act that can be done in the given circumstances. But in deciding which consequences of an act are good and which are bad, we must make judgments of intrinsic value, and these are *not* empirically verifiable. The statement that friendship, or intelligence, or pleasure is (intrinsically) good is understood by Moore in a nonnaturalistic way.

Moore analyzes such judgments of intrinsic value as follows. When we assert, for example, that pleasure is intrinsically good, we attribute the value-property of goodness to pleasure. This property is a unique, indefinable quality in the sense that it cannot be analyzed as a complex made up of other, simpler properties (in the way that "being a horse" can be analyzed in terms of being an animal having a certain shape and size, four legs, hooves, a tail, etc.). Since goodness is a simple quality in this sense, the word "good" is indefinable. We know what it means, Moore claims, because we have in our minds a particular notion or idea whenever we say that something is good, and this idea is different from other ideas we have in our minds when we use other words. Furthermore, the unique, indefinable quality of goodness that we attribute to something when we call it good is not an empirical property. Unlike the color yellow which, although a simple, indefinable property is also an empirical one, we cannot see the goodness of something with our eyes, nor can we directly perceive it by any other sense. Therefore, Moore concludes, goodness (or intrinsic value) is a "nonnatural" property. Its presence or absence in anything is not a fact that can be empirically known.

Moore assumes throughout this argument that the word "good" is the name of a property. However, as we shall see in the second and third readings of this chapter, there are other ways of conceiving of the meaning of "good." Before turning to these, let us examine Moore's criticism of naturalism.

According to naturalism value judgments are one type of factual statement. Now Moore claims that such a view results from the committing of a logical error, which he calls "the naturalistic fallacy." In order to demonstrate this fallacy he gives two arguments, which we shall consider in turn. The first argument is *the open question test,* and may be summarized as follows. Let us suppose a naturalistic definition of intrinsic value were true. A naturalistic definition of intrinsic value is any definition of a value-word (a word used as the predicate of a value judgment), such that the meaning of the word is made identical with the meaning of a word or set of words standing for *empirical* properties. Examples are: "Good" means "pleasant." "Good" means "approved of by my society." "Good" means "desired for its own sake." "Good" means "satisfies human needs." "Bad" means "unpleasant"; and so on. If any such definition were true, then whenever a value-word occurred in a sentence we could substitute for it the word or set of words that are defined as equivalent to it, *without changing the meaning of the sentence.* Thus, if "good" means "pleasant," then the two sentences "Playing tennis is a good experience" and "Playing tennis is a pleasant experience" must mean the same thing. Now consider the following two (compound) sentences:

S1: This is pleasant, but is it good?
S2: This is pleasant, but is it pleasant?

The only difference between these two sentences is that, where the word "good" occurs in one, the word "pleasant" occurs in the other. Therefore, if the definition "good" means "pleasant" were a correct definition, the two sentences should mean exactly the same thing. But, according to Moore, it is clear that they do not. The reason is that S2 is a silly sentence; no one would ever utter it, for if we already know that something is pleasant there is no point in asking whether it is pleasant. But S1 is not a silly sentence. We may know that something is pleasant and still ask seriously whether it is good. We may very well wonder, if someone finds it pleasant to kick others around, whether it is good that he do so. At least it is an *open question* whether something that is pleasant is also good. Yet if "good" just meant "pleasant," then once we knew that something was pleasant we could make no sense in asking whether it was good, for we would then be asking whether it was pleasant. Now we can apply the same argument to *any* naturalistic definition of a value-word, using S1 and S2 as our models. Thus, "This is approved of by my society, but is it good?" is a sensible question to ask, but no one would ever say such a ridiculous thing as "This is approved of by my society, but is it approved of by my society?" Yet, if "good" means "approved of by my society" these two questions must mean the same thing, so that if one is ridiculous the other must be equally ridiculous. Since one of the sentences is not ridiculous while the other is, they cannot be identical in meaning and the naturalistic definition must not be true.

There is another way to prove the same point. Let us again assume, for the moment, that a naturalistic definition is true (say, "good" means "pleasant"). Again we construct two compound sentences, differing only in the respect that, where "good" occurs in one sentence, the defining empirical term ("pleasant" in this case) occurs in the other. The two sentences are:

S3: This is pleasant, but it is not good.
S4: This is pleasant, but it is not pleasant.

Now if the naturalistic definition were true, S3 and S4 would mean exactly the same thing. But when we reflect about what they say, we notice that S4 is a self-contradiction, whereas it is at least questionable whether S3 is also a self-contradiction. And further reflection shows that S3 cannot mean the same thing as S4. For there are some people who would assert S3 and we would understand what they meant. But no one would ever assert S4. Take, for example, a Puritan who thought that pleasure is (intrinsically) evil. He might very well say S3 to himself, when he found himself enjoying something. And we all know how puritanical people condemn others for enjoying themselves. Or, to take another case, there are mystics who believe that the pleasures of the senses, though not necessarily bad, are "mere illusions" which only get in the way of achieving what is truly good, which is the mystical vision of "reality" itself. So here again it makes sense to assert S3. But neither the Puritan nor the mystic would be so foolish as to utter the contradiction expressed in S4. Therefore, S3 and S4 cannot mean the same thing, and hence the definition "good" means "pleasant," must be false. According to Moore, a similar argument can be applied to any proposed naturalistic definition, and thus there is always a fallacy in equating a value-word with a word standing for empirically determinable properties. Values, in short, can never be reduced to facts.

COGNITIVISM AND NONCOGNITIVISM

We now turn to a theory of value that is to be contrasted with both naturalism and nonnaturalism. This theory, known as noncognitivism or "the emotive theory," is propounded and defended by Professor Charles Stevenson in the second reading of this chapter. In order to understand this theory let us begin by distinguishing three uses or functions of language: the reportive or assertive function, the expressive function, and the dynamic function. When we use language to make an assertion or report a fact, we are stating what we believe about something. Thus we might say, "It is going to rain," and so communicate to our hearers a belief we have about the weather in the immediate future. We use language to do the same job when we say, "It rained yesterday," or when we say, "Rain falls when there is a change in atmospheric pressure," or when we say, "A drop of rain contains oxygen," and so on. In other words, whenever we express a matter-of-fact belief that something is so, will be so, or has been so, the language we use has a reportive or assertive function. It is only when language is used in this way that we can ask whether what we say is true or false. And only with reference to this function of language can we speak of knowing that something is or is not so.

The second function of language is exemplified most obviously in emotional ejaculations. Here we use words to express our feelings. Touching a hot stove, I yell, "Ouch!" A music lover cries out, "Bravo!" on hearing a beautifully sung aria. We shout, "Hurrah!" when our team is winning. Language in this way evinces or displays our emotion, just as our posture, facial expressions, and non-verbal actions may also reveal our feelings to others. Ejaculations are the simplest expressive use of language. Perhaps the most complex and subtlest expressive use is found in lyrical poetry. But it is important to notice that declarative sentences may also have this function. Each of the following express a certain emotion: "This is a splendid day for a picnic." "I'm so relieved they got home safely." "He was absolutely brilliant in that chess game." "It was a despicable thing to do."

The third function of language is its capacity to arouse or evoke the feelings of others, to influence their attitudes, and to change or redirect their behavior. The simplest example is a command or order, and we are all familiar with the subtle (and not so subtle!) techniques of persuasion used in advertising copy and in radio and television commercials. Other examples are proposals ("Let's go to the movies tonight."); requests ("I wish you would not walk on the lawn."); suggestions ("We suggest that you go by plane rather than by car."); advice ("My advice is that you should see a doctor."); recommendations ("I recommend leniency in this case."); prescriptions ("You ought to get more exercise."). In each instance the uttering of the statement is intended to exert an influence on the hearer, and frequently this intended effect is brought about by the utterance. Political oratory, preaching, "pep talks," and didactic literature all have this function. Language is being used to call forth some response on the part of others. Thus we name this the "dynamic" function of language.

Now where do value judgments fit into this threefold division of linguistic functions? When we utter a moral judgment, are we making an assertion that is true or false? Are we expressing our feelings? Or are we trying to guide and direct the conduct of others? The theory of noncognitivism holds that value judgments belong in the last two categories but not in the first. Statements about what is good, bad, right, wrong, desirable, undesirable are not cognitive assertions. That is to say, the person who makes such statements is not expressing a belief; he is not making a claim that is true or false. Rather, he is expressing his attitudes and trying to get others to have the same attitudes he has. Thus when a person says, "Mohandas Gandhi was a good man," he is expressing his approval of Gandhi and is trying to evoke approval of Gandhi in his hearers. Declarative sentences that express value judgments, therefore, are linguistic utterances having an expressive and dynamic function, but not a reportive or assertive ("cognitive") function. Thus they are sharply to be distinguished from declarative sentences, like "Gandhi was assassinated in 1948," that express beliefs and that accordingly are open to verification procedures. Since value judgments are neither true nor false, there is no sense in talking about their verification. Indeed, since moral statements are merely emotive expressions and dynamic instruments of language, there is no such thing as moral knowledge. Hence the name, "noncognitivism." According to the noncognitivist, we should not talk about *knowing* what is right and wrong, good and bad. However, as we shall see shortly, the noncognitivist does speak of moral *reasoning* in a special sense.

Noncognitivism differs from naturalism and nonnaturalism in that both of the latter theories conceive of value judgments as expressing beliefs, capable of being true or false. Both naturalism and nonnaturalism, consequently, are forms of "cognitivism." Both claim that there is such a thing as moral knowledge. For naturalism, value judgments are one type of factual assertion. They are verifiable empirically or scientifically, and moral knowledge is simply one branch of scientific knowledge. For nonnaturalism, a value judgment is an assertion or belief that a value-property characterizes a given object, act, or person. This belief is either true or false, and intuition is the way to find out which it is. Noncognitivists deny both of these views. They reject naturalism for the same reason given by the nonnaturalist, to wit, it commits the naturalistic fallacy. Noncognitivists, indeed, offer an explanation of why the naturalistic fallacy is a fallacy. Naturalism assumes that all declarative sentences have the same linguistic function, which is to be assertive of facts, and hence it overlooks the possibility that value judgments can be expressive and dynamic but not cognitive or assertive.

Noncognitivists deny nonnaturalism because nonnaturalists think of value judgments as assertive of beliefs about the presence or absence of value-properties in things. Thus they take the adjectives "good," "desirable," "right," and the like to be names of properties: goodness, desirability, rightness, etc. In so doing, they think of value-words as having a descriptive function, the way "yellow," "loud," "heavy," and other such adjectives are descriptive. But, the noncognitivist argues, adjectives may have any of the three different linguistic functions listed above, and value-words like "good," "desirable," and "right" are used only expressively and dynamically in sentences where they occur as predicates. Such sentences, therefore, are misconstrued if they are understood the way ordinary descriptive sentences, such as "The balloon is yellow," are understood.

Professor Stevenson, who is the foremost exponent of noncognitivism in contemporary philosophy, begins his essay by distinguishing two ways in which people can disagree with one another: disagreement in belief and disagreement in attitude. The first kind of disagreement occurs when one person makes an assertion and another denies it. Both persons are using language reportively. They are expressing opposite beliefs about the same thing. The second kind of disagreement occurs when one person expresses a favorable or positive attitude toward something and another expresses an unfavorable or negative attitude toward the same thing. (Two persons might also disagree in the strength or intensity of their attitudes, even when both attitudes are positive or when both are negative.) It is the latter kind of disagreement that occurs in ethics, according to the noncognitivist. When one person says, "This is good" and another says, "No, it is bad," each is expressing his own attitude and trying to get the other to change his attitude and agree (in attitude) with the speaker. Their disagreement is not a contradiction in the usual sense, where one person claims that a belief is true and the other claims it is false. Instead, it is a conflict of attitudes, and attitudes are neither true nor false.

Attitudes, however, are not entirely unrelated to beliefs. Sometimes we will approve of something (and so call it "good" or "desirable" or "right") when we do not have correct beliefs about its nature or consequences. Then, as we obtain more knowledge about its nature or consequences and accordingly change our beliefs, our attitudes will change, either in strength or in direction. For example, we might approve of a proposed law and then, upon learning what would be the probable consequences if it were passed, change our attitude from approval to disapproval. In this kind of situation our attitude toward something depends on our beliefs about it. If two people have a disagreement in attitude, it might then be possible for one person to change the attitude of the other by showing him that he has false beliefs about the object in question. Now since scientific method can be used to establish the truth or falsity of empirical beliefs, science has the capacity to enlighten our moral judgments. This would happen if our obtaining scientific knowledge about something caused a change in our attitudes toward it. This causal relationship between facts and values, however, is still very different from the basic thesis of naturalism, namely, that moral knowledge is itself a kind of scientific knowledge.

In the second part of his essay Stevenson attempts to show why a noncognitivist theory of value does not imply ethical relativism. His argument brings out the noncognitivist view of *moral reasoning*. We have seen above that, according to the noncognitivist, value judgments are neither true nor false. How, then, can we reason about them? To give reasons in support of a value statement would normally be understood to be a logical process of justifying someone's asserting the statement. The reasons would be such as to show that the statement is true. Likewise, giving reasons against a value statement would ordinarily be taken as a way of showing the statement to be false and hence as a way of justifying someone's denying the statement. But if value statements are mere expressions of attitude and hence neither true nor false, how can there be such a thing as giving reasons for or against them? Stevenson answers this question by distinguishing between "reasons for believing" and "reasons for approving." The kind of reasons relevant to value judgments are reasons for approving, and since such reasons can be given it is possible for attitudes to be justified or unjustified. Exactly what is involved in this noncognitivist account of moral reasoning is set forth in the second part of Stevenson's essay. It may be fruitfully compared with the last three readings of this chapter (by Hare, Foot, and Phillips and Mounce), in which other accounts of moral reasoning are presented. It will also be of interest to the reader to ask himself whether Stevenson has successfully proven that noncognitivism does not entail either normative ethical relativism or meta-ethical relativism, as these theories were discussed in Chapter 2.

STANDARDS OF EVALUATION AND THE MEANING OF "GOOD"

The third reading in this chapter, by Professor R. M. Hare, contains still another conception of value judgments. This conception differs in fundamental ways from all three views we have discussed: naturalism, nonnaturalism, and noncognitivism. Hare opens his essay with an attack on naturalism, giving his own explanation of why the naturalistic fallacy is a fallacy, and reformulating the fallacy in his own way. His basic criticism of naturalism is that, in making value judgments one kind of factual or empirical assertion, the naturalist takes away the evaluative meaning of value-words. This evaluative meaning is the *commending* function of the word. When we say, "Mohandas Gandhi was a good man," we are commending or praising him; we are not merely describing him or reporting a fact about him. Thus a value statement is not a statement of fact. In uttering the former we are *evaluating* the subject being talked about; in uttering the latter we are *describing* it.

So far, it would seem that Hare's view is just like noncognitivism. But this is not correct. Although a value-word has a commending function, this function does not consist merely in expressing a positive atttude on the part of the speaker and in evoking a similar attitude on the part of the hearer. When a person says that something is good, according to Hare, he is doing two additional things besides expressing and evoking attitudes, and these two additional things are what distinguish value judgments from ejaculations, commands, exhortations, and other expressive and dynamic uses of language. First, the person who commends something on the basis of an evaluation of it is *guiding choices by appeal to a universal principle*. Second, he is *making an assertion that must be supported by reasons, and these reasons must be of a certain sort.* Let us consider each of these points in turn.

(1) In order to understand what a value judgment is or what it means to

evaluate something, we must distinguish between the *meaning* of a value-word and its *criteria*. Take the word "good," for example. There are many kinds of things we call good: good painters, good mathematicians, good fountain pens, good cars, good books, and so on. In calling any of these things good we are evaluating them positively and hence commending them. This function or use of the word is common to all its applications, no matter what kind of thing the word is being applied to. But if we ask, concerning the thing to which the word is applied, "What makes it good? What is good about it?" we see immediately that there will be different answers, according to the different classes of things being called good. Hare names the class of things with which some object is being compared in evaluating it the "class of comparison." The characteristics or properties of a thing which we point out in answering the questions What makes it good? What is good about it? are called "good-making characteristics." Thus, while the meaning (use, function) of the word "good" remains constant throughout all classes of comparison (the commending function), the set of characteristics that are good-making vary with each class of comparison. The properties that a painter must have to be a good painter will be entirely different from the properties that make a mathematician a good mathematician. (It is possible, of course, for one individual to have both sets of properties.) Similarly, what makes a fountain pen good will be very different from what makes a car good; and so for the other classes of comparison.

For each class of comparison, how do we know which of the characteristics belonging to a member of the class are its good-making characteristics? The answer lies in the *criteria* of goodness or *standards* of evaluation which we implicitly appeal to whenever we make a value judgment. Consider, for instance, a person whom we judge to be a good mathematician. Suppose he has the following properties: blue eyes, six feet tall, born in Chicago, 190 I.Q., does not believe in God, has proven theorems in topology no one else has proven, has three children, has written a book used by other mathematicians in their research. Only three of these characteristics, we would say, are *relevant* to his being a good mathematician. How do we know that these characteristics are relevant and that the other ones are irrelevant? The answer is that these are the characteristics in virtue of which the person *satisfies our criteria* for anyone's being a good mathematician. His high I.Q., his ability to prove theorems, and his being the author of an authoritative book in his field are characteristics which, when present in a person, tend to enable him to fulfill (to some degree) the conditions that define an ideal mathematician. We may therefore speak of the criteria of the word "good" as distinct from its meaning. The criteria of a good fountain pen, to take another example, will be the standards by which we judge fountain pens to be excellent, good, mediocre, poor, terrible, and so on. A good fountain pen will be a fountain pen that fulfills the conditions of excellence to a higher degree than a mediocre or poor pen. And the good-making characteristics are those properties of a pen that enable it to fulfill these conditions to the degree indicated. Such properties are: it does not leak; it does not need frequent refilling; it does not scratch or blot; it is easy and comfortable to hold; it continues to write after many years of hard use; and so on.

We now have four concepts necessary for a complete analysis of a value judgment: (a) *the meaning of a value-word* (its commending function); (b) *the criteria of a value-word* (the standards of evaluation being referred to when the value-word is applied in each case); (c) *the good-making characteristics* (the properties of the object in virtue of which it satisfies the criteria to a certain degree); and (d) *the class of comparison* (the class of objects whose different values are determined by one set of criteria). A value judgment may consequently be defined as follows: A value judgment is the commending of an object because it has those good-making characteristics which enable it to fulfill to a certain degree, in comparison with other objects in the given class of comparison, those criteria which are accepted as standards for evaluating all members of that class of comparison.

We are now ready to see how a value judgment guides choices by appeal to a universal principle, which we said above is one of the two basic aspects of evaluation in Hare's analysis. Suppose I am trying to decide what fountain pen to buy, within a given price range. If someone points to one of the pens I am looking at and says, "That is a good pen," he is directly guiding my choice. Assuming that he and I both accept the same criteria for evaluating pens, I know that if he is telling me the truth I should buy that pen (unless he states that some other pen is even better). For in saying that it is a good pen, he is implying that it has the good-making characteristics which I also want a pen to have. Furthermore, I know that any other pen similar to this one (in relevant respects) will also be a good pen, since it will have the same good-making characteristics and so will fulfill the criteria to the same degree. The universal principle in accordance with which the value judgment is made is the principle that, if any pen in the given price range (that is, any member of the class of comparison) is like this one in the relevant respects (that is, has the same good-making characteristics), it will be a good pen. Thus, as Hare puts it, "All value judgments are covertly universal." A value judgment tells us not only the value of a particular object, but the value of any object relevantly similar to it. The judgment can guide anyone who is confronted with a choice between such an object and other objects in the class of comparison. This is one reason why the noncognitivist analysis of a value judgment is incorrect, according to Hare. For noncognitivists do not mention standards of evaluation, and do not recognize that such standards make every value judgment a universal guide to choice.

(2) A second reason why the noncognitivist theory of value is mistaken, in Hare's view, is that it fails to account for the way reasons support value judgments. On this point it is enlightening to contrast Hare's analysis of the justification of value judgments with the analysis given by Stevenson. According to Hare, whenever a person makes a value judgment it is appropriate to ask him, Why? If he says that something is good, for example, we can always demand, What are your reasons for saying it is good? or simply, Why is it good? Now

these questions can be rephrased as, What makes this good, in your judgment? or, What do you think is good about it? And these questions, we have seen, are requests for the person to specify the *good-making characteristics* of the object. Thus the reasons that support a value judgment are statements that point out the good-making characteristics of the thing that is being evaluated. These are empirical assertions concerning its properties, and here is the place where facts are related to values. Empirical statements about an object may be relevant or irrelevant to a judgment of its value. They are relevant if they are about the properties of the object in virtue of which it fulfills the standards of evaluation being applied in the given judgment; otherwise, they are irrelevant. Thus the reasons that justify the judgment that Mohandas Gandhi was a good man will not merely be those beliefs about Gandhi that have an influence on our attitudes toward him, as Stevenson would claim. They will be, instead, facts about Gandhi which show that he had those characteristics (such as benevolence, honesty, and courage) that make him a good man, according to the moral standards we are using to judge all men.

One further element in Hare's theory should be noted. The *complete* justification of any value judgment goes beyond the statement of relevant facts about the object being judged. This is only the first step in justifying a value judgment, and it consists in showing that the object does fulfill the given standards to a certain degree. But suppose someone challenges those standards. If this happens, then the person who makes a value judgment on the basis of those standards must justify his use of them in evaluating objects in the given class of comparison. This is the second step of justifying a value judgment. Thus someone might say, I agree with you that this object is good if you judge it by standards A, B, and C, but it would be bad if it were judged by standards X, Y, and Z. Unless you can show why one ought to use A, B, and C and ought not to use X, Y, and Z as standards for judging this object, you have not established the truth of your judgment that the object is good. This raises the question How can standards of evaluation be justified? What sort of reasons can be given to validate them? Professor Hare's answer is given in the last section of the reading. Here he discusses not only value judgments made by applying standards to objects but also value judgments made by applying rules of conduct to acts. While standards tell us what things are good or bad, rules of conduct tell us what acts are right or wrong. Standards and rules are collectively called "principles" by Hare. Principles serve to guide our choices and decisions, since we appeal to them whenever we want to know what is the best thing to choose, or what we ought to do when we have alternatives among which to decide.

One step of moral reasoning is the application of principles to guide our choices and decisions. Hare points out that this step of moral reasoning can be put in the form of a syllogism or deductive argument, the first or major premise being a statement of the principle, the second or minor premise being a factual statement about the act and its circumstances, and the conclusion being the value judgment about what we ought to do. An example would be:

Major premise (Principle):	Never say what is false.
Minor premise (Fact):	To say X in these circumstances would be to say what is false.
Conclusion (Value judgment):	I ought not to say X.

The same kind of reasoning takes place if we are applying a standard of evaluation to an object, thus:

Major premise (Principle):	Any man who is benevolent, honest, and courageous is a good man.
Minor premise (Fact):	Mohandas Gandhi was benevolent, honest, and courageous.
Conclusion (Value judgment):	Mohandas Gandhi was a good man.

Decisions and choices, then, are justified on the ground of principles. But how can principles (the major premises) themselves be justified? What kind of reasoning would yield good reasons for accepting one principle rather than another?

Hare explores this question in some detail. He first shows that principles are things we ourselves *decide* to use. Even if we derive them from our culture, they have no power to guide our choices unless we make a "decision of principle" to adopt them as our own. It is our own decision to accept a principle that enables it to operate as a major premise in the syllogism of moral reasoning. So the question: On what grounds do principles rest? becomes the question: What reasons would justify a person's decision to adopt a principle as a guide to his own choice and conduct? In order to answer this question, Hare examines the way principles are adopted, changed, and given up in the ordinary circumstances of life. He considers how we learn principles in childhood, and how we come to reject them, make exceptions to them, or modify them as we use them in everyday experience. In doing this he shows how it is the *effects* or *consequences* of our using principles that determine whether they are justified. When the effects of our principles are unsatisfactory in some way or are unsuitable to our changing environment, we judge these effects to be undesirable. This judgment is a value judgment and, like any other, must be made on the basis of a principle. Thus we reject or modify our original principles on the ground of new principles. These new principles, in turn, are judged by *their* effects or consequences, and so on until we have exhausted all the principles that make up our whole way of life. Hare then considers the question of whether there is any kind of reasoning by which a whole way of life can be justified. Whether his solution to this problem is an acceptable one is left for the reader's critical reflection.

THE CONNECTION BETWEEN FACTS AND VALUES

In the last two readings of this chapter the question of the relation between facts and values is reconsidered. In her essay, "Moral Beliefs," Mrs. Philippa Foot tries to show that Stevenson's separation of attitudes from beliefs and

Hare's view of the independence of the evaluative meaning of "good" from its descriptive meaning cannot be maintained. She argues that there are limits to the kinds of things toward which we can have a pro-attitude or which can meaningfully be judged to be good. The empirical evidence by which value judgments are supported is not determined by an attitude or by a "decision of principle." Mrs. Foot claims that if we examine our actual use of value terms we shall see that there is no "logical gap" between the factual premises and the evaluative conclusion of our reasoning when we are involved in arguments about values. By considering such value-concepts as "dangerous," "injury," "courage," and "justice," Mrs. Foot gives examples of how the use of these concepts depends on empirical facts. She is not claiming that value words can be defined in terms of factual words; she is not *reducing* value judgments to facts. Hence it would be misleading to call her position a form of "naturalism." But she does argue that the naturalistic fallacy does not entail a complete logical separation between values and facts.

In the last reading Professors Phillips and Mounce criticize Mrs. Foot's arguments. They attempt to show that there is a logical connection between values and facts only when a certain background of moral ideals is assumed. For example, what is to count as an "injury" and hence as something "bad" will depend, not on what human beings happen to want to avoid (a matter of fact), but rather on a whole way of life which includes moral standards regarding how we ought to live. A value judgment can be supported by empirical evidence only against the background of moral standards that determine what is to count as a benefit or a harm, a good or an evil. An argument about the value of something, therefore, cannot be settled merely by finding a set of facts about the thing that provides neutral evidence for its goodness or badness. Whether Mrs. Foot could successfully reply to this criticism is a question left for the reader's own thought.

GEORGE EDWARD MOORE
Goodness as a Simple Property

What, then, is good? How is good to be defined? Now, it may be thought that this is a verbal question. A definition does indeed often mean the expressing of one word's meaning in other words. But this is not the sort of definition I am asking for. Such a definition can never be of ultimate importance in any study except lexicography. If I wanted that kind of definition I should have to consider in the first place how people generally used the word 'good'; but my

From G. E. Moore, *Principia Ethica* (1903). Reprinted by permission of the Cambridge University Press (Cambridge, England).

business is not with its proper usage, as established by custom. I should, indeed, be foolish, if I tried to use it for something which it did not usually denote: if, for instance, I were to announce that, whenever I used the word 'good,' I must be understood to be thinking of that object which is usually denoted by the word 'table.' I shall, therefore, use the word in the sense in which I think it is ordinarily used; but at the same time I am not anxious to discuss whether I am right in thinking that it is so used. My business is solely with that object or idea, which I hold, rightly or wrongly, that the word is generally used to stand for. What I want to discover is the nature of that object or idea, and about this I am extremely anxious to arrive at an agreement.

But, if we understand the question in this sense, my answer to it may seem a very disappointing one. If I am asked 'What is good?' my answer is that good is good, and that is the end of the matter. Or if I am asked 'How is good to be defined?' my answer is that it cannot be defined, and that is all I have to say about it. But disappointing as these answers may appear, they are of the very last importance. To readers who are familiar with philosophic terminology, I can express their importance by saying that they amount to this: That propositions about the good are all of them synthetic and never analytic; and that is plainly no trivial matter. And the same thing may be expressed more popularly, by saying that, if I am right, then nobody can foist upon us such an axiom as that 'Pleasure is the only good' or that 'The good is the desired' on the pretence that this is 'the very meaning of the word.'

Let us, then, consider this position. My point is that 'good' is a simple notion, just as 'yellow' is a simple notion; that, just as you cannot, by any manner of means, explain to any one who does not already know it, what yellow is, so you cannot explain what good is. Definitions of the kind that I was asking for, definitions which describe the real nature of the object or notion denoted by a word, and which do not merely tell us what the word is used to mean, are only possible when the object or notion in question is something complex. You can give a definition of a horse, because a horse has many different properties and qualities, all of which you can enumerate. But when you have enumerated them all, when you have reduced a horse to his simplest terms, then you can no longer define those terms. They are simply something which you think of or perceive, and to any one who cannot think of or perceive them, you can never, by any definition, make their nature known. It may perhaps be objected to this that we are able to describe to others, objects which they have never seen or thought of. We can, for instance, make a man understand what a chimaera is, although he has never heard of one or seen one. You can tell him that it is an animal with a lioness's head and body, with a goat's head growing from the middle of its back, and with a snake in place of a tail. But here the object which you are describing is a complex object; it is entirely composed of parts, with which we are all perfectly familiar—a snake, a goat, a lioness; and we know what is meant by the middle of a lioness's back, and where her tail is wont to grow. And so it is with all objects, not previously known, which we are able to define: they are all complex; all composed of parts, which may themselves, in the first instance, be capable of similar definition, but which must in the end be reducible to simplest parts, which can no longer be defined. But yellow and good, we say, are not complex: they are notions of that simple kind, out of which definitions are composed and with which the power of further defining ceases.

When we say, as Webster says, 'The definition of horse is "A hoofed quadruped of the genus Equus,"' we may, in fact, mean three different things. (1) We may mean merely: 'When I say "horse," you are to understand that I am talking about a hoofed quadruped of the genus Equus.' This might be called the arbitrary verbal definition: and I do not mean that good is indefinable in that sense. (2) We may mean, as Webster ought to mean: 'When most English people say "horse," they mean a hoofed quadruped of the genus Equus.' This may be called the verbal definition proper, and I do not say that good is indefinable in this sense either; for it is certainly possible to discover how people use a word: otherwise, we could never have known that 'good' may be translated by 'gut' in German and by 'bon' in French. But (3) we may, when we define horse, mean something much more important. We may mean that a certain object, which we all of us know, is composed in a certain manner: that it has four legs, a head, a heart, a liver, etc., etc., all of them arranged in definite relations to one another. It is in this sense that I deny good to be definable. I say that it is not composed of any parts, which we can substitute for it in our minds when we are thinking of it. We might think just as clearly and correctly about a horse, if we thought of all its parts and their arrangement instead of thinking of the whole: we could, I say, think how a horse differed from a donkey just as well, just as truly, in this way, as now we do, only not so easily; but there is nothing whatsoever which we could so substitute for good; and that is what I mean, when I say that good is indefinable.

But I am afraid I have still not removed the chief difficulty which may prevent acceptance of the proposition that good is indefinable. I do not mean to say that *the* good, that which is good, is thus indefinable; If I did think so, I should not be writing on Ethics, for my main object is to help towards discovering that definition. It is just because I think there will be less risk of error in our search for a definition of 'the good,' that I am now insisting that *good* is indefinable. I must try to explain the difference between these two. I suppose it may be granted that 'good' is an adjective. Well 'the good,' 'that which is good,' must therefore be the substantive to which the adjective 'good' will apply: it must be the whole of that to which the adjective will apply, and the adjective must *always* truly apply to it. But if it is that to which the adjective will apply, it must be something different from that adjective itself; and the whole of that something different, whatever it is, will be our definition of *the* good. Now it may be that this something will have other adjectives, beside 'good,' that will apply to it. It may be full of pleasure, for example; it may be intelligent: and if these two adjectives are really part of its definition, then it will certainly be true, that pleasure and intelligence are good. And many people appear to think that, if we say 'Pleasure and intelligence are good,' or if we say 'Only pleasure and intelligence are good,' we are defining 'good.' Well, I cannot deny that propositions of this nature may sometimes be called definitions; I do not know well enough how the word is generally used to decide upon this point. I only wish it to be understood that that is not what I mean when I say there is no possible definition of good, and that I shall not mean this if I use the word again. I do most fully believe that some true proposition of the form 'Intelligence is good and intelligence alone is good' can be found; if none could be found, our definition of *the* good would be impossible. As it is, I believe *the* good to be definable; and yet I still say that good itself is indefinable.

'Good,' then, if we mean by it that quality which we assert to belong to a thing, when we say that the thing is good, is incapable of any definition, in the most important sense of that word. The most important sense of 'definition' is that in which a definition states what are the parts which invariably compose a certain whole; and in this sense 'good' has no definition because it is simple and has no parts. It is one of those innumerable objects of thought which are themselves incapable of definition, because they are the ultimate terms by reference to which whatever *is* capable of definition must be defined. That there must be an indefinite number of such terms is obvious, on reflection; since we cannot define anything except by an analysis, which, when carried as far as it will go, refers us to something, which is simply different from anything else, and which by that ultimate difference explains the peculiarity of the whole which we are defining: for every whole contains some parts which are common to other wholes also. There is, therefore, no intrinsic difficulty in the contention that 'good' denotes a simple and indefinable quality. There are many other instances of such qualities.

Consider yellow, for example. We may try to define it, by describing its physical equivalent; we may state what kind of light-vibrations must stimulate the normal eye, in order that we may perceive it. But a moment's reflection is sufficient to shew that those light-vibrations are not themselves what we mean by yellow. *They* are not what we perceive. Indeed we should never have been able to discover their existence, unless we had first been struck by the patent difference of quality between the different colours. The most we can be entitled to say of those vibrations is that they are what corresponds in space to the yellow which we actually perceive.

Yet a mistake of this simple kind has commonly been made about 'good.' It may be true that all things which are good are *also* something else, just as it is true that all things which are yellow produce a certain kind of vibration in the light. And it is a fact, that Ethics aims at discovering what are those other properties belonging to all things which are good. But far too many philosophers have thought that when they named those other properties they were actually defining good; that these properties, in fact, were simply not 'other,' but absolutely and entirely the same with goodness. This view I propose to call the 'naturalistic fallacy' and of it I shall now endeavour to dispose.

• • • • •

. . . When A says 'Good means pleasant' and B says 'Good means desired,' they may merely wish to assert that most people have used the word for what is pleasant and for what is desired respectively. And this is quite an interesting subject for discussion: only it is not a whit more an ethical discussion than the last was. Nor do I think that any exponent of naturalistic Ethics would be willing to allow that this was all he meant. They are all so anxious to persuade us that what they call the good is what we really ought to do. 'Do, pray, act so, because the word "good" is generally used to denote actions of this nature': such, on this view, would be the substance of their teaching. And in so far as they tell us how we ought to act, their teaching is truly ethical, as they mean it to be. But how perfectly absurd is the reason they would give for it! 'You are to do this, because most people use a certain word to denote conduct such as this.' 'You are to say the thing which is not, because most people call it lying.' That is an argument just as good!—My dear sirs, what we want to know from you as ethical teachers, is not how people use a word; it is not even, what kind of actions they approve, which the use of this word 'good' may certainly imply: what we want to know is simply what *is* good. We may indeed agree that what most people do think good, is actually so; we shall at all events be glad to know their opinions: but when we say their opinions about what *is* good, we do mean what we say; we do not care whether they call that thing which they mean 'horse' or 'table' or 'chair,' 'gut' or 'bon' or 'agathos'; we want to know what it is that they so call. When they say 'Pleasure is good,' we cannot believe that they merely mean 'Pleasure is pleasure' and nothing more than that.

• • • • •

In fact, if it is not the case that 'good' denotes something simple and indefinable, only two alternatives are possible: either it is a complex, a given whole, about the correct analysis of which there may be disagreement; or else it means nothing at all, and there is no such subject as Ethics. . . .

(1) The hypothesis that disagreement about the meaning of good is disagreement with regard to the correct analysis of a given whole, may be most plainly seen to be incorrect by consideration of the fact that, whatever definition be offered, it may be always asked, with significance, of the complex so defined, whether it is itself good. To take, for instance, one of the more plausible, because one of the more complicated, of such proposed definitions, it may easily be thought, at first sight, that to be good may mean to be that which we desire to desire. Thus if we apply this definition to a particular instance and say 'When we think that A is good, we are thinking that A is one of the things which we desire to desire,' our proposition may seem quite plausible. But, if we carry the investigation further, and ask ourselves 'Is it good to desire to desire A?' it is apparent, on a little reflection, that this question is itself as intelligible, as the original question 'Is A good?'—that we are, in fact, now asking for exactly the same information about the desire to desire A, for which we formerly asked with regard to A itself. But it is also apparent that the meaning of this second question cannot be correctly analysed into 'Is the desire to desire A one of the

things which we desire to desire?': we have not before our minds anything so complicated as the question 'Do we desire to desire to desire to desire A?' Moreover any one can easily convince himself by inspection that the predicate of this proposition—'good'—is positively different from the notion of 'desiring to desire' which enters into its subject: 'That we should desire to desire A is good' is *not* merely equivalent to 'That A should be good is good.' It may indeed be true that what we desire to desire is always also good; perhaps, even the converse may be true: but it is very doubtful whether this is the case, and the mere fact that we understand very well what is meant by doubting it, shews clearly that we have two different notions before our minds.

(2) And the same consideration is sufficient to dismiss the hypothesis that 'good' has no meaning whatsoever. It is very natural to make the mistake of supposing that what is universally true is of such a nature that its negation would be self-contradictory: the importance which has been assigned to analytic propositions in the history of philosophy shews how easy such a mistake is. And thus it is very easy to conclude that what seems to be a universal ethical principle is in fact an identical proposition; that, if, for example, whatever is called 'good' seems to be pleasant, the proposition 'Pleasure is the good' does not assert a connection between two different notions, but involves only one, that of pleasure, which is easily recognised as a distinct entity. But whoever will attentively consider with himself what is actually before his mind when he asks the question 'Is pleasure (or whatever it may be) after all good?' can easily satisfy himself that he is not merely wondering whether pleasure is pleasant. And if he will try this experiment with each suggested definition in succession, he may become expert enough to recognise that in every case he has before his mind a unique object, with regard to the connection of which with any other object, a distinct question may be asked. Every one does in fact understand the question 'Is this good?' When he thinks of it, his state of mind is different from what it would be, were he asked 'Is this pleasant, or desired, or approved?' It has a distinct meaning for him, even though he may not recognise in what respect it is distinct. Whenever he thinks of 'intrinsic value,' or 'intrinsic worth,' or says that a thing 'ought to exist,' he has before his mind the unique object—the unique property of things—which I mean by 'good.' Everybody is constantly aware of this notion, although he may never become aware at all that it is different from other notions of which he is also aware. But, for correct ethical reasoning, it is extremely important that he should become aware of this fact; and, as soon as the nature of the problem is clearly understood, there should be little difficulty in advancing so far in analysis.

'Good,' then, is indefinable. . . .

• • • • •

HEDONISM

In this chapter we have to deal with what is perhaps the most famous and the most widely held of all ethical principles—the principle that nothing is good but pleasure. My chief reason for treating of this principle in this place is, as I said, that Hedonism appears in the main to be a form of Naturalistic Ethics: in other words, that pleasure has been so generally held to be the sole good, is almost entirely due to the fact that it has seemed to be somehow involved in the *definition* of 'good'—to be pointed out by the very meaning of the word. If this is so, then the prevalence of Hedonism has been mainly due to what I have called the naturalistic fallacy—the failure to distinguish clearly that unique and indefinable quality which we mean by good.

•   •   •   •   •

I propose, then, to begin by an examination of Mill's *Utilitarianism.* That is a book which contains an admirably clear and fair discussion of many ethical principles and methods. Mill exposes not a few simple mistakes which are very likely to be made by those who approach ethical problems without much previous reflection. But what I am concerned with is the mistakes which Mill himself appears to have made, and these only so far as they concern the Hedonistic principle. Let me repeat what that principle is. It is, I said, that pleasure is the only thing at which we ought to aim, the only thing that is good as an end and for its own sake. And now let us turn to Mill and see whether he accepts this description of the question at issue. 'Pleasure,' he says at the outset, 'and freedom from pain, are the only things desirable as ends'; and again, at the end of his argument, 'To think of an object as desirable (unless for the sake of its consequences) and to think of it as pleasant are one and the same thing'. These statements, taken together, and apart from certain confusions which are obvious in them, seem to imply the principle I have stated; and if I succeed in shewing that Mill's reasons for them do not prove them, it must at least be admitted that I have not been fighting with shadows or demolishing a man of straw.

It will be observed that Mill adds 'absence of pain' to 'pleasure' in his first statement, though not in his second. There is, in this, a confusion, with which, however, we need not deal. I shall talk of 'pleasure' alone, for the sake of conciseness; but all my arguments will apply *à fortiori* to 'absence of pain': it is easy to make the necessary substitutions.

Mill holds, then, that 'happiness is desirable, and *the only thing desirable,* as an end; all other things being only desirable as means to that end'. Happiness he has already defined as 'pleasure, and the absence of pain'; he does not pretend that this is more than an arbitrary verbal definition; and, as *such,* I have not a word to say against it. His principle, then, is 'pleasure is the only thing desirable,' if I may be allowed, when I say 'pleasure,' to include in that word (so far as necessary) absence of pain. And now what are his reasons for holding that principle to be true? He has already told us that 'Questions of ultimate ends are not amenable to direct proof. Whatever can be proved to be good, must be so by being shewn to be a means to something *admitted to be good without proof.*' With this, I perfectly agree: indeed the chief object of my first chapter was to shew that this is so. Anything which is good as an end must be admitted to be good without proof. We are agreed so far. . . . 'How,' he says, 'is it possible to prove that health is good?' 'What proof is it possible to give that pleasure is good?' Well, in Chapter IV, in which he deals with the proof of his Utilitarian principle, Mill repeats the above statement in these words: 'It has already,' he says, 'been remarked, that questions of ultimate ends do not admit of proof, in the ordinary acceptation of the term'. 'Questions about ends,' he goes on in this same passage, 'are, in other words, questions what things are desirable.' I am quoting these repetitions, because they make it plain what otherwise might have been doubted, that Mill is using the words 'desirable' or 'desirable as an end' as absolutely and precisely equivalent to the words 'good as an end.' We are, then, now to hear, what reasons he advances for this doctrine that pleasure alone is good as an end.

'Questions about ends,' he says, 'are, in other words, questions what things are desirable. The utilitarian doctrine is, that happiness is desirable, and the only thing desirable, as an end; all other things being only desirable as means to that end. What ought to be required of this doctrine—what conditions is it requisite that the doctrine should fulfil—to make good its claim to be believed?

'The only proof capable of being given that a thing is visible, is that people actually see it. The only proof that a sound is audible, is that people hear it; and so of the other sources of our experience. In like manner, I apprehend, the sole evidence it is possible to produce that anything is desirable, is that people do actually desire it. If the end which the utilitarian doctrine proposes to itself were not, in theory and in practice, acknowledged to be an end, nothing could ever convince any person that it was so. No reason can be given why the general happiness is desirable, except that each person, so far as he believes it to be attainable, desires his own happiness. This, however, being the fact, we have not only all the proof which the case admits of, but all which it is possible to require, that happiness is a good: that each person's happiness is a good to that person, and the general happiness, therefore, a good to the aggregate of all persons. Happiness has made out its title as *one* of the ends of conduct, and consequently one of the criteria of morality.'

There, that is enough. That is my first point. Mill has made as naïve and artless a use of the naturalistic fallacy as anybody could desire. 'Good,' he tells us, means 'desirable,' and you can only find out what is desirable by seeking to find out what is actually desired. This is, of course, only one step towards the proof of Hedonism; for it may be, as Mill goes on to say, that other things beside pleasure are desired. Whether or not pleasure is the only thing desired is, as Mill himself admits, a psychological question. . . . The important step for Ethics is this one just taken, the step which pretends to prove that 'good' means 'desired.'

Well, the fallacy in this step is so obvious, that it is quite wonderful how Mill failed to see it. The fact is that 'desirable' does not mean 'able to be desired' as 'visible' means 'able to be seen.' The desirable means simply what *ought* to be desired or *deserves* to be desired; just as the detestable means not what can be but what ought to be detested and the damnable what deserves to be damned. Mill has, then smuggled in, under cover of the word 'desirable,' the very notion about which he ought to be quite clear. 'Desirable' does indeed mean 'what it is good to desire'; but when this is understood, it is no longer plausible to say that our only test of *that,* is what is actually desired. Is it merely a tautology when the Prayer Book talks of *good* desires? Are not *bad* desires also possible? Nay, we find Mill himself talking of a 'better and nobler object of desire', as if, after all, what is desired were not *ipso facto* good, and good in proportion to the amount it is desired. Moreover, if the desired is *ipso facto* the good; then the good is *ipso facto* the motive of our actions, and there can be no question of finding motives for doing it, as Mill is at such pains to do. If Mill's explanation of 'desirable' be *true,* then his statement that the rule of action may be *confounded* with the motive of it is untrue: for the motive of action will then be according to him *ipso facto* its rule; there can be no distinction between the two, and therefore no confusion, and thus he has contradicted himself flatly. These are specimens of the contradictions, which, as I have tried to shew, must always follow from the use of the naturalistic fallacy; and I hope I need now say no more about the matter.

CHARLES L. STEVENSON
Noncognitivism and Relativism

THE NATURE OF ETHICAL DISAGREEMENT

I

When people disagree about the value of something—one saying that it is good or right and another that it is bad or wrong—by what methods of argument or inquiry can their disagreement be resolved? Can it be resolved by the methods of science, or does it require methods of some other kind, or is it open to no rational solution at all?

The question must be clarified before it can be answered. And the word that is particularly in need of clarification, as we shall see, is the word "disagreement."

Let us begin by noting that "disagreement" has two broad senses: In the first sense it refers to what I shall call "disagreement in belief." This occurs when Mr. A believes *p,* when Mr. B believes *not-p,* or something incompatible

From C. L. Stevenson, "The Nature of Ethical Disagreement," *Sigma* (1948), and "Relativism and Nonrelativism in the Theory of Value," Presidential Address to the Western Division of the American Philosophical Association, *Proceedings of the American Philosophical Association* (1961–62). Reprinted by permission of the author and the American Philosophical Association.

with p, and when neither is content to let the belief of the other remain unchallenged. Thus doctors may disagree in belief about the causes of an illness; and friends may disagree in belief about the exact date on which they last met.

In the second sense the word refers to what I shall call "disagreement in attitude." This occurs when Mr. A has a favorable attitude to something, when Mr. B has an unfavorable or less favorable attitude to it, and when neither is content to let the other's attitude remain unchanged. The term "attitude" is here used in much the same sense that R. B. Perry uses "interest"; it designates any psychological disposition of being *for* or *against* something. Hence love and hate are relatively specific kinds of attitudes, as are approval and disapproval, and so on.

This second sense can be illustrated in this way: Two men are planning to have dinner together. One wants to eat at a restaurant that the other doesn't like. Temporarily, then, the men cannot "agree" on where to dine. Their argument may be trivial, and perhaps only half serious; but in any case it represents a disagreement *in attitude*. The men have divergent preferences and each is trying to redirect the preference of the other—though normally, of course, each is willing to revise his own preference in the light of what the other may say.

Further examples are readily found. Mrs. Smith wishes to cultivate only the four hundred; Mr. Smith is loyal to his old poker-playing friends. They accordingly disagree, in attitude, about whom to invite to their party. The progressive mayor wants modern school buildings and large parks; the older citizens are against these "new-fangled" ways; so they disagree on civic policy. These cases differ from the one about the restaurant only in that the clash of attitudes is more serious and may lead to more vigorous argument.

The difference between the two senses of "disagreement" is essentially this: the first involves an opposition of beliefs, both of which cannot be true, and the second involves an opposition of attitudes, both of which cannot be satisfied.

Let us apply this distinction to a case that will sharpen it. Mr. A believes that most voters will favor a proposed tax and Mr. B disagrees with him. The disagreement concerns attitudes—those of the voters—but note that A and B are *not* disagreeing in attitude. Their disagreement is *in belief about* attitudes. It is simply a special kind of disagreement in belief, differing from disagreement in belief about head colds only with regard to subject matter. It implies not an opposition of the actual attitudes of the speakers but only of their beliefs about certain attitudes. Disagreement *in* attitude, on the other hand, implies that the very attitudes of the speakers are opposed. A and B may have opposed beliefs about attitudes without having opposed attitudes, just as they may have opposed beliefs about head colds without having opposed head colds. Hence we must not, from the fact that an argument is concerned with attitudes, infer that it necessarily involves disagreement *in* attitude.

2

We may now turn more directly to disagreement about values, with particular reference to normative ethics. When people argue about what is good, do they disagree in belief, or do they disagree in attitude? A long tradition of ethical theorists strongly suggest, whether they always intend to or not, that the disagreement is one *in belief*. Naturalistic theorists, for instance, identify an ethical judgment with some sort of scientific statement, and so make normative ethics a branch of science. Now a scientific argument typically exemplifies disagreement in belief, and if an ethical argument is simply a scientific one, then it too exemplifies disagreement in belief. The usual naturalistic theories of ethics that stress attitudes—such as those of Hume, Westermarck, Perry, Richards, and so many others—stress disagreement in belief no less than the rest. They imply, of course, that disagreement about what is good is disagreement *in belief* about attitudes; but we have seen that that is simply one sort of disagreement in belief, and by no means the same as disagreement *in* attitude. Analyses that stress disagreement *in* attitude are extremely rare.

If ethical arguments, as we encounter them in everyday life, involved disagreement in belief exclusively—whether the beliefs were about attitudes or about something else—then I should have no quarrel with the ordinary sort of naturalistic analysis. Normative judgments could be taken as scientific statements and amenable to the usual scientific proof. But a moment's attention will readily show that disagreement in belief has not the exclusive role that theory has so repeatedly ascribed to it. It must be readily granted that ethical arguments usually involve disagreement in belief; but they *also* involve disagreement in attitude. And the conspicuous role of disagreement in attitude is what we usually take, whether we realize it or not, as the distinguishing feature of ethical arguments. For example:

Suppose that the representative of a union urges that the wage level in a given company ought to be higher—that it is only right that the workers receive more pay. The company representative urges in reply that the workers ought to receive no more than they get. Such an argument clearly represents a disagreement in attitude. The union is *for* higher wages; the company is *against* them, and neither is content to let the other's attitude remain unchanged. *In addition* to this disagreement in attitude, of course, the argument may represent no little disagreement in belief. Perhaps the parties disagree about how much the cost of living has risen and how much the workers are suffering under the present wage scale. Or perhaps they disagree about the company's earnings and the extent to which the company could raise wages and still operate at a profit. Like any typical ethical argument, then, this argument involves both disagreement in attitude and disagreement in belief.

It is easy to see, however, that the disagreement in attitude plays a unifying and predominating role in the argument. This is so in two ways:

In the first place, disagreement in attitude determines what beliefs are *relevant* to the argument. Suppose that the company affirms that the wage scale of fifty years ago was far lower than it is now. The union will immediately urge that this contention, even though true, is irrelevant. And it is irrelevant simply because information about the wage level of fifty years ago, maintained under totally different circumstances, is not likely to affect the present attitudes of either party. To be relevant, any belief that is introduced into the argument must be one that is likely to lead one side or the other to have a different attitude, and so reconcile disagreement in attitude. Attitudes are often functions of beliefs. We often change our attitudes to something when we change our beliefs about it; just as a child ceases to *want* to touch a live coal when he comes to *believe* that it will burn him. Thus in the present argument any beliefs that are at all likely to alter attitudes, such as those about the increasing cost of living or the financial state of the company, will be considered by both sides to be relevant to the argument. Agreement in belief on these matters may lead to agreement in attitude toward the wage scale. But beliefs that are likely to alter the attitudes of neither side will be declared irrelevant. They will have no bearing on the disagreement in attitude, with which both parties are primarily concerned.

In the second place, ethical argument usually terminates when disagreement in attitude terminates, even though a certain amount of disagreement in belief remains. Suppose, for instance, that the company and the union continue to disagree in belief about the increasing cost of living, but that the company, even so, ends by favoring the higher wage scale. The union will then be content to end the argument and will cease to press its point about living costs. It may bring up that point again, in some future argument of the same sort, or in urging the righteousness of its victory to the newspaper columnists; but for the moment the fact that the company has agreed in attitude is sufficient to terminate the argument. On the other hand: suppose that both parties agreed on all beliefs that were introduced into the argument, but even so continued to disagree in attitude. In that case neither party would feel that their dispute had been successfully terminated. They might look for other beliefs that could be introduced into the argument. They might use words to play on each other's emotions. They might agree (in attitude) to submit the case to arbitration, both feeling that a decision, even if strongly adverse to one party or the other, would be preferable to a continued impasse. Or, perhaps, they might abandon hope of settling their dispute by any peaceable means.

In many other cases, of course, men discuss ethical topics without having the strong, uncompromising attitudes that the present example has illustrated. They are often as much concerned with redirecting their own attitudes, in the light of greater knowledge, as with redirecting the attitudes of others. And the attitudes involved are often altruistic rather than selfish. Yet the above example will serve, so long as that is understood, to suggest the nature of ethical disagreement. Both disagreement in attitude and disagreement in belief are involved, but the former predominates in that (1) it determines what sort of disagreement in belief is relevantly disputed in a given ethical argument, and (2) it determines by its continued presence or its resolution whether or not the argument has been settled. We may see further how intimately the two sorts of disagreement are related: since attitudes are often functions of beliefs, an agreement in belief may lead people, as a matter of psychological fact, to agree in attitude.

3

Having discussed disagreement, we may turn to the broad question that was first mentioned, namely: By what methods of argument or inquiry may disagreement about matters of value be resolved?

It will be obvious that to whatever extent an argument involves disagreement in belief, it is open to the usual methods of the sciences. If these methods are the *only* rational methods for supporting beliefs—as I believe to be so, but cannot now take time to discuss—then scientific methods are the only rational methods for resolving the disagreement in *belief* that arguments about values may include.

But if science is granted an undisputed sway in reconciling beliefs, it does not thereby acquire, without qualification, an undisputed sway in reconciling attitudes. We have seen that arguments about values include disagreement in attitude, no less than disagreement in belief, and that in certain ways the disagreement in attitude predominates. By what methods shall the latter sort of disagreement be resolved?

The methods of science are still available for that purpose, but only in an indirect way. Initially, these methods have only to do with establishing agreement in belief. If they serve further to establish agreement in attitude, that will be due simply to the psychological fact that altered beliefs may cause altered attitudes. Hence scientific methods are conclusive in ending arguments about values only to the extent that their success in obtaining agreement in belief will in turn lead to agreement in attitude.

In other words: the extent to which scientific methods can bring about agreement on values depends on the extent to which a commonly accepted body of scientific beliefs would cause us to have a commonly accepted set of attitudes.

How much is the development of science likely to achieve, then, with regard to values? To what extent *would* common beliefs lead to common attitudes? It is, perhaps, a pardonable enthusiasm to *hope* that science will do everything —to hope that in some rosy future, when all men know the consequences of their acts, they will all have common aspirations and live peaceably in complete moral accord. But if we speak not from our enthusiastic hopes but from our present knowledge, the answer must be far less exciting. We usually *do not know*, at the beginning of any argument about values, whether an agreement in belief, scientifically established, will lead to an agreement in attitude or not. It is logically possible, at least, that two men should continue to disagree in attitude even though they had all their beliefs in common, and even though neither had made any logical or inductive error, or omitted any relevant evidence. Differences in temperament, or in early training, or in social status, might make the men retain different attitudes even though both were possessed of the complete scientific truth. Whether this logical possibility is an empirical likelihood I shall not presume to say; but it is unquestionably a possibility that must not be left out of account.

To say that science can always settle arguments about value, we have seen, is to make this assumption: Agreement in attitude will always be consequent upon complete agreement in belief, and science can always bring about the latter. Taken as purely heuristic, this assumption has its usefulness. It leads people to discover the discrepancies in their beliefs and to prolong enlightening argument that *may* lead, as a matter of fact, from commonly accepted beliefs to commonly accepted attitudes. It leads people to reconcile their attitudes in a rational, permanent way, rather than by rhapsody or exhortation. But the assumption is *nothing more,* for present knowledge, than a heuristic maxim. It is wholly without any proper foundation of probability. I conclude, therefore, that scientific methods cannot be guaranteed the definite role in the so-called normative sciences that they may have in the natural sciences. Apart from a heuristic assumption to the contrary, it is possible that the growth of scientific knowledge may leave many disputes about values permanently unsolved. Should these disputes persist, there are nonrational methods for dealing with them, of course, such as impassioned, moving oratory. But the purely intellectual methods of science, and, indeed, *all* methods of reasoning, may be insufficient to settle disputes about values even though they may greatly help to do so.

For the same reasons I conclude that normative ethics is not a branch of any science. It deliberately deals with a type of disagreement that science deliberately avoids. Ethics is not psychology, for instance; for although psychologists may, of course, agree or disagree in belief about attitudes, they need not, as psychologists, be concerned with whether they agree or disagree with one another *in* attitude. Insofar as normative ethics draws from the sciences, in order to change attitudes *via* changing people's beliefs, it *draws* from *all* the sciences; but a moralist's peculiar aim—that of *redirecting* attitudes—is a type of activity, rather than knowledge, and falls within no science. Science may study that activity and may help indirectly to forward it; but is not *identical* with that activity.

•　•　•　•　•

RELATIVISM AND NONRELATIVISM IN THE THEORY OF VALUE

. . . In its main form a relativistic theory of value is simply one that expands "X is good," for example, into "X is approved by ———." For certain cases the word "approved" may have to give place to some other attitude-designating term, such as "liked," "favored," or "esteemed"; but in all cases there is some counterpart of the blank. And for varying utterances of "good," relativism maintains, we must fill in the blank now with a reference to the speaker, now with a reference to some group to which the speaker belongs, now with reference merely to most or to many people at many or most times, now with a reference to certain people who are particularly familiar with X, and so on. The only restriction is that the people must be specified by factual terms; for the use of evaluative terms would only renew the question about their meaning and would also fail to ensure that "reduction" of values to facts which relativists, in naturalistic fashion, normally seek to establish.

It may easily happen, according to relativism, that the conditions under which "good" is uttered are not sufficient to indicate whose attitudes are in question. We must then ask the speaker to be more explicit. And this should be no more surprising, relativism implies, than the parallel situation in physics. When a man who is talking about motion leaves room for doubt about the frame of reference he is using, we must in that case too ask him to be more explicit.

I think I am correct in suggesting that my definition makes precise a sense of "relativism" that is of philosophical interest. It has no connection, of course, with the view that an action's value depends upon, and thus is "relative to," the circumstances in which it occurs; but that is as it should be, since the latter view tends to be shared by relativists and nonrelativists alike. Socrates, for instance, can scarcely be called a relativist, yet he took it for granted that the value of an act depended on the circumstances, as is evident from his remarks about returning a deposit of arms to a man who is not in his right mind.

•   •   •   •   •

The aim of this essay . . . is to contrast a relativistic theory of value with a simplified version of the view that I have worked out in my *Ethics and Language*. The latter view—i.e. the simplified version, which can conveniently be referred to as "the so-called noncognitive view"—is easily summarized:

It maintains that although a speaker normally uses "X is yellow" to express his belief about X, he normally uses "X is good" to express something else, namely his approval of X. It adds that "good," being a term of praise, usually commends X to others and thus tends to evoke their approval as well. And it makes similar remarks, *mutatis mutandis*,[1] about "right," "duty," and so on.

•   •   •   •   •

The view can be contrasted with relativism in a perfectly obvious respect. It does *not* say that the evaluative terms are relative terms, and accordingly it does *not*, in relativistic fashion, expand "this is good" into "this is approved by——." For note that the expansion maintains by implication that a speaker typically makes a value judgment in the course of expressing his belief. The belief is *about* an attitude, to be sure, and for different ways of filling in the blank will be about the attitude of different people; but it is nevertheless a belief. And the expression of a belief is precisely what the so-called noncognitive theory is rejecting. It holds that a speaker typically makes a value judgment in the course of expressing his *attitude*—his judgment and his attitude being related directly, without the mediation of a belief.

That there is *a* distinction between the two views, then, is indisputable. But it may at first seem that the distinction depends on a technicality. It may seem that the so-called noncognitive view is *almost* a form of relativism, departing from it only in ways that make no practical difference. I must now show that that is far from being true.

—————
[1] [necessary changes having been made.—Ed. note.]

In the first place, the so-called noncognitive view helps us to see that our everyday issues about value are usually genuine and are not likely (apart from possible confusions to which *all* discourse is heir) to turn out to be pseudo-issues.

Relativism can bring with it no such assurance. For—in the form that emphasizes beliefs about attitudes, and the only form I am discussing—relativism is content to purchase its scientific affiliations at a curious price. It provides a scientific solution to those issues in which all parties are talking about the same attitudes, but it leaves us with the disturbing suggestion that many cases will not be of that sort. When Mr. A, for instance, says that socialized medicine is good and Mr. B says that it is bad, there may be only a pseudo-issue—one in which Mr. A is affirming that certain people approve of socialized medicine and Mr. B is affirming that certain *other* people disapprove it. Neither need be mistaken in that case, and their discussion may continue only because they are confused by their relative terms, each failing to see *whose* attitudes the other is talking about.

The so-called noncognitive view, on the other hand, can easily avoid this paradoxical implication. It can do so simply because it points out that Mr. A and Mr. B, in an example like the above, are respectively praising and disparaging the same thing. It thus represents their issue as a disagreement in attitude—one in which the men initially express opposed attitudes rather than opposed beliefs and thus prepare the way for a discussion in which one or the other of their attitudes may come to be altered or redirected. Such an issue is far from any that can be called "pseudo" or "verbal." It is not a purely scientific issue, but it is nevertheless a genuine issue and of a sort whose importance is beyond question.

So much, then, for the first difference between the views. And beyond this there is a second difference, which I consider to be of even greater importance. It is concerned with the *reasons* by which value judgments can be supported, and I can best introduce it in the following way:

When a man expresses a belief—any belief, and hence, a fortiori, any belief about attitudes—his reasons for what he says are intended, of course, to support this belief, showing that it is well grounded, rather than capricious or arbitrary. His reasons are accordingly "reasons for believing," as studied in inductive and deductive logic. Relativism implies that the theory of value need recognize no other reasons than these. But what happens when a man expresses his approval of something? In that case his reasons for what he says are intended to support his approval, showing that *it* is well grounded rather than capricious or arbitrary. His reasons are accordingly "reasons for approving." And the interest of the so-called noncognitive view, I wish to suggest, lies in showing that the theory of value makes very little sense unless it provides for these latter reasons.

Consider once again, for instance, Mr. A's favorable evaluation of socialized medicine. According to relativism his reasons attempt to show that socialized medicine is approved by——, and are thus reasons for *believing* that it is so approved. For most ways of filling in the blank, then, Mr. A can draw his reasons entirely from that small part of psychology or social science that deals with de facto approvals. Other reasons, I must acknowledge, may sometimes be relevant and will become particularly relevant in cases where Mr. A happens to be referring, say, to the approval of some hypothetical person who knows all the consequences of socialized medicine. But relativism puts no special emphasis on such references. Value judgments remain value judgments, it implies, and can be fully supported by reasons, even when they describe the approval of those who are factually uninformed.

For the so-called noncognitive view, on the contrary, Mr. A's reasons will be reasons *for approving* of socialized medicine. So we may expect him to speak of the probable effects of socialized medicine on the improvement of public health, for instance, and to add that it frees the poorer classes from worry, that it is less expensive to taxpayers than one may initially suppose, that it doesn't appreciably diminish the number of qualified applicants to medical schools, that its administrative problems are easily solved, and so on. I cannot undertake to say, of course, whether or not these reasons are all of them true; but it will be evident that they are reasons that we shall want to take seriously and are not, like those emphasized by relativism, of the comparatively trivial sort that are used in the course of describing, rather than guiding, approval.

There is nothing new, of course, in the conception of reasons for approving, which simply remind us that the head and the heart can work together. Nor is there anything new in the so-called noncognitive theory's conception of the modus operandi of these reasons. They support an approval by reinforcing it, or in other words, by showing or attempting to show that the object of approval is connected with other objects of approval—the reasons, then, serving as intermediaries that are intended to permit various attitudes to act together. In speaking of the consequences of socialized medicine on the public health, for instance, Mr. A does so on the assumption that these consequences, being themselves approved, will by a familiar psychological principle serve to strengthen an approval of what is taken to be their cause.

What *is* new in the so-called noncognitive theory, however, is its manner of making intelligible the relation between these reasons and the judgment that they support. By taking a (favorable) judgment to express approval, it shows why the *approval* needs to be guided by reasons. Whereas relativism, together with many other views, by taking the judgment to express a *belief about* approval, leads us to suppose that this belief, and only this belief, needs to be guided by reasons.

A moment's thought will show that reasons for approving are extraordinarily complicated. They are as complicated as the causal milieu in which any evaluated object invariably stands. They are of such variety that they fall within *all* the sciences, and thus draw not from some specialized part of what we know or think we know, but draw from the whole of it. They provide the so-called noncognitive view with a cognitive richness that is virtually unlimited. It is of the utmost importance, then, to keep them from being confused with those far simpler reasons—reasons showing that people in fact approve of such and such things—that relativism is content to emphasize.

My case, however, is by no means complete. I must take further steps in showing that the methodological aspects of the so-called noncognitive view are its strength. For they may seem, in spite of what I have been saying, to be its weakness. Although they unquestionably run contrary to the relativism that I have been discussing, they may seem to do so only by introducing another and neighboring sort of relativism, and one that is equally open to objections. I think that I can fully disprove this, showing that the neighboring relativism, too, is foreign to the so-called noncognitive view. . . .

To understand the point in question we must remember that the so-called noncognitive view recognizes the possibility of giving factual reasons for evaluative conclusions. My example about socialized medicine repeatedly illustrated these reasons and will be sufficient to show that there is nothing unusual about them. But they cannot, of course, be judged by the rules of deductive or inductive logic. That is precluded by the very notion of reasons for approving, which fall outside logic simply because they require inferences (if I may call them that) from belief-expressing sentences to attitude-expressing sentences. The truth of the reasons themselves can be tested by logic, but their bearing on the evaluative conclusion is neither logical nor illogical. It is simply nonlogical.

The so-called noncognitive view must accordingly deal with the following question: "When reasons are nonlogical, on what grounds, if any, are we to accept certain reasons and reject others?" And of course the view cannot in sanity maintain that there are no grounds whatsoever. All of us, in common sense discussions, accept certain reasons as *justifying* an evaluative conclusion and reject certain others as *failing to justify* such a conclusion. Consider, for instance, the following example:

A certain state is considering the possibility of introducing a sharply progressive income tax. Mr. Pro claims that the tax would be highly desirable and gives as his reason, "it would for the most part tax the rich, and thus put less burden on the poor." Mr. Con acknowledges that the tax would indeed have that effect, but adds that no such consideration can justify Mr. Pro's favorable judgment. "Actually," he says in reply, "your reason justifies an *un*favorable judgment of the tax, since the rich are already heavily burdened." And so on.

Note that Mr. Con is rejecting Mr. Pro's reason not because he considers it false, but because it fails, he maintains, to justify the conclusion that it is alleged to justify. And regardless of whether Mr. Con is right or wrong in this contention, his remark unquestionably makes good sense. No theorist, whether he is a so-called noncognitivist or something else, could be content to hold that "justify" has no meaning in such a context.

Now it is precisely here that the so-called noncognitive view, in spite of its sharp break with relativism with regard to the meaning of "good," "right," and so on, seems to lead back to relativism by another route. For in providing a nonlogical sense of "justify," and one that allows for individual differences in the way that reasons guide approval, it seems to have no better alternative than to consider "justify" a relative term. It seems committed, accordingly, to what may be called a "methodological relativism," or in other words, to a theory that defends some such principle as this: to say that a factual reason, R, justifies the evaluation, E, is to say that a belief of R will in fact cause people of sort——to be more inclined to accept E.

The objections to methodological relativism are much the same, let me remark, as they are for any other sort of relativism with regard to values. There
will again be the possibility of pseudo-issues; for when Mr. Pro says that a certain R justifies a certain E, and Mr. Con denies this, they may neither of them
be mistaken, and think they are disagreeing only because they are confused by
their relative term. And even in cases where the issue is genuine, the evidence
showing that R justifies E will usually involve no more than a psychological or
sociological inquiry into the considerations by which such and such people are
influenced. So although methodological relativism stays off stage, as it were, it
nevertheless continues to direct the actors.

But I have been speaking, it will be remembered, about what may easily
seem to be the case. I must now make good my claim that it is not in fact the
case.

Since the question requires me to explain what "justify" means, I can best
proceed by considering what sort of problem the word is expected to handle.
Suppose, then, that we should attempt to correlate each of a certain set of value
judgments with its justifying reasons—taking care to include only the reasons
that really justify the judgments, and giving warnings about those that, though
sometimes forensically effective, really do not justify the judgments. What would
we be doing? Would we be developing only the prolegomena to an evaluative
inquiry? Or would we be in the midst of an inquiry that was itself evaluative?

It is tempting to favor the first of these alternatives. "A study of justifying
reasons," we are likely to say, "is useful because it permits us to take a non-
evaluative first step toward deciding what is right or good—a step that gives
us a methodology, with rules for making trustworthy inferences. We can then go
on, subsequently, to a second step, where by applying our methodology we can
draw our evaluative conclusions with greater security."

But such an answer, as I see it, is entirely incorrect. I suspect that its
alleged two steps are two only in appearance, the former being no more than a
mirror image of the latter. Or to speak more literally, I suspect that any inquiry
of the sort now in question—any attempt to find the factual reasons by which a
value judgment can be justified—is itself an evaluative inquiry, and indeed, one
that if fully developed would require us to take a stand on each and every
evaluative issue that could ever confront us. I have been led to this conclusion
by studying examples, of which the following are typical:

Suppose that a theorist should say: "Given any specific judgment of the
form, *X is good,* there is one and only one sort of reason that is sufficient to
justify it, and that is a reason of the form, *X leads to the general happiness.*" Is
his claim one that stands a little apart from normative ethics, being concerned
only with its methodology, or is it an ordinary ethical claim?

I think there can be no doubt about the matter. Our theorist is more than a
methodologist with utilitarian propensities. He simply *is* a utilitarian. His terms
"reason" and "justify" must not lead us to suppose that he is making a neutral,

methodological claim that is separable from utilitarianism. For how can he hold that *X leads to the general happiness* is the only reason sufficient to justify the conclusion, *X is good,* without holding that anything is good if and only if it leads to the general happiness?

My example is perhaps too general, however, to be wholly instructive, so let me turn to several that are more specific. Suppose that Mr. Asothersdo has accepted a bribe but claims that he has done nothing wrong, since many of his associates did the same thing. Most of us would deny, of course, that his reason does anything at all toward justifying his judgment, whether in this special case or in any similar case. And as I see it, our denial amounts to our saying just this: "Your accepting a bribe is no less wrong when others are doing it than when others aren't doing it." Thus what seems to be our objection to Mr. Asothersdo's logic, in some extended sense of that term, is in practice wholly indistinguishable from an ordinary ethical judgment.

Interesting cases arise when reasons are taken to strengthen a man's position without fully establishing it. Thus Mr. Lowscale says that one of his friends is industrious and therefore a good man. We shall presumably wish to reply that his reason is not *sufficient* to justify his conclusion—thus refusing to make the judgment, "he is good if industrious, regardless of his other qualities." But we shall presumably add that his reason acts as a vectorial force, as it were, in *helping* to justify his conclusion—thus, in effect, making the judgment, "industriousness is a virtue, but a good man must have other virtues as well." So both aspects of our remark about a justifying reason again raise issues that are straightforwardly evaluative.

I could multiply examples endlessly but shall be content to give only one more. Suppose that Mr. Pacifist says, "it is our duty to avoid a war even at the cost of losing our freedom," and gives as his reason, "a war, in this atomic age, would destroy the lives of millions of innocent people, with devastating effects on civilization." This is an argument that most of us are not prepared to handle with the same dispatch as we handle Mr. Asothersdo's argument or Mr. Lowscale's argument. We shall some of us have to deliberate before deciding whether Mr. Pacifist's reason justifies his conclusion or whether it doesn't. And just what will we be trying to decide? Is it some pre-ethical question that bothers us, concerned only with methodology? It seems to me obvious that we are confronted, rather, with a choice between evils—evils that we hope are only hypothetical, but are not so certain to be hypothetical that we can afford to disregard them. Which would be worse: to keep peace at the expense of our freedom or to destroy the lives of millions of innocent people with devastating effects on civilization? When we ask that we are in effect asking over again whether Mr. Pacifist's reason, if true, will justify his conclusion; and the words "reason," "justify," and "conclusion" certainly cannot blind us, in any such living context, to the fact that our question is a genuinely *ethical* question.

So the general situation is this: when we claim that the factual reason, R, if true, would justify or help to justify the evaluative conclusion, E, we are in effect making another value judgment, E', of our own—the latter serving to evaluate the situation that we shall have if the facts of the case include those that R purports to describe.

Once this has been established there is no difficulty in reading off its implications with regard to the topic of my paper. The so-called noncognitive view, in its treatment of justifying reasons, is immediately freed from any suspicion of joining forces with methodological relativism. Indeed we need only review what has been said:

A methodological inquiry, when it attempts to find the R's that will justify a given E, does not stand apart from an evaluative inquiry but simply continues it, yielding ordinary value judgments that are expressed in a different terminology. The so-called noncognitive view, then, which we have seen to be nonrelativistic with regard to ordinary value judgments, is equally so with regard to justifications. Just as it does not take "good" to be a relative term, so it does not take "justify" to be a relative term—for the latter term does no more than extend the issues introduced by the former.

Such is the simple answer to what superficially appears to be a difficult question. But to dispel any sense of perplexity that may attend the answer, let me make the following remark:

If we approach all value judgments with an initial skepticism, supposing that we somehow "must" refuse to make them until we have given a full set of reasons that justify them, then the above reduction of "R justifies E" to the further judgment, E', will indeed perplex us. For we shall never, with this approach, be able to *get started* with our evaluations. We shall withhold judgment about E until we have found the R's that justify it; but in claiming that certain R's justify it we shall, by the reduction in question, be making another judgment, E'; so we must withhold judgment about E' until we have found the R's that justify *it*—and so on. Our initial skepticism will never be dispelled. But that will be true, let me point out, only if we start with an initial skepticism, and indeed, with an initial skepticism that infects *all* our value judgments. And why should we start in any such manner as that? Why cannot we start as we do in common life? There we have attitudes that we initially trust and we proceed to express them. Reasons serve not to bring our attitudes into being but only to redirect them. And if in accepting or rejecting the reasons we are making new evaluations, and thus expressing new attitudes, that is only to say that more of our attitudes, through the mediation of the reasons, are coming into play. If we initially distrust all our attitudes, in short, our reasons will not *give* us attitudes; but an initial distrust of all our attitudes is so fantastic that we need not, surely, take it seriously.

In revealing the scope and variety of justifying reasons, then, the so-called noncognitive view implies nothing that is paradoxical. And if it makes no attempt to say which R's will justify a given E, that is only because, having shown that such an inquiry reduplicates an evaluative inquiry, it is careful not to go beyond its limited aims. As a nonnormative meta-theory of norms, its business is not to make value judgments but only to survey and clarify them.

RICHARD MERVYN HARE
What Is a Value Judgment?

Let me illustrate one of the most characteristic features of value-words in terms of a particular example. It is a feature sometimes described by saying that 'good' and other such words are the names of 'supervenient' or 'consequential' properties. Suppose that a picture is hanging upon the wall and we are discussing whether it is a good picture; that is to say, we are debating whether to assent to, or dissent from, the judgment 'P is a good picture'. It must be understood that the context makes it clear that we mean by 'good picture' not 'good likeness' but 'good work of art'—though both these uses would be value-expressions.

First let us notice a very important peculiarity of the word 'good' as used in this sentence. Suppose that there is another picture next to P in the gallery (I will call it Q). Suppose that either P is a replica of Q or Q of P, and we do not know which, but do know that both were painted by the same artist at about the same time. Now there is one thing that we cannot say; we cannot say 'P is exactly like Q in all respects save this one, that P is a good picture and Q not'. If we were to say this, we should invite the comment, 'But how can one be good and the other not, if they are exactly alike? There must be some *further* difference between them to make one good and the other not.' Unless we at least admit the relevance of the question 'What makes one good and the other not?' we are bound to puzzle our hearers; they will think that something has gone wrong with our use of the word 'good'. Sometimes we cannot specify just what it is that makes one good and the other not; but there always must be something. Suppose that in the attempt to explain our meaning we said: 'I didn't say that there *was* any other difference between them; there is just this one difference, that one is good and the other not. Surely you would understand me if I said that one was *signed* and the other not, but that there was otherwise no difference? So why shouldn't I say that one was *good* and the other not, but that there was otherwise no difference?' The answer to this protest is that the word 'good' is not like the word 'signed'; there is a difference in their logic.

The following reason might be suggested for this logical peculiarity: there is some one characteristic or group of characteristics of the two pictures on which the characteristic 'good' is logically dependent, so that, of course, one cannot be good and the other not, unless these characteristics vary too. To quote a parallel case, one picture could not be *rectangular* and the other not, unless certain other characteristics also varied, for example the size of at least one of the angles. And so a natural response to the discovery that 'good' behaves as it does,

From R. M. Hare, *The Language of Morals* (1952). Reprinted by permission of the author and The Clarendon Press, Oxford.

is to suspect that there is a set of characteristics which together *entail* a thing being good, and to set out to discover what these characteristics are. This is the genesis of that group of ethical theories which Professor Moore called 'naturalist' —an unfortunate term, for as Moore says himself, substantially the same fallacy may be committed by choosing metaphysical or suprasensible characteristics for this purpose. Talking about the supernatural is no prophylactic against 'naturalism'. The term has, unfortunately, since Moore's introduction of it, been used very loosely. It is best to confine it to those theories against which Moore's refutation (or a recognizable version of it) is valid. In this sense most 'emotive' theories are not naturalist, though they are often called so. Their error is a quite different one. I shall argue below that what is wrong with naturalist theories is that they leave out the prescriptive or commendatory element in value-judgements, by seeking to make them derivable from statements of fact. If I am right in this opinion, my own theory, which preserves this element, is not naturalist.

•   •   •   •   •

Let us then ask whether 'good' behaves in the way that we have noticed for the same reason that 'rectangular' does; in other words, whether there are certain characteristics of pictures which are defining characteristics of a good picture, in the same way as 'having all its angles 90 degrees and being a rectilinear plane figure' are defining characteristics of a rectangle. Moore thought that he could prove that there were no such defining characteristics for the word 'good' as used in morals. His argument has been assailed since he propounded it; and it is certainly true that the formulation of it was at fault. But it seems to me that Moore's argument was not merely plausible; it rests, albeit insecurely, upon a secure foundation; there is indeed something about the way in which, and the purposes for which, we use the word 'good' which makes it impossible to hold the sort of position which Moore was attacking, although Moore did not see clearly what this something was. Let us, therefore, try to restate Moore's argument in a way which makes it clear why 'naturalism' is untenable, not only for the moral use of 'good' as he thought, but also for many other uses.

Let us suppose for the sake of argument that there are some 'defining characteristics' of a good picture. It does not matter of what sort they are; they can be a single characteristic, or a conjunction of characteristics, or a disjunction of alternative characteristics. Let us call the group of these characteristics C. 'P is a good picture' will then mean the same as 'P is a picture and P is C'. For example, let C mean 'Having a tendency to arouse in people who are at that time members of the Royal Academy (or any other definitely specified group of people), a definitely recognizable feeling called "admiration"'. The words 'definitely specified' and 'definitely recognizable' have to be inserted, for otherwise we might find that words in the *definiens*[1] were being used evaluatively, and this would make the definition no longer 'naturalistic'. Now suppose that we wish to say that the members of the Royal Academy have good taste

---

[1] [The defining term, as distinct from the term that is being defined.—Ed. note.]

in pictures. To have good taste in pictures means to have this definitely recognizable feeling of admiration for those pictures, and only those pictures, which are good pictures. If therefore we wish to say that the members of the Royal Academy have good taste in pictures, we have, according to the definition, to say something which means the same as saying that they have this feeling of admiration for pictures which have a tendency to arouse in them this feeling.

Now this is not what we wanted to say. We wanted to say that they admired good pictures; we have succeeded only in saying that they admired pictures which they admired. Thus if we accept the definition we debar ourselves from saying something that we do sometimes want to say. What this something is will become apparent later; for the moment let us say that what we wanted to do was to *commend* the pictures which the members of the Royal Academy admired. Something about our definition prevented our doing this. We could no longer commend the pictures which they admired, we could only say that they admired those pictures which they admired. Thus our definition has prevented us, in one crucial case, from commending something which we want to commend. That is what is wrong with it.

Let us generalize. If 'P is a good picture' is held to mean the same as 'P is a picture and P is C', then it will become impossible to commend pictures for being C; it will be possible only to say that they are C. It is important to realize that this difficulty has nothing to do with the particular example that I have chosen. It is not because we have chosen the wrong defining characteristics; it is because, whatever defining characteristics we choose, this objection arises, that we can no longer commend an object for possessing those characteristics.

Let us illustrate this by another example. I am deliberately excluding for the moment moral examples because I want it to be clear that the logical difficulties which we are encountering have nothing to do with morals in particular but are due to the general characteristics of value-words. Let us consider the sentence 'S is a good strawberry'. We might naturally suppose that this means nothing more than 'S is a strawberry and S is sweet, juicy, firm, red, and large'. But it then becomes impossible for us to say certain things which in our ordinary talk we do say. We sometimes want to say that a strawberry is a good strawberry because it is sweet, &c. This—as we can at once see if we think of ourselves saying it—does not mean the same as saying that a strawberry is a sweet, &c., strawberry because it is sweet, &c. But according to the proposed definition this is what it would mean. Thus here again the proposed definition would prevent our saying something that we do succeed in saying meaningfully in our ordinary talk.

●   ●   ●   ●

Naturalism in ethics, like attempts to square the circle and to 'justify induction', will constantly recur so long as there are people who have not understood the fallacy involved. It may therefore be useful to give a simple procedure for exposing any new variety of it that may be offered. Let us suppose that someone claims that he can deduce a moral or other evaluative judgement from a set of purely factual or descriptive premises, relying on some definition to the effect that V (a value-word) means the same as C (a conjunction of descriptive predicates). We first have to ask him to be sure that C contains no expression that is covertly evaluative (for example 'natural' or 'normal' or 'satisfying' or 'fundamental human needs'). Nearly all so-called 'naturalistic definitions' will break down under this test—for to be genuinely naturalistic a definition must contain no expression for whose applicability there is not a definite criterion which does not involve the making of a value-judgement. If the definition satisfies this test, we have next to ask whether its advocate wishes to commend anything for being C. If he says that he does, we have only to point out to him that his definition makes this impossible, for the reasons given. And clearly he cannot say that he never wishes to commend anything for being C; for to commend things for being C is the whole object of his theory.

● ● ● ● ●

It is a characteristic of 'good' that it can be applied to any number of different classes of objects. We have good cricket-bats, good chronometers, good fire-extinguishers, good pictures, good sunsets, good men. The same is true of the word 'red'; all the objects I have just listed might be red. We have to ask first whether, in explaining the meaning of the word 'good', it would be possible to explain its meaning in all of these expressions at once, or whether it would be necessary to explain 'good cricket-bat' first, and then go on to explain 'good chronometer' in the second lesson, 'good fire-extinguisher' in the third, and so on; and if the latter, whether in each lesson we should be teaching something entirely new—like teaching the meaning of 'fast dye' after we had in a previous lesson taught the meaning of 'fast motor-car'—or whether it would be just the same lesson over again, with a different example—like teaching 'red dye' after we had taught 'red motor-car'. Or there might be some third possibility.

The view that 'good chronometer' would be a completely new lesson, even though the day before we had taught 'good cricket-bat', runs at once into difficulties. For it would mean that at any one time our learner could only use the word 'good' in speaking of classes of objects which he had learnt so far. He would never be able to go straight up to a new class of objects and use the word 'good' of one of them. When he had learnt 'good cricket-bat' and 'good chronometer', he would not be able to manage 'good fire-extinguisher'; and when he had learnt the latter, he would still be unable to manage 'good motor-car'. But in fact one of the most noticeable things about the way we use 'good' is that we are able to use it for entirely new classes of objects that we have never called 'good' before. Suppose that someone starts collecting cacti for the first time and puts one on his mantel-piece—the only cactus in the country. Suppose then that a friend sees it, and says 'I must have one of those'; so he sends for one from wherever they grow, and puts it on his mantel-piece, and when his friend comes in, he says 'I've got a better cactus than yours'. But how does he know how to apply the word in this way? He has never learnt to apply 'good' to cacti; he does not even know any *criteria* for telling a good cactus from a bad one (for as yet there are none); but he has learnt to use the word 'good', and having learnt that, he can apply it to any class of objects that he requires to place in order of merit. He and his friend may dispute about the criteria of good cacti; they may attempt to set up rival criteria; but they could not even do this unless they were from the start under no difficulty in using the word 'good'. Since, therefore, it is possible to use the word 'good' for a new class of objects without further instruction, learning the use of the word for one class of objects cannot be a different lesson from learning it for another class of objects—though learning the criteria of goodness in a new class of objects may be a new lesson each time.

* * * * *

Of all the problems raised by the preceding argument, the key problem is as follows: there are two sorts of things that we can say, for example, about strawberries; the first sort is usually called *descriptive,* the second sort *evaluative.* Examples of the first sort of remark are, 'This strawberry is sweet' and 'This strawberry is large, red, and juicy'. Examples of the second sort of remark are 'This is a good strawberry' and 'This strawberry is just as strawberries ought to be'. The first sort of remark is often given as a reason for making the second sort of remark; but the first sort does not by itself entail the second sort, nor vice versa. Yet there seems to be some close logical connexion between them. Our problem is: 'What is this connexion?'; for no light is shed by saying that there is a connexion, unless we can say what it is.

The problem may also be put in this way: if we knew all the descriptive properties which a particular strawberry had (knew, of every descriptive sentence relating to the strawberry, whether it was true or false), and if we knew also the meaning of the word 'good', then what else should we require to know, in order to be able to tell whether a strawberry was a good one? Once the question is put in this way, the answer should be apparent. We should require to know, what are the criteria in virtue of which a strawberry is to be called a good one, or what are the characteristics that make a strawberry a good one, or what is the standard of goodness in strawberries. We should require to be given the major premiss. We have already seen that we can know the meaning of 'good strawberry' without knowing any of these latter things—though there is also a sense of the sentence 'What does it mean to call a strawberry a good one?' in which we should not know the answer to it, unless we also knew the answer to these other questions. It is now time to elucidate and distinguish these two ways in which we can be said to know what it means to call an object a good member of its class. This will help us to see more clearly both the differences and the similarities between 'good' and words like 'red' and 'sweet'.

Since we have been dwelling for some time on the differences, it will do no harm now to mention some of the similarities. For this purpose, let us consider the two sentences 'M is a red motor-car' and 'M is a good motor-car'. It will be noticed that 'motor-car', unlike 'strawberry', is a functional word, as defined in the preceding chapter. Reference to the *Shorter Oxford English Dictionary* shows that a motor-car is a carriage, and a carriage a means of conveyance. Thus, if a motor-car will not convey anything, we know from the definition of motor-car that it is not a good one. But when we know this, we know so little, compared with what is required in order to know the full criteria of a good motor-car, that I propose in what follows to ignore, for the sake of simplicity, this complicating factor. I shall treat 'motor-car' as if it did not have to be defined functionally: that is to say, I shall assume that we could learn the meaning of 'motor-car' (as in a sense we can) simply by being shown examples of motor-cars. It is, of course, not always easy to say whether or not a word is a functional word; it depends, like all questions of meaning, on how the word is taken by a particular speaker.

The first similarity between 'M is a red motor-car' and 'M is a good motor-car' is that both can be, and often are, used for conveying information of a purely factual or descriptive character. If I say to someone 'M is a good motor-car', and he himself has not seen, and knows nothing of M, but does on the other hand know what sorts of motor-car we are accustomed to call 'good' (knows what is the accepted standard of goodness in motor-cars), he undoubtedly receives information from my remark about what sort of motor-car it is. He will complain that I have misled him, if he subsequently discovers that M will not go over 30 m.p.h., or uses as much oil as petrol, or is covered with rust, or has large holes in the roof. His reason for complaining will be the same as it would have been if I had said that the car was red and he subsequently discovered that it was black. I should have led him to expect the motor-car to be of a certain description when in fact it was of a quite different description.

The second similarity between the two sentences is this. Sometimes we use them, not for actually conveying information, but for putting our hearer into a position subsequently to use the word 'good' or 'red' for giving or getting information. Suppose, for example, that he is utterly unfamiliar with motor-cars in the same sort of way as most of us are unfamiliar with horses nowadays, and knows no more about motor-cars than is necessary in order to distinguish a motor-car from a hansom cab. In that case, my saying to him 'M is a good motor-car' will not give him any information about M, beyond the information that it is a motor-car. But if he is able then or subsequently to examine M, he will have learnt something. He will have learnt that some of the characteristics which M has, are characteristics which make people—or at any rate me—call it a good motor-car. This may not be to learn very much. But suppose that I make judgements of this sort about a great many motor-cars, calling some good and some not good, and he is able to examine all or most of the motor-cars about which I am speaking; he will in the end learn quite a lot, always presuming that I observe a consistent standard in calling them good or not good. He will eventually, if he pays careful attention, get into the position in which he knows, after I have said that a motor-car is a good one, what sort of a motor-car he may expect it to be—for example fast, stable on the road, and so on.

Now if we were dealing, not with 'good', but with 'red', we should call this process 'explaining the meaning of the word'—and we might indeed, in a sense, say that what I have been doing is explaining what one means by 'a good motor-car'. This is a sense of 'mean' about which, as we have seen, we must be on our guard. The processes, however, are very similar. I might explain the meaning of 'red' by continually saying of various motor-cars 'M is a red motor-car', 'N is not a red motor-car', and so on. If he were attentive enough, he would soon get into a position in which he was able to use the word 'red' for giving or getting information, at any rate about motor-cars. And so, both with 'good' and with 'red', there is this process, which in the case of 'red' we may call 'explaining the meaning', but in the case of 'good' may only call it so loosely and in a secondary sense; to be clear we must call it something like 'explaining or conveying or setting forth the standard of goodness in motor-cars'.

The standard of goodness, like the meaning of 'red', is normally something which is public and commonly accepted. When I explain to someone the meaning of 'red motor-car', he expects, unless I am known to be very eccentric, that he will find other people using it in the same way. And similarly, at any rate with objects like motor-cars where there is a commonly accepted standard, he will expect, having learnt from me what is the standard of goodness in motor-cars, to be able, by using the expression 'good motor-car', to give information to other people, and get it from them, without confusion.

A third respect in which 'good motor-car' resembles 'red motor-car' is the following: both 'good' and 'red' can vary as regards the exactitude or vagueness of the information which they do or can convey. We normally use the expression 'red motor-car' very loosely. Any motor-car that lies somewhere between the unmistakably purple and the unmistakably orange could without abuse of language be called a red motor-car. And similarly, the standard for calling motor-cars good is commonly very loose. There are certain characteristics, such as inability to exceed 30 m.p.h., which to anyone but an eccentric would be sufficient conditions for refusing to call it a good motor-car; but there is no precise set of accepted criteria such that we can say 'If a motor-car satisfies these conditions, it is a good one; if not, not'. And in both cases we could be precise if we wanted to. We could, for certain purposes, agree not to say that a motor-car was 'really red' unless the redness of its paint reached a certain measurable degree of purity and saturation; and similarly, we might adopt a very exact standard of goodness in motor-cars. We might refuse the name 'good motor-car' to any car that would not go round a certain race-track without mishap in a certain limited time, that did not conform to certain other rigid specifications as regards accommodation, &c. This sort of thing has not been done for the expression 'good motor-car'; but . . . it has been done by the Ministry of Agriculture for the expression 'super apple'.

It is important to notice that the exactness or looseness of their criteria does absolutely nothing to distinguish words like 'good' from words like 'red'. Words in both classes may be descriptively loose or exact, according to how rigidly the criteria have been laid down by custom or convention. It certainly is not true that value-words are distinguished from descriptive words in that the former are looser, descriptively, than the latter. There are loose and rigid examples of both sorts of word. Words like 'red' can be extremely loose, without becoming to the least degree evaluative; and expressions like 'good sewage effluent' can be the subject of very rigid criteria, without in the least ceasing to be evaluative.

It is important to notice also, how easy it is, in view of these resemblances between 'good' and 'red', to think that there are no differences—to think that to set forth the standard of goodness in motor-cars is to set forth the meaning, in all senses that there are of that word, of the expression 'good motor-car'; to think that 'M is a good motor-car' means neither more nor less than 'M has certain characteristics of which "good" is the name'.

It is worth noticing here that the functions of the word 'good' which are concerned with information could be performed equally well if 'good' had no commendatory function at all. This can be made clear by substituting another word, made up for the purpose, which is to be supposed to lack the commendatory force of 'good'. Let us use 'doog' as this new word. 'Doog', like 'good', can be used for conveying information only if the criteria for its application are known; but this makes it, unlike 'good', altogether meaningless until these criteria are made known. I make the criteria known by pointing out various motor-cars, and saying 'M is a doog motor-car', 'N is not a doog motor-car', and so on. We must imagine that, although 'doog' has no commendatory force, the criteria for doogness in motor-cars which I am employing are the same as those which, in the previous example, I employed for goodness in motor-cars. And so, as in the previous example, the learner, if he is sufficiently attentive, becomes able to use the word 'doog' for giving or getting information; when I say to him 'Z is a doog motor-car', he knows what characteristics to expect it to have; and if he wants to convey to someone else that a motor-car Y has those same characteristics, he can do so by saying 'Y is a doog motor-car'.

Thus the word 'doog' does (though only in connexion with motor-cars) half the jobs that the word 'good' does—namely, all those jobs that are concerned with the giving, or learning to give or get, information. It does not do those jobs which are concerned with commendation. Thus we might say that 'doog' functions just like a descriptive word. First my learner learns to use it by my giving him examples of its application, and then he uses it by applying it to fresh examples. It would be quite natural to say that what I was doing was teaching my learner the *meaning* of 'doog'; and this shows us again how natural it is to say that, when we are learning a similar lesson for the expression 'good motor-car' (i.e. learning the criteria of its application), we are learning its meaning. But with the word 'good' it is misleading to say this; for the meaning of 'good motor-car' (in another sense of 'meaning') is something that might be known by someone who did not know the criteria of its application; he would know, if someone said that a motor-car was a good one, that he was commending it; and to know that, would be to know the meaning of the expression. Further, as we saw earlier, someone might know about 'good' all the things which my learner learnt about the word 'doog' (namely, how to apply the word to the right objects, and use it for giving and getting information) and yet be said not to know its meaning; for he might not know that to call a motor-car good was to commend it.

• • • • •

It is now time to inquire into the reasons for the logical features of 'good' that we have been describing, and to ask why it is that it has this peculiar combination of evaluative and descriptive meaning. The reason will be found in the purposes for which it, like other value-words, is used in our discourse. The examination of these purposes will reveal the relevance of the matters discussed in the first part of this book to the study of evaluative language.

I have said that the primary function of the word 'good' is to commend. We have, therefore, to inquire what commending is. When we commend or condemn anything, it is always in order, at least indirectly, to guide choices, our own or other people's, now or in the future. Suppose that I say 'The South Bank Exhibition is very good'. In what context should I appropriately say this, and what would be my purpose in so doing? It would be natural for me to say it to someone who was wondering whether to go to London to see the Exhibition, or, if he was in London, whether to pay it a visit. It would, however, be too much to say that the reference to choices is always as direct as this. An American returning from London to New York, and speaking to some people who had no intention of going to London in the near future, might still make the same remark. In order, therefore, to show that critical value-judgements are all ultimately related to choices, and would not be made if they were not so related, we require to ask, for what purpose we have standards.

It has been pointed out by Mr. Urmson that we do not speak generally of 'good' wireworms. This is because we never have any occasion for choosing between wireworms, and therefore require no guidance in so doing. We therefore need to have no standards for wireworms. But it is easy to imagine circumstances in which this situation might alter. Suppose that wireworms came into use as a special kind of bait for fishermen. Then we might speak of having dug up a very good wireworm (one, for example, that was exceptionally fat and attractive to fish), just as now, no doubt, seafishermen might talk of having dug up a very good lug-worm. We only have standards for a class of objects, we only talk of the virtues of one specimen as against another, we only use value-words about them, when occasions are known to exist, or are conceivable, in which we, or someone else, would have to choose between specimens. We should not call pictures good or bad if no one ever had the choice of seeing them or not seeing them (or of studying them or not studying them in a way that art students study pictures, or of buying them or not buying them). Lest, by the way, I should seem to have introduced a certain vagueness by specifying so many alternative kinds of choices, it must be pointed out that the matter can, if desired, be made as precise as we require; for we can specify, when we have called a picture a good one, within what class we have called it good; for example, we can say 'I meant a good picture to study, but not to buy'.

Some further examples may be given. We should not speak of good sunsets, unless sometimes the decision had to be made, whether to go to the window to look at the sunset; we should not speak of good billiard-cues, unless sometimes we had to choose one billiard-cue in preference to another; we should not speak of good men unless we had the choice, what sort of men to try to become. Leibniz, when he spoke of 'the best of all possible worlds', had in mind a creator choosing between the possibilities. The choice that is envisaged need not ever occur, nor even be expected ever to occur; it is enough for it to be envisaged as occurring, in order that we should be able to make a value-judgement with reference to it. It must be admitted, however, that the most useful value-judgements are those which have reference to choices that we might very likely have to make.

It should be pointed out that even judgements about past choices do not refer merely to the past. As we shall see, all value-judgements are covertly universal in character, which is the same as to say that they refer to, and express acceptance of, a standard which has an application to other similar instances. If I censure someone for having done something, I envisage the possibility of him, or someone else, or myself, having to make a similar choice again; otherwise there would be no point in censuring him. Thus, if I say to a man whom I am teaching to drive 'You did that manœuvre badly' this is a very typical piece of driving-instruction; and driving-instruction consists in teaching a man to drive not in the past but in the future; to this end we censure or commend past pieces of driving, in order to impart to him the standard which is to guide him in his subsequent conduct.

When we commend an object, our judgement is not solely about that particular object, but is inescapably about objects like it. Thus, if I say that a certain motor-car is a good one, I am not merely saying something about that particular motor-car. To say something about that particular car, merely, would not be to commend. To commend, as we have seen, is to guide choices. Now for guiding a particular choice we have a linguistic instrument which is not that of commendation, namely, the singular imperative. If I wish merely to tell someone to choose a particular car, with no thought of the kind of car to which it belongs, I can say 'Take that one'. If instead of this I say 'That is a good one', I am saying something more. I am implying that if any motor-car were just like that one, it would be a good one too; whereas by saying 'Take that one', I do not imply that, if my hearer sees another car just like that one, he is to take it too. But further, the implication of the judgement 'That is a good motor-car' does not extend merely to motor-cars *exactly* like that one. If this were so, the implication would be for practical purposes useless; for nothing is exactly like anything else. It extends to every motor-car that is like that one in the *relevant* particulars; and the relevant particulars are its virtues—those of its characteristics for which I was commending it, or which I was calling good about it. Whenever we commend, we have in mind something about the object commended which is the reason for our commendation. It therefore always makes sense, after someone has said 'That is a good motor-car', to ask 'What is good about it?' or 'Why do you call it good?' or 'What features of it are you commending?' It may not always be easy to answer this question precisely, but it is always a legitimate question. If we did not understand why it was always a legitimate question, we should not understand the way in which the word 'good' functions.

We may illustrate this point by comparing two dialogues:

(1) X. Jones' motor-car is a good one.

     Y. What makes you call it good?

     X. Oh, just that it's good.

     Y. But there must be some *reason* for your calling it good, I mean some property that it has in virtue of which you call it good.

     X. No; the property in virtue of which I call it good is just its goodness and nothing else.

     Y. But do you mean that its shape, speed, weight, manœuvrability &c., are irrelevant to whether you call it good or not?

     X. Yes, quite irrelevant; the only relevant property is that of goodness, just as, if I called it yellow, the only relevant property would be that of yellowness.

(2) The same dialogue, only with 'yellow' substituted for 'good' and 'yellowness' for 'goodness' throughout, and the last clause ('just as . . . yellowness') omitted.

The reason why X's position in the first dialogue is eccentric is that since, as we have already remarked, 'good' is a 'supervenient' or 'consequential' epithet, one may always legitimately be asked when one has called something a good something, 'What is good about it?' Now to answer this question is to give the properties in virtue of which we call it good. Thus, if I have said, 'That is a good motor-car' and someone asks 'Why? What is good about it?' and I reply 'Its high speed combined with its stability on the road', I indicate that I call it good in virtue of its having these properties or virtues. Now to do this is *eo ipso* to say something about other motor-cars which have these properties. If any motor-car whatever had these properties, I should have, if I were not to be inconsistent, to agree that it was, *pro tanto*, a good motor-car; though of course it might, although it had these properties in its favour, have other countervailing disadvantages, and so be, taken all in all, not a good motor-car.

This last difficulty can always be got over by specifying in detail why I called the first motor-car a good one. Suppose that a second motor-car were like the first one in speed and stability, but gave its passengers no protection from the rain, and proved difficult to get into and out of. I should not then call it a good motor-car, although it had those characteristics which led me to call the first one good. This shows that I should not have called the first one good either, if it too had had the bad characteristics of the second one; and so in specifying what was good about the first one, I ought to have added '. . . and the protection it gives to the passengers and the ease with which one can get into and out of it'. This process could be repeated indefinitely until I had given a complete list of the characteristics of the first motor-car which were required to make me allow it to be a good one. This, in itself, would not be saying all that there was to be said about my standards for judging motor-cars—for there might be other motor-cars which, although falling short to a certain extent in these characteristics, had other countervailing good characteristics; for example, soft upholstery, large accommodation, or small consumption of petrol. But it would be at any rate some help to my hearer in building up an idea of my standards in motor-cars; and in this lies the importance of such questions and answers, and the importance of recognizing their relevance, whenever a value-judgement has been made. For one of the purposes of making such judgements is to make known the standard.

When I commend a motor-car I am guiding the choices of my hearer not merely in relation to that particular motor-car but in relation to motor-cars in general. What I have said to him will be of assistance to him whenever in the future he has to choose a motor-car or advise anyone else on the choice of a motor-car or even design a motor-car (choose what sort of motor-car to have made) or write a general treatise on the design of motor-cars (which involves choosing what sort of motor-cars to advise other people to have made). The method whereby I give him this assistance is by making known to him a stand-ard for judging motor-cars.

This process has, as we have noticed, certain features in common with the process of defining (making known the meaning or application of) a descriptive word, though there are important differences. We have now to notice a further resemblance between showing the usage of a word and showing how to choose between motor-cars. In neither case can the instruction be done successfully unless the instructor is consistent in his teaching. If I use 'red' for objects of a wide variety of colours, my hearer will never learn from me a consistent usage of the word. Similarly, if I commend motor-cars with widely different or even contrary characteristics, what I say to him will not be of assistance to him in choosing motor-cars subsequently, because I am not teaching him any consistent standard—or any standard at all, for a standard is by definition consistent. He will say, 'I don't see by what standards you are judging these motor-cars; please explain to me why you call them all good, although they are so different'. Of course, I might be able to give a satisfactory explanation. I might say, 'There are different sorts of motor-cars, each good in its way; there are sports cars, whose prime requisites are speed and manœuvrability; and family cars, which ought rather to be capacious and economical; and taxis, and so on. So when I say a car is good which is fast and manœuvrable, although it is neither capacious nor economical, you must understand that I am commending it as a sports car, not as a family car'. But suppose that I did not recognize the relevance of his ques-tion; suppose that I was just doling out the predicate 'good' entirely haphazard, as the whim took me. It is clear that in this case I should teach him no standard at all.

We thus have to distinguish two questions that can always be asked in elucidation of a judgement containing the word 'good'. Suppose that someone says 'That is a good one'. We can then always ask (1) 'Good what—sports car or family car or taxi or example to quote in a logic-book?' Or we can ask (2)

'What makes you call it good?' To ask the first question is to ask for the class within which evaluative comparisons are being made. Let us call it the class of comparison. To ask the second question is to ask for the virtues or 'good-making characteristics'. These two questions are, however, not independent; for what distinguishes the class of comparison 'sports car' from the class 'family car' is the set of virtues which are to be looked for in the respective classes. This is so in all cases where the class of comparison is defined by means of a functional word— for obviously 'sports car', 'family car', and 'taxi' are functional to a very much higher degree than plain 'motor-car'. Sometimes, however, a class of comparison may be further specified without making it more functional; for example, in explaining the phrase 'good wine' we might say 'I mean good wine for this district, not good wine compared with all the wines that there are'.

Now since it is the purpose of the word 'good' and other value-words to be used for teaching standards, their logic is in accord with this purpose. We are therefore in a position at last to explain the feature of the word 'good' which I pointed out at the beginning of this investigation. The reason why I cannot apply the word 'good' to one picture, if I refuse to apply it to another picture which I agree to be in all other respects exactly similar, is that by doing this I should be defeating the purpose for which the word is designed. I should be commending one object, and so purporting to teach my hearers one standard, while in the same breath refusing to commend a similar object, and so undoing the lesson just imparted. By seeking to impart two inconsistent standards, I should be imparting no standard at all. The effect of such an utterance is similar to that of a contradiction; for in a contradiction, I say two inconsistent things, and so the effect is that the hearer does not know what I am trying to say.

What I have said so far may also be put into another terminology, that of principles. . . . To teach a person—or to decide on for oneself—a standard for judging the merits of objects of a certain class is to teach or decide on principles for choosing between objects of that class. To know the principles for choosing motor-cars is to be able to judge between motor-cars or to tell a good one from a bad one. If I say 'That isn't a good motor-car' and am asked what virtue it is, the lack of which makes me say this, and reply 'It isn't stable on the road', then I am appealing to a principle.

• • • • •

It is time now to ask whether 'good', as used in moral contexts, has any of the features to which I have drawn attention in non-moral ones. It will no doubt be thought by some readers that all that I have said hitherto is entirely irrelevant to ethics. To think this is to miss the enlightenment of some very interesting parallels; but I have no right on my part to assume that 'good' behaves in at all the fashion that I have described when it is used in morals. To this problem we must now address ourselves; but first something more must be said about another distinction of which I may seem to have made light, that between the so-called 'intrinsic' and 'instrumental' uses of 'good'.

There has been a disposition among philosophers to do one of two opposite things. The first is to suppose that all value-judgements whatever relate to the performance by an object of a function distinct from the object itself. The second is to suppose that, because there are some objects which are commended for their own sakes, and do not have an obvious function beyond their mere existence, to commend such an object is to do something quite different from commending an object which does have a function. It will help us to avoid doing either of these things if we avail ourselves of the general notions of 'virtue' and 'standard' which I have been using in the preceding chapters.

When we are dealing with objects which are evaluated solely in virtue of their performance of a function, the virtues of such objects will consist in those characteristics which either promote, or themselves constitute, the good performance of the function. The matter can be made clear by supposing that what we are judging is the *performance* of the object, not the object itself. Imagine that we are judging a fire-extinguisher. To do so we watch it being used to put out a fire, and then judge its performance. Certain characteristics of the performance count as virtues (e.g. putting out the fire quickly, causing little damage to property, emitting no dangerous fumes, small consumption of expensive chemicals, &c.). Note that certain of the expressions used in specifying the standard (e.g. 'damage' and 'dangerous') are themselves value-expressions; these indicate that the specification of the standard is not in itself complete, but includes 'cross-references' to standards for evaluating, respectively, the state of repair of property, and the effect of gases on the human body. It would be impossible to specify the standard completely without having for purposes of reference a specification of all the other standards to which it is necessary to refer. Aristotle[2] gives examples of such cross-references in which the standards are arranged hierarchically, the cross-references being all in the same direction. It does not seem obvious that they need be so arranged, though it would be tidy if they were.

Now what we must notice, for our present purposes, about the above list of virtues of the fire-extinguisher's performance, is that it is just a list of virtues, not differing logically from the list of virtues of a class of objects not having a function. Compare it, for example, with the list of virtues of a good bath. A good bath is good both instrumentally (in that it is conducive to cleanliness) and intrinsically (for we should not have nearly so many baths if our only purpose in having them were to become clean). Let us for the moment ignore the instrumental goodness of the bath, and concentrate on its intrinsic goodness. To be good intrinsically, a bath must be within a certain range of temperature, which must be maintained throughout its duration; the vessel must be above a certain minimum size, which varies with that of the bather; it must be of a certain shape; and it must be full of soft clean water; there must be soap above a certain degree of fineness (e.g. not containing abrasives or free caustics)—and the reader may add to the list according to his taste. In this specification I have tried to avoid cross-references to other standards, but I have not been entirely successful; e.g. 'clean water' means 'water in which there is no dirt', and what is to count as dirt is a matter for evaluation. Thus even where we are dealing with intrinsic goodness we cannot avoid cross-references, and therefore it is not the necessity for cross-references which makes goodness instrumental.

We notice that in both cases—the fire-extinguisher and the bath—we have a standard or list of virtues, and commend objects which possess these virtues. In the case of the fire-extinguisher we commend directly its performance, and the object only indirectly; in the case of the bath we might be said to commend the object directly. But this is really a distinction without a difference; are we to say that 'inducing heat in my skin' is a performance of the bath, or are we to say that 'being hot' is a quality of the bath? Similarly, one of the virtues required in a good pineapple is that it should be sweet; is its sweetness an intrinsic quality of the pineapple, or is it the disposition to produce certain desirable sensations in me? When we can answer such questions, we shall be able to draw a precise distinction between intrinsic and instrumental goodness.

It would, however, be a mistake to say that there is *no* difference between what we do when we commend a fire-extinguisher and what we do when we commend a sunset. We commend them for entirely different reasons, and in the case of the fire-extinguisher these reasons all refer to what it is intended to do. We saw above that if 'good' is followed by a functional word (e.g. the name of an instrument), this word itself gives us a partial specification of the virtues required; whereas in other cases this specification is absent. All that I am maintaining is that the logical apparatus of virtues and standards which I have been elaborating is sufficiently general to cover both instrumental and intrinsic goodness. And to see this is to make the first step towards seeing that it may be general enough to cover moral goodness too. To this question we must now turn.

Let us review some of the reasons that have led people to hold that the use of the word 'good' in moral contexts is totally different from its use in non-moral ones. The first reason is connected with the difference between intrinsic and instrumental good, and we have already dealt with it. The second reason is that the properties which make a man morally good are obviously different from those which make a chronometer good. It is therefore easy to think that the *meaning* of the word 'good' is different in the two cases. But this can now be seen to be a mistaken conclusion. The descriptive meaning is certainly different, as the descriptive meaning of 'good' in 'good apple' is different from its meaning in 'good cactus'; but the evaluative meaning is the same—in both cases we are commending. We are commending as a man, not as a chronometer. If we insisted on calling the meaning of 'good' different, because the virtues required in objects of different classes are different, we should end up with what Mr. Urmson calls 'a homonym with as many punning meanings as the situations it applied to'.

The third reason is this: it is felt that somehow 'moral goodness' is more august, more important, and therefore deserves to have a logic all its own. This plea seldom comes out into the open; but it lies behind much of the argument, and in itself has something to recommend it. We do attach more importance to a man's being a good man than to a chronometer's being a good chronometer. We do not *blame* chronometers for being bad (though we do blame their makers). We get stirred up about moral goodness in a way that few people get stirred up about technical or other sorts of goodness. This is why many readers will have been irritated by my supposing that the behaviour of 'good' in 'good sewage effluent' can have any interest for the moral philosopher. We have to ask, therefore, why it is that we feel this way, and whether the fact that we do makes it necessary for us to give an entirely different account of the logic of 'good' in the two cases.

We get stirred up about the goodness of men because we are men. This means that the acceptance of a judgement, that such and such a man's act is good in circumstances of a certain sort, involves the acceptance of the judgement that it would be good, were we ourselves placed in similar circumstances, to do likewise. And since we might *be* placed in similar circumstances, we feel deeply about the question. We feel less deeply, it must be admitted, about the question, whether it was a bad act of Agamemnon to sacrifice Iphigenia, than about the question, whether it was a bad act of Mrs. Smith to travel on the railway without paying her fare; for we are not likely to be in Agamemnon's position, but most of us travel on railways. Acceptance of a moral judgement about Mrs. Smith's act is likely to have a closer bearing upon our future conduct than acceptance of one about Agamemnon's. But we never envisage ourselves turning into chronometers.

These observations are to a certain extent confirmed by the behaviour of technicians and artists. As Hesiod pointed out, these people do get stirred up about their respective non-moral goodnesses, in the way that ordinary people get stirred up about moral questions: 'Potters get angry with potters, and carpenters with carpenters, and beggars with beggars, and poets with poets'. Commercial competition is not the only reason—for it is possible to compete without malice. When an architect, for example, says of another architect's house, with feeling, 'That is a thoroughly badly designed house', the reason for the feeling is that if he were to admit that the house was well designed, he would be admitting that in avoiding in his own work features like those of the design in question, he had been wrong; and this might mean altering his whole way of designing houses, which would be painful.

Further, we cannot get out of being men, as we can get out of being architects or out of making or using chronometers. Since this is so, there is no avoiding the (often painful) consequences of abiding by the moral judgments that we make. The architect who was forced to admit that a rival's house was better than anything he had ever produced or could produce, might be upset; but in the last resort he could become a barman instead. But if I admit that the life of St. Francis was morally better than mine, and really mean this as an evaluation, there is nothing for it but to try to be more like St. Francis, which is arduous. That is why most of our 'moral judgements' about the saints are merely conventional—we never intend them to be a guide in determining our own conduct.

Moreover, in the case of differences about morals it is very difficult, and, in cases where the effect on our own life is profound, impossible, to say 'It's all a matter of taste; let's agree to differ'; for to agree to differ is only possible when we can be sure that we shall not be forced to make choices which will radically affect the choices of other people. This is especially true where choices have to be made cooperatively; it must be pointed out, however, that though most moral choices are of this kind, this sort of situation is not peculiar to morals. The members of the Kon-tiki expedition could not have agreed to differ about how to build their raft, and families sharing a kitchen cannot agree to differ about its organization. But although we can usually get out of building rafts or sharing kitchens, we cannot easily get out of living in societies with other people. Perhaps men living in complete isolation could agree to differ about morals. It would at any rate seem that communities not in close contact with one another could agree to differ about some moral questions without actual inconvenience. To say this, of course, is not necessarily to maintain any kind of moral relativism, for communities could agree to differ about whether the earth was round. To agree to differ is to say, in effect, 'We will differ about this question, but let us not be angry or fight about it'; it is not to say 'we will differ, but let us not differ'; for the latter would be a logical impossibility. And so if two communities agreed to differ about, say, the moral desirability of legalized gambling in their respective territories, what would happen would be this; they would say 'We will continue to hold, one of us that it is wrong to legalize gambling, and the other that it is not wrong; but we will not get angry about each other's laws, or seek to interfere in each other's administration of them'. And the same thing might be done about other matters than gambling, provided that what each community did had slight effect outside its own borders. Such agreements will not work, however, if one community holds it to be a moral duty to prevent certain practices taking place wherever they occur.

Such a case is worth considering in order to contrast with it the more usual state of affairs; normally the moral judgements that we make, and hold to, deeply affect the lives of our neighbours; and this in itself is enough to explain the peculiar place that we assign to them. If we add to this the logical point, already mentioned, that moral judgements always have a possible bearing on our own conduct, in that we cannot in the fullest sense accept them without conforming to them, . . . then no further explanation is needed of the special status of morals. This special status does not require a special logic to back it up; it results from the fact that we are using the ordinary apparatus of value-language in order to commend or condemn the most intimate actions of ourselves and those like us. We may add that the 'emotivity' of much moral utterance, which some have thought to be of the essence of evaluative language, is only a symptom—and a most unreliable one—of an evaluative use of words. Moral language is frequently emotive, simply because the situations in which it is typically used are situations about which we often feel deeply. One of the chief uses of the comparison which I have been drawing between moral and non-moral value-language is to make it clear that the essential logical features of value-words can be present where the emotions are not markedly involved.

It might be objected that my account of the matter gives no means of distinguishing prudential judgements like 'It is never a good thing to volunteer for anything in the Army' from properly moral judgements like 'It is not good to break one's promises'. But the considerations given earlier enable us to distinguish satisfactorily between these two classes of judgement. It is clear from the context that in the second case we are commending within a different class of comparison, and requiring a different set of virtues. Sometimes we commend an act within the class of acts having an effect upon the agent's future happiness; sometimes we commend an act within the class of acts indicative of his moral character, that is to say, those acts which show whether or not he is a good man—and the class of comparison 'man' in this context is the class 'man to try to become like'. Which of these we are doing is always clear from the context, and there is nearly always a further verbal difference too, as in the example quoted. It must be admitted, however, that a great deal of research has still to be done on the different classes of comparison within which we commend people and acts.

DECISIONS AND PRINCIPLES

There are two factors which may be involved in the making of any decision to do something. Of these, the first may at any rate theoretically be absent, the second is always present to some degree. They correspond to the major and minor premisses of the Aristotelian practical syllogism. The major premiss is a principle of conduct; the minor premiss is a statement, more or less full, of what we should in fact be doing if we did one or other of the alternatives open to us. Thus if I decide not to say something, because it is false, I am acting on a principle, 'Never (or never under certain conditions) say what is false', and I must know that this, which I am wondering whether to say, is false.

Let us take the minor premiss first, since it presents less difficulty. We plainly cannot decide what to do unless we know at least something about what we should be doing if we did this or that. For example, suppose that I am an employer, and am wondering whether or not to sack a clerk who habitually turns up at the office after the hour at which he has undertaken to turn up. If I sack him I shall be depriving his family of the money on which they live, perhaps giving my firm a reputation which will lead clerks to avoid it when other jobs are available, and so on; if I keep him, I shall be causing the other clerks to do work which otherwise would be done by this clerk; and the affairs of the office will not be transacted so quickly as they would if all the clerks were punctual. These would be the sorts of consideration that I should take into account in making my decision. They would be the effects on the total situation of the alternative actions, sacking him or not sacking him. It is the effects which determine what I should be doing; it is between the two sets of effects that I am deciding. The whole point about a decision is that it makes a difference to what happens; and this difference is the difference between the effects of deciding one way, and the effects of deciding the other.

It sometimes seems to be implied by writers on ethics that it is immoral, on certain sorts of occasion, to consider the effects of doing something. We ought, it is said, to do our duty no matter what the effects of doing it. As I am using the word 'effects', this cannot be maintained. I am not making a claim for 'expediency' (in the bad sense) as against 'duty'. Even to do our duty—in so far as it is *doing* something—is effecting certain changes in the total situation. It is quite true that, of the changes that it is possible to effect in the total situation, most people would agree that we ought to consider certain kinds more relevant than others (which than which, it is the purpose of moral principles to tell us). I do not think that the immediacy or remoteness of the effects makes any difference, though their certainty or uncertainty does. The reason why it is considered immoral to fail to right an injustice whose effects will maximize pleasure, is not that in such a choice the effects are considered when they should not have been; it is that certain of the effects—namely, the maximization of pleasure—are given a relevance which they should not have, in view of the prior claim of those other effects which would have consisted in the righting of the injustice.

•　•　•　•　•

. . . To learn to do anything is never to learn to do an individual act; it is always to learn to do acts of a certain kind in a certain kind of situation; and this is to learn a principle. Thus, in learning to drive, I learn, not to change gear *now*, but to change gear when the engine makes a certain kind of noise. If this were not so, instruction would be of no use at all; for if all an instructor could do were to tell us to change gear *now*, he would have to sit beside us for the rest of our lives in order to tell us just when, on each occasion, to change gear.

Thus without principles we could not learn anything whatever from our elders. This would mean that every generation would have to start from scratch and teach itself. But even if each generation were able to teach itself, it could not do so without principles; for self-teaching, like all other teaching, is the teaching of principles. . . .

There is a limit in practice to the amount that can be taught to someone by someone else. Beyond this point, self-teaching is necessary. The limit is set by the variety of conditions which may be met with in doing whatever is being taught; and this variety is greater in some cases than in others. A sergeant can teach a recruit almost all there is to be known about fixing bayonets on parade, because one occasion of fixing bayonets on parade is much like another; but a driving instructor cannot do more than begin to teach his pupil the art of driving, because the conditions to be met with in driving are so various. In most cases, teaching cannot consist in getting the learner to perform faultlessly a fixed drill. One of the things that has to be included in any but the most elementary kinds of instruction is the opportunity for the learner to make decisions for himself, and in so doing to examine, and even modify to suit particular types of case, the principles which are being taught. The principles that are taught us initially are of a provisional kind (very like the principle 'Never say what is false' which I discussed in the last chapter). Our training, after the initial stages, consists in taking these principles, and making them less provisional; we do this by using them continually in our own decisions, and sometimes making exceptions to them; some of the exceptions are made because our instructor points out to us that certain cases are instances of classes of exceptions to the principle; and some of the exceptions we decide on for ourselves. . . . If we learn from experiment that to follow a certain principle would have certain effects, whereas to modify it in a certain way would have certain other effects, we adopt whichever form of the principle leads to the effects which we choose to pursue.

We may illustrate this process of modifying principles from the example already used, that of learning to drive. I am told, for instance, always to draw into the side of the road when I stop the car; but later I am told that this does not apply when I stop before turning into a side-road to the off-side—for then I must stop near the middle of the road until it is possible for me to turn. Still later I learn that in this manœuvre it is not necessary to stop at all if it is an uncontrolled junction and I can see that there is no traffic which I should obstruct by turning. When I have picked up all these modifications to the rule, and the similar modifications to all the other rules, and practice them habitually as so modified, then I am said to be a good driver, because my car is always in the right place on the road, travelling at the right speed, and so on. The good driver is, among other things, one whose actions are so exactly governed by principles which have become a habit with him, that he normally does not have to *think* just what to do. But road conditions are exceedingly various, and therefore it is unwise to let all one's driving become a matter of habit. One can never be certain that one's principles of driving are perfect—indeed, one can be very sure that they are not; and therefore the good driver not only drives well from habit, but constantly attends to his driving habits, to see whether they might not be improved; he never stops learning.

•   •   •   •   •

Drivers often know just what to do in a certain situation without being able to enunciate in words the principle on which they act. This is a very common state of affairs with all kinds of principles. Trappers know just where to set their traps, but often cannot explain just why they have put a trap in a particular place. We all know how to use words to convey our meaning; but if a logician presses us for the exact definition of a word we have used, or the exact rules for its use, we are often at a loss. This does not mean that the setting of traps or the use of words or the driving of cars does not proceed according to principles. One may know how, without being able to say how—though if a skill is to be taught, it is easier if we *can* say how.

We must not think that, if we can decide between one course and another without further thought (it seems self-evident to us, which we should do), this necessarily implies that we have some mysterious intuitive faculty which tells us what to do. A driver does not know when to change gear by intuition; he knows it because he has learnt and not forgotten; what he knows is a principle, though he cannot formulate the principle in words. The same is true of moral decisions which are sometimes called 'intuitive'. We have moral 'intuitions' because we have learnt how to behave, and have different ones according to how we have learnt to behave.

It would be a mistake to say that all that had to be done to a man to make him into a good driver was to tell him, or otherwise inculcate into him, a lot of general principles. This would be to leave out the factor of decision. Very soon after he begins to learn, he will be faced with situations to deal with which the provisional principles so far taught him require modification; and he will then have to decide what to do. He will very soon discover which decisions were right and which wrong, partly because his instructor tells him, and partly because having seen the effects of the decisions he determines in future not to bring about such effects. On no account must we commit the mistake of supposing that decisions and principles occupy two separate spheres and do not meet at any point. All decisions except those, if any, that are completely arbitrary are to some extent decisions of principle. We are always setting precedents for ourselves. It is not a case of the principle settling everything down to a certain point, and decision dealing with everything below that point. Rather, decision and principles interact throughout the whole field. Suppose that we have a principle to act in a certain way in certain circumstances. Suppose then that we find ourselves in circumstances which fall under the principle, but which have certain other peculiar features, not met before, which make us ask 'Is the principle really intended to cover cases like this, or is it incompletely specified— is there here a case belonging to a class which should be treated as exceptional?' Our answer to this question will be a decision, but a decision of principle, as is shown by the use of the value-word 'should'. If we decide that this should be an exception, we thereby modify the principle by laying down an exception to it.

Suppose, for example, that in learning to drive I have been taught always to signal before I slow down or stop, but have not yet been taught what to do when stopping in an emergency; if a child leaps in front of my car, I do not signal, but keep both hands on the steering-wheel; and thereafter I accept the former principle with this exception, that in cases of emergency it is better to steer than to signal. I have, even on the spur of the moment, made a decision of principle. To understand what happens in cases like this is to understand a great deal about the making of value-judgements.

I do not wish to seem to be pressing too far my comparison, in respect of the way in which they are learnt, between principles of driving and principles of conduct. It is necessary also to bear in mind some distinctions. In the first place, the expression 'good driver' is itself ambiguous in that it is not immediately clear what standard is being applied. It might be simply a standard of expertness; we might call a person a good driver if he were able to do just what he wanted with his car; we might say 'Although a very good driver, he is most inconsiderate to other road users'. On the other hand, we sometimes expect a good driver to have moral qualities as well; we do not, according to this criterion, call a man a good driver if he drives expertly, but without the slightest heed for the convenience or safety of other people. The line between these two standards of good driving is not easy to draw in practice. There is also a third standard, according to which a driver is said to be good if he conforms to the accepted principles of good driving as laid down, for example, in the *Highway Code*. Since the *Highway Code* is compiled with a definite purpose in view, this standard coincides to a great extent with the second.

Secondly, there are two ways of looking at driving instruction:

(1) We establish at the beginning certain ends, for example the avoidance of collisions, and instruction consists in teaching what practices are conducive to those ends. According to this way of looking at them, the principles of good driving are hypothetical imperatives.

(2) We teach at first simple rules of thumb, and the learner only gradually comes to see what the ends are, at which the instruction is aimed.

It must not be thought that either (1) or (2) by itself gives a complete account of our procedure. Which method we adopt depends to a great extent on the maturity and intelligence of the learner. In teaching African soldiers to drive, we might incline more to the second method; if I had to teach my two-year-old son to drive, I should have to adopt the same methods as I now adopt for teaching him to refrain from interfering with the controls when I am driving myself. With a highly intelligent learner, on the other hand, we may adopt a method which has more of (1) in it than of (2).

It must not be thought, however, that method (2) is ever entirely without a place even in the case of the most rational of learners. It may be that the desirability of avoiding collisions is at once understood and accepted even by comparatively stupid learners; but there are a great many more ends than this which a good driver has to aim at. He has to avoid causing many kinds of avoidable inconvenience both to himself and to others; he has to learn not to do things which result in damage to his vehicle, and so on. It is of no use to establish at the beginning a general end, 'the avoidance of avoidable inconven- ience'; for 'inconvenience' is a value-word, and until he has had experience of driving, the learner will not know what sorts of situation are to count as avoidable inconvenience. The general end or principle is vacuous until by our detailed instruction we have given it content. Therefore it is always necessary to start, to some extent, by teaching our learner *what* to do, and leaving it for him to find out later *why*. We may therefore say that although moral principles, which are normally taught us when we are immature, are taught largely by method (2), and principles of driving preponderantly by method (1), there is not an absolute division between the two sorts of principle in this respect. What I have just said about first learning *what* to do, and about the initial vacuity of the general end, is borrowed from Aristotle.[3] The one fundamental distinction between principles of driving and principles of conduct is that the latter are, in

---

[3] *Nicomachean Ethics*, i. 4.

Aristotle's term, 'architectonic' of the former; for the ends of good driving (safety, the avoidance of inconvenience to others, the preservation of property, and so on) are justified ultimately, if justification is sought, by appeal to moral considerations.

It would be folly, however, to say that there is only one way of learning a skill or any other body of principles, or of justifying a particular decision made in the practice of it. There are many ways, and I have tried to make the above account sufficiently general to cover all of them. It is sometimes said by writers on morals that we have to justify an act by reference to its effects, and that we tell which effects are to be sought, which avoided, by reference to some principle. Such a theory is that of the utilitarians, who bid us look at the effects, and examine these in the light of the principle of utility, to see which effects would maximize pleasure. Sometimes, on the other hand, it is said . . . that an act is justified directly by reference to the principles which it observes, and these principles in their turn by reference to the effects of always observing them. Sometimes it is said that we should observe principles and ignore the effects—though for the reason given above 'effects' cannot be here intended in the sense in which I have been using it. What is wrong with these theories is not what they say, but their assumption that they are telling us the only way to justify actions, or decide what actions to do. We do, indeed, justify and decide on actions in all these ways; for example, sometimes, if asked why we did A, we say, 'Because it was a case falling under principle P', and if asked to justify P in turn, we go into the effects of observing it and of not observing it. But sometimes, when asked the same question 'Why did you do A?' we say 'Because if I hadn't, E would have happened', and if asked what was wrong about E happening, we appeal to some principle.

The truth is that, if asked to justify as completely as possible any decision, we have to bring in both effects—to give content to the decision—and principles, and the effects in general of observing those principles, and so on, until we have satisfied our inquirer. Thus a complete justification of a decision would consist of a complete account of its effects, together with a complete account of the principles which it observed, and the effects of observing those principles—for, of course, it is the effects (what obeying them in fact consists in) which give content to the principles too. Thus, if pressed to justify a decision completely, we have to give a complete specification of the way of life of which it is a part. This complete specification it is impossible in practice to give; the nearest attempts are those given by the great religions, especially those which can point to historical persons who carried out the way of life in practice. Suppose, however, that we can give it. If the inquirer still goes on asking 'But why *should* I live like that?' then there is no further answer to give him, because we have already, *ex hypothesi*, said everything that could be included in this further answer. We can only ask him to make up his own mind which way he ought to live; for in the end everything rests upon such a decision of principle. He has to decide whether to accept that way of life or not; if he accepts it, then we can proceed to justify the decisions that are based upon it; if he does not accept it, then let him accept some other, and try to live by it. The sting is in the last clause. To describe such ultimate decisions as arbitrary, because *ex hypothesi* everything which could be used to justify them has already been included in the decision, would be like saying that a complete description of the universe was utterly unfounded, because no further fact could be called upon in corroboration of it. This is not how we use the words 'arbitrary' and 'unfounded'. Far from being arbitrary, such a decision would be the most well-founded of decisions, because it would be based upon a consideration of everything upon which it could possibly be founded.

It will be noticed how, in talking of decisions of principle, I have inevitably started talking value-language. Thus we decide that the principle *should* be modified, or that it is *better* to steer than to signal. This illustrates the very close relevance of what I have been saying in the first part of this book to the problems of the second part; for to make a value-judgement is to make a decision of principle. To ask whether I ought to do A in these circumstances is (to borrow Kantian language with a small though important modification) to ask whether or not I will that doing A in such circumstances should become a universal law. It may seem a far cry from Kant to Professor Stevenson; but the same question could be put in other words by asking 'What attitude shall I adopt and recommend towards doing A in such circumstances?'; for 'attitude', if it means anything, means a principle of action. Unfortunately Stevenson, unlike Kant, devotes very little space to the examination of this first-person question; had he paid due attention to it, and avoided the dangers of the word 'persuasive', he might have reached a position not unlike that of Kant.

As Kant points out in the important passage on the Autonomy of the Will, . . . we have to make our own decisions of principle. Other people cannot make them for us unless we have first decided to take their advice or obey their orders. There is an interesting analogy here with the position of the scientist, who also has to rely on his own observations. It might be said that there is a difference here between decisions and observations, to the detriment of the former, in that an observation, once made, is public property, whereas decisions have to be made by the agent himself on each occasion. But the difference is only apparent. A scientist would not have become a scientist unless he had convinced himself that the observations of other scientists were in general reliable. He did this by making some observations of his own. When we learnt elementary chemistry at school, we had some theoretical periods and some practical. In the theoretical periods we studied books; in the practical periods we made experiments, and found, if we were lucky, that the results tallied with what the books said. This showed us that what the books said was not all nonsense; so that even if, by reason of disturbing factors ignored by us, our experiments came out wrong, we were inclined to trust the books and acknowledge that we had made a mistake. We were confirmed in this assumption by the fact that we often discovered later what the mistake had been. If our observations, however carefully we did them, were always at variance with the textbooks, we should not be tempted to make science our profession. Thus the confidence of the scientist in other people's observations is ultimately based, among other things, on his own observations and his own judgements about what is reliable. He has in the end to rely on himself.

The case of the moral agent is not dissimilar. When in our early days we are given our elementary moral instruction, there are some things that we are told, and some things that we do. If, when we did as we were told, the total effects of our so doing, when they happened, were always such as we would not have chosen had we known, then we should seek better advice, or, if prevented from so doing, either work out our own salvation or become moral defectives. If we are in general given what we subsequently come to see to have been good advice, we decide in general to follow the advice and adopt the principles of those who have given us this good advice in the past. This is what happens to any child who is well brought up. Just as the scientist does not try to rewrite all that is in the textbooks, but takes that for granted and sticks to his own particular researches, so this fortunate child will take over bodily the principles of his elders and adapt them in detail, by his own decisions, to suit his own circumstances from time to time. This is how in a well-ordered society morality remains stable, and at the same time gets adapted to changing circumstances.

There are, however, many ways in which this happy state of affairs can deteriorate. Let us consider a process that seems to occur quite often in history; it occurred in Greece during the fifth and fourth centuries, and it has occurred in our own time. Suppose that the people of a certain generation—I will call it the first generation—have got very settled principles, inherited from their fathers. Suppose that they have become so settled as to be second nature, so that generally speaking people act on the principles without thinking and their power of making considered decisions of principle becomes atrophied. They act always by the book, and come to no harm, because the state of the world in their time remains much the same as that for which the principles were thought out. But their sons, the second generation, as they grow up, find that conditions have changed (e.g. through a protracted war or an industrial revolution), and that the principles in which they have been brought up are no longer adequate. Since, in their education, much stress has been laid on observing principles, and very little on making the decisions on which these principles are ultimately based, their morality has no roots, and becomes completely unstable. Books on 'The Whole Duty of Man' are no longer written or read. Often, when they do what it says in such books, they subsequently find cause to regret their decisions; and there are too many cases of this kind for any confidence in the old principles, as a body, to remain. No doubt there are among these old principles certain very general ones, which will remain acceptable unless human nature and the state of the world undergo a most fundamental change; but the second generation, not having been brought up to make decisions of principle, but to do what it says in the book, will not, most of them, be able to make those crucial decisions which would determine which principles to keep, which to modify, and which to abandon. Some people, the Polemarchuses of the second generation, will have been so steeped in the old principles that they just follow them come what may; and these will on the whole be more fortunate than the others, for it is better to have some principles, even if they sometimes lead to decisions which we regret, than to be morally adrift. The bulk of the second generation, and still more perhaps of the third, will not know which of the principles to keep and which to reject; and so they will come more and more to live from day to day—not a bad thing, because it trains their powers of decision, but it is an unpleasant and dangerous state to be in. A few among them, the rebels, will shout from the housetops that some or all of the old moral principles are worthless; some of these rebels will advocate new principles of their own; some will have nothing to offer. Though they increase the confusion, these rebels perform the useful function of making people decide between their rival principles; and if they not only advocate new principles, but sincerely try to live by them, they are conducting a moral experiment which may be of the utmost value to man (in which case they go down in history as great moral teachers), or may, on the other hand, prove disastrous both to them and to their disciples.

It may take several generations for this disease to play itself out. Morality regains its vigour when ordinary people have learnt afresh to decide for themselves what principles to live by, and more especially what principles to teach their children. Since the world, though subject to vast material changes, changes only very slowly in matters that are fundamental from the moral point of view, the principles which win the acceptance of the mass of people are not likely to differ enormously from those which their fathers came to distrust. The moral principles of Aristotle resemble those of Aeschylus more than they differ from them, and we ourselves shall perhaps come back to something recognizably like the morality of our grandfathers. But there will be some changes; some of the principles advocated by the rebels will have been adopted. That is how morality progresses—or retrogresses. The process is, as we shall see, reflected by very subtle changes in the uses of value-words; the impossibility of translating Aristotle's catalogue of virtues into modern English may serve as an example, and the disappearance without trace of the word 'righteous' may serve as another.

The question 'How shall I bring up my children?' which we have mentioned, is one to the logic of which, since ancient times, few philosophers have given much attention. A child's moral upbringing has an effect upon him which will remain largely untouched by anything that happens to him thereafter. If he has had a stable unbringing, whether on good principles or on bad ones, it will be extremely difficult for him to abandon those principles in later life—difficult but not impossible. They will have for him the force of an objective moral law; and his behaviour will seem to give much evidence in support of intuitionist ethical theories, provided that it is not compared with the behaviour of those who stick just as firmly to quite different principles. But nevertheless, unless our education has been so thorough as to transform us into automata, we can come to doubt or even reject these principles; that is what makes human beings, whose moral systems change, different from ants, whose 'moral system' does not. Therefore, even if for me the question 'What shall I do in such and such a situation?' is almost invariably answered without ambiguity by the moral intuition which my upbringing has given me, I may, if I ask myself 'How shall I bring up my children?' pause before giving an answer. It is here that the most fundamental moral decisions of all arise; and it is here, if only moral philosophers would pay attention to them, that the most characteristic uses of moral words are to be found. Shall I bring up my children *exactly* as I was brought up, so that they have the same intuitions about morals as I have? Or have circumstances altered, so that the moral character of the father will not provide a suitable equipment for the children? Perhaps I shall try to bring them up like their father, and shall fail; perhaps their new environment will be too strong for me, and they will come to repudiate my principles. Or I may have become so bewildered by the strange new world that, although I still act from force of habit on the principles that I have learnt, I simply do not know what principles to impart to my children, if, indeed, one in my condition can impart any settled principles at all. On all these questions, I have to make up my mind; only the most hide-bound father will try to bring up his children, without thinking, in exactly the way that he himself was brought up; and even he will usually fail disastrously.

Many of the dark places of ethics become clearer when we consider this dilemma in which parents are liable to find themselves. We have already noticed that, although principles have in the end to rest upon decisions of principle, decisions as such cannot be taught; only principles can be taught. It is the powerlessness of the parent to make for his son those many decisions of principle which the son during his future career will make, that gives moral language its characteristic shape. The only instrument which the parent possesses is moral education—the teaching of principles by example and precept, backed up by chastisement and other more up-to-date psychological methods. Shall he use these means, and to what extent? Certain generations of parents have had no doubts about this question. They have used them to the full; and the result has been to turn their children into good intuitionists, able to cling to the rails, but bad at steering round corners. At other times parents—and who shall blame them?—suffer from lack of confidence; they are not sure enough what they themselves think, to be ready to impart to their children a stable way of life. The children of such a generation are likely to grow up opportunists, well able to make individual decisions, but without the settled body of principles which is the most priceless heritage that any generation can leave to its successors. For, though principles are in the end built upon decisions of principle, the building is the work of many generations, and the man who has to start from the beginning is to be pitied; he will not be likely, unless he is a genius, to achieve many conclusions of importance, any more than the average boy, turned loose without instruction upon a desert island, or even in a laboratory, would be likely to make any of the major scientific discoveries.

The dilemma between these two extreme courses in education is plainly a false one. Why it is a false one is apparent, if we recall what was said earlier about the dynamic relation between decisions and principles. It is very like learning to drive. It would be foolish, in teaching someone to drive, to try to inculcate into him such fixed and comprehensive principles that he would never have to make an independent decision. It would be equally foolish to go to the other extreme and leave it to him to find his own way of driving. What we do, if we are sensible, is to give him a solid basis of principles, but at the same time ample opportunity of making the decisions upon which these principles are based, and by which they are modified, improved, adapted to changed circumstances, or even abandoned if they become entirely unsuited to a new environment. To teach only the principles, without giving the opportunity of subjecting them to the learner's own decisions of principle, is like teaching science exclusively from textbooks without entering a laboratory. On the other hand, to abandon one's child or one's driving-pupil to his own self-expression is like putting a boy into a laboratory and saying 'Get on with it'. The boy may enjoy himself or kill himself, but will probably not learn much science.

The moral words, of which we may take 'ought' as an example, reflect in their logical behaviour this double nature of moral instruction—as well they may, for it is in moral instruction that they are most typically used. The sentences in which they appear are normally the expression of decisions of principle—and it is easy to let the decisions get separated, in our discussion of the subject, from the principles. This is the source of the controversy between the 'objectivists', as intuitionists sometimes call themselves, and the 'subjectivists', as they often call their opponents. The former lay stress on the fixed principles that are handed down by the father, the latter on the new decisions which have to be made by the son. The objectivist says 'Of course you know what you ought to do; look at what your conscience tells you, and if in doubt go by the consciences of the vast majority of men.' He is able to say this, because our consciences are the product of the principles which our early training has indelibly planted in us, and in one society these principles do not differ much from one person to another. The subjectivist, on the other hand, says 'But surely, when it comes to the point—when I have listened to what other people say, and given due weight to my own intuitions, the legacy of my upbringing—I have in the end to decide for myself what I ought to do. To deny this is to be a conventionalist; for both common moral notions and my own intuitions are the legacy of tradition, and—apart from the fact that there are so many different traditions in the world—traditions cannot be started without someone doing what I now feel called upon to do, decide. If I refuse to make my own decisions, I am, in merely copying my fathers, showing myself a lesser man than they; for whereas they must have initiated, I shall be merely accepting.' This plea of the subjectivist is quite justified. It is the plea of the adolescent who wants to be adult. To become morally adult is to reconcile these two apparently conflicting positions by learning to make decisions of principle; it is to learn to use 'ought'-sentences in the realization that they can only be verified by reference to a standard or set of principles which we have by our own decision accepted and made our own. This is what our present generation is so painfully trying to do.

PHILIPPA FOOT
Moral Beliefs

To many people it seems that the most notable advance in moral philosophy during the past fifty years or so has been the refutation of naturalism; and they are a little shocked that at this late date such an issue should be reopened. It is easy to understand their attitude: given certain apparently unquestionable assumptions, it would be about as sensible to try to reintroduce naturalism as to try to square the circle. Those who see it like this have satisfied themselves that they know in advance that any naturalistic theory must have a catch in it somewhere, and are put out at having to waste more time exposing an old fallacy. This paper is an attempt to persuade them to look critically at the premises on which their arguments are based.

It would not be an exaggeration to say that the whole of moral philosophy, as it is now widely taught, rests on a contrast between statements of fact and evaluations, which runs something like this: 'The truth or falsity of statements of fact is shown by means of evidence; and what counts as evidence is laid down in the meaning of the expressions occurring in the statement of fact. (For instance, the meaning of "round" and "flat" made Magellan's voyages evidence for the roundness rather than the flatness of the Earth; someone who went on questioning whether the evidence was evidence could eventually be shown to have made some linguistic mistake.) It follows that no two people can make the same statement and count completely different things as evidence; in the end one at least of them could be convicted of linguistic ignorance. It also follows that if a man is given good evidence for a factual conclusion he cannot just refuse to accept the conclusion on the ground that in his scheme of things this evidence is not evidence at all. With evaluations, however, it is different. An evaluation is not connected logically with the factual statements on which it is based. One man may say that a thing is good because of some fact about it, and another may refuse to take that fact as any evidence at all, for nothing is laid down in the meaning of "good" which connects it with one piece of "evidence" rather than another. It follows that a moral eccentric could argue to moral conclusions from quite idiosyncratic premises; he could say, for instance, that a man was a good man because he clasped and unclasped his hands, and never turned NNE after turning SSW. He could also reject someone else's evaluation simply by denying that his evidence was evidence at all.

'The fact about "good" which allows the eccentric still to use this term

From P. Foot, "Moral Beliefs," *Proceedings of the Aristotelian Society*, LIX (1958–59), 83–104. Reprinted by courtesy of the author and the Editor of The Aristotelian Society. © 1958 The Aristotelian Society.

without falling into a morass of meaninglessness, is its "action-guiding" or "practical" function. This it retains; for like everyone else he considers himself bound to choose the things he calls "good" rather than those he calls "bad". Like the rest of the world he uses "good" in connection only with a "pro-attitude"; it is only that he has pro-attitudes to quite different things, and therefore calls them good.'

There are here two assumptions about 'evaluations', which I will call assumption (1) and assumption (2).

Assumption (1) is that some individual may, without logical error, base his beliefs about matters of value entirely on premises which no one else would recognise as giving any evidence at all. Assumption (2) is that, given the kind of statement which other people regard as evidence for an evaluative conclusion, he may refuse to draw the conclusion because *this* does not count as evidence for *him*.

Let us consider assumption (1). We might say that this depends on the possibility of keeping the meaning of 'good' steady through all changes in the facts about anything which are to count in favour of its goodness. (I do not mean, of course, that a man can make changes as fast as he chooses; only that, whatever he has chosen, it will not be possible to rule him out of order.) But there is a better formulation, which cuts out trivial disputes about the meaning which 'good' happens to have in some section of the community. Let us say that the assumption is that the evaluative function of 'good' can remain constant through changes in the evaluative principle; on this ground it could be said that even if no one can call a man *good* because he clasps and unclasps his hands, he can commend him or express his *pro-attitude* towards him, and if necessary can invent a new moral vocabulary to express his unusual moral code.

Those who hold such a theory will naturally add several qualifications. In the first place, most people now agree with Hare, against Stevenson, that such words as 'good' only apply to individual cases through the application of general principles, so that even the extreme moral eccentric must accept principles of commendation. In the second place 'commending', 'having a pro-attitude', and so on, are supposed to be connected with doing and choosing, so that it would be impossible to say, e.g. that a man was a good man only if he lived for a thousand years. The range of evaluation is supposed to be restricted to the range of possible action and choice. I am not here concerned to question these supposed restrictions on the use of evaluative terms, but only to argue that they are not enough.

The crucial question is this. Is it possible to extract from the meaning of words such as 'good' some element called 'evaluative meaning' which we can think of as externally related to its objects? Such an element would be represented, for instance, in the rule that when any action was 'commended' the speaker must hold himself bound to accept an imperative 'let me do these things'. This is externally related to its object because, within the limitation which we noticed earlier, to possible actions, it would make sense to think of anything as the subject of such 'commendation'. On this hypothesis a moral eccentric could be described as commending the clasping of hands as the action of a good man, and we should not have to look for some background to give the supposition sense. That is to say, on this hypothesis the clasping of hands could be commended without any explanation; it could be what those who hold such theories call 'an ultimate moral principle'.

I wish to say that this hypothesis is untenable, and that there is no describing the evaluative meaning of 'good', evaluation, commending, or anything of the sort, without fixing the object to which they are supposed to be attached. Without first laying hands on the proper object of such things as evaluation, we shall catch in our net either something quite different, such as accepting an order or making a resolution, or else nothing at all.

Before I consider this question, I shall first discuss some other mental attitudes and beliefs which have this internal relation to their object. By this I hope to clarify the concept of internal relation to an object, and incidentally, if my examples arouse resistance, but are eventually accepted, to show how easy it is to overlook an internal relation where it exists.

Consider, for instance, pride.

People are often surprised at the suggestion that there are limits to the things a man can be proud of, about which indeed he can feel pride. I do not know quite what account they want to give of pride; perhaps something to do with smiling and walking with a jaunty air, and holding an object up where other people can see it; or perhaps they think that pride is a kind of internal sensation, so that one might naturally beat one's breast and say 'pride is something I feel *here*'. The difficulties of the second view are well known; the logically private object cannot be what a name in the public language is the name of.[1] The first view is the more plausible, and it may seem reasonable to say that given certain behaviour a man can be described as showing that he is proud of something, whatever that something may be. In one sense this is true, and in another sense not. Given any description of an object, action, personal characteristic, etc., it is not possible to rule it out as an object of pride. Before we can do so we need to know what would be said about it by the man who is to be proud of it, or feels proud of it; but if he does not hold the right beliefs about it then whatever his attitude is it is not pride. Consider, for instance, the suggestion that someone might be proud of the sky or the sea: he looks at them and what he feels is *pride*, or he puffs out his chest and gestures with *pride* in their direction. This makes sense only if a special assumption is made about his beliefs, for instance, that he is under some crazy delusion and believes that he has saved the sky from falling, or the sea from drying up. The characteristic object of pride is something seen (*a*) as in some way a man's own, and (*b*) as some sort of achievement or advantage; without this object pride cannot be described. To see that the second condition is necessary, one should try supposing that a man happens to feel proud because he has laid one of his hands on the other, three times in an hour. Here again the supposition that it is pride that he feels will

---

[1] See L. Wittgenstein, *Philosophical Investigations* (1953), especially sections 243–315.

make perfectly good sense if a special background is filled in. Perhaps he is ill, and it is an achievement even to do this; perhaps this gesture has some religious or political significance, and he is a brave man who will so defy the gods or the rulers. But with no special background there can be no pride, not because no one could psychologically speaking feel pride in such a case, but because whatever he did feel could not logically be pride. Of course, people can see strange things as achievements, though not just anything, and they can identify themselves with remote ancestors, and relations, and neighbours, and even on occasions with Mankind. I do not wish to deny there are many far-fetched and comic examples of pride.

We could have chosen many other examples of mental attitudes which are internally related to their object in a similar way. For instance, fear is not just trembling, and running, and turning pale; without the thought of some menacing evil no amount of this will add up to fear. Nor could anyone be said to feel dismay about something he did not see as bad; if his thoughts about it were that it was altogether a good thing, he could not say that (oddly enough) what he felt about it was dismay. 'How odd, I feel dismayed when I ought to be pleased' is the prelude to a hunt for the adverse aspect of the thing, thought of as lurking behind the pleasant façade. But someone may object that pride and fear and dismay are feelings or emotions and therefore not a proper analogy for 'commendation', and there will be an advantage in considering a different kind of example. We could discuss, for instance, the belief that a certain thing is dangerous, and ask whether this could logically be held about anything whatsoever. Like 'this is good', 'this is dangerous' is an assertion, which we should naturally accept or reject by speaking of its truth or falsity; we seem to support such statements with evidence, and moreover there may seem to be a 'warning function' connected with the word 'dangerous' as there is supposed to be a 'commending function' connected with the word 'good'. For suppose that philosophers, puzzled about the property of dangerousness, decided that the word did not stand for a property at all, but was essentially a practical or action-guiding term, used for *warning*. Unless used in an 'inverted comma sense' the word 'dangerous' was used to warn, and this meant that anyone using it in such a sense committed himself to avoiding the things he called dangerous, to preventing other people from going near them, and perhaps to running in the opposite direction. If the conclusion were not obviously ridiculous, it would be easy to infer that a man whose application of the term was different from ours throughout might say that the oddest things were dangerous without fear of disproof; the idea would be that he could still be described as 'thinking them dangerous', or at least as 'warning', because by his attitude and actions he would have fulfilled the conditions for these things. This is nonsense because without its proper object *warning*, like *believing dangerous*, will not be there. It is logically impossible to warn about anything not thought of as threatening evil, and for danger we need a particular kind of serious evil such as injury or death.

There are, however, some differences between thinking a thing dangerous and feeling proud, frightened or dismayed. When a man says that something is dangerous he must support his statement with a special kind of evidence; but when he says that he feels proud or frightened or dismayed the description of the object of his pride or fright or dismay does not have quite this relation to his original statement. If he is shown that the thing he was proud of was not his after all, or was not after all anything very grand, he may have to say that his pride was not justified, but he will not have to take back the statement that he was proud. On the other hand, someone who says that a thing is dangerous, and later sees that he made a mistake in thinking that an injury might result from it, has to go back on his original statement and admit that he was wrong. In neither case, however, is the speaker able to go on as before. A man who discovered that it was not his pumpkin but someone else's which had won the prize could only say that he still felt proud, if he could produce some other ground for pride. It is in this way that even feelings are logically vulnerable to facts.

It will probably be objected against these examples that for part of the way at least they beg the question. It will be said that indeed a man can only be proud of something he thinks a good action, or an achievement, or a sign of noble birth; as he can only feel dismay about something which he sees as bad, frightened at some threatened evil; similarly he can only warn if he is also prepared to speak, for instance, of injury. But this will only limit the range of possible objects of those attitudes and beliefs if the range of these terms is limited in its turn. To meet this objection I shall discuss the meaning of 'injury' because this is the simplest case. Anyone who feels inclined to say that anything could be counted as an achievement, or as the evil of which people were afraid, or about which they felt dismayed, should just try this out. I wish to consider the proposition that anything could be thought of as dangerous, because if it causes injury it is dangerous, and anything could be counted as an injury. I shall consider bodily injury because this is the injury connected with danger; it is not correct to put up a notice by the roadside reading 'Danger!' on account of bushes which might scratch a car. Nor can a substance be labelled 'dangerous' on the ground that it can injure delicate fabrics; although we can speak of the danger that it may do so, that is not the use of the word which I am considering here.

When a body is injured it is changed for the worse in a special way, and we want to know which changes count as injuries. First of all, it matters how an injury comes about; e.g. it cannot be caused by natural decay. Then it seems clear that not just any kind of thing will do, for instance, any unusual mark on the body, however much trouble a man might take to have it removed. By far the most important class of injuries are injuries to a part of the body, counting as injuries because there is interference with the function of that part; injury to a leg, an eye, an ear, a hand, a muscle, the heart, the brain, the spinal cord. An injury to an eye is one that affects, or is likely to affect, its sight; an injury to a hand one which makes it less well able to reach out and grasp, and perform other operations of this kind. A leg can be injured because its movements and supporting power can be affected; a lung because it can become too weak to draw in the proper amount of air. We are most ready to speak of an injury where the function of a part of the body is to perform a characteristic operation, as in these examples. We might hesitate to say that a skull can be injured, and might prefer to speak of damage to it, since although there is indeed a function (a protective function) there is no operation. But thinking of the protective function of the skull we may want to speak of injury here. In so far as the concept of *injury* depends on that of *function* it is narrowly limited, since not even every use to which a part of the body is put will count as its function. Why is it that, even if it is the means by which they earn their living, we would never consider the removal of the dwarf's hump or the bearded lady's beard as a bodily injury? It will be tempting to say that these things are disfigurements, but this is not the point; if we suppose that a man who had some invisible extra muscle made his living as a court jester by waggling his ears, the ear would not have been injured if this were made to disappear. If it were natural to men to communicate by movements of the ear, then ears would have the function of signalling (we have no word for this kind of 'speaking') and an impairment of this function would be an injury; but things are not like this. This court jester would use his ears to make people laugh, but this is not the function of ears.

No doubt many people will feel impatient when such facts are mentioned, because they think that it is quite unimportant that this or that *happens* to be the case, and it seems to them arbitrary that the loss of the beard, the hump, or the ear muscle would not be called an injury. Isn't the loss of that by which one makes one's living a pretty catastrophic loss? Yet it seems quite natural that these are not counted as injuries if one thinks about the conditions of human life, and contrasts the loss of a special ability to make people gape or laugh with the ability to see, hear, walk, or pick things up. The first is only needed for one very special way of living; the other in any foreseeable future for any man. This restriction seems all the more natural when we observe what other threats besides that of injury can constitute danger: of death, for instance, or mental derangement. A shock which could cause mental instability or impairment of memory would be called dangerous, because a man needs such things as intelligence, memory, and concentration as he needs sight or hearing or the use of hands. Here we do not speak of injury unless it is possible to connect the impairment with some physical change, but we speak of danger because there is the same loss of a capacity which any man needs.

There can be injury outside the range we have been considering; for a man may sometimes be said to have received injuries where no part of his body has had its function interfered with. In general, I think that any blow which disarranged the body in such a way that there was lasting pain would inflict an injury, even if no other ill resulted, but I do not know of any other important extension of the concept.

It seems therefore that since the range of things which can be called injuries is quite narrowly restricted, the word 'dangerous' is restricted in so far as it is connected with injury. We have the right to say that a man cannot decide to call just anything dangerous, however much he puts up fences and shakes his head.

So far I have been arguing that such things as pride, fear, dismay, and the thought that something is dangerous have an internal relation to their object, and hope that what I mean is becoming clear. Now we must consider whether those attitudes or beliefs which are the moral philosopher's study are similar, or whether such things as 'evaluation' and 'thinking something good' and 'commendation' could logically be found in combination with any object whatsoever. All I can do here is to give an example which may make this suggestion seem implausible, and to knock away a few of its supports. The example will come from the range of trivial and pointless actions such as we were considering in speaking of the man who clasped his hands three times an hour, and we can point to the oddity of the suggestion that this can be called a good action. We are bound by the terms of our question to refrain from adding any special background, and it should be stated once more that the question is about what can count in favour of the goodness or badness of a man or an action, and not what could be, or be thought, good or bad with a special background. I believe that the view I am attacking often seems plausible only because the special background is surreptitiously introduced.

Someone who said that clasping the hands three times in an hour was a good action would first have to answer the question 'How do you mean?' For the sentence 'this is a good action' is not one which has a clear meaning. Presumably, since our subject is moral philosophy, it does not here mean 'that was a good thing to do' as this might be said of a man who had done something sensible in the course of any enterprise whatever; we are to confine our attention to 'the moral use of "good"'. I am not clear that it makes sense to speak of a 'moral use of "good"', but we can pick out a number of cases which raise moral issues. It is because these are so diverse and because 'this is a good action' does not pick out any one of them, that we must ask 'How do you mean?' For instance, some things that are done fulfil a duty, such as the duty of parents to children or children to parents. I suppose that when philosophers speak of good actions they would include these. Some come under the heading of a virtue such as charity, and they will be included too. Others again are actions which require the virtues of courage or temperance, and here the moral aspect is due to the fact that they are done in spite of fear or the temptation of pleasure; they must indeed be done for the sake of some real or fancied good, but not necessarily what philosophers would want to call a moral good. Courage is not *particularly* concerned with saving other people's lives, or temperance with leaving them their share of the food and drink, and the goodness of *what is done* may here be all kinds of usefulness. It is because there are these very diverse cases included (I suppose) under the expression 'a good action' that we should refuse to consider applying it without asking what is meant, and we should now ask what is intended when someone is supposed to say that 'clasping the hands three times in an hour is a good action'. Is it supposed that this action fulfils a duty? Then in virtue of what does a man have this duty, and to whom does he owe it? We have promised not to slip in a special background, but he cannot possibly have a *duty* to clasp his hands unless such a background exists. Nor could it be an act of charity, for it is not thought to do anyone any good, nor again a gesture of humility unless a special assumption turns it into this. The action could be courageous, but only if it were done both in the face of fear and for the sake of a good; and we are not allowed to put in special circumstances which could make this the case.

I am sure that the following objection will now be raised. 'Of course clasping one's hands three times in an hour cannot be brought under one of the virtues which we recognise, but that is only to say that it is not a good action by our current moral code. It is logically possible that in a quite different moral code quite different virtues should be recognised, for which we have not even got a name.' I cannot answer this objection properly, for that would need a satisfactory account of the concept of a virtue. But anyone who thinks it would be easy to describe a new virtue connected with clasping the hands three times in an hour should just try. I think he will find that he has to cheat, and suppose that in the community concerned the clasping of hands has been given some special significance, or is thought to have some special effect. The difficulty is obviously connected with the fact that without a special background there is no possibility of answering the question 'What's the point?' It is no good saying that here would be a point in doing the action because the action was a morally good action: the question is how it can be given any such description if we cannot first speak about the point. And it is just as crazy to suppose that we can call *anything* the point of doing something without having to say what the point of *that* is. In clasping one's hands one may make a slight sucking noise, but what is the point of that? It is surely clear that moral virtues must be connected with human good and harm, and that it is quite impossible to call anything you like good or harm. Consider, for instance, the suggestion that a man might say he had been harmed because a bucket of water had been taken out of the sea. As usual it would be possible to think up circumstances in which this remark would make sense; for instance, when coupled with a belief in magical influences; but then the harm would consist in what was done by the evil spirits, not in the taking of the water from the sea. It would be just as odd if someone were supposed to say that harm had been done to him because the hairs of his head had been reduced to an even number.[2]

I conclude that assumption (1) is very dubious indeed, and that no one should be allowed to speak as if we can understand 'evaluation', 'commendation' or 'pro-attitude', whatever the actions concerned.

II

I propose now to consider what was called assumption (2), which said that a man might always refuse to accept the conclusion of an argument about values, because what counted as evidence for other people did not count for him. Assumption (2) could be true even if assumption (1) were false, for it might be

[2] In face of this sort of example many philosophers take refuge in the thicket of aesthetics. It would be interesting to know if they are willing to let their whole case rest on the possibility that there might be aesthetic objections to what was done.

that once a particular question of values—say a moral question—had been accepted, any disputant was bound to accept particular pieces of evidence as relevant, the same pieces as everyone else, but that he could always refuse to draw any moral conclusions whatsoever or to discuss any questions which introduced moral terms. Nor do we mean 'he might refuse to draw the conclusion' in the trivial sense in which anyone can perhaps refuse to draw *any* conclusion; the point is that any statement of value always seems to go beyond any statement of fact, so that he might have a reason for accepting the factual premises but refusing to accept the evaluative conclusion. That this is so seems to those who argue in this way to follow from the practical implications of evaluation. When a man uses a word such as 'good' in an 'evaluative' and not an 'inverted comma' sense, he is supposed to commit his will. From this it has seemed to follow inevitably that there is a logical gap between fact and value; for is it not one thing to say that a thing is so, and another to have a particular attitude towards its being so; one thing to see that certain effects will follow from a given action, and another to care? Whatever account was offered of the essential feature of evaluation—whether in terms of feelings, attitudes, the acceptance of imperatives or what not—the fact remained that with an evaluation there was a committal in a new dimension, and that this was not guaranteed by any acceptance of facts.

I shall argue that this view is mistaken; that the practical implication of the use of moral terms has been put in the wrong place, and that if it is described correctly the logical gap between factual premises and moral conclusion disappears.

In this argument it will be useful to have as a pattern the practical or 'action-guiding' force of the word 'injury', which is in some, though not all, ways similar to that of moral terms. It is clear I think that an injury is necessarily something bad and therefore something which as such anyone always has a reason to avoid, and philosophers will therefore be tempted to say that anyone who uses 'injury' in its full 'action-guiding' sense commits himself to avoiding the things he calls injuries. They will then be in the usual difficulties about the man who says he knows he ought to do something but does not intend to do it; perhaps also about weakness of the will. Suppose that instead we look again at the kinds of things which count as injuries, to see if the connection with the will does not start here. As has been shown, a man is injured whenever some part of his body, in being damaged, has become less well able to fulfil its ordinary function. It follows that he suffers a disability, or is liable to do so; with an injured hand he will be less well able to pick things up, hold on to them, tie them together or chop them up, and so on. With defective eyes there will be a thousand other things he is unable to do, and in both cases we should naturally say that he will often be unable to get what he wants to get or avoid what he wants to avoid.

Philosophers will no doubt seize on the word 'want', and say that if we suppose that a man happens to want the things which an injury to his body prevents him from getting, we have slipped in a supposition about a 'pro-attitude' already; and that anyone who does not happen to have these wants can still refuse to use 'injury' in its prescriptive, or 'action-guiding' sense. And so it may seem that the only way to make a *necessary* connection between 'injury' and the things that are to be avoided, is to say that it is only used in an 'action-guiding sense' when applied to something the speaker intends to avoid. But we should look carefully at the crucial move in that argument, and query the suggestion that someone might happen not to want anything for which he would need the use of hands or eyes. Hands and eyes, like ears and legs, play a part in so many operations that a man could only be said not to need them if he had no wants at all. That such people exist, in asylums, is not to the present purpose at all; the proper use of his limbs is something a man has reason to want if he wants anything.

I do not know just what someone who denies this proposition could have in mind. Perhaps he is thinking of changing the facts of human existence, so that merely wishing, or the sound of the voice, will bring the world to heel? More likely he is proposing to rig the circumstances of some individual's existence within the framework of the ordinary world, by supposing for instance that he is a prince whose servants will sow and reap and fetch and carry for him, and so use their hands and eyes in his service that he will not need the use of his. Let us suppose that such a story could be told about a man's life; it is wildly implausible, but let us pretend that it is not. It is clear that in spite of this we could say that any man had a reason to shun injury; for even if at the end of his life it could be said that by a strange set of circumstances he had never needed the use of his eyes, or his hands, this could not possibly be foreseen. Only by once more changing the facts of human existence, and supposing every vicissitude foreseeable, could such a supposition be made.

This is not to say that an injury might not bring more incidental gain than necessary harm; one has only to think of times when the order has gone out that able-bodied men are to be put to the sword. Such a gain might even, in some peculiar circumstances, be reliably foreseen, so that a man would have even better reason for seeking than for avoiding injury. In this respect the word 'injury' differs from terms such as 'injustice'; the practical force of 'injury' means only that anyone has *a* reason to avoid injuries, not that he has an overriding reason to do so.

It will be noticed that this account of the 'action-guiding' force of 'injury' links it with reasons for acting rather than with actually doing something. I do not think, however, that this makes it a less good pattern for the 'action-guiding' force of moral terms. Philosophers who have supposed that actual action was required if 'good' were to be used in a sincere evaluation have got into difficulties over weakness of will, and they should surely agree that enough has been done if we can show that any man has reason to aim at virtue and avoid vice. But is this impossibly difficult if we consider the kinds of things that count as virtue and vice? Consider, for instance, the cardinal virtues, prudence, temperance, courage and justice. Obviously any man needs prudence, but does he not also need to resist the temptation of pleasure when there is harm involved? And how could it be argued that he would never need to face what was fearful for the sake of some good? It is not obvious what someone would mean if he said that temperance or courage were not good qualities, and this not because of the 'praising' sense of these *words,* but because of the things that courage and temperance are.

I should like to use these examples to show the artificiality of the notions of 'commendation' and of 'pro-attitudes' as these are commonly employed. Philosophers who talk about these things will say that after the facts have been accepted—say that X is the kind of man who will climb a dangerous mountain, beard an irascible employer for a rise in pay, and in general face the fearful for the sake of something he thinks worth while—there remains the question of 'commendation' or 'evaluation'. If the word 'courage' is used they will ask whether or not the man who speaks of another as having courage is supposed to have commended him. If we say 'yes' they will insist that the judgement about courage *goes beyond the facts,* and might therefore be rejected by someone who refused to do so; if we say 'no' they will argue that 'courage' is being used in a purely descriptive or 'inverted commas sense', and that we have not got an example of the evaluative use of language which is the moral philosopher's special study. What sense can be made, however, of the question 'does he commend?' What is this extra element which is supposed to be present or absent after the facts have been settled? It is not a matter of liking the man who has courage, or of thinking him altogether good, but of 'commending him for his courage'. How are we supposed to do that? The answer that will be given is that we only commend someone else in speaking of him as courageous if we accept the imperative 'let me be courageous' for ourselves. But this is quite unnecessary. I can speak of someone else as having the virtue of courage, and of course recognise it as a virtue in the proper sense, while knowing that I am a complete coward, and making no resolution to reform. I know that I should be better off if I were courageous, and so have a reason to cultivate courage, but I may also know that I will do nothing of the kind.

If someone were to say that courage was not a virtue he would have to say that it was not a quality by which a man came to act well. Perhaps he would be thinking that someone might be worse off for his courage, which is true, but only because an incidental harm might arise. For instance, the courageous man might have underestimated a risk, and run into some disaster which a cowardly man would have avoided because he was not prepared to take any risk at all. And his courage, like any other virtue, could be the cause of harm to him because possessing it he fell into some disastrous state of pride.[3] Similarly, those who question the virtue of temperance are probably thinking not of the virtue itself but of men whose temperance has consisted in resisting pleasure for the sake of some illusory good, or those who have made this virtue their pride.

But what, it will be asked, of justice? For while prudence, courage and temperance are qualities which benefit the man who has them, justice seems

[3] Cf. Aquinas, *Summa Theologica,* I–II, q. 55, Art. 4.

rather to benefit others, and to work to the disadvantage of the just man him-self. Justice as it is treated here, as one of the cardinal virtues, covers all those things owed to other people: it is under injustice that murder, theft and lying come, as well as the withholding of what is owed for instance by parents to children and by children to parents, as well as the dealings which would be called unjust in everyday speech. So the man who avoids injustice will find him-self in need of things he has returned to their owner, unable to obtain an ad-vantage by cheating and lying; involved in all those difficulties painted by Thrasymachus in the first book of the Republic, in order to show that injustice is more profitable than justice to a man of strength and wit. We will be asked how, on our theory, justice can be a virtue and injustice a vice, since it will surely be difficult to show that any man whatsoever must need to be just as he needs the use of his hands and eyes, or needs prudence, courage and temper-ance?

Before answering this question I shall argue that if it cannot be answered, then justice can no longer be recommended as a virtue. The point of this is not to show that it must be answerable, since justice is a virtue, but rather to sug-gest that we should at least consider the possibility that justice is not a virtue. This suggestion was taken seriously by Socrates in the Republic, where it was assumed by everyone that if Thrasymachus could establish his premise—that injustice was more profitable than justice—his conclusion would follow: that a man who had the strength to get away with injustice had reason to follow this as the best way of life. It is a striking fact about modern moral philosophy that no one sees any difficulty in accepting Thrasymachus' premise and rejecting his conclusion, and it is because Nietzsche's position is at this point much closer to that of Plato that he is remote from academic moralists of the present day.

In the Republic it is assumed that if justice is not a good to the just man, moralists who recommend it as a virtue are perpetrating a fraud. Agreeing with this, I shall be asked where exactly the fraud comes in; where the untruth that justice is profitable to the individual is supposed to be told? As a preliminary answer we might ask how many people are prepared to say frankly that injus-tice is more profitable than justice? Leaving aside, as elsewhere in this paper, religious beliefs which might complicate the matter, we will suppose that some tough atheistical character has asked 'Why should I be just?' (Those who be-lieve that this question has something wrong with it can employ their favourite device for sieving out 'evaluating meaning', and suppose that the question is 'Why should I be "just"?') Are we prepared to reply 'As far as you are con-cerned you will be better off if you are unjust, but it matters to the rest of us that you should be just, so we are trying to get you to be just'? He would be likely to enquire into our methods, and then take care not to be found out, and I do not think that many of those who think that it is not necessary to show that justice is profitable to the just man would easily accept that there was nothing more they could say.

The crucial question is: 'Can we give anyone, strong or weak, a reason why he should be just?'—and it is no help at all to say that since 'just' and 'unjust' are 'action-guiding words' no one can even ask 'Why should I be just?' Confronted with that argument the man who wants to do unjust things has only to be careful to avoid the *word*, and he has not been given a reason why he should not do the things which other people call 'unjust'. Probably it will be argued that he has been given a reason so far as anyone can ever be given a reason for doing or not doing anything, for the chain of reasons must always come to an end somewhere, and it may seem that one man may always reject the reason which another man accepts. But this is a mistake; some answers to the question 'why should I?' bring the series to a close and some do not. Hume showed how *one* answer closed the series in the following passage:

'Ask a man *why he uses exercise;* he will answer, *because he desires to keep his health.* If you then enquire, *why he desires health,* he will readily reply, *because sickness is painful.* If you push your enquiries further, and desire a reason *why he hates pain,* it is impossible he can ever give any. This is an ultimate end, and is never referred to any other object.' (*Enquiries,* appendix I, para. v.) Hume might just as well have ended this series with boredom: sickness often brings boredom, and no one is required to give a reason why he does not want to be bored, any more than he has to give a reason why he does want to pursue what interests him. In general, anyone is given a reason for acting when he is shown the way to something he wants; but for some wants the question 'Why do you want that?' will make sense, and for others it will not.[4] It seems clear that in this division justice falls on the opposite side from pleasure and interest and such things. 'Why shouldn't I do that?' is not answered by the words 'because it is unjust' as it is answered by showing that the action will bring boredom, loneliness, pain, discomfort or certain kinds of incapacity, and this is why it is not true to say that 'it's unjust' gives a reason in so far as any reasons can ever be given. 'It's unjust' gives a reason only if the nature of justice can be shown to be such that it is necessarily connected with what a man wants.

This shows why a great deal hangs on the question of whether justice is or is not a good to the just man, and why those who accept Thrasymachus' premise and reject his conclusion are in a dubious position. They recommend justice to each man, as something he has a reason to follow, but when challenged to show why he should do so they will not always be able to reply. This last assertion does not depend on any 'selfish theory of human nature' in the philosophical sense. It is often possible to give a man a reason for acting by showing him that someone else will suffer if he does not; someone else's good may really be more to him than his own. But the affection which mothers feel for children, and lovers for each other, and friends for friends, will not take us far when we are asked for reasons why a man should be just; partly because it will not extend far enough, and partly because the actions dictated by benevolence and justice are not always the same. Suppose that I owe someone money; '. . . what if he be my enemy, and has given me just cause to hate him? What if he be a vicious man, and deserves the hatred of all mankind? What if he be a miser, and can

[4] For an excellent discussion of reasons for action, see G. E. M. Anscombe, *Intention* (Oxford 1957) sections 34–40.

make no use of what I would deprive him of? What if he be a profligate de-bauchee, and would rather receive harm than benefit from large possessions?' [5] Even if the general practice of justice could be brought under the motive of universal benevolence—the desire for the greatest happiness of the greatest num-ber—many people certainly do not have any such desire. So that if injustice is only to be recommended on these grounds a thousand tough characters will be able to say that they have been given no reason for practising justice, and many more would say the same if they were not too timid or too stupid to ask ques-tions about the code of behaviour which they have been taught. Thus, given Thrasymachus' premise Thrasymachus' point of view is reasonable; we have no particular reason to admire those who practise justice through timidity or stu-pidity.

It seems to me, therefore, that if Thrasymachus' thesis is accepted things cannot go on as before; we shall have to admit that the belief on which the status of justice as a virtue was founded is mistaken, and if we still want to get people to be just we must recommend justice to them in a new way. We shall have to admit that injustice is more profitable than justice, at least for the strong, and then do our best to see that hardly anyone can get away with being unjust. We have, of course, the alternative of keeping quiet, hoping that for the most part people will follow convention into a kind of justice, and not ask awkward questions, but this policy might be overtaken by a vague scepticism even on the part of those who do not know just what is lacking; we should also be at the mercy of anyone who was able and willing to expose our fraud.

Is it true, however, to say that justice is not something a man needs in his dealings with his fellows, supposing only that he be strong? Those who think that he can get on perfectly well without being just should be asked to say ex-actly how such a man is supposed to live. We know that he is to practise injus-tice whenever the unjust act would bring him advantage; but what is he to say? Does he admit that he does not recognise the rights of other people, or does he pretend? In the first case even those who combine with him will know that on a change of fortune, or a shift of affection, he may turn to plunder them, and he must be as wary of their treachery as they are of his. Presumably the happy unjust man is supposed, as in Book II of the *Republic*, to be a very cunning liar and actor, combining complete injustice with the appearance of justice: he is prepared to treat others ruthlessly, but pretends that nothing is further from his mind. Philosophers often speak as if a man could thus hide himself even from those around him, but the supposition is doubtful, and in any case the price in vigilance would be colossal. If he lets even a few people see his true attitude he must guard himself against them; if he lets no one into the secret he must al-ways be careful in case the least spontaneity betray him. Such facts are impor-tant because the need a man has for justice in dealings with other men depends on the fact that they are men and not inanimate objects or animals. If a man only needed other men as he needs household objects, and if men could be

[5] Hume, *Treatise*, III. ii. I.

manipulated like household objects, or beaten into a reliable submission like donkeys, the case would be different. As things are, the supposition that injustice is more profitable than justice is very dubious, although like cowardice and intemperance it might turn out incidentally to be profitable.

The reason why it seems to some people so impossibly difficult to show that justice is more profitable than injustice is that they consider in isolation particular just acts. It is perfectly true that if a man is just it follows that he will be prepared, in the event of very evil circumstances, even to face death rather than to act unjustly—for instance, in getting an innocent man convicted of a crime of which he has been accused. For him it turns out that his justice brings disaster on him, and yet like anyone else he had good reason to be a just and not an unjust man. He could not have it both ways and while possessing the virtue of justice hold himself ready to be unjust should any great advantage accrue. The man who has the virtue of justice is not ready to do certain things, and if he is too easily tempted we shall say that he was ready after all.

D. Z. PHILLIPS AND H. O. MOUNCE
On Morality's Having a Point

• • • •

I

It has come to be thought important once again in ethics to ask for the point of morality. Why does it matter whether one does one thing rather than another? Surely, it is argued, if one wants to show someone why it is his duty to do something, one must be prepared to point out the importance of the proposed action, the harm involved in failing to do it, and the advantage involved in performing it. Such considerations simply cannot be put aside. On the contrary, the point of moral conduct must be elucidated in terms of the reasons for performing it. Such reasons separate moral arguments from persuasion and coercion, and moral judgements from likes and dislikes; they indicate what constitutes human good and harm.

If we take note of the role of reasons in morality, we shall see that not anything can count as a moral belief. After all, why does one regard some rules as

From D. Z. Phillips and H. O. Mounce, "On Morality's Having a Point," *Philosophy*, XL, No. 154 (1965), 308–319. Reprinted by permission of the authors and the editor of *Philosophy*.

moral principles, and yet never regard others as such? Certainly, we *can* see the point of some rules as moral principles, but in the case of other rules we cannot. How is the point seen? There is much in the suggestion that it is to be appreciated in terms of the backgrounds which attend moral beliefs and principles. When rules which claim to be moral rules are devoid of these backgrounds we are puzzled. We do not know what is being said when someone claims that the given rule is a moral rule.

Normally, we do not speak of these backgrounds when we express and discuss moral opinions. It is only when we are asked to imagine their absence that we see how central they must be in any account we try to give of morality. Consider the rules, 'Never walk on the lines of a pavement', and 'Clap your hands every two hours'. If we saw people letting such rules govern their lives in certain ways, taking great care to observe them, feeling upset whenever they or other people infringe the rules, and so on, we should be hard put to understand what they were doing. We fail to see any point in it. On the other hand, if backgrounds are supplied for such rules, if further descriptions of the context in which they operate are given, sometimes, they can begin to look like moral principles. Given the background of a religious community, one can begin to see how the rule, 'Never walk on the lines of a pavement', could have moral significance. Think of, 'Take off thy shoes for thou art on holy ground', and its connections with the notions of reverence and disrespect. It is more difficult, though we do not say it is impossible, to think of a context in which the rule, 'Clap your hands every two hours', could have moral significance. Our first example shows how we can be brought to some understanding of a moral view when it is brought under a concept with which we are familiar. By linking disapproval of walking on the lines of a pavement with lack of reverence and disrespect, even those not familiar with the religious tradition in question may see that a *moral* view is being expressed. Such concepts as sincerity, honesty, courage, loyalty, respect, and, of course, a host of others, provide the kind of background necessary in order to make sense of rules as moral principles. It does not follow that all the possible features of such backgrounds need be present in every case. The important point to stress is that unless the given rule has *some* relation to such backgrounds, we would not know what is meant by calling it a moral principle.

The above conclusion follows from a more extensive one, namely, that commendation is internally related to its object. Mrs Foot, for example, suggests that there is an analogy between commendation on the one hand, and mental attitudes such as pride and beliefs such as 'This is dangerous' on the other. One cannot feel proud of *anything*, any more than one can say that *anything* is dangerous. Similarly in the case of commendation: how can one say that clapping one's hands every two hours is a good action? The answer is that one cannot, unless the context in which the action is performed, for example, recovery from paralysis, makes its point apparent.

Certainly, those who have insisted on the necessity of a certain conceptual background in order to make sense of moral beliefs and moral judgements have done philosophy a service. They have revealed the artificiality of locating what is characteristically moral in a mental attitude such as a pro-attitude, or in a mental activity such as commending. They have shown the impossibility of making sense of something called 'evaluative meaning' which is thought of as being externally or contingently related to its objects. One could have a pro-attitude towards clapping one's hands every two hours, and one could commend one's never walking on the lines of a pavement, but neither pro-attitude nor commendation would, in themselves, give a point to such activities.

If the point of virtues is not to be expressed in terms of pro-attitudes or commendations, how is it to be brought out? It has been suggested that this could be done by showing the connection between virtues and human good and harm. But this is where the trouble starts, for if we are not careful, we may, in our eagerness to exorcise the spirit of evaluative meaning, fall under the spell of the concept of human good and harm, which is an equally dangerous idea. Unfortunately, this has already happened, and much of the current talk about human good and harm is as artificial as the talk about 'attitudes' in moral philosophy which it set out to criticise.

The point of calling an action (morally) good, it is suggested, is that it leads to human good and avoids harm. Further, what is to count as human good and harm is said to be a *factual* matter. Thus, one must try to show that there is a logical connection between statements of fact and statements of value, and that the logical gap supposed to exist between them can be closed. Men cannot pick and choose which facts are relevant to a moral conclusion, any more than they can pick and choose which facts are relevant in determining a physical ailment. Admittedly, the notion of a fact is a complex one, but this makes it all the more important to exercise care in the use of it. Let us try to appreciate this complexity in terms of an example.

Someone might think that pushing someone roughly is rude, and that anyone who denies this is simply refusing to face the facts. But this example, as it stands, is worthless, since it tells one nothing of the context in which the pushing took place. The reference to the context is all important in giving an account of the action, since not any kind of pushing can count as rudeness. Consider the following examples:

(a) One man pushing another person violently in order to save his life.

(b) A doctor pushing his way through a football-match crowd in response to an urgent appeal.

(c) The general pushing which takes place in a game of rugby.

(d) A violent push as a customary form of greeting between close friends.

In all these cases, pushing someone else is not rude. If someone took offence at being pushed, he might well see in the light of the situation that no offence had been caused. But what of situations where there is general agreement that an offence *has* been caused? Is the offence a fact from which a moral conclusion can be deduced? Clearly not, since what this suggestion ignores is the fact that *standards already prevail* in the context in which the offence is recognised. If one wants to call the offence a fact, one must recognise that it is a fact which already has moral import. The notion of 'offence' is parasitic on the notion of a

standard or norm, although these need not be formulated. The person who wishes
to say that the offence is a 'pure fact' from which a moral conclusion can be deduced is simply confused. What are the 'pure facts' relating to the pushing and
the injury it is supposed to cause? A physiological account of the pushing (which
might be regarded as pure enough) would not enable one to say what was going
on, any more than a physiological account of the injury would tell us anything
about what moral action (if any) is called for as a result. It makes all the difference morally whether the grazed ankle is caused by barging in the line-out
or by barging in the bus queue. Any attempt to characterise the fact that an
offence has been caused as a non-evaluative fact from which a moral conclusion
can be deduced begs the question, since in asserting that a *kind of offence* has
been caused, a specific background and the standards inherent in it have already
been invoked.

But our opponent is still not beaten. He might give way on the confusion
involved in the talk about deducing moral conclusions from 'pure facts', and
agree that 'pushing' does not constitute rudeness in all contexts. Nevertheless,
he might argue, where the circumstances *are* appropriate, it is possible to determine the rudeness of an action in a way which will settle any disagreement.
But, again, this is clearly not the case. Whenever anyone says, 'That action is
rude', there is no logical contradiction involved in denying the assertion, since
although two people may share a moral concept such as rudeness, they may still
differ strongly in its application. This is possible because views about rudeness
do not exist *in vacuo,* but are often influenced by *other* moral beliefs. A good
example of disagreement over the application of the concept of rudeness can be
found in Malcolm's Memoir of Wittgenstein. Wittgenstein had lost his temper
in a philosophical discussion with Moore, and would not allow Moore sufficient
time to make his point. Moore thought that Wittgenstein's behaviour was rude,
holding that good manners should always prevail, even in philosophical discussion. Wittgenstein, on the other hand, thought Moore's view of the matter
absurd: philosophy is a serious business, important enough to justify a loss of
temper; to think this rudeness is simply to misapply the judgement. Here, one
can see how standards of rudeness have been influenced by wider beliefs; in
other words, how the judgement, 'That is rude', is not entailed by the facts.

The position we have arrived at does not satisfy a great many contemporary
moral philosophers. They are not prepared to recognise the possibility of permanent radical moral disagreement. They want to press on towards ultimate
agreement, moral finality, call it what you will. They propose to do this by considering certain non-moral concepts of goodness in the belief that they will throw
light on the notion of human good and harm. The non-moral example, 'good
knife', has been popular in this respect. The word 'knife' names an object in
respect of its function. Furthermore, the function is involved in the meaning
of the word, so that if we came across a people who possessed objects which
looked exactly like knives, but who never used these objects as we use them,
we should refuse to say that they had the concept of a knife. Now when a thing
has a function, the main criterion for its goodness will be that it serves that

function well. Clearly, then, not anything can count as a good knife. But how does this help our understanding of moral goodness? Moral concepts are not functional. One can see what is to count as a good knife by asking what a knife is *for*, but can one see the point of generosity in the same way? To ask what generosity is *for* is simply to vulgarise the concept; it is like thinking that 'It is more blessed to give than to receive' is some kind of policy!

Yet, although moral concepts are not functional words, they are supposed to resemble them in important respects. The interesting thing, apparently, about many non-functional words, is that when they are linked with 'good' they yield criteria of goodness in much the same way as 'good knife' and other functional words do. For example, it seems as if 'good farmer' might yield criteria of goodness in this way. After all, farming is an activity which has a certain point. To call someone a good farmer will be to indicate that he has fulfilled the point of that activity. What 'the point' amounts to can be spelled out in terms of healthy crops and herds, and a good yield from the soil. The philosophical importance of these examples is that they show that the range of words whose meaning provides criteria of goodness extends beyond that of functional words. But what if the range is even wider than these examples suggest? It is clear what the philosophers who ask this question have in mind: what if the meaning of moral concepts could yield criteria of goodness in the same way? If this were possible, one need not rest content with expounding 'good knife' or 'good farmer'; 'good man' awaits elucidation. The goal is to find out what constitutes human flourishing. Furthermore, once these greater aims are achieved, all moral disputes would be, in principle at least, resolvable. Anyone claiming to have a good moral argument would have to justify it by showing its point in terms of human good and harm. And, once again, not anything could count as human good and harm.

The programme is nothing if not ambitious. Unfortunately, it will not work. The reason why is no minor defect: the whole enterprise is misconceived almost from the start. As far as land farming is concerned, the confusion could have been avoided had one asked why 'farming' yields criteria when joined with 'good'. To say that this type of farming is an activity which has a point, that farming serves some end, and that to call someone a good farmer is to say that he achieves this end, is only to tell part of the story. The most important part is left out, namely, *that the end in question is not in dispute.* That is why it makes sense to talk of experts in farming, and why problems in farming can be solved by technical or scientific means. For example, farmers might disagree over which is the best method of growing good wheat, but there is no disagreement over what is to count as good wheat. On the other hand, the situation is different where animal farming is concerned. Suppose it were established that the milk yield was not affected by keeping the cattle indoors in confined quarters, and by cutting their food supply.[1] Many people would say that no good farmer would be prepared to do this, despite the economic factors involved. Others may disagree and see nothing wrong in treating animals in this way. The point to note

[1] We owe this example to Dr. H. S. Price.

is that here one has a *moral* dispute. We recognise it as such because of the issues of cruelty, care, and expediency involved in it. The dispute cannot be settled by reference to the point of farming in this instance, since it is agreed that whichever side one takes, the milk yield remains the same. One must recognise that there are different conceptions of what constitutes good farming. Similarly, we shall find that there is no common agreement on what constitutes human good and harm. We shall argue presently that human good is not independent of the moral beliefs people hold, but is determined by them. In short, what must be recognised is that there are different conceptions of human good and harm.

II

The above argument would not satisfy the philosophers we have in mind. For them, moral views are founded on facts, the facts concerning human good and harm. We shall argue, on the other hand, that moral viewpoints determine what is and what is not to count as a relevant fact in reaching a moral decision. This philosophical disagreement has important consequences, for if we believe that moral values can be justified by appeal to *the* facts, it is hard to see how one man can reject another man's reasons for his moral beliefs, since these reasons too, presumably, refer to the facts. If, on the other hand, we hold that the notion of factual relevance is parasitic on moral beliefs, it is clear that deadlock in ethics will be a common occurrence, simply because of what some philosophers have unwisely regarded as contingent reasons, namely, the different moral views people hold.

Many philosophers are not convinced that there need be a breakdown in moral argument. It is tempting to think that anyone who has heard *all* the arguments in favour of a moral opinion cannot still ask why he ought to endorse it, any more than anyone who has heard all there is to say about the earth's shape can still ask why he ought to believe that the earth is round. Anyone who has heard *all* the reasons for a moral opinion has, it seems, heard all the facts. Sometimes the facts are difficult to discern, but there is in principle no reason why moral disagreement should persist. Therefore, it is difficult to see how 'x is good' can be a well-founded moral argument when 'x is bad' is said to be equally well founded. So runs the argument.

Certainly, it is difficult for philosophers who argue in this way to account for moral disagreement, since for them, moral judgements are founded on the facts of human good and harm, and the facts are incontrovertible. It is not surprising to find Bentham being praised in this context, since he too alleged that there is a common coinage into which 'rival' moral views could be cashed. The rivalry is only apparent, since the felicific calculus soon discovers the faulty reasoning. On this view, moral opinions are hypotheses whose validity is tested by reference to some common factor which is the sole reason for holding them. Bentham said the common factor was pleasure; nowadays it is called human good and harm. Whether one's moral views are 'valid' depends on whether they lead to human good and harm. But how does one arrive at these facts? One is said to do so by asking the question, 'What is the point?' often enough.

Philosophers are led to argue in this way by misconstruing the implications of the truth that a certain conceptual background is necessary in order for beliefs to have moral significance. Instead of being content to locate the point of such beliefs in their moral goodness, they insist on asking further what the point of *that* is. If one does not give up questioning too soon, one will arrive at the incontrovertible facts of human good and harm which do not invite any further requests for justification. Injury seems to be thought of as one such final halting place. To ask what is the point of calling injury a bad thing is to show that one has not grasped the concept of injury. To say that an action leads to injury is to give *a* reason for avoiding it. Injury may not be an overriding reason for avoiding the action which leads to it, as injustice is, but its being *a* reason is justified because injury is necessarily a bad thing. Even if we grant the distinction between reasons and overriding reasons, which is difficult enough if one asks who is to say which are which, is it clear that injury is always a reason for avoiding the action which leads to it?

The badness of injury, it is argued, is made explicit if one considers what an injury to hands, eyes, or ears, prevents a man from doing and getting; the badness is founded on what all men want. Mrs Foot, for example, expounds the argument as follows,

. . . the proper use of his limbs is something a man has reason to want if he wants anything.

I do not know just what someone who denies this proposition could have in mind. Perhaps he is thinking of changing the facts of human existence, so that merely wishing, or the sound of the voice, will bring the world to heel? More likely he is proposing to rig the circumstances of some individual's existence within the framework of the ordinary world, by supposing for instance that he is a prince whose servants will sow and reap and fetch and carry for him, and so use their hands and eyes in his service that he will not need the use of his.[2]

But, Mrs Foot argues, not even this supposition will do, since the prince cannot foresee that his circumstances will not change. He still has good reason to avoid injury to his hands and eyes, since he may need them some day. But there was no need to have thought up such an extravagant example to find objections to the view that injury is necessarily bad. There are more familiar ones close at hand which are far more difficult to deal with than the case of the fortunate prince. For example, consider the following advice,

And if thine eye offend thee, pluck it out, and cast it from thee: it is better to enter into life with one eye, rather than having two eyes to be cast into hell fire. (Matt. xviii. 9.)

[2] Above, p. 420.

Or again, consider how Saint Paul does not think 'the thorn in the flesh' from which he suffered to be a bad thing. At first, he does so regard it, and prays that it be taken away. Later, however, he thanks God for his disability, since it was a constant reminder to him that he was not sufficient unto himself. Another example is worth quoting.[3] Brentano was blind at the end of his life. When friends commiserated with him over the harm that had befallen him, he denied that his loss of sight was a bad thing. He explained that one of his weaknesses had been a tendency to cultivate and concentrate on too many diverse interests. Now, in his blindness, he was able to concentrate on his philosophy in a way which had been impossible for him before. We may not want to argue like Saint Paul or Brentano, but is it true that we have no idea what they have in mind?

A readiness to admit that injury might result in incidental gain will not do as an answer to the above argument. True, there would be a gain in being injured if an order went out to put all able-bodied men to the sword, but are we to regard the examples of Saint Paul and Brentano as being in this category? In some peculiar circumstances where this gain could be foreseen, we might even imagine a person seeking injury rather than trying to avoid it. But is this the way we should account for saints who prayed to be partakers in the sufferings of Christ? Obviously not. It is clear that Paul himself does not regard his ailment as something which happens to be useful in certain circumstances. But in any case, why speak of *incidental* gain in any of these contexts, and why speak of the contexts themselves as *peculiar*? In doing so, is not the thesis that injury is necessarily bad being defended by calling any examples which count against it incidental or peculiar? In so far as moral philosophers argue in this way, they lay themselves open to the serious charge which Sorel has made against them:

The philosophers always have a certain amount of difficulty in seeing clearly into these ethical problems, because they feel the impossibility of harmonising the ideas which are current at a given time in a class, and yet imagine it to be their duty to reduce everything to a unity. To conceal from themselves the fundamental heterogeneity of all this civilised morality, they have recourse to a great number of subterfuges, sometimes relegating to the rank of exceptions, importations, or survivals, everything which embarrasses them. . . .[4]

Is it not the case that we cannot understand Brentano's attitude to his blindness unless we understand the kind of dedication to intellectual enquiry of which he was an example, and the virtues which such dedication demands in the enquirer? Again, we cannot understand Saint Paul's attitude to his ailment unless we understand something of the Hebrew-Christian conception of man's relationship to God, and the notions of insufficiency, dependence, and divine succour, involved in it. These views of personal injury or physical harm

[3] We owe it to Mr Rush Rhees.
[4] Georges Sorel, *Reflections on Violence*, trans. T. E. Hulme (Collier-Macmillan, 1961) pp. 229–30.

cannot be cast in terms of what all men want. On the contrary, it is the specific contexts concerned, namely, dedication to enquiry and dedication to God, which determine what is to constitute goodness and badness. We can deny this only by elevating one concept of harm as being paradigmatic in much the same way as Bentham elevated one of the internal sentiments. We can say that injury is necessarily bad at the price of favouring one idea of badness.

In so far as philosophers construct a paradigm in their search for 'the unity of the facts of human good and harm', they are not far removed from the so-called scientific rationalists and their talk of proper functions, primary purpose, etc. One of these, in an argument with a Roman Catholic housewife over birth control, stressed the harm which could result from having too many children. He obviously thought that the reference to physical harm clinched the matter. The housewife, on the other hand, stressed the honour a mother has in bringing children into the world. It seems more likely that the scientific rationalist was blind to what the housewife meant by honour, than that she was blind to what he meant by harm. Are we for that reason to call the honour incidental gain?

How would the scientific rationalist and the housewife reach the agreement which some philosophers seem to think inevitable if all the facts were known? It is hard to see how they could without renouncing what they believe in. Certainly, one cannot regard their respective moral opinions as hypotheses which the facts will either confirm or refute, for what would the evidence be? For the rationalist, the possibility of the mother's death or injury, the economic situation of the family, the provision of good facilities for the children, and so on, would be extremely important. The housewife too agrees about providing the good things of life for children, but believes that one ought to begin by allowing them to enter the world. For her, submission to the will of God, the honour of motherhood, the creation of a new life, and so on, are of the greatest importance. But there is no settling of the issue in terms of some supposed common evidence called human good and harm, since what they differ over is precisely the question of what constitutes human good and harm. The same is true of all fundamental moral disagreements, for example, the disagreement between a pacifist and a militarist. The argument is unlikely to proceed very far before deadlock is reached.

Deadlock in ethics, despite philosophical misgivings which have been voiced, does not entail liberty to argue as one chooses. The rationalist, the housewife, the pacifist, or the militarist, cannot say what they like. Their arguments are rooted in different moral traditions within which there are rules for what can and what cannot be said. Because philosophers believe that moral opinions rest on common evidence, they are forced to locate the cause of moral disagreement in the evidence's complexity: often, experience and imagination are necessary in assessing it. One can imagine someone versed in the views we have been attacking, and sympathetic with them, saying to an opponent in a moral argument, 'If only you could see how wrong you are. If only you had the experience and the imagination to appreciate the evidence for the goodness of the view I am advocating, evidence, which, unfortunately, is too complex for you to master, you would see that what I want is good for you too, since really, all men want it'. Such appeals to 'the common good' or to 'what all men want' are based on conscious or unconscious deception. It may be admitted that the majority of mothers nowadays want to plan the birth of their children, to fit in with the Budget if possible, and regard the rearing of their children as a pause in their careers. But this will not make the slightest difference to the housewife of our previous example. She believes that what the majority wants is a sign of moral decadence, and wants different things. But she does not believe because she wants; she wants because she believes.

The view that there are ways of demonstrating goodness by appeal to evidence which operate *independently* of the various moral opinions people hold is radically mistaken. Sometimes, philosophers seem to suggest that despite the moral differences which separate men, they are really pursuing the same end, namely, what all men want. The notion of what all men want is as artificial as the common evidence which is supposed to support it. There are no theories of goodness.

Supplementary Paperback Reading

Two excellent paperback books concerned with the problem of values and facts are:

W. D. Hudson, *The Is/Ought Question*. (St. Martin's Press)

G. J. Warnock, *Contemporary Moral Philosophy*. (St. Martin's Press)

The following list includes articles and books in paperback dealing with various aspects of the problem:

G. E. M. Anscombe, "On Brute Facts," in J. J. Thomson and G. Dworkin, *Ethics*. (Harper and Row)

G. E. M. Anscombe, "Modern Moral Philosophy," in J. J. Thomson and G. Dworkin, *Ethics*. (Harper and Row)

A. J. Ayer, *Language, Truth and Logic*, Ch. VI. (Dover Publications)

A. J. Ayer, "On the Analysis of Moral Judgements." (Bobbs-Merrill Reprint Series in Philosophy)

J. Dewey, *Theory of Valuation*. (University of Chicago Press)

P. Edwards, *The Logic of Moral Discourse*. (Free Press)

A. C. Ewing, *Ethics*, Ch. VI and VII. (Free Press)

W. D. Falk, "Goading and Guiding," in R. Ekman, *Readings in the Problems of Ethics*. (Scribner's)

P. Foot, "Goodness and Choice." (Bobbs-Merrill Reprint Series in Philosophy) Also in W. D. Hudson, *The Is/Ought Question.* (St. Martin's Press)

P. Foot, "Moral Arguments," in J. Margolis, *Contemporary Ethical Theory* (Random House) and in J. J. Thomson and G. Dworkin, *Ethics.* (Harper and Row)

N. Fotion, *Moral Situations.* (Antioch Press)

W. K. Frankena, "The Naturalistic Fallacy," in P. Foot, *Theories of Ethics* (Oxford University Press) and in J. Margolis, *Contemporary Ethical Theory.* (Random House)

P. T. Geach, "Good and Evil," in P. Foot, *Theories of Ethics* (Oxford University Press) and in Bobbs-Merrill Reprint Series in Philosophy.

S. Hampshire, "Fallacies in Moral Philosophy," in J. Margolis, *Contemporary Ethical Theory.* (Random House)

R. M. Hare, *The Language of Morals.* (Oxford University Press)

R. M. Hare, *Freedom and Reason.* (Oxford University Press)

R. M. Hare, "The Promising Game," in P. Foot, *Theories of Ethics* (Oxford University Press) and in W. D. Hudson, *The Is/Ought Question.* (St. Martin's Press)

R. M. Hare, "Geach: Good and Evil," in P. Foot, *Theories of Ethics* (Oxford University Press) and in Bobbs-Merrill Reprint Series in Philosophy.

W. D. Hudson, *Ethical Intuitionism.* (St. Martin's Press)

C. I. Lewis, *An Analysis of Knowledge and Valuation.* (Open Court)

G. E. Moore, *Principia Ethica,* Preface and Ch. I and II. (Cambridge University Press)

G. E. Moore, "A Reply to My Critics," in P. Foot, *Theories of Ethics.* (Oxford University Press)

G. Nakhnikian, "On the Naturalistic Fallacy," in H. N. Castaneda and G. Nakhnikian, *Morality and the Language of Conduct.* (Wayne State University Press)

P. H. Nowell-Smith, *Ethics,* Ch. 1–8, 11–16. (Penguin Books)

A. N. Prior, "The Naturalistic Fallacy: The Logic of Its Refutation," in R. Ekman, *Readings in the Problems of Ethics.* (Scribner's)

J. Rawls, "Outline of a Decision Procedure for Ethics," in J. J. Thomson and G. Dworkin, *Ethics.* (Harper and Row)

N. Rescher, *Introduction to Value Theory.* (Prentice-Hall)

J. R. Searle, "How to Derive 'Ought' from 'Is'," in P. Foot, *Theories of Ethics* (Oxford University Press) and in W. D. Hudson, *The Is/Ought Question* (St. Martin's Press). Also in Bobbs-Merrill Reprint Series in Philosophy.

A. Sesonske, *Value and Obligation.* (Oxford University Press)

C. L. Stevenson, *Ethics and Language.* (Yale University Press)

C. L. Stevenson, *Facts and Values.* (Yale University Press)

C. L. Stevenson, "Moore's Arguments Against Certain Forms of Naturalism," in P. Foot, *Theories of Ethics.* (Oxford University Press)

J. O. Urmson, *The Emotive Theory of Ethics.* (Oxford University Press)

C. Wellman, "Ethical Naturalism," in R. Ekman, *Readings in the Problems of Ethics.* (Scribner's)

8

INTRINSIC

VALUE

Introduction

One of the central issues in ethics, as we have seen in Chapters 4 and 5, is whether an act is right because of its consequences or because of the kind of act that it is. Act-utilitarians maintain the first position, deontologists the second. When, according to the first position, an act is judged by its utility, there is always presupposed some standard by which its consequences are evaluated as good or bad. A right act is an act that has good consequences, or better consequences than any alternative act would have. Here the moral value of the act is *extrinsic,* since it depends on the value of something else, namely, the act's consequences. The value of some of these consequences may also be extrinsic, since they may in turn be judged on the basis of still further consequences. Finally, however, the act-utilitarian must arrive at consequences that are judged, not on the basis of their further consequences, but on the basis of their intrinsic nature. In other words, the extrinsic value of an act *ultimately* depends on the *intrinsic* value of its effects.

For the deontologist, on the other hand, the moral value of an act (or of a kind of act) is intrinsic. We can know whether an act is right without considering what its consequences will be. So here again a judgment of intrinsic value must be made.

Finally, the position known as rule-utilitarianism also presupposes some standard of intrinsic value. According to this position, the moral value of an act depends on its conformity to a valid moral rule, and a moral rule is valid if it has utility, that is, if its being followed leads to intrinsically good consequences.

We are thus confronted with the problem What is intrinsic value and how can it be known? In order to deal with this problem in the clearest way possible, we shall understand the term "intrinsic value" within the framework of a certain kind of value judgment. Thus we shall distinguish judgments of intrinsic value (that is, a judgment that something is intrinsically good or intrinsically bad) from judgments of extrinsic value (that something is extrinsically good or extrinsically bad). In the light of our discussion of value judgments in Chapter 7, we can then clarify our problem in the following way. Instead of asking, "What is intrinsic value?" we inquire, "When someone judges an object to be intrinsically good or bad, what *standards of evaluation* does he refer to, and what *good-making or bad-making characteristics* would he cite in support of his judgment?" And instead of asking, "How can intrinsic value be known?" we inquire, "By what method can judgments of intrinsic value be justified?" or

"What reasons are good reasons for claiming that something is intrinsically good or bad?"

TYPES OF VALUE JUDGMENTS

Let us begin with a classification of different types of value judgments. For convenience we shall use R. M. Hare's analysis of a value judgment as presented in the preceding chapter. Accordingly, we shall assume that all value judgments, no matter of what type, have the following four elements in common: (i) a *value-predicate* or word whose function is to commend or condemn the object being evaluated; (ii) a *standard of evaluation* which sets the conditions that must be fulfilled for the object to be judged as good (or the conditions that an object fails to fulfill when it is judged as bad); (iii) the *good-making or bad-making characteristics,* which are the empirical properties of the object in virtue of which it fulfills or fails to fulfill the given standard and so is evaluated positively or negatively; and (iv) a *class of comparison,* or the class of objects within which the given object is placed in an order of merit and which delimits the appropriate range for applying the standard.

We now proceed to our classification of different types of value judgments. (A similar classification is set forth by Professor C. A. Baylis in the third reading of this chapter.) Value judgments are divided into two basic types, the first of which is subdivided into three categories, as follows:

(A) Judgments of extrinsic value.
    (1) Judgments of instrumental value.
    (2) Judgments of contributive value.
    (3) Judgments of inherent value.
(B) Judgments of intrinsic value.

We shall examine what differentiates each group, beginning with the three subdivisions of judgments of extrinsic value.

(1) *Judgments of instrumental value.* When an object or act is judged to be good because it brings about, or helps to bring about, some future state of affairs which is itself judged to have instrumental, contributive, inherent, or intrinsic value, then the object or act is said to have instrumental value. As we shall see, the same object or act that has instrumental value may also have contributive and inherent value. An example of an object having *only* instrumental value would be a house key. This is judged to be a good thing just because it is a useful instrument in bringing about some end or purpose we consider to be good. A judgment of instrumental disvalue (that something is instrumentally bad, harmful, dangerous, etc.) occurs when the act or object is thought to bring about, or to tend to bring about, a state of affairs judged to be instrumentally, contributively, inherently, or intrinsically bad. If an object or act had some consequences that were judged to be good and some that were judged to be bad, then it would have both instrumental value and instrumental disvalue. It would

be instrumentally good in some respects and instrumentally bad in others. An example would be the act of buying a dog as a pet. This may bring about much pleasure to the owner but may also at times involve trouble and inconvenience for him.

(2) *Judgments of contributive value.* Sometimes an object which is part of a larger spatial whole or an event which is part of a longer temporal process will be judged to be good in so far as its presence in the whole contributes to the value of the whole. Thus the sparkplugs in the motor of a car have contributive value because their functioning is necessary to the functioning of the whole motor. By themselves, they have no value. Sometimes, however, a part of a whole may not only have contributive value (in so far as its presence contributes to the value of the whole) but, in addition, some other kind of value. For example, the solo portion of a piano concerto will of course contribute to the aesthetic value of the entire piece. But that portion may have value (that is, may be judged to be good) even when played by itself. This additional value would be inherent, not contributive. It should be added that an object or event has contributive disvalue when it tends to lessen or destroy the value of the whole of which it is a part.

The main difference between instrumental and contributive value may be stated thus. If X and Y are related as earlier cause to later effect, and if Y is judged to be good, then X has instrumental value when its good-making characteristics are those in virtue of which it is a cause of Y. If X and Y are related, spatially or temporally, as part to whole, and if Y is judged to be good, then X has contributive value when the value of Y is increased or maintained by the fact that X has the good-making characteristics it has. It is important to note that, for both types of value judgment, if there were no Y related to X in the ways indicated, or if, though there was such a Y it was judged to have no value, then X would have no value. Consequently, we say that in these cases the value of X is *derivative* from the value of something else.

(3) *Judgments of inherent value.* An object or event in public space-time has inherent value if and only if it is experienced by people in such a way that, however different may be their manner of experiencing it, their experiences of it have intrinsic value to them. When several people experience an object or event in a given set of circumstances, one person's experience may be intrinsically good and another's may be intrinsically bad, due to differences in their taste, attitudes, personalities, etc. When this occurs the object or event is both inherently good and inherently bad. Let us take an example. A man who loves the music of Handel goes to a performance of *The Messiah* and enjoys it thoroughly. His experience of the music (the actual sounds as he hears them) is of intrinsic value to him. Another person who attends the same concert is irritated and bored by the music (as *he* hears it). His experience of it is intrinsically bad. Now the public performance made up of the complex of events of the musicians' playing their various instruments, the singers' singing, and the conductor's conducting, is the space-time event having (in this case) inherent

value and also inherent disvalue. If everyone in the audience had liked the performance, then the event would have had only inherent value. If everyone who heard it disliked it, it would have had inherent disvalue only. Notice that we are not here concerned with the effects or consequences of the performance that occurred after it was finished (such as the paying of the musicians for their evening's work, or the fact that the manager of the concert hall was encouraged to have a similar performance played at a later date, etc.). Nor are we concerned with a larger whole—such as the entire series of concerts of which this was one, or the whole musical life of the city where it took place. We are only concerned with the relation between this particular event and the way it was experienced by the persons present at it, who "lived through" it. It should be noted that events having inherent value need not be human acts like playing musical instruments, singing, or conducting. A rainbow appearing after a storm may have inherent value for all who happen to see it. An object, as distinct from an event, has inherent value when those who perceive it (e.g., looking at a painting) or do something with it (e.g., building a model ship) find satisfaction in such perception or activity.

The concept of inherent value may be schematically explained thus. If Y is a person's experience of object or event X, and if Y has intrinsic value for the person, then X has inherent value. We may then distinguish *actual* and *potential* inherent value in the following way. X has actual inherent value to the extent that the actual experience of it by anyone has intrinsic value. X has potential inherent value when it is the case that, *if* people *were* to experience it, they would find their experiences intrinsically good. A painting hidden in a closet may therefore have (potential) inherent value, even when no one is looking at it. In either case, however, the object X would have no inherent value if no one's actual or possible experience of it had intrinsic value. Here again the value of X is *derivative* from the value of something else.

(A) and (B). We are now in a position to understand the difference between extrinsic value (whether instrumental, contributive, or inherent) and intrinsic value. The difference is this. If something has intrinsic value, its value is not derivative from the value of anything else, while the opposite is true of extrinsic value. It does not matter what *standard* of intrinsic value is being used. As long as something—which, in the case of intrinsic value, is always someone's experience that he actually "lives through"—is judged to be good (or bad) without requiring any reference to the value of something else, the judgment that it is good (or bad) is a judgment of intrinsic value. Otherwise, it is one of the three kinds of judgment of extrinsic value.

It can now be seen that, if all value is either extrinsic or intrinsic, then all value is ultimately derived from intrinsic value or is itself intrinsic value. Nothing can be good extrinsically unless something is good intrinsically, and nothing can be good at all without reference to intrinsic value. Thus intrinsic value is the source and foundation of all value.

THE CONCEPT OF INTRINSIC VALUE

There are five ideas in terms of which the concept of intrinsic value has been understood by philosophers:

(i) To say that something has intrinsic value is to say that it is sought or desired *for its own sake,* or *as an end in itself.*

(ii) To say that something has intrinsic value is to say that it has value and that its value depends on its *nature* rather than on its consequences or on its relation to other things.

(iii) To say that something has intrinsic value is to say that it would have value even if it were *the only thing existing in the universe.*

(iv) To say that something has intrinsic value is to say that there is an *objective, non-natural property* inhering in (belonging to) it.

(v) To say that something has intrinsic value is to say that it has *non-derivative* value.

(i) The Greek philosopher Plato was among the first to point out that all the things people desire fall into three classes: things that they desire as ends in themselves, things that they desire merely as means to ends, and things that they desire both as ends in themselves and as means to further ends. Sometimes, for example, a person will want to attain an end because he expects that he will find the end enjoyable, regardless of any further purposes it might serve to bring about. He wants it for its own sake. Other things he will desire because without them he cannot attain his ends. They are things he would never want to have if he were able to attain his ends without them. Such things are sought not for their own sake but for the sake of something else. Another way to put it is that they are *valued* not as ends in themselves but merely as means to ends.

This way of thinking leads to the distinction between what is "good as an end" and what is "good as a means," and this in turn is made the basis for the distinction between intrinsic and extrinsic value. Intrinsic value thus becomes identified with being-sought-for-its-own-sake. In order to discover what things have intrinsic value, all we have to do is to see what things people desire as ends in themselves or, in other words, what they seek for its own sake and not for the sake of something else. A clear example of this procedure is given in John Stuart Mill's *Utilitarianism.* (See Chapter 4.) Mill tried to prove that happiness is the only thing intrinsically *desirable* by showing that the only thing people *desire,* other than as a means to happiness or as a part of happiness, is happiness itself.

The difficulty with this procedure is that it overlooks the difference between fact and value. The statement "So-and-so desires X for its own sake," is a factual assertion, verifiable in ordinary empirical ways. The statement "X is intrinsically good (or desirable)" is a value judgment. If the naturalistic fallacy is a genuine fallacy (see Chapter 7), then the second statement cannot be deduced from the first, nor can it mean the same thing as the first. Yet there would seem to be some logical connection between the two. To say that something has intrinsic value may not be to *say* that it is (desired as) an end in itself, but it would seem that the fact that something is desired as an end in itself could at least provide *evidence* in support of the judgment that it has intrinsic value. This possibility is explored in some detail by Professor C. A. Baylis in the third reading of this chapter.

(ii) The second way of looking at intrinsic value is linked with the first way. Let us suppose that someone finds great satisfaction in playing tennis. He does not play the game to make money, or as a means to keep physically fit, or as a matter of social prestige, or for any reason other than that he simply enjoys it. Since he does it not as a means to some further end but entirely for its own sake, we can say that he finds tennis playing to be a worthwhile pursuit or a good thing to do as an end in itself. Now this means that the consequences resulting from his playing tennis are *not* reasons for his considering it to be good, nor is any relation between the game and other things (such as the social life at his tennis club, or his reputation as a good player among his friends). The sole reason why he desires to play the game is that it is the kind of game it is. The reason for his liking to play tennis, the reason he would give if asked why he found it so enjoyable, would be simply that it is tennis. Or else he might point to certain aspects of tennis which are not found in other games and which he finds especially interesting, exciting, challenging, or fulfilling to him. In neither case, be it noted, is he citing any effects or consequences that come after his playing a game. From considerations like these, some philosophers have concluded that the game of tennis has *intrinsic* value for this person because he values it (likes it, wants to play it) for being the kind of game it is, and not for its consequences or its relation to anything else. To generalize: Something has intrinsic value if and only if it is valued (desired, sought) because of its "intrinsic" nature and not because of any factors "extrinsic" to it. When we come to point (v), we shall see why this view of intrinsic value is a plausible one.

(iii) In the first reading of this chapter Professor G. E. Moore presents an argument against the hedonistic criterion of intrinsic value, that is, against the view that the sole standard of intrinsic value is pleasure. We shall later consider this view in detail. For the present, it should be noted that at certain points in his argument Moore is concerned with the concept of intrinsic value as the value anything would have if it existed alone in the universe or, in other words, if the entire universe consisted of nothing but the object itself. Thus in one passage he states, "By saying that a thing is intrinsically good . . . means that it would be a good thing that the thing in question should exist, even if it existed *quite alone,* without any further accompaniments or effects whatever." It is not difficult to see how this concept of intrinsic value is connected with the preceding one. For if, as concept (ii) asserts, the intrinsic value of an object is based on its "intrinsic" nature (the kind of thing it is "in itself"), then that value must remain attached to it even if it had no relation—causal, spatial, or temporal—to anything else. And this means that the object would have value, or would be judged to be good, even if it were the only thing in existence.

Notice, however, that in our example under (ii) the thing that has intrinsic value to a person is one of his own experiences (namely, playing the game of tennis). And we saw earlier that one difference between intrinsic value and inherent value is that the former is attributable to experiences of persons, while the latter is attributable to public space-time objects and events. If this is so, then nothing can have intrinsic value unless it is an experience in some person's consciousness. So in order for a thing to be intrinsically good there must at least exist a person who is capable of having a conscious experience of some kind. However, Moore's point can be put in a slightly different way. To say that something is intrinsically good is to say, first, that it is an experience and, second, that it would be a good thing for someone to have the experience even if nothing else than the person and his experience were to exist in the universe.

(iv) The word "intrinsic" has sometimes led philosophers to view intrinsic value as an objective property belonging to things in the same way that empirical properties belong to them. If we characterize a flower as being scarlet in color, having thin petals, and being the size of a quarter when in full bloom, we think of these characteristics or properties as "inhering in" the flower. Our descriptive statements about the flower are true when it in fact does have the properties we attribute to it. So also, according to this view, if our statement that the flower has intrinsic value is true, then the flower's value must be another property inhering in it. This property, however, is a "non-natural" one, since its presence in an object cannot be determined empirically.

Those who have read the essay by G. E. Moore in Chapter 7 will immediately recognize this view as the nonnaturalistic or intuitionist theory of value. Intrinsic value, in this view, may be defined as the non-natural property of an object that would have to be included in any complete, true description of the object. However, as we shall see below, it is quite possible to conceive of intrinsic value as non-derivative value, without having to accept the particular view of a value judgment propounded by nonnaturalism or intuitionism.

(v) The final concept of intrinsic value we shall consider here may be stated thus: Whenever the value of something does not depend, wholly or in part, on the value of something else, it has intrinsic value. It may be the case that anything having intrinsic value also has extrinsic value; that is to say, some of its total value may be *derived from* the value of its consequences or from the value of other things to which it is spatially or temporally related. But its intrinsic value is whatever value we judge it to have *over and above its derivative value*. To say that something is intrinsically good, then, is to say that at least some of its goodness is non-derivative. We have seen earlier how judgments of intrinsic value in this way can be differentiated from judgments of extrinsic (derivative) value. Let us now examine how this view of intrinsic value compares with some of the others we have been considering.

First, what is the relation between desiring something as an end in itself and judging it to have non-derivative value? We cannot say they are identical, since the value judgment "X is intrinsically good" cannot mean the same thing as the factual statement "X is desired as an end in itself." Yet it would seem that, whenever we desire to have a certain experience for its own sake, we think of it as *worth* having regardless of its consequences. Hence the two are correlated. Perhaps it will help to recall that a positive value judgment always expresses a pro-attitude on the part of the judge toward the object being judged, and a negative judgment expresses a con-attitude. In the case of a judgment of intrinsic value, the pro- or con-attitude being expressed by it is a disposition on the part of the judge to want to have, or to want to avoid, an experience as an end in itself, or else it is a disposition to like, or dislike, the experience when and as it is being "lived through." So this is one way a judgment of intrinsic value may be seen to be related to the desire for something as an end in itself. Another way of relating them is suggested by Professor C. A. Baylis in the third reading of this chapter. He argues that desiring, wanting, or prizing something for its own sake or as an end in itself is *evidence for* the intrinsic value of that which is so desired, wanted, or prized. We shall consider this argument further toward the end of this introduction.

The concept of intrinsic value as the value of something that rests on its nature and not on its effects or relations to other things can be shown to be one implication of the concept of intrinsic value as non-derivative value. In a judgment of non-derivative value, whatever might be the standard of evaluation referred to, one condition must be satisfied. The good-making characteristics determined by that standard must not be properties belonging to the consequences of the thing or properties belonging to its relation to other things. For if they were, then what would *make* the thing good would be some "extrinsic" fact about its consequences or its relation to other things, and hence its goodness or value would be derivative. What makes something intrinsically good, therefore, must be a property or set of properties belonging to the thing itself. In this sense the intrinsic value of something must be grounded on its nature.

Could something have non-derivative value if it existed alone in the universe? The question is to be answered in the negative if "existing alone" excludes the presence of a person who can "live through" the conscious experience that has the value. If the presence of such a person is not excluded, then it is not clear what the question means. Since we do not know exactly what conditions must hold for the question to be correctly answered either way, we do not know what is being asked. One possible meaning can be given by reference to the idea of inherent value stated earlier. We could say that, if no person existed in the universe, objects could still be said to have *potential* inherent value. This would simply mean that, if a person were to experience such objects, his experience of them would be intrinsically good. It should be noted, however, that the idea of the value of something existing alone in the universe is used by Moore in the context of an important argument concerning the hedonistic criterion of intrinsic value, which we shall discuss below.

Finally, it should be clear that it is not necessary to think of intrinsic value as an objective property of something if it is defined as non-derivative value. Of course there must be some empirical property or set of properties of the thing judged to be intrinsically good which constitute its good-making characteristics. But the intrinsic goodness or value itself is not a property that inheres in anything. It is not a property at all. (For a defense of this view, see the reading by

R. M. Hare in Chapter 7.) To call the value "intrinsic" is simply to deny that it is derived from the value of anything else. It is not to affirm that it somehow exists "in" the thing which is judged to be intrinsically good.

HEDONISM

We come now to the problem of the *criterion* or *standard* of intrinsic value. So far we have not considered what possible standards of evaluation might be applied in making judgments of intrinsic value; we have only been concerned with the general nature of such judgments. But all three of the readings included in this chapter deal with this further subject. Indeed, two of them are mainly concerned with defending or attacking one particular standard of intrinsic value. This is the standard of pleasure, and the position that holds this to be the sole valid criterion of intrinsic value is called "hedonism" (from the Greek word meaning "pleasure"). Hedonism has been angrily attacked by some philosophers and vigorously defended by others since the very beginning of Western philosophy. Let us take a closer look at it.

We have defined hedonism as the view that the sole valid standard of intrinsic value is pleasure. This view has four implications:

(a) All pleasures are intrinsically good.

(b) Only pleasure is intrinsically good.

(c) A thing is intrinsically good to the extent that it is pleasurable.

(d) What makes anything intrinsically good is the pleasure it gives to someone.

Proposition (a) means that there are no bad pleasures. Immediately someone will question the hedonist: But what about a sadist who gets pleasure out of torturing people? Are not the pleasures of a sadist bad? The hedonist's reply is that his pleasures are *extrinsically* bad, because they cause pain (the opposite of pleasure) to others. That is, they have intrinsically bad consequences. But the very thing that makes those consequences intrinsically bad makes the sadist's experience itself intrinsically good, namely, the fact that he finds it pleasurable. It would be much better (where "better" refers to the total, over-all value of the situation) if he found pleasure in bringing pleasure to others, or at least in lessening their pain. But, argues the hedonist, if we consider only the non-derivative value of his experience, we must admit it to be good. For we are then disregarding its consequences and its relation to other things. In judging intrinsic value it is necessary to abstract an experience from its context. We must not consider its effects either on the person himself or on others. It is only within this limited (but highly important) frame of reference that the sadist's experience is judged to be good.

Proposition (b) means that there is nothing intrinsically good but pleasure. Immediately someone will object, But surely there are many good things in human life besides pleasure. What about knowledge? beauty? friendship? moral virtue? The hedonist will reply, "Yes, I agree that these things are good, but what is it that makes them good? Why do we value them so highly? Is it not that they either tend to increase the amount of pleasure in the world or are them-selves great sources of pleasure for those who experience them? Suppose no one liked to know the truth and suppose that knowledge was used only to make the lives of men more miserable. Would we then consider knowledge something worth having? Suppose no one found pleasure in the experience of beauty, or ever enjoyed having friends. Aren't these good things held to be good precisely because they are such deep sources of pleasure for practically everyone? And if we consider moral virtue, we do not have to be utilitarians to see that, whether we take it as a means to an end or as an end in itself, it would have no value if it did not yield pleasure to someone." The hedonist would claim that, though a man may be morally admirable because he seeks to do his duty for its own sake, the inherent value of such a "good will" lies in the fact that an impartial spec-tator does find pleasure in contemplating it. If such a spectator disliked the contemplation of moral virtue, and if the virtuous person himself found no sat-isfaction in doing his duty for its own sake, and if no pleasant consequences of any sort resulted from his being virtuous, would we not withdraw all value from moral virtue?

Proposition (c) means that the degree of intrinsic value in any experience is directly proportional to the amount or quantity of pleasure it brings to the person who has it. This view was held by Jeremy Bentham. It was vehemently attacked by John Stuart Mill, who thought that the quality of a pleasure as well as its quantity should be taken into account in judging its intrinsic value. The readings by Bentham and Mill in Chapter 4 include all the important aspects of this dispute, and should be consulted for a full consideration of the pro's and con's regarding this third proposition of hedonism. We shall find a further ar-gument in opposition to it set forth by G. E. Moore in the first reading of the present chapter.

Proposition (d) states that the only intrinsically good-making characteristic of anything is pleasure. This follows from the principle that pleasure is the only standard of evaluation to be used in judgments of intrinsic value, since a stand-ard determines what characteristics of a thing are good-making. To say that pleas-ure is an intrinsically good-making characteristic of X is to say that, so far as the intrinsic value of X is concerned, it is good in virtue of the fact that it is pleasant to someone. Thus it is not a mere accident that every pleasure is in-trinsically good, that only pleasure is intrinsically good, and that the intrinsic goodness of something is directly proportional to its pleasantness. Proposition (d) is the logical ground for propositions (a), (b), and (c). The hedonist's justification for proposition (d) is the same as his argument for his basic prin-ciple. This principle may be stated thus. In judging whether any experience is intrinsically good or bad we apply only one test, namely, to ask how pleasant or unpleasant the experience is to the person who "lives through" it. In order to be clearer about the nature of this hedonistic standard, and in order to better understand the arguments given in support of it, we must make certain distinc-tions with regard to the concept of pleasure.

First it is necessary to distinguish two meanings of the term "pleasure." One meaning equates pleasure with *bodily pleasure* or *pleasure of the senses*. When "pleasure" is used in this sense, it is the name of a certain class of sensations or feelings which we get when our bodily organs and nerve endings are stimulated in various ways. Sometimes the terms "animal pleasure" and "sensual pleasure" are used to denote all such sensations and feelings. When "pleasure" is used in this way, its opposite is bodily pain.

The second meaning of pleasure is *any pleasant experience*. We can think of this in the following way. Suppose we were asked to place all of our experiences on a scale, ranging from those which were most pleasant through those which were somewhat pleasant, slightly pleasant, neither pleasant nor unpleasant, mildly unpleasant, quite unpleasant, to extremely unpleasant. Perhaps many of our daily experiences would fall near the neutral center of the scale. These would be experiences that, as far as their pleasure (pleasantness or unpleasantness) was concerned, were indifferent to us. But there would be other experiences that we would unhesitatingly place on either side of the neutral line. Now the word "pleasure" in its second sense is taken to denote the entire class of experiences that fall on the positive side of the neutral line, no matter how they might vary in degree or amount of pleasantness, and no matter what may be the source of their pleasantness. What one person finds to be pleasant another will find to be unpleasant or indifferent; what one person derives great pleasure from another will derive only mild pleasure from, or none at all. Thus the *sources* of pleasure may vary considerably from person to person. But the *hedonic tone* of different people's experiences is common to them all. That is to say, everyone knows the difference among pleasant, indifferent, and unpleasant experiences, however great may be their disagreement concerning the particular things they find to be pleasant, indifferent, or unpleasant.

In common usage we have four terms for referring to the hedonic tone of our experiences: "enjoyment," "liking," "satisfaction," and "pleasure." Examples of typical phrases in which these terms are employed are: "He enjoys X"; "He finds X enjoyable"; "He likes (doing) X"; "He finds satisfaction in (doing) X"; "X gives him pleasure"; "X is pleasant to him." When the word "pleasure" is used in its second sense, it is understood to cover all four of these ways of speaking. It is the name of the entire class of experiences which any person enjoys, likes, finds satisfying, or finds pleasant.

In this second sense of the word, the opposite of pleasure is not bodily pain but rather the unpleasantness of any experience, whatever its source. Thus it is possible for bodily pain (that is, the sensations resulting from the stimulation of certain nerve endings) to be pleasant. A certain type of masochist, for example, finds the experience of being whipped pleasant. Here we can say without contradiction that the person finds pleasure in having pain-sensations. This means simply that, because of his abnormal emotions (extreme guilt, the need for punishment, etc.), the person gets satisfaction—even thrills—from the experience of bodily pain. A *source* of pleasantness, for him, is for most of us a source of great unpleasantness. It might also be possible—though perhaps it is very rare in actual occurrence—for a person to find bodily pleasure (that is, "pleasure" in the first sense) to be an unpleasant experience. This might happen to a person who was sexually aroused but had extreme guilt feelings about sex. At any rate, if we are careful to keep the two meanings of "pleasure" separate in our minds, we need not think that it is somehow gross or animalistic, and hence degrading or ignoble, to be a hedonist. For a hedonist may advocate, as the sole valid standard of intrinsic value, pleasure in the second sense and not in the first. And this is the sort of hedonism we shall be concerned with here.

It is important not to confuse the sources of pleasure with pleasure itself. The hedonist claims only that pleasure itself (meaning, now, the positive hedonic tone of any experience) is the standard of intrinsic value. He does not claim that intrinsic value depends on any particular source of pleasure. For the hedonist *any* pleasant experience is intrinsically good just *because* it is pleasant, no matter what it is that gives pleasure to the person concerned. There is no reason why the most exalted kinds of experiences, such as reading poetry or attaining a mystical vision, should not be included as sources of pleasure. The hedonist does not say that everyone ought to be a pure sensualist and try to have as much bodily pleasure as possible. Indeed, as R. M. Blake points out in the second reading of this chapter, the so-called "hedonic paradox" is perfectly consistent with hedonism. The "hedonic paradox" states that those who seek pleasure as a conscious goal in life are often those who gain very little pleasure from life. A person who deliberately sought to maximize his bodily pleasures would probably end up having experiences that were less pleasant over the long run than those of a person who found pleasure in a variety of sources and who did not even pursue "a life of pleasure" as a deliberate goal.

ARGUMENTS FOR AND AGAINST HEDONISM

The first two readings in this chapter present arguments in opposition to, and in defense of, the hedonistic criterion of intrinsic value. It should be noted that in the first reading G. E. Moore is not only attacking hedonism as a theory of intrinsic value. He is also attacking the normative ethical system which is properly designated as "hedonistic act-utilitarianism." This is the view that the act which a person ought to do in any situation is the act which, in comparison with all the alternatives in the situation, will bring about the greatest balance of pleasure over pain (pleasantness over unpleasantness) in the world. Similarly, R. M. Blake in the second reading sometimes argues in support of this position as well as in support of the hedonistic criterion of intrinsic value. It is helpful to keep these two theories distinct in our minds. For although hedonistic act-utilitarianism implies the truth of the hedonistic theory of intrinsic value, the converse does not hold. It is possible to accept pleasure as the sole valid standard of intrinsic value and not accept an act-utilitarian theory of right conduct. Rule-utilitarianism (see Chapter 5) might be accepted instead, or even ethical egoism (see Chapter 2).

A word should be added concerning the arguments given by Professor C. A. Baylis in the last reading of this chapter. After distinguishing various types of value judgment, Baylis takes up the problem of justifying the criteria or standards to be used in judgments of intrinsic value. He here makes the distinction between an "identifying property" of intrinsic value and a "conferring property." The latter corresponds to what has been called a "good-making characteristic" in this and the preceding chapter. For hedonism there is only one such conferring property or good-making characteristic—namely, pleasure. According to Baylis, whether the hedonist's position is true is an empirical question which, he says, can be deferred "for later scientific resolution." The important philosophical question—as distinct from that empirical question—concerns the *identifying* property of intrinsic value. For once we know this property, we can pick out things that have intrinsic value from all other things. Having done this we can examine intrinsically valuable things and see what property or properties confer their value upon them. This would then tell us the conferring property or properties of intrinsic value.

Now Baylis argues that the identifying property of intrinsic value (that is, the criterion by which we distinguish things having intrinsic value from all other things) is the property of "being prized for its own sake," which is explained as follows. When we guard against certain kinds of error in trying to identify intrinsically valuable things (Baylis lists three such kinds of error), we discover that intrinsically valuable things are experiences "that we find ourselves prizing . . . , *i.e.* liking, approving, desiring, preferring, and commending . . . for their own qualities (rather than because of their relations to other valuable things). . . ." Thus intrinsic value occurs when someone has correct knowledge of his experience, does not confuse it with its consequences or surrounding circumstances (that is, he disregards its relation to other things), and he finds himself seeking or wanting to have this experience in preference to other experiences he might have instead. Given this way of identifying intrinsically good experiences, we can then make empirical tests to confirm or disconfirm hedonism. As Baylis puts it, "We can submit to scientific test procedures the Hedonist's claim that pleasant experiences and only pleasant experiences are intrinsically good. For with both intrinsic goods and pleasant experiences identifiable it becomes a factual question, testable by empirical methods, what the relations between these two groups of things are." Whether such a method for establishing the truth or falsity of hedonism is valid is a matter for the reader's consideration.

GEORGE EDWARD MOORE

Utility and Intrinsic Value

[The theory we are considering asserts:] That, if we had to choose between two actions, one of which would have as its sole or total effects, an effect or set of effects, which we may call A, while the other would have as its sole or total effects, an effect or set of effects, which we may call B, then, *if* A contained more pleasure than B, it always would be our duty to choose the action which caused A rather than that which caused B. This, it asserts, would be absolutely *always* true, *no matter what A and B might be like in other respects.* And to assert this is (it now goes on to say) *equivalent* to asserting that any effect or set of effects which contains more pleasure is always *intrinsically* better than one which contains less.

By calling one effect or set of effects *intrinsically better* than another it means that it is better *in itself,* quite apart from any accompaniments or further effects which it may have. That is to say: To assert of any one thing, A, that it is *intrinsically* better than another, B, is to assert that if A existed *quite alone,* without any accompaniments or effects whatever—if, in short, A constituted the whole Universe, it would be better that such a Universe should exist, than that a Universe which consisted solely of B should exist instead. In order to discover whether any one thing is *intrinsically* better than another, we have always thus to consider whether it would be better that the one should exist *quite alone* than that the other should exist *quite alone.* No one thing or set of things, A, ever can be *intrinsically* better than another, B, unless it would be better that A should exist quite alone than that B should exist quite alone. . . .

It is plain, then, that this theory assigns a quite unique position to pleasure and pain in two respects; or possibly only in one, since it is just possible that the two propositions which it makes about them are not merely equivalent, but absolutely identical—that is to say, are merely different ways of expressing exactly the same idea. The two propositions are these. (1) That if any one had to choose between two actions, one of which would, in its total effects, cause more pleasure than the other, it always would be his duty to choose the former; and that it never could be any one's duty to choose one action rather than another, unless its total effects contained more pleasure. (2) That any Universe, or part of a Universe, which contains more pleasure, is always intrinsically better than one which contains less; and that nothing can be intrinsically better than anything else, unless it contains more pleasure. It does seem to be just possible

From G. E. Moore, *Ethics* (1912). Reprinted by permission of Oxford University Press (London).

that these two propositions are merely two different ways of expressing exactly the same idea. The question whether they are so or not simply depends upon the question whether, when we say, 'It would be better that A should exist quite alone than that B should exist quite alone', we are or are not saying exactly the same thing, as when we say, 'Supposing we had to choose between an action of which A would be the sole effect, and one of which B would be the sole effect, it would be our duty to choose the former rather than the latter'. And it certainly does seem, at first sight, as if the two propositions were not identical; as if we should not be saying exactly the same thing in asserting the one, as in asserting the other. But, even if they are not identical, our theory asserts that they are certainly *equivalent*: that, whenever the one is true, the other is certainly also true. And, if they are not identical, this assertion of equivalence amounts to the very important proposition that: An action is right, only if no action, which the agent could have done instead, would have had intrinsically better results: while an action is wrong, only if the agent *could* have done some other action instead whose total results would have been intrinsically better. It certainly seems as if this proposition were not a mere tautology. And, if so, then we must admit that our theory assigns a unique position to pleasure and pain in two respects, and not in one only. It asserts, first of all, that they have a unique relation to right and wrong; and secondly, that they have a unique relation to *intrinsic value*.

Our theory asserts, then, that any whole which contains a greater amount of pleasure, is always intrinsically better than one which contains a smaller amount, no matter what the two may be like in other respects; and that no whole can be intrinsically better than another unless it contains more pleasure. But it must be remembered that throughout this discussion, we have, for the sake of convenience, been using the phrase 'contains more pleasure' in an inaccurate sense. . . . I should say of one whole, A, that it contained more pleasure than another, B, whenever A and B were related to one another in either of the five following ways: namely (1) when A and B both contain an excess of pleasure over pain, but A contains a greater excess than B; (2) when A contains an excess of pleasure over pain, while B contains no excess either of pleasure over pain or of pain over pleasure; (3) when A contains an excess of pleasure over pain, while B contains an excess of pain over pleasure; (4) when A contains no excess either of pleasure over pain or of pain over pleasure, while B does contain an excess of pain over pleasure; and (5) when both A and B contain an excess of pain over pleasure, but A contains a smaller excess than B. Whenever in stating this theory, I have spoken of one whole, or effect, or set of effects, A, as containing more pleasure than another, B, I have always meant merely that A was related to B *in one or other of these five ways*. And so here, when our theory says that every whole which contains a greater amount of pleasure is always intrinsically better than one which contains less, and that nothing can be intrinsically better than anything else unless it contains more pleasure, this must be understood to mean that any whole, A, which stands to another, B, in *any one* of these five relations, is always intrinsically better than B, and that no one thing can be intrinsically better than another, unless it stands to it in *one or other* of these five relations. And it becomes important to remember this, when we go on to take account of another fact.

It is plain that when we talk of one thing being 'better' than another we may mean any one of five different things. We may mean either (1) that while both are positively good, the first is better; or (2) that while the first is positively good, the second is neither good nor bad, but indifferent; or (3) that while the first is positively good, the second is positively bad; or (4) that while the first is indifferent, the second is positively bad; or (5) that while both are positively bad, the first is less bad than the second. We should, in common life, say that one thing was 'better' than another, whenever it stood to that other in any one of these five relations. Or, in other words, we hold that among things which stand to one another in the relation of better and worse, some are positively good, others positively bad, and others neither good nor bad, but indifferent. And our theory holds that this is, in fact, the case, with things which have a place in the scale of *intrinsic* value: some of them are intrinsically good, others intrinsically bad, and others indifferent. And it would say that a whole is intrinsically good, whenever and only when it contains an excess of pleasure over pain; intrinsically bad, whenever and only when it contains an excess of pain over pleasure; and intrinsically indifferent, whenever and only when it contains neither.

In addition, therefore, to laying down precise rules as to what things are intrinsically *better* or *worse* than others, our theory also lays down equally precise ones as to what things are intrinsically *good* and *bad* and *indifferent*. By saying that a thing is intrinsically good it means that it would be a good thing that the thing in question should exist, even if it existed *quite alone,* without any further accompaniments or effects whatever. By saying that it is intrinsically bad, it means that it would be a bad thing or an evil that it should exist, even if it existed quite alone, without any further accompaniments or effects whatever. And by saying that it is intrinsically indifferent, it means that, if it existed *quite alone,* its existence would be neither a good nor an evil in any degree whatever. And just as the conceptions 'intrinsically better' and 'intrinsically worse' are connected in a perfectly precise manner with the conceptions 'right' and 'wrong', so, it maintains, are these other conceptions also. To say of anything, A, that it is 'intrinsically good', is equivalent to saying that, if we had to choose between an action of which A would be the sole or total effect, and an action, which would have absolutely no effects at all, it would always be our duty to choose the former, and wrong to choose the latter. And similarly to say of anything, A, that it is 'intrinsically bad', is equivalent to saying that, if we had to choose between an action of which A would be the sole effect, and an action which would have absolutely no effects at all, it would always be our duty to choose the latter and wrong to choose the former. And finally, to say of anything, A, that it is 'intrinsically indifferent', is equivalent to saying that, if we had to choose between an action, of which A would be the sole effect, and an action which would have absolutely no effects at all, it would not matter which we chose: either choice would be equally right.

To sum up, then, we may say that . . . our theory lays down three principles. It asserts (1) that anything whatever, whether it be a single effect, or a whole set of effects, or a whole Universe, is *intrinsically good,* whenever and only when it either is or contains an excess of pleasure over pain; that anything whatever is *intrinsically bad,* whenever and only when it either is or contains an excess of pain over pleasure; and that all other things, no matter what their nature may be, are intrinsically indifferent. It asserts (2) that any one thing, whether it be a single effect, or a whole set of effects, or a whole Universe, is intrinsically *better* than another, whenever and only when the two are related to one another in one or other of the five following ways: namely, when either (*a*) while both are intrinsically good, the second is not so good as the first; or (*b*) while the first is intrinsically good, the second is intrinsically indifferent; or (*c*) while the first is intrinsically good, the second is intrinsically bad; or (*d*) while the first is intrinsically indifferent, the second is intrinsically bad; or (*e*) while both are intrinsically bad, the first is not so bad as the second. And it asserts (3) that, if we had to choose between two actions one of which would have intrinsically better total effects than the other, it always would be our duty to choose the former, and wrong to choose the latter; and that no action ever can be right *if* we could have done anything else instead which would have had intrinsically better total effects, nor wrong, *unless* we could have done something else instead which would have had intrinsically better total effects. From these three principles taken together, the whole theory follows. And whether it be true or false, it is, I think, at least a perfectly clear and intelligible theory. Whether it is or is not of any practical importance is, indeed, another question. But, even if it were of none whatever, it certainly lays down propositions of so fundamental and so far-reaching a character, that it seems worth while to consider whether they are true or false. There remain, I think, only two points which should be noticed with regard to it, before we go on to consider the principal objections which may be urged against it.

It should be noticed, first, that, though this theory asserts that nothing is *intrinsically* good, unless it is or contains an excess of pleasure over pain, it is very far from asserting that nothing is *good,* unless it fulfils this condition. By saying that a thing is *intrinsically good,* it means, as has been explained, that the existence of the thing in question *would* be a good, even if it existed quite alone, without any accompaniments or effects whatever; and it is quite plain that when we call things 'good' we by no means always mean this: we by no means always mean that they *would* be good, even if they existed quite alone. Very often, for instance, when we say that a thing is 'good', we mean that it is good *because of its effects;* and we should not for a moment maintain that it *would* be good, even if it had no effects at all. We are, for instance, familiar with the idea that it is sometimes a good thing for people to suffer pain; and yet we should be very loth to maintain that in all such cases their suffering *would* be a good thing, even if nothing were gained by it—if it had no further effects. We do, in general, maintain that suffering is good, only *where* and *because* it has further good effects. And similarly with many other things. Many things, therefore, which are *not* 'intrinsically' good, may nevertheless be 'good' in some one or other of the senses in which we use that highly ambiguous word. And hence our theory can and would quite consistently maintain that, while nothing is *intrinsically* good except pleasure or wholes which contain pleasure, many other things really are 'good'; and similarly that, while nothing is *intrinsically* bad except pain or wholes which contain it, yet many other things are really 'bad'. It would, for instance, maintain that it is *always* a good thing to act rightly, and a bad thing to act wrongly; although it would say at the same time that, since actions, strictly speaking, do not *contain* either pleasure or pain, but are only accompanied by or causes of them, a right action is *never intrinsically* good, nor a wrong one *intrinsically* bad. And similarly it would maintain that it is perfectly true that some men are 'good', and others 'bad', and some better than others; although no man can strictly be said to *contain* either pleasure or pain, and hence none can be either intrinsically good or intrinsically bad or intrinsically better than any other. It would even maintain (and this also it can do quite consistently), that events which are *intrinsically* good are nevertheless very often bad, and intrinsically bad ones good. It would, for instance, say that it is often a very bad thing for a man to enjoy a particular pleasure on a particular occasion, although the event, which consists in his enjoying it, may be intrinsically good, since it contains an excess of pleasure over pain. It may often be a very bad thing that such an event should happen, because it *causes* the man himself or other beings to have less pleasure or more pain in the future, than they would otherwise have had. And for similar reasons it may often be a very good thing that an intrinsically bad event should happen.

It is important to remember all this, because otherwise the theory may appear much more paradoxical than it really is. It may, for instance, appear, at first sight, as if it denied all value to anything except pleasure and wholes which contain it—a view which would be extremely paradoxical if it were held. But it does *not* do this. It does not deny all value to other things, but only all *intrinsic* value—a very different thing. It only says that none of them *would* have any value if they existed quite alone. But, of course, as a matter of fact, none of them do exist quite alone, and hence it may quite consistently allow that, as it is, many of them do have very great value. Concerning kinds of value, other than intrinsic value, it does not profess to lay down any general rules at all. And its reason for confining itself to intrinsic value is because it holds that this and this alone is related to right and wrong in the perfectly definite manner explained above. Whenever an action is right, it is right only if and because the total effects of no action, which the agent could have done instead, would have had more intrinsic value; and whenever an action is wrong, it is wrong only if and because the total effects of some other action, which the agent could have done instead, would have had more *intrinsic* value. This proposition, which is true of *intrinsic* value, is not, it holds, true of value of any other kind.

And a second point which should be noticed about this theory is the following. It is often represented as asserting that pleasure is the only thing which is *ultimately* good or desirable, and pain the only thing which is *ulti-*

mately bad or undesirable; or as asserting that pleasure is the only thing which is good *for its own sake*, and the pain the only thing which is bad *for its own sake*. And there is, I think, a sense in which it does assert this. But these expressions are not commonly carefully defined; and it is worth noticing that, if our theory does assert these propositions, the expressions '*ultimately* good' or 'good *for its own sake*' must be understood in a different sense from that which has been assigned above to the expression '*intrinsically* good'. We must not take '*ultimately* good' or 'good *for its own sake*' to be synonyms for '*intrinsically* good'. For our theory most emphatically does *not* assert that pleasure is the only thing *intrinsically* good, and pain the only thing *intrinsically* evil. On the contrary, it asserts that any whole which *contains* an excess of pleasure over pain is *intrinsically* good, no matter how much else it may contain besides; and similarly that any whole which contains an excess of pain over pleasure is *intrinsically* bad. This distinction between the conception expressed by '*ultimately* good' or '*good for its own sake*', on the one hand, and that expressed by '*intrinsically* good', on the other, is not commonly made; and yet obviously we must make it, if we are to say that our theory does assert that pleasure is the only *ultimate* good, and pain the only *ultimate* evil. The two conceptions, if used in this way, have one important point in common, namely, that both of them will only apply to things whose existence *would* be good, even if they existed quite alone. Whether we assert that a thing is 'ultimately good' or 'good for its own sake' or 'intrinsically good', we are always asserting that it would be good, even if it existed quite alone. But the two conceptions differ in respect of the fact that, whereas a whole which is 'intrinsically good' may contain parts which are *not* intrinsically good, i.e. *would* not be good, if they existed quite alone; anything which is 'ultimately good' or 'good for its own sake' can contain no such parts. This, I think, is the meaning which we must assign to the expressions 'ultimately good' or 'good for its own sake', if we are to say that our theory asserts pleasure to be the *only* thing 'ultimately good' or 'good for its own sake'. We may, in short, divide intrinsically good things into two classes: namely (1) those which, while as wholes they are intrinsically good, nevertheless contain some parts which are not intrinsically good; and (2) those, which either have no parts at all, or, if they have any, have none but what are themselves intrinsically good. And we may thus, if we please, confine the terms 'ultimately good' or 'good for their own sakes' to things which belong to the second of these two classes. We may, of course, make a precisely similar distinction between two classes of intrinsically bad things. And it is only if we do this that our theory can be truly said to assert that nothing is 'ultimately good' or 'good for its own sake', except pleasure; and nothing 'ultimately bad' or 'bad for its own sake', except pain.

Such is the ethical theory which I have chosen to state, because it seems to me particularly simple, and hence to bring out particularly clearly some of the main questions which have formed the subject of ethical discussion.

•　•　•　•　•

[Criticism of the Theory]

It *may* . . . *possibly* be the case that quantity of pleasure *is*, as a matter of fact, a correct *criterion* of right and wrong, even if intrinsic value is *not* always in proportion to quantity of pleasure contained. But it is impossible to *prove* that it is a correct criterion, except by assuming that intrinsic value always *is* in proportion to quantity of pleasure. And most of those who have held the former view have, I think, in fact made this assumption, even if they have not definitely realized that they were making it.

Is this assumption true, then? Is it true that one whole will be intrinsically better than another, whenever and only when it contains more pleasure, no matter what the two may be like in other respects? It seems to me almost impossible that any one, who fully realizes the consequences of such a view, can possibly hold that it *is* true. It involves our saying, for instance, that a world in which absolutely nothing except pleasure existed—no knowledge, no love, no enjoyment of beauty, no moral qualities—must yet be intrinsically better—better worth creating—provided only the total quantity of pleasure in it were the least bit greater, than one in which all these things existed *as well as* pleasure. It involves our saying that, even if the total quantity of pleasure in each was exactly equal, yet the fact that all the beings in the one possessed in addition knowledge of many different kinds and a full appreciation of all that was beautiful or worthy of love in their world, whereas *none* of the beings in the other possessed any of these things, would give us no reason whatever for preferring the former to the latter. It involves our saying that, for instance, the state of mind of a drunkard, when he is intensely pleased with breaking crockery, is just as valuable, in itself—just as well worth having, as that of a man who is fully realizing all that is exquisite in the tragedy of King Lear, provided only the mere quantity of pleasure in both cases is the same. Such instances might be multiplied indefinitely, and it seems to me that they constitute a *reductio ad absurdum* of the view that intrinsic value is always in proportion to quantity of pleasure. Of course, here again, the question is quite incapable of proof either way. And if anybody, after clearly considering the issue, does come to the conclusion that no one kind of enjoyment is ever intrinsically better than another, provided only that the pleasure in both is equally intense, and that, if we *could* get as much pleasure in the world, without needing to have any knowledge, or any moral qualities, or any sense of beauty, as we can get *with* them, then all these things would be entirely superfluous, there is no way of proving that he is wrong. But it seems to me almost impossible that anybody, who does really get the question clear, should take such a view; and, if anybody were to, I think it is self-evident that he would be wrong.

It may, however, be asked: If the matter is as plain as this, how has it come about that anybody ever has adopted the view that intrinsic value *is* always in proportion to quantity of pleasure, or has ever argued, as if it were so? And I think one chief answer to this question is that those who have done so have *not* clearly realized all the consequences of their view, partly because they have been too exclusively occupied with the particular question as to whether, in the case of *the total consequences* of *actual* voluntary actions, degree of intrinsic value is not always in proportion to quantity of pleasure—a question which, as has been admitted, is, in itself, much more obscure. But there is, I think, another reason, which is worth mentioning, because it introduces us to a principle of great importance. It may, in fact, be held, with great plausibility, that no whole can ever have any intrinsic value *unless* it contains some pleasure; and it might be thought, at first sight, that this reasonable, and perhaps true, view could not possibly lead to the wholly unreasonable one that intrinsic value is always *in proportion* to quantity of pleasure: it might seem obvious that to say that nothing can be valuable *without* pleasure is a very different thing from saying that intrinsic value is always *in proportion* to pleasure. And it is, I think, in fact true that the two views are really as different as they seem, and that the latter does not at all follow from the former. But, if we look a little closer, we may, I think, see a reason why the latter should very naturally have been *thought* to follow from the former.

The reason is as follows. If we say that no whole can ever be intrinsically good, *unless* it contains some pleasure, we are, of course, saying that if from any whole, which is intrinsically good, we were to subtract all the pleasure it contains, the remainder, whatever it might be, would have no intrinsic goodness at all, but must always be either intrinsically *bad,* or else intrinsically indifferent: and this (if we remember our definition of intrinsic value) is the same thing as to say that this remainder actually *has* no intrinsic goodness at all, but always *is* either positively bad or indifferent. Let us call the pleasure which such a whole contains, A, and the whole remainder, whatever it may be, B. We are then saying that the whole A + B is intrinsically good, but that B is *not* intrinsically good at all. Surely it seems to follow that the intrinsic value of A + B cannot possibly be greater than that of A by itself? How, it may be asked, could it possibly be otherwise? How, by adding to A something, namely B, which has *no* intrinsic goodness at all, could we possibly get a whole which has *more* intrinsic value than A? It may naturally seem to be self-evident that we could not. But, if so, then it absolutely follows that we can never increase the value of any whole whatever except by adding *pleasure* to it: we may, of course, *lessen* its value, by adding other things, e.g. by adding pain; but we can never *increase* it except by adding pleasure.

Now from this it does not, of course, follow strictly that the intrinsic value of a whole is always *in proportion* to the quantity of pleasure it contains in the special sense in which we have throughout been using this expression—that is to say as meaning that it is in proportion to the *excess* of pleasure over pain. . . . But it is surely very natural to think that it does. And it *does* follow that we must be wrong in the reasons we gave for disputing this proposition. It does follow that we must be wrong in thinking that by adding such things as knowledge or a sense of beauty to a world which contained a certain amount of pleasure, without adding any more pleasure, we could increase the intrinsic value of that world. If, therefore, we are to dispute the proposition that intrinsic value *is* always in proportion to quantity of pleasure we must dispute this argument. But the argument may seem to be almost indisputable. It has, in fact, been used as an argument in favour of the proposition that intrinsic value *is* always in proportion to quantity of pleasure, and I think it has probably had much influence in inducing people to adopt that view, even if they have not expressly put it in this form.

How, then, can we dispute this argument? We might, of course, do so, by rejecting the proposition that no whole can ever be intrinsically good, *unless* it contains some pleasure; but, for my part, though I don't feel certain that this proposition *is* true, I also don't feel at all certain that it is *not* true. The part of the argument which it seems to me certainly can and ought to be disputed is another part—namely, the assumption that, where a whole contains two factors, A and B, and one of these, B, has no intrinsic goodness at all, the intrinsic value of the whole cannot be *greater* than that of the other factor, A. This assumption, I think, obviously rests on a still more general assumption, of which it is only a special case. The general assumption is: That where a whole consists of two factors, A and B, the amount by which its intrinsic value exceeds that of one of these two factors must always be equal to that of the other factor. Our special case will follow from this general assumption: because it will follow that if B be intrinsically *indifferent,* that is to say, if its intrinsic value = o, then the amount by which the value of the whole A + B exceeds the value of A must also = o, that is to say, the value of the whole must be precisely *equal* to that of A; while if B be intrinsically *bad,* that is to say, if its intrinsic value is less than o, then the amount by which the value of A + B will exceed that of A will also be less than o, that is to say, the value of the whole will be *less* than that of A. Our special case does then follow from the general assumption; and nobody, I think, would maintain that the special case was true without maintaining that the general assumption was also true. The general assumption may, indeed, very naturally seem to be self-evident: it has, I think, been generally assumed that it is so: and it may seem to be a mere deduction from the laws of arithmetic. But, so far as I can see, it is *not* a mere deduction from the laws of arithmetic, and, so far from being self-evident, is certainly untrue.

Let us see exactly what we are saying, if we deny it. We are saying that the fact that A and B *both* exist together, together with the fact that they have to one another any relation which they do happen to have (when they exist together, they always must have *some* relation to one another; and the precise nature of the relation certainly may in some cases make a great difference to the value of the whole state of things, though, perhaps, it need not in all cases)— that these two facts *together* must have a certain amount of intrinsic value, that is to say, must be either intrinsically good, or intrinsically bad, or intrinsically indifferent, and that the amount by which this value exceeds the value which the existence of A would have, if A existed quite alone, *need* not be equal to the value which the existence of B would have, if B existed quite alone. This is all that we are saying. And can any one pretend that such a view necessarily contradicts the laws of arithmetic? or that it is self-evident that it cannot be true? I cannot see any ground for saying so; and if there is no ground, then the argument which sought to show that we can never add to the value of any whole *except* by adding pleasure to it, is entirely baseless.

If, therefore, we reject the theory that intrinsic value is always in proportion to quantity of pleasure, it does seem as if we may be compelled to accept the principle that *the amount by which the value of a whole exceeds that of one of its factors is not necessarily equal to that of the remaining factor*—a principle which, if true, is very important in many other cases. But, though at first sight this principle may seem paradoxical, there seems to be no reason why we should not accept it; while there are other independent reasons why we should accept it. And, in any case, it seems quite clear that the degree of intrinsic value of a whole is *not* always in proportion to the quantity of pleasure it contains.

But, if we do reject this theory, what, it may be asked, can we substitute for it? How can we answer the question, what kinds of consequences are intrinsically better or worse than others?

We may, I think, say, first of all, that for the same reason for which we have rejected the view that intrinsic value is always in proportion to quantity of pleasure, we must also reject the view that it is always in proportion to the quantity of any other *single* factor whatever. Whatever single kind of thing may be proposed as a measure of intrinsic value, instead of pleasure—whether knowledge, or virtue, or wisdom, or love—it is, I think, quite plain that it is not such a measure; because it is quite plain that, however valuable any one of these things may be, we may always add to the value of a whole which contains any one of them, not only by adding more of that one, but also *by adding something else instead*. Indeed, so far as I can see, there is no characteristic whatever which always distinguishes every whole which has greater intrinsic value from every whole which has less, *except* the fundamental one that it would always be the duty of every agent to prefer the better to the worse, if he had to choose between a pair of actions, of which they would be the *sole* effects. And similarly, so far as I can see, there is no characteristic whatever which belongs to all things that are intrinsically *good* and only to them—except simply the one that they all *are* intrinsically good and *ought* always to be preferred to *nothing at all*, if we had to choose between an action whose sole effect would be one of them and one which would have no effects whatever. The fact is that the view which seems to me to be true is the one which, apart from theories, I think everyone would naturally take, namely, that there are an *immense variety* of different things, *all* of which are intrinsically good; and that though all these things may perhaps have some characteristic *in common*, their variety is so great that they have none, which, *besides* being common to them all, is also *peculiar* to them—that is to say, which never belongs to anything which is intrinsically bad or indifferent. All that can, I think, be done by way of making plain what kinds of things are intrinsically good or bad, and what are better or worse than others, is to classify some of the chief kinds of each, pointing out what the factors are upon which their goodness or badness depends. And I think this is one of the most profitable things which can be done in Ethics, and one which has been too much neglected hitherto. But I have not space to attempt it here.

I have only space for two final remarks. The first is that there do seem to be two important characteristics, which are *common* to absolutely all intrinsic goods, though not peculiar to them. Namely (1) it does seem as if nothing can be an intrinsic good unless it contains *both* some feeling and *also* some other form of consciousness; and, as we have said before, it seems possible that amongst the feelings contained must always be some amount of pleasure. And (2) it does also seem as if every intrinsic good must be a complex whole containing a considerable variety of different factors—as if, for instance, nothing so simple as pleasure by itself, however intense, could ever be any good. But it is important to insist (though it is obvious) that neither of these characteristics is *peculiar* to intrinsic goods: they may obviously *also* belong to things bad and indifferent. Indeed, as regards the first, it is not only true that many wholes which contain both feeling and some other form of consciousness are intrinsically bad; but it seems also to be true that nothing can be intrinsically bad, *unless* it contains some feeling.

The other final remark is that we must be very careful to distinguish the two questions (1) whether, and in what degree, a thing is *intrinsically* good and bad, and (2) whether, and in what degree, it is capable of adding to or subtracting from the intrinsic value of a whole of which it forms a part, from a third, entirely different question, namely (3) whether, and in what degree, a thing is *useful* and has good *effects,* or *harmful* and has *bad* effects. All three questions are very liable to be confused, because, in common life, we apply the names 'good' and 'bad' to things of all three kinds indifferently: when we say that a thing is 'good' we may mean either (1) that it is intrinsically good or (2) that it adds to the value of many intrinsically good wholes or (3) that it is useful or has good effects; and similarly when we say that a thing is bad we may mean any one of the three corresponding things. And such confusion is very liable to lead to mistakes, of which the following are, I think, the commonest. In the first place, people are apt to assume with regard to things, which really are very good indeed in senses (1) or (2), that they are scarcely any good at all, simply because they do not seem to be of much *use*—that is to say, to lead to *further* good effects; and similarly, with regard to things which really are very bad in senses (1) or (2), it is very commonly assumed that there cannot be much, if any, harm in them, simply because they do not seem to lead to *further* bad results. Nothing is commoner than to find people asking of a good thing: What *use* is it? and concluding that, if it is no use, it cannot be any good; or asking of a bad thing: What harm does it do? and concluding that if it *does* no harm, there cannot be any harm *in* it. Or, again, by a converse mistake, of things which really are very useful, but are not good at all in senses (1) and (2), it is very commonly assumed that they *must* be good in one or both of these two senses. Or again, of things, which really are very good in senses (1) and (2), it is assumed that, because they are good, they cannot possibly do harm. Or finally, of things, which are neither intrinsically good nor useful, it is assumed that they cannot be any good at all, although in fact they are very good in sense (2). All these mistakes are liable to occur, because, in fact, the degree of goodness or badness of a thing in any one of these three senses is by no means always in proportion to the degree of its goodness or badness in either of the other two; but if we are careful to distinguish the three different questions, they can, I think, all be avoided.

RALPH MASON BLAKE
Why Not Hedonism?

Let it first be clearly understood . . . that in attempting to defend hedonism from its critics I am by no means concerned with the *integral* defense of any historical hedonistic system. By hedonism I do not mean Epicureanism, or Benthamism, or the doctrines of J. S. Mill. There is not the slightest difficulty in showing, and it has in fact been demonstrated *ad nauseam*,[1] that these historic theories are one and all infected with serious fallacies and gross errors. I believe, however, that there is a set of fundamental principles which, whether or not it has ever been held in this precise form by any of the classical proponents of hedonism, at any rate seems to have been more or less approximated by each of them; that this set, moreover, will be recognized as undoubtedly constituting *a* hedonistic system; and, finally, that *this* hedonistic system is by no means to be disposed of by the simple device of showing that it has usually been inadequately stated, defended by fallacious arguments, and combined with inconsistent or erroneous principles.

This central core of hedonistic doctrine has been most clearly and completely disengaged from its various historical accompaniments not by any advocate of the theory, but, oddly enough, precisely by its acutest critic, Mr. G. E. Moore (in his *Ethics*). Ignoring all complications and refinements of interpretation, the bare essentials of this view can be stated in a highly compressed form in seven propositions. Of these the first two are simply preliminary definitions of terms. They are as follows: (1) To say of a thing that it is *intrinsically* good means that it would be good even if it existed quite alone, without any accompaniments or effects whatever; and (2) to say of a thing that it is *ultimately* good, or good *for its own sake*, means (*a*) that it is intrinsically good, and (*b*)

Reprinted from "Why Not Hedonism? A Protest," by R. M. Blake, *International Journal of Ethics*, XXXVII, No. 1 (1926), 1–18, by permission of The University of Chicago Press. Copyright, 1926, by The University of Chicago Press.

[1] [To the point of nausea.—Ed. note.]

that it contains no part which is not intrinsically good. The next three propositions are definitions of moral concepts. They are not peculiar to hedonism, as such, but characterize it as a *teleological*, rather than a *formalistic*, system of ethics. These propositions are as follows: (3) To call a voluntary act *wrong* means that the total consequences of some other action possible to the agent under the circumstances form a whole which is intrinsically better than the whole formed by the total consequences of the act in question. (4) To call a voluntary act *right* means that it is not wrong. (5) To call a voluntary act a *duty* for a given agent, or to say that the agent *ought* to perfom it, means that, among the acts possible to the agent under the circumstances, the total consequences of the act in question form a whole which is intrinsically better than the whole formed by the total consequences of any of the other possible acts. The next proposition also is not necessarily peculiar to hedonism as such. It amounts to a denial of Mr. Moore's principle of "organic unity" (cf. his *Principia Ethica*), and might form a part of a non-hedonistic system. This principle is as follows: (6) The intrinsic value of a whole is always in proportion to the amount of ultimate value which it contains. The last proposition is the characteristic and peculiar thesis of hedonism, viz., (7) pleasurable consciousness is always ultimately good (or good for its own sake); and nothing else is ever ultimately good.

And now for the current objections. Most of these, I think it will readily be seen, simply do not touch at all the theory previously stated. So far as it is concerned, they are completely beside the mark. For example, much ink is still expended upon the refutation of "psychological hedonism," i.e., the once fashionable theory that the sole human motive is the desire for pleasure. . . . The doctrine was, of course, accepted by most of the hedonists of the past, and was indeed frequently put forward by them as a proof of the truth of their ethical theory. Its falsity is, however, now generally recognized, and its uselessness as a basis for demonstration of the ethical theory fully admitted. It evidently forms no part of the doctrine previously stated, and is in no way implied thereby. Discussion of it is therefore wholly irrelevant to any living issue.

But even those who recognize the irrelevance of psychological hedonism sometimes formulate and criticize ethical hedonism in a way which is almost equally irrelevant. Hedonists hold—so the matter is frequently put—that even though the desire for pleasure is not actually the sole human motive, yet nevertheless it *ought* to be. . . . "Although other things besides pleasure may be desired, pleasure is the only thing that ought to be desired." Now, whether or not such a doctrine has actually formed a part of hedonistic systems in the past, it certainly ought to be plain that it is by no means an *essential* feature of such a system. Not only is it not in any way implied in the foregoing propositions, but on any reasonable view of things would seem even to be definitely excluded thereby. For according to these principles to say that no man *ought* ever to desire anything other than pleasure means that the total consequences of a desire for something other than pleasure *never* form a whole which contains more pleasurable experience than does the whole formed by the total consequences of any other possible desire; and to most observers of human life this statement seems to be plainly false. Hence, indeed, the familiar "hedonistic paradox" to the effect that "pleasure to be got must be forgot"—a paradox which may certainly be quite consistently accepted by hedonists. The fact that hedonists judge the value of acts by reference to their consequences in pleasure by no means commits them to the view that such consequences are best attained by making them directly the sole human motive and the sole object of human desire. Nobody makes any scruple of admitting that such a valuable end as health, for example, is not best attained by making it a direct and constant object of conscious concern. It should therefore not surprise us to find that the like is true also of other valuable ends. In fact, I am not familiar with any system of ethics in which it is held that desire for the ultimate end proposed by the system should be made the sole human desire. Why then should it be supposed that hedonists alone are bound to maintain such a doctrine?

As for the connection of hedonism with egoism, it might seem superfluous at this late date to insist that hedonists need in no way be adherents of egoism. Yet this confusion still to some extent persists, even among writers who ought to know very much better. Thus Professor Münsterberg seems to have supposed that a hedonist can consistently regard any given act as constituting for him a duty only provided he can view it as resulting in a preponderance of pleasure for *himself*; for he argues against hedonism as follows: "When we will the morally good, we do indeed wish that the good also give us joy, but we know that it is not good simply because it gives us pleasure. . . . Even if we acknowledge the pleasure in the minds of other human beings as goal for our moral action, the moral self is not therefore based on pleasure. . . . We feel it our duty to serve the pleasure of others, but this duty cannot itself come into question as a pleasure. We may submit to it with pleasure, but we do not submit to it because it gives us pleasure." But need a hedonist maintain that our duty must needs be a pleasure in the doing?

Mr. Joad also thinks it an inconsistency in a hedonist to admit "that the individual can, and ought to, desire something which may have no relation to his own pleasure, namely, the good of the community"; for he tells us not only that Mill's implicit admission of this doctrine involved him in inconsistencies, but also that "these inconsistencies in Mill are important, and I have dwelt on them at some length because they demonstrate the impracticability of maintaining, even with the best will in the world, that pleasure is the only thing of value. . . . They reveal themselves most completely in Mill's work, but they are implied in any form of utilitarian hedonism." I should very much like to have it pointed out just *how* the rejection of egoism implies any inconsistency in such a form of utilitarian hedonism as that outlined above.

Another classical line of attack upon hedonism consists in elaborate criticism of the so-called "hedonistic calculus." If the rightness and wrongness of actions depend upon the degree to which a greater or less "quantity of pleasure" is realized in their consequences, then, in order definitely to determine upon the rightness or wrongness of any action, we must be able somehow to predict the consequences of various actions and to estimate the relative "quantities of pleasure" involved. Now no one would deny, I suppose, that it is no easy matter to forecast the future, especially in such a complicated sphere as that of human conduct and its effects; nor will any one be disposed to doubt that there are grave difficulties involved in the determination and comparison of quantities of pleasure and displeasure. I cannot here enter into the details of this question, but it ought to be clearly understood that precisely similar difficulties affect any teleological system of ethics whatsoever. Every such system makes the value of actions depend upon the quantity of good which they succeed in realizing; every such system holds that some actions are better than others, that some realize more and some less good. In every such system, therefore, some sort of "calculus" is necessary, and I find it very difficult to understand how it can be any easier to determine such quantitative questions as are here involved in terms of "satisfaction of desire" or "harmony" or "self-realization" than it is in terms of pleasure and displeasure. Hedonists have at least made a resolute attempt to deal with this aspect of the matter. I fail to see how any teleological system can view such an attempt as superfluous; and I am not aware that any system has made the attempt with more earnestness or with greater success than hedonism.

Professor Dewey is one of those who make much of the defects of the "calculus" as an objection to hedonism. But I cannot help thinking that he interprets the doctrine in a manner that is highly artificial and unreal. He seems to suppose that in the view of hedonists the calculus can be applied with perfect mathematical precision to the determination of the results of individual acts severally, and that, too, with absolute accuracy and certainty of result. This seems to me something of a caricature of the hedonistic view. I venture to think that even Bentham and Mill, who no doubt entertained somewhat exaggerated notions with regard to the applicability of the calculus, never went to anything like such lengths.

•   •   •   •   •

Professor Albee puts the argument a little differently:

A direct computation of the consequences of actions, in terms of happiness and unhappiness, can never afford the foundation for a scientific Ethics, not merely, or principally, because experience shows that individuals derive pleasure and pain, as the case may be, from very different things; but because it is absolutely certain, on general principles, that every advance in morality involves a shifting of the scale of hedonistic values. Otherwise expressed, individuals and nations are constantly, if generally slowly, discarding one scale of hedonistic values for another, previously assumed to be ultimate, and this in proportion to the development of moral character. Reduced to its lowest terms, this means that hedonistic values vary as moral character varies.

It is difficult to see that this way of stating the matter makes things really any harder for the hedonist. It is true that men's judgments regarding the sources or causes of pleasure are subject to frequent change, but so are their judgments with regard to the sources of any sort of ultimate value. It is true that as men change they derive pleasure from different things and in different degrees than formerly. But whatever theory of ultimate value is adopted, it seems likely that changes in human thought and character or in other conditions of life will bring with them similar alterations in the sources of value. The mere fact that changes in *moral character* constitute one cause of such alterations in the sources of value seems to introduce no essentially novel difficulty into the argument; and in any case the fact would remain the same and the difficulty equal on any teleological theory whatever.

But arguments based on the difficulties of the calculus do not exhaust the case against hedonism. There is no stopping the chorus of objections. "A state of unbroken pleasure would not really be pleasant. A continuous heaven of constant enjoyment would be intolerable boredom." Such an objection surely represents mere confusion of thought. How can pleasure be unpleasant? How can enjoyment be boredom? "But uninterrupted pleasure is an ideal which is impossible of attainment in any actual human life. It is a mere chimera." Or, as Professor Rogers puts the point: "That at which a sensible human being aims is no unimaginable state of the intensest possible pleasure unaccompanied by pain. . . . Rational satisfaction is no dream of an undisturbed and impossibly complete state of felicity." But what hedonist has asserted the attainability of such an ideal? Are hedonists, then, wholly ignorant of the conditions of human life? In truth they are not so foolish as to maintain the attainability of any such perfect consummation, or to counsel attempts to realize the impossible. What they hold is simply that the intrinsic value of any state of affairs is in proportion to the amount of pleasurable experience it contains, and that human effort should be so directed as to make this amount *as great as possible*. No overstrained idealism is implied. A hedonist may, indeed, consistently also be a pessimist. We should not forget that the truth of pessimism has often been argued from hedonistic premises.

But then, says Professor Rogers, "in practice the only clear meaning, therefore, that a 'sum of pleasures' carries is this, that I want my life to be a continuous series of satisfied moments lasting as long as possible. But this is pretty much an empty platitude, which throws almost no light at all on what constitutes satisfaction at any given moment." But is it to be expected of any theory of the nature of the ultimate end that it should automatically reveal the particular means to that end? For Professor Rogers "that at which a sensible human being aims is . . . the realization that he is making the most of life that it is possible for him, with his particular interests and limitations, to make, considering the means at his disposal." How much light does *this* way of formulating the end throw upon "what constitutes satisfaction at any given moment"?

The interesting feature of Professor Rogers' case is that *de facto* he comes very near, despite his protests, to being a hedonist himself—if only he were not so desperately afraid of the name. "Only when we can point to pleasure," he writes, "is the judgment of value felt to be *justified*." "No aim will be called reflectively a *good* aim unless it tends to result in pleasure." But still he will not be called hedonist. He does not "intend to say that mere pleasurableness by itself is a good. Pleasantness as such is not good because pleasantness does not exist by itself; a good is concrete, and pleasantness merely an abstract quality." But, may we ask, what hedonist attaches any value to mere "pleasantness" as an abstract universal? It is, of course, only concrete pleasurable experience which he values.

•   •   •   •   •

Many criticisms of hedonism reduce to most elementary misunderstandings of the hedonistic distinction between pleasurable experience as intrinsic and ultimate good, and moral value as a species of extrinsic or instrumental good. Thus A. E. Taylor writes: "A man is not morally good because his career has been marked by extraordinary cases of unexpected good luck, nor is the life of one of the lower animals to be reckoned morally good because it may contain a vast number of pleasant moments." But hedonists, of course, do not say that *moral* goodness consists in enjoyment of pleasure; for them moral goodness is an *extrinsic* value derived from the fact that certain actions and dispositions *result in* consequences which are more pleasurable than the results of other acts and dispositions. The same confusion is apparent also in Taylor's treatment of the question, Is the good always pleasant? He interprets this to mean "Is the morally good or *right* act always accompanied by more pleasure than a wrong act?" To the question so stated no hedonist would dream of giving an affirmative answer. Professor Fullerton also gives a criticism of hedonism based on this same misunderstanding. After quoting Bentham to the effect that all pleasure is in itself a good, even the pleasure a malicious man "takes at the thought of the pain which he sees, or expects to see, his adversary undergo," he asks, "Can the pleasure of a malignant act properly be called *morally* good at all?" This question being answered in the negative, Bentham's position is considered to be refuted. But, as we have seen, no hedonist dreams of maintaining that pleasant experience is *in itself* a *moral* good. In fact, for hedonism nothing whatever is in itself, i.e., intrinsically, a moral good.

Another favorite procedure of the critics is based upon the fact that hedonists have often professed to give demonstrative *proofs* of the truth of their theory. These attempted demonstrations are examined and found to be inconclusive, or positively fallacious. Hedonism, it is thus discovered, has "failed to prove its case," and we pass on to consider the alternative theories. Now let us admit at once that the fundamental principles of hedonism are incapable of demonstration. So far as I can see, the critics are quite right in rejecting all the alleged proofs that have ever been offered, and I know of nothing that can be set in their place. But how stands the case with the alternative theories? Is it possible to give a demonstration of *their* fundamental principles? Their advocates scarcely pretend that it is. These alternatives are accepted, not because of any rigorous proof of their truth, but on quite other grounds. The fact that hedonism "fails to prove its case" in itself certainly constitutes no proof of the truth of any other theory. The truth of the matter seems to be that no theory of ethics, in so far as it is a question of ultimate ends, is susceptible of "proof" in the strict sense. In fact, even Bentham and Mill were on occasion prepared to admit as much. Thus Bentham says of the fundamental principle of hedonism, "Is it susceptible of any direct proof? It should seem not: for that which is used to prove everything else, cannot itself be proved: a chain of proofs must have their commencement somewhere." And Mill also remarks: "To be incapable of proof by reasoning is common to all first principles." Unfortunately, however, Mill nevertheless attempted, in his fourth chapter, precisely such a proof as he had here stated to be impossible. His lack of success is certainly not surprising.

Fundamental ethical principles, in fact, as Mr. Moore so properly insists, are accepted or rejected on intuitive grounds. The most that any adherent of any ethical system can do by way of persuading another to accept his theory is to state its fundamental principles as clearly and adequately as possible, to take care that these are properly interpreted, and that the issues are not obscured by any confusion with irrelevant or inconsistent doctrines, to exhibit the implications of these principles and their consistency or inconsistency with other human beliefs, and then simply to appeal to the reflective judgment of his hearer. . . .

For my own part, when I subject to such a test the fundamental principles of hedonistic ethics, they appear to me to ring true. Indeed, it seems to me to be actually self-evident that all pleasurable experience is ultimately good. It does *not* seem to me self-evident that *nothing but* pleasurable experience is ever ultimately good; but much careful reflection has hithetro failed to reveal anything else which *does* seem to me ultimately good. Again, it is not self-evident to me that the intrinsic value of a whole is necessarily always in proportion to the amount of ultimate good which it contains; but in every instance which I have ever considered it has always seemed to me that this is actually the case. Consequently I am forced to adopt a hedonistic position. If other men judge these matters differently I know of no way of "refuting" them; but, on the other hand, I have never been able to see that any of the considerations advanced in opposition to hedonism constitute a refutation of *it*.

From what has been said, however, it is obvious that there may be perfectly *legitimate* criticisms of hedonism—those, namely, which consist simply in presenting for judgment "hard cases" concerning which it is thought that the only conclusion consistent with hedonistic principles will nevertheless, on careful reflection, be rejected. But such criticisms, however legitimate in method, have never actually seemed to me in the least conclusive. Such force as they at first sight sometimes appear to have always turns out to arise, so far as I can see, from some confusion of thought which still clouds the issue. Once these confusions are cleared away, I never seem to find in these "hard cases" anything incompatible with the truth of hedonism.

Any adequate consideration of this phase of the matter would lead us too far afield to allow of our undertaking it on the present occasion with any degree of fullness. I shall therefore simply illustrate the way in which it seems to me possible to dispose of such hard cases by the examination of a few upon which Mr. Moore chiefly depends, and which I hope will be more or less typical. The following is an instance which he believes will persuade us that even wholes containing no pleasure may be intrinsically valuable: "Let us imagine one world exceedingly beautiful. Imagine it as beautiful as you can . . . and then imagine the ugliest world you can possibly conceive. Imagine it simply one heap of filth," and then suppose that no one ever can or does receive pleasure or displeasure from either world in any respect or degree whatever. "Would it not be well to do what we could to produce [the beautiful world] rather than the other?" Would not the former be intrinsically better than the latter? Now I ask myself whether this case does not derive most of its apparent force from the circumstance that the reader who makes this imaginative comparison very naturally revolts from the image of the ugly world and at the same time takes pleasure in the thought of the beautiful world, and that he neglects explicitly to notice and to discount this fact. I also ask myself whether the reader is not influenced, and his judgment unconsciously perverted, by the fact that we can scarcely compare these two imaginary worlds without the thought that the beautiful world obviously possesses greater pleasure-producing *potentialities* than the ugly one; by the fact that it is difficult to compare these two imaginary worlds without reference to the consideration that the one world provides, for any conscious being that might sometime be introduced upon the scene, a better basis for enjoyment than does the other. Once I carefully notice and discount such sources of bias, I entirely fail, for my own part, to see any superior value in the beautiful world.

Another of Mr. Moore's examples—one of those which to his mind "constitute a *reductio ad absurdum* of the view that intrinsic value is always in proportion to quantity of pleasure," is as follows. If this hedonistic principle is true, it "involves our saying . . . that a world in which absolutely nothing except pleasure existed—no knowledge, no love, no enjoyment of beauty, no moral qualities—must yet be intrinsically better—better worth creating—provided only the total quantity of pleasure in it were the least bit greater, than one in which all these things existed *as well as* pleasure." This instance seems almost deliberately framed to confuse the issue; for it is very difficult in considering the matter to remember that, if we are not illegitimately to introduce into our second world an additional increment of pleasure, by "enjoyment of beauty" we must here distinctly mean merely *contemplation* of beauty, wholly divorced from any element of pleasure. Moreover, it is difficult to keep our minds wholly free from the thought of the greater hedonic potentialities of a world possessing so many elements which in our experience are fruitful sources of enjoyment, as compared with a world from which these sources are eliminated. Once I clear my mind from such confusing associations, however, I feel no further difficulty in reaching the hedonistic conclusion.

Mr. Moore also points out that the hedonistic theory compels us to assert that "the state of mind of a drunkard, when he is intensely pleased with breaking crockery, is just as valuable, in itself—just as well worth having, as that of a man who is fully realizing all that is exquisite in the tragedy of King Lear, provided only the mere quantity of pleasure in both cases is the same." Here again, once I carefully abstract from all tacit reference to the differing promise and potentiality of these two states of mind, from all larger thought of their vastly differing significance for the total lives of these men and of their fellows, I find myself quite clearly committed to the hedonistic view of the matter.

I thus do quite clearly embrace the conclusion which Mr. Moore thinks self-evidently mistaken, "that if we *could* get as much pleasure in the world, without needing to have any knowledge, or any moral qualities, or any sense of beauty, as we can yet *with* them, then all these things would be entirely su-perfluous." But I also quite as heartily agree with Mr. Moore that "the question is quite incapable of proof either way," and that "if anybody, after clearly con-sidering the issue, does come" to the contrary conclusion, "there is no way of proving that he is wrong." My point simply is that there is no short and easy way with hedonism, and that the cavalier way in which it is commonly treated is wholly unreasonable and unjust.

CHARLES A. BAYLIS
Grading, Values, and Choice

The stalemate in ethics among naturalists, intuitionists, emotivists and linguistic analysts remains unbroken. Each has criticized the others vigorously but none has succeeded in showing how either value statements or obligation statements can provide us with good reasons for choice. To mention but one example, R. M. Hare, in *The Language of Morals*, proposes that "You ought to tell him the truth" is more clearly rendered as, "If you do not tell him the truth you will be breaking a general *'ought'* principle [*i.e.* "a proper universal imperative"] to which I hereby subscribe." But surely the fact that an action we are thinking of doing violates an universal imperative to which the utterer of that imperative subscribes does not give us a good reason for deciding against that action unless we have other reasons for believing that he is in some sense correct in subscrib-ing to this imperative.

Ethical principles that merely persuade and do not provide grounds for choice are a failure, because they do not do the job we want them to do. In this paper I attempt some positive suggestions for discovering principles which will provide sound reasons for our choices. I take as my point of departure Mr. J. O. Urmson's article "On Grading".

From C. A. Baylis, "Grading, Values, and Choice," *Mind*, LXVII, No. 268 (1958), 485–501. Reprinted by permission of the author and the editor of *Mind*.

Urmson begins with the concrete example of the grading of apples in England as *Super, Extra Fancy, Fancy,* and so on, according to criteria fixed by the Ministry of Agriculture and Fisheries. We can and do, of course, grade many other things. Trainers grade race horses; officials at a dog show grade dogs; real estate appraisers grade houses; teachers grade their students; women grade other women's clothes and husbands; and all of us grade our fellow human beings in a number of respects, one of the most interesting and difficult being the grading of them as to moral character. In each of these cases the grading criteria are different. In some cases, such as the commercial ones, they are very precise and well agreed upon. In others, such as the moral cases, the criteria tend to be vague and incomplete (open-textured) and acceptance of them is likely to be much less widespread. Sometimes we use only positive grading labels, such as 'good', 'better', and 'best'; in other cases we like negative ones as well, and perhaps a neutral one.

Urmson makes the point that people could be trained to do the mechanics of physical grading, *e.g.* sorting apples by grade, so that they could do an excellent job without knowing that they are grading. They might think they are merely classifying in accordance with the criteria given them. They might neither know nor care what the purpose behind the classifying might be. If the grading labels used were not recognized grading ones, such as *Excellent, Very Good,* and *Good,* but emotively neutral *ad hoc*[1] labels such as X, Y, Z, an outsider might not know whether grading or some other form of classifying were going on. But the grader does know. Urmson gives this as one reason for insisting that grading and classifying are two different operations, even though to an external observer they might seem indistinguishable.

Another reason for distinguishing the two is noted by a commentator, Karl Britton, who points out that the same grading might well result from applying a different set of criteria. To apply criteria is one thing and to grade by doing so is something else again.

An even more basic reason for distinguishing the two is noted by another commentator, M. J. Baker, who calls attention to the simple fact that whereas to classify is merely to sort things by certain criteria, to grade is to use certain criteria as a means of classifying according to merit, real or alleged. "To grade is to rank objects, actions, events, states of affairs, etc., in order of merit and demerit . . . and this ranking signifies the degrees of merit which we may expect can be manifested."

Urmson raises the important question, "Is the relation between the criteria and the grade analytic or synthetic?" We might be tempted to say that all we mean by assigning a grading label say, 'good', to an object is that it has objective criteria A, B, and C. But aside from the distinctions already mentioned between sorting by means of objective criteria and grading, to say that the relation between grade and criteria is analytic would result in "the absurd situation that 'good' was a homonym with as many punning meanings as the situations it

[1] [Literally, "to this," that is, chosen for use in the given case without intending them to be applied in other cases.—Ed. note.]

applied to." It would have a different meaning when used of an apple, a cabbage, a theatrical performance, a man, and so on, whereas as a matter of fact it has a common meaning in many different cases, that of a grade label, ranking say between fair and excellent. On the other hand, Urmson urges, to regard the relation between grade and criteria as synthetic is equally absurd. Where there is agreement as to the necessary and sufficient criteria for applying a certain grade, to say that something meets all these criteria but does not merit that grade, "would not merely be empirically surprising; it would involve a breakdown in communication." Urmson does not resolve this difficulty save by suggesting that the dichotomy 'analytic or synthetic' applies only to descriptive predicates and not to value predicates. But this tells us only that value predicates have a strange nature without specifying what it is.

There is another important problem that Urmson leaves essentially unresolved. That is the problem of justifying the criteria used as a basis for assigning grades. He remarks, correctly enough, that where there is agreement about the criteria to be used for a given bit of grading there is no practical problem. But where there is disagreement about the criteria he is unable to suggest a solution unless there is agreement at a higher level about the criteria for the grading criteria. But to take this view is to adopt essentially the sceptical view according to which value statements carry an implicit reference to some standard, *i.e.* criteria, but that the choice among criteria is logically arbitrary. All you need, and indeed, all you can get, according to Urmson, is *de facto*[2] agreement. To be sure, such agreement has the practical merit of preventing conflict for as long as it lasts. But it provides little or no ground for the correctness of the value judgments which rest on it.

The unsatisfactoriness of Urmson's treatment of these two problems, of the relation between a value grade and the criteria for that grade, and of the grounds for choosing grading criteria, makes it desirable both to supplement his account and to depart from it. I begin by distinguishing various types of grading labels; those for entities which are (1) good of a kind, (2) extrinsically (or derivatively) good, and (3) intrinsically (or non-derivatively) good. Among extrinsic goods I distinguish (2a) instrumental goods, (2b) contributive goods, and (2c) inherent goods.

(1) Often when we apply the label 'good' to something we mean only that it is a good thing of a certain kind, that it is good in one or more respects. When we speak of good apples, we may mean that they are good looking or good tasting, or good sources of nourishment or vitamins, or perhaps good in several of these respects, good perhaps in all the major respects in which apples can be good rather than bad. Similarly we sometimes speak of good guns or good blackjacks, or even of good lies. In labelling something good of its kind, we do not commit ourselves to the assertion that the kind of thing concerned is itself good. In labelling something good in one or more respects we do not thereby label it good on the whole. Consequently it does not follow from 'X is a good

thing of kind Y' or 'X is good in respect Y' that 'X is a good thing'. The kind of results which a lie tends to have makes most lies bad deeds, with good lies tending to be worse deeds than bad ones. Since the uses to which a gun may be put are so varied, some good, some bad, we hesitate to label an object of that kind as in general a good thing or a bad thing. Often when we label something merely as good of a kind, or good in a certain respect, we mark our reluctance to labelling it a good thing.

(2a) When by contrast to such a carefully qualified assertion, we want to assert that something is a good means to something good, we say of it that it is *instrumentally good*. In such an assertion we are predicating goodness of it, we are saying that it is a good thing, rather than making the limited claim that it is a thing good of a certain kind. Anything is instrumentally good in so far as it is a causal factor in the production of something which is good, that is, it is a condition or a cause or a contributing cause of something good. Instrumentally good things derive their value from the value of that to which they are a means. Their instrumental value is thus extrinsic to them. Instrumental goods are one species of *extrinsic goods,* that is, of goods whose value is derived from their relation to something else of value.

(2b) Another species of extrinsic goods consists of those things which are necessary parts of a good whole. Thus a spark plug may have little or no value by itself but may nevertheless be a good thing because it is a necessary part of something good, for example, a gasoline motor. An essential part of a good whole derives merit from being just that. It contributes to a whole something which is necessary for that thing's goodness as a whole. We may call things which are good in this way *contributive goods.*

The difference between instrumental and contributive goods is that the former are means to a good end, the latter necessary parts of a good whole. A description that will fit either is "something that is good in virtue of being conducive, whether through a causal relation or a part-whole relation, to something good, whether that good be an end or a whole". There may well be other relations to good objects or events which generate additional sub-classes of extrinsic goods. If so, the account given here could be extended to them. The same principles would be involved, for all extrinsic goods are such precisely to the extent that they derive their value from their relations to other things of value.

(2c) One especially interesting sub-class of extrinsic goods consists of inherent goods. They derive their value from being objects of experiences which are intrinsically good. C. I. Lewis defines them as follows: "Those values which are resident in objects in such wise that they are realizable in experience through presentation of the object itself to which they are attributed, we propose to call *inherent* values." The experience of something inherently good is normally an intrinsic good. A Hedonist, for example, would go further and expand this account by saying that an object is inherently good to the extent that the experience of it has a pleasant hedonic tone. On his view pleasant experiences are intrinsically good; pleasant objects, namely objects the experience of which is pleasant, are inherently good. On the other hand, one who holds a conative theory, like R. B. Perry, could say that an object is inherently good to the extent that it is an object of an interest, the intrinsic source of this value being the interest. The value of inherent goods, like that of instrumental and contributive goods, is extrinsic. It is derived from the value that is realized when they are apprehended in the appropriate manner by some sentient being. The chief difference between instrumental and contributive goods on the one hand and inherent goods on the other, is that the former are good in virtue of being conducive to other good things, the latter in so far as the experience of them is intrinsically good. When unexperienced, an inherently good object's value is merely potential or latent. It normally becomes manifest when a sentient creature becomes aware of the object in the appropriate way. Under abnormal circumstances inherent value may remain latent even when the inherently good object is experienced. Thus a beautiful painting may arouse neither pleasure nor interest in a person lost in grief. Yet it would still have the capacity to give a satisfying experience to observers under more normal circumstances. That inherent value is none the less derivative is shown by the fact that it ceases to be latent and is realized only when an appropriate experience of it is intrinsically good.[3]

(3) For any entity to be *intrinsically good* it must have a non-derivative positive worth; it must be good in itself; it must have positive value over and above any extrinsic value it may have. It must not owe all its value to its relations to other valuable things. If an experience, or anything else, has intrinsic value this value belongs to it in virtue of its own nature and is independent of any derivative value it may possess.

Some writers, *e.g.* John Dewey, have denied that there are any intrinsic goods; others, *e.g.* Urmson and Hare, have objected to the extrinsic-intrinsic distinction as applied to values. I consider their objections in turn. Perhaps Dewey's denial of intrinsic goods is motivated in part by his behaviouristic trends. Looking for intrinsic goods among physical objects or occurrences, he naturally finds none. A physical event or object would be of no value, positive or negative, were it never to affect any sentient creature directly or indirectly. A beautiful vase, buried forever in the sands of Carthage (to use Moore's example), has now only latent inherent value, an aesthetic value which could be

---

[3] We may characterize extrinsic goods as *actual* when the good which is the source from which the extrinsic value is derived is actual. Thus X is instrumentally good to the extent that it is a causal factor in the production of an actual Y which is good. Similarly, X is contributively good if it is a necessary part of an actual good Y. Again, X is inherently good to the extent that actual experiences of it occur and are intrinsically good. An entity has potential (or latent) *extrinsic* value in so far as it has the capacity to be a means or a part of something good or to be the object of an intrinsically good experience. An entity is *normally extrinsically good* if normally its results are good, or if normally the wholes of which it is a necessary part are good, or if normally an experience of it is intrinsically good.

It is to be noted that the proximate sources of instrumental or contributive value need not be intrinsically good. It is enough that they be good, whether intrinsically or extrinsically. But for an object to be inherently good the experience of it must be intrinsically good.

realized only if, contrary to the hypothesis, it were again to be contemplated aesthetically. If objects or events, as contrasted with experiences, have any value it is only because they are either themselves inherently valuable or are instrumental or contributive to other things which are inherently valuable. And the value of inherently valuable things is realized and becomes actual only when they are experienced. It is derived from the intrinsic value of the experience of them. All these extrinsic values are thus ultimately derivative from intrinsic ones. Unless somewhere along the chain of derivatively valuable things there is something which has intrinsic value, nothing would be a good thing. For example, part at least of the goodness of apples rests on the fact that the eating of them is pleasant. It is in virtue of their capacity to bring about intrinsically good experiences that we term apples good. The same is true of other inherently good things. Similarly, instrumental and contributive goods are good only because sooner or later they are conducive to intrinsic goods. Thus, money is instrumentally good because we can buy with it other good things and thus acquire inherently good things which we enjoy directly. The value of objects in every case seems to reside in their effects, direct or indirect, on sentient creatures.

Satisfying experiences, pleasant experiences, happy experiences, all hedonically toned states of consciousness, I urge, are intrinsically good. Some such experiences have good consequences, some have bad ones, but all have a value or a merit of their own, distinct from any value, positive or negative, which their consequences have. This value, which they owe to their own nature and not to their relations to other things of value, is intrinsic value. I need not, and do not, claim here that pleasant experiences are the only things which are intrinsically good, but they are thus good whether anything else is or not. They are worth having for their own sakes; other things being equal it is better that they should exist rather than not; they are worthy of existence for their own sake; they are good in themselves, they are intrinsically good.

Dewey objects to intrinsic goods on the ground that nothing is an end and merely an end. Life and time and fortune march on and whatever is a result has a result. This seems true enough, but it is no ground for denying intrinsic values. A richly satisfying experience does indeed have consequences. Very likely it will aid our digestion. But it would be very odd indeed of anyone other than a victim of ulcers or some similar trouble to prefer it to a neutral or dissatisfying experience primarily because of that effect. Its primary worth lies in its own satisfyingness. Dewey appears to have overlooked, or perhaps never to have realized, that to say of anything that it is intrinsically good is not to deny that it is extrinsically good. It is rather to affirm that it possesses a value over and above any extrinsic value it may have.

Urmson objects to dividing valuable things into two main classes, those good as means and those good in themselves, or as he says, "as ends". His objections seem to be three: . . . (1) Most things that we value are good partly as means and partly as ends. (2) He sees "no reason for thinking that there is more than one sense of the word 'good'". (3) He holds that the criteria of goodness "are different in each situation". The facts require "different criteria for goodness in apples and cabbages (and *a fortiori*[4] in men and guns)".

None of these comments seem to raise serious difficulties. (1) That some things are good both as means and as end, does not belie the fact that they are good as means, nor the fact that they are good as ends. (2) The fact that 'good' has a single meaning common to its different applications seems to be true, but leaves open the possibility, on which Urmson rightly insists, that some things are good in some respects, *e.g.* as means, and the same or other things are good in other respects, *e.g.* as ends. (3) Urmson's third objection seems to amount to pointing out that some things are good of their kind, that when we call something 'good' we don't always mean that it is intrinsically or extrinsically good. But this I have not merely admitted but emphasized. Urmson makes the additional point that farmers value their products not only as a means to certain ends, but also for their own sake. But this is, I think, to confuse intrinsic goods with inherent goods. The latter are those the experience of which is intrinsically good. For example, things which are normally satisfying because of their own nature and not merely because they are conducive to other satisfying things are inherently good. Thus farmers take satisfaction in their produce itself and not merely in the market value of that produce. But to say this is not to assert that the produce has intrinsic value apart from such satisfaction.

Hare's objections to the distinction between intrinsic and instrumental values rest apparently on this same confusion of inherent goods and intrinsic goods. For example, he gives a good bath as an example of something not only instrumentally but intrinsically good, and then mentions as a criterion of its intrinsic goodness that it must remain within a certain temperature range during a certain temporal interval. But we can see at once that a bath having these and other virtues would still have no actual value if left unused or if used only by a person devoid of affective and conative states. A bath is normally a source of a satisfactory experience for the bather, and is for this reason inherently good. It is a pleasant thing. But it is the pleasant experience of bathing that is intrinsically good.

Hare says that the point of his discussion here is to show that the criteria for intrinsic value and for instrumental value are of the same general kind. He does not of course show this since he does not use an example of a genuinely intrinsic good. But in any case I point to fundamental differences between criteria for the two kinds of goodness below.

Urmson's failure to delineate a method for choosing the criteria for grading labels appears to arise in part from unwillingness to distinguish things good of a kind from extrinsically good things, and inherently good things from intrinsically good experiences. Since the criteria are different in the different types of cases these or similar distinctions seem a prerequisite for the task.

The criteria for extrinsic goods are primarily scientific ones. We grade as

[4] [That is, even more so, for evaluating men and guns.—Ed. note.]

instrumental goods those things which are causally productive of something good, and the causal relations are excellent examples of relations which are investigated by scientific methods. We grade as contributive goods those things which are necessary parts of good wholes, and the relation necessary-part-of is again one which is testable by scientific procedures. We grade as inherently good those things the experience of which is intrinsically good. To discover their criteria we have but to observe the distinguishing characteristics of those kinds of objects which yield intrinsically good experiences when one is aware of them in an appropriate way. The criteria which mark such kinds of objects will be present in each normal experience of an object of that kind, and can be remarked by the usual observational and other scientific methods. For each kind of extrinsic goods the criteria will be different, as Urmson remarks, but they will share the characteristics of being indicative of a causal or part-whole relation to something good or of being such that the experience of them is intrinsically good. And since these various criteria will themselves be selected by scientific criteria, they will have high predictive power and high reliability.

Similar remarks apply to criteria for things good of a kind, save that we do not have to ask whether the kind concerned is itself good or bad, as we do in identifying something as extrinsically good.

What about the something good from which extrinsic goods derive their value? How can we recognize cases of it? Something instrumentally or contributively good may be such because it is conducive to something else extrinsically good. But eventually, if it is to be a good thing at all, it must be conducive to something either inherently or intrinsically good. And inherent goods to be such must yield experiences which are intrinsically good. There remains the question "What are the criteria of intrinsically good experiences?"

One difficulty with Urmson's discussion of "criteria" is that he fails to distinguish between two related concepts. They are suggested by P. B. Rice's terms, 'identifying property' and 'conferring property'. I would modify his account of them to the following: an *identifying property* of anything to which the term 'intrinsically good' properly applies is a discoverable characteristic the presence of which in anything is a reliable sign of the intrinsic goodness of that thing. A *conferring property* of anything intrinsically good is that "value-making" characteristic of it which confers upon it the value-characteristic of being intrinsically good. A hedonist would say that the pleasantness of an experience is such a value-making characteristic. It confers intrinsic goodness of any experience that it characterizes. Other value theorists would describe the property which confers intrinsic goodness in other ways. But, fortunately, for our present purposes, we need not here settle such disagreements. We can defer them for later scientific resolution. If we find an identifying property of intrinsic goods then we can examine such goods at leisure for those empirical properties which confer the intrinsic goodness. Once a conferring property of intrinsic goodness has been found it can serve also as an identifying property. But to find it requires the prior use of some other identifying property. What such properties are there?

We have said that for anything to be intrinsically good it must be worthy of existence entirely apart from any extrinsic value it may have, and we have explained what we mean by 'worthy of existence' by saying that anything which has this characteristic ought, *ceteris paribus*,[5] to exist rather than not, that it would be better for it to exist, and that anyone who can bring it into being ought to do so unless there is something preferable he can do instead. We can further describe this concept by adding that we ought, other things being equal, to prefer the existence of an intrinsically good thing to its nonexistence, we ought to choose its presence rather than its absence, we ought, on suitable occasions to approve of it ourselves and commend it to others, and so on. *The intrinsic goodness of anything both demands and justifies such action and attitudes on our part.* It should be obvious that this analysis of the meaning of 'intrinsically good' does not commit the so called "naturalistic fallacy" but, on the contrary, specifically preserves "the normative force" of the term. The crucial question is what kind of empirical criteria, *i.e.* identifying properties will serve as reliable evidence of the presence of something intrinsically good, in this normative sense?

When we judge things of certain kinds, *e.g.* pleasant experiences, to be intrinsically good, the best initial evidence for this that we could have, I submit, is that we find ourselves *prizing* things of that kind, *i.e.* liking, approving, desiring, preferring, and commending them, for their own qualities (rather than because of their relations to other valuable things) in circumstances where to the best of our searching knowledge we are making no mistake in our cognition of them. Such evidence gives us an initial probability that what we thus prize is intrinsically good. We can increase this probability by making repeated examinations of things of the same kind under circumstances which vary just enough to guard against the kinds of cognitive error which might occur.

The types of error which might occur when we conscientiously try to discover whether or not something, *e.g.* a pleasant experience, is intrinsically good are three:

(1) We might mistake some extrinsic value of our alleged intrinsic good for an intrinsic value of it. But this we can guard against by attending explicitly to its extrinsic value and discounting it, or by seeking intrinsic goods of the same kind where there is evidence that their extrinsic value is negligible.

(2) Through inadvertence we might fail to take account of some relevant feature of the alleged intrinsic good. But this we can guard against by focusing our attention more carefully on it, or by examining other cases of the same sort of thing. To overlook a relevant feature of anything, even of an experience thought to be intrinsically good, is always possible, but it could be due only to inattention, and this with care is avoidable. Again, since we are examining an experience and not an "external" object, we need not worry about errors of perception. If our perceptual apparatus were out of order we might be having some other experience, better or worse as the case may be, but what we are

---

[5] [Other things being equal.—Ed. note.]

asking about is the experience we are actually having, no matter how we came to have it. And since it is the intrinsic value of this experience which we are attempting to assess we need not look for the causal properties of it, for its results will be relevant only to its extrinsic value. We can concentrate our attention on its own manifest characteristics, on its qualities rather than its relational properties.

(3) The possibilities of making an error of judgment are more numerous. A judgment of appraisal might be wrong because we made it while under the influence of some disability such as fatigue or alcohol or passion or prejudice. But such errors can be avoided, allowed for, or corrected. Often our experience contains clues which would lead us to suspect the presence of one or more of these disabilities. We sometimes know when we are tired or drunk; we occasionally recognize that we are engulfed by rage or some other passion, and once in a while we can even spot some of our own prejudices. But where there is doubt we can always seek the evidence of others about our condition and, if desirable, the evidence of professional experts. Mistakes due to errors of these sorts can be detected and corrected.

We know the typical causes of such mistakes and we can take precautions to avoid them.

More startlingly, it might be alleged that, unknown to us, our whole ability to reason correctly has been virtually destroyed. Perhaps we have a brain tumor which makes it impossible for us to tell a valid inference from an invalid one. Perhaps we are unknowingly sinking into a pre-mortem coma. Such wild hypotheses have the minimal antecedent probability of Cartesian logical possibilities but little more than that. Just because such conditions would be serious, clues to them would scarcely fail to be insistently present. The remote possibility of such extraordinary contingencies should no more cause us anguished doubt about our value judgments than perpetual worry over our ability to do a simple sum correctly or to draw the simplest scientific inference.

In short, there seem to be no unavoidable sources of incorrigible error in our judgment that experiences of certain kinds, e.g. the enjoyment of a symphony, are intrinsically good. We have only to note that we consistently prize certain kinds of experience even though careful precautions are taken against the various sources of error. In support of such a judgment as that pleasant experiences are intrinsically good, we can check and recheck in case after case, and we can check our own judgments against those of others who are making similar tests. It seems, therefore, that with due caution we can make some statements attributing intrinsic value which can be known to be true with a probability that approximates "moral certainty".

It might be objected that, even though some judgments about intrinsic value have a high probability, it is always possible that in expressing these judgments in the form of statements, we might choose an inappropriate term or statement form to express our meaning. Our tongue or pen might slip. But such errors, too, are detectable and correctable. They provide no more difficulty in theory than a slip of a typist's or telegraphist's finger.

The identifying properties of intrinsic goods are, then, the prizings, etc., which occur in our search for intrinsic goods when extrinsic value is discounted, and when the evidence indicates the high probability of the absence of relevant cognitive error. Prizings under these circumstances are reliable indices of intrinsic value in the sense that the balance of probabilities favours the occurrence of intrinsic value when these cautious prizings are present. And the degree of their reliability increases toward certainty as more and more precautions are taken. No scientific judgment can claim a better kind of support.

If the above account is substantially correct the relation between the statements 'X is intrinsically good' and 'X has the observed identifying property of being prized for its own sake by Y' is synthetic rather than analytic. Neither entails the other. If the former is true there is some antecedent probability that the latter is true. If the latter is true and reasonable precautions have been taken in guarding the prizing against various possible types of errors, then the former is confirmed to some degree. The attribution of intrinsic goodness to an experience is like the attribution of an ideally defined, but not actually observable physical property, e.g. weighing precisely one pound, to an object. Though neither the value characteristic nor the physical weight is directly observable, where either characteristic is present it is probable that under certain conditions certain related characteristics of the entity in question will be observed and reported.

Consider the statement 'This book weighs precisely one kilogram'. This means that the book has exactly the same weight as a certain platinum-iridium cylinder in the International Bureau of Weights and Measures. The precise meaning of 'has exactly the same weight as' may be further specified in some such way as this: if this book were placed on one balance of a perfect scale, and the standard one kilogram cylinder on the other, and the whole scale placed on a perfectly level surface and shielded from all forces which might operate on one pan of the balance and not the other, and if the scale with the 'o' point on it is located with exact symmetry with reference to the two halves of the balance, and if the lighting conditions are ideal, and if an ideal observer is placed so that one perfect eye is in a line perpendicular to both the pointer and the scale and at optimal visual distance, and if all other requirements of a perfect observation and report are met, then the observer will report that the tip of the pointer conceals the centre of the 'o' mark on the scale.

The catch-all requirement that all the other conditions of a perfect scale, perfect circumstances, perfect observer, and perfect observation and report be met, indicates that the list of requirements which have been specifically mentioned is incomplete. Further, many of those mentioned, such as an ideal observer and ideal conditions, are indefinite and require further specification, and so on. In any case it seems quite clear that these ideal requirements can not be known with certainty to have been satisfied. At most, we can know that they have been approximated.

● ● ● ● ●

The situation is similar with regard to value statements, for example, with regard to the value statement, 'This pleasant experience of hearing this Mozart symphony is intrinsically good', *i.e.* 'is worthy of being prized for its own sake'. If this experience were prized for its own sake by an ideal observer acquainted with all the relevant data and making no mistake in judgment, the favourable result of such an ideal test would establish conclusively the intrinsic goodness of this experience and of the value statement asserting it. But, no actual appraising can be known to meet these ideal requirements. We have indeed for any actual test good grounds for believing that we have only approximated the ideal. But the more closely our actual conditions are known to approximate to the ideal test conditions, the more confirmation does a favourable test report give to the value statement being tested. As more and more possible sources of error are guarded against, the probability of the statement increases, often to the point where disbelief in it would be unreasonable.

•   •   •   •   •

May we not conclude then that the occurrence under the controlled conditions specified of what we have called generically "prizings" yields probable knowledge of the existence of intrinsic goods? If these prizings are, thus, identifying properties of intrinsic goods they enable us to recognize particular intrinsic goods and various kinds of intrinsic goods with relatively high reliability. With the aid of this knowledge and knowledge of causal and part-whole relations we can fairly readily gain probable knowledge of extrinsic goods. By combining these results with our knowledge of intrinsic goods we can identify instrumental, contributive and inherent goods.

Further, with the aid of our knowledge of intrinsic values, we can examine more carefully the various rival claims that have been made about the properties which confer intrinsic goodness. We can submit to scientific test procedures the Hedonist's claim that pleasant experiences and only pleasant experiences are intrinsically good. For with both intrinsic goods and pleasant experiences identifiable it becomes a factual question, testable by empirical methods, what the relations between these two groups of things are. If we confirm the general Hedonist thesis mentioned and also the more specific claim that the amount of intrinsic goodness varies directly with the intensity and duration of the pleasantness, then we shall have established the probable truth of a simple quantitative Hedonism. But if the facts show that intrinsic goodness varies with different qualities of pleasantness, then we shall be led to a qualitative Hedonism. If they show that characteristics other than pleasantness confer intrinsic goodness we shall have to accept some pluralistic account of intrinsic goods. In any event, these will become scientific rather than philosophical problems. As good philosophers we must follow the evidence that is obtained regarding them.

More important still, our probable knowledge of values provides us with good grounds for choice, for we were careful not to sacrifice the normative force of value terms in order to gain knowledge of the empirical properties which enable us to apply those terms correctly. It is an analytic consequence of something's being good, we have maintained, that, other things being equal, it is normatively preferable to seek it rather than avoid it, and that indeed we ought to seek it unless there is something preferable we can do instead. That is why it would be logically odd to make such statements as: "Eating that would be very bad for you. You'd better have some." Or, "Eating that would be very good for you. By all means avoid it." For to say that something is good is to say that it is worth seeking, that we ought to seek it unless there is some good reason to the contrary, and to say that something is bad is to say that other things being equal it is worth avoiding. We do have probable knowledge about values. And this gives us good reasons for choice.

Supplementary Paperback Reading

J. Austin, "Pleasure and Happiness," in J. M. Smith and E. Sosa, *Mill's* Utilitarianism: *Text and Criticism.* (Wadsworth)

K. Baier, "Good Reasons," in J. J. Thomson and G. Dworkin, *Ethics.* (Harper and Row)

F. H. Bradley, "Pleasure for Pleasure's Sake," in J. M. Smith and E. Sosa, *Mill's* Utilitarianism: *Text and Criticism.* (Wadsworth)

J. Dewey, *Theory of the Moral Life,* Ch. II and IV. (Holt, Rinehart and Winston)

W. K. Frankena, *Ethics,* Ch. 5. (Prentice-Hall)

R. M. Hare, "Pain and Evil," in J. Feinberg, *Moral Concepts.* (Oxford University Press)

A. Kenny, "Happiness," in J. Feinberg, *Moral Concepts.* (Oxford University Press)

C. I. Lewis, *An Analysis of Knowledge and Valuation,* Ch. XII–XV. (Open Court)

G. E. Moore, *Principia Ethica,* Ch. III and VI. (Cambridge University Press)

P. H. Nowell-Smith, *Ethics,* Ch. 10. (Penguin Books)

N. Rescher, *Introduction to Value Theory.* (Prentice-Hall)

G. Ryle, "Pleasure," in J. Feinberg, *Moral Concepts.* (Oxford University Press)

M. Schlick, *Problems of Ethics,* Ch. VI and VIII. (Dover Publications)

A. Sesonske, *Value and Obligation.* (Oxford University Press)

C. L. Stevenson, *Ethics and Language,* Ch. VIII. (Yale University Press)

R. Taylor, *Good and Evil,* Ch. 6, 7. (Macmillan)

9

MORALITY,

SELF-INTEREST,

AND JUSTICE

Introduction

There is one problem of moral philosophy that perhaps deserves, more than any other, to be called the Ultimate Question. It is the question of the rationality of the moral life itself. It may be expressed thus: Is the commitment to live by moral principles a decision grounded on reason or is it, in the final analysis, an arbitrary choice?

The Ultimate Question is not itself a moral question. That is to say, it is not a question about what we morally ought to do or even about how we can discover what moral principles we ought to follow. It is, instead, a question about the justification of morality as a whole. Why, it asks, should we be concerned with morality at all? If living by moral principles is such an arduous task, if our moral integrity sometimes requires the sacrifice of our happiness or even our life, why not simply reject the whole moral "game" and live amorally? In short, why be moral?

This demand for a justification of being moral was first stated in its classic form in Plato's *Republic*. Glaucon and Adeimantus, two of the figures participating in the dialogue, challenge Socrates, the protagonist, to justify the living of a morally upright life. Their challenge is presented in the form of the following story, which is known as The Myth of Gyges.

According to the tradition, Gyges was a shepherd in the service of the king of Lydia; there was a great storm, and an earthquake made an opening in the earth at the place where he was feeding his flock. Amazed at the sight, he descended into the opening, where, among other marvels, he beheld a hollow brazen horse, having doors, at which he stooping and looking in saw a dead body of stature, as appeared to him, more than human, and having nothing on but a gold ring; this he took from the finger of the dead and reascended. Now the shepherds met together, according to custom, that they might send their monthly report about the flocks to the king; into their assembly he came having the ring on his finger, and as he was sitting among them he chanced to turn the collet of the ring inside his hand, when instantly he became invisible to the rest of the company and they began to speak of him as if he were no longer present. He was astonished at this, and again touching the ring he turned the collet outwards and reappeared; he made several trials of the ring, and always with the same result—when he turned the collet inwards he became invisible, when outwards he reappeared. Whereupon he contrived to be chosen one of the messengers who were sent to the court; where as soon as he arrived he seduced the queen, and with her help conspired against the king and slew him, and took the kingdom. Suppose now that there were two such magic rings, and the just put on one of them and the unjust the other; no man can be imagined to be of such an iron nature that he would stand fast in justice. No man would keep his hands off what was not his own when he could safely take what he liked out of the market, or go into houses and lie with any one at his pleasure, or kill or release from prison whom he would, and in all respects be like a God among men. Then the actions of the just would be as the actions of the unjust; they would both come at last to the same point. And this we may truly affirm to be a great proof that a man is just, not willingly or because he thinks that justice is any good to him individually, but of necessity, for wherever any one thinks that he can safely be unjust, there he is unjust. For all men believe in their hearts that injustice is far more profitable to the individual than justice, and he who argues as I have been supposing, will say that they are right. If you could imagine any one obtaining this power of becoming invisible, and never doing any wrong or touching what was another's, he would be thought by the lookers-on to be a most wretched idiot, although they would praise him to one another's faces, and keep up appearances with one another from a fear that they too might suffer injustice. (Plato, *Republic,* Book II. Translated by B. Jowett.)

Here is a classic statement of the case against morality. Socrates' attempt to reply to it, which forms the main argument of Plato's *Republic,* consists in trying to show that moral virtue is its own reward and that only the just (morally upright) man is truly happy. Thus in effect Socrates claims that in the long run there is no real conflict between duty and self-interest. Philosophers have been disputing about this ever since, and in this chapter we are presented with various contemporary discussions of the problem.

In order to see exactly what is at stake in trying to answer the question: Why be moral? we must recognize how it differs from a question about the nature of moral reasoning. For the question: Why be moral? arises the moment when someone realizes that, if he commits himself to the principles of moral reasoning, he may find himself in circumstances where his reasoning leads to the conclusion that he ought to do an act which entails some inconvenience, unpleasantness, or frustration for himself. It might even lead to the conclusion that in the given situation confronting him he must give up his life. He then wants to know why he should follow the rules of moral reasoning.

It should be noted that this problem does not arise for the ethical egoist, who *identifies* moral reasoning with prudential reasoning. As we saw in Chapter 3 ethical egoism is the view that each person ought to do whatever will most further his self-interest in the long run. If this is taken as an ultimate moral principle then the question: Why be moral? becomes the question: Why seek the furtherance of my self-interest in the long run? Such a question would only be asked by someone who did not want to give up his pleasures or who was satisfied with pursuing short-range goals in life, and who realized at the same time that his long-range interests might not be furthered by his continuing to live in the way he had been living. The answer to his question, of course, would be that, if he is not willing to put up with inconveniences and discomforts and if he is not able to discipline himself to sacrifice his short-range goals when his pursuit of them prevents him from achieving lasting satisfactions in life, then he will not in fact be happy. But for the ethical egoist, no sacrifice of his self-interest *as a whole* would ever be justified and no such sacrifice would ever be morally required of him.

Since the Ultimate Question arises only when it is logically possible for there to be a conflict between the demands of morality and the pursuit of self-interest, we shall be concerned from this point on with non-egoist moral principles only. We are not assuming that morality is superior to self-interest, but only that it is possible for them to be in conflict. Under this assumption, then, the next point to realize is that the Ultimate Question lies outside the framework of the logic of moral reasoning itself. For the logic of moral reasoning tells us what a good reason in ethics is. It defines the method of reasoning a person should use *if* he were to commit himself to trying to find out what he morally ought to do. In asking: Why be moral? on the other hand, one is challenging the reasonableness of being committed to trying to find out what one morally ought to do. It is a challenge to the whole enterprise of moral reasoning and moral conduct. The challenge can be put this way: Suppose there is a valid method of moral reasoning and suppose, by following it, I do find out what I morally ought to do. Why should I bother to act in accordance with this knowledge? Why shouldn't I follow my self-interest instead? In other words, granted that there is a logic of moral reasoning, why should I choose to let this logic outweigh the logic of self-interest or prudence when there is a conflict between them? In making this challenge the person is not questioning the validity of moral reasoning. Rather, he is asking why such reasoning should guide his conduct when he could just as well choose to have his conduct guided by another set of rules of reasoning, namely, the furtherance of his own self-interest. Thus he is demanding a justification for morality (the commitment to use moral reasoning as a guide to conduct) *as a whole*.

In order to find an acceptable answer to the Ultimate Question it is necessary first to consider the logic of moral reasoning. Only then can we determine whether there are reasons of some kind that justify anyone's decision to follow that logic in thought and action.

THE LOGIC OF MORAL REASONING

Moral reasoning takes place whenever someone deliberates about whether he morally ought to do one thing rather than another in a situation of choice, and whenever someone tries to show that another's action, or a past action of his own, was the morally right (or wrong) thing to do, given the circumstances that held at that time. There are, in other words, two contexts in which moral reasoning occurs: deliberation and justification.

We deliberate when we are uncertain about what we should do when confronted with alternative courses of action. The aim of deliberation is to arrive at a true answer to the question: What ought I to do? Our deliberation consists in thinking about the reasons for, or against, doing each of the alternatives. A reason *for* doing an act will be a reason which, in our own judgment, would justify anyone's doing the act in circumstances like those in the present case.

It will be a reason in support of the moral judgment "This is a right act (or a good act)." Similarly, a reason *against* doing an act will be such that it justifies a person's refraining from doing it in the same sort of circumstances. It will be a reason in support of the moral judgment "This is a wrong act (or a bad act)." Thus moral deliberation is the process of going over the pro's and con's concerning each alternative open to choice with the purpose of arriving at a conclusion about what one ought to do in the given situation, after all the pro's and con's have been taken into account.

Moral deliberation is one context in which moral reasoning takes place. The other context is that of moral justification, and the reasoning process is exactly the same. Whereas we *deliberate* about acts open to our own choice, we *justify* the acts of others, or acts done by ourselves in the past, or the acts that anyone who is in a certain set of circumstances ought to do. The term "justification" is here used to cover not only reasons for doing an act but also reasons against doing an act. To show that an act is justified, whether done by ourselves or by others, we must give reasons in support of the moral judgment that the act is right or good. To show that an act is unjustified (and that refraining from it is justified) we must give reasons in support of the judgment that the act is wrong or bad. To state *why* an act is right or wrong, good or bad, is to give reasons for or against doing it. Thus moral reasoning is the same whether we are justifying the acts of others or are deliberating about what we ourselves ought to do in a situation of choice.

What is meant by the "logic" of moral reasoning? We can best answer this question if we first realize that all reasoning is guided by certain principles. In a course on logic one studies the principles of deductive and inductive reasoning. These principles are rules of inference or forms of argument which tell us when we are reasoning correctly (following the rules) or incorrectly (breaking the rules). We sometimes think we are reasoning correctly in everyday life when in fact we are not, and we can test whether our reasoning is sound by applying the principles or "laws of logic" that govern the kind of reasoning we are engaged in. The logic of moral reasoning is the set of principles that governs our reasoning in moral deliberation and justification, when we are not only giving reasons for and against different acts, but are trying to give *good* reasons—reasons that actually do show that an act is justified or unjustified. When this is the case, our aim is to reason correctly, and we must then appeal to a set of principles of valid reasoning. These principles are such that, if our reasoning is carried on in accordance with them, we can claim that we are rationally justified in making the moral judgments which we draw as our conclusions. We can claim to *know* that a certain act is the right or wrong thing to do in a given situation. Moral knowledge is possible only when there is a method for giving good reasons in justification of moral beliefs or, in other words, only when there is a logic of moral reasoning.

Any method of moral reasoning must be intersubjectively valid. This means that its principles must be binding universally, so that if R is a good reason for one person to accept moral judgment M it must also be a good reason for everyone else to accept M. Of course there may be good reasons for rejecting M as well as good reasons for accepting M. In that case the principles that constitute the logic of moral reasoning must enable anyone to decide which of these reasons outweigh others. But here again intersubjective validity must hold. If in one man's thinking reason R1 outweighs reason R2 and if his thinking conforms to the logic of moral reasoning, then in anyone else's thinking R1 should outweigh R2. Furthermore, the intersubjective validity of moral reasoning requires that it be logically independent of moral beliefs. That is, it must always be possible for a moral belief which is tested by the method to turn out false. If a person were to set up principles of moral reasoning that he could control in such a way as always to justify his own beliefs, it would not be a genuine method of reasoning. Let us suppose, for example, that we are trying to decide whether it was right for President Truman to have ordered the dropping of an atomic bomb on Hiroshima. First we notice that, though this is a case of moral justification and not moral deliberation, nevertheless the very same reasons that now show his decision to have been justified (or unjustified) are reasons that he should have taken into account in deliberating about the alternatives confronting him. What *we* want to know is whether his decision was right or wrong; what *he* wanted to know was which decision would be right for him to make. If R is a good reason for *us* to believe he was right in ordering the bomb to be dropped, then R was a good reason for *him* to decide to give the order. And it would be a good reason for a Japanese living in Hiroshima at that time (however unlikely it would be for him to accept it as a good reason). Similarly, suppose we now have a good reason to think that President Truman made the wrong decision. Then this would have been a good reason at that time for President Truman not to order the dropping of the bomb, regardless of whether he ever thought of this reason or, if he did, whether he accepted it as a reason. And however strongly one might now be convinced that his decision was wrong (or that it was right), one must be willing to "follow the argument wherever it may lead" and accept the outcome of reasoning about the decision, even if the conclusion turns out to be contrary to one's present convictions. For the process of reasoning about the decision is the process of trying to determine which judgment is true: "President Truman's decision was right." "President Truman's decision was wrong." We engage in this process when we seek knowledge about what was morally right or wrong in the given case. Now to seek such knowledge is to presuppose that such knowledge is possible; that is, that there is a method of reasoning which is intersubjectively valid in the domain of ethics. This means that anyone who is willing to be rational in seeking the truth about the morality of President Truman's decision is bound by the rules which define the method.

There have been moral philosophers, however, who have denied any intersubjectively valid method of reasoning in ethics. They have taken the position either of ethical scepticism or of ethical relativism. Ethical scepticism makes the double claim that there is no such thing as genuine moral knowledge and that it is impossible for there to be such knowledge. Ethical relativism (when understood as either normative ethical relativism or meta-ethical relativism, as defined in the Introduction to Chapter 2) holds that moral knowledge is relative to a given culture, in the sense that, although we can justify moral judgments by reference to the standards and rules of conduct adopted in a given culture, no (cross-cultural) reasons can be found to justify those standards and rules. This amounts to a denial of intersubjective validity at a cultural level.

We can now see that the problem of the logic of moral reasoning is twofold. There is, first, the problem of showing that there is such a thing as a logic of moral reasoning, and second, there is the problem of specifying its principles. This twofold aspect of the problem was mentioned in the introduction to the first chapter of this book, where the general nature of ethics was discussed. One task of ethics, it was there said, is the analysis of moral reasoning. A sequence of questions was given to explain what is involved in such an analysis. This sequence is repeated below because these questions are relevant to the subject matter of the present chapter. It is to be noticed that the questions are listed in pairs. The first question in each pair concerns the possibility of moral truth, moral knowledge, and moral reasoning. The second question in each pair concerns the method for obtaining moral truth and knowledge and the method for carrying on moral reasoning. The second question always assumes an affirmative answer to the first. For if the answer to the first were negative (as an ethical sceptic would hold), then moral knowledge and reasoning would be impossible and the question of methods for achieving them would not arise. Thus this sequence of questions clearly brings out the twofold aspect of the problem of the logic of moral reasoning.

Is there a valid method by which the truth or falsity of moral beliefs can be established?

If so, what is this method and on what grounds does its validity rest?

Are moral statements verifiable?

If so, what is their method of verification?

Is there such a thing as knowledge of good and evil, right and wrong?

If so, how can such knowledge be obtained?

Is there a way of reasoning by which moral judgments can be justified?

If so, what is the logic of such reasoning?

Can we claim that the reasons we give in support of our moral judgments are good (sound, valid, acceptable, warranted) reasons?

If so, on what grounds can we make this claim? What are the criteria for the goodness (soundness, validity, etc.) of a reason?

We have already studied a number of different answers to these questions in earlier chapters of this book. In his *Utilitarianism* (Chapter 4) John Stuart Mill was not only propounding the ultimate norm of morality as he saw it, but was also giving an account of moral reasoning. For him, this consisted of two stages: application of the "greatest happiness principle" to rules of conduct in the various circumstances of life, and a "proof" of this principle itself. Another view of moral reasoning was set forth by Immanuel Kant (Chapter 5). In moral deliberation and justification, Kant thought that the categorical imperative in its various forms provided a valid test for a justifying ground of action and hence for a good reason in ethical thinking. In Chapter 7 we studied Professor Stevenson's "noncognitivist" theory of moral reasoning, according to which a justifying reason is conceived as a "belief" that supports an "attitude." In that chapter we also examined various theories about the relation between empirical facts and value judgments. We saw that there is considerable dispute among philosophers with regard to the precise role of facts in the justification of value judgments. Finally, the intuitionist view of moral knowledge was presented in two essays, one by the deontologist W. D. Ross (Chapter 5) and the other by the utilitarian G. E. Moore (Chapter 7).

In the present chapter we are going to take a fresh look at the whole problem of the logic of moral reasoning because we want to consider what we have called the Ultimate Question: the question of whether a person's decision to *use* the logic of moral reasoning as a guide to his life is itself a decision based on reason. Are we in the last analysis justified in striving for moral integrity, or is the whole practice of thinking and living morally an absurd "game"? Let us now briefly consider how the readings of this chapter deal with the problem.

THE MORAL POINT OF VIEW

In the first reading Professor Kurt Baier begins with an account of deliberative reasoning in general. We deliberate, he says, when we are confronted with alternatives open to our choice and we want to know which alternative is the best, that is, which one we ought to choose. Our deliberation, according to Baier, consists of two steps of reasoning: the surveying of the facts and the weighing of the reasons. In the first step, we begin with certain "rules of reason" or "consideration-making beliefs" that we have learned from our society. These are statements of the form: The fact that an act has such-and-such a characteristic is a reason for, or against, doing it. Rules of reason may be moral or nonmoral. An example of the first is: The fact that an act involves the breaking of a promise is a (moral) reason against doing it. An example of the second would be: The fact that an act is likely to be harmful to myself is a (nonmoral) reason against my doing it. Rules of reason are like Hare's "principles" in that they function as major premises in practical syllogisms, thus:

Major premise (Rule of reason):	The fact that an act involves breaking a promise is a reason against doing it.
Minor premise (Fact):	This act involves breaking my promise.

Conclusion (Practical judgment):	In the fact that this act involves breaking my promise I have a reason against doing it.

The first step of deliberation or practical reasoning (the surveying of the facts) consists in specifying all the rules of reason—moral and nonmoral—that are applicable to each of the alternatives open to a person's choice. As a result of this step, the person surveys all the relevant considerations, the pro's and con's, re-garding his decision.

Now in many cases there will be some reasons for doing a given act and other reasons against doing it. In order to arrive at a decision about what he finally ought to do, the person must go through a second step of deliberation. He must determine which reasons are more important than others; in other words, he must weigh the various pro's and con's. This second step requires reference to "rules of superiority," which state what reasons outweigh, or are outweighed by, other reasons. Given these rules, the person can then draw a conclusion as to what is the best alternative open to him, all things considered.

Our next problem is: How can the two sets of principles of reasoning (rules of reason and rules of superiority) be justified? Before taking up that question directly, Baier sets forth a concept of the moral point of view. He does this in order to make clear how moral rules of reason differ from nonmoral ones, for unless this is made clear, no sound argument can be given to show why moral rules of reason are superior to nonmoral ones (which is itself a rule of superi-ority). However, once the moral point of view has been analyzed, Baier believes he is in a position to show that moral rules of reason are "supreme," that is, that moral reasons outweigh all other kinds of reasons in practical deliberation. Let us look at his argument.

He begins with the "fundamental" rule of reason (a nonmoral one): The fact that a person would enjoy doing something is a reason for his doing it. Baier argues that it is better to follow this rule rather than its contrary or contradictory because the very purpose of reasoning (in *any* society) is to gain satisfaction and to avoid frustration, and this purpose would not be served by the use of the contrary or contradictory rule of reason. Indeed, anyone who thought he had a reason for doing an act when it would be something he disliked doing or when it would not be enjoyable to him (assuming no other kind of reason was brought into consideration) would be the very paradigm of an irrational person. He would be mad, because he would be seeking self-frustration for its own sake.

Baier then turns to a proof of the superiority of moral reasons over reasons of self-interest. He now endeavors to justify the rule of superiority: Moral rea-sons outweigh nonmoral reasons. It is to be noted that he equates the question: Why are moral reasons superior to all others? with the question: Why should we be moral? For the answer to both questions, he claims, lies in the reasons why a society would be justified in having all its members give greater weight to moral than to any other reasons whenever they deliberate. According to Baier the final reason for everyone's adopting the logic of moral reasoning as supreme is to be found in the social function of morality itself. Baier compares what life in society would be like without this rule of superiority with what it is like with it. In comparing these "two alternative worlds," he uses an argument similar to that given by Thomas Hobbes to establish the legitimate ground of moral and political obligation. It will be of interest to the reader to review Hobbes' argu-ment as stated in the first reading of Chapter 3 and then compare it with Baier's.

JUSTICE AND SOCIAL ADVANTAGE

In the second and third readings of this chapter a different approach to the Ultimate Question is taken. In his essay "Justice As Fairness" Professor John Rawls (whose views on rule-utilitarianism were presented in Chapter 5) argues that the reason why an individual should be moral lies in the nature of his relation to other individuals under a system of moral rules that are fair to everyone. To decide not to follow such rules and still gain the benefits that result from one's continuing to live in a society is to be *unfair* to those who make those benefits possible by following the rules. It is true that unless everyone in a society had reason mutually to acknowledge the bindingness of the rules, the rules would not be just. But if it is reasonable for everyone to give such mutual acknowledgment, then each person is obligated by what Professor Rawls calls "the duty of fair play" to abide by the rules. Thus justice as fairness is the ground of each individual's moral obligation.

How do we know when the rules of a society are just? Rawls suggests two criteria at the beginning of his essay in answer to this question. If it is then asked: Why are these to be accepted as true criteria of justice? the answer given by Rawls is that these are in fact the criteria that would be satisfied by any system of social rules which each person living in a society had good reason to acknowledge as binding upon him and everyone else. It should be noted that in arguing this point Rawls assumes that each individual is rational and self-interested. Thus he conceives of a moral system of just rules as arising when a group of rational self-interested persons get together to maintain or to evaluate a set of social practices from which they all expect to benefit.

Once such mutual acknowledgment is made and the rules are agreed upon, the restraints of morality form a framework in which each person is morally related to every other person. To be a moral being is to have such a relation to others. Thus for an individual to deny in those circumstances that he has a duty to be moral is for him to deny a relation that holds between himself and others. It is to deny his membership in a moral community, a membership which he has himself acknowledged publicly by participating in the adoption and evaluation of the rules.

In the last part of his essay Rawls considers the relation between justice and utility. The standard of justice as fairness, he argues, is a standard not only different from the principle of utility but also a standard that may sometimes be in conflict with utility. For example, a utilitarian set of rules might permit the treatment of a person as a means to social ends if the advantage to society outweighed the frustration of the individual. But such rules would violate justice since the individual so used would not have reason to acknowledge them as binding upon himself. We can infer from this that a normative ethical system which fulfilled Rawls's standard of justice would be deontological rather than purely teleological. (See the Introduction to Chapter 5 for definitions of these terms.)

In the third reading of this chapter Professor David P. Gauthier makes three basic points concerning the Ultimate Question, when the Ultimate Question is understood as an inquiry into the rationality of morality itself. First, he argues that a set of social rules constitutes a moral system only if it is advantageous for all to accept them and at the same time requires some sacrifice of an individual's self-interest for *him* to accept them. Professor Gauthier shows how this can come about in practical life by means of an example taken from the contemporary international situation. His second point is based on a distinction between the question: Why should we (collectively) be moral? and the question: Why should I (as an individual) be moral? According to Professor Gauthier when these two questions are clearly distinguished it will be seen that moral reasons can be given in answer to the first question but that no reasons, moral or nonmoral, can provide a satisfactory answer to the second. His third point is that the "thesis" which he states and defends in his first point is a necessary but not a sufficient condition of morality. There are two reasons why it is not a sufficient condition: It does not require any kind of trustworthiness (or fidelity in keeping one's word) other than what will serve the mutual advantage of everyone as a whole, and it does not include a principle of justice or fairness. It will be of interest to the reader to see whether Rawls's account of morality in the preceding reading can be used to supplement Gauthier's account here.

WHY BE MORAL?

The last reading of this chapter, by Professor Kai Nielsen, is a thorough search into the meaning and possibility of answering the Ultimate Question when it is asked outside the framework of the moral point of view, and when considerations of justice and social advantage are not accepted as relevant to it. Professor Nielsen grants that if we interpret the question: Why be moral? to mean Why should a society have a moral code? or Why should people in general be moral? it can be answered in much the same way as is done by Thomas Hobbes and by Professor Baier. But this will not give us an answer to the question of why any particular individual should be moral, and it is this question that Professor Nielsen is mainly concerned with.

There is another important distinction to keep in mind with regard to the meaning of the question: Why be moral? This distinction is pointed out by Nielsen at the beginning of his essay. The question may be taken as a demand for *motivating* reasons for being moral, or it may be taken as a demand for *justifying* reasons for being moral. In the former case we respond by trying to get the questioner to desire to be moral. We try to persuade or influence him so that he will be inspired to do what is right. We try to strengthen his moral motives and instil in him a sense of justice. If he is a child we give him a moral upbringing, teaching him how to behave and at the same time developing his capacity and inclination to carry on moral reasoning for himself. If we are successful in this, he will not feel the need to ask the question: Why be moral?

in later life. For he will have been motivated to be moral and thus not need to *ask* to be motivated.

It is the second way of understanding the question, however, that concerns the moral philosopher. He wants to know what justification can be given for moral conduct and for moral reasoning, if these practices are challenged *in toto* (i.e., all together). The first answer to *this* question, considered by Nielson in Section I of his article, is: We should be moral because it is our duty to be moral, or because it would be wrong not to be moral. Nielson rejects this answer on the ground that it *presupposes* that moral reasons outweigh reasons of self-interest, and this is the very thing in question. We cannot give moral reasons for being moral, since moral reasons are accepted as valid or warranted only by those who are *not* challenging the validity of moral reasoning as a whole. But this is precisely what *is* being challenged by the person who demands a justification for being moral. His question is not: What, morally, ought I to do?, for this question could be answered by giving him moral reasons for, or against, various alternatives open to him. He is not asking for moral reasons, but is demanding why moral reasons should guide his decisions and conduct at all. He is saying: "I know what moral reasoning tells me to do, but why should I do what moral reasoning tells me? It is true that *if* I take the moral point of view and so place myself under the guidance and direction of moral norms, then I know what I ought to do and why I ought to do it. But why should I take the moral point of view in the first place?"

Some philosophers have claimed that it is absurd to say, "I know what my moral duty is—now tell me why I ought to do my moral duty." For if a person acknowledges that something is his duty, then he knows why he ought to do it, namely, just because it *is* his duty. But this misses the point of his question, for he could reply, "Yes, I know I ought to do it if it is my duty *and* if moral duty takes precedence over self-interest. But why should moral reasons outweigh reasons of self-interest?" As we saw above, we cannot answer *this* question in terms of moral reasons. To give moral reasons would be to beg the question.

Well, if we can't give moral reasons for being moral, perhaps we can give reasons of self-interest. This is, indeed, what Socrates tried to do in Plato's *Republic.* Professor Nielsen argues, however, that no philosopher has so far succeeded in showing that it is to a person's interest to be moral, or in short, that morality pays. He discusses the position originated by Thomas Hobbes and developed by Kurt Baier (in the first reading of this chapter), that morality can be justified from the point of view of society as a whole. Accepting this argument, Nielsen goes on to show in the second section of his essay that the same argument cannot be used to justify morality to the *individual.* We are left, then, with the problem posed by the person who wants to have it shown that he, as an individual, should be moral rather than be an ethical egoist. (For an explanation of ethical egoism, see Chapter 2.)

As a way of approaching this problem, Nielsen first considers, in Section II, the position of the "subjectivist," who claims that no reasons can be given to justify being moral to an individual. It is simply a matter of the individual's deciding arbitrarily whether to be committed to following the logic of moral reasoning or not to be so committed. The choice between being moral and being an egoist is an ultimate normative commitment, or what R. M. Hare would call a "decision of principle" involving the choice of a whole way of life. According to the subjectivist, there is no method of reasoning by which such a decision can be justified, one way or the other. It is therefore completely arbitrary.

Against the subjectivist view several arguments have been proposed. Nielsen considers two such arguments in Section III of his article, one by Professor Baier and another by Professor John Hospers. After criticizing these arguments Nielsen develops his own case against subjectivism. We shall now examine his argument, which is set forth in Section IV of his essay.

The first step in Nielsen's argument involves the distinction between acting selfishly (that is, acting without regard for the interests of others) and intelligently pursuing the long-range goal of living as happily as possible in this life. The selfish man might well not be as happy as one who is unselfish—that is, as one who is kind, affectionate, and considerate of the welfare of others. But here again we cannot reply to the person who asks, Why be moral? by saying that being moral will in fact be conducive to his long-range happiness. For this in effect denies any basic conflict between moral duty and self-interest, and anyone who takes the moral point of view admits that such a conflict can and does occur in human life. Otherwise, as we saw earlier, the problem of justifying morality would not arise.

Nielsen next considers, and rejects, the argument that being moral is fulfilling the purpose of human nature or being "fully human." He then takes up the following challenge of the rational egoist: "It is true that if I appear selfish to others they will dislike me and I shall not be happy. But suppose I keep my policy of self-interest a secret. Then I shall gain the advantages of being liked by others and at the same time not give up the pursuit of my own happiness." To this the reply is made, "Your conscience will bother you, so you will really be unhappy inwardly." If the egoist then objects, "Since I do not accept the bindingness of moral reasons, I simply refuse to recognize the authority of my conscience," the reply is, "It is not so easy to get rid of one's conscience, for it is deeply ingrained in one's personality from early childhood conditioning." Now suppose this is countered by the egoist as follows: "But at least I can make a deliberate effort to minimize the feelings of a bad conscience and perhaps I can eventually come to disregard them when they do occur. After all, they are not likely to bother me very much when I realize they make no claim on me. Since I do not acknowledge the validity of moral demands, I look at my conscience as an irrational carry-over from childhood. Recognizing this, I can then pursue my self-interest without a qualm." At this stage of the argument, Nielsen holds, the egoist has imagined a very unrealistic situation, which is similar to the "desert island" examples sometimes used in ethics. We must remember that when the egoist asks, "Why should I be moral?" he is speaking as a real person in the real world. He is not on a desert island or in some other possible world where the psychological laws of personality development are entirely different. Thus the last reply of the egoist is simply not relevant to his original question.

Of course, if the conditions of the possible but unrealistic world were accepted, then Nielsen admits that the subjectivist position would hold. Under those conditions, the decision to be moral (that is, the decision to commit ourselves to the validity of moral reasoning and to the obligatoriness of moral conduct) and the decision to be an egoist would, in each case, reflect the kind of person we were. Either a person is the sort who takes the moral point of view about himself and others, or else he is the sort who puts his own happiness above that of everyone else. Which way of life we ultimately choose just shows what kind of men we are. One cannot *condemn* the person who chooses egoism unless one takes the moral point of view and hence presupposes that the moral way of life is more justified than the egoistic way of life. The egoist could just as well condemn the moral person as a stupid fool, by taking the egoistic point of view and judging him to be foolish for not considering his own self-interest as the final standard for good and bad behavior.

But is it the case that the moral life has no more reasons to justify it than the egoistic life? In Section V of his article, Nielsen again raises the point that the subjectivist position is plausible only under extremely unrealistic, hypothetical conditions. The Myth of Gyges itself is a case of "desert island" thinking, where a problem seems difficult only because it is not stated in terms of the conditions that hold in the real world. A consistent and thoroughgoing policy of egoism, *when carried out in the world as we know it,* would, according to Neilsen, have consequences for the person who adopted it such that he would prefer not to continue to live that way of life. He would, sooner or later, make a different "decision of principle" when he became enlightened about the actual consequences of his egoism.

There remains one possibility still to be considered, and Nielsen takes this up in Section VI of his article. Suppose a person realizes that, given his personality and the world as it is, he might make himself quite unhappy by *consistently* and *systematically* living as an egoist *every moment* of his life. Being an intelligent and rational person, suppose he then decides *not* to make egoism a consistent, undeviating policy, but only to be egoistic now and then, when the circumstances allow him to get away with avoiding his moral duty. Won't he be happier than the person who is consistently moral under all circumstances? And if so, then why be *consistently* or *thoroughly* moral? The question: Why be moral? becomes the question: Why should I *always* be moral, even when it is clear that the circumstances are such that I can successfully pursue my own happiness by being immoral? In dealing with this final question Nielsen discusses three cases that appear to satisfy the conditions stipulated, namely, circumstances in which an individual might be made happier by doing what is morally wrong, even considering the realities of the world as it is. These are "hard core" cases—the toughest challenges that can be presented to the philosopher who wishes to defend the justifiability of *always* taking the moral point of view, no matter what the circumstances may be.

Must we accept the subjectivist view here and admit that no reasons can be given for being *consistently* and *thoroughly* moral? Must this be a completely arbitrary decision for an individual to make? Professor Nielsen makes the following reply: First, such a decision does depend on the sort of person the individual is. Secondly, even if the subjectivist were correct on this point, it would not mean that people generally would become immoral or lose their sense of obligation upon hearing this argument. Thirdly, society will see to it that these circumstances where immorality pays will be kept to a minimum. This will be true even of a society that has come to accept the subjectivist position regarding cases of this sort. Finally, the individual who does act immorally in such circumstances will have, as a matter of self-interest, a desire not to have others follow his own example, since he might some day be the victim of such an act done by another. He will thus try to get others to adopt the moral point of view in every circumstance and to live a moral life consistently and thoroughly.

This last point raises the question (not considered by Professor Nielsen) of whether an egoist—even a part-time egoist—does not contradict himself. If he approves of himself doing something which he disapproves of others doing in the same circumstances, can he not be charged with inconsistency? If an act is right for one person to do, it would seem that it must be right for anyone else to do in similar circumstances, unless there is a relevant difference between them. And what difference between himself and others can an egoist claim to be relevant, since he admits that he would not want to have someone else take advantage of him, even if that other person could get away with it? This question brings us back to the principle of universalizability, which we discussed in Chapter 5. The egoist seems to be making an exception in his own favor, and this violates the consistent use of *any* standard or rule of conduct, moral or nonmoral. Yet in claiming that his act is right (or even that it is not wrong), the egoist must implicitly appeal to a standard or rule, and this standard or rule would make it right (or not wrong) for anyone to do the same act in the same circumstances. Since the egoist is not willing to say this, he stands condemned on the logical ground of inconsistency. Whether this is a sound argument for rejecting egoism is a problem for the further reflection of everyone interested in the foundations of moral philosophy.

The Moral Point of View

THE BEST THING TO DO

. . . 'What shall I do?' is a value question, that is, one requiring a value judgement for an answer. More exactly, 'What shall I do?' means the same as 'What
is *the best* thing I can do?' That this is so is obvious from the reply 'I know this
would be the best thing to do, but that is not what I want to know. I want to
know, *what shall I* do?' A man who says this obviously does not know what he
is asking. He may want to query the truth of what he is told, but he cannot
claim that his question has yet to be answered.

• • • • •

Granted, then, that 'What shall I do?' is a request for a value judgment,
namely, 'What is the *best* thing to do?' we have to ask ourselves by what criteria
we are supposed to judge which of the courses open to the agent is the best. It
is natural to think that just as a manufactured article is judged by its power to
serve the purpose for which it has been made, and for which it is normally used,
so a line of action is judged by its ability to serve the purpose for which it is
entered upon by the agent. But this is only a provisional judgment, for we can
always ask whether what the agent is aiming at is the best thing to aim at.
Frequently, when someone asks, 'What shall I do?' he is not merely asking which
is the better course of action, *given a certain aim or end,* but which of several
ends or aims is the best.

It is unfortunate that the means-end model has dominated philosophical
thinking in this field. It has led some philosophers, maintaining (rightly) that
we can ask which is the best thing to aim at in these circumstances, to conclude
(wrongly) that there must be an *ultimate* aim or end, a *summum bonum,* to
which all ordinary aims or ends are merely means. Hence, they claim, whether
this or that is the better end to aim at must be judged by its serving the ultimate
end or *summum bonum.* Other philosophers, maintaining (rightly) that there
can be no such ultimate end or *summum bonum,* have concluded (wrongly)
that we cannot ask which is the better end to aim at. They have claimed that
reason can tell us only about what are the best means to given ends, but that ends
themselves cannot be determined or judged by reason. However, 'being a good
means to a certain end' is not the only criterion of the merit of a course of action.

The error which this means-end model of the evaluation of lines of action forces on us is this. It compels us to think that what is a reason for (or against) doing something is determined by what we are aiming at. Since different people aim at different things and since they frequently argue about what to aim at, either we are compelled to assume that there is one objectively determined end or aim which we must aim at if we are to follow reason, or, if we reject objective ends as absurd, we are compelled to renounce all reasoning about ends. However, it is not true that our ends determine what is a reason for doing something, but, on the contrary, reasons determine what we ought to, and frequently do, aim at. What is a reason for doing this, or against doing that, is independent of what this or that man is actually aiming at. The best course of action is not that course which most quickly, least painfully, least expensively, etc., leads to the gaining of our ends, but *it is the course of action which is supported by the best reasons.* And the best reasons may require us to abandon the aim we actually have set our heart on.

Our next question must, therefore, be concerned with what it is that makes something a reason for (or against) entering on a certain line of action. When we are deliberating about alternative courses of action before us, our deliberation progresses through two distinct stages, first, the surveying of the facts with a view to determining which of them are relevant considerations and, secondly, the determination of the relative "weight" of these considerations with a view to deciding which course of action has the full weight of reason behind it.

•   •   •   •   •

The Surveying of the Facts
What facts must I survey? How do I tell that a given fact is a relevant consideration? What makes a fact a pro or a con, a reason for or against?

Suppose I have been in the United States for some time and have just come back to Australia, bringing with me a brand-new Chevrolet which I am importing duty-free. My friend, Paddy Concannan, offers me £3,000 for it, although he knows quite well it cost me only £1,000 new. I am eager to accept the offer. Have I a good reason for doing so? One at least is quite obvious. In selling the car I would be making a profit of 200 per cent. That would normally be regarded as a consideration, a reason for selling. How can I show that it is? The proof might be set out in the following way.

  (i) The fact that doing something would yield a high profit is a good reason for doing it.
 (ii) It would yield a high profit to sell my car to Paddy now.
(iii) Therefore, the fact that it would yield a high profit to sell my car to Paddy now is a reason for selling it now.

Another way of putting the conclusion would be to say that *in the fact* that it would yield a high profit to sell it now *I* have a good reason for selling it now.

My wife, on the other hand, advises against selling. She says that, having brought the car into the country as my personal possession, I was exempted from paying duty on condition that I would not sell it for three years. Her argument could be put in this way.

(i) The fact that doing something is illegal is a reason against doing it.
(ii) It would be illegal to sell my car to Paddy now.
(iii) Hence the fact that selling it to Paddy now would be illegal is a reason against selling it now.

How did we make sure that certain facts were considerations? We examined the proposed line of action with a view to discovering whether it was of certain well-known sorts, for example, lawful or unlawful or yielding profit or loss. For we believe that these features provide us with reasons for or against entering on the proposed line of action. We begin with certain beliefs; let us call them "consideration-making beliefs" or "rules of reason." These are propositions to the effect that if a line of action is of a certain sort then the agent has a reason for or against entering on it. Consideration-making beliefs can function as major premises in our arguments or as inference-licenses in our inferences. The minor premises are the facts which, in accordance with the consideration-making beliefs, we conclude to be reasons.

It is, of course, possible to make mistakes in these deliberations. Our major premises may be wrong: we may believe wrongly that the fact that a proposed line of action is illegal is a reason against entering on it, that the fact that it would yield a high profit is a reason for entering on it. Or the major premise may not *apply* to the facts we have discovered about the proposed line of action: it may not be correct to say that a profit of 200 per cent is a high profit or that selling a car imported duty-free is illegal. Lastly, what we take to be a fact about the proposed line of action may not be a fact: it may not be true that selling to Paddy would yield 200 per cent, for Paddy, being a shrewd businessman and knowing the transaction to be illegal, may refuse to pay as much as £3,000 once he has got hold of the car.

There is no mystery about how to avoid or correct the second and third type of error, but it is not at all apparent how we guard against the first. We learn the consideration-making beliefs prevalent in our community as part of our education. They are taught us not as beliefs but as facts. Later we come to realize that they are only group convictions and that they may be wrong. But we are not at all clear about how to detect errors in this field. I shall deal with this problem in Chapter Twelve.* For the time being, we shall simply accept our consideration-making beliefs as true.

To sum up. In reply to the question 'What are reasons?' or 'What are considerations?' or 'What are pros and cons?' we must answer, 'They are certain facts.' What *makes* these facts considerations? That certain (true) consideration-making beliefs apply to them. What follows from the fact that something is a consideration? That someone who is planning to do something of a certain sort has, in the fact that it is of this sort, a reason for or against doing it. That something is a reason, therefore, of necessity always involves some possible agent. That some fact is a consideration always implies the context of a course of action planned by someone.

Does this mean that what is a reason for me is not necessarily a reason for you? In the most obvious interpretation of this question, it certainly does mean that. The fact that Mrs. Smith has died is a good reason for Mr. Smith to wear mourning, but not for Mr. Jones to do so. There is another less natural interpretation of the above question. Mr. Jones may consider the illegality of some course of action a good reason against doing it, and Mr. Smith may believe that it is not a good reason. The view that what is a reason for me is not necessarily a reason for you may be interpreted to mean that neither Mr. Smith nor Mr. Jones need be wrong—that what Mr. Smith rightly thinks to be a good reason for doing something Mr. Jones may rightly believe not to be so. In other words, the popular view that the same facts are reasons for some people but not for others can be interpreted in two different ways. It may be taken to mean that the conclusions, or that the major premises, of the arguments set out above are 'speaker-relative,' 'true for some, false for others.' The latter view is false. Consideration-making beliefs, the major premises of the above arguments, are not relative to particular situations or particular persons. It is either true, or it is false, that the fact that some course of action is illegal is a good reason against entering on it. It cannot be true for me, false for you.

This may be readily admitted for consideration-making beliefs, such as that it would be illegal or bad manners to do something. But it might be denied for others, such as that it would not be in my interest or that I would not enjoy it. For it might be said that the fact that some course of action is in my interest is a reason *for me* to do it, but *not for you*.

This objection is based on a simple confusion connected with the use of the personal pronoun. 'That doing something is in *my* interest' can be read in two quite different ways: (a) that doing something is in *Baier's* interest; (b) that doing something is in *one's* interest. That something is in Baier's interest is indeed only a reason for Baier to do it. But then no one would hold that '(a) is a reason for doing it' is a consideration-making belief of our society. We are not, all of us, taught to regard as a reason for entering on it the fact that some line of action is in Baier's interest. What we are taught is that (b) is a reason for doing something. And against (b) we cannot raise the objection that it is person-relative. For it is simply true or simply false, not true for me and false for you, that the fact that doing something would be in *one's* interest is a reason for doing it.

Set out formally, the argument runs as follows.

(i) The fact that doing something is in *one's* interest is a reason for doing it.

(ii) Being polite to my boss is in *my* interest.

(iii) Therefore, that it is in my interest to be polite to my boss is a reason for my being polite to my boss: or, put differently,

Therefore, in the fact that it is in my interest to be polite to my boss I have a reason for being polite to my boss.

Some readers may still feel that there are some reasons which are person-relative. For instance, they might say, the fact that there is good fishing at Port Fairie is a good reason for one person to take a holiday there, but not for another. But here again, they would be confusing the conclusion of the argument with its major premise. The conclusion, like all such conclusions, is indeed person-relative, but the major premise is not.

(i) The fact that *one* enjoys a certain activity is a reason for taking a holiday in a place where there are good opportunities for engaging in it.

(ii) *I* enjoy fishing and there is good fishing at Port Fairie.

(iii) Hence in the fact that there is good fishing at Port Fairie *I* have a reason for taking my holiday there.

On the other hand, on the basis of the same major premise someone else may argue in this way.

(ii) I do not enjoy fishing.

(iii) Hence in the fact that there is good fishing at Port Fairie I do not have a reason for taking my holiday there.

There is admittedly an important difference between the last two types of reason and the others, but the difference does not lie in the fact that the consideration-making beliefs are not equally person-neutral. It lies rather in the place where one must look for the facts which are the considerations. In the case of illegality, bad manners, unconventionality, and so on, I have to look for features of my proposed line of action which would contravene *some kind of rule holding for everyone*. In the case of self-interest and enjoyment, it is not enough to find out that people generally are, or that this or that person is, benefited by or enjoys this sort of thing. I must find out whether the particular line of action is in *the agent's interest* or would be enjoyed by *him*. Only then has *he* a reason for entering on it, and no one else has.

Although there are these differences, there is also the following identity. In both cases, *anyone* proposing to enter on an action of a certain sort has in the fact that it is of this sort a reason for or against entering on it. In the case of illegal and unconventional actions, the sort can be stated without reference to the agent; in the case of self-interest and enjoyment, the *sort* is agent-relative. We must say, 'in *one's* interest,' 'if *one* enjoys it.' But when put in this form, it is true for any and every agent, not true for some and false for others.

Our conclusion is this. All consideration-making beliefs are person-neutral. They are simply true or false, not true for me and false for you or vice versa. On the other hand, all considerations or reasons are considerations or reasons for someone in some particular context or situation and may not be reasons for someone else or for the same person in another context or situation. For a given fact is a reason only because it is a reason for a particular person when deliberating about a number of alternative lines of action open to him. Considerations or reasons are not propositions laid up in heaven or universal truths, but they are particular facts to which, in particular contexts, universally true (or false) consideration-making beliefs apply.

The Weighing of the Reasons

Our first step in deliberation, the surveying of the facts, as we have seen, brings to light the pros and cons, those among the many facts which are relevant, those in which we have reasons for or against. Let us, then, turn to the second step, the *weighing* of the pros and cons. Our question now is 'Which consideration, or combination of considerations, is the weightiest?' Just as in the answer to our first series of questions we employed consideration-making beliefs, so here we employ *beliefs about the superiority of one type of reason over another*. These "rules of superiority" tell us which reasons *within a given type*, and *which types*, are superior to which. We all think, for instance, that the fact that we would enjoy fishing and that we would enjoy tennis are reasons of the same sort. They may conflict on a particular occasion for it may be impossible to do both. We then ask, 'Which would we enjoy most?' If we enjoy tennis more than fishing, then in the fact that we would enjoy tennis we have a better, weightier reason than in the fact that we would enjoy fishing.

Similarly, we employ principles of the superiority of one type of reason over another. We all believe that reasons of self-interest are superior to reasons of mere pleasure, that reasons of long-range interest outbalance reasons of short-range interest, and reasons of law, religion, and morality outweigh reasons of self-interest. On the other hand, there is considerable uncertainty about whether and when law is superior to morality, religion to law, and morality to religion.

. . . It is most important to remember that the question 'Which type of consideration is superior to which?' is not identical with the question 'What sorts of fact tend to move most people or the agent most?' This is easily overlooked because . . . considerations are facts and in being moved by considerations we are, therefore, moved by facts. But we can be said to be moved by considerations only if we are moved by these facts not merely in virtue of their intrinsic moving power but in virtue of the power we attribute to them *qua* considerations. The same fact may move different people in different ways. We can always ask whether people *ought* to be moved by a fact in the way in which they actually are moved by it.

We are, for instance, convinced that legal considerations are superior to considerations of self-interest, that the reason *against* selling my Chevrolet to Paddy (the reason which I have in the fact that doing so would be illegal) is better than the one *for* selling it (which I have in the fact that it would produce a very high profit). Yet we are quite ready to concede that many people would yield to the temptation to make such a high profit, for the fact that they would make it has perhaps a greater moving power than the fact that they would be doing something illegal. 'How great is the power of these facts to move various people?' is an empirical question. Answers to it will vary from person to person and from society to society, but these answers are logically independent of the answer to the question 'Which reason or type of reason is superior or better?'

Suppose it is granted, then, that the main considerations involved in our problems are considerations of self-interest and illegality. The second step of my deliberation, leading to the final answer, can then be set out as follows.

(i) (In the fact that selling now would be illegal) I have a reason *against* selling now.

(ii) (In the fact that selling now would yield a high profit) I have a reason *for* selling now.

(iii) My reason against selling is a reason of law.

(iv) My reason for selling is a reason of self-interest.

(v) Reasons of law are superior to reasons of self-interest.

(vi) Hence my reason against selling is superior to my reason for selling.

(vii) Therefore, in the fact that selling now would be illegal I have an over-riding reason against selling now.

The correctness of the final outcome of my deliberation thus depends on the correctness and completeness of the first step, the finding of the considerations relevant, and on the correctness of the second step, the ascertaining of the relative weights of the considerations involved. It has already been explained how we guard against errors at the first stage. How can we guard against making mistakes at the second stage? The important steps here are (iii), (iv), and (v). Together (iii) and (iv) consist in the correct classification of the reasons we have. This step is important because our beliefs about the superiority of one reason over another may be formulated in terms of the types of reason there are. Moral reasons have a very high reputation. That is to say, we think that moral reasons are superior to most or all other types. Hence, many reasons are claimed to be moral which are not. For if they are believed to be moral, then in virtue of the high reputation they enjoy, these reasons will tend to be given a correspondingly great weight. All sorts of reasons, from self-interest to the wildest superstitions, are therefore passed off as moral reasons. Hence, too, moral reasons are beginning to lose their deservedly high reputation, for people accept many reasons as moral which are not and which they clearly see do not deserve to be evaluated highly. Moreover, we can evaluate correctly the popular beliefs about the superiority of one type of reason over another only if we are quite clear what are the criteria for saying that a reason is of a certain sort, for only then can we tell whether giving a certain weight to that sort of consideration is justified. In Chapter Twelve,* I shall deal more fully with this particular problem.

Step (v) raises no special difficulties, for it consists merely in the correct application of the principles of superiority, and this involves merely the difficulties inherent in all cases of applying general rules to particular instances.

Prima-facie Reasons and Reasons on Balance

We can now review the whole procedure of deliberation. We are setting out to answer the question 'Which course of action has the weight of reason behind it?' or, what comes to the same thing, 'What ought I to do?' In answering this question, we are going through a preliminary stage of setting out those facts about the proposed line of action which are pros and those which are cons, respectively. Every fact which is a pro sets up a presumption that I ought, and

---

* [Beginning on page 510 below.—Ed. note.]

every fact which is a con sets up a presumption that I ought not, to do the thing in question. Any one of these presumptions can be rebutted or confirmed later *by the weighing* of the various pros and cons. A given presumption is rebutted if some other reason or combination of reasons is found *weightier* than the one which has given rise to the original presumption. In other words, the fact that I have a reason for or against entering on the proposed line of action *does not entail* that I ought or ought not to enter on it—it merely "presumptively implies" it. That is to say, it must be taken to imply that I ought or ought not to enter on it unless, later on, in the weighing of considerations, I find some that are weightier than this one. In that case, the original presumptive implication has been rebutted.

The term 'presumption' is borrowed from legal language, and 'presumptive implication' is based on it. To give an example from legal reasoning: Concerning the life of any person, a court does not presume anything. However, one or the other of the interested parties can establish a presumption that the person in question is dead if it can be shown that his closest relative or any other person who, from the nature of the case, would be expected to hear from him has not in fact heard from him in seven years. In the absence of any further information, it must be accepted that this person is dead. But further evidence can be produced to rebut this presumption of death. Someone, for instance, may produce a witness who testifies that he has seen the person recently. In the absence of any further evidence, the original presumption has then been rebutted and replaced by the opposite, that he is now alive. But this presumption can again be rebutted, and indeed conclusively refuted, if a reliable witness testifies that he has seen the person die.

To say that a certain fact is a consideration, a pro or a con, is to say that this fact gives rise to a presumption, namely, that the agent ought or ought not to enter on the course of action in relation to which the fact is a pro or a con. Exactly the same point is made when it is claimed that some reasons are only *prima-facie* reasons, or reasons *other things being equal*. All that is meant is that the facts which are the reasons give rise merely to a presumption that the agent ought or ought not to enter on the line of action contemplated. Similarly, the claim that sometimes the word 'ought' is only a 'prima-facie ought' can be explained as follows. 'Because selling the car would be illegal, you ought not to sell it' means no more than that, other things being equal, the person addressed ought not to sell it, that unless he has some overriding reason to the contrary he ought not to sell it.

In contrast with this, someone might say to me that I ought not to sell the car now, meaning thereby that, *all things considered,* I ought not to sell it, that in his view no other contrary reason could be offered capable of overriding the reason or reasons on which he bases his judgment. We may call such a reason or such "an ought" a reason or "ought" *on balance* or, following Ross, a reason *sans phrase.*

·   ·   ·   ·   ·

Summary

Summing up, we can say that deliberating is a subsidiary calculative procedure. It is subsidiary because we engage in it for the sake of getting certain results which are intended to determine our conduct. Decision is deliberately postponed and made dependent on the outcome of deliberation. I might instead have spun a coin and determined to act in one way if heads, in another if tails, came top. But I have resolved to act in whichever way is supported by the outcome of my deliberation, that is, in that way which has the weight of reason behind it. Finding what is supported by the best reasons is a rule-guided and somewhat formalized activity consisting of two steps, surveying the facts and weighing the reasons. The facts are surveyed with a view to determining those which are relevant reasons. I do this by bearing in mind my convictions about what constitute good reasons, my consideration-making beliefs, for example, that doing something would be enjoyable to me, or in my interest, or harmful to someone else, or against the law, or immoral, and so on. This primary deliberation may at any moment become an examination of the question whether my consideration-making beliefs are true. This latter question will be discussed in Chapter Twelve.*

The second step in my deliberation consists in weighing those facts which my first step has revealed as relevant. It is not enough to know which reasons speak for and which against entering on a certain course of action; I must also know which are the strongest or best reasons. Here, too, I am helped by certain beliefs, the rules of priority which I take over from my social environment. It is generally agreed in our society that moral reasons are superior to reasons of self-interest, reasons of long-range interest superior to reasons of short-range interest, and reasons of self-interest superior to mere pleasure or pain. I must postpone until Chapter Twelve* the discussion of the question whether the beliefs prevalent in our society are correct or not.

●　　●　　●　　●　　●

THE MORAL POINT OF VIEW

Morality Involves Doing Things on Principle

[One] feature of consistent egoism is that the rules by which a consistent egoist abides are merely rules of thumb. A consistent egoist has only one supreme principle, to do whatever is necessary for the realization of his one aim, the promotion of his interest. He does not have *principles,* he has only an aim. If one has adopted the moral point of view, then one acts on principle and not merely on rules of thumb designed to promote one's aim. This involves conforming to the rules whether or not doing so favors one's own or anyone else's aim.

Kant grasped this point even if only obscurely. He saw that adopting the moral point of view involves acting on principle. It involves conforming to rules even when doing so is unpleasant, painful, costly, or ruinous to oneself. . . .

●　　●　　●　　●　　●

* [Beginning on page 510 below.—Ed. note.]

. . . This follows from the very nature of moral principles. They are binding on everyone alike quite irrespective of what are the goals or purposes of the person in question. Hence self-interest cannot be the moral point of view, for it sets every individual one supreme goal, his own interest, which overrules all his other maxims.

Moral Rules Are Meant for Everybody

The point of view of morality is inadequately characterized by saying that *I* have adopted it if *I* act on principles, that is, on rules to which I do not make exceptions whenever acting on them would frustrate one or the other of my purposes or desires. It is characterized by greater universality than that. It must be thought of as a standpoint from which principles are considered as being acted on *by everyone*. Moral principles are not merely principles on which a person must always act without making exceptions, but they are principles *meant for everybody*.

It follows from this that the teaching of morality must be completely universal and open. Morality is meant to be taught to all members of the group in such a way that everyone can and ought always to act in accordance with these rules. It is not the preserve of an oppressed or privileged class or individual. People are neglecting their duties if they do not teach the moral rules to their children. Children are removed from the homes of criminals because they are not likely to be taught the moral rules there. Futhermore, moral rules must be taught quite openly and to everybody without discrimination. An esoteric code, a set of precepts known only to the initiated and perhaps jealously concealed from outsiders, can at best be a religion, not a morality. 'Thou shalt not eat beans and this is a secret' or 'Always leave the third button of your waistcoat undone, but don't tell anyone except the initiated members' may be part of an esoteric religion, but not of a morality. 'Thou shalt not kill, but it is a strict secret' is absurd. 'Esoteric morality' is a contradiction in terms. It is no accident that the so-called higher religions were imbued with the missionary spirit, for they combine the beliefs of daemons and gods and spirits characteristic of primitive religions with *a system of morality*. Primitive religions are not usually concerned to proselytize. On the contrary, they are imbued with the spirit of the exclusive trade secret. If one thinks of one's religion as concentrated wisdom of life revealed solely to the *chosen* people, one will regard it as the exclusive property of the club, to be confined to the elect. If, on the other hand, the rules are thought to be for everyone, one must in consistency want to spread the message.

The condition of universal teachability yields three other criteria of moral rules. They must not, in the first place, be 'self-frustrating.' They are so if their purpose is frustrated as soon as everybody acts on them, if they have a point only when a good many people act on the opposite principle. Someone might, for instance, act on the maxim 'When you are in need, ask for help, but never help another man when he is in need.' If everybody adopted this principle, then their adoption of the second half would frustrate what obviously is the point of the adoption of the first half, namely, to get help when one is in need. Although such a principle is not self-contradictory—for anybody could consistently adopt it—it is nevertheless objectionable from the moral point of view, for it could not be taught openly to everyone. It would then lose its point. It is a parasitic principle, useful to anyone only if many people act on its opposite.

The same is true of 'self-defeating' and 'morally impossible' rules. A principle is self-defeating if its point is defeated as soon as a person lets it be known that he has adopted it, for example, the principle 'Give a promise even when you know or think that you can never keep it, or when you don't intend to keep it.' The very point of giving promises is to reassure and furnish a guarantee to the promisee. Hence any remark that throws doubt on the sincerity of the promiser will defeat the purpose of making a promise. And clearly to *let it be known* that one gives promises even when one knows or thinks one cannot, or when one does not intend to keep them, is to raise such doubts. And to say that one acts on the above principle is to imply that one may well give promises in these cases. Hence to reveal that one acts on this principle will tend to defeat one's own purpose.

It has already been said that moral rules must be capable of being taught openly, but this rule is self-defeating when taught openly, for then everyone would be known to act on it. Hence it cannot belong to the morality of any group.

Lastly, there are some rules which it is literally impossible to teach in the way the moral rules of a group must be capable of being taught, for example, the rule 'Always assert what you think not to be the case.' Such *morally impossible* rules differ from self-frustrating and self-defeating rules in that the latter could have been taught in this way, although it would have been quite senseless to do so, where as the former literally cannot be so taught. The reason why the above rule cannot be taught in this way is that the only possible case of acting on it, doing so secretly, is ruled out by the conditions of *moral teaching*.

• • • • •

These points are of general interest in that they clarify some valuable remarks contained in Kant's doctrine of the categorical imperative. In particular they clarify the expression 'can will' contained in the formulation 'Act so that thou *canst will* thy maxim to become a universal law of nature.' 'Canst will' in one sense means what I have called 'morally possible.' Your maxim must be a formula which is morally possible, that is, which is logically capable of being a rule belonging to the morality of some group, as the maxim 'Always lie' is not. No one *can* wish that maxim to be a rule of *some morality*. To say that one is wishing it is to contradict oneself. One cannot wish it any more than one can wish that time should move backwards.

The second sense of 'can will' is that in which no rational person can will certain things. Self-frustrating and self-defeating moral rules are not morally impossible, they are merely senseless. No rational person could wish such rules to become part of any morality. That is to say, anyone wishing that they should, would thereby expose himself to the charge of irrationality, like the person who wishes that he should never attain his ends or that he should (for no reason at all) be plagued by rheumatic pains throughout his life.

The points just made also show the weakness of Kant's doctrine. For while it is true that someone who acts on the maxim 'Always lie' acts on a morally impossible one, it is not true that every liar necessarily acts on that maxim. If he acts on a principle at all, it may, for instance, be 'Lie when it is the only way to avoid harming someone,' or 'Lie when it is helpful to you and harmful to no one else,' or 'Lie when it is entertaining and harmless.' Maxims such as these can, of course, be willed in either of the senses explained.

Moral Rules Must Be for the Good of Everyone Alike
The conditions so far mentioned are merely formal. They exclude certain sorts of rule as not coming up to the formal requirements. But moral rules should also have a certain sort of content. Observation of these rules should be *for the good of everyone alike*. Thrasymachus' view that justice is the advantage of the stronger, if true of the societies of his day, is an indictment of their legal systems from the moral point of view. It shows that what goes by the name of morality in these societies is no more than a set of rules and laws which enrich the ruling class at the expense of the masses. But this is wrong because unjust, however much the rules satisfy the formal criteria. For given certain initial social conditions, formal equality before the law may favor certain groups and exploit others.

There is one obvious way in which a rule may be for the good of everyone alike, namely, if it furthers the common good. When I am promoted and my salary is raised, this is to my advantage. It will also be to the advantage of my wife and my family and possibly of a few other people—it will not be to the advantage of my colleague who had hoped for promotion but is now excluded. It may even be to his detriment if his reputation suffers as a result. If the coal miners obtain an increase in their wages, then this is to the advantage of coal miners. It is for their common good. But it may not be to the advantage of anyone else. On the other hand, if production is raised and with it everyone's living standard, that is literally to everyone's advantage. The rule 'Work harder,' if it has these consequences, is for the common good of all.

Very few rules, if any, will be for the common good of everyone. But a rule may be in the interest of everyone alike, even though the results of the observation of the rule are not for the common good in the sense explained. Rules such as 'Thou shalt not kill,' 'Thou shalt not be cruel,' 'Thou shalt not lie' are obviously, in some other sense, for the good of everyone alike. What is this sense? It becomes clear if we look at these rules from the moral point of view, that is, that of an independent, unbiased, impartial, objective, dispassionate, disinterested observer. Taking such a God's-eye point of view, we can see that it is in the interest of everyone alike that everyone should abide by the rule 'Thou shalt not kill.' From the moral point of view, it is clear that it is in the interest of everyone alike if everyone alike should be allowed to pursue his own interest provided this does not adversely affect someone else's interests. Killing someone in the pursuit of my interests would interfere with his.

There can be no doubt that such a God's-eye point of view is involved in the moral standpoint. The most elementary teaching is based on it. The negative version of the so-called Golden Rule sums it up: 'Don't do unto others as you would not have them do unto you.' When we teach children the moral point of view, we try to explain it to them by getting them to put themselves in another person's place: 'How would you like to have that done to you!' 'Don't do evil,' the most readily accepted moral rule of all, is simply the most general form of stating this prohibition. For doing evil is the opposite of doing good. Doing good is doing for another person what, if he were following (self-interested) reason, he would do for himself. Doing evil is doing to another person what it would be contrary to reason for him to do to himself. Harming another, hurting another, doing to another what he dislikes having done to him are the specific forms this takes. Killing, cruelty, inflicting pain, maiming, torturing, deceiving, cheating, rape, adultery are instances of this sort of behavior. They all violate the condition of 'reversibility,' that is, that the behavior in question must be acceptable to a person whether he is at the 'giving' or 'receiving' end of it.

It is important to see just what is established by this condition of being for the good of everyone alike. In the first place, anyone is doing wrong who engages in nonreversible behavior. It is irrelevant whether he knows that it is wrong or not, whether the morality of his group recognizes it or not. Such behavior is 'wrong in itself,' irrespective of individual or social recognition, irrespective of the consequences it has. Moreover, every single act of such behavior is wrong. We need not consider the whole group or the whole of humanity engaging in this sort of behavior, but only a single case. Hence we can say that all nonreversible behavior is morally wrong; hence that anyone engaging in it is doing what, prima facie, he ought not to do. We need not consider whether this sort of behavior has harmful consequences, whether it is forbidden by the morality of the man's group, or whether he himself thinks it wrong.

The principle of reversibility does not merely impose certain prohibitions on a moral agent, but also certain positive injunctions. It is, for instance, wrong —an omission—not to help another person when he is in need and when we are in a position to help him. The story of the Good Samaritan makes this point. The positive version of the Golden Rule makes the same point more generally: 'Do unto others as you would have them do unto you.' Note that it is wrong— not merely not meritorious—to omit to help others when they are in need and when you are in a position to help them. It does not follow from this, however, that it is wrong not to promote the greatest good of the greatest number, or not to promote the greatest amount of good in the world. Deontologists and utilitarians alike make the mistake of thinking that it is one, or the only one, of our moral duties to 'do the optimific act.' Nothing could be further from the truth. We do not have a duty to do good to others or to ourselves, or to others and/or to ourselves in a judicious mixture such that it produces the greatest possible amount of good in the world. We are morally required to do good only to those who are actually in need of our assistance. The view that we always ought to do the optimific act, or whenever we have no more stringent duty to perform, would have the absurd result that we are doing wrong whenever we are relaxing, since on those occasions there will always be opportunities to produce greater good than we can by relaxing. For the relief of suffering is always a greater good than mere enjoyment. Yet it is quite plain that the worker who, after a tiring day, puts on his slippers and listens to the wireless is not doing anything he ought not to, is not neglecting any of his duties, even though it may be perfectly true that there are things he might do which produce more good in the world, even for himself, than merely relaxing by the fireside.

•   •   •   •   •

WHY SHOULD WE BE MORAL?*

We are now in a position to deal with the various problems we shelved earlier. . . . We had to postpone the examination of how we verify those fundamental propositions which serve as major premises in our practical arguments. We must now deal with this. The examination of the prevailing consideration-making beliefs used at the first stage of our practical deliberations leads naturally to the examination of our rules of superiority used at the second stage. This in turn involves our investigating whether moral reasons are superior to all others and . . . whether and why we should be moral. . . .

The Truth of Consideration-making Beliefs

Let us begin with our most elementary consideration-making belief: the fact that if I did x I would enjoy doing x is a reason for me to do x. There can be little doubt that this is one of the rules of reason recognized in our society. Most people would use the knowledge of the fact that they would enjoy doing something as a pro in their deliberations whether to do it. When we wonder whether to go to the pictures or to a dinner dance, the fact that we would enjoy the dinner dance but not the pictures is regarded as a reason for going to the dinner dance rather than to the pictures. We are now asking whether this widely held belief is true, whether this fact really is a reason or is merely and falsely believed to be so.

•   •   •   •   •

Our practical argument runs as follows:
   (i) The fact that if I did x I would enjoy doing x is a reason for me to do x.
   (ii) I would enjoy doing x if I did x.
   (iii) Therefore I ought to do x (other things being equal).

•   •   •   •   •

* [Here Chapter Twelve begins.—Ed. note.]

The problem of the truth or falsity of consideration-making beliefs is . . . reduced to the question whether it is better that they, rather than their contraries or contradictories, should be used as rules of reason, that is, as major premises in practical arguments. How would we tell?

It is not difficult to see that the contrary of our rule of reason is greatly inferior to it. For if, instead of the presently accepted belief (see above (i)), its contrary became the prevailing rule, then anyone trying to follow reason would have to conclude that whenever there is something that he would enjoy doing if he did it then he ought *not* to do it. "Reason" would counsel everyone always to refrain from doing what he enjoys, from satisfying his desires. "Reason" would counsel self-frustration for its own sake.

It is important to note that such an arrangement is possible. To say that we would not now *call* it 'following reason' is not enough to refute it. We can imagine two societies in which English is spoken and which differ only in this, that in one society (i) is accepted, in the other the contrary of (i). It would then be correct to say in one society that doing what one would enjoy doing was following reason, in the other society that it was acting contrary to it. The 'tautologousness' of the first remark *in our society* is not incompatible with the 'tautologousness' of the contrary remark *in another society*. From the fact that the proposition 'Fathers are male' is analytic, we can infer that 'fathers are male' is necessarily true. But this is so only because we would not correctly *call* anything 'father' that we would correctly call 'not male.' And it is perfectly in order to say that in any society in which English was spoken but in which the words 'father' and/or 'male' were not used in this way those words did not mean quite the same as in our society. And with this, the matter is ended, for we are not concerned to settle the question which verbal arrangement, ours or theirs, is the better. Nothing at all follows from the fact that a society has our usage of 'father' and 'male' or theirs. But in the case of the use of 'reason,' much depends on which usage is accepted. The real difficulty only begins when we have concluded, correctly, that the word 'reason' is used in a different sense in that other society. For the practical implications of the word 'reason' are the same in both societies, namely, that people are encouraged to follow reason rather than act contrary to it. However, *what* is held in one society to be in accordance with reason is held to be contrary to it in the other. Hence, we must say that in practical matters nothing fundamental can be settled by attention to linguistic proprieties or improprieties.

What, then, is relevant? We must remember what sort of a 'game' the game of reasoning is. We ask the question 'What shall I do?' or 'What is the best course of action?' Following reasons is following those hints which are most likely to make the course of action the best in the circumstances. The criteria of 'best course of action' are linked with what we mean by 'the good life.' In evaluating a life, one of the criteria of merit which we use is how much satisfaction and how little frustration there is in that life. Our very purpose in 'playing the reasoning game' is to maximize satisfactions and minimize frustrations. Deliberately to frustrate ourselves and to minimize satisfaction would certainly be to go counter to the very purpose for which we deliberate and weigh the pros and cons. These criteria are, therefore, necessarily linked with the very purpose of the activity of reasoning. Insofar as we enter on that 'game' at all, we are therefore bound to accept these criteria. Hence we are bound to agree that the consideration-making belief which is prevalent in our society is better than its contrary.

But need we accept that purpose? Is this not just a matter of taste or preference? Could not people with other tastes choose the opposite purpose, namely, self-frustration and self-denial rather than satisfaction of desires and enjoyment? The answer is No, it is not just a matter of taste or preference. Whether we like or don't like oysters, even whether we prefer red ink to claret, is a matter of taste, though to prefer red ink is to exhibit a very eccentric taste. Whether we prefer to satisfy our desires or to frustrate them is not, however, a matter of taste or preference. It is not an eccentricity of taste to prefer whatever one does *not* enjoy doing to whatever one does enjoy doing. It is perverse or crazy if it is done every now and then, mad if it is done always or on principle.

•   •   •   •   •

The contradictory of our most fundamental consideration-making belief is also less satisfactory than *it* is. If it were to be believed that the fact that one would enjoy doing x was not a reason for doing it (a belief which is the contradictory of our most fundamental consideration-making belief), then people wishing to follow reason would be neither advised to do what they would enjoy doing nor advised not to do it. Reason would simply be silent on this issue. Never to do what one would enjoy doing would be as much in accordance with reason (other things being equal) as always to do it. In such a world, "following reason" might be less rewarding than following instinct or inclination. Hence this cannot *be* following reason, for it *must* pay to follow reason at least as much as to follow instinct or inclination, or else it is not reason.

To sum up. People who replace our most fundamental consideration-making belief by its contrary or contradictory will not do as well as those who adhere to it. Those who adopt its contrary must even be said to be mad. This seems to me the best possible argument for the preferability of our fundamental consideration-making belief to its contrary and contradictory. And this amounts to a proof of its truth. I need not waste any further time on examining whether the other consideration-making beliefs prevalent in our society are also true. Everyone can conduct this investigation for himself.

The Hierarchy of Reasons

•   •   •   •   •

. . . It has often been thought that enlightened egoism is a possible rational way of running things. Sidgwick,[1] for instance, says that the principle of egoism,

[1] Henry Sidgwick, *The Methods of Ethics*, 7th ed. (London: Macmillan and Co., 1907), concluding chapter, par. 1.

to have as one's ultimate aim one's own greatest happiness, and the principle of universal benevolence, to have as one's ultimate aim the greatest happiness of the greatest number, are equally rational. Sidgwick then goes on to say that these two principles may conflict and anyone who admits the rationality of both may go on to maintain that it is rational not to abandon the aim of one's own greatest happiness. On his view, there is a fundamental and ultimate contradiction in our apparent intuitions of what is reasonable in conduct. He argues that this can be removed only by the assumption that the individual's greatest happiness and the greatest happiness of the greatest number are both achieved by the rewarding and punishing activity of a perfect being whose sanctions would suffice to make it always everyone's interest to promote universal happiness to the best of his knowledge.

The difficulty which Sidgwick here finds is due to the fact that he regards reasons of self-interest as being no stronger and no weaker than moral reasons. This, however, is not in accordance with our ordinary convictions. It is generally believed that when reasons of self-interest conflict with moral reasons, then moral reasons override those of self-interest. It is our common conviction that moral reasons are superior to all others. Sidgwick has simply overlooked that although it is prima facie in accordance with reason to follow reasons of self-interest and also to follow moral reasons nevertheless, when there is a conflict between these two types of reason, when we have a self-interested reason for doing something and a moral reason against doing it, there need not be an ultimate and fundamental contradiction in what it is in accordance with reason to do. For one type of reason may be *stronger* or *better* than another so that, when two reasons of different types are in conflict, it is in accordance with reason to follow the stronger, contrary to reason to follow the weaker.

The Supremacy of Moral Reasons

Are moral reasons really superior to reasons of self-interest as we all believe? Do we really have reason on our side when we follow moral reasons against self-interest? What reasons could there be for being moral? Can we really give an answer to 'Why should we be moral?' It is obvious that all these questions come to the same thing. When we ask, 'Should we be moral?' or 'Why should we be moral?' or 'Are moral reasons superior to all others?' we ask to be shown the reason for being moral. What is this reason?

Let us begin with a state of affairs in which reasons of self-interest are supreme. In such a state everyone keeps his impulses and inclinations in check when and only when they would lead him into behavior detrimental to his own interest. Everyone who follows reason will discipline himself to rise early, to do his exercises, to refrain from excessive drinking and smoking, to keep good company, to marry the right sort of girl, to work and study hard in order to get on, and so on. However, it will often happen that people's interests conflict. In such a case, they will have to resort to ruses or force to get their own way. As this becomes known, men will become suspicious, for they will regard one another as scheming competitors for the good things in life. The universal supremacy of the rules of self-interest must lead to what Hobbes called the state of nature. At the same time, it will be clear to everyone that universal obedience to certain rules overriding self-interest would produce a state of affairs which serves everyone's interest much better than his unaided pursuit of it in a state where everyone does the same. Moral rules are universal rules designed to override those of self-interest when following the latter is harmful to others. 'Thou shalt not kill,' 'Thou shalt not lie,' 'Thou shalt not steal' are rules which forbid the inflicting of harm on someone else even when this might be in one's interest.

The very *raison d'être* of a morality is to yield reasons which overrule the reasons of self-interest in those cases when everyone's following self-interest would be harmful to everyone. Hence moral reasons are superior to all others.

'But what does this mean?' it might be objected. 'If it merely means that we do so regard them, then you are of course right, but your contention is useless, a mere point of usage. And how could it mean any more? If it means that we not only do so regard them, but *ought* so to regard them, then there must be *reasons* for saying this. But there could not be any reasons for it. If you offer reasons of self-interest, you are arguing in a circle. Moreover, it cannot be true that it is always in my interest to treat moral reasons as superior to reasons of self-interest. If it were, self-interest and morality could never conflict, but they notoriously do. It is equally circular to argue that there are moral reasons for saying that one ought to treat moral reasons as superior to reasons of self-interest. And what other reasons are there?'

The answer is that we are now looking at the world from the point of view of *anyone*. We are not examining particular alternative courses of action before this or that person; we are examining two alternative worlds, one in which moral reasons are always treated by everyone as superior to reasons of self-interest and one in which the reverse is the practice. And we can see that the first world is the better world, because we can see that the second world would be the sort which Hobbes describes as the state of nature.

This shows that I ought to be moral, for when I ask the question 'What ought I to do?' I am asking, 'Which is the course of action supported by the best reasons?' But since it has just been shown that moral reasons are superior to reasons of self-interest, I have been given a reason for being moral, for following moral reasons rather than any other, namely, they are better reasons than any other.

But is this always so? Do we have a reason for being moral whatever the conditions we find ourselves in? Could there not be situations in which it is not true that we have reasons for being moral, that, on the contrary, we have reasons for ignoring the demands of morality? Is not Hobbes right in saying that in a state of nature the laws of nature, that is, the rules of morality, bind only *in foro interno?**

Hobbes argues as follows:

(i) To live in a state of nature is to live outside society. It is to live in

---

* [That is, within the conscience of those who have reason to accept the laws of nature as binding upon them.—Ed. note.]

conditions in which there are no common ways of life and, therefore, no reliable expectations about other people's behavior other than that they will follow their inclination or their interest.

(ii) In such a state reason will be the enemy of co-operation and mutual trust. For it is too risky to hope that other people will refrain from protecting their own interests by the preventive elimination of probable or even possible dangers to them. Hence reason will counsel everyone to avoid these risks by preventive action. But this leads to war.

(iii) It is obvious that everyone's following self-interest leads to a state of affairs which is desirable from no one's point of view. It is, on the contrary, desirable that everybody should follow rules overriding self-interest whenever that is to the detriment of others. In other words, it is desirable to bring about a state of affairs in which all obey the rules of morality.

(iv) However, Hobbes claims that in the state of nature it helps nobody if a single person or a small group of persons begins to follow the rules of morality, for this could only lead to the extinction of such individuals or groups. In such a state, it is therefore contrary to reason to be moral.

(v) The situation can change, reason can support morality, only when the presumption about other people's behavior is reversed. Hobbes thought that this could be achieved only by the creation of an absolute ruler with absolute power to enforce his laws. . . . This is not true and . . . it is quite different if people live in a society, that is, if they have common ways of life, which are taught to all members and somehow enforced by the group. Its members have reason to expect their fellows generally to obey its rules, that is, its religion, morality, customs, and law, even when doing so is not, on certain occasions, in their interest. Hence they too have reason to follow these rules.

Is this argument sound? One might, of course, object to step (i) on the grounds that this is an empirical proposition for which there is little or no evidence. For how can we know whether it is true that people in a state of nature would follow only their inclinations or, at best, reasons of self-interest, when nobody now lives in that state or has ever lived in it?

However, there is some empirical evidence to support this claim. For in the family of nations, individual states are placed very much like individual persons in a state of nature. The doctrine of the sovereignty of nations and the absence of an effective international law and police force are a guarantee that nations live in a state of nature, without commonly accepted rules that are somehow enforced. Hence it must be granted that living in a state of nature leads to living in a state in which individuals act either on impulse or as they think their interest dictates. For states pay only lip service to morality. They attack their hated neighbors when the opportunity arises. They start preventive wars in order to destroy the enemy before he can deliver his knockout blow. Where interests conflict, the stronger party usually has his way, whether his claims are justified or not. And where the relative strength of the parties is not obvious, they usually resort to arms in order to determine "whose side God is on." Treaties are frequently concluded but, morally speaking, they are not worth the paper they are written on. Nor do the partners regard them as contracts binding in the ordinary way, but rather as public expressions of the belief of the governments concerned that for the time being their alliance is in the interest of the allies. It is well understood that such treaties may be canceled before they reach their predetermined end or simply broken when it suits one partner. . . .

It is, moreover, difficult to justify morality in international affairs. For suppose a highly moral statesman were to demand that his country adhere to a treaty obligation even though this meant its ruin or possibly its extinction. Suppose he were to say that treaty obligations are sacred and must be kept whatever the consequences. How could he defend such a policy? Perhaps one might argue that someone has to make a start in order to create mutual confidence in international affairs. Or one might say that setting a good example is the best way of inducing others to follow suit. But such a defense would hardly be sound. The less skeptical one is about the genuineness of the cases in which nations have adhered to their treaties from a sense of moral obligation, the more skeptical one must be about the effectiveness of such examples of virtue in effecting a change of international practice. Power politics still govern in international affairs.

We must, therefore, grant Hobbes the first step in his argument and admit that in a state of nature people, as a matter of psychological fact, would not follow the dictates of morality. But we might object to the next step that knowing this psychological fact about other people's behavior constitutes a reason for behaving in the same way. Would it not still be immoral for anyone to ignore the demands of morality even though he knows that others are likely or certain to do so, too? Can we offer as a justification for morality the fact that no one is entitled to do wrong just because someone else is doing wrong? This argument begs the question whether it *is* wrong for anyone in this state to disregard the demands of morality. It cannot be wrong to break a treaty or make preventive war if we have no reason to obey the moral rules. For to say that it is wrong to do so is to say that we ought not to do so. But if we have no reason for obeying the moral rule, then we have no reason overruling self-interest, hence no reason for keeping the treaty when keeping it is not in our interest, hence it is not true that we have a reason for keeping it, hence not true that we ought to keep it, hence not true that it is wrong not to keep it.

I conclude that Hobbes's argument is sound. Moralities are systems of principles whose acceptance by everyone as overruling the dictates of self-interest is in the interest of everyone alike, though following the rules of a morality is not of course identical with following self-interest. If it were, there could be no conflict between a morality and self-interest and no point in having moral rules overriding self-interest. Hobbes is also right in saying that the application of this system of rules is in accordance with reason only in social conditions, that is, when there are well-established ways of behavior.

The answer to our question 'Why should we be moral?' is therefore as follows. We should be moral because being moral is following rules designed to overrule self-interest whenever it is in the interest of everyone alike that everyone should set aside his interest. It is not self-contradictory to say this, because it may be in one's interest *not* to follow one's interest at times. We have already seen that enlightened self-interest acknowledges this point. But while enlightened self-interest does not require any genuine sacrifice from anyone, morality does. In the interest of the possibility of the good life for everyone, voluntary sacrifices are sometimes required from everybody. Thus, a person might do better for himself by following enlightened self-interest rather than morality. It is not possible, however, that *everyone* should do better for himself by following enlightened self-interest rather than morality. The best possible life *for everyone* is possible only by everyone's following the rules of morality, that is, rules which quite frequently may require individuals to make genuine sacrifices.

It must be added to this, however, that such a system of rules has the support of reason only where people live in societies, that is, in conditions in which there are established common ways of behavior. Outside society, people have no reason for following such rules, that is, for being moral. In other words, outside society, the very distinction between right and wrong vanishes.

JOHN RAWLS
Justice as Fairness

I

It might seem at first sight that the concepts of justice and fairness are the same, and that there is no reason to distinguish them, or to say that one is more fundamental than the other. I think that this impression is mistaken. In this paper I wish to show that the fundamental idea in the concept of justice is fairness; and I wish to offer an analysis of the concept of justice from this point of view. To bring out the force of this claim, and the analysis based upon it, I shall then argue that it is this aspect of justice for which utilitarianism, in its classical form, is unable to account, but which is expressed, even if misleadingly, by the idea of the social contract.

To start with I shall develop a particular conception of justice by stating and commenting upon two principles which specify it, and by considering the circumstances and conditions under which they may be thought to arise. The principles defining this conception, and the conception itself, are, of course, familiar. It may be possible, however, by using the notion of fairness as a

From John Rawls, "Justice as Fairness," *Philosophical Review,* LXVII, No. 2 (1958), 164–194. Reprinted by permission of the author and the editor of *The Philosophical Review.*

framework, to assemble and to look at them in a new way. Before stating this conception, however, the following preliminary matters should be kept in mind.

Throughout I consider justice only as a virtue of social institutions, or what I shall call practices. The principles of justice are regarded as formulating restrictions as to how practices may define positions and offices, and assign thereto powers and liabilities, rights and duties. Justice as a virtue of particular actions or of persons I do not take up at all. It is important to distinguish these various subjects of justice, since the meaning of the concept varies according to whether it is applied to practices, particular actions, or persons. These meanings are, indeed, connected, but they are not identical. I shall confine my discussion to the sense of justice as applied to practices, since this sense is the basic one. Once it is understood, the other senses should go quite easily.

Justice is to be understood in its customary sense as representing but *one* of the many virtues of social institutions, for these may be antiquated, inefficient, degrading, or any number of other things, without being unjust. Justice is not to be confused with an all-inclusive vision of a good society; it is only one part of any such conception. It is important, for example, to distinguish that sense of equality which is an aspect of the concept of justice from that sense of equality which belongs to a more comprehensive social ideal. There may well be inequalities which one concedes are just, or at least not unjust, but which, nevertheless, one wishes, on other grounds, to do away with. I shall focus attention, then, on the usual sense of justice in which it is essentially the elimination of arbitrary distinctions and the establishment, within the structure of a practice, of a proper balance between competing claims.

Finally, there is no need to consider the principles discussed below as *the* principles of justice. For the moment it is sufficient that they are typical of a family of principles normally associated with the concept of justice. The way in which the principles of this family resemble one another, as shown by the background against which they may be thought to arise, will be made clear by the whole of the subsequent argument.

2

The conception of justice which I want to develop may be stated in the form of two principles as follows: first, each person participating in a practice, or affected by it, has an equal right to the most extensive liberty compatible with a like liberty for all; and second, inequalities are arbitrary unless it is reasonable to expect that they will work out for everyone's advantage, and provided the positions and offices to which they attach, or from which they may be gained, are open to all. These principles express justice as a complex of three ideas: liberty, equality, and reward for services contributing to the common good.

The term "person" is to be construed variously depending on the circumstances. On some occasions it will mean human individuals, but in others it may refer to nations, provinces, business firms, churches, teams, and so on. The principles of justice apply in all these instances, although there is a certain logical priority to the case of human individuals. As I shall use the term "person," it will be ambiguous in the manner indicated.

The first principle holds, of course, only if other things are equal: that is, while there must always be a justification for departing from the initial position of equal liberty (which is defined by the pattern of rights and duties, powers and liabilities, established by a practice), and the burden of proof is placed on him who would depart from it, nevertheless, there can be, and often there is, a justification for doing so. Now, that similar particular cases, as defined by a practice, should be treated similarly as they arise, is part of the very concept of a practice; it is involved in the notion of an activity in accordance with rules. The first principle expresses an analogous conception, but as applied to the structure of practices themselves. It holds, for example, that there is a presumption against the distinctions and classifications made by legal systems and other practices to the extent that they infringe on the original and equal liberty of the persons participating in them. The second principle defines how this presumption may be rebutted.

It might be argued at this point that justice requires only an equal liberty. If, however, a greater liberty were possible for all without loss or conflict, then it would be irrational to settle on a lesser liberty. There is no reason for circumscribing rights unless their exercise would be incompatible, or would render the practice defining them less effective. Therefore no serious distortion of the concept of justice is likely to follow from including within it the concept of the greatest equal liberty.

The second principle defines what sorts of inequalities are permissible; it specifies how the presumption laid down by the first principle may be put aside. Now by inequalities it is best to understand not *any* differences between offices and positions, but differences in the benefits and burdens attached to them either directly or indirectly, such as prestige and wealth, or liability to taxation and compulsory services. Players in a game do not protest against there being different positions, such as batter, pitcher, catcher, and the like, nor to there being various privileges and powers as specified by the rules; nor do the citizens of a country object to there being the different offices of government such as president, senator, governor, judge, and so on, each with their special rights and duties. It is not differences of this kind that are normally thought of as inequalities, but differences in the resulting distribution established by a practice, or made possible by it, of the things men strive to attain or avoid. Thus they may complain about the pattern of honors and rewards set up by a practice (e.g., the privileges and salaries of government officials) or they may object to the distribution of power and wealth which results from the various ways in which men avail themselves of the opportunities allowed by it (e.g., the concentration of wealth which may develop in a free price system allowing large entrepreneurial or speculative gains).

It should be noted that the second principle holds that an inequality is allowed only if there is reason to believe that the practice with the inequality, or resulting in it, will work for the advantage of *every* party engaging in it. Here it is important to stress that *every* party must gain from the inequality. Since the principle applies to practices, it implies that the representative man in every office or position defined by a practice, when he views it as a going concern, must find it reasonable to prefer his condition and prospects with the inequality to what they would be under the practice without it. The principle excludes, therefore, the justification of inequalities on the grounds that the disadvantages of those in one position are outweighed by the greater advantages of those in another position. This rather simple restriction is the main modification I wish to make in the utilitarian principle as usually understood. When coupled with the notion of a practice, it is a restriction of consequence, and one which some utilitarians, e.g., Hume and Mill, have used in their discussions of justice without realizing apparently its significance, or at least without calling attention to it. Why it is a significant modification of principle, changing one's conception of justice entirely, the whole of my argument will show.

Further, it is also necessary that the various offices to which special benefits or burdens attach are open to all. It may be, for example, to the common advantage, as just defined, to attach special benefits to certain offices. Perhaps by doing so the requisite talent can be attracted to them and encouraged to give its best efforts. But any offices having special benefits must be won in a fair competition in which contestants are judged on their merits. If some offices were not open, those excluded would normally be justified in feeling unjustly treated, even if they benefited from the greater efforts of those who were allowed to compete for them. Now if one can assume that offices are open, it is necessary only to consider the design of practices themselves and how they jointly, as a system, work together. It will be a mistake to focus attention on the varying relative positions of particular persons, who may be known to us by their proper names, and to require that each such change, as a once for all transaction viewed in isolation, must be in itself just. It is the system of practices which is to be judged, and judged from a general point of view: unless one is prepared to criticize it from the standpoint of a representative man holding some particular office, one has no complaint against it.

3

Given these principles one might try to derive them from a priori principles of reason, or claim that they were known by intuition. These are familiar enough steps and, at least in the case of the first principle, might be made with some success. Usually, however, such arguments, made at this point, are unconvincing. They are not likely to lead to an understanding of the basis of the principles of justice, not at least as principles of justice. I wish, therefore, to look at the principles in a different way.

Imagine a society of persons amongst whom a certain system of practices is *already* well established. Now suppose that by and large they are mutually self-interested; their allegiance to their established practices is normally founded on the prospect of self-advantage. One need not assume that, in all senses of the term "person," the persons in this society are mutually self-interested. If the characterization as mutually self-interested applies when the line of division is the family, it may still be true that members of families are bound by ties of sentiment and affection and willingly acknowledge duties in contradiction to self-interest. Mutual self-interestedness in the relations between families, nations, churches, and the like, is commonly associated with intense loyalty and devotion on the part of individual members. Therefore, one can form a more realistic conception of this society if one thinks of it as consisting of mutually self-interested families, or some other association. Further, it is not necessary to suppose that these persons are mutually self-interested under all circumstances, but only in the usual situations in which they participate in their common practices.

Now suppose also that these persons are rational: they know their own interests more or less accurately; they are capable of tracing out the likely consequences of adopting one practice rather than another; they are capable of adhering to a course of action once they have decided upon it; they can resist present temptations and the enticements of immediate gain; and the bare knowledge or perception of the difference between their condition and that of others is not, within certain limits and in itself, a source of great dissatisfaction. Only the last point adds anything to the usual definition of rationality. This definition should allow, I think, for the idea that a rational man would not be greatly downcast from knowing, or seeing, that others are in a better position than himself, unless he thought their being so was the result of injustice, or the consequence of letting chance work itself out for no useful common purpose, and so on. So if these persons strike us as unpleasantly egoistic, they are at least free in some degree from the fault of envy.

Finally, assume that these persons have roughly similar needs and interests, or needs and interests in various ways complementary, so that fruitful cooperation amongst them is possible; and suppose that they are sufficiently equal in power and ability to guarantee that in normal circumstances none is able to dominate the others. This condition (as well as the others) may seem excessively vague; but in view of the conception of justice to which the argument leads, there seems no reason for making it more exact here.

Since these persons are conceived as engaging in their common practices, which are already established, there is no question of our supposing them to come together to deliberate as to how they will set these practices up for the first time. Yet we can imagine that from time to time they discuss with one another whether any of them has a legitimate complaint against their established institutions. Such discussions are perfectly natural in any normal society. Now suppose that they have settled on doing this in the following way. They first try to arrive at the principles by which complaints, and so practices themselves, are to be judged. Their procedure for this is to let each person propose the principles upon which he wishes his complaints to be tried with the understanding that, if acknowledged, the complaints of others will be similarly tried, and that no complaints will be heard at all until everyone is roughly of one mind as to how complaints are to be judged. They each understand further that the principles proposed and acknowledge on this occasion are binding on future occasions. Thus each will be wary of proposing a principle which would give him a peculiar advantage, in his present circumstances, supposing it to be accepted. Each person knows that he will be bound by it in future circumstances the peculiarities of which cannot be known, and which might well be such that the principle is then to his disadvantage. The idea is that everyone should be required to make *in advance* a firm commitment, which others also may reasonably be expected to make, and that no one be given the opportunity to tailor the canons of a legitimate complaint to fit his own special condition, and then to discard them when they no longer suit his purpose. Hence each person will propose principles of a general kind which will, to a large degree, gain their sense from the various applications to be made of them, the particular circumstances of which being as yet unknown. These principles will express the conditions in accordance with which each is the least unwilling to have his interests limited in the design of practices, given the competing interests of the others, on the supposition that the interests of others will be limited likewise. The restrictions which would so arise might be thought of as those a person would keep in mind if he were designing a practice in which his enemy were to assign him his place.

The two main parts of this conjectural account have a definite significance. The character and respective situations of the parties reflect the typical circumstances in which questions of justice arise. The procedure whereby principles are proposed and acknowledged represents constraints, analogous to those of having a morality, whereby rational and mutually self-interested persons are brought to act reasonably. Thus the first part reflects the fact that questions of justice arise when conflicting claims are made upon the design of a practice and where it is taken for granted that each person will insist, as far as possible, on what he considers his rights. It is typical of cases of justice to involve persons who are pressing on one another their claims, between which a fair balance or equilibrium must be found. On the other hand, as expressed by the second part, having a morality must at least imply the acknowledgment of principles as impartially applying to one's own conduct as well as to another's, and moreover principles which may constitute a constraint, or limitation, upon the pursuit of one's own interests. There are, of course, other aspects of having a morality: the acknowledgment of moral principles must show itself in accepting a reference to them as reasons for limiting one's claims, in acknowledging the burden of providing a special explanation, or excuse, when one acts contrary to them, or else in showing shame and remorse and a desire to make amends, and so on. It is sufficient to remark here that having a morality is analogous to having made a firm commitment in advance; for one must acknowledge the principles of morality even when to one's disadvantage. A man whose moral judgments always coincided with his interests could be suspected of having no morality at all.

Thus the two parts of the foregoing account are intended to mirror the kinds of circumstances in which questions of justice arise and the constraints which having a morality would impose upon persons so situated. In this way one can see how the acceptance of the principles of justice might come about, for given all these conditions as described, it would be natural if the two principles of justice were to be acknowledged. Since there is no way for anyone to win special advantages for himself, each might consider it reasonable to acknowledge equality as an initial principle. There is, however, no reason why they should regard this position as final; for if there are inequalities which satisfy the second principle, the immediate gain which equality would allow can be considered as intelligently invested in view of its future return. If, as is quite likely, these inequalities work as incentives to draw out better efforts, the members of this society may look upon them as concessions to human nature: they, like us, may think that people ideally should want to serve one another. But as they are mutually self-interested, their acceptance of these inequalities is merely the acceptance of the relations in which they actually stand, and a recognition of the motives which lead them to engage in their common practices. *They* have no title to complain of one another. And so provided that the conditions of the principle are met, there is no reason why they should not allow such inequalities. Indeed, it would be short-sighted of them to do so, and could result, in most cases, only from their being dejected by the bare knowledge, or perception, that others are better situated. Each person will, however, insist on an advantage to himself, and so on a common advantage, for none is willing to sacrifice anything for the others.

These remarks are not offered as a rigorous proof that persons conceived and situated as the conjectural account supposes, and required to adopt the procedure described, would settle on the two principles of justice. For such a proof a more elaborate and formal argument would have to be given: there remain certain details to be filled in, and various alternatives to be ruled out. The argument should, however, be taken as a proof, or a sketch of a proof; for the proposition I seek to establish is a necessary one, that is, it is intended as a theorem: namely, that when mutually self-interested and rational persons confront one another in typical circumstances of justice, and when they are required by a procedure expressing the constraints of having a morality to jointly acknowledge principles by which their claims on the design of their common practices are to be judged, they will settle on these two principles as restrictions governing the assignment of rights and duties, and thereby accept them as limiting their rights against one another. It is this theorem which accounts for these principles as principles of justice, and explains how they come to be associated with this moral concept. Moreover, this theorem is analogous to those about human conduct in other branches of social thought. That is, a simplified situation is described in which rational persons pursuing certain ends and related to one another in a definite way, are required to act subject to certain limitations; then, given this situation, it is shown that they will act in a certain manner. Failure so to act would imply that one or more of the assumptions does not obtain. The foregoing account aims to establish, or to sketch, a theorem in this sense; the aim of the argument is to show the basis for saying that the principles of justice may be regarded as those principles which arise when the constraints of having a morality are imposed upon rational persons in typical circumstances of justice.

•   •   •   •   •

5

That the principles of justice may be regarded as arising in the manner described illustrates an important fact about them. Not only does it bring out the idea that justice is a primitive moral notion in that it arises once the concept of morality is imposed on mutually self-interested agents similarly circumstanced, but it emphasizes that, fundamental to justice, is the concept of fairness which relates to right dealing between persons who are cooperating with or competing against one another, as when one speaks of fair games, fair competition, and fair bargains. The question of fairness arises when free persons, who have no authority over one another, are engaging in a joint activity and amongst themselves settling or acknowledging the rules which define it and which determine the respective shares in its benefits and burdens. A practice will strike the parties as fair if none feels that, by participating in it, they or any of the others are taken advantage of, or forced to give in to claims which they do not regard as legitimate. This implies that each has a conception of legitimate claims which he thinks it reasonable for others as well as himself to acknowledge. If one thinks of the principles of justice as arising in the manner described, then they do define this sort of conception. A practice is just or fair, then, when it satisfies the principles which those who participate in it could propose to one another for mutual acceptance under the afore-mentioned circumstances. Persons engaged in a just, or fair, practice can face one another openly and support their respective positions, should they appear questionable, by reference to principles which it is reasonable to expect each to accept.

It is this notion of the possibility of mutual acknowledgment of principles by free persons who have no authority over one another which makes the concept of fairness fundamental to justice. Only if such acknowledgment is possible can there be true community between persons in their common practices; otherwise their relations will appear to them as founded to some extent on force. If, in ordinary speech, fairness applies more particularly to practices in which there is a choice whether to engage or not (e.g., in games, business competition), and justice to practices in which there is no choice (e.g., in slavery), the element of necessity does not render the conception of mutual acknowledgment inapplicable, although it may make it much more urgent to change unjust than unfair institutions. For one activity in which one can always engage is that of proposing and acknowledging principles to one another supposing each to be similarly circumstanced; and to judge practices by the principles so arrived at is to apply the standard of fairness to them.

Now if the participants in a practice accept its rules as fair, and so have no complaint to lodge against it, there arises a prima facie duty (and a corresponding prima facie right) of the parties to each other to act in accordance with the practice when it falls upon them to comply. When any number of persons engage in a practice, or conduct a joint undertaking according to rules, and thus restrict their liberty, those who have submitted to these restrictions when required have the right to a similar acquiescence on the part of those who have benefited by their submission. These conditions will obtain if a practice is correctly acknowledged to be fair, for in this case all who participate in it will benefit from it. The rights and duties so arising are special rights and duties in that they depend on previous actions voluntarily undertaken, in this case on the parties having engaged in a common practice and knowingly accepted its benefits. It is not, however, an obligation which presupposes a deliberate performative act in the sense of a promise, or contract, and the like. An unfortunate mistake of proponents of the idea of the social contract was to suppose that political obligation does require some such act, or at least to use language which suggests it. It is sufficient that one has knowingly participated in and accepted the benefits of a practice acknowledged to be fair. This prima facie obligation may, of course, be overridden: it may happen, when it comes one's turn to follow a rule, that other considerations will justify not doing so. But one cannot, in general, be released from this obligation by denying the justice of the practice only when it falls on one to obey. If a person rejects a practice, he should, so far as possible, declare his intention in advance, and avoid participating in it or enjoying its benefits.

This duty I have called that of fair play, but it should be admitted that to refer to it in this way is, perhaps, to extend the ordinary notion of fairness. Usually acting unfairly is not so much the breaking of any particular rule, even if the infraction is difficult to detect (cheating), but taking advantage of loopholes or ambiguities in rules, availing oneself of unexpected or special circumstances which make it impossible to enforce them, insisting that rules be enforced to one's advantage when they should be suspended, and more generally, acting contrary to the intention of a practice. It is for this reason that one speaks of the sense of fair play: acting fairly requires more than simply being able to follow rules; what is fair must often be felt, or perceived, one wants to say. It is not, however, an unnatural extension of the duty of fair play to have it include the obligation which participants who have knowingly accepted the benefits of their common practice owe to each other to act in accordance with it when their performance falls due; for it is usually considered unfair if someone accepts the benefits of a practice but refuses to do his part in maintaining it. Thus one might say of the tax-dodger that he violates the duty of fair play: he accepts the benefits of government but will not do his part in releasing resources to it; and members of labor unions often say that fellow workers who refuse to join are being unfair: they refer to them as "free riders," as persons who enjoy what are the supposed benefits of unionism, higher wages, shorter hours, job security, and the like, but who refuse to share in its burdens in the form of paying dues, and so on.

The duty of fair play stands beside other prima facie duties such as fidelity and gratitude as a basic moral notion; yet it is not to be confused with them.

These duties are all clearly distinct, as would be obvious from their definitions. As with any moral duty, that of fair play implies a constraint on self-interest in particular cases; on occasion it enjoins conduct which a rational egoist strictly defined would not decide upon. So while justice does not require of anyone that he sacrifice his interests in that *general position* and procedure whereby the principles of justice are proposed and acknowledged, it may happen that in particular situations, arising in the context of engaging in a practice, the duty of fair play will often cross his interests in the sense that he will be required to forego particular advantages which the peculiarities of his circumstances might permit him to take. There is, of course, nothing surprising in this. It is simply the consequence of the firm commitment which the parties may be supposed to have made, or which they would make, in the general position, together with the fact that they have participated in and accepted the benefits of a practice which they regard as fair.

Now the acknowledgment of this constraint in particular cases, which is manifested in acting fairly or wishing to make amends, feeling ashamed, and the like, when one has evaded it, is one of the forms of conduct by which participants in a common practice exhibit their recognition of each other as persons with similar interests and capacities. In the same way that, failing a special explanation, the criterion for the recognition of suffering is helping one who suffers, acknowledging the duty of fair play is a necessary part of the criterion for recognizing another as a person with similar interests and feelings as oneself. A person who never under any circumstances showed a wish to help others in pain would show, at the same time, that he did not recognize that they were in pain; nor could he have any feelings of affection or friendship for anyone; for having these feelings implies, failing special circumstances, that he comes to their aid when they are suffering. Recognition that another is a person in pain shows itself in sympathetic action; this primitive natural response of compassion is one of those responses upon which the various forms of moral conduct are built.

Similarly, the acceptance of the duty of fair play by participants in a common practice is a reflection in each person of the recognition of the aspirations and interests of the others to be realized by their joint activity. Failing a special explanation, their acceptance of it is a necessary part of the criterion for their recognizing one another as persons with similar interests and capacities, as the conception of their relations in the general position supposes them to be. Otherwise they would show no recognition of one another as persons with similar capacities and interests, and indeed, in some cases perhaps hypothetical, they would not recognize one another as persons at all, but as complicated objects involved in a complicated activity. To recognize another as a person one must respond to him and act towards him in certain ways; and these ways are intimately connected with the various prima facie duties. Acknowledging these duties in *some* degree, and so having the elements of morality, is not a matter of choice, or of intuiting moral qualities, or a matter of the expression of feelings or attitudes (the three interpretations between which philosophical opinion frequently oscillates); it is simply the possession of one of the forms of conduct in which the recognition of others as persons is manifested.

· · · · ·

Now one consequence of this conception is that, where it applies, there is no moral value in the satisfaction of a claim incompatible with it. Such a claim violates the conditions of reciprocity and community amongst persons, and he who presses it, not being willing to acknowledge it when pressed by another, has no grounds for complaint when it is denied; whereas he against whom it is pressed can complain. As it cannot be mutually acknowledged it is a resort to coercion; granting the claim is possible only if one party can compel acceptance of what the other will not admit. But it makes no sense to concede claims the denial of which cannot be complained of in preference to claims the denial of which can be objected to. Thus in deciding on the justice of a practice it is not enough to ascertain that it answers to wants and interests in the fullest and most effective manner. For if any of these conflict with justice, they should not be counted, as their satisfaction is no reason at all for having a practice. It would be irrelevant to say, even if true, that it resulted in the greatest satisfaction of desire. In tallying up the merits of a practice one must toss out the satisfaction of interests the claims of which are incompatible with the principles of justice.

6

The discussion so far has been excessively abstract. While this is perhaps un-avoidable, I should now like to bring out some of the features of the conception of justice as fairness by comparing it with the conception of justice in classical utilitarianism as represented by Bentham and Sidgwick, and its counterpart in welfare economics. This conception assimilates justice to benevolence and the latter in turn to the most efficient design of institutions to promote the general welfare. Justice is a kind of efficiency.

Now it is said occasionally that this form of utilitarianism puts no restric-tions on what might be a just assignment of rights and duties in that there might be circumstances which, on utilitarian grounds, would justify institutions highly offensive to our ordinary sense of justice. But the classical utilitarian conception is not totally unprepared for this objection. Beginning with the notion that the general happiness can be represented by a social utility function consisting of a sum of individual utility functions with identical weights (this being the meaning of the maxim that each counts for one and no more than one), it is commonly assumed that the utility functions of individuals are similar in all essential respects. Differences between individuals are ascribed to acci-dents of education and upbringing, and they should not be taken into account. This assumption, coupled with that of diminishing marginal utility, results in a prima facie case for equality, e.g., of equality in the distribution of income during any given period of time, laying aside indirect effects on the future. But even if utilitarianism is interpreted as having such restrictions built into the

utility function, and even if it is supposed that these restrictions have in practice much the same result as the application of the principles of justice (and appear, perhaps, to be ways of expressing these principles in the language of
mathematics and psychology), the fundamental idea is very different from the
conception of justice as fairness. For one thing, that the principles of justice
should be accepted is interpreted as the contingent result of a higher order
administrative decision. The form of this decision is regarded as being similar
to that of an entrepreneur deciding how much to produce of this or that com-
modity in view of its marginal revenue, or to that of someone distributing goods
to needy persons according to the relative urgency of their wants. The choice
between practices is thought of as being made on the basis of the allocation of
benefits and burdens to individuals (these being measured by the present
capitalized value of their utility over the full period of the practice's existence),
which results from the distribution of rights and duties established by a practice.

Moreover, the individuals receiving these benefits are not conceived as
being related in any way: they represent so many different directions in which
limited resources may be allocated. The value of assigning resources to one
direction rather than another depends solely on the preferences and interests
of individuals as individuals. The satisfaction of desire has its value irrespective
of the moral relations between persons, say as members of a joint undertaking,
and of the claims which, in the name of these interests, they are prepared to
make on one another; and it is this value which is to be taken into account by
the (ideal) legislator who is conceived as adjusting the rules of the system from
the center so as to maximize the value of the social utility function.

It is thought that the principles of justice will not be violated by a legal
system so conceived provided these executive decisions are correctly made. In
this fact the principles of justice are said to have their derivation and explanation; they simply express the most important general features of social institutions in which the administrative problem is solved in the best way. These
principles have, indeed, a special urgency because, given the facts of human
nature, so much depends on them; and this explains the peculiar quality of
the moral feelings associated with justice. This assimilation of justice to a higher
order executive decision, certainly a striking conception, is central to classical
utilitarianism; and it also brings out its profound individualism, in one sense
of this ambiguous word. It regards persons as so many *separate* directions in
which benefits and burdens may be assigned; and the value of the satisfaction
or dissatisfaction of desire is not thought to depend in any way on the moral
relations in which individuals stand, or on the kinds of claims which they are
willing, in the pursuit of their interests, to press on each other.

7

Many social decisions are, of course, of an administrative nature. Certainly this
is so when it is a matter of social utility in what one may call its ordinary sense:
that is, when it is a question of the efficient design of social institutions for the

use of common means to achieve common ends. In this case either the benefits and burdens may be assumed to be impartially distributed, or the question of distribution is misplaced, as in the instance of maintaining public order and security or national defense. But as an interpretation of the basis of the principles of justice, classical utilitarianism is mistaken. It *permits* one to argue, for example, that slavery is unjust on the grounds that the advantages to the slaveholder as slaveholder do not counterbalance the disadvantages to the slave and to society at large burdened by a comparatively inefficient system of labor. Now the conception of justice as fairness, when applied to the practice of slavery with its offices of slaveholder and slave, would not allow one to consider the advantages of the slaveholder in the first place. As that office is not in accordance with principles which could be mutually acknowledged, the gains accruing to the slaveholder, assuming them to exist, cannot be counted as in *any* way mitigating the injustice of the practice. The question whether these gains outweigh the disadvantages to the slave and to society cannot arise, since in considering the justice of slavery these gains have no weight at all which requires that they be overridden. Where the conception of justice as fairness applies, slavery is *always* unjust.

I am not, of course, suggesting the absurdity that the classical utilitarians approved of slavery. I am only rejecting a type of argument which their view allows them to use in support of their disapproval of it. The conception of justice as derivative from efficiency implies that judging the justice of a practice is always, in principle at least, a matter of weighing up advantages and disadvantages, each having an intrinsic value or disvalue as the satisfaction of interests, irrespective of whether or not these interests necessarily involve acquiescence in principles which could not be mutually acknowledged. Utilitarianism cannot account for the fact that slavery is always unjust, nor for the fact that it would be recognized as irrelevant in defeating the accusation of injustice for one person to say to another, engaged with him in a common practice and debating its merits, that nevertheless it allowed of the greatest satisfaction of desire. The charge of injustice cannot be rebutted in this way. If justice were derivative from a higher order executive efficiency, this would not be so.

•   •   •   •   •

DAVID P. GAUTHIER
Morality and Advantage

I

Hume asks, rhetorically, "what theory of morals can ever serve any useful purpose, unless it can show, by a particular detail, that all the duties which it recommends, are also the true interest of each individual?" But there are many to whom this question does not seem rhetorical. Why, they ask, do we speak the language of morality, impressing upon our fellows their duties and obligations, urging them with appeals to what is right and good, if we could speak to the same effect in the language of prudence, appealing to considerations of interest and advantage? When the poet, Ogden Nash, is moved by the muse to cry out:

> O Duty,
> Why hast thou not the visage of a sweetie or a cutie?

we do not anticipate the reply:

> O Poet,
> I really am a cutie and I think you ought to know it.

The belief that duty cannot be reduced to interest, or that morality may require the agent to subordinate all considerations of advantage, is one which has withstood the assaults of contrary-minded philosophers from Plato to the present. Indeed, were it not for the conviction that only interest and advantage can motivate human actions, it would be difficult to understand philosophers contending so vigorously for the identity, or at least compatibility, of morality with prudence.

Yet if morality is not true prudence it would be wrong to suppose that those philosophers who have sought some connection between morality and advantage have been merely misguided. For it is a truism that we should all expect to be worse off if men were to substitute prudence, even of the most enlightened kind, for morality in all of their deliberations. And this truism demands not only some connection between morality and advantage, but a seemingly paradoxical connection. For if we should all expect to suffer, were men to be prudent instead of moral, then morality must contribute to advantage in a unique way, a way in which prudence—following reasons of advantage—cannot.

From David P. Gauthier, "Morality and Advantage," *Philosophical Review*, LXXVI, No. 4 (1967), 460–475. Reprinted by permission of the author and the editors of *The Philosophical Review*.

Thomas Hobbes is perhaps the first philosopher who tried to develop this seemingly paradoxical connection between morality and advantage. But since he could not admit that a man might ever reasonably subordinate considerations of advantage to the dictates of obligation, he was led to deny the possibility of real conflict between morality and prudence. So his argument fails to clarify the distinction between the view that claims of obligation reduce to considerations of interest and the view that claims of obligation promote advantage in a way in which considerations of interest cannot.

More recently, Kurt Baier has argued that "being moral is following rules designed to overrule self-interest whenever it is in the interest of everyone alike that everyone should set aside his interest." Since prudence is following rules of (enlightened) self-interest, Baier is arguing that morality is designed to overrule prudence when it is to everyone's advantage that it do so—or, in other words, that morality contributes to advantage in a way in which prudence cannot.

Baier does not actually demonstrate that morality contributes to advantage in this unique and seemingly paradoxical way. Indeed, he does not ask how it is possible that morality should do this. It is this possibility which I propose to demonstrate.

II

Let us examine the following proposition, which will be referred to as "the thesis": *Morality is a system of principles such that it is advantageous for everyone if everyone accepts and acts on it, yet acting on the system of principles requires that some persons perform disadvantageous acts.*

What I wish to show is that this thesis *could be true*, that morality could possess those characteristics attributed to it by the thesis. I shall not try to show that the thesis is true—indeed, I shall argue in Section V that it presents at best an inadequate conception of morality. But it is plausible to suppose that a modified form of the thesis states a necessary, although not a sufficient, condition for a moral system.

Two phrases in the thesis require elucidation. The first is "advantageous for everyone." I use this phrase to mean that *each* person will do better if the system is accepted and acted on than if *either* no system is accepted and acted on *or* a system is accepted and acted on which is similar, save that it never requires any person to perform disadvantageous acts.

Clearly, then, the claim that it is advantageous for everyone to accept and act on the system is a very strong one; it may be so strong that no system of principles which might be generally adopted could meet it. But I shall consider in Section V one among the possible ways of weakening the claim.

The second phrase requiring elucidation is "disadvantageous acts." I use this phrase to refer to acts which, in the context of their performance, would be less advantageous to the performer than some other act open to him in the same context. The phrase does not refer to acts which merely impose on the performer some short-term disadvantage that is recouped or outweighed in the long run.

Rather it refers to acts which impose a disadvantage that is never recouped. It follows that the performer may say to himself, when confronted with the requirement to perform such an act, that it would be better *for him* not to perform it.

It is essential to note that the thesis, as elucidated, does not maintain that morality is advantageous for everyone in the sense that each person will do *best* if the system of principles is accepted and acted on. Each person will do better than if no system is adopted, or than if the one particular alternative mentioned above is adopted, but not than if any alternative is adopted.

Indeed, for each person required by the system to perform some disadvantageous act, it is easy to specify a better alternative—namely, the system modified so that it does not require *him* to perform any act disadvantageous to himself. Of course, there is no reason to expect such an alternative to be better than the moral system for everyone, or in fact for anyone other than the person granted the special exemption.

A second point to note is that each person must gain more from the disadvantageous acts performed by others than he loses from the disadvantageous acts performed by himself. If this were not the case, then some person would do better if a system were adopted exactly like the moral system save that it never requires *any* person to perform disadvantageous acts. This is ruled out by the force of "advantageous for everyone."

This point may be clarified by an example. Suppose that the system contains exactly one principle. Everyone is always to tell the truth. It follows from the thesis that each person gains more from those occasions on which others tell the truth, even though it is disadvantageous to them to do so, than he loses from those occasions on which he tells the truth even though it is disadvantageous to him to do so.

Now this is not to say that each person gains by telling others the truth in order to ensure that in return they tell him the truth. Such gains would merely be the result of accepting certain short-term disadvantages (those associated with truth-telling) in order to reap long-term benefits (those associated with being told the truth). Rather, what is required by the thesis is that those disadvantages which a person incurs in telling the truth, when he can expect neither short-term nor long-term benefits to accrue to him from truth-telling, are outweighed by those advantages he receives when others tell him the truth when they can expect no benefits to accrue to them from truth-telling.

The principle enjoins truth-telling in those cases in which whether one tells the truth or not will have no effect on whether others tell the truth. Such cases include those in which others have no way of knowing whether or not they are being told the truth. The thesis requires that the disadvantages one incurs in telling the truth in these cases are less than the advantages one receives in being told the truth by others in parallel cases; and the thesis requires that this holds for everyone.

Thus we see that although the disadvantages imposed by the system on any person are less than the advantages secured him through the imposition of disadvantages on others, yet the disadvantages are real in that incurring them is *unrelated* to receiving the advantages. The argument of long-term prudence, that I ought to incur some immediate disadvantage *so that* I shall receive compensating advantages later on, is entirely inapplicable here.

III

It will be useful to examine in some detail an example of a system which possesses those characteristics ascribed by the thesis to morality. This example, abstracted from the field of international relations, will enable us more clearly to distinguish, first, conduct based on immediate interest; second, conduct which is truly prudent; and third, conduct which promotes mutual advantage but is not prudent.

A and *B* are two nations with substantially opposed interests, who find themselves engaged in an arms race against each other. Both possess the latest in weaponry, so that each recognizes that the actual outbreak of full scale war between them would be mutually disastrous. This recognition leads *A* and *B* to agree that each would be better off if they were mutually disarming instead of mutually arming. For mutual disarmament would preserve the balance of power between them while reducing the risk of war.

Hence *A* and *B* enter into a disarmament pact. The pact is advantageous for both if both accept and act on it, although clearly it is not advantageous for either to act on it if the other does not.

Let *A* be considering whether or not to adhere to the pact in some particular situation, whether or not actually to perform some act of disarmament. *A* will quite likely consider the act to have disadvantageous consequences. *A* expects to benefit, not by its own acts of disarmament, but by *B*'s acts. Hence if *A* were to reason simply in terms of immediate interest, *A* might well decide to violate the pact.

But *A*'s decision need be neither prudent nor reasonable. For suppose first that *B* is able to determine whether or not *A* adheres to the pact. If *A* violates, then *B* will detect the violation and will then consider what to do in the light of *A*'s behavior. It is not to *B*'s advantage to disarm alone; *B* expects to gain, not by its own acts of disarmament, but by *A*'s acts. Hence *A*'s violation, if known to *B*, leads naturally to *B*'s counterviolation. If this continues, the effect of the pact is entirely undone, and *A* and *B* return to their mutually disadvantageous arms race. *A*, foreseeing this when considering whether or not to adhere to the pact in the given situation, must therefore conclude that the truly prudent course of action is to adhere.

Now suppose that *B* is unable to determine whether or not *A* adheres to the pact in the particular situation under consideration. If *A* judges adherence to be in itself disadvantageous, then it will decide, both on the basis of immediate interest and on the basis of prudence, to violate the pact. Since *A*'s decision is unknown to *B*, it cannot affect whether or not *B* adheres to the pact, and so the advantage gained by *A*'s violation is not outweighed by any consequent loss.

Therefore if *A* and *B* are prudent they will adhere to their disarmament pact whenever violation would be detectable by the other, and violate the pact whenever violation would not be detectable by the other. In other words, they will adhere openly and violate secretly. The disarmament pact between A and B thus possesses two of the characteristics ascribed by the thesis to morality. First, accepting the pact and acting on it is more advantageous for each than making no pact at all. Second, in so far as the pact stipulates that each must disarm even when disarming is undetectable by the other, it requires each to perform disadvantageous acts—acts which run counter to considerations of prudence.

One further condition must be met if the disarmament pact is to possess those characteristics ascribed by the thesis to a system of morality. It must be the case that the requirement that each party perform disadvantageous acts be essential to the advantage conferred by the pact; or, to put the matter in the way in which we expressed it earlier, both A and B must do better to adhere to this pact than to a pact which is similar save that it requires no disadvantageous acts. In terms of the example, A and B must do better to adhere to the pact than to a pact which stipulates that each must disarm only when disarming is detectable by the other.

We may plausibly suppose this condition to be met. Although A will gain by secretly retaining arms itself, it will lose by B's similar acts, and its losses may well outweigh its gains. B may equally lose more by A's secret violations than it gains by its own. So, despite the fact that prudence requires each to violate secretly, each may well do better if both adhere secretly than if both violate secretly. Supposing this to be the case, the disarmament pact is formally analogous to a moral system, as characterized by the thesis. That is, acceptance of and adherence to the pact by A and B is more advantageous for each, either than making no pact at all or than acceptance of and adherence to a pact requiring only open disarmament, and the pact requires each to perform acts of secret disarmament which are disadvantageous.

•   •   •   •   •

IV

We may now return to the connection of morality with advantage. Morality, if it is a system of principles of the type characterized in the thesis, requires that some persons perform acts genuinely disadvantageous to themselves, as a means to greater mutual advantage. Our example shows sufficiently that such a system is possible, and indicates more precisely its character. In particular, by an argument strictly parallel to that which we have pursued, we may show that men who are merely prudent will not perform the required disadvantageous acts. But in so violating the principles of morality, they will disadvantage themselves. Each will lose more by the violations of others than he will gain by his own violations.

Now this conclusion would be unsurprising if it were only that no man can gain if he alone is moral rather than prudent. Obviously such a man loses, for he adheres to moral principles to his own disadvantage, while others violate them also to his disadvantage. The benefit of the moral system is not one which any individual can secure for himself, since each man gains from the sacrifices of others.

What is surprising in our conclusion is that no man can ever gain if he is moral. Not only does he not gain by being moral if others are prudent, but he also does not gain by being moral if others are moral. For although he now receives the advantage of others' adherence to moral principles, he reaps the disadvantage of his own adherence. As long as his own adherence to morality is independent of what others do (and this is required to distinguish morality from prudence), he must do better to be prudent.

If all men are moral, all will do better than if all are prudent. But any one man will always do better if he is prudent than if he is moral. There is no real paradox in supposing that morality is advantageous, even though it requires the performance of disadvantageous acts.

On the supposition that morality has the characteristics ascribed to it by the thesis, is it possible to answer the question "Why should we be moral?" where "we" is taken distributively, so that the question is a compendious way of asking, for each person, "Why should I be moral?" More simply, is it possible to answer the question "Why should I be moral?"

I take it that this question, if asked seriously, demands a reason for being moral other than moral reasons themselves. It demands that moral reasons be shown to be reasons for acting by a noncircular argument. Those who would answer it, like Baier, endeavor to do so by the introduction of considerations of advantage.

Two such considerations have emerged from our discussion. The first is that if all are moral, all will do better than if all are prudent. This will serve to answer the question "Why should we be moral?" if this question is interpreted rather as "Why should we all be moral—rather than all being something else?" If we must all be the same, then each person has a reason—a prudential reason— to prefer that we all be moral.

But, so interpreted, "Why should we be moral?" is not a compendious way of asking, for each person, "Why should I be moral?" Of course, if everyone is to be whatever I am, then I should be moral. But a general answer to the question "Why should I be moral?" cannot presuppose this.

The second consideration is that any individual always does better to be prudent rather than moral, provided his choice does not determine other choices. But in so far as this answers the question "Why should I be moral?" it leads to the conclusion "I should not be moral." One feels that this is not the answer which is wanted.

We may put the matter otherwise. The individual who needs a reason for being moral which is not itself a moral reason cannot have it. There is nothing surprising about this; it would be much more surprising if such reasons could be found. For it is more than apparently paradoxical to suppose that considerations of advantage could ever of themselves justify accepting a real disadvantage.

V

I suggested in Section II that the thesis, in modified form, might provide a necessary, although not a sufficient, condition for a moral system. I want now to consider how one might characterize the man who would qualify as moral according to the thesis—I shall call him the "moral" man—and then ask what would be lacking from this characterization, in terms of some of our commonplace moral views.

The rationally prudent man is incapable of moral behavior, in even the limited sense defined by the thesis. What difference must there be between the prudent man and the "moral" man? Most simply, the "moral" man is the prudent but trustworthy man. I treat trustworthiness as the capacity which enables its possessor to adhere, and to judge that he ought to adhere, to a commitment which he has made, without regard to considerations of advantage.

The prudent but trustworthy man does not possess this capacity completely. He is capable of trustworthy behavior only in so far as he regards his *commitment* as advantageous. Thus he differs from the prudent man just in the relevant respect; he accepts arguments of the form "If it is advantageous for me to agree[1] to do x, and I do agree to do x, then I ought to do x, whether or not it then proves advantageous for me to do x."

Suppose that A and B, the parties to the disarmament pact, are prudent but trustworthy. A, considering whether or not secretly to violate the agreement, reasons that its advantage in making and keeping the agreement, provided B does so as well, is greater than its advantage in not making it. If it can assume that B reasons in the same way, then it is in a position to conclude that it ought not to violate the pact. Although violation would be advantageous, consideration of this advantage is ruled out by A's trustworthiness, given the advantage in agreeing to the pact.

The prudent but trustworthy man meets the requirements implicitly imposed by the thesis for the "moral" man. But how far does this "moral" man display two characteristics commonly associated with morality—first, a willingness to make sacrifices, and second, a concern with fairness?

Whenever a man ignores his own advantage for reasons other than those of greater advantage, he may be said to make some sacrifice. The "moral" man, in being trustworthy, is thus required to make certain sacrifices. But these are extremely limited. And—not surprisingly, given the general direction of our

---

[1] The word "agree" requires elucidation. It is essential not to confuse an advantage in agreeing to do x with an advantage in saying that one will do x. If it is advantageous for me to agree to do x, then there is some set of actions open to me which includes both saying that I will do x and doing x, and which is more advantageous to me than any set of actions open to me which does not include saying that I will do x. On the other hand, if it is advantageous for me to say that I will do x, then there is some set of actions open to me which includes saying that I will do x, and which is more advantageous to me than any set which does not include saying that I will do x. But this set need not include doing x.

argument—it is quite possible that they limit the advantages which the "moral" man can secure.

Once more let us turn to our example. A and B have entered into a disarmament agreement and, being prudent but trustworthy, are faithfully carrying it out. The government of A is now informed by its scientists, however, that they have developed an effective missile defense, which will render A invulnerable to attack by any of the weapons actually or potentially at B's disposal, barring unforeseen technological developments. Futhermore, this defense can be installed secretly. The government is now called upon to decide whether to violate its agreement with B, install the new defense, and, with the arms it has retained through its violation, establish its dominance over B.

A is in a type of situation quite different from that previously considered. For it is not just that A will do better by secretly violating its agreement. A reasons not only that it will do better to violate no matter what B does, but that it will do better if both violate than if both continue to adhere to the pact. A is now in a position to gain from abandoning the agreement; it no longer finds mutual adherence advantageous. . . .

. . . Now had this situation obtained at the outset, no agreement would have been made, for A would have had no reason to enter into a disarmament pact. And of course had A expected this situation to come about, no agreement —or only a temporary agreement—would have been made; A would no doubt have risked the short-term dangers of the continuing arms race in the hope of securing the long-run benefit of predominance over B once its missile defense was completed. On the contrary, A expected to benefit from the agreement, but now finds that, because of its unexpected development of a missile defense, the agreement is not in fact advantageous to it.

The prudent but trustworthy man is willing to carry out his agreements, and judges that he ought to carry them out, in so far as he considers them advantageous. A is prudent but trustworthy. But is A willing to carry out its agreement to disarm, now that it no longer considers the agreement advantageous?

If A adheres to its agreement in this situation, it makes a sacrifice greater than any advantage it receives from the similar sacrifices of others. It makes a sacrifice greater in kind than any which can be required by a mutually advantageous agreement. It must, then, possess a capacity for trustworthy behavior greater than that ascribed to the merely prudent but trustworthy man (or nation). This capacity need not be unlimited; it need not extend to a willingness to adhere to any commitment no matter what sacrifice is involved. But it must involve a willingness to adhere to a commitment made in the expectation of advantage, should that expectation be disappointed.

I shall call the man (or nation) who is willing to adhere, and judges that he ought to adhere, to his prudentially undertaken agreements even if they prove disadvantageous to him, the trustworthy man. It is likely that there are advantages available to trustworthy men which are not available to merely prudent but trustworthy men. For there may be situations in which men can make agreements which each expects to be advantageous to him, provided he can count on the others' adhering to it whether or not their expectation of advantage is realized. But each can count on this only if all have the capacity to adhere to commitments regardless of whether the commitment actually proves advantageous. Hence, only trustworthy men who know each other to be such will be able rationally to enter into, and so to benefit from, such agreements.

Baier's view of morality departs from that stated in the thesis in that it requires trustworthy, and not merely prudent but trustworthy, men. Baier admits that "a person might do better for himself by following enlightened self-interest rather than morality." This admission seems to require that morality be a system of principles which each person may expect, initially, to be advantageous to him, if adopted and adhered to by everyone, but not a system which actually is advantageous to everyone.

Our commonplace moral views do, I think, support the view that the moral man must be trustworthy. Hence, we have established one modification required in the thesis, if it is to provide a more adequate set of conditions for a moral system.

But there is a much more basic respect in which the "moral" man falls short of our expectations. He is willing to temper his single-minded pursuit of advantage only by accepting the obligation to adhere to prudentially undertaken commitments. He has no real concern for the advantage of others, which would lead him to modify his pursuit of advantage when it conflicted with the similar pursuits of others. Unless he expects to gain, he is unwilling to accept restrictions on the pursuit of advantage which are intended to equalize the opportunities open to all. In other words, he has no concern with fairness.

We tend to think of the moral man as one who does not seek his own well-being by means which would deny equal well-being to his fellows. This marks him off clearly from the "moral" man, who differs from the prudent man only in that he can overcome the apparent paradox of prudence and obtain those advantages which are available only to those who can display real restraint in their pursuit of advantage.

Thus a system of principles might meet the conditions laid down in the thesis without taking any account of considerations of fairness. Such a system would contain principles for ensuring increased advantage (or expectation of advantage) to everyone, but no further principle need be present to determine the distribution of this increase.

It is possible that there are systems of principles which, if adopted and adhered to, provide advantages which strictly prudent men, however rational, cannot attain. These advantages are a function of the sacrifices which the principles impose on their adherents.

Morality may be such a system. If it is, this would explain our expectation that we should all be worse off were we to substitute prudence for morality in our deliberations. But to characterize morality as a system of principles advantageous to all is not to answer the question "Why should I be moral?" nor is it to provide for those considerations of fairness which are equally essential to our moral understanding.

KAI NIELSEN

Why Should I Be Moral?

I

Why . . . be moral? We need initially to note that this question actually ought to be broken down into two questions, namely, 1) 'Why should people be moral?' or 'Why should there be a morality at all?' and 2) 'Why should I be moral?' As will become evident, these questions ought not in the name of clarity, to be confused. But they have been run together; in asking for a justification for the institution of morality both questions are relevant and easily confused. 'Why be Moral?' nicely straddles these questions. In this section I shall first examine some traditional, and I believe unhelpful, answers to the above general questions. There the general question is not broken down as it should be and in examining these views I shall not break it down either. After noting the difficulties connected with these approaches, I shall state what I believe to be a satisfactory answer to the question, 'Why should there be a morality at all?' and indicate why it leaves untouched the harder question, 'Why should I be moral?'

There is a prior consideration that we must first dispose of. In considering both of these questions we must be careful to distinguish the *causes* of a man's being moral from the *reasons* he gives for being moral. If one is a little careful about the implications of the word 'likes', Bradley seems perfectly right in saying: 'A man is moral because he likes being moral; and he likes it, partly because he has been brought up to the habit of liking it, and partly because he finds it gives him what he wants, while its opposite does not do so'. In other words people are moral primarily because they have been conditioned to be moral. The human animal is a social animal and (as Butler and Hume observed) people normally tend to consider the welfare of others as well as their own welfare. People indeed act selfishly but they also take out life insurance, feel anxiety over the troubles of others, and even have moments of mild discomfort at the thought that life on this planet may some day be impossible. People react in this way because they have been taught or conditioned to so react. But, the 'because' here is explanatory and *not* justificatory. It explains in a very general way what *makes* or *causes* people to be moral. But the question I am concerned with here is a quite different one. In asking 'Why should people be moral?', I am asking the question, 'What good reasons do people have for

From K. Nielsen, "Why Should I Be Moral?" *Methodos*, XV, No. 59–60 (1963), 275–306. Reprinted by permission of the author and Marsilio Editori, Publishers of *Methodos* (Padova, Italy).

being moral?' In asking about the justification for acting morally, I am only incidentally concerned with an explanation of the causes of moral behavior.

What good reasons are there for being moral? And if there are good reasons for being moral are they sufficient or decisive reasons?

There is a short, snappy answer to my question. The plain man might well say: 'People ought to be moral because it is wicked, evil, morally reprehensible not to be moral. We have the very best reasons for being moral, namely that it is immoral not to be moral'. The plain man (or at the very least the plain Western Man and not *just* the ordinary Oxford Don) would surely agree with Bradley "that consciousness, when unwarped by selfishness and not blinded by sophistry is convinced that to ask for the Why? is simple immorality. . .". The correct answer to the question: 'Why Be Moral?' is simply that this is what we ought to do.

This short answer will not do, for the plain man has failed to understand the question. A clear-headed individual could not be asking for *moral* justification for being moral. This would be absurd. Rather he is asking the practical question: why should people be bound by the conventions of morality at all? He would not dispute Baier's contention that "it is generally believed that when reasons of self-interest conflict with moral reasons, then moral reasons override those of self-interest". It is perfectly true that the plain man regards moral reasons as superior to all others and it is, of course, in accordance with reason to follow superior or overriding reasons, but if a clear-headed man asks 'Why should we be moral?' he is challenging the very grading criteria those ordinary convictions rest on. He would acknowledge that it is indeed morally reprehensible or wicked not to act morally. But he would ask: 'So what?' And he might even go on to query: 'What is the good of all this morality anyway? Are not those Marxists and Freudians right who claim that the whole enterprise of morality is nothing but an ideological device to hoodwink people into *not* seeking what they really want? Why should people continue to fall for this conjuring trick? To call someone "wicked" or "evil" is to severely grade them down, but why should people accept any *moral* grading criteria at all?'

There are several traditional replies to this. But all of them are unsatisfactory.

One traditional approach advocated by Plato and Bishop Butler, among others, claims that people should be moral because they will not be happy otherwise. Being moral is at least a necessary condition for being happy.

For Butler the argument takes the following form. Human beings are so constituted that they will, generally speaking, act morally. When they don't act morally they will clearly recognize they were mistaken in not doing so. The human animal has a conscience and this conscience not only causes people to act in a certain way, but is in fact a *norm* of action. Conscience guides as well as goads; the deliverances of conscience are both action-evoking and a source of moral knowledge. Conscience tells the moral agent what to do even in specific situations. It clearly and unequivocally tells him to always act morally and he is so constituted that if he ignores the dictates of his conscience he will not be happy. In other words, Butler agrees with Plato in claiming that Thrasymachus and other amoralists are fundamentally mistaken about the true interests of a human being.

That it is in the human animal's best interest to live virtuously is no more established by Butler than it is by Plato. Plato is reduced to analogy, myth and mystagogy and, as Duncan-Jones points out, Butler is finally pushed to concede that "full acceptance of the conclusion that human nature is satisfiable and only satisfiable by virtue depends on revelation". In the face of what clearly seem to be genuine exceptions to the claim that it is in the individual's self-interest always to act morally, Butler is driven to remark: "All shall be set right at the final distribution of things".

· · · · ·

There is a more defensible answer to the question: 'Why should people be moral?' It was first urged (in the Western World, at least) by Epicurus; later it was developed and given its classical forceful statement by Hobbes. Bertrand Russell elaborates it in his own way in his *Human Society in Ethics and Politics* (1955) and Kurt Baier has clearly elucidated and defended Hobbes' argument in his *The Moral Point of View* (1958). This Hobbesian argument, which within its proper scope seems to me conclusive, can readily be used to meet the objections of those "tough-minded" Marxists and Freudians who do not want the usual fare of "sweetness and light".

Hobbes points out that as a matter of fact the restless, malcontent, foraging human animal wants "The commodious life"; that is, he wants above all peace, security, freedom from fear. He wants to satisfy his desires to the maximum extent, but one of the very strongest and most persistent of these desires is the desire to be free from the "tooth and claw" of a life in which each man exclusively seeks his own interest and totally neglects to consider the interests of others. In such a situation life would indeed be "nasty, brutish and short". We could not sleep at night without fear of violent death; we could not leave what we possessed without well-warranted anxiety over its being stolen or destroyed. Impulses and inclinations would be held in check only when they would lead to behavior detrimental to the individual's own interest. Where people's interests conflict, each man would (without the institution of morality) resort to subterfuge or violence to gain his own ends. A pervasive Dobuan-like suspicion would be normal and natural . . . even rational in such a situation. Every individual would be struggling for the good things of life and no rule except that of his own self-interest would govern the struggle. The universal reign of the rule of exclusive self-interest would lead to the harsh world that Hobbes called "the state of nature". And, as Baier puts it, "At the same time, it will be clear to everyone that universal obedience to certain rules overriding self-interest would produce a state of affairs which serves everyone's interest much better than his unaided pursuit of it in a state where everyone does the same". Baier goes on to point out that "the very *raison d'être* of a morality is to yield reasons which override the reasons of self-interest in those cases when everyone's following self-interest would be harmful to everyone".

When we ask: why should we have a morality—any morality, even a completely conventional morality—we answer that if everyone acts morally, or generally acts morally, people will be able to attain more of what they want. It is obvious that in a moral community more good will be realized than in a non-moral collection of people. Yet in the interest of realizing a commodious life for all, voluntary self-sacrifice is sometimes necessary; but the best possible life for everyone is attainable only if people act morally; the greatest possible good is realizable only when everyone puts aside his own self-interest when it conflicts with the common good.

•   •   •   •   •

II

Yet an answer to the question 'Why should people be moral?' does not meet one basic question that the thorough-going sceptic may feel about the claims of morality. The "existing individual" may want to know why *he,* as an individual, ought to accept the standards of morality when it is not in *his* personal interest to do so. He may have no doubt at all about the general utility of the moral enterprise. But *his* not recognizing the claims of morality will not greatly diminish the total good. Reflecting on this, he asks himself: 'Why should *I* be moral when I will not be caught or punished for not acting morally?'

Recall how Glaucon and Adeimantus* readily agreed that Socrates has established that morality is an indispensable social practice. But their perplexity over morals is not at an end. They want Socrates to go on and prove that the individual ought to be moral even when he is perfectly safe in not acting morally. Someone might readily agree that the Hobbesian arguments establish that the greatest total good will be realized if people act morally, but he still wants to know 'Why should I be moral in those cases where acting morally will not be in *my* rational self-interest?' He might say to himself—though certainly if he were wise he would not proclaim it—'There is no reason why I should act morally'.

Such an individual egoist cannot be refuted by indicating that his position cannot be a moral position. He may grant the overall social good of morality and he may be fully aware that 'Why should I do my duty?' cannot be a moral question—there is indeed no room at all for that question as a moral question, but an individual egoist is not trying to operate within the bounds of morality. He is trying to decide whether or not he should *become* a moral agent or he may —in a more theoretical frame of mind—wonder if any *reason* can be given for his remaining a moral agent. Prichard is quite right in arguing that the *moral*

* [In telling Socrates the Myth of Gyges. See page 483.—Ed. note.]

agent has no choice here. To assert 'I'll only be moral when being moral is in my rational interest' is to rule out, in a quite *a priori* fashion, the very possibility of one's being moral as long as one has such an intention. To be a moral agent entails that one gives up seriously entertaining whether one should deliberately adopt a policy of individual egoism. 'X is moral' entails 'X will try to do his duty even when so acting is not in his personal interest'. Thus we must be very *careful* how we take the individual egoist's question: his question is, 'Should I become moral and give up my individual egoism or shall I remain such an egoist?'. If he decides to remain an individual egoist he will have made the decision that *he* ought to behave like a man of good morals when and only when such behavior is in his own personal interest. Now what grounds (if any) have we for saying that a man who makes such a decision is mistaken or irrational? What (if any) intellectual mistake has he made? Remember, he doesn't challenge Prichard's remarks about the logical relations of duty to interest or the Hobbesian argument that morality is an essential social device if we are to have a commodius life. But he still wants to know why *he* should be moral rather than non-moral.

The individual egoist may well believe that those who insist on being moral even when it is not in their self-interest are really benighted fools duped by the claims of society. A "really clever man" will take as his own personal norm of action the furtherance of his own good. Everything else must give pride of place to this. He will only endeavor to make it seem perfectly obvious that he is a staunch pillar of the community so as to avoid reprisals from his society.

Can such an individual egoist be shown to be wrong or to be asking a senseless question? What arguments can be given for an affirmative answer to the question: 'Should I be moral?'

•　　•　　•　　•

Medlin* . . . comments: "If the good fellow wants to know how he should justify conventional morality to the individual egoist, the answer is that he *shouldn't* and *can't*. Buy your car elsewhere, blackguard him whenever you meet, and let it go at that". A philosopher, Medlin goes on to comment, is "not a rat-catcher" and it is not his "job to dig vermin out of such burrows as individual egoism". Inasmuch as Medlin is pointing out that the individual egoist's position isn't and can't be a moral alternative to conventional morality, he is perfectly right in his strictures; but as an answer to the question as I have posed it, Medlin's reply is simply irrelevant.

Must we say at this juncture that practical reasoning has come to an end and that we must simply *decide* for ourselves how to act? Is it just that, depending on what attitudes I actually happen to have, I strive to be one sort of a person rather than another without any sufficient rational guides to tell me what I am to do? Does it come to just that—finally? Subjectivists say (at such a juncture) that there are no such guides. And this time there seems to be a strong

* [See the reading by Brian Medlin in Chapter Three.—Ed. note.]

strand of common sense or hardheaded street wisdom to back up the subjectivists' position.

I do not believe that we are that bad off. There are weighty considerations of a mundane sort in favor of the individual's taking the moral point of view. But I think the subjectivists are right in claiming that it is a mistake to argue that a man is simply irrational if he does not at all times act morally. It is indeed true that if a man deliberately refuses to do what he acknowledges as morally required of him, we do say he is irrational or better unreasonable. But here 'irrational' and 'unreasonable' have a distinctively *moral* use. There are other quite standard employments of the word in which we would not say that such a man is irrational. In all contexts the word "irrational" has the evaluative force of strongly condemning something or other. In different contexts the criteria for what is to be called 'irrational' differ. In Toulmin's terms the criteria are field-dependent and the force of the word is field-independent. In saying a man acts irrationally in not assenting to any moral considerations whatsoever we need not be claiming that he makes any mistakes in observation or deduction. Rather we are condemning him for not accepting the moral point of view. But he is asking why he, as an individual in an ongoing community, should always act as a moral agent. He is not asking for *motivation* but for a *reason* for being a morally good man. He wants to know what intellectual mistake the man who acts non-morally must make. To be told such a man is immoral and in *that sense* is unreasonable or irrational is not to the point.

The subjectivist I am interested in contends that in the nature of the case there can be no reasons here for being moral rather than non-moral. One must just *decide* to act one way or another without reasons. There is much to be said for the subjectivist's claim here but even here I think there are rational considerations in favor of an individual's opting for morality.

III

Before I state and examine those considerations I would like to show how two recent tantalizingly straight-forward answers will not do. Baier has offered one and Hospers the other.

Baier says that when we ask 'Why should I be moral?' we are asking 'Which is the course of action supported by the best reasons?' Since we can show along Hobbesian lines that men generally have better reasons for being moral than for being non-moral the individual has "been given a reason for being moral, for following moral reasons rather than any other. . .". The reason is simply that "they are better reasons than any other". *But in the above type situation,* when I am asking, 'Why should I be moral?', I am not concerned with which course of action is supported by the best reasons *sans phrase* or with what is the best thing to do for all concerned. I am only concerned with what is a good reason *for me.* I want to know what is the best thing *for me* to do; that is, I want to know what will make for *my* greatest good.

Baier might point out that an individual has the best reasons for acting morally because by each man's acting morally the greatest possible good will be realized. Yet, if the reference is to men severally and not to them as a group, it might well be the case that an individual's acting immorally might in effect further the total good, for his bad example might spur others on to greater acts of moral virtue. But be that as it may, the individual egoist could still legitimately reply to Baier: 'All of what you say is irrelevant unless realization of the greatest total good serves *my* best interests. When and only when the reasons for all involved are also the best reasons for me am I personally justified in adopting the moral point of view'.

We can, of course, criticize a so-called ethical egoist for translating the question 'What is the best thing to do' into the question 'What is the best thing *for me* to do'. In morality we are concerned with what is right, what is good and what is supported by the best reasons, *period*; but recall that the *individual* egoist is challenging the sufficiency of moral reasons which we, as social beings, normally grant to the moral enterprise. (We need to reflect on the sense of 'sufficiency' here. The egoist is not challenging the point of having moral codes. He is challenging the sufficiency of the moral life as a device to enhance *his* happiness. But is this "a goal of morality"? It is not.) He is asking for reasons for *his* acting morally and unfortunately Baier's short answer does not meet the question Baier sets out to answer, though as I have already indicated it does answer the question, 'Why should people be moral?'

Hospers has a different argument which, while wrong, carries a crucial insight that takes us to the very heart of our argument. Like Baier, Hospers does not keep apart the question 'Why should I be moral?' from 'Why should people be moral?' After giving a psychological explanation of what motivates people to be moral, Hospers considers what *reasons* there are for being moral.

Virtue is its own reward and if an act is indeed right this is a sufficient reason for performing the act. We have been operating on the wrong assumption—an assumption that we inherited from Plato—namely, that if it isn't in our interest to behave morally we have no reason to do it. But it does not follow that if a right action is not in our interest we have no reason for doing it. If we ask 'Why should we do this act rather than other acts we might have done instead' the answer 'Because it is the right act' is, says Hospers, "the best answer and ultimately the only answer".[1]

It is indeed true that *if we are reasoning from the moral point of view* and if an act is genuinely the right act to do in a given situation, then it is the act we should do. Once a moral agent knows that such and such an action is the right *one to do in* these circumstances he has *eo ipso* been supplied with the reason for doing it. But in asking 'Why should I be moral?' an individual is asking why *he* should (non-moral sense of 'should') reason as a moral agent. He is asking, and *not* as a moral agent, what reason there is for his doing what is right.

[1] John Hospers, *Human Conduct: An Introduction to the Problems of Ethics* (New York, 1961), p. 194.

It is at this point that Hospers' reply—and his implicit defense of his simple answer—exhibits insight. It will, Hospers points out, be natural for an individual to ask this question only when "the performance of the act is *not* to his own interest".[2] It is also true that *any* reason we give other than a reason which will show that what is right is in his rational self-interest will be rejected by him. Hospers remarks "What he wants, and he will accept no other answer, is a self-interested reason" for acting as a moral agent.[3] But this is like asking for the taste of pink for "the situation is *ex hypothesi* one in which the act required of him is contrary to his interest. Of course it is impossible to give him a reason *in accordance with his interest for acting contrary* to his interest".[4] 'I have a reason for acting in accordance with my interest which is contrary to my interests' is a contradiction. The man who requests an answer to 'Why should I do what is right when it is not in my interest?' is making a "self-contradictory request". We come back once more to Prichard and Bradley and see that after all our "question" is a logically absurd one—no real question at all. The person asking "the question" cannot "without self-contradiction, accept a reason of self-interest for doing what is contrary to his interest and yet he will accept no reason except one of self-interest".[5]

His "question" is no real question at all but at best a non-rational expression of a personal predicament. Our problem has been dissolved—the "common sense core of subjectivism" has turned out to be the core of the onion.

But has it really? Is any further question here but a confused request for *motivation* to do what we know we have the best reasons for doing? Let us take stock. Hospers has in effect shown us: 1) That x's being right entails *both* x should be done (where 'should' has a moral use) and there is (from the moral point of view) a *sufficient reason* for doing x ('I ought to do what is right' is a tautology where 'ought' is used morally); 2) That from the point of view of self-interest the only reasons that can be sufficient reasons for acting are self-interested reasons. This again is an obvious tautology. The man asking 'Why should I do what is right when it is not in my self-interest?' has made a self-contradictory request *when he is asking this question as a self-interested question.*

These two points must be accepted, but what if an individual says: As I see it, there are two alternatives: either I act from the moral point of view, where logically speaking I must try to do what is right, or I act from the point of view of rational self-interest, where again I must seek to act according to my rational self-interest. But is there any *reason* for me always to act from one point of view rather than another when I am a member in good standing in a moral community? True enough, Hospers has shown me that *from the moral point of view* I have no alternative but to try to do what is right and from a *self-interested point of view* I have no rational alternative but to act according to what I judge to be

[2] *Ibid.*, p. 194.
[3] *Ibid.*
[4] *Ibid.*
[5] *Ibid.*, p. 195.

in my rational self-interest. But what I want to know is what I am to do: Why adopt one point of view rather than another? Is there a good reason *for me,* placed as I am, to adopt the moral point of view or do I just arbitrarily choose, as the subjectivist would argue?

I do not see that Hospers' maneuver has shown this question to be senseless or an expression of a self-contradictory request. Rather his answer in effect brings the question strikingly to the fore by showing how from the moral point of view 'Because it's right' must be a sufficient answer, and how it cannot possibly be a sufficient answer from the point of view of self-interest or from the point of view of an individual challenging the sufficiency of the whole moral point of view, as a personal guide for his actions. It seems that we have two strands of discourse here with distinct criteria and distinct canons of justification. We just have to make up our minds which point of view we wish to take. The actual effect of Hospers' argument is to display in fine rational order the common sense core of subjectivism: *at this point* we just choose and there can be no reasons for our choice.

It will not do for Hospers to argue that an individual could not rationally choose a non-moral way of life or ethos, for in choosing to act from a self-interested vantage point an individual is not choosing a way of life; he is, instead, adopting a personal policy of action in a very limited area for himself alone. Such an individual might well agree with Hospers that a rational way of life is one, the choice of which, is (1) free, (2) enlightened, and (3) impartial.[6] This remark, he could contend, is definitive of what we *mean* by 'a rational way of life'. An intelligent egoist would even urge that such a way of life be adopted but he could still ask himself (it wouldn't be prudent to ask others) what *reason* there would be for *him* or any single individual, living in a community committed to such a way of life to act in accordance with it. (This need not be a question which logically speaking requires a self-interested answer. An existing individual is trying to make up his mind what he is to do.)

To reply, 'If it's rational then it should be done', is to neglect the context-dependent criteria of both 'rational' and 'should'. There are both moral and non-moral uses of 'should' and 'rational'. In the above example Hospers is using 'rational' in a moralistic sense; as Hospers puts it, "Let me first define 'rationality' with regard to a way of life" and while a way of life is not exhausted by moral considerations it essentially includes them. Only if 'rational' and 'should' belong to the same strand of discourse is 'If it is rational then it should be done' analytic. Something could be rational from the moral point of view (morally reasonable) and yet imprudent (irrational from the point of view of self-interest). If we were asking what we should do in terms of self-interest, it would not follow in this case that we should do what is rational in the sense of 'morally reasonable'. Conversely, where 'What is rational' means 'What is prudent' it would not follow that what is rational is what, morally speaking, we ought to do.

[6] *Ibid.,* p. 585.

Thus, it seems to me that neither Baier's nor Hospers' answers will do. We are left with our original question, now made somewhat more precise, 'Is there a good reason for me as an individual in a moral community to always act morally no matter how I am placed?'. There is no room *in morality* for this question but this question can arise when we think about how to act and when, as individuals, we reflect on what ends of action to adopt. But as a result of Hospers' analysis, must we now say that here we must 1) simply make a choice concerning how to act or 2) where there is no live question concerning how to act it is still the case that there can be no non-question begging justification for an individual, were he faced with such a choice, to act one way rather than another? (Of course there is the very best *moral* justification for his acting as a moral agent. But that is not our concern here, for here we are asking: why reason morally?)

Here the pull of subjectivism is strong—and at this point it has an enlightened common sense on its side. But I think there is something more to be said that will take the bite out of such subjectivism. In trying to bring this out, I am in *one sense* going back to Plato. It is, of course, true that we can't ask for a self-interested reason for doing what is right where *ex hypothesi* the action is not in our self-interest. But in actual moral situations it is not so clear what is in our self-interest and what is not, and often what is *apparently* in our self-interest is really not. Part of my counter to the subjectivist, and *here* I am with Plato, is that if a man decides *repeatedly* to act non-morally where he thinks he can get away with it, he will not, as a very general rule, be happy.

This isn't the whole of my case by any means, but I shall start with this consideration.

IV

Suppose that I, in a fully rational frame of mind, am trying to decide whether or not to adopt individual egoism as my personal policy of action. I ask myself: 'Should I pursue a selfish policy or should I consider others as well even when in my best judgment it doesn't profit me?'. In my deliberation I might well ask myself: 'Will I really be happy if I act without regard for others?'. And here it is natural to consider the answer of the ancients. Plato and Aristotle believe that only the man who performs just actions has a well-ordered soul. And only the man with a well-ordered soul will be "truly happy". If I am thrown off course by impulse and blind action I will not have a well-ordered soul; I will not be genuinely happy. But the alternative I am considering is not between impulsive blind action and rational, controlled action, but between two forms of deliberate, rationally controlled activity. Why is my soul any less well-ordered or why do I realize myself (to shift to Bradley's idiom) any the less if I act selfishly than if I act morally? If it is replied, 'You will "realize yourself more" because most people have found that they are happiest when they are moral', I can again ask: 'But what has that to do with me? Though I am one man among men, I may not in this respect be like other men. Most people have neurotic compulsions about duties and are prey to customary taboos and tribal loyalties. If I can free myself from such compulsions and superstitions will I be any the less happy if I am selfish? I should think that I would be happier by being intelligently selfish. I can forget about others and single-mindedly go after what I want'.

To this last statement Plato and Aristotle would reply that by always acting selfishly a man will not fully realize his distinctively human *areté*.[7] By so acting, he simply will not be responding in a fully human way. We say of a man that he is a 'good man, a truly happy man' when he performs his function well, just as we say a tranquilizer is a 'good tranquilizer' when it performs its function well; that is to say, when the tranquilizer relaxes the tense, harassed individual. But can we properly talk about human beings this way? We do speak of a surgeon as 'a good surgeon' when he cures people by deftly performing operations when and only when people need operations. Similarly, a teacher is 'a good teacher' if he stimulates his students to thought and to assimilate eagerly "the best that has been thought and said in the world". We can indeed speak of the *areté* or "virtue" of the teacher, fireman, preacher, thief or even . . . of the wife or unmarried girl. People have certain social roles and they can perform them ill or well. "In this sense we can speak of 'a good husband', 'a good father', 'a good Chancellor of the Exchequer' . . .", but . . . hardly of "a good man". People, *qua* human beings, do not seem to have a function, purpose, or role. A child can sensibly ask: 'What are hammers for?', 'What are aspirins for?', 'What are dentists for?', but if a child asks 'What are people for?', we must point out to him that this question is not really like the others. 'Daddie, what are people for?' is foolish or *at the very least*—even for the Theist—an extremely amorphous question. At best we must quickly strike some religious attitude and some disputed cosmology must be quickly brought in, but no such exigency arises for the cosmologically neutral question, 'Daddie, what are napkins for?' or 'Daddie, what are policemen for?'. After all, what is the function of man *as such*? In spite of all his hullabalo about it, is not Sartre correct in claiming that man has no "essence"—no *a priori* nature—but that human beings are what human beings make of themselves? If a human being acts in an eccentric or non-moral way are we really entitled to say he is any less of a human being?

If we counter that we are indeed entitled to say this, and we then go on to say, 'By not acknowledging that we are so entitled, we are in effect overriding or ignoring man's "distinctively human qualities"' are we not now using 'distinctively human qualities' primarily as a grading label? In such contexts, isn't its actual linguistic function primarily moral? We are disapproving of a way of acting and attempting to guide people away from patterns of behavior that are like this. If we say the consistently selfish man is less human than the moral man, are we not here using 'less human' as a moral grading label and not just as a phrase to describe men? 'More human', on such a use, would not be used to

---

[7] [Excellence or virtue.—Ed. note.]

signify those qualities (if there are any) which are common to and distinctive of the human animal; but would be used as an honorific moral label. And *if* it is used *only* to describe how people have behaved then it is perfectly possible for me to ask, 'Why should I be more human rather than less?'.

Most moderns would not try to meet the question 'Why should I be moral?' in this Greek way, though they still would be concerned with that ancient problem, 'How should I live in order to be truly happy?'. A rational man might make this elementary prudential reflection: 'If I am thoroughly and consistently selfish and get caught people will treat me badly. I will be an outcast, I will be unloved, all hands will be on guard against me. I may even be retaliated against or punished as an "irredeemable moral beast". All of this will obviously make me suffer. Thus, I better not take up such a selfish policy or I will surely be unhappy'.

At this point it is natural to take a step which, if pushed too far, cannot but lead to a "desert-island example". It is natural to reply: 'Clearly it would be irrational to *appear* selfish. But I don't at all propose to do that. I only propose to look out for "number one" and only "number one". I will do a good turn for others when it is likely, directly or indirectly, to profit me. I will strive to appear to be a man of good morals and I will do a good deed when and only when it is reasonable to believe there will be some personal profit in it. Surely, a policy of unabashed, outright selfishness would be disastrous to me. Obviously, this is something I will strive to avoid. But I shall keep as the maxim of *my* actions: Always consider yourself first. Only do things for others, when by so acting, it will profit you, and do not be frankly selfish or openly aggressive except in those situations where no harm is likely to befall you for so acting. Take great pains to see that your selfishness is undetected by those who might harm you'.

But, at this point our hypothetical rational egoist would need to consider the reply: 'You will regret acting this way. The pangs of conscience will be severe, your superego will punish you. Like Plato's tyrant you will be a miserable, disordered man. Your very mental health will be endangered'.

Imperceptibly drawing nearer to a desert-island example, the egoist might reply: 'But the phrase "mental health" is used to describe those well adjusted people who keep straight on the tracks no matter what. I don't intend to be "healthy" *in that sense*. And, I do not recognize the *authority* of conscience. My conscience is just the internalized demands of Father and Tribe. But why should I assent to those demands, when it doesn't serve my interests? They are irrational, compulsive moralistic demands, and I shall strive to free myself from them'.

To this it might be countered, 'Granted that conscience has no moral or even rational authority over *you*, you unfortunate man, but practically speaking, you cannot break these bonds so easily. Consciously you may recognize their lack of authority but unconsciously they have and always will continue to have —in spite of all your ratiocination—a dominating grip on you. If you flaunt them, go against them, ignore them, it will cost you your peace of mind, you will pay in psychic suffering, happiness will be denied you. But as a rational egoist happiness is supposedly your goal. And it is wishful thinking to think some psychiatrist will or can take you around this corner. Neither psychoanalysis nor any other kind of therapy can obliterate the "voice of the superego". It can at best diminish its demands when they are *excessive*. Your conditioning was too early and too pervasive to turn your back on it now. If you are rational you will not struggle in such a wholesale fashion against these ancient, internalized demands. Thus, you should not act without regard to the dictates of morality if you really want to be happy'.

It is at this stage that the rational egoist is likely to use his visa to Desert Island. He might say: 'But if I had the power of Gyges[8] and that power included the power to still the nagging voice of my superego, would it not then be reasonable for me to always act in my own self-interest no matter what the effect on others? If there was some non-harmful pill—some moral tranquilizer —that I could take that would "kill" my conscience but allow me to retain my prudence and intelligence why then, under those circumstances, should I act morally rather than selfishly? What good reason is there for me in that situation to act morally if I don't *want* to?'

It is not sufficient to be told that if most people had Gyges' ring (or its modern, more streamlined, equivalent) they would go on acting as they do now. The question is not 'What would most people do if they had Gyges' ring?' or even 'What would I do if I had Gyges' ring?' The question is rather, 'What should I do?'. At this point can *reasons* be found which would convince an intelligent person that even in this kind of situation, he ought to act morally? That is, would it serve his "true interests" (as Plato believes) for him to be moral, even in the event these conditions obtained?

It is just here, I believe, that subjectivism quite legitimately raises its ugly head. If the above desert-island situation did in fact obtain, I think we would have to say that whether it would or would not be in your "true interests" to be moral or non-moral would depend on the sort of person you are. With the possible exception of a few St. Anthony's, we are, as a matter *of fact,* partly egoistic and partly other-regarding in our behaviour. There can be no complete non-personal, objective justification for acting morally rather than non-morally. In certain circumstances a person of one temperament would find it in his interests to act one way and a person of another temperament to act in another. We have two policies of action to choose from, with distinct criteria of appropriateness and which policy of action will make us happy will depend on the sort of person we *happen* to be.

It is here that many of us feel the "existential bite" of our question. Students, who are reasonably bright and not a little versed in the ways of the world, are often (and rightly) troubled by the successive destruction of first psychological egoism and then ethical egoism. They come to see that individual egoism can't be a moral view, but they feel somehow cheated; somehow, in some way, they sense that something has been put over on them. And I think

---

[8] [See the Myth of Gyges, page 483.—Ed. Note.]

there is a point to this rather common and persistent feeling and I have tried, in effect, to show what this is. I would *not,* of course, claim that it is always the "Why-should-I-be-moral?" question that troubles a reflective student at this juncture but frequently, like Glaucon and Adeimantus, the student wants to know why, as a solitary flesh and blood individual, he should be moral. He *feels* that he should be moral, but is he somehow being duped? He wants a *reason* that will be a good and sufficient reason for his being moral, quite apart from *his* feelings or attitudes about the matter. He does not want to be in the position of finally having to decide, albeit after reflection, what sort of person to strive to be. It seems to me that the subjectivists are right in suggesting that this is just what he finally can't avoid doing, that he doesn't have and can't have *the kind* of objectivity he demands here. We need not have existentialist dramatics here, but we do need to recognize the logical and practical force of this point. Most rationalistic and theological ethical theories seem to me myth-making devices to disguise this *prima facie* uncomfortable fact.

V

But need we despair of the rationality of the moral life once we have dug out and correctly placed this irreducible element of choice in reasoning about human conduct? Perhaps some will despair but since it is not the job of a philosopher to be a kind of universal Nannie I don't think he need concern himself to relieve this despair. But, I think, if he will remind people of the exact point on the logical map where this subjectivism correctly enters and make them once more aware of the map as a whole they will—now able to see the forest as well as the trees—be less inclined to despair about the rationality of their acting morally. If one is willing to reason morally, nothing we have said here need upset the objectivity and rationality of moral grading criteria. More importantly here, to admit subjectivism at this point does not at all throw into doubt the Hobbesian defense of the value of morality as a social practice. It only indicates that *in the situation* in which an *individual* is 1) very unlikely to be caught, 2) so rationally in control that he will be very unlikely to develop habits which would lead to his punishment, and 3) is free from the power of his conscience, it might, just might (if he were a certain kind of person), make him happier to be non-moral than moral. But this is not the usual bad fellow we meet on the streets and the situation is anything but typical.

A recognition of the irrelevance of desert-island examples will provide further relief from moral anxiety, over such subjectivism. Critics of utilitarianism invent situations in which a social practice is, as we use moral language, regarded as obligatory even though there is no advantage in acting in accordance with it in this particular kind of circumstance. They construct desert-island examples and then crucify the utilitarian with them. They point out, for example, that promises made on desert-islands to a dying man to dispose of his effects in a certain way are considered obligatory even if it is clear that 1) some other disposal of his effects would be more beneficial and 2) that there is no reasonable chance that the breach in trust would be detected. The usual utilitarian answer is that disregarding promises of this sort would weaken our moral character; and, in addition, we cannot be quite sure that such a breach in trust would not be detected or that it would really do more good than harm. Further, to ignore a promise of this sort is bad, for it would tend to weaken the utility of the social *practice* of promise-keeping.

Nowell-Smith, however, is quite correct in saying: "The relentless desert-islander can always break such utilitarian moves by adding stipulations to the terms of the original problem". That is, he will say to the utilitarian, 'But what would you say *if* breaking a trust in situations of this type would not weaken the utility of the practice of promise-keeping? Surely it is *intelligible* to suppose that such acts would not weaken people's moral fiber, would not be detected, and would not do more total good than harm.' To this the utilitarian can only say that this statement of the desert-islander is a very "iffy proposition", indeed. Nowell-Smith rightly remarks: "The force of these desert-island arguments . . . depend expressly on the improbability of the case supposed". "It is difficult to assess their force precisely because the case *is* improbable and therefore not catered for in our ordinary language". The language of human conduct has the structure it has because the world is as it is and not otherwise. If people and things were very different, the structure of moral codes and the uses of evaluative language presumably would be different. The very form of our talk about human conduct "reflects empirical truths that are so general and obvious that we can afford to ignore exceptions". If through desert-island examples we withdraw that pervasive contextual background it is difficult to know what is the logically proper thing to say. The logic of the language of human conduct did not develop with such wildly improbable situations in view. It, after all, has a wide range of distinct, practical uses, and it only has application in a certain type of setting. If one of these desert-island situations were to obtain, we would have a good reason, as Wittgenstein clearly saw, to make a linguistic stipulation, that is, we would have to decide what is to be *said* here and our linguistic decision would indeed be an intervention in the world, it would indeed have normative import. But it is neither possible nor necessary that we make all such stipulations in advance and we can hardly reasonably accuse the language of conduct of inadequacy because it does not cater to desert-island cases. It would be like saying that "the language of voting" is inadequate because it does not tell us what to do in a situation in which a senior class, consisting of a thousand, tries to elect a president from four candidates and each time a vote is taken each candidate gets exactly 250 votes. This indeed is a logical possibility, but that *this* logical possibility is not considered in setting out the procedures for voting does not at all indicate an inadequacy in our voting procedures.

Our "Gyges-ring situations" are just such desert-island cases. In fact, Nowell-Smith is quite correct in remarking that the Gyges-ring example in the *Republic* is a paradigm of all such desert-island arguments.

'Would I be happier if I were intelligently selfish in a situation in which I could free myself from guilt feelings, avoid punishment, loss of love, contempt of family and friends, social ostracism, etc.?' To ask this is to ask a desert-island question. Surely we can and do get away with occasional selfish acts—though again note the usual burden of guilt—but given the world as it is, a deliberate, persistent though cunning policy of selfishness is very likely to bring on guilt feelings, punishment, estrangement, contempt, ostracism and the like. A clever man might avoid one or another of these consequences but it would be very unlikely that he could avoid them all or even most of them. And it is truistic to remark that we all want companionship, love, approval, comfort, security and recognition. It is very unlikely that the consistently selfish man can get those things he wants. At this point, it may be objected: 'But suppose someone doesn't want those things, then what are we to say?' But this is only to burgeon forth with another desert-island example. The proper thing to reply is that people almost universally are not that way and that in reasoning about whether I should or should not be selfish, I quite naturally appeal to certain very pervasive facts (including facts about attitudes) and do not, and need not, normally, try to find an answer that would apply to all conceivable worlds and all *possible* human natures. To think that one must do so is but to exhibit another facet of the genuinely irrational core of rationalism.

VI

It seems to me that the above considerations count heavily against adopting a thoroughly consistent policy of individual egoism. But do such considerations at all touch the individual who simply, on occasion, when his need is great, acts in a way that is inconsistent with the dictates of morality? Will such a person always be happier—in the long run—if he acts conscientiously or is this a myth foisted on us, perhaps for good social reasons, by our religions and moralities? Are all the situations desert-island situations in which we can reasonably claim that there could be rational men who would be happier if they acted non-morally rather than morally or in which we would have to say that any decision to act one way rather than another is a matter of arbitrary choice? Are there paradigm cases which establish the subjectivist's case—establish that it is altogether likely that some clear-headed people will be happier if, in some non-desert-island circumstances, they deliberately do what they acknowledge is wrong and or in some non-desert-island circumstances some people must just decide in such circumstances what they are to do?

Let us examine three *prima facie* cases.

Suppose a man, believing it to be wrong, decides to be unfaithful to his wife when it is convenient, non-explosive and unlikely to be discovered. Usually it is not, on the part of the knight-errant husband, a deliberate and systematic policy but it might be and sometimes is. Bored husbands sometimes day-dream that this is a return to paradise; that is to say, it might earn, at least in anticipation, a good score in a felicific calculus. In order to make the example sufficiently relevant to the argument, we must exclude those cases in which the husband believes there is nothing wrong in this behavior and/or gives reasons or rationalizations to excuse his behavior. I must also exclude the guilty weak-willed man with the Pauline syndrome. The case demands a man who deliberately—though with sufficiently prudent moderation—commits adultery. It is important for our case that he believes adultery to be immoral. Nonetheless, while believing people ought not to be adulterers, he asks himself, 'Should I continue to live this way anyway? Will I really be happier if I go the way of St. Paul?' He does not try to universalize his decision. He believes that to choose to remain an adulterer is immoral, but the immoral choice remains for him a live option. Though people may not put all this to themselves so explicitly, such a case is not an impossibility. People may indeed behave in this way. My example is not a desert-island one. I admit there is something odd about my adulterer that might make him seem like a philosophical *papier maché* figure. There is also something conceptually odd about saying that a man believes x to be wrong and yet, without guilt or ambivalence and without excusing conditions, rationally decides to do x. With good reason we say, 'If he knows it to be wrong or really believes it to be wrong, he will (everything else being equal) try to avoid it'. Still there is a sense in which he could say he believes x to be wrong even though he seeks x. The sense is this: he would not wish that people generally choose or seek x. When this is the case he says 'x is wrong' even though he makes a frank exception of himself without attempting to morally justify this exception. It is important to note that this is a *special* though perfectly intelligible use on my part of 'He believes it to be wrong'. While it withdraws one essential feature, namely that non-universalisable exceptions are inadmissable, it retains something of the general sense of what we mean by calling something morally wrong.

Yet, for the sake of the argument at least, let us assume that we do not have a desert-island case. Assuming then that there are such men, is their doing what is wrong here also for *them* the personally disadvantageous thing? Can any individual who acts in such a way ever be reasonably sure he won't be caught—that one of the girls won't turn up and make trouble, that he won't run into an acquaintance at the wrong time? Even if these seem to be remote possibilities, can he ever be free enough from them in his dream life? And if his dreams are bothersome, if he develops a rather pervasive sense of uneasiness, is it really worth it? He must again consider the power of his conscience (superego) even though he rationally decided to reject its authority. Will it give him peace? Will the fun be worth the nagging of his conscience? It is difficult to *generalize* here. Knowledge of oneself, of people, of human psychology and of imaginative literature is all extremely relevant here. I think the individual egoist can correctly argue that it is not *always* clear that he would be unhappier in such a situation if he did what was wrong. A great deal depends on the individual and the exact particular circumstance but the moralist who says it is never, or hardly ever, the case that a person will be happier by pursuing a selfish policy certainly overstates his case.

Let me now take a different paradigm for which much the same thing must be said. It is important to consider this new case because most people would label this man a "veritable moral beast" yet he stands to gain very much from acting immorally. The case I have in mind is that of a very intelligent, criminally experienced, well-equipped, non-masochistic but ruthless kidnapper. He is a familiar type in the movies and thrillers. Now, Hollywood to the contrary, why should it not sometimes be the case that such a kidnapper will be happier if he is successful? Indeed, he may have a murder on his hands but the stakes are very high and when he is successful he can live in luxury for the rest of his life. With good reason our *folklore* teaches he would not be happier. It is of the utmost value to society that such behavior be strenuously disapproved. And given the long years of conditioning we are all subject to, it remains the case that most people (placed in the position of the kidnapper) would not be happier with the successful completion of such a kidnapping if it involved murdering the kidnapped child. But then most people are not kidnappers. They have very different personalities. Such brutalities together with fear of detection would haunt them and it is probably the case that they also haunt many kidnappers. But if the kidnapper were utterly non-moral, very, very clever, etc., why wouldn't *he* really be happier? He could live in comfort; he could marry, have children and attain companionship, love, approval, etc. 'Well', we would say, 'his conscience would always bother him'. But, particularly with modern medical help, which he could now well afford, would it bother him enough? 'Well, there would always be the awful possibility of detection and the punishment that might follow'. But, if the stakes were high enough and if he were clever enough might it not be better than a life of dull routine, poverty or near poverty? And think of the "kicks" he would get in outwitting the police? We all have a little adventure in our souls. 'But'—the dialogue might go on—'if he were intelligent enough to pull off this job successfully, he would certainly be intelligent enough to avoid poverty and to avoid making his living in a routine, boring way'. The dialogue could go on interminably but I think it is clear enough again that even here there is no one decisive clearcut answer to be given. The case for morality here is stronger than in the previous paradigm, but it is still not decisive. Yet there are paradigms in which doing what is clearly wrong (and understood by the individual in question to be wrong) is in the rational self-interest of some individuals. Our first more typical paradigm is not completely clear, but the following third and less typical paradigm given by Hospers is a clearer example of a case in which it is in a man's self-interest not to do what is right.

There is a young bank clerk who decides, quite correctly, that he can embezzle $50,000 without his identity ever being known. He fears that he will be underpaid all his life if he doesn't embezzle, that life is slipping by without his ever enjoying the good things of this world; his fiancee will not marry him unless he can support her in the style to which she is accustomed; he wants to settle down with her in a suburban house, surround himself with books, stereo hi-fi set, and various *objets d'art,* and spend a pleasant life, combining culture with sociability; he never wants to commit a similar act again. He does just what he wanted to do: he buys a house, invests the remainder of the money wisely so as to enjoy a continued income from it, marries the girl, and lives happily ever after; he doesn't worry about detection because he has arranged things so that no blame could fall on him; anyway he doesn't have a worrisome disposition and is not one to dwell on past misdeeds; he is blessed with a happy temperament, once his daily comforts are taken care of. The degree of happiness he now possesses would not have been possible had he not committed the immoral act.[9]

Clearly it was in his rational self-interest to do what is wrong.

Someone might claim that it is too much to expect that he could arrange things so that no blame would fall on him. This could happen only in desert-island type situations. But unless we began to have the doubts characteristic of traditional epistemologists about 'the blame could not fall on him', there are plenty of cases in which crimes of this general sort are carried out with success. There is no good reason to think such an individual in such circumstances would not be happier.

But it is also crucial to recall that our cases here only involve certain specific acts that do go against the requirements of morality. The cultured despiser of morals, we described in the last section, is a man who rejects the authority of *all* moral considerations and systematically pursues a selfish policy in all things. Thus, we would need to project risks similar to those of the wayward husband and the kidnapper through his entire life. But are there really any realistic paradigms for such generalized egoistic behavior that would hold any attraction at all for a rational man? I doubt very much that there are. Yet, our three paradigms indicate that for *limited patterns of behavior,* no decisively good reasons can be given to some individuals that would justify their doing the moral thing in such a context. (It would be another thing again if they repeatedly acted in that way. Here the case for morality would be much stronger.)

In pointing this out, the subjectivist is on solid ground. But it is also true that even here it is not just a matter of "paying your money and taking your choice", for what it would be rational for you to do depends, in large measure, on what sort of person you are and on the particular circumstances into which you are cast.

There is a further more general and more important consideration. Even if large groups of people read and accepted my argument as correct, even if it got favorable billing by Luce publications, it still remains very unlikely that kidnapping and crime would increase one iota. For the most part, people get their standards not from ethical treatises or even scriptural texts or homely sayings but by idealizing and following the example of some living person or persons. Morality or immorality does not typically (or perhaps even ever) arise from precept or argument but from early living examples. The foundations of one's character are developed through unconscious imitation way before perplexity over morality can possibly arise. Unless a man is already ready to run amuck, he will not be morally derailed by the recognition that in deliberating about how

[9] John Hospers, *Human Conduct: An Introduction to the Problems of Ethics,* pages 180–81.

to act one finally must simply decide what sort of a person one wishes to be. Since most people are not ready to go amuck, the truth of my argument will not cause a housing shortage in hell.

There are further considerations that will ameliorate this subjectivism. It seems reasonable to say that in different societies the degree of subjectivism will vary. All societies are interested in preserving morality; they have a quite natural and rationally justifiable vested interest in their moral codes. Now, as societies gain a greater know-how, and particularly as they come to understand man and the structure of society better, it seems reasonable to assume they can more effectively protect their vested interests. In other words, I believe, it is reasonable to assume that it will become increasingly difficult to be successfully non-moral as a society gains more knowledge about itself and the world.

This also poses a puzzle for the intelligent individual egoist. In such advancing culture-studying cultures, it will become increasingly more difficult for *him* to be non-moral. But it is in his rational interest for *others* to be moral so he should not oppose this more efficient enforcement of morality. And if he does choose to oppose it, it is very probable that he will suffer a fate not unlike Camus' stranger.

More generally, it will not be in the interest of the individual egoist to oppose morality and even if he, and others like him, do find that it pays to act non-morally their failure to act morally will of necessity be so moderate that the set of social practices that help make up morality will not be disturbed in any extensive way. (This puts the point very modestly.) And, if too many go the way of the rational individual egoist, then it will no longer pay to be non-moral so that large numbers of individual egoists, if they are rational, will become men of good morals.

Though the plain man committed to the moral point of view will probably not jump with joy over this state of affairs, I think the considerations in the last three paragraphs give him genuine grounds for being sanguine. The subjectivism I have pin-pointed need not create a generation of "despairing philosophers" even if my argument is accepted as completely sound.

Supplementary Paperback Reading

K. Baier, "The Point of View of Morality." (Bobbs-Merrill Reprint Series in Philosophy)

H. Bedau, *Justice and Equality*. (Prentice-Hall)

F. H. Bradley, "Why Should I Be Moral?" in R. Ekman, *Readings in the Problems of Ethics*. (Scribner's)

J. Feinberg, "Justice and Personal Desert." (Bobbs-Merrill Reprint Series in Philosophy)

W. K. Frankena, *Ethics,* Ch. 6. (Prentice-Hall)

D. P. Gauthier, *Morality and Rational Self-Interest*. (Prentice-Hall)

R. M. Hare, *Freedom and Reason*. (Oxford University Press)

H. L. A. Hart, "Are There Any Natural Rights?" in A. Quinton, *Political Philosophy*. (Oxford University Press)

W. G. Maclagan, "How Important Is Moral Goodness?" in J. J. Thomson and G. Dworkin, *Ethics*. (Harper and Row)

A. I. Melden, *Human Rights*. (Wadsworth)

K. Nielsen, "Is 'Why Should I Be Moral' an Absurdity?" in R. Ekman, *Readings in the Problems of Ethics*. (Scribner's)

Ch. Perelman, *Justice*. (Random House)

D. Z. Phillips, "Does It Pay To Be Good?" in J. J. Thomson and G. Dworkin, *Ethics*. (Harper and Row)

J. Rawls, "The Sense of Justice," in J. Feinberg, *Moral Concepts*. (Oxford University Press)

N. Rescher, *Distributive Justice: A Constructive Critique of the Utilitarian Theory of Distribution*. (Bobbs-Merrill)

A. Sesonske, *Value and Obligation*. (Oxford University Press)

W. T. Stace, "Why Should I Be Moral?" in R. Ekman, *Readings in the Problems of Ethics*. (Scribner's)

S. E. Toulmin, *The Place of Reason in Ethics*, Ch. 10–14. (Cambridge University Press)

G. Vlastos, "Human Worth, Merit, and Equality," in J. Feinberg, *Moral Concepts*. (Oxford University Press)

B. Williams, "The Idea of Equality," in J. Feinberg, *Moral Concepts*. (Oxford University Press)

10

ETHICS AND GOD

Introduction

THE RELATIONSHIP BETWEEN MORALITY AND RELIGION

Does morality depend on religion? Must ethical standards and rules have religious foundations to be validly binding? If God did not exist, would that mean that there is no right or wrong? An affirmative answer to these questions has traditionally been held by the established organized religions of Western civilization (Judaism, Christianity, and Islam). According to this tradition, God, the all-good, all-powerful, all-knowing Creator of the universe, is the ground and source of moral duty as well as the ground and source of existence. Without God there would be no universally valid rules of conduct, but only the varying norms each society adopts as its own moral code. What is more, according to the traditional religious view, our knowledge of right and wrong is dependent on our knowledge of God's will. It is only because we know what God wants us to do that we know what is morally required of us.

This way of understanding the relation between morality and religion is based on the conception of God as the spiritual father and loving creator of all human beings. The appropriate human response to such a Being is one of gratitude and love. Since God is also conceived to have infinite goodness, knowledge, and power, He alone is the proper object of worship. The divine Being is thought of as a transcendent Person who has every perfection to the highest degree. To worship such a Being is to acknowledge His authority over all human concerns and interests. It involves placing one's whole trust in Him, remaining loyal to Him by letting one's will be constantly governed by His will, and finding one's rightful living and supreme fulfillment in obedience to His commands out of love for Him. For those who make such a commitment, to live in harmony with the Divine Law constitutes the highest moral ideal of human life.

This, then, is one way to conceive of the relation between morality and religion. A quite different way of understanding that relationship has arisen in recent times with the development of studies in the sociology and psychology of religion. According to this view moral norms are not based on religious foundations but are grounded in human nature and human society. The function of religious beliefs, attitudes, and practices is to deepen and strengthen a people's commitment to its whole way of life, including its moral code. Religion is a cultural institution serving a specific social purpose. It gives support to a society's norms, unifying and preserving its way of life, and reinforcing people's adherence to its common values. The concept of God is a symbolic personification of the highest moral ideals of the culture, and images of divine power and divine law signify the legitimacy of those ideals. Under this conception, stories about God are ways in which a society's basic values are given mythical and dramatic expression. The traditions and standards of conduct shared by a people, the general world-view and outlook on life held by the group, as well as the meaning of its history, are all embodied in the poetic and imaginative forms of its religious life.

Unlike the traditional view, this way of understanding the relation between religion and morality does not make the moral duty of human beings dependent upon a supernatural or transcendent source. Although the authoritativeness of a society's moral code is given symbolic representation in the *concept* of a Supreme Being, the validity of that code is not derived from the actual existence and nature of such a Being. Indeed, within the framework of this second view, there is no reason why the foundations of morality could not be understood according to one of the ethical theories that have been presented in this book. Consider, as an example, the beliefs of a religious rule-utilitarian. Such a person would hold that the rightness or wrongness of any act is based on its conformity or nonconformity to valid rules of conduct, and that the greatest happiness principle determines the validity of those rules. At the same time, the religious rule-utilitarian might justify religious beliefs and practices as ways of developing attitudes in people that deepen their commitment to the utilitarian ethical code.

In the present chapter we shall not be concerned with this second, human-centered way of regarding religion and morality. We will consider, instead, one important and widely accepted ethical theory that stems from the first view, according to which the ultimate ground of moral duty is to be found in the will or commands of an existent God. This theory has come to be known as the Divine Command Theory of Ethics.

THE DIVINE COMMAND THEORY OF ETHICS

Given the traditional conception of God as the loving creator of all human beings, it follows that whatever God commands people to do is right and whatever is right is something that God commands people to do. To express this in logical terms, there is an *extensional equivalence* between the class of right acts and the class of acts commanded by God. Extensional equivalence simply means that every member of the first class is also a member of the second, and every member of the second is also a member of the first. Any ethical theory in which such an extensional equivalence holds is a Divine Command Theory of Ethics. (This definition is intended to cover wrong acts as well as right ones. Thus every wrong act is an act that God commands us *not* to do, and every act so commanded is wrong.)

There are three different forms which a Divine Command Theory may take. These three forms may be thought of as alternative ways to *account for* the extensional equivalence between the class of right acts and the class of acts God commands us to do.

(I) According to the first form of the theory, God knows which acts are right and which are wrong and, since He is perfectly good, He always commands us to do right acts and to refrain from wrong ones. God's moral knowledge and moral goodness *guarantee* that what He commands us to do is always what we ought to do. The extensional equivalence between right acts and what God commands is not accidental or coincidental. There is a necessary connection between the two. What God commands *must* be right and what is right *must* be commanded by God. God, being omniscient, knows what acts are right, and being perfectly good, necessarily wills that His creatures do what is right.

(II) According to the second form of the theory, every right act is an act commanded by God because God's commanding us to do an act is the very thing that *makes* it right. The reason why an act is right is simply the fact that God has commanded us to do it. Similarly, everything God forbids us to do is necessarily wrong, since God's forbidding it is precisely what *makes* it wrong.

(III) The third form of the theory explains the extensional equivalence between right acts and acts commanded by God as follows. To say that an act is right and to say that God commands us to do the act are one and the same thing. The meaning of "Act X is right" is also the meaning of "God commands us to do X." There are not two different ideas being expressed here that are somehow correlated with each other, but one idea expressed in two different ways. The two statements are exactly synonymous. Now if two statements do mean exactly the same thing, then whenever one is true the other must be true and whenever one is false so is the other. Hence whenever it is true that an act is right it is also true that God commands us to do it, and whenever God commands us to do something it must be true that the act so commanded is right.

In this chapter these three forms of the Divine Command Theory will be critically examined. They all presuppose the existence of God, but our study of them will not directly be concerned with arguing for or against God's existence. Our interest here centers on *the implications of God's existence for ethics*. For even if it is the case that there is a God as understood by the Judaic-Christian-Islamic tradition, there remains the question: What has the existence of such a Being got to do with human conduct? Suppose, in other words, that there is indeed a creator of the universe who is all-knowing, all-powerful, and all-good. Why should we take this fact into consideration in our search for a valid normative ethical system? Does our knowledge of right and wrong require that we know the will of such a Being? Just what is the relevance of God's existence (if God does exist) to the moral life of human beings on Earth? These are the problems that will concern us in this chapter.

SOCRATES AND EUTHYPHRO

The first reading of the chapter is one of the dialogues of the Greek philosopher, Plato (427–347 B.C.). In this dialogue Plato presents us with a discussion between two men of Athens: Socrates, who was Plato's teacher, and a priest named Euthyphro. Although written outside the Western religious tradition, it is a classic statement of a basic problem underlying the Divine Command Theory of Ethics. The problem may be stated thus: Is an action right because God commands it, or does God command it because it is right? Those who answer with the first claim are committed to form (II) of the Divine Command Theory. Those who accept the second claim are committed to form (I).

It is to be noted that this question is stated somewhat differently in Plato's dialogue, since Socrates and Euthyphro, being citizens of ancient Athens, do not conceive of God in the Judaic-Christian-Islamic way. The question arises when Euthyphro claims that he is doing a pious act (that is, a religiously proper or upright act) in bringing his father to trial for murder. Socrates asks him what piety is. The importance of the ensuing discussion for our question is brought out when Euthyphro asserts that pious acts are acts that are loved by the gods. In doing an act of piety, Euthyphro claims, he is doing what the gods approve of. Socrates then asks: "Is the pious loved by the gods because it is pious, or is it pious because it is loved by the gods?" Thus he raises the central question of the Divine Command Theory of Ethics.

Neither Euthyphro nor Socrates himself answers the question, but the dialogue between them brings out the perplexity of holding either side of the issue. If it is said on the one hand that the gods love what is pious *because* it is pious, then the property of being god-beloved cannot be the same property as being pious. Furthermore, piety would not in that case depend on the love of the gods. What, then, does it depend on? What makes all pious acts pious? Unless we know the answer to this, we cannot know whether Euthyphro's act is or is not pious. On the other hand, if it is said that an act is pious *because* the gods love it, then whatever the gods love, for whatever reason, must be pious. Thus any kind of act could become pious, depending entirely on what attitudes the gods happen to take toward the act. Socrates' examination of Euthyphro's statements in this discussion reveals Euthyphro's failure to confront this dilemma.

A CONTEMPORARY CRITIQUE OF THE DIVINE COMMAND THEORY
OF ETHICS

In the second reading Jonathan Harrison, who is professor of philosophy at the University of Nottingham, England, systematically explores the relation between God's commands and human duties in the religious ethics of the Western tradition. Professor Harrison points out that if it is God's commands that make acts right or wrong (form (II) of the Divine Command Theory), it follows that no acts would be right—nor would any be wrong—if God does not exist. Another consequence of this view is that no matter what God commanded us to do it would be right, even if He commanded us to be cruel to one another. Suppose, however, we adopt form (I) of the Divine Command Theory to avoid this consequence. In that case God would know that cruelty is wrong and therefore would not command our being cruel but on the contrary would forbid it. This position means that even God must recognize the wrongness of cruelty, and this implies that cruelty would be wrong whether God existed or not. Thus God's existence would not be needed as a ground for human morality.

It might be argued (again in accordance with form (I) of the theory) that it is God's goodness which guarantees that He would not command human beings to be cruel. Since God is perfectly good, it might then be concluded, His will can rightly be held to impose moral duties upon human agents. This argument, Professor Harrison claims, is open to the same objection as that arising from the dilemma concerning right acts and God's commands. The dilemma in the present case is this: Is God good because His character fulfills a standard independent of His will, or is the fact that God approves of a certain kind of character itself the standard of goodness? One might reply that God is good because He is benevolent, merciful, and just. The question then arises: Are benevolence, mercy, and justice valid grounds for judging a being to be good, and if so, are they not standards by which we human beings are judging God? But for people to judge God seems to contradict God's ultimate authority over His creatures. Furthermore, if such standards of good character are valid, then we people can know what is good without relying on God's knowledge or goodness. On the other hand, if benevolence, mercy, and justice are proper standards of goodness because God approves of what is benevolent, merciful, and just, then it is possible that, if God were to approve of malevolence, ruthlessness, and injustice, these would automatically become proper standards of good character. So we are left with the same dilemma we previously confronted in connection with right acts.

Professor Harrison then discusses several additional difficulties in the theory that ethics must have religious foundations. First there is the problem of evil. If there is a morally perfect Being who is all-powerful and who created this universe, why is there so much evil (undeserved suffering) in the universe He created? Next there is the problem of how we can know what God commands us to do. If one appeals to the Bible or the Koran as authoritative sources of knowledge, one assumes that statements made in the Bible or the Koran about God's revelations are true. Suppose it is then claimed that such statements are true because they were revealed by God to the writers of the Bible or the Koran. This way of arguing is logically circular. The Bible or Koran is being taken as the true source of our knowledge of God's revelations, while at the same time God's revelations are being taken as the basis for the truth of the Bible or Koran. Finally, if it is necessary to use human reason to judge whether someone's claim to have a revelation from God is genuine or fraudulent, then human reason is being given the final authority to decide the acceptability of such a claim. This seems to be contrary to the idea that revelation provides knowledge that is absolutely certain because it comes directly from God.

A PHILOSOPHICAL DEFENSE OF ONE FORM OF THE
DIVINE COMMAND THEORY

In the last reading of the chapter, Robert Merrihew Adams, professor of philosophy at the University of California, Los Angeles, defends a modified form of the Divine Command Theory. This form of the theory, he argues, successfully avoids many of the difficulties with other versions. The most serious objection to forms (II) and (III) of the traditional theory, he says, is the following. Suppose God were to command that we be cruel. Then it would follow from the theory that, since it is wrong for us to disobey God, it would be wrong for us not to be cruel. Yet, Professor Adams asserts, any ethical theory which would make it possible for cruelty to be right is philosophically unacceptable.

To avoid this problem, Professor Adams proposes a modified Divine Command Theory, according to which both of the following entailments hold true:

(1) "It is wrong to do X" entails "It is contrary to God's commands to do X."

(2) "It is contrary to God's commands to do X" and "God loves his human creatures" together entail "It is wrong to do X."

When these two principles are both accepted, certain consequences follow. First, if an action is wrong then it is true that God commands us not to do it. But God's love for His creatures leads Him to command only right actions and to forbid only wrong ones. Thus given God's love and the fact that an action is contrary to what God wills for His creatures, the action in question must be wrong. It is not wrong *merely* because it is contrary to God's will. Now since no loving Creator would command His creatures to be cruel, it is not wrong to refrain from cruelty.

One implication of this modified Divine Command Theory, Professor Adams points out, is that ethical judgments are *objective* and *nonnatural*. To say that they are objective is to say that they are true or false and that their truth or falsity does not depend on human feelings, attitudes, or beliefs. Thus if an action is wrong it is not wrong simply because people disapprove of it or think it is wrong. It is wrong because it is contrary to the will of the loving Creator of humanity.

To say that ethical judgments are nonnatural is to say that they are true or false and that their truth or falsity is not discoverable by scientific ways of thinking. Such judgments express objective facts about the commands of God, and since we cannot have scientific knowledge of God's commands, ethical judgments are assertions of nonnatural fact.

Although Professor Adams does not discuss in his essay how ethical judgments are known to be true or false, he does analyze the framework within which such knowledge can alone be obtained. This framework is the moral experience of human beings as realized in the context of a religious life. He begins by considering the difference in meaning between "X is wrong" and "X is contrary to God's commands." Although both statements *refer to* the same objective state of affairs, it is possible for them to have different *meanings* because the emotions and attitudes expressed by them can become divergent under certain conditions. Take, for example, the hypothetical case of God's commanding us to be cruel. Here doing a certain action would be contrary to God's commands—an act of helping another in distress, for instance—yet the moral attitude of disapproval normally experienced with regard to any action opposed to God's commands would not be experienced in this situation. Although the religious believer would have to judge the action wrong, he could not take a moral attitude of condemnation toward it. Similarly, under this hypothetical condition the words "That action is wrong" would not have their normal meaning for the believer, since he uses these words normally both to express his own negative attitude toward the action in question and to express that attitude, as Professor Adams puts it, "clothed in the majesty of a divine authority." Consequently in this hypothetical situation a breakdown would occur in the believer's moral and religious life, within the framework of which it is unthinkable that God would command us to be cruel.

Another important element in Professor Adams' theory is that religious believers can value some things independently of God's commands. Thus a believer might place positive value on kindness and negative value on cruelty, without reference to God's commands. But such valuation is not to be identified with moral judgment. The goodness and badness being attributed to kindness and cruelty are not the ethical properties of right and wrong (which are always related to God's commands). Thus, according to the Modified Divine Command Theory, worship of a Creator whose will is the ultimate criterion of right and wrong is not blind obedience to an arbitrary moral dictator. Rather, it is based on the believer's attributing goodness to a loving Creator and so conceiving of Him as a being worthy of one's absolute loyalty and devotion.

In the last part of his essay Professor Adams takes up a problem raised by Professor Harrison in the preceding reading. The problem is that both believers and nonbelievers assume that they use moral terms like "right" and "wrong" in the same way and with the same meaning. But if an essential aspect of the use of these terms in the believer's discourse involves a reference to God's commands, then the nonbeliever cannot be understanding these terms in the same way as the believer. The result is that whenever they discuss an ethical question, the believer and nonbeliever are talking at cross purposes, using the same words with different meanings. The solution to this problem, according to the Modified Divine Command Theory, is to realize that, though there are some differences in the uses of "right" and "wrong" as spoken by the believer and the nonbeliever, there are also certain elements they have in common. It is because of this common meaning, which Professor Adams analyzes in his essay, that moral discourse between believer and nonbeliever is possible.

Although Professor Adams does not attempt to prove that the truth of moral judgments is grounded on the commands of a Supreme Being, he does show how his Modified Divine Command Theory provides a way of understanding the relation between morality and religion that is in harmony with the Western religious tradition.

PLATO
Euthyphro

Euthyphro: [1] What's new, Socrates, to make you leave your usual haunts in the Lyceum and spend your time here by the king-archon's court? Surely you are not prosecuting any one before the king archon as I am?

Socrates: The Athenians do not call this a prosecution but an indictment, Euthyphro.

E: What is this you say? Someone must have indicted you, for you are not going to tell me that you have indicted someone else.

S: No indeed.

E: But someone else has indicted you?

S: Quite so.

E: Who is he?

S: I do not really know him myself, Euthyphro. He is apparently young and unknown. They call him Meletus, I believe. He belongs to the Pitthean deme, if you know anyone from that deme called Meletus, with long hair, not much of a beard, and a rather aquiline nose.

E: I don't know him, Socrates. What charge does he bring against you?

S: What charge? A not ignoble one I think, for it is no small thing for a young man to have knowledge of such an important subject. He says he knows how our young men are corrupted and who corrupts them. He is likely to be wise, and when he sees my ignorance corrupting his contemporaries, he proceeds to accuse me to the city as to their mother. I think he is the only one of our

From Plato, *Euthyphro*, translated and edited, with notes, by G. M. A. Grube. This translation first published in G. M. A. Grube, ed., *The Trial and Death of Socrates* (1975). Reprinted by permission of George M. A. Grube and Hackett Publishing Company, Inc., P. O. Box 55573, Indianapolis, Indiana, 46205.

NOTE: All footnotes are by G. M. A. Grube, the editor and translator.

[1] We know nothing about Euthyphro except what we can gather from this dialogue. He is obviously a professional priest who considers himself an expert on ritual and on piety generally, and, it seems, is generally so considered.

public men to start out the right way, for it is right to care first that the young should be as good as possible, just as a good farmer is likely to take care of the young plants first, and of the others later. So, too, Meletus first gets rid of us who corrupt the growth of the young, as he says, and then afterwards he will obviously take care of the older and become a source of great blessings for the city, as seems likely to happen to one who started out this way.

E: I could wish this were true, Socrates, but I fear the opposite may happen. He seems to me to start out by harming the very heart of the city by attempting to wrong you. Tell me, what does he say you do to corrupt the young?

S: Strange things, to hear him tell it, for he says that I am a maker of gods, that I create new gods while not believing in the old gods, and he has indicted me for this very reason, as he puts it.

E: I understand, Socrates. This is because you say that the divine sign keeps coming to you.[2] So he has written this indictment against you as one who makes innovations in religious matters, and he comes to court to slander you, knowing that such things are easily misrepresented to the crowd. The same is true in my case. Whenever I speak of divine matters in the assembly and foretell the future, they laugh me down as if I were crazy; and yet I have foretold nothing that did not happen. Nevertheless, they envy all of us who do this. One need not give them any thought, but carry on just the same.

S: My dear Euthyphro, to be laughed at does not matter perhaps, for the Athenians do not mind anyone they think clever, as long as he does not teach his own wisdom, but if they think that he makes others to be like himself they get angry, whether through envy, as you say, or for some other reason.

E: I have certainly no desire to test their feelings towards me in this matter.

S: Perhaps you seem to make yourself but rarely available, and not to be willing to teach your own wisdom, but my liking for people makes them think that I pour out to anybody anything I have to say, not only without charging a fee but appearing glad to reward anyone who is willing to listen. If then they were intending to laugh at me, as you say they laugh at you, there would be nothing unpleasant in their spending their time in court laughing and jesting, but if they are going to be serious, the outcome is not clear except to you prophets.

E: Perhaps it will come to nothing, Socrates, and you will fight your case as you think best, as I think I will mine.

S: What is your case, Euthyphro? Are you the defendant or the prosecutor?

E: The prosecutor.

S: Whom do you prosecute?

---

[2] In Plato, Socrates always speaks of his divine sign or voice as intervening to prevent him from doing or saying something (e.g., *Apology* 31 d), but never positively. The popular view was that it enabled him to foretell the future, and Euthyphro here represents that view. Note, however that Socrates dissociates himself from "you prophets."

E: One whom I am thought crazy to prosecute.

S: Are you pursuing someone who will easily escape you?

E: Far from it, for he is quite old.

S: Who is it?

E: My father.

S: My dear sir! Your own father?

E: Certainly.

S: What is the charge? What is the case about?

E: Murder, Socrates.

S: Good heavens! Certainly, Euthyphro, most men would not know how they could do this and be right. It is not the part of anyone to do this, but of one who is far advanced in wisdom.

E: Yes by Zeus, Socrates, that is so.

S: Is then the man your father killed one of your relatives? Or is that obvious, for you would not prosecute your father for the murder of a stranger.

E: It is ridiculous, Socrates, for you to think that it makes any difference whether the victim is a stranger or a relative. One should only watch whether the killer acted justly or not; if he acted justly, let him go, but if not, one should prosecute, even if the killer shares your hearth and table. The pollution is the same if you knowingly keep company with such a man and do not cleanse yourself and him by bringing him to justice. The victim was a dependent of mine, and when we were farming in Naxos he was a servant of ours. He killed one of our household slaves in drunken anger, so my father bound him hand and foot and threw him in a ditch, then sent a man here to enquire from the priest what should be done. During that time he gave no thought or care to the bound man, as being a killer, and it was no matter if he died, which he did. Hunger and cold and his bonds caused his death before the messenger came back from the seer. Both my father and my other relatives are angry that I am prosecuting my father for murder on behalf of a murderer, as he did not even kill him. They say that such a victim does not deserve a thought and that it is impious for a son to prosecute his father for murder. But their ideas of the divine attitude to piety and impiety are wrong, Socrates.

S: Whereas, by Zeus, Euthyphro, you think that your knowledge of the divine, and of piety and impiety, is so accurate that, when those things happened as you say, you have no fear of having acted impiously in bringing your father to trial?

E: I should be of no use, Socrates, and Euthyphro would not be superior to the majority of men, if I did not have accurate knowledge of all such things.

S: It is indeed most important, my admirable Euthyphro, that I should become your pupil, and as regards this indictment challenge Meletus about these very things and say to him: that in the past too I considered knowledge about the divine to be most important, and that now that he says that I improvise and innovate about the gods I have become your pupil. I would say to him: "If, Meletus, you agree that Euthyphro is wise in these matters, consider me, too, to have the right beliefs and do not bring me to trial. If you do not think so, then prosecute that teacher of mine for corrupting the older men, me and his own father, by teaching me and by exhorting and punishing him. If he is not convinced, does not discharge me, or indicts you instead of me, I shall repeat the same challenge in court.

E: Yes by Zeus, Socrates, and, if he should try to indict me, I think I would find his weak spots and the talk in court would be about him rather than about me.

S: It is because I realize this that I am eager to become your pupil, my dear friend. I know that other people as well as this Meletus do not even seem to notice you, whereas he sees me so sharply and clearly that he indicts me for ungodliness. So tell me now, by Zeus, what you just now maintained you clearly knew: what kind of thing do you say that godliness and ungodliness are, both as regards murder and other things; or is the pious not the same and alike in every action, and the impious the opposite of all that is pious and like itself, and everything that is to be impious presents us with one form [3] or appearance in so far as it is impious.

E: Most certainly, Socrates.

S: Tell me then, what is the pious, and what the impious, do you say?

E: I say that the pious is to do what I am doing now, to prosecute the wrongdoer, be it about murder or temple robbery or anything else, whether the wrongdoer is your father or your mother or anyone else; not to prosecute is impious. And observe, Socrates, that I can quote the law as a great proof that this is so. I have already said to others that such actions are right, not to favour the ungodly, whoever they are. These people themselves believe that Zeus is the best and most just of the gods, yet they agree that he bound his father because he unjustly swallowed his sons, and that he in turn castrated his father for similar reasons. But they are angry with me because I am prosecuting my father for his wrongdoing. They contradict themselves in what they say about the gods and about me.

S: Indeed, Euthyphro, this is the reason why I am a defendant in the case, because I find it hard to accept things like that being said about the gods, and it is likely to be the reason why I shall be told I do wrong. Now, however, if you, who have full knowledge of such things, share their opinions, then we must agree with them too, it would seem. For what are we to say, we who agree that we ourselves have no knowledge? Tell me, by the god of friendship, do you really believe these things are true?

---

[3] This is the kind of passage that makes it easier for us to follow the transition from Socrates' universal definitions to the Platonic theory of separately existent eternal universal Forms. The words *eidos* and *idea*, the technical terms for the Platonic Forms, commonly mean physical stature or bodily appearance. As we apply a common epithet, in this case pious, to different actions or things, these must have a common characteristic, present a common appearance or form, to justify the use of the same term, but in the early dialogues, as here, it seems to be thought of as immanent in the particulars and without separate existence. The same is true . . . where the word "Form" is also used.

E: Yes, Socrates, and so are even more surprising things, of which the majority has no knowledge.

S: And do you believe that there really is war among the gods, and terrible emnities and battles, and other such things as are told by the poets, and other sacred stories such as are embroidered by good writers and by representations of which the robe of the goddess is adorned when it is carried up to the Acropolis. Are we to say these things are true, Euthyphro?

E: Not only these, Socrates, but, as I was saying just now, I will, if you wish, relate many other things about the gods which I know will amaze you.

S: I should not be surprised, but you will tell me these at leisure some other time. For now, try to tell me more clearly what I was asking just now, for, my friend, you did not teach me adequately when I asked you what the pious was, but you told me that what you are doing now, to prosecute your father for murder, is pious.

E: And I told the truth, Socrates.

S: Perhaps. You agree, however, that there are many other pious actions.

E: There are.

S: Bear in mind then that I did not bid you tell me one or two of the many pious actions but that form itself that makes all pious actions pious, for you agreed that all impious actions are impious and all pious actions pious through one form, or don't you remember?

E: I do.

S: Tell me then what form itself is, so that I may look upon it, and using it as a model, say that any action of yours or another's that is of that kind is pious, and if it is not that it is not.

E: If that is how you want it, Socrates, that is how I will tell you.

S: That is what I want.

E: Well then, what is dear to the gods is pious, what is not is impious.

S: Splendid, Euthyphro! You have now answered in the way I wanted. Whether your answer is true I do not know yet, but you will obviously show me that what you say is true.

E: Certainly.

S: Come then, let us examine what we mean. An action or a man dear to the gods is pious, but an action or a man hated by the gods is impious. They are not the same, but opposites, the pious and the impious. Is that not so?

E: It is indeed.

S: And that seems to be a good statement?

E: I think so, Socrates.

S: We have also stated that the gods are in a state of discord, that they are at odds with each other, Euthyphro, and that they are at enmity with each other. That too has been said.

E: It has.

S: What are the subjects of difference that cause hatred and anger? Let us look at it this way. If you and I were to differ about numbers as to which is the greater, would this difference make us enemies and angry with each other, or would we proceed to count and soon resolve our difference about this?

E: We would certainly do so.

S: Again, if we differed about the larger and the smaller, we would turn to measurement and soon cease to differ.

E: That is so.

S: And about the heavier and the lighter, we would resort to weighing and be reconciled.

E: Of course.

S: What subject of difference would make us angry and hostile to each other if we were unable to come to a decision? Perhaps you do not have an answer ready, but examine as I tell you whether these subjects are the just and the unjust, the beautiful and the ugly, the good and the bad. Are these not the subjects of difference about which, when we are unable to come to satisfactory decision, you and I and other men become hostile to each other whenever we do.

E: That is the difference, Socrates, about those subjects.

S: What about the gods, Euthyphro? If indeed they have differences, will it not be about these same subjects?

E: It certainly must be so.

S: Then according to your argument, my good Euthyphro, different gods consider different things to be just, beautiful, ugly, good and bad, for they would not be at odds with one another unless they differed about these subjects, would they?

E: You are right.

S: And they like what each of them considers beautiful, good, and just, and hate the opposites of these?

E: Certainly.

S: But you say that the same things are considered just by some gods and unjust by others, and as they dispute about these things they are at odds and at war with each other. Is that not so?

E: It is.

S: The same things then are loved by the gods and hated by the gods, both god-loved and god-hated.

E: It seems likely.

S: And the same things would be both pious and impious, according to this argument?

E: I'm afraid so.

S: So you did not answer my question, you surprising man. I did not ask you what same thing is both pious and impious, and it appears that what is loved by the gods is also hated by them. So it is in no way surprising if your present action, namely punishing your father, may be pleasing to Zeus but displeasing to Kronos and Ouranos, pleasing to Hephaestus but displeasing to Hera, and so with any other gods who differ from each other on this subject.

E: I think, Socrates, that on this subject no gods would differ from one another, that whoever has killed anyone unjustly should pay the penalty.

S: Well now, Euthyphro, have you ever heard any man maintaining that one who has killed or done anything else unjustly should not pay the penalty?

E: They never cease to dispute on this subject, both elsewhere and in the courts, for when they have committed many wrongs they do and say anything to avoid the penalty.

S: Do they agree they have done wrong, Euthyphro, and in spite of so agreeing do they nevertheless say they should not be punished?

E: No, they do not agree on that point.

S: So they do not say or do anything. For they do not venture to say this, or dispute that they must not pay the penalty if they have done wrong, but I think they deny doing wrong. Is that not so?

E: That is true.

S: Then they do not dispute that the wrongdoer must be punished, but they may disagree as to who the wrongdoer is, what he did and when.

E: You are right.

S: Do not the gods have the same experience, if indeed they are at odds with each other about the just and the unjust, as your argument maintains? Some assert that they wrong one another, while others deny it, but no one among gods or men ventures to say that the wrongdoer must not be punished.

E: Yes, that is true, Socrates, as to the main point.

S: And those who disagree, whether men or gods, dispute about each action, if indeed the gods disagree. Some say it is done justly, others unjustly. Is that not so?

E: Yes indeed.

S: Come now, my dear Euthyphro, tell me, too, that I may become wiser, what proof you have that all the gods consider that man to have been killed unjustly who became a murderer while in your service, was bound by the master of his victim, and died in his bonds before the one who bound him found out from the seers what was to be done with him, and that it is right for a son to denounce and to prosecute his father on behalf of such a man. Come, try to show me a clear sign that all the gods definitely believe this action to be right. If you can give me adequate proof of this, I shall never cease to extol your wisdom.

E: This is perhaps no light task, Socrates, though I could show you very clearly.

S: I understand that you think me more dull-witted than the jury, as you will obviously show them that these actions were unjust and that all the gods hate such actions.

E: I will show it to them clearly, Socrates, if only they will listen to me.

S: They will listen if they think you show them well. But this thought came to me as I was speaking, and I am examining it, saying to myself: "If Euthyphro shows me conclusively that all the gods consider such a death unjust, to what greater extent have I learned from him the nature of piety and impiety? This action would then, it seems, be hated by the gods, but the pious and the impious were not thereby now defined, for what is hated by the gods has also been shown to be loved by them." So I will not insist on this point; let us assume, if you wish, that all the gods consider this unjust and that they all hate it. However, is this the correction we are making in our discussion, that what all the gods hate is impious, and what they all love is pious, and that what some gods love and others hate is neither or both? Is that how you now wish us to define piety and impiety?

E: What prevents us from doing so, Socrates?

S: For my part nothing, Euthyphro, but you look whether on your part this proposal will enable you to teach me most easily what you promised.

E: I would certainly say that the pious is what all the gods love, and the opposite, which all the gods hate, is the impious.

S: Then let us again examine whether that is a sound statement, or do we let it pass, and if one of us, or someone else, merely says that this is so, do we accept that it is so? Or should we examine what the speaker means?

E: We must examine it, but I certainly think that this is now a fine statement.

S: We shall soon know better whether it is. Consider this: Is the pious loved by the gods because it is pious, or is it pious because it is loved by the gods?

E: I don't know what you mean, Socrates.

S: I shall try to explain more clearly; we speak of something being carried [4] and something carrying, of something being led and something leading, of something being seen and something seeing, and you understand that these things are all different from one another and how they differ?

E: I think I do.

S: So there is something being loved and something loving, and the loving is a different thing.

E: Of course.

S: Tell me then whether that which it is (said to be) being carried is being carried because someone carries it or for some other reason.

E: No, that is the reason.

S: And that which is being led is so because someone leads it, and that which is being seen because someone sees it?

E: Certainly.

S: It is not seen by someone because it is being seen but on the contrary it is being seen because someone sees it, nor is it because it is being led that

[4] This is the present participle form of the verb *pheromenon,* literally *being-carried.* The following passage is somewhat obscure, especially in translation, but the general meaning is clear. Plato points out that this participle simply indicates the object of an action of carrying, seeing, loving, etc. It follows from the action and adds nothing new, the action being prior to it, not following from it, and a thing is said to be loved because someone loves it, not vice versa. To say therefore that the pious is being loved by the gods says no more than that the gods love it. Euthyphro, however, also agrees that the pious is loved by the gods because of its nature (because it is pious), but the fact of its being loved by the gods does not define that nature, and as a definition is therefore unsatisfactory. It only indicates a quality or affect of the pious, and the pious is therefore still to be defined.

someone leads it but because someone leads it that it is being led; it is not because it is being seen that someone sees it, but it is being seen because someone sees it; nor does someone carry an object because it is being carried, but it is being carried because someone carries it. Is what I want to say clear, Euthyphro? I want to say this, namely, that if anything comes to be, or is affected, it does not come to be because it is coming to be, but it is coming to be because it comes to be; nor is it affected because it is being affected but because something affects it. Or do you not agree?

E: I do.

S: What is being loved is either something that comes to be or something that is affected by something?

E: Certainly.

S: So it is in the same case as the things just mentioned; it is not loved by those who love it because it is being loved, but it is being loved because they love it?

E: Necessarily.

S: What then do we say about the pious, Euthyphro? Surely that it is loved by all the gods, according to what you say?

E: Yes.

S: It is loved because it is pious, or for some other reason?

E: For no other reason.

S: It is loved then because it is pious, but it is not pious because it is loved? [5]

E: Apparently.

S: And because it is loved by the gods it is being loved and is dear to the gods?

E: Of course.

S: The god-beloved is then not the same as the pious, Euthyphro, nor the pious the same as the god-beloved, as you say it is, but one differs from the other.

E: How so, Socrates?

S: Because we agree that the pious is beloved for the reason that it is pious, but it is not pious because it is loved. Is that not so?

E: Yes.

S: And that the god-beloved, on the other hand, is so because it is loved

[5] I quote an earlier comment of mine on this passage: ". . . it gives in a nutshell a point of view from which Plato never departed. Whatever the gods may be, they must by their very nature love the right because it is right." They have no choice in the matter. "This separation of the dynamic power of the gods from the ultimate reality, this setting up of absolute values above the gods themselves was not as unnatural to a Greek as it would be to us. . . . The gods who ruled on Olympus . . . were not creators but created beings. As in Homer, Zeus must obey the balance of Necessity, so the Platonic gods must conform to an eternal scale of values. They did not create them, cannot alter them, cannot indeed wish to do so." (*Plato's Thought*, Boston, Beacon Press, 1958, pp. 152-3.)

by the gods, by the very fact of being loved, but it is not loved because it is god-beloved.

E: True.

S: But if the god-beloved and the pious were the same, my dear Euthyphro, and the pious were loved because it was pious, then the god-beloved would be loved because it was god-beloved, and if the god-beloved was god-beloved because it was loved by the gods, then the pious would also be pious because it was loved by the gods; but now you see that they are in opposite cases as being altogether different from each other: the one is of a nature to be loved because it is loved, the other is loved because it is of a nature to be loved. I'm afraid, Euthyphro, that when you were asked what piety is, you did not wish to make its nature clear to me, but you told me an affect or quality of it, that the pious has the quality of being loved by all the gods, but you have not yet told me what the pious is. Now, if you will, do not hide things from me but tell me again from the beginning what piety is, whether loved by the gods or having some other quality —we shall not quarrel about that—but be keen to tell me what the pious and the impious are.

E: But Socrates, I have no way of telling you what I have in mind, for whatever proposition we put forward goes around and refuses to stay put where we establish it.

S: Your statements, Euthyphro, seem to belong to my ancestor, Daedalus. If I were stating them and putting them forward, you would perhaps be making fun of me and say that because of my kinship with him my conclusions in discussion run away and will not stay where one puts them. As these propositions are yours, however, we need some other jest, for they will not stay put for you, as you say yourself.

E: I think the same jest will do for our discussion, Socrates, for I am not the one who makes them go round and not remain in the same place; it is you who are the Daedalus; for as far as I am concerned they would remain as they were.

S: It looks as if I was cleverer than Daedalus in using my skill, my friend, in so far as he could only cause to move the things he made himself, but I can make other people's move as well as my own. And the smartest part of my skill is that I am clever without wanting to be, for I would rather have my arguments remain unmoved than possess the wealth of Tantalus as well as the cleverness of Daedalus. But enough of this. Since I think you are making unnecessary difficulties, I am as eager as you are to find a way to teach me about piety, and do not give up before you do. See whether you think all that is pious is of necessity just.

E: I think so.

S: And is then all that is just pious? Or is all that is pious just, but not all that is just pious, but some of it is and some is not?

E: I do not follow what you are saying, Socrates.

S: Yet you are younger than I by as much as you are wiser. As I say, you are making difficulties because of your wealth of wisdom. Pull yourself together, my dear sir, what I am saying is not difficult to grasp. I am saying the opposite of what the poet said who wrote:

You do not wish to name Zeus, who had done it, and who made all things grow, for where there is fear there is also shame.

I disagree with the poet. Shall I tell you why?

E: Please do.

S: I do not think that "where there is fear there is also shame," for I think that many people who fear disease and poverty and many other such things feel fear, but are not ashamed of the things they fear. Do you not think so?

E: I do indeed.

S: But where there is shame there is also fear. Does anyone feel shame at something who is not also afraid at the same time of a reputation for wickedness?

E: He is certainly afraid.

S: It is then not right to say "where there is fear there is also shame," but that where there is shame there is also fear, for fear covers a larger area than shame. Shame is a part of fear just as odd is a part of number, with the result that it is not true that where there is number there is also oddness, but that where there is oddness there is also number. Do you follow me now?

E: Surely.

S: This is the kind of thing I was asking before, whether where there is piety there is also justice, but where there is justice there is not always piety, for the pious is a part of justice. Shall we say that, or do you think otherwise?

E: No, but like that, for what you say appears to be right.

S: See what comes next; if the pious is a part of the just, we must, it seems, find out what part of the just it is. Now if you asked me something of what we mentioned just now, such as what part of number is the even, and what number that is, I would say it is the number that is divisible into two equal, not unequal, parts. Or do you not think so?

E: I do.

S: Try in this way to tell me what part of the just the pious is, in order to tell Meletus not to wrong us any more and not to indict me for ungodliness, since I have learned from you sufficiently what is godly and pious and what is not.

E: I think, Socrates, that the godly and pious is the part of the just that is concerned with the care of the gods, while that concerned with the care of men is the remaining part of justice.

S: You seem to me to put that very well, but I still need a bit of information. I do not know yet what you mean by care, for you do not mean it in the same sense as the care of other things, as, for example, not everyone knows how to care for horses, but the horse breeder does.

E: Yes, I do mean it that way.

S: So horse breeding is the care of horses.

E: Yes.

S: Nor does everyone know how to care for dogs, but the hunter does.

E: That is so.

S: So hunting is the care of dogs.

E: Yes.

S: And cattle raising is the care of cattle.

E: Quite so.

S: While piety and godliness is the care of the gods, Euthyphro. Is that what you mean?

E: It is.

S: Now care in each case has the same effect; it aims at the good and the benefit of the object cared for, as you can see that horses cared for by horse breeders are benefited and become better. Or do you not think so?

E: I do.

S: So dogs are benefited by dog breeding, cattle by cattle raising, and so with all the others. Or do you think that care aims to harm the object of its care?

E: By Zeus, no.

S: It aims to benefit the object of its care.

E: Of course.

S: Is piety then, which is the care of the gods, also to benefit the gods and make them better? Would you agree that when you do something pious you make someone of the gods better?

E: By Zeus, no.

S: Nor do I think that this is what you mean—far from it—but that is why I asked you what you meant by the care of gods, because I did not believe you meant this kind of care.

E: Quite right, Socrates, that is not the kind of care I mean.

S: Very well, but what kind of care of the gods would piety be?

E: The kind of care, Socrates, that slaves take of their masters.

S: I understand. It is likely to be the service of the gods.

E: Quite so.

S: Could you tell me to the achievement of what goal service to doctors tends? Is it not, do you think, to achieving health?

E: I think so.

S: What about service to shipbuilders? To what achievement is it directed?

E: Clearly, Socrates, to the building of a ship.

S: And service to housebuilders to the building of a house?

E: Yes.

S: Tell me then, my good sir, to the achievement of what aim does service to the gods tend? You obviously know since you say that you, of all men, have the best knowledge of the divine.

E: And I am telling the truth, Socrates.

S: Tell me then, by Zeus, what is that excellent aim that the gods achieve, using us as their servants?

E: Many fine things, Socrates.

S: So do generals, my friend. Nevertheless you could tell me their main concern, which is to achieve victory in war, is it not?

E: Of course.

S: The farmers too, I think, achieve many fine things, but the main point of their efforts is to produce food from the earth.

E: Quite so.

S: Well then, how would you sum up the many fine things that the gods achieve?

E: I told you a short while ago, Socrates, that it is a considerable task to acquire any precise knowledge of these things, but, to put it simply, I say that if a man knows how to say and do what is pleasing to the gods at prayer and sacrifice, those are pious actions such as preserve both private houses and public affairs of state. The opposite of these pleasing actions are impious and overturn and destroy everything.

S: You could tell me in far fewer words, if you were willing, the sum of what I asked, Euthyphro, but you are not keen to teach me, that is clear. You were on the point of doing so, but you turned away. If you had given that answer, I should now have acquired from you sufficient knowledge of the nature of piety. As it is, the lover of inquiry must follow it wherever it may lead him. Once more then, what do you say that piety and the pious are, and also impiety? Are they a knowledge of how to sacrifice and pray?

E: They are.

S: To sacrifice is to make a gift to the gods, whereas to pray is to beg from the gods?

E: Definitely, Socrates.

S: It would follow from this statement that piety would be a knowledge of how to give to, and beg from, the gods.

E: You understood what I said very well, Socrates.

S: That is because I am so desirous of your wisdom, and I concentrate my mind on it, so that no word of yours may fall to the ground. But tell me, what is this service to the gods? You say it is to beg from them and to give to them?

E: I do.

S: And to beg correctly would be to ask from them things that we need?

E: What else?

S: And to give correctly is to give them what they need from us, for it would not be skillful to bring gifts to anyone that are in no way needed.

E: True, Socrates.

S: Piety would then be a sort of trading skill between gods and men?

E: Trading yes, if you prefer to call it that.

S: I prefer nothing, unless it is true. But tell me, what benefit do the gods derive from the gifts they receive from us? What they give us is obvious to all. There is for us no good that we do not receive from them, but how are they benefited by what they receive from us? Or do we have such an advantage over them in the trade that we receive all our blessings from them and they receive nothing from us?

E: Do you suppose, Socrates, that the gods are benefited by what they receive from us?

S: What could those gifts from us to the gods be, Euthyphro?

E: What else, you think, than honour, reverence, and what I mentioned before, gratitude.

S: The pious is then, Euthyphro, pleasing to the gods, but not beneficial or dear to them?

E: I think it is of all things most dear to them.

S: So the pious is once again what is dear to the gods.

E: Most certainly.

S: When you say this, will you be surprised if your arguments seem to move about instead of staying put? And will you accuse me of being Daedalus who makes them move, though you are yourself much more skillful than Daedalus and make them go round in a circle? Or do you not realize that our argument has moved around and come once again to the same place? You surely remember that earlier the pious and the god-beloved were shown not to be the same but different from each other. Or do you not remember?

E: I do.

S: Do you then not realize that when you say now that that what is dear to the gods is the pious? Is this not the same as the god-beloved? Or is it not?

E: It certainly is.

S: Either we were wrong when we agreed before, or, if we were right then, we are wrong now.

E: That seems to be so.

S: So we must investigate again from the beginning what piety is, as I shall not willingly give up before I learn this. Do not think me unworthy, but concentrate your attention and tell the truth. For you know it, if any man does, and I must not let you go, like Proteus, before you tell me. If you had no clear knowledge of piety and impiety you would never have ventured to prosecute your old father for murder on behalf of a servant. For fear of the gods you would have been afraid to take the risk lest you should not be acting rightly, and would have been ashamed before me, but now I know well that you believe you have clear knowledge of piety and impiety. So tell me, my good Euthyphro, and do not hide what you believe.

E: Some other time, Socrates, for I am in a hurry now, and it is time for me to go.

S: What a thing to do, my friend! By going you have cast me down from a great hope I had, that I would learn from you the nature of the pious and the impious and so escape Meletus' indictment by showing that I had acquired wisdom in divine matters from Euthyphro, and my ignorance would no longer cause me to be careless and inventive about such things, and that I would be better for the rest of my life.

JONATHAN HARRISON
God's Commands and Man's Duties

When we consider the relation between God's commands and man's duties, it seems to be a fairly good rough approximation to the truth to say that there are three possible views about the nature of this relation. In the *first* place, it is possible to say that God, since he is omniscient, always knows what is right and wrong, and, since he is perfectly good, always commands us to do what is right and prohibits us from doing what is wrong; he is pleased with us when we obey his commands, and do what is right, and displeased with us when we disobey his commands, and do what is wrong.[1] On this view, God's will is determined by his knowledge of right and wrong. *Secondly,* it is possible to say that what makes right actions right and what makes wrong actions wrong is that God has commanded the right actions and prohibited the wrong ones, and that being commanded by God is the *only* thing which makes an action right and being prohibited by God is the *only* thing which makes an action wrong. On this view, it is impossible for God, in commanding some actions and prohibiting others, to be guided by the fact that the actions he commands are right and the actions he prohibits are wrong, because, before he has commanded them, no actions are right, and before he has prohibited them, no actions are wrong. The *third* possible view is that there are not two pairs of different facts, being commanded by God and being right, and being prohibited by God and being wrong: to say that an action is right just *means* that it is commanded by God, and to say that an action is wrong just *means* that it is prohibited by God. Hence it is impossible to raise the question, which the first view answered in one way and the second view in another, whether it is the fact that an action is right that causes God to command it or whether, conversely it is the fact that an action is commanded by God that makes it right. On the third view there are not two different facts, being commanded by God and being right, such that we can ask whether the first is dependent upon the second or whether the second is dependent upon the first. There is just one single fact, which may be put indifferently by saying either that God has commanded something or that it is right.

From Jonathan Harrison, *Our Knowledge of Right and Wrong* (1971). Reprinted by permission of the author and George Allen & Unwin Ltd., London. Footnotes edited.
[1] This appears to have been the view of Aquinas and Bishop Butler.

Which of these three theories one holds does not necessarily make any difference to what one thinks is right and wrong. It is perfectly possible, for example, for theologians who hold each of these three theories to agree that it is right for us to love one another, but the first kind of theologian will think that, though loving actions are both right and commanded by God, they are commanded by God because they are right. The second kind of theologian will think that though loving actions are both commanded by God and right, they are right because God has commanded them. The third theologian will think that, though it is true to say of loving actions that they are commanded by God and true to say of them that they are right, to say these things is not to make two different statements about loving actions, but to make one and the same statement in two different ways.

However, though which of these three theories one holds *need* not make any difference to what actions one actually thinks are right and wrong, there is one possible circumstance in which it *will* make a very great deal of difference. If there is no God, then, if you accept the second theory, that only what God commands is right, you are logically bound to say that there are no right and wrong actions, for, according to your theory, only one thing can make an action right, namely, that God commands it, and, if there is no God, nothing can be commanded by him. If you hold the third theory, and think that to say that an action is right just *means* that God has commanded it and that to say that an action is wrong just *means* that God has prohibited it, you will also, if you think that there is no God, be logically committed to holding that nothing is right and nothing is wrong, for, of course, if there is no God there will be no actions which God commands and no actions which he prohibits. If, however, you hold the first theory, it is possible for you to think both that there is no God and also to think that some actions are right and others wrong. Since, on this view, actions are right for some reason other than that God commands them—though God does command or prohibit them in fact—it is possible for actions which are right to go on being right, even if there is no God.

The three theories, though they need not make any difference to one's views about what actions are right and wrong, are nevertheless very different kinds of theory. One might describe the first as a sort of *psychological* theory about God's policy of action. It states that it is God's policy, in directing the behaviour of his creatures, always to command right actions and to prohibit wrong ones. The second theory is not a psychological theory about what makes God command some actions and prohibit others. It says nothing about what causes God to command a certain class of action, but simply says that, if God does command any class of action, it is right for us to perform actions of this class. Hence it is a theory not about God's policy of action, but a *moral* theory about what makes right actions right. The third theory says nothing about what makes actions right or wrong, nor anything about what makes God command some actions and prohibit others. It is simply a *linguistic* theory about the meanings of the words 'right' and 'wrong.' It says that the word 'right' simply means 'commanded by God,' and that the word 'wrong' simply means 'prohibited by God.' Hence these three theories, though they do not necessarily—while they may—make any difference to one's views about what actions are right and what actions are wrong, are theories of very different kinds. . . . Odd though it may seem, there is even no logical connection between which of these three views one holds and whether one believes that there actually is a God or not, though perhaps the first of the three is the most *natural* view for an atheist or an agnostic, since it is the only one of the three which can be adopted by someone who both wants to hold that some things are right and wrong and at the same time wants to hold that there is no God—and most atheists and agnostics do appear to wish to hold that some things are right and others wrong. One can hold the second view or the third and at the same time believe that there is not a God, provided, of course, one is prepared to embrace the logical conclusion that, in that event, nothing is right and nothing is wrong. It is presumably partly extreme reluctance to accept that nothing is right and wrong which has driven most who think that there is no God, or that it cannot be decided whether there is a God or not, to embrace the first of the three views we have distinguished. . . .

Whether one holds the first view or the second, though it may not make any difference to the actions one thinks are right and wrong, does make a difference to whether one thinks that one finds out *first* what God commands, or whether one thinks that one finds out *first* what is right or wrong. If the second view is correct, one must find out first what God commands, and then argue that, since everything God commands is right, this kind of thing, which God is supposed to command, is right. It is not, on the second view, possible to find out what is right or wrong first, without previously having determined whether or not God commands it; hence, on the second view, ignorance of God's commands or of his existence must imply an equal degree of ignorance concerning what actions are right and what wrong.

On the first view it is perfectly possible to argue from an antecedent knowledge of right and wrong as a premise to a conclusion about what God commands or prohibits. We may, on this view, argue that, since it is wrong for us to harm one another, and since God forbids us to perform any action which is wrong, God must forbid us to harm one another, or more accurately, that if he exists at all, he must forbid us to harm one another. That, if God exists (and there is a right and wrong which neither consists in the fact that he commands some things and forbids others, nor is *determined* by the fact that he commands some things and forbids others) he always commands what is right and forbids what is wrong would seem to follow from the fact that God is, by definition, perfectly good. If he sometimes commanded what was wrong or forbade what is right, this would be inconsistent with the way in which we would expect a perfectly good being to behave.

There are difficulties with each of these three views. The first view has difficulty in explaining how, if it is true, God can be omnipotent. If we accept the first view, we must suppose that God's will, and in particular what actions God commands men to perform and what actions he commands them to refrain from performing, is determined by a moral law which is not identical with his commands, as it is on the third view, nor determined by his commands, as it would be on the second view. This seems to imply that the fact that certain things are wrong and other things are right is something over which God has no control. If he could control it, then it would be extremely odd to suppose that his will was subsequently determined by what he had himself brought about. It would be a very extraordinary situation if, though God's will was determined by the moral law, he himself decided what the moral law which determined his actions should be. God's will might just as well not be determined by any law at all, as be determined by a law which he himself decided upon. . . .

The second and third views apparently have no difficulty in accounting for God's omnipotence. On the second view, God, by deciding what actions he will command and what actions he will prohibit, actually decides what the moral law shall be, for whatever he commands becomes right for us, and whatever he prohibits becomes wrong. On the third view, he decides what shall be right for us and what wrong, for the fact that something is right just is the fact that he commands it, and the fact that it is wrong just is the fact that he prohibits it, and, presumably, he commands and prohibits what he pleases.

The difficulty the second and third view have is to explain how God can be good at all, let alone how he can be perfectly good. For one thing, the conclusion, which each of these two views entails, that whatever God were to command would be right for us, even if he commanded homicide, cannibalism or incest, is one which many people find shocking. For another thing, it seems reasonable to ask how, if the second or third views are true, can it even make sense to raise the question whether God is good or not, for, to say that a rational being is good is to say that his will accords with the moral law. God, however, could be neither good nor not good in this sense, for the moral law, on both the second view and the third, is something which he himself lays down or determines; hence his will could not be determined by the moral law, for there simply is no moral law, independent of what he himself decides, to determine it. Though there is nothing immoral in his commanding anything he pleases—for he himself determines what shall and shall not be immoral—many find the idea that God is in that way above morality repulsive.

Quite apart from the fact that there is nothing, however outrageous human beings may find it, which God may not, so far as moral considerations go, do, there is also a logical difficulty involved in saying that God is perfectly good on these two views. For God cannot be perfectly good, in the sense that whatever he does is right, if what he does is not determined by his knowledge of what is right, as it would be on the first of the three views. Indeed, it may be argued that it is even circular to define God as a being who is, among other things, perfectly good, if we also want to say that a being is good if he does what is right, and that he does what is right if he does what God commands. We are, in other words, first defining, or partly defining, God in terms of *goodness,* and then subsequently defining goodness in terms of what is commanded by *God.* . . .

It is possible to combine a variant of the second view with the first if one says that one thing, but not the *only* thing, which makes right actions right is that God has commanded them. Some actions, say Sabbath observance, are right simply because God has commanded them, but other actions, say actions of promise-keeping, are not right simply because God has commanded them, but for some other reason. On this view, being commanded by God is just one of a number of things which make it right for us to do something, but not the only thing which makes right actions right. It is then possible to argue that, since things like promise-keeping and honesty are right, and can be known to be right without its first being known whether or not God commands them, and since God is perfectly good, and will command us to perform actions which are right, he will command us to perform actions like keeping our promises and telling the truth. Since, on this view, being commanded by God is one thing which makes an action right, actions which are right for some reason other than that they are commanded by God now become right for *two* reasons; since they are right for whatever reason, God will command them, and since they are commanded by God, they will also become right because it is also right for us to obey his commands. Since God may also command some actions which are not antecedently right, there are some actions which are right only because God has commanded them; it will be impossible to infer that God has commanded *these* actions from a prior knowledge of the fact that they are right because, where these actions are concerned, they are not right until God has commanded them.

It might even be possible, on this view, to have a conflict of duties, a conflict between our duty to obey God's commands and our duty to perform an action which is right for some reason other than that God has commanded it. One might say that, when God commanded Abraham to sacrifice Isaac, Abraham was faced with a conflict of duties, a duty to preserve human life and to take care of his offspring, and a duty to obey God's commands. It might seem suitably pious to say that, in the event of such a conflict, one's duty to obey God's commands would take precedence over any other duty.

If there were no God, all the actions which were right for some reason other than that they were commanded by God, might still be right, though in this case they would be right for one reason only, instead of two. They would be right for whatever reason made them right in the first place—say that not to have performed them would have caused other people unnecessary suffering—but they would no longer be right because God, who commands us to perform every action that is right, has commanded us to perform them, for God does not exist. Hence, on this view, or combination of views, there will still be some right actions, if God does not exist, though not so many as there would be if God does exist. One will also have motives, if God exists, for doing what is right, which one will not have, if God does not exist. If God exists, one may wish to do what is right not simply because it is right, but to please the God who has commanded it, and possibly also because one believes that ill will befall one in this world or the next as a result of a persistent adherence to wrong-doing. . . .

If there is a God, and he is omnipotent and omniscient, as by definition he is, then everything that happens in the universe, with the possible exception, already mentioned, of the free actions of human beings, must be something which he has intended or has allowed to happen, and has intended or allowed to happen for some reason. Hence, if something that happens is beneficial to mankind, God must have intended it to be so, and if something that happens is harmful to mankind, God must have intended this to be so also. Now, of course, a great deal of what happens in the world is of benefit to mankind; men are usually born with the tendency to develop abilities, in particular their intelligence, which are useful to them; they have been made sociable to quite a high degree, which enables them to augment their power and their productivity by co-operating with one another; in nature there is a not wholly inadequate supply of the raw materials which they need; and man is quite well adapted to the environment in which he lives. All this, on the assumption that there is a God who is responsible for every contingent matter of fact about the world being as it is, points to the fact that God is well-disposed to mankind. On the other hand, much of what happens in the world does not point to a God who is well-disposed to man. Man would be happier and more successful if he were even more intelligent than God has made him, if he were less prone to quarrel with his fellow men, less prone to physical and mental illness and deformity, had a more adequate supply of the commodities he needs, and was better adapted to his environment. Hence, on the assumption that there is a God, an investigation of the natural world would point to the fact that he is reasonably benevolently disposed to mankind, but by no means wholly so, and, moreover, to the fact that he is much more well-disposed to some men than he is to others. To some men, indeed, he would appear to behave in a manner worse than any human malevolence could possibly imagine or contrive.

Many attempts have been made to reconcile the apparent evil and imperfection in the world with God's benevolence, but they have not been very successful. It has been suggested that some evil in the world enhances the goodness of the whole, much as a discord in music may enhance the beauty of the music or an ugly colour in a painting may enhance the beauty of the painting; it may be argued, however, that the dreadful suffering endured by many is too high a price to pay for this aesthetic beauty. It has also been suggested that the appearance of evil in the world may be due to the fact that man, being finite, sees only a small part of the whole, and that, were he to see the whole, he would realize that the evil in the part he does see is a necessary means to some overriding good. But though this *may* be so, that it is so is simply a possibility—and a remote one, at that—which we have no means of testing unless we do view the whole that we cannot see. It has been suggested, too, that the causal laws which govern the universe make evil a necessary concomitant, and sometimes a necessary means, to a greater good. For example, the function of pain is to warn the person who feels it of something that will do him damage, and, though pain could be dispensed with, it would be at the price of endangering the organism which it is the function of pain to preserve. It is argued that even useless pain is still part of that price which mankind, or rather, sentient creatures in general, have to pay for their preservation, for it would be impossible to have the physiological mechanism which causes us to feel pain unless we also felt pain sometimes when it was too late or impossible for us to take the necessary avoiding action. The difficulty with this defence is that one cannot argue that the causal laws which govern the universe make it inevitable that we should experience pain if we are to be warned of danger, when God is himself supposed to have created the universe and made these causal laws what they are, and so must have the power to alter them at will. It has been suggested that man himself brings evil into the world by his own free will, and that the only way God could have prevented this was by creating men without free will; but a man without free will would be a less admirable being than a man with free will; hence evil is the necessary price we have to pay for freedom. The reply to this is obvious. Not all the evil in the world *is* the result of the operation of man's free will. Earthquake, famine and pestilence are not. It might even be argued that God could, if he had wished to do so, have created man both free and good. What we freely choose to do is to an enormous extent dependent upon the physical state of our brain and nervous system. A woman taking therapeutic drugs for mental illness may freely choose to do many things which the same woman not taking drugs will not freely choose to do. Hence if an ordinary doctor, by giving someone drugs or some other form of treatment, can change the pattern of a person's free and voluntary activity for the better, it is difficult to see how God could find it difficult to have made people better than they are, and at the same time free. Hence, even if we concede that there is a God who for some reason or other brings about or permits everything that happens in the universe, it is difficult to see how one can arrive by the unaided use of reason, at the conclusion that he is perfectly benevolent. (If you say, as I have suggested you should, that God is by definition perfectly benevolent, you must then say that it is difficult to see how you can arrive at the conclusion that the being who governs the universe is God.) For all these reasons one cannot, even granted that there is a God, or at least that the universe is ruled by an omnipotent and omniscient being, come to the conclusion that necessarily he commands us to perform those actions which it would be to our good to perform, for a God who will allow suffering might very well command actions which are *not* conducive to the happiness of his creatures.

If one does *not* allow oneself to assume that there *is* a God, it is still more difficult to produce any reason for thinking that God commands men to perform those actions which further their own happiness. In this case, we are not allowed to assume that there is a God, and simply show that he is benevolent; we must show that there is a God, and that he is benevolent. All the difficulties with the first argument, for the benevolence of God on the assumption that he exists, are also difficulties with the second argument, which purports to show that there is a God who is benevolent; and there are more as well. The hypothesis that the world is governed by an unobserved but benevolent God is very unlike the hypothesis that there is an unobserved magnet in my pocket, which is causing a compass needle to behave in an unusual way, or that there is an unobserved planet, the existence of which is modifying the behaviour of other planets, even leaving aside the difficulty that it is in principle possible to observe the magnet and the planet, though they are at the moment unobserved, while it may be argued that God is in principle something which it is impossible to observe. Where the hypotheses that there is an unobserved magnet in my pocket or an unobserved planet in the solar system are concerned, one argues to their existence from an apparent irregularity in the normal course of nature, an irregularity in the behaviour of the compass needle or in the behaviour of other planets, which irregularity can be shown to be only apparent if the magnet or the extra planet are postulated. The argument in fact goes as follows: something which happens appears to go against what we expect from what we know of the laws which govern nature; if however, there were an unobserved magnet or an unobserved planet situated in a certain position in space, we could explain what is happening without abandoning any of the laws which we already accept; hence there is very likely an unobserved magnet or an unobserved planet. In the case of the argument to the existence of a benevolent God, however, there *is* no interruption to the normal laws of nature. The fact that man is intelligent and is adapted to his environment can be perfectly well explained without the hypothesis that there is a God. If we discount, for the sake of simplicity, miracles, which are in any case sporadic, unpredictable and imperfectly attested, the argument to the existence of God takes as its premise not apparent irregularities in the course of nature, but the fact that nature is uniform. There is no need, however, to postulate anything at all to explain the fact that nature is uniform. Indeed, it would be impossible to have any explanation of this. For normally the question 'Why' means 'Why in this case but not in that?' and it is impossible to ask the question 'Why is nature uniform in this case but not in that?'—which question *might* be answered by saying there is a God responsible for the uniformity in this case, though there is not in that—for, where the universe is concerned, the universe is the sum total of everything that there is, and hence there are no other cases. Hence, if we are not allowed to assume that there is a God, it is still more difficult to argue to the existence of a benevolent God who makes laws which it is in man's interest to obey.

Perhaps, however, we are wrong to try to make our argument to the nature of God's laws rest upon his benevolence. Perhaps we should argue, instead, that what God intends is the normal or the 'natural', and that deviations from the normal or 'natural' are contrary to his intentions, and so wrong. Hence suicide is wrong because God must have intended man to live out his normal life-span, unless this is shortened by illness which man has no power to control, and contraception is wrong because this is contrary to the normal or natural manner of having sexual intercourse, and sexual perversion is wrong for the same reason.

There are a number of difficulties with this manner of arguing. For one thing, it is very difficult to find any standard of normality other than what is usual or what happens most, and what happens most is obviously quite often wrong. For another thing, if God is omnipotent and omniscient, then he must have intended everything that happens, and be as much responsible for deviations from the norm as he is for the norm itself; hence we cannot argue that the norm is what he intends, but the deviations are not what he intends. And it is very difficult to argue that it is wrong to interfere with the normal course of nature by committing suicide or using contraceptives while stopping short of arguing that it must also be wrong to interfere with the normal course of nature by curing disease or using artificial fertilizers. In any case, the argument would at most allow us to argue to God's intentions given the assumption that there is a God, not at all to the *existence* of a God.

If we cannot argue to the nature of God's commands for man from a consideration of the nature of the world, perhaps we are able to know about him from what we are told about him in the Bible or in some other holy book. Certainly in the Bible we are told things about God, and what he intends, and what he expects of his creatures. The most serious difficulty is that part of the appeal of the Bible is a moral appeal. Christ, for example, is presented not simply as a man who worked miracles and who claimed to be, or to be in a special relationship to, God. He behaved in certain ways which most people regard with at least qualified approval and enunciated certain moral precepts which commend themselves to many people at least in some degree. But for the appeal of Christ to be a moral appeal, it must be presupposed that we have some standards of right and wrong already, by which Christ's behaviour can be morally assessed. For his precepts to commend themselves to us, we must have some insight into what is right and wrong which is independent of his testimony. I personally have no doubt that, if Christ behaved in ways which we would consider quite reprehensible, and enunciated precepts which most people would regard as being outrageous, the claims which he made on his own behalf and on behalf of the religion which he founded would command no serious attention.

It is true that, given that Christ's behaviour appeals to the standards of morality we already have, and given that many of his moral precepts commend themselves to the degree of moral enlightenment we possess at the moment, we may well be prepared to accept some *other* of his precepts simply on his authority, that is, on the authority of someone who has already shown himself to possess moral insight and to be in practice good. But such precepts would supplement the knowledge of right and wrong we already possess, rather than be the sole means of our having any knowledge of right and wrong. Hence the view that we acquire all our knowledge of right and wrong—that is, on the view that 'right' simply means 'commanded by God', all our knowledge of God's commands—upon the authority of some divine being, revealed in some divine book, must be rejected.

In any case, . . . all knowledge based upon testimony presupposes knowledge not based upon testimony. We may know that there are black swans in Australia or that Pythagoras's theorem is true because we have been told, and the person who told us may himself have been told by yet another person, but the chain of testimony must end at some point by someone's having observed the black swans in Australia, or worked out Pythagoras's theorem, for himself. Hence, though we may believe things about God's commands or man's duties on the authority of some holy person or book, there still remains the question how this holy person or the men who wrote the holy book themselves came to know what they claim to know.

Many people believe that our consciences provide a way of knowing what it is that God commands us to perform, and what kind of thing he wishes us to do. I believe that, for many people, conscience presents itself as of divine authority. These people, when they have a guilty conscience, feel as if God is actively displeased with their conduct, and, when they have a clear conscience, feel as if he is not displeased or is positively approving of them. Hence they imagine, if this is not too question-begging a word, their conduct to be under the perpetual review of a being who demands that they do what he enjoins, and that they refrain from doing what he prohibits. I doubt, however, whether conscience does provide us with any means of knowing what God's wishes for us are. For one thing, I do not think it is a universal phenomenon that conscience presents itself as the voice of God. Many who do not even believe in God have a conscience which demands that they behave in some ways and refrain from behaving in others.

For another thing, it is unclear whether conscience is supposed to provide us with a means of inferring what God's commands are, or whether it provides us with some form of direct acquaintance with the wishes of the divinity. If it were to provide us with a means of inferring the commands of the divinity, the argument would, again, have either to be one which rested *upon the assumption* that there is a God who causes us to feel guilty or self-approving in the way we do, and to have the conscientious scruples we do have, or it must itself provide us with a reason for thinking that there *is* a God who causes our consciences to operate as it does. The latter argument would only be plausible if the operations of conscience could not be explained in any other way, but these operations can already be partially explained as being a reaction to the pressures of our environment and the demands made upon us by our community, and it seems quite possible that psychologists will be able to produce a full explanation of the working of conscience in the course of time. And the argument that, *if* there is a God, he must intend us to refrain from performing those actions which are such that they would cause us to have an uneasy conscience if we did perform them is highly precarious. Conscience is moulded by social influences which often seem to have little to do with divine action, and is highly fallible, both because the person who possesses the conscience is mistaken about or ignorant of relevant matters of fact, and also because it appears to enjoin at one time things which we subsequently reject as being wrong. God, if he is omnipotent and omniscient, must be responsible for the deliverances of our conscience when these err just as much as when they do not err.

Perhaps, however, it is not so much a case of arguing to the existence of God, using facts about our consciences as premises, as that, through our consciences, we are brought into some form of direct contact with the divine will, and hence know what he commands not by inference but by something more like direct acquaintance with his commands. It is certainly true that, in many people, though not in all, conscience does present itself as if it were a form of immediate awareness, as if we did not need to infer, from the deliverances of conscience, what God's commands are, but knew them in some more intimate, less discursive way. If this were so, it is important to realize how very different would be our awareness of God's commands from our knowledge of the commands of our human superiors. Where these latter are concerned, we hear words, the meaning of which we understand, and which we believe to emanate from the bodies of the people who are commanding us, which bodies we suppose to be animated by minds, whatever being animated by a mind consists of. Hence we are not directly aware of some entity called a command; what we are directly aware of is a noise, or possibly ink marks on paper, and we infer from the occurrence of the noise or the ink marks that there is some being with a mind like ours who is doing what we are doing when we ourselves command others. In the case of our alleged *acquaintance* with God's commands, however, there can be no question of written marks being made on paper by some divine being, or of sound waves emanating from his vocal chords. We must, if we are aware of his commands at all, and especially if this awareness is supposed not to involve our making any inference, be directly aware of the commands without the intermediary of ink marks on paper producing light waves which modify the retina of our eyes or of noises produced by sound waves affecting our ears.

Personally I find it very difficult to conceive of what such an awareness, the awareness of a command of some being, which does not consist in the first instance of an awareness of symbols the meaning of which we understand, could possibly be. It is true that I am familiar with the experience of imagining myself disapproved of by some superhuman being, as I am with the experience of imagining myself disapproved of by other human beings, but *imagining* oneself disapproved of, even if it is accompanied by a tendency to believe that one actually is disapproved of, is a very different matter from being aware, in some unusual way, of the disapproval which these other beings are supposed to feel.

It is often the case that people who believe that there is some intimate connection between God's commands and man's duties hold their moral opinions with much greater firmness, a firmness which in some cases amounts to an intolerant dogmatism, than people who believe that moral beliefs are not beliefs about God's commands, whether or not these latter people also believe that there is a God who commands them to perform actions which they think are right. I cannot personally see any reason why the belief that actions are right because they are commanded by God, or the belief that 'right' simply means 'commanded by God' should by itself produce dogmatism or intolerance, but there is a reason why the belief that one arrives at least at some of one's moral tenets upon God's *authority* should produce such dogmatism. The reason, I think, is this. An omniscient being can scarcely be supposed to be mistaken about what is right and wrong; hence, if we are told that something is right upon the authority of an omniscient being, it is natural to suppose that we ourselves cannot be mistaken about this thing's being right. Though this is natural, however, it is mistaken. Though God's 'beliefs' may be superhuman and infallible, our beliefs, even when they are beliefs which we think that God has revealed to us, are all human and fallible. Hence, though God may know that adultery is wrong, and may have told us that adultery is wrong, it does not follow that we ourselves know that adultery is wrong, and it does not follow, therefore, that we are justified in maintaining that adultery is wrong with supreme confidence. For our belief that adultery is wrong, if we believe this because we believe God has revealed it to us, can be no better warranted than our belief that God *has* revealed it to us, and this belief is simply a human fallible belief of ours. We may feel that God has not only revealed to us that adultery is wrong, but has also revealed to us the fact that he has revealed to us that adultery is wrong, and hence that our belief that God has revealed to us that adultery is wrong has a divine backing which justifies us in holding it with a confidence which we would not have in it if we thought it was merely a human belief of our own; but this, again, is a mistake. To argue that we know that God has revealed some fact to us because God has revealed to us the fact that he has revealed this fact would be rather like the notorious argument that God exists because this is revealed in the Bible, which must be infallible, because it is the word of God. Any doubt about whether God has revealed something must imply a like doubt about whether he has revealed to us that he has revealed this: If God does not exist, for example, not only can he not have revealed to us that adultery is wrong; he also cannot have revealed to us that he has revealed that adultery is wrong. In any case, it is a peculiar kind of revelation which requires another and prior revelation of the fact that it is revelation. . . .

In the foregoing argument in this chapter I have spoken as if God were, though not actually part of the furniture of the world, at least like a piece of furniture, though, perhaps, a piece of transcendent furniture, transcendent because lying outside space and outside time. God, though transcendent, is treated as an actual entity, and the possessor of attributes (human or quasi-human attributes) and a list of everything there was that left out God would to that extent be incomplete. This perhaps simple-minded view of the divinity is now considered old-fashioned by many philosophers of religion, if not by ordinary people or even by philosophers of religion when they turn from speculation to actual devotion. If we reject it, the sentence 'God exists', which by almost everyone until quite recently had been supposed to be used to assert that, among or transcending the furniture of the universe there was an actual entity, answering to a certain description, must be considered to be used for doing something different, for example, for expressing one's intention to lead a certain kind of life.[2]

If God is not an actually existing entity, then he cannot be an actually existing entity of the sort which issues commands, and hence the question of the relation between God's commands and man's duties cannot arise. The most we can do is to *believe* we have duties, and think that faith in God, in a sense which does not involve believing that the proposition that he exists is true, manifests itself in their performance. Perhaps all that having faith in God consists of is doing one's duty, or in doing one's duty and at the same time telling oneself certain stories, stories to the effect that one is being watched over by a loving God, who is pained by one's transgressions and delighted by one's good actions; stories, however, which one is not expected to *believe*, though one may *pretend* that they are true if one finds this encouraging.

For myself, however, I find it difficult to believe that, when one says that God exists, one is not asserting the existence of a being who actually has the attributes of being omnipotent, omniscient and benevolent. Faith itself may not consist in *believing* that such a being exists, so much as assiduously and perserveringly acting as if there were such a being, and certainly this is the most, if it is not too much, that could be required of one as a duty; nevertheless, when one asserts that God exists, one is actually asserting the proposition that there is in the universe or 'beyond' it an actual being who possesses certain characteristics. It is very difficult to make sense of the religious attitude if all possibility of such an assertion's being a genuine proposition, and so of being true, is removed.

[2] See R. B. Braithwaite, *An Empiricist's View of the Nature of Religious Belief* (Cambridge University Press, 1955).

ROBERT MERRIHEW ADAMS

A Modified Divine Command Theory of Ethical Wrongness

I

It is widely held that all those theories are indefensible which attempt to explain in terms of the will or commands of God what it is for an act to be ethically right or wrong. In this paper I shall state such a theory, which I believe to be defensible; and I shall try to defend it against what seem to me to be the most important and interesting objections to it. I call my theory a *modified* divine command theory because in it I renounce certain claims that are commonly made in divine command analyses of ethical terms. (I should add that it is *my* theory only in that I shall state it, and that I believe it is defensible—not that I am sure it is correct.) I present it as a theory of ethical *wrongness* partly for convenience. It could also be presented as a theory of the nature of ethical obligatoriness or of ethical permittedness. Indeed, I will have occasion to make some remarks about the concept of ethical permittedness. But as we shall see (in Section IV) I am not prepared to claim that the theory can be extended to all ethical terms; and it is therefore important that it not be presented as a theory about ethical terms in general.

It will be helpful to begin with the statement of a simple, *un*-modified divine command theory of ethical wrongness. This is the theory that ethical wrongness *consists in* being contrary to God's commands, or that the word "wrong" in ethical contexts *means* "contrary to God's commands." It implies that the following two statement forms are logically equivalent.

(1) It is wrong (for A) to do X.
(2) It is contrary to God's commands (for A) to do X.

Of course that is not all that the theory implies. It also implies that (2) is conceptually prior to (1), so that the meaning of (1) is to be explained in terms of (2), and not the other way round. It might prove fairly difficult to state or

This is a major part of the essay, "A Modified Divine Command Theory of Ethical Wrongness," by Robert Merrihew Adams. From *Religion and Morality: A Collection of Essays,* edited by Gene Outka and John P. Reeder, Jr., copyright © 1973 by Gene Outka and John P. Reeder, Jr. Reprinted by permission of the author, the editors, and Doubleday & Company, Inc. Footnotes edited.

explain in what that conceptual priority consists, but I shall not go into that here. I do not wish ultimately to defend the theory in its unmodified form, and I think I have stated it fully enough for my present purposes.

I have stated it as a theory about the meaning of the word "wrong" in ethical contexts. The most obvious objection to the theory is that the word "wrong" is used in ethical contexts by many people who cannot mean by it what the theory says they must mean, since they do not believe that there exists a God. This objection seems to me sufficient to refute the theory if it is presented as an analysis of what *everybody* means by "wrong" in ethical contexts. The theory cannot reasonably be offered except as a theory about what the word "wrong" means as used by *some but not all* people in ethical contexts. Let us say that the theory offers an analysis of the meaning of "wrong" in Judeo-Christian religious ethical discourse. This restriction of scope will apply to my modified divine command theory too. This restriction obviously gives rise to a possible objection. Isn't it more plausible to suppose that Judeo-Christian believers use "wrong" with the same meaning as other people do? This problem will be discussed in Section VI. . . .

II

The following seems to me to be the gravest objection to the divine command theory of ethical wrongness, in the form in which I have stated it. Suppose God should command me to make it my chief end in life to inflict suffering on other human beings, for no other reason than that He commanded it. (For convenience I shall abbreviate this hypothesis to "Suppose God should command cruelty for its own sake.") Will it seriously be claimed that in that case it would be wrong for me not to practice cruelty for its own sake? I see three possible answers to this question.

(1) It might be claimed that it is logically impossible for God to command cruelty for its own sake. In that case, of course, we need not worry about whether it would be wrong to disobey if He did command it. It is senseless to agonize about what one should do in a logically impossible situation. This solution to the problem seems unlikely to be available to the divine command theorist, however. For why would he hold that it is logically impossible for God to command cruelty for its own sake? Some theologians (for instance, Thomas Aquinas) have believed (a) that what is right and wrong is independent of God's will, *and* (b) that God always does right by the necessity of His nature. Such theologians, if they believe that it would be wrong for God to command cruelty for its own sake, have reason to believe that it is logically impossible for Him to do so. But the divine command theorist, who does not agree that what is right and wrong is independent of God's will, does not seem to have such a reason to deny that it is logically possible for God to command cruelty for its own sake.

(2) Let us assume that it is logically possible for God to command cruelty for its own sake. In that case the divine command theory seems to imply that it would be wrong not to practice cruelty for its own sake. There have been at least a few adherents of divine command ethics who have been prepared to accept this consequence. William Ockham held that those acts which we call "theft," "adultery," and "hatred of God" would be meritorious if God had commanded them. He would surely have said the same about what I have been calling the practice of "cruelty for its own sake."

This position is one which I suspect most of us are likely to find somewhat shocking, even repulsive. We should therefore be particularly careful not to misunderstand it. We need not imagine that Ockham disciplined himself to be ready to practice cruelty for its own sake if God should command it. It was doubtless an article of faith for him that God is unalterably opposed to any such practice. The mere logical possibility that theft, adultery, and cruelty might have been commanded by God (and therefore meritorious) doubtless did not represent in Ockham's view any real possibility.

(3) Nonetheless, the view that if God commanded cruelty for its own sake it would be wrong not to practice it seems unacceptable to me; and I think many, perhaps most, other Jewish and Christian believers would find it unacceptable too. I must make clear the sense in which I find it unsatisfactory. It is not that I find an internal inconsistency in it. And I would not deny that it may reflect, accurately enough, the way in which some believers use the word "wrong." I might as well frankly avow that I am looking for a divine command theory which at least might possibly be a correct account of how *I* use the word "wrong." I do not use the word "wrong" in such a way that I would say that it would be wrong not to practice cruelty if God commanded it, and I am sure that many other believers agree with me on this point.

But now have I not rejected the divine command theory? I have assumed that it would be logically possible for God to command cruelty for its own sake. And I have rejected the view that if God commanded cruelty for its own sake, it would be wrong not to obey. It seems to follow that I am committed to the view that in certain logically possible circumstances it would not be wrong to disobey God. This position seems to be inconsistent with the theory that "wrong" means "contrary to God's commands."

I want to argue, however, that it is still open to me to accept a modified form of the divine command theory of ethical wrongness. According to the modified divine command theory, when I say, "It is wrong to do X," (at least part of) what I *mean* is that it is contrary to God's commands to do X. "It is wrong to do X" *implies* "It is contrary to God's commands to do X." But "It is contrary to God's commands to do X" implies "It is wrong to do X" only if certain conditions are assumed—namely, only if it is assumed that God has the character which I believe Him to have, of loving His human creatures. If God were really to command us to make cruelty our goal, then He would not have that character of loving us, and I would not say it would be wrong to disobey Him.

But do I say that it would be wrong to obey Him in such a case? This is the point at which I am in danger of abandoning the divine command theory completely. I do abandon it completely if I say both of the following things.

(A) It would be wrong to obey God if He commanded cruelty for its own sake.

(B) In (A), "wrong" is used in what is for me its normal ethical sense.

If I assert both (A) and (B), it is clear that I cannot consistently maintain that "wrong" in its normal ethical sense for me means or implies "contrary to God's commands."

But from the fact that I deny that it would be wrong to disobey God if He commanded cruelty for its own sake, it does not follow that I must accept (A) and (B). Of course someone might claim that obedience and disobedience would both be ethically permitted in such a case; but that is not the view that I am suggesting. If I adopt the modified divine command theory as an analysis of my present concept of ethical wrongness (and if I adopt a similar analysis of my concept of ethical permittedness), I will not hold either that it would be wrong to disobey, or that it would be ethically permitted to disobey, or that it would be wrong to obey, or that it would be ethically permitted to obey, if God commanded cruelty for its own sake. For I will say that my concept of ethical wrongness (and my concept of ethical permittedness) would "break down" if I really believed that God commanded cruelty for its own sake. Or to put the matter somewhat more prosaically, I will say that my concepts of ethical wrongness and permittedness could not serve the functions they now serve, because using those concepts I could not call any action ethically wrong or ethically permitted, if I believed that God's will was so unloving. This position can be explained or developed in either of two ways, each of which has its advantages.

I could say that by "X is ethically wrong" I mean "X is contrary to the commands of a *loving* God" (i.e., "There is a *loving* God and X is contrary to His commands") and by "X is ethically permitted" I mean "X is in accord with the commands of a *loving* God" (i.e., "There is a *loving* God and X is not contrary to His commands"). On this analysis we can reason as follows. If there is only one God and He commands cruelty for its own sake, then presumably there is not a *loving* God. If there is not a loving God then neither "X is ethically wrong" nor "X is ethically permitted" is true of any X. Using my present concepts of ethical wrongness and permittedness, therefore, I could not (consistently) call any action ethically wrong or permitted if I believed that God commanded cruelty for its own sake. This way of developing the modified divine command theory is the simpler and neater of the two, and that might reasonably lead one to choose it for the construction of a theological ethical theory. On the other hand, I think it is also simpler and neater than ordinary religious ethical discourse, in which (for example) it may be felt that the statement that a certain act is wrong is *about* the will or commands of God in a way in which it is not about His love.

In this essay I shall prefer a second, rather similar, but somewhat untidier, understanding of the modified divine command theory, because I think it may lead us into some insights about the complexities of actual religious ethical discourse. According to this second version of the theory, the statement that something is ethically wrong (or permitted) says something about the will or commands of God, but not about His love. Every such statement, however, *presupposes* that certain conditions for the applicability of the believer's concepts of ethical right and wrong are satisfied. Among these conditions is that God does not command cruelty for its own sake—or, more generally, that God loves His human creatures. It need not be assumed that God's love is the only such condition.

The modified divine command theorist can say that the possibility of God commanding cruelty for its own sake is not provided for in the Judeo-Christian religious ethical system as he understands it. The possibility is not provided for, in the sense that the concepts of right and wrong have not been developed in such a way that actions could be correctly said to be right or wrong if God were believed to command cruelty for its own sake. The modified divine command theorist agrees that it is logically possible that God should command cruelty for its own sake; but he holds that it is unthinkable that God should do so. To have *faith* in God is not just to believe that He exists, but also to trust in His love for mankind. The believer's concepts of ethical wrongness and permittedness are developed within the framework of his (or the religious community's) religious life, and therefore within the framework of the assumption that God loves us. The concept of the will or commands of God has a certain function in the believer's life, and the use of the words "right" (in the sense of "ethically permitted") and "wrong" is tied to that function of that concept. But one of the reasons why the concept of the will of God can function as it does is that the love which God is believed to have toward men arouses in the believer certain attitudes of love toward God and devotion to His will. If the believer thinks about the unthinkable but logically possible situation in which God commands cruelty for its own sake, he finds that in relation to that kind of command of God he cannot take up the same attitude, and that the concept of the will or commands of God could not then have the same function in his life. For this reason he will not say that it would be wrong to disobey God, or right to obey Him, in that situation. At the same time he will not say that it would be wrong to obey God in that situation, because he is accustomed to use the word "wrong" to say that something is contrary to the will of God, and it does not seem to him to be the right word to use to express his own personal revulsion toward an act against which there would be no divine authority. Similarly, he will not say that it would be "right," in the sense of "ethically permitted," to disobey God's command of cruelty; for that does not seem to him to be the right way to express his own personal attitude toward an act which would not be in accord with a divine authority. In this way the believer's concepts of ethical rightness and wrongness would break down in the situation in which he believed that God commanded cruelty for its own sake—that is, they would not function as they now do, because he would not be prepared to use them to say that any action was right or wrong.

III

It is clear that according to this modified divine command theory, the meaning of the word "wrong" in Judeo-Christian ethical discourse must be understood in terms of a complex of relations which believers' use of the word has, not only to their beliefs about God's commands, but also to their attitudes toward certain types of action. I think it will help us to understand the theory better if we can give a brief but fairly comprehensive description of the most important features of the Judeo-Christian ethical use of "wrong," from the point of view of the modified divine command theory. That is what I shall try to do in this section.

(1) "Wrong" and "contrary to God's commands" at least contextually imply each other in Judeo-Christian ethical discourse. "It is wrong to do X" will be assented to by the sincere Jewish or Christian believer if and only if he assents to "It is contrary to God's commands to do X." This is a fact sufficiently well known that the known believer who says the one commits himself publicly to the other.

Indeed "wrong" and such expressions as "against the will of God" seem to be used interchangeably in religious ethical discourse. If a believer asks his pastor, "Do you think it's always against the will of God to use contraceptives?" and the pastor replies, "I don't see anything wrong with the use of contraceptives in many cases," the pastor has answered the same question the inquirer asked.

(2) In ethical contexts, the statement that a certain action is wrong normally expresses certain volitional and emotional attitudes toward that action. In particular it normally expresses an intention, or at least an inclination, not to perform the action, and/or dispositions to feel guilty if one has performed it, to discourage others from performing it, and to react with anger, sorrow, or diminished respect toward others if they have performed it. I think this is true of Judeo-Christian ethical discourse as well as of other ethical discourse.

The interchangeability of "wrong" and "against the will of God" applies in full force here. It seems to make no difference to the expressive function of an ethical statement in a Judeo-Christian context which of these expressions is used. So far as I can see, the feelings and dispositions normally expressed by "It is wrong to commit suicide" in a Judeo-Christian context are exactly the same as those normally expressed by "It is against God's will to commit suicide," or by "Suicide is a violation of the commandments of God." . . .

(3) In a Judeo-Christian context, moreover, the attitudes expressed by a statement that something is wrong are normally quite strongly affected and

colored by specifically religious feelings and interests. They are apt to be motivated in various degrees by, and mixed in various proportions with, love, devotion, and loyalty toward God, and/or fear of God. Ethical wrongdoing is seen and experienced as *sin*, as rupture of personal or communal relationship with God. The normal feelings and experience of guilt for Judeo-Christian believers surely cannot be separated from beliefs, and ritual and devotional practices, having to do with God's judgment and forgiveness.

In all sin there is offense against a person (God), even when there is no offense against any other human person—for instance, if I have a vice which harms me but does not importantly harm any other human being. Therefore in the Judeo-Christian tradition reactions which are appropriate when one has offended another person are felt to be appropriate reactions to any ethical fault, regardless of whether another human being has been offended. I think this affects rather importantly the emotional connections of the word "wrong" in Judeo-Christian discourse.

(4) When a Judeo-Christian believer is trying to decide, in an ethical way, whether it would be wrong for him to do a certain thing, he typically thinks of himself as trying to determine whether it would be against God's will for him to do it. His deliberations may turn on the interpretation of certain religiously authoritative texts. They may be partly carried out in the form of prayer. It is quite possible, however, that his deliberations will take forms more familiar to the nonbeliever. Possibly his theology will encourage him to give some weight to his own intuitions and feelings about the matter, and those of other people. Such encouragement might be provided, for instance, by a doctrine of the leading of the Holy Spirit. Probably the believer will accept certain very general ethical principles as expressing commandments of God, and most of these may be principles which many nonbelievers would also accept (for instance, that it is always, or with very few exceptions, wrong to kill another human being). The believer's deliberation might consist entirely of reasoning from such general principles. But he would still regard it as an attempt to discover God's will on the matter.

(5) Typically, the Judeo-Christian believer is a nonnaturalist objectivist about ethical wrongness. When he says that something is (ethically) wrong, he means to be stating what he believes to be a fact of a certain sort—what I shall call a "nonnatural objective fact." Such a fact is objective in the sense that whether it obtains or not does not depend on whether any human being thinks it does. It is harder to give a satisfactory explanation of what I mean by "nonnatural" here. Let us say that a nonnatural fact is one which does not consist simply in any fact or complex of facts which can be stated entirely in the languages of physics, chemistry, biology, and human psychology. That way of putting it obviously raises questions which it leaves unanswered, but I hope it may be clear enough for present purposes.

That ethical facts are objective and nonnatural has been believed by many people, including some famous philosophers—for instance, Plato and G. E.

Moore. The term "nonnaturalism" is sometimes used rather narrowly, to refer to a position held by Moore, and positions closely resembling it. Clearly, I am using "nonnaturalist" in a broader sense here.

Given that the facts of wrongness asserted in Judeo-Christian ethics are non-natural in the sense explained above, and that they accordingly do not consist entirely in facts of physics, chemistry, biology, and human psychology, the question arises, in what they do consist. According to the divine command theory (even the modified divine command theory), in so far as they are nonnatural and objective, they consist in facts about the will or commands of God. I think this is really the central point in a divine command theory of ethical wrongness. This is the point at which the divine command theory is distinguished from alternative theological theories of ethical wrongness, such as the theory that facts of ethical rightness and wrongness are objective, nonnatural facts about ideas or essences subsisting eternally in God's understanding, not subject to His will but guiding it.

The divine command account of the nonnatural fact-stating function of Judeo-Christian ethical discourse has at least one advantage over its competitors. It is clear, I think, that in stating that X is wrong a believer normally commits himself to the view that X is contrary to the will or commands of God. And the fact (if it is a fact) that X is contrary to the will or commands of God is surely a nonnatural objective fact. But it is not nearly so clear that in saying that X is wrong, the believer normally commits himself to belief in any *other* nonnatural objective fact. . . .

(6) The modified divine command theorist cannot consistently claim that "wrong" and "contrary to God's commands" have exactly the same meaning for him. For he admits that there is a logically possible situation which he would describe by saying, "God commands cruelty for its own sake," but not by saying, "It would be wrong not to practice cruelty for its own sake." If there were not at least some little difference between the meanings with which he actually, normally uses the expressions "wrong" and "contrary to God's commands," there would be no reason for them to differ in their applicability or inapplicability to the far-out unthinkable case. We may now be in a position to improve somewhat our understanding of what the modified divine command theorist can suppose that difference in meaning to be, and of why he supposes that the believer is unwilling to say that disobedience to a divine command of cruelty for its own sake would be wrong.

We have seen that the expressions "It is wrong" and "It is contrary to God's commands" or "It is against the will of God" have virtually the same uses in religious ethical discourse, and the same functions in the religious ethical life. No doubt they differ slightly in the situations in which they are most likely to be used and the emotional overtones they are most apt to carry. But in all situations experienced or expected by the believer as a believer they at least contextually imply each other, and normally express the same or extremely similar emotional and volitional attitudes.

There is also a difference in meaning, however, a difference which is normally of no practical importance. All three of the following are aspects of the normal use of "it is wrong" in the life and conversation of believers. (a) It is used to state what are believed to be facts about the will or commands of God. (b) It is used in formulating decisions and arguments about what to do (i.e., not just in deciding what one *ought* to do, but in deciding *what to do*). (c) It expresses certain emotional and volitional attitudes toward the action under discussion. "It is wrong" is commonly used to do all three of those things at once.

The same is true of "It is contrary to God's commands" and "It is against the will of God." They are commonly used by believers to do the same three things, and to do them at once. But because of their grammatical form and their formal relationships with other straightforwardly descriptive expressions about God, they are taken to be, first and last, descriptive expressions about God and His relation to whatever actions are under discussion. They can therefore be used to state what are supposed to be facts about God, even when one's emotional and decision-making attitude toward those supposed facts is quite contrary to the attitudes normally expressed by the words "against the will of God."

In the case of "It is wrong," however, it is not clear that one of its functions, or one of the aspects of its normal use, is to be preferred in case of conflict with the others. I am not willing to say, "It would be wrong not to do X," when both my own attitude and the attitude of most other people toward the doing of X under the indicated circumstances is one of unqualified revulsion. On the other hand, neither am I willing to say, "It would be wrong to do X," when I would merely be expressing my own personal revulsion (and perhaps that of other people as well) but nothing that I could regard as clothed in the majesty of a divine authority. The believer's concept of ethical wrongness therefore breaks down if one tries to apply it to the unthinkable case in which God commands cruelty for its own sake.

None of this seems to me inconsistent with the claim that part of what the believer normally means in saying "X is wrong" is that X is contrary to God's will or commands.

IV

The modified divine command theory clearly conceives of believers as valuing some things independently of their relation to God's commands. If the believer will not say that it would be wrong not to practice cruelty for its own sake if God commanded it, that is because he values kindness, and has a revulsion for cruelty, in a way that is at least to some extent independent of his belief that God commands kindness and forbids cruelty. This point may be made the basis of both philosophical and theological objections to the modified divine command theory, but I think the objections can be answered.

The philosophical objection is, roughly, that if there are some things I value independently of their relation to God's commands, then my value concepts cannot rightly be analyzed in terms of God's commands. According to the modified divine command theory, the acceptability of divine command ethics depends in part on the believer's independent positive valuation of the sorts of things that God is believed to command. But then, the philosophical critic objects, the believer must have a prior, nontheological conception of ethical right and wrong, in terms of which he judges God's commandments to be acceptable—and to admit that the believer has a prior, nontheological conception of ethical right and wrong is to abandon the divine command theory.

The weakness of this philosophical objection is that it fails to note the distinctions that can be drawn among various value concepts. From the fact that the believer values some things independently of his beliefs about God's commands, the objector concludes, illegitimately, that the believer must have a conception of ethical right and wrong that is independent of his beliefs about God's commands. This inference is illegitimate because there can be valuations which do not imply or presuppose a judgment of ethical right or wrong. For instance, I may simply like something, or want something, or feel a revulsion at something.

What the modified divine command theorist will hold, then, is that the believer values some things independently of their relation to God's commands, but that these valuations are not judgments of ethical right and wrong and do not of themselves imply judgments of ethical right and wrong. He will maintain, on the other hand, that such independent valuations are involved in, or even necessary for, judgments of ethical right and wrong which also involve beliefs about God's will or commands. The adherent of a divine command ethics will normally be able to give reasons for his adherence. Such reasons might include: "Because I am grateful to God for His love"; "Because I find it the most satisfying form of ethical life"; "Because there's got to be an objective moral law if life isn't to fall to pieces, and I can't understand what it would be if not the will of God." As we have already noted, the modified divine command theorist also has reasons why he would not accept a divine command ethics in certain logically possible situations which he believes not to be actual. All of these reasons seem to me to involve valuations that are independent of divine command ethics. The person who has such reasons wants certain things—happiness, certain satisfactions—for himself and others; he hates cruelty and loves kindness; he has perhaps a certain unique and "numinous" awe of God. And these are not attitudes which he has simply because of his beliefs about God's commands. They are not attitudes, however, which presuppose judgments of moral right and wrong. . . .

This version of the divine command theory may seem *theologically* objectionable to some believers. One of the reasons, surely, why divine command theories of ethics have appealed to some theologians is that such theories seem especially congruous with the religious demand that God be the object of our highest allegiance. If our supreme commitment in life is to doing what is right just because it is right, and if what is right is right just because God wills or commands it, then surely our highest allegiance is to God. But the modified divine command theory seems not to have this advantage. For the modified divine command theorist is forced to admit, as we have seen, that he has reasons for his adherence to a divine command ethics, and that his having these reasons implies that there are some things which he values independently of his beliefs about God's commands. It is therefore not correct to say of him that he is committed to doing the will of God *just* because it is the will of God; he is committed to doing it partly because of other things which he values independently. Indeed it appears that there are certain logically possible situations in which his present attitudes would not commit him to obey God's commands (for instance, if God commanded cruelty for its own sake). This may even suggest that he values some things, not just independently of God's commands, but more than God's commands.

We have here a real problem in religious ethical motivation. The Judeo-Christian believer is supposed to make God the supreme focus of his loyalties; that is clear. One possible interpretation of this fact is the following. Obedience to whatever God may command is (or at least ought to be) the one thing that the believer values for its own sake and more than anything and everything else. Anything else that he values, he values (or ought to) only to a lesser degree and as a means to obedience to God. This conception of religious ethical motivation is obviously favorable to an *un*modified divine command theory of ethical wrongness.

But I think it is not a realistic conception. Loyalty to God, for instance, is very often explained, by believers themselves, as motivated by gratitude for benefits conferred. And I think it is clear in most cases that the gratitude presupposes that the benefits are valued, at least to some extent, independently of loyalty to God. Similarly, I do not think that most devout Judeo-Christian believers would say that it would be wrong to disobey God if He commanded cruelty for its own sake. And if I am right about that I think it shows that their positive valuation of (emotional/volitional pro-attitude toward) doing *whatever* God may command is not clearly greater than their independent negative valuation of cruelty.

In analyzing ethical motivation in general, as well as Judeo-Christian ethical motivation in particular, it is probably a mistake to suppose that there is (or can be expected to be) one only thing that is valued supremely and for its own sake, with nothing else being valued independently of it. The motivation for a person's ethical orientation in life is normally much more complex than that, and involves a plurality of emotional and volitional attitudes of different sorts which are at least partly independent of each other. At any rate, I think the modified divine command theorist is bound to say that that is true of his ethical motivation.

In what sense, then, can the modified divine command theorist maintain that God is the supreme focus of his loyalties? I suggest the following interpretation of the single-hearted loyalty to God which is demanded in Judeo-Christian religion. In this interpretation the crucial idea is *not* that some one thing is valued for its own sake and more than anything else, and nothing else valued independently of it. It is freely admitted that the religious person will have a plurality of motives for his ethical position, and that these will be at least partly independent of each other. It is admitted further that a desire to obey the commands of God (*whatever* they may be) may not be the strongest of these motives. What will be claimed is that certain beliefs about God enable the believer to integrate or focus his motives in a loyalty to God and His commands. Some of these beliefs are about what God commands or wills (contingently—that is, although He could logically have commanded or willed something else instead).

Some of the motives in question might be called egoistic; they include desires for satisfactions for oneself—which God is believed to have given or to be going to give. Other motives may be desires for satisfaction for other people; these may be called altruistic. Still other motives might not be desires for anyone's satisfaction, but might be valuations of certain kinds of action for their own sakes; these might be called idealistic. I do not think my argument depends heavily on this particular classification, but it seems plausible that all of these types, and perhaps others as well, might be distinguished among the motives for a religious person's ethical position. Obviously such motives might pull one in different directions, conflicting with one another. But in Judeo-Christian ethics beliefs about what God does in fact will (although He could have willed otherwise) are supposed to enable one to *fuse* these motives, so to speak, into one's devotion to God and His will, so that they all pull together. Doubtless the believer will still have some motives which conflict with his loyalty to God. But the religious ideal is that these should all be merely momentary desires and impulses, and kept under control. They ought not to be allowed to influence voluntary action. The deeper, more stable, and controlling desires, intentions, and psychic energies are supposed to be fused in devotion to God. As I interpret it, however, it need not be inconsistent with the Judeo-Christian ethical and religious ideal that this fusion of motives, this integration of moral energies, depends on belief in certain propositions which are taken to be contingent truths about God.

Lest it be thought that I am proposing unprecedented theological positions, or simply altering Judeo-Christian religious beliefs to suit my theories, I will call to my aid on this point a theologian known for his insistence on the sovereignty of God. Karl Barth seems to me to hold a divine command theory of ethics. But when he raises the question of why we should obey God, he rejects with scorn the suggestion that God's *power* provides the basis for His claim on us. "By deciding for God [man] has definitely decided not to be obedient to power as power." God's claim on us is based rather on His grace. "God calls us and orders us and claims us by being gracious to us in Jesus Christ." I do not mean to suggest that Barth would agree with everything I have said about motivation, or that he offers a lucid account of a divine command theory. But he does agree with the position I have proposed on this point, that the believer's loyalty is not to be construed as a loyalty to God *as* all-powerful, nor to God *whatever* He might conceivably have willed. It is a loyalty to God *as* having a certain attitude toward us, a certain will for us, which God was free not to have, but to which, in Barth's view, He has committed Himself irrevocably in Jesus Christ. The believer's devotion is not to merely possible commands of God as such, but to God's actual (and gracious) will.

V

The ascription of moral qualities to God is commonly thought to cause problems for divine command theories of ethics. It is doubted that God, as an agent, can properly be called "good" in the moral sense if He is not subject to a moral law that is not of His own making. For if He is morally good, mustn't He do what is right *because* it is right? And how can He do that, if what's right is right because He wills it? Or it may be charged that divine command theories trivialize the claim that God is good. If "X is (morally) good" means roughly "X does what God wills," then "God is (morally) good" means only that God does what He wills—which is surely much less than people are normally taken to mean when they say that God is (morally) good. In this section I will suggest an answer to these objections.

Surely no analysis of Judeo-Christian ethical discourse can be regarded as adequate which does not provide for a sense in which the believer can seriously assert that God is good. Indeed an adequate analysis should provide a plausible account of what believers do in fact mean when they say, "God is good." I believe that a divine command theory of ethical (rightness and) wrongness can include such an account. I will try to indicate its chief features.

(1) In saying "God is good" one is normally expressing a favorable emotional attitude toward God. I shall not try to determine whether or not this is part of the meaning of "God is good"; but it is normally, perhaps almost always, at least one of the things one is doing if one says that God is good. If we were to try to be more precise about the type of favorable emotional attitude normally expressed by "God is good," I suspect we would find that the attitude expressed is most commonly one of *gratitude*.

(2) This leads to a second point, which is that when God is called "good" it is very often meant that He is *good to us,* or *good to* the speaker. "Good" is sometimes virtually a synonym for "kind." And for the modified divine command theorist it is not a trivial truth that God is kind. In saying that God is good in the sense of "kind," one presupposes, of course, that there are some things which the beneficiaries of God's goodness value. We need not discuss here whether the beneficiaries must value them independently of their beliefs about God's will. For the modified divine command theorist does admit that there are some things which believers value independently of their beliefs about God's commands. Nothing that the modified divine command theorist says about the meaning of

("right" and) "wrong" implies that it is a trivial truth that God bestows on His creatures things that they value.

(3) I would not suggest that the descriptive force of "good" as applied to God is exhausted by the notion of kindness. "God is good" must be taken in many contexts as ascribing to God, rather generally, qualities of character which the believing speaker regards as virtues in human beings. Among such qualities might be faithfulness, ethical consistency, a forgiving disposition, and, in general, various aspects of love, as well as kindness. Not that there is some definite list of qualities, the ascription of which to God is clearly implied by the claim that God is good. But saying that God is good normally commits one to the position that God has some important set of qualities which one regards as virtues in human beings.

(4) It will not be thought that God has *all* the qualities which are virtues in human beings. Some such qualities are logically inapplicable to a being such as God is supposed to be. For example, aside from certain complications arising from the doctrine of the incarnation, it would be logically inappropriate to speak of God as controlling His sexual desires. (He doesn't have any.) And given some widely held conceptions of God and his relation to the world, it would hardly make sense to speak of Him as *courageous*. For if He is impassible and has predetermined absolutely everything that happens, He has no risks to face and cannot endure (because He cannot suffer) pain or displeasure. . . .

(5) If we accept a divine command theory of ethical rightness and wrongness, I think we shall have to say that *dutifulness* is a human virtue which, like sexual chastity, is logically inapplicable to God. God cannot either do or fail to do His duty, since He does not have a duty—at least not in the most important sense in which human beings have a duty. For He is not subject to a moral law not of His own making. Dutifulness is one virtuous disposition which men can have that God cannot have. But there are other virtuous dispositions which God can have as well as men. Love, for instance. It hardly makes sense to say that God does what He does *because* it is right. But it does not follow that God cannot have any reason for doing what He does. It does not even follow that He cannot have reasons of a type on which it would be morally virtuous for a man to act. For example, He might do something because He knew it would make His creatures happier.

(6) The modified divine command theorist must deny that in calling God "good" one presupposes a standard of moral rightness and wrongness superior to the will of God, by reference to which it is determined whether God's character is virtuous or not. And I think he can consistently deny that. He can say that morally virtuous and vicious qualities of character are those which agree and conflict, respectively, with God's commands, and that it is their agreement or disagreement with God's commands that makes them virtuous or vicious. But the believer normally thinks he has at least a general idea of what qualities of character are in fact virtuous and vicious (approved and disapproved by God). Hav-

ing such an idea, he can apply the word "good" descriptively to God, meaning that (with some exceptions, as I have noted) God has the qualities which the believer regards as virtues, such as faithfulness and kindness. . . .

VI

As I noted at the outset, the divine command theory of ethical wrongness, even in its modified form, has the consequence that believers and nonbelievers use the word "wrong" with different meanings in ethical contexts, since it will hardly be thought that nonbelievers mean by "wrong" what the theory says believers mean by it. This consequence gives rise to an objection. For the phenomena of common moral discourse between believers and nonbelievers suggest that they mean the same thing by "wrong" in ethical contexts. In the present section I shall try to explain how the modified divine command theorist can account for the facts of common ethical discourse.

I will first indicate what I think the troublesome facts are. Judeo-Christian believers enter into ethical discussions with people whose religious or anti-religious beliefs they do not know. It seems to be possible to conduct quite a lot of ethical discourse, with apparent understanding, without knowing one's partner's views on religious issues. Believers also discuss ethical questions with persons who are known to them to be nonbelievers. They agree with such persons, disagree with them, and try to persuade them, about what acts are morally wrong. (Or at least it is normally *said*, by the participants and others, that they agree and disagree about such issues.) Believers ascribe, to people who are known not to believe in God, beliefs that certain acts are morally wrong. Yet surely believers do not suppose that nonbelievers, in calling acts wrong, mean that they are contrary to the will or commandments of God. Under these circumstances how can the believer really mean "contrary to the will or commandments of God" when he says "wrong"? If he agrees and disagrees with nonbelievers about what is wrong, if he ascribes to them beliefs that certain acts are wrong, must he not be using "wrong" in a nontheological sense?

What I shall argue is that in some ordinary (and I fear imprecise) sense of "mean," what believers and nonbelievers mean by "wrong" in ethical contexts may well be partly the same and partly different. There are agreements between believers and nonbelievers which make common moral discourse between them possible. But these agreements do not show that the two groups mean exactly the same thing by "wrong." They do not show that "contrary to God's will or commands" is not part of what believers mean by "wrong."

Let us consider first the agreements which make possible common moral discourse between believers and nonbelievers. (1) One important agreement, which is so obvious as to be easily overlooked, is that they use many of the same ethical terms—"wrong," "right," "ought," "duty," and others. And they may utter many of the same ethical sentences, such as "Racial discrimination is morally wrong." In determining what people believe we rely very heavily on what they say (when they seem to be speaking sincerely)—and that means in large part, on the words that they use and the sentences they utter. If I know that somebody says, with apparent sincerity, "Racial discrimination is morally wrong," I will normally ascribe to him the belief that racial discrimination is morally wrong, even if I also know that he does not mean *exactly* the same thing as I do by "racial discrimination" or "morally wrong." Of course if I know he means something *completely* different, I would not ascribe the belief to him without explicit qualification.

I would not claim that believers and nonbelievers use *all* the same ethical terms. "Sin," "law of God," and "Christian," for instance, occur as ethical terms in the discourse of many believers, but would be much less likely to occur in the same way in nonbelievers' discourse.

(2) The shared ethical terms have the same basic grammatical status for believers as for nonbelievers, and at least many of the same logical connections with other expressions. Everyone agrees, for instance, in treating "wrong" as an adjective and "Racial discrimination is morally wrong" as a declarative sentence. "(All) racial discrimination is morally wrong" would be treated by all parties as expressing an A-type (universal affirmative) proposition, from which consequences can be drawn by syllogistic reasoning or the predicate calculus. All agree that if X is morally wrong, then it isn't morally right and refraining from X is morally obligatory. Such grammatical and formal agreements are important to common moral discourse.

(3) There is a great deal of agreement, among believers and nonbelievers, as to what types of action they call "wrong" in an ethical sense and I think that that agreement is one of the things that make common moral discourse possible. It is certainly not complete agreement. Obviously there is a lot of ethical disagreement in the world. Much of it cuts right across religious lines, but not all of it does. There are things which are typically called "wrong" by members of some religious groups, and not by others. Nonetheless there are types of action which everyone or almost everyone would call morally wrong—such as torturing someone to death because he accidentally broke a small window in your house. Moreover any two people (including any one believer and one nonbeliever) are likely to find some actions they both call wrong that not everyone does. I imagine that most ethical discussion takes place among people whose area of agreement in what they call wrong is relatively large.

There is probably much less agreement about the most basic issues in moral theory than there is about many ethical issues of less generality. There is much more unanimity in what people (sincerely) say in answer to such questions as "Was what Hitler did to the Jews wrong?" or "Is it normally wrong to disobey the laws of one's country?" than in what they (sincerely) say in answer to such questions as "Is it always right to do the act which will have the best results?" or "Is pleasure the only thing that is good for its own sake?" The issue between adherents and nonadherents of divine command ethics is typical of basic issues in ethical and metaethical theory in this respect.

(4) The emotional and volitional attitudes normally expressed by the statement that something is "wrong" are similar in believers and nonbelievers. They are not exactly the same; the attitudes typically expressed by the believer's statement that something is "wrong" are importantly related to his religious practice and beliefs about God, and this doubtless makes them different in some ways from the attitudes expressed by nonbelievers uttering the same sentence. But the attitudes are certainly similar, and that is important for the possibility of common moral discourse.

(5) Perhaps even more important is the related fact that the social functions of a statement that something is (morally) "wrong" are similar for believers and nonbelievers. To say that something someone else is known to have done is "wrong" is commonly to attack him. If you say that something you are known to have done is "wrong," you abandon certain types of defense. To say that a public policy is "wrong" is normally to register oneself as opposed to it, and is sometimes a signal that one is willing to be supportive of common action to change it. These social functions of moral discourse are extremely important. It is perhaps not surprising that we are inclined to say that two people agree with each other when they both utter the same sentence and thereby indicate their readiness to take the same side in a conflict.

Let us sum up these observations about the conditions which make common moral discourse between believers and nonbelievers possible. (1) They use many of the same ethical terms, such as "wrong." (2) They treat those terms as having the same basic grammatical and logical status, and many of the same logical connections with other expressions. (3) They agree to a large extent about what types of action are to be called "wrong." To call an action "wrong" is, among other things, to classify it with certain other actions, and there is considerable agreement between believers and nonbelievers as to what actions those are. (4) The emotional and volitional attitudes which believers and nonbelievers normally express in saying that something is "wrong" are similar, and (5) saying that something is "wrong" has much the same social functions for believers and nonbelievers.

So far as I can see, none of this is inconsistent with the modified divine command theory of ethical wrongness. According to that theory there are several things which are true of the believer's use of "wrong" which cannot plausibly be supposed to be true of the nonbeliever's. In saying, "X is wrong," the believer commits himself (subjectively, at least, and publicly if he is known to be a believer) to the claim that X is contrary to God's will or commandments. The believer will not say that anything would be wrong, under any possible circumstances, if it were not contrary to God's will or commandments. In many contexts he uses the term "wrong" interchangeably with "against the will of God" or "against the commandments of God." The heart of the modified divine command theory, I have suggested, is the claim that when the believer says, "X is wrong," one thing he means to be doing is stating a nonnatural objective fact about X, and the nonnatural objective fact he means to be stating is that X is contrary to the will or commandments of God. This claim may be true even though the uses of "wrong" by believers and nonbelievers are similar in all five of the ways pointed out above. . . .

Supplementary Paperback Reading

Aquinas, St. Thomas, *Introduction to St. Thomas Aquinas,* ed. A. C. Pegis (Random House, N. Y.)

K. Barth, *Church Dogmatics: A Selection,* ed. G. W. Bromiley (Harper Torchbooks, N. Y.)

W. W. Bartley III, *Morality and Religion* (St. Martin's Press, N. Y.)

H. Bettinson, ed. and trans., *The Early Christian Fathers: A Selection from the Writings of the Fathers from St. Clement of Rome to St. Athanasius* (Oxford University Press, N. Y.)

M. Buber, *Eclipse of God: Studies in the Relation between Religion and Philosophy* (Harper Torchbooks, N. Y.)

M. Buber, *I and Thou,* trans. W. Kaufmann (Charles Scribner's Sons, N. Y.)

M. Buber, *Pointing the Way: Collected Essays by Martin Buber,* ed. and trans. Maurice S. Friedman (Schocken Books, N. Y.)

M. Friedman, *Martin Buber: The Life of Dialogue,* third rev. ed. (University of Chicago Press)

J. M. Gustafson, *Christ and the Moral Life* (University of Chicago Press)

W. Kaufmann, *Existentialism, Religion and Death: Thirteen Essays* (New American Library, N. Y.)

W. Kaufmann, ed., *Religion from Tolstoy to Camus* (Harper Torchbooks, N. Y.)

S. Kierkegaard, *Fear and Trembling and The Sickness Unto Death,* ed. and trans., W. Lowrie (Princeton University Press)

S. Kierkegaard, *Purity of Heart and To Will One Thing,* trans. D. V. Steere (Harper Torchbooks, N.Y.)

C. S. Lewis, *Mere Christianity* (Macmillan, N. Y.)

D. Little and S. B. Twiss, Jr., *Comparative Religious Ethics* (Harper and Row, N. Y.)

H. Richard Niebuhr, *The Meaning of Revelation* (Macmillan, N. Y.)

Reinhold Niebuhr, *The Nature and Destiny of Man,* Vols. I and II (Charles Scribner's Sons, N. Y.)

G. Outka and J. P. Reeder, Jr., eds., *Religion and Morality: A Collection of Essays* (Anchor Books, N. Y.)

R. E. Santoni, ed., *Religious Language and the Problem of Religious Knowledge* (Indiana University Press, Bloomington)

W. T. Stace, *Religion and the Modern Mind* (J. B. Lippincott, Philadelphia)

G. F. Thomas, *Christian Ethics and Moral Philosophy* (Charles Scribner's Sons, N. Y.)

P. Tillich, *Systematic Theology,* Vols. I, II, and III (University of Chicago Press)

11

THE ETHICS OF

EXISTENTIALISM

Introduction

EXISTENTIALISM, NIHILISM, AND AMORALISM

The rise of the philosophy of existentialism in the twentieth century has brought a radically new perspective to bear on the problems of normative and analytic ethics. Existentialists do not believe that any actions are inherently right or wrong. Nor do they think it is possible to justify moral principles on rational grounds. All standards and rules of conduct are open to our choice, and each of us must simply decide what norms we shall live by. This choice is made by each of us at every moment of our existence, and we are absolutely free to make whatever choice we wish. Nothing that could serve as the validating ground for our choices is discoverable by rational inquiry.

It has been claimed that existentialism inevitably leads to nihilism and amoralism in human life. Nihilism (literally, belief in nothing) is an outlook on life in which human existence is seen to be utterly meaningless and absurd, without order or direction. Daily living becomes a kind of pointless game in which every "move" is completely arbitrary. This game is played against the background of an indifferent universe. From the standpoint of reality-as-a-whole, it does not matter what human beings do with their lives.

Amoralism is the doctrine that there are no valid principles to guide human conduct and that therefore no one need abide by any moral standards. We have no duties or obligations. Nothing we do can be right or wrong. Thus the amoral person declines to make any moral judgments either about himself or about others, believing that all such judgments are totally without foundation.

The claim that existentialism entails both nihilism and amoralism—a claim we shall be examining critically in this chapter—has been defended in the following way. According to existentialism there is no rational ground for any moral standards or rules. The choice of one set of standards or rules is no more justified than the choice of another. Thus we have total freedom to choose any standards or rules we please. Indeed, we have the freedom to decide to do away with all standards and rules if we wish. As far as reason is concerned, an unprincipled life is just as good as one based on principles. Now if it is the case that there is no rational justification for any standard or rule, then it makes no sense to speak of an ethical system that is validly binding upon everyone as a moral agent. Existentialism, it is then concluded, makes life a moral vacuum, taking away all motivation to strive for a better world. There being no reason to abide by moral standards, one might as well live amorally. But even then one's actions will be totally groundless. Thus whether we choose to live according to moral principles or to live amorally, our decision is absurd and the lives we live are meaningless. To choose without reason is to choose arbitrarily, and in a situation of this sort nothing in life can have any significance.

Whether these conclusions do necessarily follow from the existentialist view of "the human condition" is a question that will be our central concern in this chapter. Each of the three readings included in the chapter expresses a certain position on this issue. The first reading contains selections from the works of Friedrich Nietzsche (1844–1900), who was not strictly speaking an existentialist himself but an important forerunner of existentialism. His writings had a major influence on all existentialist thought and provide a background for understanding that thought. In the second reading a fully developed existentialist position is presented by the French dramatist, novelist, and philosopher, Jean-Paul Sartre (born 1905). Sartre argues that the existentialist's conception of "the human condition" does provide a basis for moral responsibility and an ethical life. A recent interpretation of existentialism by the contemporary American philosopher, Frederick Olafson, is set forth in the third reading. Professor Olafson tries to show how a theory of moral obligation can be based on the existentialist view of human freedom and the responsibility that goes with it. Thus both Sartre and Olafson attempt to refute the charge that existentialism entails nihilism and amoralism.

ESSENCE AND EXISTENCE

What does it mean to exist as a human being? This question can be answered in a number of ways, of which existentialism is but one. Any philosophy that takes this question to be the most fundamental one for our understanding of reality may be called an "existence-philosophy" (from the German *Existenzphilosophie*). Some of the important existence-philosophers of the nineteenth and twentieth centuries are Soren Kierkegaard, Martin Heidegger, Karl Jaspers, and Gabriel Marcel, as well as Jean-Paul Sartre. It is primarily Sartre, however, and those thinkers such as Simone de Beauvoir and Albert Camus who share his philosophical outlook, who are properly spoken of as "existentialists." For existentialism is one type of existence-philosophy (just as utilitarianism is one type of ethical theory). Let us look more closely at the central question of existence-philosophy.

What is the difference between human existence and the kind of existence mere objects have? To say that an object exists means that it occupies space and is made up of matter or some form of energy. But to exist as a human being is not merely to be "out there" in the universe as a material body in space. Even our human bodies are not mere physical objects when we understand them to belong to ourselves, since identifying them as our own bodies already presupposes that *we* exist as the human beings who have those bodies. The question for existence-philosophy has to do with how *our* existence is to be understood and analyzed.

Perhaps each of us exists only insofar as we are conscious beings, capable of being aware of a world around us in a way that a chair, a stone, or a drop of water are not. But then the question of human existence becomes: What does it mean to exist as a conscious being which can be aware of a world?

The answer given by the philosophy of existentialism is this: Humans are those beings, and only those beings, of whom it is true to say that their existence precedes their essence. This answer is stated and explained by Sartre in the second reading of this chapter. A few words about how the terms "essence" and "existence" are being used here will help us to grasp the full significance of Sartre's assertion. The essence of a thing is the set of properties in virtue of which it is the kind of thing it is. What makes a chair a chair and not a table or a bed? If we examine a chair we can notice the various properties it has: its size, shape, color, what it is made of, how much it weighs, what it is normally used for, and so on. Many of these properties are not part of the essence of a chair because they are not what make it a chair rather than something else. Its color, for example, is irrelevant to its being a chair, since another object could have the same color and not be a chair and an object could be a chair without having that color. Now if we could specify those properties in virtue of which, or on the basis of which, a chair is a chair, we would then understand what (the essence of) a chair is. Thus one might consider its shape and the uses to which it is normally put as being essential to its being a chair. By knowing its essential nature we would know *what it means for something to exist as a chair*.

Can we not say the same thing about a human being? If we could know what set of properties make human beings human and not mere things or physical objects, it would seem we would have an answer to our question, *What does it mean for something to exist as a human being?* But existentialists argue that this parallel does not hold. Human beings have no essence in the way an object like a chair has an essence. Something cannot exist as a chair, cannot exist and *be* a chair, unless it has the essential nature of chairness. But human beings are entities of an entirely different sort. There is no specific set of properties that make all humans human rather than something else. Indeed, humans are precisely those beings which exist *as* humans prior to their having an essence.

To say that for human beings "existence precedes essence" means that whatever properties are exemplified by persons or by the lives they lead are the products of their own choice. This choice has been made by them in absolute, unconditional freedom. They are guided by no laws or rules, no norms or standards, other than those of their own making. And they can make new ones any time they wish. Thus to be human is to be confronted at every moment with the choice of what kind of being to be. To exist as a human is nothing else but to choose to be one kind of entity rather than another. It follows that the characteristics people have they alone are responsible for. They have defined themselves by giving themselves a nature. Even when they have more or less unchanging properties that constitute a stable, recognizable character that persists over time, they are in fact choosing to remain as they are from moment to moment, and so are just as responsible for their nature as they would be if they had changed themselves.

Thus Sartre's answer to the question, What does it mean to exist as a human being? is that to exist is an activity of choosing one's nature in absolute freedom. Before considering Sartre's philosophy in greater detail, it will be helpful to examine one of the main influences on that philosophy: the thought and outlook of Friedrich Nietzsche.

NIETZSCHE'S CRITIQUE OF TRADITIONAL ETHICS

Friedrich Nietzsche was a professor of classical philology at the University of Basel, Switzerland. His poor health forced him to retire in 1879, and from then until he became insane in 1889 he wrote a number of revolutionary books that have had a profound effect upon twentieth century European thought and literature. In these books Nietzsche does not develop a systematic philosophy, but gives expression to a certain way of looking at human existence and a certain conception of human values. He critically examines the foundations of the traditional moral outlook that had come to shape European civilization, rejects it completely, and advocates the adoption of an entirely new ethical viewpoint to replace it. The reading in this chapter consists of selected passages from a number of these revolutionary works.

For Nietzsche the end of belief in God in modern times was an event of overwhelming significance. Without God it is no longer possible to rely on or appeal to a source of moral standards higher than human life itself. Thus a great opportunity arises for people to free themselves once and for all from what Nietzsche saw as the self-denying, antinatural, life-negating values of the Judeo-Christian tradition. He called for a "revaluation of all values" in which a new morality could be created. This new morality would involve a radical transformation in the lives of those individuals who had the will to create it. It would be a new way of existing as a human being. The new morality is not a system of moral principles to be followed by everyone. On the contrary, it is only when individuals give expression to their will to become fully developed, integrated, autonomous, and self-creating beings that they make it possible for the new morality to be realized in their lives. The *content* of that morality will vary from person to person, but all those who live by it will achieve a kind of inner freedom and wholeness and strength that comes from being the true masters of their own lives. Nietzsche holds that each of us must do this in his own way. Our values and ideals must be the genuine embodiment of our own longings and desires, unfettered by the conventional ties that in the past have bound us to others and forced us to deny our deepest wants.

The reading begins with the idea that the philosopher is the person who, in every culture and in every age, has the task of trying to see through the self-deception and dishonesty underlying the conventional morality and of affirming the true greatness of each individual. This is the task Nietzsche, as a philosopher himself, then attempts to carry out for his own culture and time. There follows the famous passage on the distinction between "master-morality" and "slave-morality," in which Nietzsche identifies the Judeo-Christian ethics as one kind of slave-morality.

It should be noted that Nietzsche is not claiming that there are two human races, in the sense in which "race" means a genetic type, a nationality, or an ethnic group within a larger society. He uses the term "race" to refer to a certain kind of person. The two types (races) of human beings are distinguished by the presence or absence of the *will* to be an autonomous creator of one's own values and by the presence or absence of the *capacity* for living a life of greatness. Corresponding to these two types of individuals are two levels of inherent worth. Those who lack the will and the capacity for a life of greatness are by their very nature inferior to those of the other "race" who possess such will and capacity. In other words, a certain kind of life—that designated by the term "slave-morality"—is inherently less worthy of being lived by humans than the kind of life designated by the term "master-morality." Nietzsche accordingly believed that some people live inferior lives while others attain a higher level of human existence. It is inaccurate, however, to think of Nietzsche as a "racist" in the current meaning of that word. For he believed that those who have the will and the capacity for the superior kind of life may belong to any genetic type, any nationality, or any ethnic community. But he does deny the fundamental egalitarian principle that all human beings have the same inherent worth simply as human beings.

Another reason Nietzsche should not be considered a "racist" is his extreme individualism. Each individual is responsible for the kind of life he or she lives, since it is up to each of us to develop the will and the capacity for a life of greatness. We all have the potentialities for such a life. What keeps most people from realizing those potentialities, Nietzsche holds, is the habit of self-deception, of lying to ourselves, that has resulted from the traditional religious view of human nature and human values. Once we free ourselves from the falsifications and distortions propagated by religious institutions, we can through our own efforts achieve the will and the power to create "the new morality." Thus Nietzsche urges us to get "beyond good and evil" by transcending the conventional ethics of our culture.

Nietzsche's individualism is also in evidence when he argues that the realization of the higher life cannot be brought about through institutional means (education, the family, law, or a new religion). In Nietzsche's view, societies deceive themselves into thinking that they can "breed" a race of morally good beings or that they can "improve" human beings by some process of moral conditioning. Such attempts are bound to fail because "the new morality" must come from an affirmation of life and a "will to power" within each individual, if it ever does come. This individualistic aspect of Nietzsche's philosophy was to have a profound influence on existentialist thought.

THE EXISTENTIALIST ETHICS OF JEAN-PAUL SARTRE

Although Sartre has written a number of novels and plays expressing his philosophical ideas, the most complete and systematic statement of his existentialism is contained in the long and difficult book, *Being and Nothingness* (*L'Etre et le Néant*, 1943). A more concise presentation of his views, especially as they bear on ethics, is given in the second reading of this chapter. It is taken from his essay, *The Humanism of Existentialism* (*L'Existentialisme est une Humanisme*, 1946). In this essay Sartre explains what he means by the idea that, for humans, existence precedes essence. As we saw earlier, Sartre denies that there is an essential human nature. A person exists as a human being by choosing his or her own nature. "Man," says Sartre, "is nothing else but what he makes of himself."

Correlative with the absolute freedom we exercise in choosing our own natures is an absolute responsibility for what we choose to be. We cannot excuse ourselves for being what we are, since we are what we have decided to be. This responsibility, Sartre adds, involves not only ourselves but the whole of humanity. When we choose to define ourselves in a certain way, we are defining for ourselves what it means to be human. Our choice is not merely to exist as a particular human being, but to be a particular *kind* of person. It is as if we were choosing a certain model of humanity to exemplify in our lives, a model that others, too, might exemplify. In this sense, Sartre claims, "I am responsible for myself and for everyone else."

To bring out the ethical implications of his position, Sartre describes the situation of a young man faced with the choice between joining the Free French Forces and so leaving his mother to live alone, or staying with her and not participating in the struggle against the German occupation. Sartre argues that in this situation, as in all situations of moral choice, there are no rules of conduct or ethical principles that the young man can appeal to as a basis for making the *right* choice. He must decide what shall be the right choice. Even if he were to go to someone for advice about what he should do, he would still be making a decision about the sort of person whose advice he will listen to. He cannot avoid personal responsibility by following someone else's advice.

Sartre intends this to be an example of moral choice in general as it applies to everyone's life. Just as we must all choose our own natures, so we must all make moral choices by deciding what shall be the right thing to do. And just as there is no essence of being human that places a requirement on the way we define ourselves, so there are no valid moral principles that can tell us how we must act.

Certain criticisms have been levelled at this view of moral decisions. It has been pointed out that the situation of the young man is in fact a rather unique one and should not be taken as typical. It is a situation in which ordinary moral principles are in conflict. The young man has an obligation to take care of his mother and also an obligation to do what he can in the struggle for social justice. If he follows one principle he fails to follow the other. But, it is argued, most moral situations are not like this. Typically our choice is not between two conflicting principles both of which are acknowledged as applicable to us, but between abiding by a principle that we acknowledge applies to us and failing to abide by it. Thus we may be confronted with a decision to steal or not to steal, to help another in distress or to turn our backs, and so on. Here it seems reasonable to guide our choice by principles that we believe are validly binding. We are not forced to choose between principles themselves.

A second criticism is that moral rules need not be free of all vagueness to be useful as guides to conduct. Sartre claims that no moral rule can be stated in a precise, unambiguous way and that therefore we must arbitrarily decide when and how they apply. If we accept the rule, "Thou shalt not kill," we must *decide* whether any given act that involves the death of someone falls under the rule and so *decide* whether the act is wrong. Is killing in self-defense prohibited? Is suicide? Is mercy-killing? Is abortion? The simple rule against killing will not answer these questions for us. Thus we must still make a choice of what specific actions are forbidden by the rule. But if we do this in every situation involving someone's death we are not using a moral rule as a guide at all. We are deciding how to act in each particular case without reference to any rule.

This argument has been criticized on the ground that its conclusion does not follow from the reasons given in it. The fact that moral rules are to a degree imprecise, leaving us uncertain about their exact range of application, does not mean that they are entirely useless as guides to conduct. After all, the laws of a state are also somewhat ambiguous and vague, but they are nevertheless validly binding upon all citizens. It is true that when we find ourselves in circumstances where it is doubtful whether a given moral rule applies, we must make a decision. This is inevitable, since the conditions of life are too complex to have clearly delineated rules covering them all. Yet moral rules can still function as general guides in normal circumstances and can help us in determining what are the most important moral considerations to be taken into account when we are deciding what we should do.

Even if these points are accepted, however, the basic concept of Sartre's existentialist ethics remains in full force. Rules and principles cannot guide our conduct unless we *choose* to place ourselves under their governance. We must *adopt* them as our own normative standards. This decision to make a rule our own rule is itself a free choice, unrestricted by any other rules or principles. And since there is no essential human nature that requires us to choose in a certain way, we define our humanity in the very exercise of that freedom. We remain fully responsible for whatever rules and principles guide us, for it is we alone who, as it were, give them the authority to guide us. To regard them as *validly binding* is simply to accept our responsibility for placing ourselves under their direction. We thereby give our own answer to the question: What does it mean to exist as a human being?

A NEW INTERPRETATION OF EXISTENTIALIST ETHICS

In his book, *Principles and Persons: An Ethical Interpretation of Existentialism,* Professor Frederick Olafson attempts to show how a theory of moral obligation can be based on the existentialist view of human existence. He begins with a discussion of ethical intellectualism, a theory of human values explicitly rejected by existentialism. The ethics of existentialism, Olafson holds, can best be understood as a reaction against all forms of ethical intellectualism in the history of western philosophy. Ethical intellectualism consists of three basic ideas. First, value judgments can be true or false. Second, such judgments are objective in the sense that their truth or falsity does not depend on human feelings, attitudes, choices, or volitions. Third, it is possible to obtain knowledge of objective values, that is, to know what value judgments are true or false. Various forms of this theory, discussed by Olafson in the beginning of the reading, were propounded by Ancient Greek and Medieval philosophers.

As a transition from these intellectualistic theories to the fully developed "ontological voluntarism" of existentialism, Olafson briefly considers Nietzsche's rejection of the objectivity of values (the view that there are real value-qualities of goodness or rightness to be found in things) and Nietzsche's own conception of evaluation. According to this conception, to judge something to be good or bad is not a function of our reason but of our will. Evaluating is a volitional act in which we place value on things. We do not discover their value, we create their value, and such valuing activity is an expression of our "will to power."

There follows a close examination of the conception of values set forth by Martin Heidegger and Jean-Paul Sartre. Here Olafson is arguing that, for these philosophers, value concepts have a practical function, not a cognitive one, in human life. Such concepts as right, wrong, desirable, undesirable, and the like are action-guiding. When we make value judgments we apply these action-guiding concepts to situations in which we are confronted with a choice. We are trying to decide which action among the alternative possibilities open to us is the one to be performed. When we say that a certain act is right, we are deciding what action is appropriate to do in the given situation. We are not asserting some objective relation of rightness or appropriateness as holding between the action in question and the given situation.

Professor Olafson then analyzes the existentialist views of human freedom and choice. He here shows how existentialists account for the place of general rules in the guidance of conduct. According to his interpretation, rules cannot function as guides to a person's conduct unless that person not only chooses to follow rules but also chooses what rules to follow. Only then can the rules tell the person what features of an action are reasons for (or against) performing the action. In choosing to follow those rules, the person is in fact choosing to *make* those features relevant reasons-for-action in situations of the given kind. The rules merely embody the individual's choice and so can have no validity independently of that choice.

In the final section of the reading Professor Olafson presents his main thesis and gives a careful argument in its defense. His thesis is that, when human existence is analyzed in terms of the foregoing concepts of value, freedom, and choice, we are provided with the foundations for a theory of moral community that includes all humans. The argument for this thesis consists in showing that moral relationships of reciprocity among persons can be based on mutually accepted obligations that are freely chosen by each autonomous individual. The general duty to fulfill these mutual obligations arises from each individual's recognition of the autonomy of every other individual. Such recognition involves the acknowledgment that the autonomy of others is necessary for their very existence as human beings, just as one's own autonomy is necessary for one's humanity. It is this capacity of human beings to take a standpoint from which they view the autonomy of others in the same light in which they view their own autonomy that enables them to place obligations upon themselves and so form a moral community.

If Professor Olafson's argument is sound, he has refuted the claim that existentialism entails nihilism and amoralism. Whether his argument is sound is left to the reader's judgment.

FRIEDRICH NIETZSCHE
Critique of Traditional Ethics

THE PHILOSOPHER'S TASK

(From *Beyond Good and Evil*, 1886)

It seems to me more and more that the philosopher, as a *necessary* man of to-morrow and the day after tomorrow, has always found himself, and always had to find himself, in opposition to his today: the ideal of the day was always his enemy. Hitherto all these extraordinary promoters of man, who are called philosophers, and who rarely have felt themselves to be friends of wisdom, but rather disagreeable fools and dangerous question marks, have found their task, their hard, unwanted, inescapable task, but finally also the greatness of their task, in being the bad conscience of their time. By applying the knife vivisectionally to the very *virtues of the time* they betrayed their own secret: to know of a *new* greatness of man, of a new untrodden way to his enhancement. Each time they have uncovered how much hypocrisy, comfortableness, letting oneself go and letting oneself drop, how many lies, were concealed under the most honored type of their contemporary morality, how much virtue was *outlived*. Each time they said: "We must proceed there, that way, where today you are least at home."

Confronted with a world of "modern ideas," which would banish everybody into a corner and a "specialty," a philosopher—if there could be any philosophers today—would be forced to define the greatness of man, the concept of "greatness," in terms precisely of man's comprehensiveness and multiplicity, his wholeness in manifoldness: he would even determine worth and rank according to how much and how many things a person could bear and take upon himself, how far a person could extend his responsibility. Today the taste and virtue of the time weaken and thin out the will; nothing is more timely than weakness of the will. Therefore, according to the philosopher's ideal, it is precisely strength of will, hardness, and the capacity for long-range decisions which must form part of the concept of "greatness"—with as much justification as the opposite doctrine, and the ideal of a dumb, renunciatory, humble, selfless humanity, was suitable for an opposite age, one which, like the sixteenth century, suffered from its accumulated will power and the most savage floods and tidal waves of selfishness. . . .

Today, conversely, when only the herd animal is honored and dispenses honors in Europe, and when "equality of rights" could all too easily be converted into an equality in violating rights—by that I mean, into a common war on all that is rare, strange, or privileged, on the higher man, the higher soul, the higher duty, the higher responsibility, and on the wealth of creative power and mastery —today the concept of "greatness" entails being noble, wanting to be by oneself, being capable of being different, standing alone, and having to live independently; and the philosopher will betray something of his own ideal when he posits: "He shall be the greatest who can be the loneliest, the most hidden, the most deviating, the human being beyond good and evil, the master of his virtues, he that is overrich in will. Precisely this shall be called *greatness*: to be capable of being as manifold as whole, as wide as full." And to ask this once more: today —is greatness *possible*?

MASTER MORALITY AND SLAVE MORALITY

(From *Beyond Good and Evil*, 1886)

Wandering through the many subtler and coarser moralities which have so far been prevalent on earth, or still are prevalent, I found that certain features recurred regularly together and were closely associated—until I finally discovered two basic types and one basic difference.

There are *master morality* and *slave morality*—I add immediately that in all the higher and more mixed cultures there also appear attempts at mediation between these two moralities, and yet more often the interpenetration and mutual misunderstanding of both, and at times they occur directly alongside each other —even in the same human being, within a *single* soul.[1] The moral discrimination of values has originated either among a ruling group whose consciousness of its difference from the ruled group was accomplished by delight—or among the ruled, the slaves and dependents of every degree.

In the first case, when the ruling group determines what is "good," the exalted, proud states of the soul are experienced as conferring distinction and determining the order of rank. The noble human being separates from himself

---

[1] These crucial qualifications, though added immediately, have often been overlooked. "Modern" moralities are clearly mixtures; hence their manifold tensions, hypocrisies, and contradictions.

those in whom the opposite of such exalted, proud states finds expression: he despises them. It should be noted immediately that in this first type of morality the opposition of "good" and *"bad"* means approximately the same as "noble" and "contemptible." (The opposition of "'good" and *"evil"* has a different origin.) One feels contempt for the cowardly, the anxious, the petty, those intent on narrow utility; also for the suspicious with their unfree glances, those who humble themselves, the doglike people who allow themselves to be maltreated, the begging flatterers, above all the liars: it is part of the fundamental faith of all aristocrats that the common people lie. "We truthful ones"—thus the nobility of ancient Greece referred to itself.

It is obvious that moral designations were everywhere first applied to *human beings* and only later, derivatively, to actions. Therefore it is a gross mistake when historians of morality start from such questions as: why was the compassionate act praised? The noble type of man experiences *itself* as determining values; it does not need approval; it judges, "what is harmful to me is harmful in itself"; it knows itself to be that which first accords honor to things; it is *value-creating*. Everything it knows as part of itself it honors: such a morality is self-glorification. In the foreground there is the feeling of fullness, of power that seeks to overflow, the happiness of high tension, the consciousness of wealth that would give and bestow: the noble human being, too, helps the unfortunate, but not, or almost not, from pity, but prompted more by an urge begotten by excess of power. The noble human being honors himself as one who is powerful, also as one who has power over himself, who knows how to speak and be silent, who delights in being severe and hard with himself and respects all severity and hardness. "A hard heart Wotan put into my breast," says an old Scandinavian saga: a fitting poetic expression, seeing that it comes from the soul of a proud Viking. Such a type of man is actually proud of the fact that he is *not* made for pity, and the hero of the saga therefore adds as a warning: "If the heart is not hard in youth it will never harden." Noble and courageous human beings who think that way are furthest removed from that morality which finds the distinction of morality precisely in pity, or in acting for others, or in *désintéressement;* [2] faith in oneself, pride in oneself, a fundamental hostility and irony against "selflessness" belong just as definitely to noble morality as does a slight disdain and caution regarding compassionate feelings and a "warm heart."

It is the powerful who *understand* how to honor; this is their art, their realm of invention. The profound reverence for age and tradition—all law rests on this double reverence—the faith and prejudice in favor of ancestors and disfavor of those yet to come are typical of the morality of the powerful; and when the men of "modern ideas," conversely, believe almost instinctively in "progress" and "the future" and more and more lack respect for age, this in itself would sufficiently betray the ignoble origin of these "ideas."

A morality of the ruling group, however, is most alien and embarrassing

[2] [Literally, disinterestedness. Nietzsche here uses the French word *désintéressement* to refer to the principle that one must disregard all of one's own interests in doing what is morally right.]

to the present taste in the severity of its principle that one has duties only to one's peers; that against beings of a lower rank, against everything alien, one may behave as one pleases or "as the heart desires," and in any case "beyond good and evil"—here pity and like feelings may find their place.[3] The capacity for, and the duty of, long gratitude and long revenge—both only among one's peers—refinement in repaying, the sophisticated concept of friendship, a certain necessity for having enemies (as it were, as drainage ditches for the affects of envy, quarrelsomeness, exuberance—at bottom, in order to be capable of being good *friends*): all these are typical characteristics of noble morality which, as suggested, is not the morality of "modern ideas" and therefore is hard to empathize with today, also hard to dig up and uncover.

It is different with the second type of morality, *slave morality*. Suppose the violated, oppressed, suffering, unfree, who are uncertain of themselves and weary, moralize: what will their moral valuations have in common? Probably, a pessimistic suspicion about the whole condition of man will find expression, perhaps a condemnation of man along with his condition. The slave's eye is not favorable to the virtues of the powerful: he is skeptical and suspicious, *subtly* suspicious, of all the "good" that is honored there—he would like to persuade himself that even their happiness is not genuine. Conversely, those qualities are brought out and flooded with light which serve to ease existence for those who suffer: here pity, the complaisant and obliging hand, the warm heart, patience, industry, humility, and friendliness are honored—for here these are the most useful qualities and almost the only means for enduring the pressure of existence. Slave morality is essentially a morality of utility.

Here is the place for the origin of that famous opposition of "good" and "evil": into evil one's feelings project power and dangerousness, a certain terribleness, subtlety, and strength that does not permit contempt to develop. According to slave morality, those who are "evil" thus inspire fear; according to master morality it is precisely those who are "good" that inspire, and wish to inspire, fear, while the "bad" are felt to be contemptible.

The opposition reaches its climax when, as a logical consequence of slave morality, a touch of disdain is associated also with the "good" of this morality—this may be slight and benevolent—because the good human being has to be *undangerous* in the slaves' way of thinking: he is good-natured, easy to deceive, a little stupid perhaps, *un bonhomme*.[4] Wherever slave morality becomes preponderant, language tends to bring the words "good" and "stupid" closer together.

One last fundamental difference: the longing for *freedom*, the instinct for happiness and the subtleties of the feeling of freedom belong just as necessarily to slave morality and morals as artful and enthusiastic reverence and devotion are the regular symptom of an aristocratic way of thinking and evaluating. . . .

---

[3] The final clause that follows the dash, omitted in the Cowan translation, is crucial and qualifies the first part of the sentence: a noble person has no *duties* to animals but treats them in accordance with his feelings, which means, if he is noble, with pity. . . .

[4] Literally "a good human being," the term is used for precisely the type described here.

THE END OF BELIEF IN GOD

(From *The Gay Science*, Book Five, 1887)

The background of our cheerfulness. The greatest recent event—that "God is dead," that the belief in the Christian God has ceased to be believable—is even now beginning to cast its first shadows over Europe. For the few, at least, whose eyes, whose *suspicion* in their eyes, is strong and sensitive enough for this spectacle, some sun seems to have set just now. . . . In the main, however, this may be said: the event itself is much too great, too distant, too far from the comprehension of the many even for the tidings of it to be thought of as having *arrived* yet, not to speak of the notion that many people might know what has really happened here, and what must collapse now that this belief has been undermined—all that was built upon it, leaned on it, grew into it; for example, our whole European morality. . . .

Even we born guessers of riddles who are, as it were, waiting on the mountains, put there between today and tomorrow and stretched in the contradiction between today and tomorrow, we firstlings and premature births of the coming century, to whom the shadows that must soon envelop Europe really *should* have appeared by now—why is it that even we look forward to it without any real compassion for this darkening, and above all without any worry and fear for *ourselves*? Is it perhaps that we are still too deeply impressed by the first consequences of this event—and these first consequences, the consequences for *us*, are perhaps the reverse of what one might expect: not at all sad and dark, but rather like a new, scarcely describable kind of light, happiness, relief, exhilaration, encouragement, dawn? Indeed, we philosophers and "free spirits" feel as if a new dawn were shining on us when we receive the tidings that "the old god is dead"; our heart overflows with gratitude, amazement, anticipation, expectation. At last the horizon appears free again to us, even granted that it is not bright; at last our ships may venture out again, venture out to face any danger; all the daring of the lover of knowledge is permitted again; the sea, *our* sea, lies open again; perhaps there has never yet been such an "open sea."

GOOD AND EVIL VERSUS GOOD AND BAD

(From *Toward a Genealogy of Morals*, 1887)

The slaves' revolt in morals begins with this, that *ressentiment* [5] itself becomes creative and gives birth to values: the *ressentiment* of those who are denied the real reaction, that of the deed, and who compensate with an imaginary revenge.

---

[5] [Literally, resentment. Nietzsche uses the French word *ressentiment* to mean an impotent rage arising from injuries done by others. He takes *ressentiment* as a sign of weakness in a person.]

Whereas all noble morality grows out of a triumphant affirmation of oneself, slave morality immediately says No to what comes from outside, to what is different, to what is not oneself: and *this* No is its creative deed. This reversal of the value-positing glance—this *necessary* direction outward instead of back to oneself—is of the nature of *ressentiment*: to come into being, slave morality requires an outside world, a counterworld; physiologically speaking, it requires external stimuli in order to react at all: its action is at bottom always a reaction.

The reverse is true of the noble way of evaluating: it acts and grows spontaneously, it seeks out its opposite only in order to say Yes to itself still more gratefully, still more jubilantly; and its negative concept, "base," "mean," "bad," is only an after-born, pale, contrasting image in relation to the positive basic concept, which is nourished through and through with life and passion: "we who are noble, good, beautiful, happy!"

. . . To be unable to take one's own enemies, accidents, and misdeeds seriously for long—that is the sign of strong and rich natures. . . . Such a man simply shakes off with one shrug much vermin that would have buried itself deep in others; here alone is it also possible—assuming that it is possible at all on earth —that there be real *"love of one's enemies."* How much respect has a noble person for his enemies! And such respect is already a bridge to love. After all, he demands his enemy for himself, as his distinction; he can stand no enemy but one in whom there is nothing to be despised and *much* to be honored. Conversely, imagine "the enemy" as conceived by a man of *ressentiment*—and here precisely is his deed, his creation: he has conceived "the evil enemy," *"the evil one"*—and indeed as the fundamental concept from which he then derives, as an after-image and counterinstance, a "good one"—himself.

MORALITY AS ANTI-NATURE
(From *Twilight of the Idols*, 1889)

I

All passions have a phase when they are merely disastrous, when they drag down their victim with the weight of stupidity—and a later, very much later phase when they wed the spirit, when they "spiritualize" themselves. Formerly, in view of the element of stupidity in passion, war was declared on passion itself, its destruction was plotted; all the old moral monsters are agreed on this: *il faut tuer les passions.*[6] The most famous formula for this is to be found in the New Testament, in that Sermon on the Mount, where, incidentally, things are by no means looked at from a height. There it is said, for example, with particular reference to sexuality: "If thy eye offend thee, pluck it out." Fortunately, no Christian acts in accordance with this precept. *Destroying* the passions and cravings, merely as

---

[6] "One must kill the passions."

a preventive measure against their stupidity—today this itself strikes us as merely another acute form of stupidity. We no longer admire dentists who "pluck out" teeth so that they will not hurt any more.

To be fair, it should be admitted, however, that on the ground out of which Christianity grew, the concept of the *"spiritualization* of passion" could never have been formed. After all the first church, as is well known, fought *against* the "intelligent" in favor of the "poor in spirit." How could one expect from it an intelligent war against passion? The church fights passion with excision in every sense: its practice, its "cure," is *castration*. It never asks: "How can one spiritualize, beautify, deify a craving?" It has at all times laid the stress of discipline on extirpation (of sensuality, of pride, of the lust to rule, of avarice, of vengefulness). But an attack on the roots of passion means an attack on the roots of life: the practice of the church is *hostile to life*.

2

The same means in the fight against a craving—castration, extirpation—is instinctively chosen by those who are too weak-willed, too degenerate, to be able to impose moderation on themselves; by those who are so constituted that they require *La Trappe*,[7] to use a figure of speech, or (without any figure of speech) some kind of definitive declaration of hostility, a *cleft* between themselves and the passion. Radical means are indispensable only for the degenerate; the weakness of the will—or, to speak more definitely, the inability *not* to respond to a stimulus—is itself merely another form of degeneration. The radical hostility, the deadly hostility against sensuality, is always a symptom to reflect on: it entitles us to suppositions concerning the total state of one who is excessive in this manner.

This hostility, this hatred, by the way, reaches its climax only when such types lack even the firmness for this radical cure, for this renunciation of their "devil." One should survey the whole history of the priests and philosophers, including the artists: the most poisonous things against the senses have been said not by the impotent, nor by ascetics, but by the impossible ascetics, by those who really were in dire need of being ascetics.

3

The spiritualization of sensuality is called *love:* it represents a great triumph over Christianity. Another triumph is our spiritualization of *hostility*. It consists in a profound appreciation of the value of having enemies: in short, it means acting and thinking in the opposite way from that which has been the rule. The

[7] The Trappist Order.

church always wanted the destruction of its enemies; we, we immoralists and Antichristians, find our advantage in this, that the church exists. In the political realm too, hostility has now become more spiritual—much more sensible, much more thoughtful, much more *considerate*. Almost every party understands how it is in the interest of its own self-preservation that the opposition should not lose all strength; the same is true of power politics. A new creation in particular—the new *Reich*,[8] for example—needs enemies more than friends: in opposition alone does it *feel* itself necessary, in opposition alone does it *become* necessary.

Our attitude to the "internal enemy" is no different: here too we have spiritualized hostility; here too we have come to appreciate its value. The price of fruitfulness is to be rich in internal opposition; one remains young only as long as the soul does not stretch itself and desire peace. Nothing has become more alien to us than that desideratum of former times, "peace of soul," the *Christian* desideratum; there is nothing we envy less than the moralistic cow and the fat happiness of the good conscience. One has renounced the *great* life when one renounces war.

In many cases, to be sure, "peace of soul" is merely a misunderstanding—something else, which lacks only a more honest name. Without further ado or prejudice, a few examples. "Peace of soul" can be, for one, the gentle radiation of a rich animality into the moral (or religious) sphere. Or the beginning of weariness, the first shadow of evening, of any kind of evening. Or a sign that the air is humid, that south winds are approaching. Or unrecognized gratitude for a good digestion (sometimes called "love of man"). Or the attainment of calm by a convalescent who feels a new relish in all things and waits. Or the state which follows a thorough satisfaction of our dominant passion, the well-being of a rare repletion. Or the senile weakness of our will, our cravings, our vices. Or laziness, persuaded by vanity to give itself moral airs. Or the emergence of certainty, even a dreadful certainty, after long tension and torture by uncertainty. Or the expression of maturity and mastery in the midst of doing, creating, working, and willing—calm breathing, *attained* "freedom of the will." *Twilight of the Idols*—who knows? perhaps also only a kind of "peace of soul."

4

I reduce a principle to a formula. Every naturalism in morality—that is, every healthy morality—is dominated by an instinct of life; some commandment of life is fulfilled by a determinate canon of "shalt" and "shalt not"; some inhibition and hostile element on the path of life is thus removed. *Anti-natural* morality—that is, almost every morality which has so far been taught, revered, and preached—turns, conversely, *against* the instincts of life: it is *condemnation* of these instincts, now secret, now outspoken and impudent. When it says, "God

[8] [Empire; state power.]

looks at the heart," it says No to both the lowest and the highest desires of life, and posits God as the *enemy of life*. The saint in whom God delights is the ideal eunuch. Life has come to an end where the "kingdom of God" begins.

5

Once one has comprehended the outrage of such a revolt against life as has become almost sacrosanct in Christian morality, one has, fortunately, also comprehended something else: the futility, apparentness, absurdity, and *mendaciousness* of such a revolt. A condemnation of life by the living remains in the end a mere symptom of a certain kind of life: the question whether it is justified or unjustified is not even raised thereby. One would require a position *outside* of life, and yet have to know it as well as one, as many, as all who have lived it, in order to be permitted even to touch the problem of the *value* of life: reasons enough to comprehend that this problem is for us an unapproachable problem. When we speak of values, we speak with the inspiration, with the way of looking at things, which is part of life: life itself forces us to posit values; life itself values through us when we posit values. From this it follows that even that anti-natural morality which conceives of God as the counter-concept and condemnation of life is only a value judgment of life—but of what life? of what kind of life? I have already given the answer: of declining, weakened, weary, condemned life. Morality, as it has so far been understood—as it has in the end been formulated once more by Schopenhauer, as "negation of the will to life"— is the very *instinct of decadence,* which makes an imperative of itself. It says: "*Perish!*" It is a condemnation pronounced by the condemned.

6

Let us finally consider how naïve it is altogether to say: "Man *ought* to be such and such!" Reality shows us an enchanting wealth of types, the abundance of a lavish play and change of forms—and some wretched loafer of a moralist comments: "No! Man ought to be different." He even knows what man should be like, this wretched bigot and prig: he paints himself on the wall and comments, "*Ecce homo!*" [9] But even when the moralist addresses himself only to the single human being and says to him, "You ought to be such and such!" he does not cease to make himself ridiculous. The single human being is a piece of *fatum* [10] from the front and from the rear, one law more, one necessity more for all that is yet to come and to be. To say to him, "Change yourself!" is to demand that everything be changed, even retroactively. And indeed there have been con-

---

[9] ["Behold man."]
[10] [Fate; necessity; what must be as it is.]

sistent moralists who wanted man to be different, that is, virtuous—they wanted him remade in their own image, as a prig: to that end, they *negated* the world! No small madness! No modest kind of immodesty!

Morality, insofar as it *condemns* for its own sake, and *not* out of regard for the concerns, considerations, and contrivances of life, is a specific error with which one ought to have no pity—an *idiosyncrasy of degenerates* which has caused immeasurable harm.

We others, we immoralists, have, conversely, made room in our hearts for every kind of understanding, comprehending, and *approving*. We do not easily negate; we make it a point of honor to be *affirmers*. More and more, our eyes have opened to that economy which needs and knows how to utilize all that the holy witlessness of the priest, of the *diseased* reason in the priest, rejects—that economy in the law of life which finds an advantage even in the disgusting species of the prigs, the priests, the virtuous. *What* advantage? But we ourselves, we immoralists, are the answer.

7

The error of free will. Today we no longer have any pity for the concept of "free will": we know only too well what it really is—the foulest of all theologians' artifices, aimed at making mankind "responsible" in their sense, that is, *dependent upon them*. Here I simply supply the psychology of all "making responsible."

Wherever responsibilities are sought, it is usually the instinct of wanting to judge and punish which is at work. Becoming has been deprived of its innocence when any being-such-and-such is traced back to will, to purposes, to acts of responsibility: the doctrine of the will has been invented essentially for the purpose of punishment, that is, because one wanted to impute guilt. The entire old psychology, the psychology of will, was conditioned by the fact that its originators, the priests at the head of ancient communities, wanted to create for themselves the right to punish—or wanted to create this right for God. Men were considered "free" so that they might be judged and punished—so that they might become *guilty*: consequently, every act had to be considered as willed, and the origin of every act had to be considered as lying within the consciousness (and thus the most fundamental counterfeit *in psychologicis* was made the principle of psychology itself).

Today, as we have entered into the reverse movement and we immoralists are trying with all our strength to take the concept of guilt and the concept of punishment out of the world again, and to cleanse psychology, history, nature, and social institutions and sanctions of them, there is in our eyes no more radical opposition than that of the theologians, who continue with the concept of a "moral world-order" to infect the innocence of becoming by means of "punishment" and "guilt." Christianity is a metaphysics of the hangman.

8

What alone can be *our* doctrine? That no one *gives* man his qualities—neither God, nor society, nor his parents and ancestors, nor he himself. (The nonsense of the last idea was taught as "intelligible freedom" by Kant—perhaps by Plato already.) No one is responsible for man's being there at all, for his being such-and-such, or for his being in these circumstances or in this environment. The fatality of his essence is not to be disentangled from the fatality of all that has been and will be. Man is not the effect of some special purpose, of a will, and end; nor is he the object of an attempt to attain an "ideal of humanity" or an "ideal of happiness" or an "ideal of morality." It is absurd to wish to devolve one's essence on some end or other. We have invented the concept of "end": in reality there is no end.

One is necessary, one is a piece of fatefulness, one belongs to the whole, one is in the whole; there is nothing which could judge, measure, compare, or sentence our being, for that would mean judging, measuring, comparing, or sentencing the whole. But there is nothing besides the whole. That nobody is held responsible any longer, that the mode of being may not be traced back to a *causa prima*,[11] that the world does not form a unity either as a sensorium or as "spirit"—that alone is the great liberation; with this alone is the innocence of becoming restored. The concept of "God" was until now the greatest objection to existence. We deny God, we deny the responsibility in God: only thereby do we redeem the world.

THE "IMPROVERS" OF MANKIND

(From *Twilight of the Idols*, 1889)

I

My demand upon the philosopher is known, that he take his stand *beyond* good and evil and leave the illusion of moral judgment *beneath* himself. This demand follows from an insight which I was the first to formulate: that *there are altogether no moral facts*. Moral judgments agree with religious ones in believing in realities which are no realities. Morality is merely an interpretation of certain phenomena—more precisely, a misinterpretation. Moral judgments, like religious ones, belong to a stage of ignorance at which the very concept of the real and the distinction between what is real and imaginary, are still lacking; thus "truth," at this stage, designates all sorts of things which we today call "imaginings." Moral judgments are therefore never to be taken literally: so understood, they always contain mere absurdity. Semeiotically, however, they

---

[11] [First cause.]

remain invaluable: they reveal, at least for those who know, the most valuable realities of cultures and inwardnesses which did not know enough to "understand" themselves. Morality is mere sign language, mere symptomatology: one must know what it is all about to be able to profit from it.

2

A first example, quite provisional. At all times they have wanted to "improve" men: this above all was called morality. Under the same word, however, the most divergent tendencies are concealed. Both the *taming* of the beast, man, and the *breeding* of a particular kind of man have been called "improvement." Such zoological terms are required to express the realities—realities, to be sure, of which the typical "improver," the priest, neither knows anything, nor wants to know anything.

To call the taming of an animal its "improvement" sounds almost like a joke to our ears. Whoever knows what goes on in menageries doubts that the beasts are "improved" there. They are weakened, they are made less harmful, and through the depressive effect of fear, through pain, through wounds, and through hunger they become sickly beasts. It is no different with the tamed man whom the priest has "improved." In the early Middle Ages, when the church was indeed, above all, a menagerie, the most beautiful specimens of the "blond beast" were hunted down everywhere; and the noble Teutons, for example, were "improved." But how did such an "improved" Teuton who had been seduced into a monastery look afterward? Like a caricature of man, like a miscarriage: he had become a "sinner," he was stuck in a cage, imprisoned among all sorts of terrible concepts. And there he lay, sick, miserable, malevolent against himself: full of hatred against the springs of life, full of suspicion against all that was still strong and happy. In short, a "Christian."

Physiologically speaking: in the struggle with beasts, to make them sick *may* be the only means for making them weak. This the church understood: it *ruined* man, it weakened him—but it claimed to have "improved" him.

3

Let us consider the other case of so-called morality, the case of *breeding* a particular race and kind. The most magnificent example of this is furnished by Indian morality, sanctioned as religion in the form of "the law of Manu." Here the task set is to breed no less than four races at once: one priestly, one warlike, one for trade and agriculture, and finally a race of servants, the Sudras. Obviously, we are here no longer among animal tamers: a kind of man that is a hundred times milder and more reasonable is the condition for even conceiving such a plan of breeding. One heaves a sigh of relief at leaving the Christian atmosphere of disease and dungeons for this healthier, higher, and *wider* world. How wretched is the New Testament compared to Manu, how foul it smells!

Yet this organization too found it necessary to be *terrible*—this time not in the struggle with beasts, but with their counter-concept, the unbred man, the mish-mash man, the chandala. And again it had no other means for keeping him from being dangerous, for making him weak, than to make him *sick*—it was the fight with the "great number." Perhaps there is nothing that contradicts our feeling more than *these* protective measures of Indian morality. The third edict, for example (Avadana-Sastra I), "on impure vegetables," ordains that the only nourishment permitted to the chandala shall be garlic and onions, seeing that the holy scripture prohibits giving them grain or fruit with grains, or water or fire. The same edict orders that the water they need may not be taken from rivers or wells, nor from ponds, but only from the approaches to swamps and from holes made by the footsteps of animals. They are also prohibited from washing their laundry and *from washing themselves,* since the water they are conceded as an act of grace may be used only to quench thirst. Finally, a prohibition that Sudra women may not assist chandala women in childbirth, and a prohibition that the latter may not *assist each other* in this condition.

The success of such sanitary police measures was inevitable: murderous epidemics, ghastly venereal diseases, and thereupon again "the law of the knife," ordaining circumcision for male children and the removal of the internal labia for female children. Manu himself says: "The chandalas are the fruit of adultery, incest, and crime (these, the *necessary* consequences of the concept of breeding). For clothing they shall have only rags from corpses; for dishes, broken pots; for adornment, old iron; for divine services, only evil spirits. They shall wander without rest from place to place. They are prohibited from writing from left to right, and from using the right hand in writing: the use of the right hand and of from-left-to-right is reserved for the virtuous, for the people of *race*."

4

These regulations are instructive enough: here we encounter for once *Aryan* humanity, quite pure, quite primordial—we learn that the concept of "pure blood" is the opposite of a harmless concept. On the other hand, it becomes clear in which people the hatred, the chandala hatred, against this "humaneness" has eternalized itself, where it has become religion, where it has become *genius.* Seen in this perspective, the Gospels represent a document of prime importance; even more, the Book of Enoch. Christianity, sprung from Jewish roots and comprehensible only as a growth on this soil, represents the counter-movement to any morality of breeding, of race, of privilege: it is the *anti-Aryan* religion par excellence. Christianity—the revaluation of all Aryan values, the victory of chandala values, the gospel preached to the poor and base, the general revolt of all the downtrodden, the wretched, the failures, the less favored, against "race": the undying chandala hatred as the *religion of love.*

5

The morality of *breeding* and the morality of *taming* are, in the means they use, entirely worthy of each other: we may proclaim it as the supreme principle that, to *make* morality, one must have the unconditional will to its opposite. This is the great, the uncanny problem which I have been pursuing the longest: the psychology of the "improvers" of mankind. A small, and at bottom modest, fact—that of the so-called *pia fraus* [12]—offered me the first approach to this problem: the *pia fraus,* the heirloom of all philosophers and priests who "improved" mankind. Neither Manu nor Plato nor Confucius nor the Jewish and Christian teachers have ever doubted their *right* to lie. They have not doubted that they had very different rights too. Expressed in a formula, one might say: *all* the means by which one has so far attempted to make mankind moral were through and through *immoral.*

6

EGOISM AND MORALITY

(From *Twilight of the Idols,* 1889)

The natural value of egoism. Self-interest is worth as much as the person who has it: it can be worth a great deal, and it can be unworthy and contemptible. Every individual may be scrutinized to see whether he represents the ascending or the descending line of life. Having made that decision, one has a canon for the worth of his self-interest. If he represents the ascending line, then his worth is indeed extraordinary—and for the sake of life as a whole, which takes a step farther through him, the care for his preservation and for the creation of the best conditions for him may even be extreme. The single one, the "individual," as hitherto understood by the people and the philosophers alike, is an error after all: he is nothing by himself, no atom, no "link in the chain," nothing merely inherited from former times; he is the whole single line of humanity up to himself. If he represents the descending development, decay, chronic degeneration, and sickness (sicknesses are, in general, the consequences of decay, not its causes), then he has small worth, and the minimum of decency requires that he take away as little as possible from those who have turned out well. He is merely their parasite.

Christian and anarchist. When the anarchist, as the mouthpiece of the declining strata of society, demands with a fine indignation what is "right,"

[12] [The pious fraud. A lie considered to be justified on religious grounds.]

"justice," and "equal rights," he is merely under the pressure of his own un-cultured state, which cannot comprehend the real reason for his suffering—what it is that he is poor in: life. A causal instinct asserts itself in him: it must be somebody's fault that he is in a bad way.

Also, the "fine indignation" itself soothes him; it is a pleasure for all wretched devils to scold: it gives a slight but intoxicating sense of power. Even plaintiveness and complaining can give life a charm for the sake of which one endures it: there is a fine dose of revenge in every complaint; one charges one's own bad situation, and under certain circumstances even one's own badness, to those who are different, as if that were an injustice, a forbidden privilege. "If I am canaille,[13] you ought to be too"—on such logic are revolutions made.

Complaining is never any good: it stems from weakness. Whether one charges one's misfortune to others or to oneself—the socialist does the former; the Christian, for example, the latter—really makes no difference. The common and, let us add, the unworthy, thing is that it is supposed to be somebody's fault that one is suffering; in short, that the sufferer prescribes the honey of revenge for himself against his suffering. The objects of this need for revenge, as a need for pleasure, are mere occasions: everywhere the sufferer finds oc-casions for satisfying his little revenge. If he is a Christian—to repeat it once more—he finds them in himself. The Christian and the anarchist are both decadents. When the Christian condemns, slanders, and besmirches "the world," his instinct is the same as that which prompts the socialist worker to condemn, slander, and besmirch *society*. The "last judgment" is the sweet comfort of revenge—the revolution, which the socialist worker also awaits, but conceived as a little farther off. The "beyond"—why a beyond, if not as a means for besmirching *this* world?

Critique of the morality of decadence. An "altruistic" morality—a morality in which self-interest wilts away—remains a bad sign under all circumstances. This is true of individuals; it is particularly true of nations. The best is lacking when self-interest begins to be lacking. Instinctively to choose what is harmful for *oneself,* to feel attracted by "disinterested" motives, that is virtually the formula of decadence. "Not to seek one's own advantage"—that is merely the moral fig leaf for quite a different, namely, a physiological, state of affairs: "I no longer know how to *find* my own advantage." Disgregation of the instincts! Man is finished when he becomes altruistic. Instead of saying naïvely, "*I* am no longer worth anything," the moral lie in the mouth of the decadent says, "Nothing is worth anything, life is not worth anything." Such a judgment always remains very dangerous, it is contagious: throughout the morbid soil of society it soon proliferates into a tropical vegetation of concepts—now as a religion (Christianity), now as a philosophy (Schopenhauerism). Sometimes the poisonous vegetation which has grown out of such decomposition poisons life itself for millennia with its fumes.

[13] [Of the masses; the mob.]

Morality for physicians. The sick man is a parasite of society. In a certain state it is indecent to live longer. To go on vegetating in cowardly dependence on physicians and machinations, after the meaning of life, the right to life, has been lost, that ought to prompt a profound contempt in society. The physicians, in turn, would have to be the mediators of this contempt—not prescriptions, but every day a new dose of nausea with their patients. To create a new responsibility, that of the physician, for all cases in which the highest interest of life, of ascending life, demands the most inconsiderate pushing down and aside of degenerating life—for example, for the right of procreation, for the right to be born, for the right to live.

To die proudly when it is no longer possible to live proudly. Death freely chosen, death at the right time, brightly and cheerfully accomplished amid children and witnesses: then a real farewell is still possible, as the one who is taking leave is still there; also a real estimate of what one has achieved and what one has wished, drawing the sum of one's life—all in opposition to the wretched and revolting comedy that Christianity has made of the hour of death. One should never forget that Christianity has exploited the weakness of the dying for a rape of the conscience; and the manner of death itself, for value judgments about man and the past.

Here it is important to defy all the cowardices of prejudice and to establish, above all, the real, that is, the physiological, appreciation of so-called *natural* death—which is in the end also "unnatural," a kind of suicide. One never perishes through anybody but oneself. But usually it is death under the most contemptible conditions, an unfree death, death *not* at the right time, a coward's death. From love of *life,* one should desire a different death: free, conscious, without accident, without ambush.

THE REVALUATION OF ALL VALUES

(From *Revaluation of All Values, Part One: The Antichrist,* 1889)

What is good? Everything that heightens the feeling of power in man, the will to power, power itself.

What is bad? Everything that is born of weakness.

What is happiness? The feeling that power is *growing,* that resistance is overcome.

Not contentedness but more power; not peace but war; not virtue but fitness (Renaissance virtue, *virtù,* virtue that is moraline [14]-free).

The weak and the failures shall perish: first principle of *our* love of man. And they shall even be given every possible assistance.

What is more harmful than any vice? Active pity for all the failures and all the weak: Christianity.

[14] The coinage of a man who neither smoked nor drank coffee.

The problem I thus pose is not what shall succeed mankind in the sequence of living beings (man is an *end*), but what type of man shall be *bred*, shall be *willed*, for being higher in value, worthier of life, more certain of a future.

Even in the past this higher type has appeared often—but as a fortunate accident, as an exception, never as something *willed*. In fact, this has been the type most dreaded—almost *the* dreadful—and from dread the opposite type was willed, bred, and *attained*: the domestic animal, the herd animal, the sick human animal—the Christian.

Mankind does *not* represent a development toward something better or stronger or higher in the sense accepted today. "Progress" is merely a modern idea, that is, a false idea. The European of today is vastly inferior in value to the European of the Renaissance: further development is altogether *not* according to any necessity in the direction of elevation, enhancement, or strength.

In another sense, success in individual cases is constantly encountered in the most widely different places and cultures: here we really do find a *higher type*, which is, in relation to mankind as a whole, a kind of overman. Such fortunate accidents of great success have always been possible and *will* perhaps always be possible. And even whole families, tribes, or peoples may occasionally represent such a *bull's-eye*.

Christianity should not be beautified and embellished: it has waged deadly war against this higher type of man; it has placed all the basic instincts of this type under the ban; and out of these instincts it has distilled evil and the Evil One: the strong man as the typically reprehensible man, the "reprobate." Christianity has sided with all that is weak and base, with all failures; it has made an ideal of whatever *contradicts* the instinct of the strong life to preserve itself; it has corrupted the reason even of those strongest in spirit by teaching men to consider the supreme values of the spirit as something sinful, as something that leads into error—as temptations. The most pitiful example: the corruption of Pascal, who believed in the corruption of his reason through original sin when it had in fact been corrupted only by his Christianity.

It is a painful, horrible spectacle that has dawned on me: I have drawn back the curtain from the *corruption* of man. In my mouth, this word is at least free from one suspicion: that it might involve a moral accusation of man. It is meant—let me emphasize this once more—*moraline-free*. So much so that I experience this corruption most strongly precisely where men have so far aspired most deliberately to "virtue" and "godliness." I understand corruption, as you will guess, in the sense of decadence: it is my contention that all the values in which mankind now sums up its supreme desiderata are *decadence-values*.

I call an animal, a species, or an individual corrupt when it loses its instincts, when it chooses, when it prefers, what is disadvantageous for it. A history of "lofty sentiments," of the "ideals of mankind"—and it is possible that

I shall have to write it—would almost explain too *why* man is so corrupt. Life itself is to my mind the instinct for growth, for durability, for an accumulation of forces, for *power*: where the will to power is lacking there is decline. It is my contention that all the supreme values of mankind *lack* this will—that the values which are symptomatic of decline, *nihilistic* values, are lording it under the holiest names.

Christianity is called the religion of *pity*. Pity stands opposed to the tonic emotions which heighten our vitality: it has a depressing effect. We are deprived of strength when we feel pity. That loss of strength which suffering as such inflicts on life is still further increased and multiplied by pity. Pity makes suffering contagious. Under certain circumstances, it may engender a total loss of life and vitality out of all proportion to the magnitude of the cause (as in the case of the death of the Nazarene). That is the first consideration, but there is a more important one.

Suppose we measure pity by the value of the reactions it usually produces; then its perilous nature appears in an even brighter light. Quite in general, pity crosses the law of development, which is the law of *selection*. It preserves what is ripe for destruction; it defends those who have been disinherited and condemned by life; and by the abundance of the failures of all kinds which it keeps alive, it gives life itself a gloomy and questionable aspect.

Some have dared to call pity a virtue (in every *noble* ethic it is considered a weakness); and as if this were not enough, it has been made *the* virtue, the basis and source of all virtues. To be sure—and one should always keep this in mind—this was done by a philosophy that was nihilistic and had inscribed the *negation of life* upon its shield. Schopenhauer was consistent enough: pity negates life and renders it *more deserving of negation*.

Pity is the *practice* of nihilism. To repeat: this depressive and contagious instinct crosses those instincts which aim at the preservation of life and at the enhancement of its value. It multiplies misery and conserves all that is miserable, and is thus a prime instrument of the advancement of decadence: pity persuades men to *nothingness!* Of course, one does not say "nothingness" but "beyond" or "God," or "*true* life," or Nirvana, salvation, blessedness.

This innocent rhetoric from the realm of the religious-moral idiosyncrasy appears much less innocent as soon as we realize which tendency it is that here shrouds itself in sublime words: *hostility against life*. Schopenhauer was hostile to life; therefore pity became a virtue for him.

Aristotle, as is well known, considered pity a pathological and dangerous condition, which one would be well advised to attack now and then with a purge: he understood tragedy as a purge. From the standpoint of the instinct of life, a remedy certainly seems necessary for such a pathological and dangerous accumulation of pity as is represented by the case of Schopenhauer (and unfortunately by our entire literary and artistic decadence from St. Petersburg to Paris, from Tolstoi to Wagner)—to puncture it and make it *burst*.

In our whole unhealthy modernity there is nothing more unhealthy than Christian pity. To be physicians *here,* to be inexorable *here,* to wield the scalpel *here*—that is *our* part, that is *our* love of man, that is how *we* are philosophers. . . .

THE WILL TO POWER

(A selection from Nietzsche's notebooks of the years 1883–1888)

In the tremendous multiplicity of events within an organism, the part which becomes conscious to us is a mere means: and the little bit of "virtue," "selflessness," and similar fictions are refuted radically by the total balance of events. We should study our organism in all its immorality—

The animal functions are, as a matter of principle, a million times more important than all our beautiful moods and heights of consciousness: the latter are a surplus, except when they have to serve as tools of those animal functions. The entire *conscious* life, the spirit along with the soul, the heart, goodness, and virtue—in whose service do they labor? In the service of the greatest possible perfection of the means (means of nourishment, means of enhancement) of the basic animal functions: above all, the enhancement of life.

What one used to call "body" and "flesh" is of such unspeakably greater importance: the remainder is a small accessory. The task of spinning on the chain of life, and in such a way that the thread grows ever more powerful— that is the task.

But consider how heart, soul, virtue, spirit practically conspire together to subvert this systematic task—as if *they* were the end in view!— The degeneration of life is conditioned essentially by the extraordinary proneness to error of consciousness: it is held in check by instinct the least of all and therefore blunders the longest and the most thoroughly.

To measure whether existence has value according to the pleasant or unpleasant feelings aroused in this consciousness: can one think of a madder extravagance of vanity? For it is only a means—and pleasant or unpleasant feelings are also only means!

What is the objective measure of value? Solely the quantum of enhanced and organized power.

Man does *not* seek pleasure and does not avoid displeasure: one will realize which famous prejudice I am contradicting. Pleasure and displeasure are mere consequences, mere epiphenomena—what man wants, what every smallest part of a living organism wants, is an increase of power. Pleasure or displeasure follow from the striving after that; driven by that will it seeks resistance, it needs something that opposes it— Displeasure, as an obstacle to its will to power, is therefore a normal fact, the normal ingredient of every organic event; man does not avoid it, he is rather in continual need of it; every victory, every feeling of pleasure, every event, presupposes a resistance overcome.

Let us take the simplest case, that of primitive nourishment: the protoplasm extends it pseudopodia in search of something that resists it—not from hunger but from will to power. Thereupon it attempts to overcome, appropriate, assimilate what it encounters: what one calls "nourishment" is merely a derivative phenomenon, an application of the original will to become *stronger*.

Displeasure thus does not merely not have to result in a diminution of our feeling of power, but in the average case it actually stimulates this feeling of power—the obstacle is the stimulus of this will to power.

One has confused displeasure with one *kind* of displeasure, with exhaustion; the latter does indeed represent a profound diminution and reduction of the will to power, a measurable loss of force. That is to say: there exists (a) displeasure as a means of stimulating the increase of power, and (b) displeasure following an overexpenditure of power; in the first case a stimulus, in the second the result of an excessive stimulation— Inability to resist is characteristic of the latter kind of displeasure: a challenge to that which resists belongs to the former— The only pleasure still felt in the condition of exhaustion is falling asleep; victory is the pleasure in the other case—

The great confusion on the part of psychologists consisted in not distinguishing between these two kinds of pleasure—that of falling asleep and that of victory. The exhausted want rest, relaxation, peace, calm—the happiness of the nihilistic religions and philosophies; the rich and living want victory, opponents overcome, the overflow of the feeling of power across wider domains than hitherto. All healthy functions of the organism have this need—and the whole organism [15] is such a complex of systems struggling for an increase of the feeling of power—

How does it happen that the basic articles of faith in psychology are one and all the most arrant misrepresentations and counterfeits? "Man strives after happiness," e.g.—how much of that is true? In order to understand what "life" is, what kind of striving and tension life is, the formula must apply as well to trees and plants as to animals. "What does a plant strive after?"—but here we have already invented a false unity which does not exist: the fact of a millionfold growth with individual and semi-individual initiatives is concealed and denied if we begin by positing a crude unity "plant." That the very smallest "individuals" cannot be understood in the sense of a "metaphysical individuality" and atom, that their sphere of power is continually changing—that is the first thing that becomes obvious; but does each of them strive after happiness when it changes in this way?—

But all expansion, incorporation, growth means striving against something that resists; motion is essentially tied up with states of displeasure; that which is here the driving force must in any event desire something else if it desires dis-

[15] The words that immediately follow in the MS have been omitted in all editions: "up to the age of puberty."

pleasure in this way and continually looks for it.— For what do the trees in a jungle fight each other? For "happiness"?— *For power!*—

Man, become master over the forces of nature, master over his own savagery and licentiousness (the desires have learned to obey and be useful)—man, in comparison with a pre-man—represents a tremendous quantum of *power—not* an increase in "happiness"! How can one claim that he has *striven* for happiness?—

As I say this I see above me, glittering under the stars, the tremendous rat's tail of errors that has hitherto counted as the highest inspiration of humanity: "All happiness is a consequence of virtue, all virtue is a consequence of free will!"

Let us reverse the values: all fitness the result of fortunate organization, all freedom the result of fitness (—freedom here understood as facility in self-direction. Every artist will understand me).

"The value of life."— Life is a unique case; one must justify all existence and not only life—the justifying principle is one that explains life, too.

Life is only a *means* to something; it is the expression of forms of the growth of power.

The "*conscious* world" cannot serve as a starting point for values: need for an "*objective*" positing of values.

In relation to the vastness and multiplicity of collaboration and mutual opposition encountered in the life of every organism, the *conscious* world of feelings, intentions, and valuations is a small section. We have no right whatever to posit this piece of consciousness as the aim and wherefore of this total phenomenon of life: becoming conscious is obviously only one more means toward the unfolding and extension of the power of life. Therefore it is a piece of naiveté to posit pleasure or spirituality or morality or any other particular of the sphere of consciousness as the highest value—and perhaps even to justify "the world" by means of this.

This is my *basic objection* to all philsophic-moralistic cosmologies and theodicies, to all *wherefores* and *highest values* in philosophy and theology hitherto. One kind of means has been misunderstood as an end; conversely, life and the enhancement of its power has been debased to a means.

If we wished to postulate a goal adequate to life, it could not coincide with any category of conscious life; it would rather have to explain all of them as a means to itself—

The "denial of life" as an aim of life, an aim of evolution! Existence as a great stupidity! Such a lunatic interpretation is only the product of measuring life by aspects of consciousness (pleasure and displeasure, good and evil). Here the means are made to stand against the end—the "unholy," absurd, above all unpleasant means—: how can an end that employs such means be worth anything! But the mistake is that, instead of looking for a purpose that explains the *necessity* of such means, we presuppose in advance a goal that actually *excludes* such means; i.e., we take a desideratum in respect of certain means (namely pleasant, rational, and virtuous ones) as a norm, on the basis of which we posit what general purpose would be desirable—

The fundamental mistake is simply that, instead of understanding consciousness as a tool and particular aspect of the total life, we posit it as the standard and the condition of life that is of supreme value: it is the erroneous perspective of *a parte ad totum* [16]—which is why all philosophers are instinctively trying to imagine a total consciousness, a consciousness involved in all life and will, in all that occurs, a "spirit," "God." But one has to tell them that precisely this turns life into a monstrosity; that a "God" and total sensorium would altogether be something on account of which life would have to be condemned— Precisely that we have *eliminated* the total consciousness that posited ends and means, is our great relief—with that we are no longer *compelled* to be pessimists— *Our* greatest *reproach* against existence was the *existence of God*—

And do you know what "the world" is to me? Shall I show it to you in my mirror? This world: a monster of energy, without beginning, without end; a firm, iron magnitude of force that does not grow bigger or smaller, that does not expend itself but only transforms itself; as a whole, of unalterable size, a household without expenses or losses, but likewise without increase or income; enclosed by "nothingness" as by a boundary; not something blurry or wasted, not something endlessly extended, but set in a definite space as a definite force, and not a space that might be "empty" here or there, but rather as force throughout, as a play of forces and waves of forces, at the same time one and many, increasing here and at the same time decreasing there; a sea of forces flowing and rushing together, eternally changing, eternally flooding back, with tremendous years of recurrence, with an ebb and a flood of its forms; out of the simplest forms striving toward the most complex, out of the stillest, most rigid, coldest forms toward the hottest, most turbulent, most self-contradictory, and then again returning home to the simple out of this abundance, out of the play of contradictions back to the joy of concord, still affirming itself in this uniformity of its courses and its years, blessing itself as that which must return eternally, as a becoming that knows no satiety, no disgust, no weariness: this, my *Dionysian* world of the eternally self-creating, the eternally self-destroying, this mystery world of the twofold voluptuous delight, my "beyond good and evil," without goal, unless the joy of the circle is itself a goal; without will, unless a ring feels good toward itself—do you want a *name* for this world? A *solution* for all its riddles? A *light* for you, too, you best-concealed, strongest, most intrepid, most midnightly men?—*This world is the will to power—and nothing besides!* And you yourselves are also this will to power—and nothing besides!

[16] From a part to the whole.

JEAN-PAUL SARTRE

The Humanism of Existentialism

I should like on this occasion to defend existentialism against some charges which have been brought against it.

First, it has been charged with inviting people to remain in a kind of desperate quietism because, since no solutions are possible, we should have to consider action in this world as quite impossible. We should then end up in a philosophy of contemplation; and since contemplation is a luxury, we come in the end to a bourgeois philosophy. The communists in particular have made these charges.

On the other hand, we have been charged with dwelling on human degradation, with pointing up everywhere the sordid, shady, and slimy, and neglecting the gracious and beautiful, the bright side of human nature; for example, according to Mlle. Mercier, a Catholic critic, with forgetting the smile of the child. Both sides charge us with having ignored human solidarity, with considering man as an isolated being. The communists say that the main reason for this is that we take pure subjectivity, the Cartesian *I think,* as our starting point; in other words, the moment in which man becomes fully aware of what it means to him to be an isolated being; as a result, we are unable to return to a state of solidarity with the men who are not ourselves, a state which we can never reach in the *cogito.*

From the Christian standpoint, we are charged with denying the reality and seriousness of human undertakings, since, if we reject God's commandments and the eternal verities, there no longer remains anything but pure caprice, with everyone permitted to do as he pleases and incapable, from his own point of view, of condemning the points of view and acts of others.

I shall today try to answer these different charges. Many people are going to be surprised at what is said here about humanism. We shall try to see in what sense it is to be understood. In any case, what can be said from the very beginning is that by existentialism we mean a doctrine which makes human life possible and, in addition, declares that every truth and every action implies a human setting and a human subjectivity.

As is generally known, the basic charge against us is that we put the emphasis on the dark side of human life. Someone recently told me of a lady

From Jean-Paul Sartre, *The Humanism of Existentialism,* translated by Bernard Frechtman. Published in Jean-Paul Sartre, *The Philosophy of Existentialism,* ed. Wade Baskin (1965). Reprinted by permission of Philosophical Library, Inc., New York.

who, when she let slip a vulgar word in a moment of irritation, excused herself by saying, "I guess I'm becoming an existentialist." Consequently, existentialism is regarded as something ugly; that is why we are said to be naturalists; and if we are, it is rather surprising that in this day and age we cause so much more alarm and scandal than does naturalism, properly so called. The kind of person who can take in his stride such a novel as Zola's *The Earth* is disgusted as soon as he starts reading an existentialist novel; the kind of person who is resigned to the wisdom of the ages—which is pretty sad—finds us even sadder. Yet, what can be more disillusioning than saying "true charity begins at home" or "a scoundrel will always return evil for good"?

We know the commonplace remarks made when this subject comes up, remarks which always add up to the same thing: we shouldn't struggle against the powers-that-be; we shouldn't resist authority; we shouldn't try to rise above our station; any action which doesn't conform to authority is romantic; any effort not based on past experience is doomed to failure; experience shows that man's bent is always toward trouble, that there must be a strong hand to hold him in check, if not, there will be anarchy. There are still people who go on mumbling these melancholy old saws, the people who say, "It's only human!" whenever a more or less repugnant act is pointed out to them, the people who glut themselves on *chansons réalistes;* these are the people who accuse existentialism of being too gloomy, and to such an extent that I wonder whether they are complaining about it, not for its pessimism, but much rather its optimism. Can it be that what really scares them in the doctrine I shall try to present here is that it leaves to man a possibility of choice? To answer this question, we must re-examine it on a strictly philosophical plane. What is meant by the term *existentialism?*

Most people who use the word would be rather embarrassed if they had to explain it, since, now that the word is all the rage, even the work of a musician or painter is being called existentialist. A gossip columnist in *Clartés* signs himself *The Existentialist,* so that by this time the word has been so stretched and has taken on so broad a meaning, that it no longer means anything at all. It seems that for want of an advanced-guard doctrine analogous to surrealism, the kind of people who are eager for scandal and flurry turn to this philosophy which in other respects does not at all serve their purposes in this sphere.

Actually, it is the least scandalous, the most austere of doctrines. It is intended strictly for specialists and philosophers. Yet it can be defined easily. What complicates matters is that there are two kinds of existentialists; first, those who are Christian, among whom I would include Jaspers and Gabriel Marcel, both Catholic; and on the other hand the atheistic existentialists among whom I class Heidegger, and then the French existentialists and myself. What they have in common is that they think that existence precedes essence, or, if you prefer, that subjectivity must be the starting point.

Just what does that mean? Let us consider some object that is manufactured, for example, a book or a paper-cutter: here is an object which has been made by an artisan whose inspiration came from a concept. He referred to the concept of what a paper-cutter is and likewise to a known method of production, which is part of the concept, something which is, by and large, a routine. Thus, the paper-cutter is at once an object produced in a certain way and, on the other hand, one having a specific use; and one can not postulate a man who produces a paper-cutter but does not know what it is used for. Therefore, let us say that, for the paper-cutter, essence—that is, the ensemble of both the production routines and the properties which enable it to be both produced and defined—precedes existence. Thus, the presence of the paper-cutter or book in front of me is determined. Therefore, we have here a technical view of the world whereby it can be said that production precedes existence.

When we conceive God as the Creator, He is generally thought of as a superior sort of artisan. Whatever doctrine we may be considering, whether one like that of Descartes or that of Leibniz, we always grant that will more or less follows understanding or, at the very least, accompanies it, and that when God creates He knows exactly what He is creating. Thus, the concept of man in the mind of God is comparable to the concept of a paper-cutter in the mind of the manufacturer, and, following certain techniques and a conception, God produces man, just as the artisan, following a definition and a technique, makes a paper-cutter. Thus, the individual man is the realization of a certain concept in the divine intelligence.

In the eighteenth century, the atheism of the *philosophers* discarded the idea of God, but not so much for the notion that essence precedes existence. To a certain extent, this idea is found everywhere; we find it in Diderot, in Voltaire, and even in Kant. Man has a human nature; this human nature, which is the concept of the human, is found in all men, which means that each man is a particular example of a universal concept, man. In Kant, the result of this universality is that the wild-man, the natural man, as well as the bourgeois, are circumscribed by the same definition and have the same basic qualities. Thus, here too the essence of man precedes the historical existence that we find in nature.

Atheistic existentialism, which I represent, is more coherent. It states that if God does not exist, there is at least one being in whom existence precedes essence, a being who exists before he can be defined by any concept, and that this being is man, or, as Heidegger says, human reality. What is meant here by saying that existence precedes essence? It means that, first of all, man exists, turns up, appears on the scene, and, only afterwards, defines himself. If man, as the existentialist conceives him, is indefinable, it is because at first he is nothing. Only afterward will he be something, and he himself will have made what he will be. Thus, there is no human nature, since there is no God to conceive it. Not only is man what he conceives himself to be, but he is also only what he wills himself to be after this thrust toward existence.

Man is nothing else but what he makes of himself. Such is the first principle of existentialism. It is also what is called subjectivity, the name we are labeled with when charges are brought against us. But what do we mean by this, if not that man has a greater dignity than a stone or table? For we mean that man first exists, that is, that man first of all is the being who hurls himself toward a future and who is conscious of imagining himself as being in the future. Man is at the start a plan which is aware of itself, rather than a patch of moss, a piece of garbage, or a cauliflower; nothing exists prior to this plan; there is nothing in heaven; man will be what he will have planned to be. Not what he will want to be. Because by the word "will" we generally mean a conscious decision, which is subsequent to what we have already made of ourselves. I may want to belong to a political party, write a book, get married; but all that is only a manifestation of an earlier, more spontaneous choice that is called "will." But if existence really does precede essence, man is responsible for what he is. Thus, existentialism's first move is to make every man aware of what he is and to make the full responsibility of his existence rest on him. And when we say that a man is responsible for himself, we do not only mean that he is responsible for his own individuality, but that he is responsible for all men.

The word subjectivism has two meanings, and our opponents play on the two. Subjectivism means, on the one hand, that an individual chooses and makes himself; and, on the other, that it is impossible for man to transcend human subjectivity. The second of these is the essential meaning of existentialism. When we say that man chooses his own self, we mean that every one of us does likewise; but we also mean by that that in making this choice he also chooses all men. In fact, in creating the man that we want to be, there is not a single one of our acts which does not at the same time create an image of man as we think he ought to be. To choose to be this or that is to affirm at the same time the value of what we choose, because we can never choose evil. We always choose the good, and nothing can be good for us without being good for all.

If, on the other hand, existence precedes essence, and if we grant that we exist and fashion our image at one and the same time, the image is valid for everybody and for our whole age. Thus, our responsibility is much greater than we might have supposed, because it involves all mankind. If I am a workingman and choose to join a Christian trade-union rather than be a communist, and if by being a member I want to show that the best thing for man is resignation, that the kingdom of man is not of this world, I am not only involving my own case—I want to be resigned for everyone. As a result, my action has involved all humanity. To take a more individual matter, if I want to marry, to have children; even if this marriage depends solely on my own circumstances or passion or wish, I am involving all humanity in monogamy and not merely myself. Therefore, I am responsible for myself and for everyone else. I am creating a certain image of man of my own choosing. In choosing myself, I choose man.

This helps us understand what the actual content is of such rather grandiloquent words as anguish, forlornness, despair. As you will see, it's all quite simple.

First, what is meant by anguish? The existentialists say at once that man is anguish. What that means is this: the man who involves himself and who realizes that he is not only the person he chooses to be, but also a lawmaker who is, at the same time, choosing all mankind as well as himself, can not help escape the feeling of his total and deep responsibility. Of course, there are many people who are not anxious; but we claim that they are hiding their anxiety, that they are fleeing from it. Certainly, many people believe that when they do something, they themselves are the only ones involved, and when someone says to them, "What if everyone acted that way?" they shrug their shoulders and answer, "Everyone doesn't act that way." But really, one should always ask himself, "What would happen if everybody looked at things that way?" There is no escaping this disturbing thought except by a kind of double-dealing. A man who lies and makes excuses for himself by saying "Not everybody does that," is someone with an uneasy conscience, because the act of lying implies that a universal value is conferred upon the lie.

Anguish is evident even when it conceals itself. This is the anguish that Kierkegaard called the anguish of Abraham. You know the story: an angel has ordered Abraham to sacrifice his son; if he really were an angel who has come and said, "You are Abraham, you shall sacrifice your son," everything would be all right. But everyone might first wonder, "Is it really an angel, and am I really Abraham? What proof do I have?"

There was a madwoman who had hallucinations; someone used to speak to her on the telephone and give her orders. Her doctor asked her, "Who is it who talks to you?" She answered, "He says it's God." What proof did she really have that it was God? If an angel comes to me, what proof is there that it's an angel? And if I hear voices, what proof is there that they come from heaven and not from hell, or from the subconscious, or a pathological condition? What proves that they are addressed to me? What proof is there that I have been appointed to impose my choice and my conception of man on humanity? I'll never find any proof or sign to convince me of that. If a voice addresses me, it is always for me to decide that this is the angel's voice; if I consider that such an act is a good one, it is I who will choose to say that it is good rather than bad.

Now, I'm not being singled out as an Abraham, and yet at every moment I'm obliged to perform exemplary acts. For every man, everything happens as if all mankind had its eyes fixed on him and were guiding itself by what he does. And every man ought to say to himself, "Am I really the kind of man who has the right to act in such a way that humanity might guide itself by my actions?" And if he does not say that to himself, he is masking his anguish.

There is no question here of the kind of anguish which would lead to quietism, to inaction. It is a matter of a simple sort of anguish that anybody who has had responsibilities is familiar with. For example, when a military officer takes the responsibility for an attack and sends a certain number of men to death, he chooses to do so, and in the main he alone makes the choice. Doubtless, orders come from above, but they are too broad; he interprets them, and on this interpretation depend the lives of ten or fourteen or twenty men. In making a decision he can not help having a certain anguish. All leaders know this anguish. That doesn't keep them from acting; on the contrary, it is the very condition of their action. For it implies that they envisage a number of possibilities, and when they choose one, they realize that it has value only because it is chosen. We shall see that this kind of anguish, which is the kind that existentialism describes, is explained, in addition, by a direct responsibility to the other men whom it involves. It is not a curtain separating us from action, but is part of action itself.

When we speak of forlornness, a term Heidegger was fond of, we mean only that God does not exist and that we have to face all the consequences of this. The existentialist is strongly opposed to a certain kind of secular ethics which would like to abolish God with the least possible expense. About 1880, some French teachers tried to set up a secular ethics which went something like this: God is a useless and costly hypothesis; we are discarding it; but, meanwhile, in order for there to be an ethics, a society, a civilization, it is essential that certain values be taken seriously and that they be considered as having an *a priori* existence. It must be obligatory, *a priori,* to be honest, not to lie, not to beat your wife, to have children, etc., etc. So we're going to try a little device which will make it possible to show that values exist all the same, inscribed in a heaven of ideas, though otherwise God does not exist. In other words—and this, I believe, is the tendency of everything called reformism in France— nothing will be changed if God does not exist. We shall find ourselves with the same norms of honesty, progress, and humanism, and we shall have made of God an outdated hypothesis which will peacefully die off by itself.

The existentialist, on the contrary, thinks it very distressing that God does not exist, because all possibility of finding values in a heaven of ideas disappears along with Him; there can no longer be an *a priori* Good, since there is no infinite and perfect consciousness to think it. Nowhere is it written that the Good exists, that we must be honest, that we must not lie; because the fact is we are on a plane where there are only men. Dostoievsky said, "If God didn't exist, everything would be possible." That is the very starting point of existentialism. Indeed, everything is permissible if God does not exist, and as a result man is forlorn, because neither within him nor without does he find anything to cling to. He can't start making excuses for himself.

If existence really does precede essence, there is no explaining things away by reference to a fixed and given human nature. In other words, there is no determinism, man is free, man is freedom. On the other hand, if God does not exist, we find no values or commands to turn to which legitimize our conduct. So, in the bright realm of values, we have no excuse behind us, nor justification before us. We are alone, with no excuses.

That is the idea I shall try to convey when I say that man is condemned to be free. Condemned, because he did not create himself, yet, in other respects is free; because, once thrown into the world, he is responsible·for everything he does. The existentialist does not believe in the power of passion. He will never agree that a sweeping passion is a ravaging torrent which fatally leads a man to certain acts and is therefore an excuse. He thinks that man is responsible for his passion.

The existentialist does not think that man is going to help himself by finding in the world some omen by which to orient himself. Because he thinks that man will interpret the omen to suit himself. Therefore, he thinks that man, with no support and no aid, is condemned every moment to invent man. Ponge, in a very fine article, has said, "Man is the future of man." That's exactly it. But if it is taken to mean that this future is recorded in heaven, that God sees it, then it is false, because it would really no longer be a future. If it is taken to mean that, whatever a man may be, there is a future to be forged, a virgin future before him, then this remark is sound. But then we are forlorn.

To give you an example which will enable you to understand forlornness better, I shall cite the case of one of my students who came to see me under the following circumstances: his father was on bad terms with his mother, and, moreover, was inclined to be a collaborationist; his older brother had been killed in the German offensive of 1940, and the young man, with somewhat immature but generous feelings, wanted to avenge him. His mother lived alone with him, very much upset by the half-treason of her husband and the death of her older son; the boy was her only consolation.

The boy was faced with the choice of leaving for England and joining the Free French Forces—that is, leaving his mother behind—or remaining with his mother and helping her to carry on. He was fully aware that the woman lived only for him and that his going-off—and perhaps his death— would plunge her into despair. He was also aware that every act that he did for his mother's sake was a sure thing, in the sense that it was helping her to carry on, whereas every effort he made toward going off and fighting was an uncertain move which might run aground and prove completely useless; for example, on his way to England he might, while passing through Spain, be detained indefinitely in a Spanish camp; he might reach England or Algiers and be stuck in an office at a desk job. As a result, he was faced with two very different kinds of action: one, concrete, immediate, but concerning only one individual; the other concerned an incomparably vaster group, a national collectivity, but for that very reason was dubious, and might be interrupted en route. And, at the same time, he was wavering between two kinds of ethics. On the one hand, an ethics of sympathy, of personal devotion; on the other, a broader ethics, but one whose efficacy was more dubious. He had to choose between the two.

Who could help him choose? Christian doctrine? No. Christian doctrine says, "Be charitable, love your neighbor, take the more rugged path, etc., etc." But which is the more rugged path? Whom should he love as a brother? The fighting man or his mother? Which does the greater good, the vague act of fighting in a group, or the concrete one of helping a particular human being to go on living? Who can decide *a priori?* Nobody. No book of ethics can tell him. The Kantian ethics says, "Never treat any person as a means, but as an end." Very well, if I stay with mother, I'll treat her as an end and not as a means; but by virtue of this very fact, I'm running the risk of treating the people around me who are fighting, as means; and, conversely, if I go to join those who are fighting, I'll be treating them as an end, and, by doing that, I run the risk of treating my mother as a means.

If values are vague, and if they are always too broad for the concrete and specific case that we are considering, the only thing left for us is to trust our instincts. That's what this young man tried to do; and when I saw him, he said, "In the end, feeling is what counts. I ought to choose whichever pushes me in one direction. If I feel that I love my mother enough to sacrifice everything else for her—my desire for vengeance, for action, for adventure—then I'll stay with her. If, on the contrary, I feel that my love for my mother isn't enough, I'll leave."

But how is the value of a feeling determined? What gives his feeling for his mother value? Precisely the fact that he remained with her. I may say that I like so-and-so well enough to sacrifice a certain amount of money for him, but I may say so only if I've done it. I may say "I love my mother well enough to remain with her" if I have remained with her. The only way to determine the value of this affection is, precisely, to perform an act which confirms and defines it. But, since I require this affection to justify my act, I find myself caught in a vicious circle.

On the other hand, Gide has well said that a mock feeling and a true feeling are almost indistinguishable; to decide that I love my mother and will remain with her, or to remain with her by putting on an act, amount somewhat to the same thing. In other words, the feeling is formed by the acts one performs; so, I can not refer to it in order to act upon it. Which means that I can neither seek within myself the true condition which will impel me to act, nor apply to a system of ethics for concepts which will permit me to act. You will say, "At least, he did go to a teacher for advice." But if you seek advice from a priest, for example, you have chosen this priest; you already knew, more or less, just about what advice he was going to give you. In other words, choosing your adviser is involving yourself. The proof of this is that if you are a Christian, you will say, "Consult a priest." But some priests are collaborating, some are just marking time, some are resisting. Which to choose? If the young man chooses a priest who is resisting or collaborating, he has already decided on the kind of advice he's going to get. Therefore, in coming to see me he knew the answer I was going to give him, and I had only one answer to give: "You're free, choose, that is, invent." No general ethics can show you what is to be done; there are no omens in the world. The Catholics will reply, "But there are." Granted—but, in any case, I myself choose the meaning they have.

When I was a prisoner, I knew a rather remarkable young man who was a Jesuit. He had entered the Jesuit order in the following way: he had had a number of very bad breaks; in childhood, his father died, leaving him in poverty, and he was a scholarship student at a religious institution where he was constantly made to feel that he was being kept out of charity; then, he failed to get any of the honors and distinctions that children like; later on, at about eighteen, he bungled a love affair; finally, at twenty-two, he failed in military training, a childish enough matter, but it was the last straw.

This young fellow might well have felt that he had botched everything. It was a sign of something, but of what? He might have taken refuge in bitterness or despair. But he very wisely looked upon all this as a sign that he was not made for secular triumphs, and that only the triumphs of religion, holiness, and faith were open to him. He saw the hand of God in all this, and so he entered the order. Who can help seeing that he alone decided what the sign meant?

Some other interpretation might have been drawn from this series of set-backs; for example, that he might have done better to turn carpenter or revolutionist. Therefore, he is fully responsible for the interpretation. Forlorn-ness implies that we ourselves choose our being. Forlornness and anguish go together.

As for despair, the term has a very simple meaning. It means that we shall confine ourselves to reckoning only with what depends upon our will, or on the ensemble of probabilities which make our action possible. When we want something, we always have to reckon with probabilities. I may be count-ing on the arrival of a friend. The friend is coming by rail or street-car; this supposes that the train will arrive on schedule, or that the street-car will not jump the track. I am left in the realm of possibility; but possibilities are to be reckoned with only to the point where my action comports with the ensemble of these possibilities, and no further. The moment the possibilities I am con-sidering are not rigorously involved by my action, I ought to disengage myself from them, because no God, no scheme, can adapt the world and its possibilities to my will. When Descartes said, "Conquer yourself rather than the world," he meant essentially the same thing.

The Marxists to whom I have spoken reply, "You can rely on the support of others in your action, which obviously has certain limits because you're not going to live forever. That means: rely on both what others are doing else-where to help you, in China, in Russia, and what they will do later on, after your death, to carry on the action and lead it to its fulfillment, which will be the revolution. You even *have* to rely upon that, otherwise you're immoral." I reply at once that I will always rely on fellow-fighters insofar as these comrades are involved with me in a common struggle, in the unity of a party or a group in which I can more or less make my weight felt; that is, one whose ranks I am in as a fighter and whose movements I am aware of at every moment. In such a situation, relying on the unity and will of the party is exactly like counting on the fact that the train will arrive on time or that the car won't jump the track. But, given that man is free and that there is no human nature for me to depend on, I can not count on men whom I do not know by relying on human goodness or man's concern for the good of society. I don't know what will become of the Russian revolution; I may make an example of it to the extent that at the present time it is apparent that the proletariat plays a part in Russia that it plays in no other nation. But I can't swear that this will inevitably lead to a triumph of the proletariat. I've got to limit myself to what I see.

Given that men are free and that tomorrow they will freely decide what man will be, I can not be sure that, after my death, fellow-fighters will carry on my work to bring it to its maximum perfection. Tomorrow, after my death, some men may decide to set up Fascism, and the others may be cowardly and muddled enough to let them do it. Fascism will then be the human reality, so much the worse for us.

Actually, things will be as man will have decided they are to be. Does that mean that I should abandon myself to quietism? No. First, I should involve myself; then, act on the old saw, "Nothing ventured, nothing gained." Nor does it mean that I shouldn't belong to a party, but rather that I shall have no illusions and shall do what I can. For example, suppose I ask myself, "Will socialization, as such, ever come about?" I know nothing about it. All I know is that I'm going to do everything in my power to bring it about. Beyond that, I can't count on anything. Quietism is the attitude of people who say, "Let others do what I can't do." The doctrine I am presenting is the very opposite of quietism, since it declares, "There is no reality except in action." Moreover, it goes further, since it adds, "Man is nothing else than his plan; he exists only to the extent that he fulfills himself; he is therefore nothing else than the ensemble of his acts, nothing else than his life."

According to this, we can understand why our doctrine horrifies certain people. Because often the only way they can bear their wretchedness is to think, "Circumstances have been against me. What I've been and done doesn't show my true worth. To be sure, I've had no great love, no great friendship, but that's because I haven't met a man or woman who was worthy. The books I've written haven't been very good because I haven't had the proper leisure. I haven't had children to devote myself to because I didn't find a man with whom I could have spent my life. So there remains within me, unused and quite viable, a host of propensities, inclinations, possibilities, that one wouldn't guess from the mere series of things I've done."

Now, for the existentialist there is really no love other than one which manifests itself in a person's being in love. There is no genius other than one which is expressed in works of art; the genius of Proust is the sum of Proust's works; the genius of Racine is his series of tragedies. Outside of that, there is nothing. Why say that Racine could have written another tragedy, when he didn't write it? A man is involved in life, leaves his impress on it, and outside of that there is nothing. To be sure, this may seem a harsh thought to someone whose life hasn't been a success. But, on the other hand, it prompts people to understand that reality alone is what counts, that dreams, expectations, and hopes warrant no more than to define a man as a disappointed dream, as miscarried hopes, as vain expectations. In other words, to define him negatively and not positively. However, when we say, "You are nothing else than your life," that does not imply that the artist will be judged solely on the basis of his works of art; a thousand other things will contribute toward summing him up. What we mean is that a man is nothing else than a series of undertakings, that he is the sum, the organization, the ensemble of the relationships which make up these undertakings.

When all is said and done, what we are accused of, at bottom, is not our pessimism, but an optimistic toughness. If people throw up to us our works of fiction in which we write about people who are soft, weak, cowardly, and sometimes even downright bad, it's not because these people are soft, weak, cowardly, or bad; because if we were to say, as Zola did, that they are that way because of heredity, the workings of environment, society, because of biological or psychological determinism, people would be reassured. They would say, "Well, that's what we're like, no one can do anything about it." But when the existentialist writes about a coward, he says that this coward is responsible for his cowardice. He's not like that because he has a cowardly heart or lung or brain; he's not like that on account of his physiological make-up; but he's like that because he has made himself a coward by his acts. There's no such thing as a cowardly constitution; there are nervous constitutions; there is poor blood, as the common people say, or there are strong constitutions. But the man whose blood is poor is not a coward on that account, for what makes cowardice is the act of renouncing or yielding. A constitution is not an act; the coward is defined on the basis of the acts he performs. People feel, in a vague sort of way, that this coward we're talking about is guilty of being a coward, and the thought frightens them. What people would like is that a coward or a hero be born that way. . . .

Besides, if it is impossible to find in every man some universal essence which would be human nature, yet there does exist a universal human condition. It's not by chance that today's thinkers speak more readily of man's condition than of his nature. By condition they mean, more or less definitely, the *a priori* limits which outline man's fundamental situation in the universe. Historical situations vary; a man may be born a slave in a pagan society or a feudal lord or a proletarian. What does not vary is the necessity for him to exist in the world, to be at work there, to be there in the midst of other people, and to be mortal there. The limits are neither subjective nor objective, or, rather, they have an objective and a subjective side. Objective because they are to be found everywhere and are recognizable everywhere; subjective because they are *lived* and are nothing if man does not live them, that is, freely determine his existence with reference to them. And though the configurations may differ, at least none of them are completely strange to me, because they all appear as attempts either to pass beyond these limits or recede from them or deny them or adapt to them. Consequently, every configuration, however individual it may be, has a universal value.

Every configuration, even the Chinese, the Indian, or the Negro, can be understood by a Westerner. "Can be understood" means that by virtue of a situation that he can imagine, a European of 1945 can, in like manner, push himself to his limits and reconstitute within himself the configuration of the Chinese, the Indian, or the African. Every configuration has universality in the sense that every configuration can be understood by every man. This does not at all mean that this configuration defines man forever, but that it can be met with again. There is always a way to understand the idiot, the child, the savage, the foreigner, provided one has the necessary information.

In this sense we may say that there is a universality of man; but it is not given, it is perpetually being made. I build the universal in choosing myself; I build it in understanding the configuration of every other man, whatever age he might have lived in. This absoluteness of choice does not do away with the relativeness of each epoch. At heart, what existentialism shows is the connection between the absolute character of free involvement, by virtue of which every man realizes himself in realizing a type of mankind, an involvement always comprehensible in any age whatsoever and by any person whosoever, and the relativeness of the cultural ensemble which may result from such a choice. . . .

This does not entirely settle the objection to subjectivism. In fact, the objection still takes several forms. First, there is the following: we are told, "So you're able to do anything, no matter what!" This is expressed in various ways. First we are accused of anarchy; then they say, "You're unable to pass judgment on others, because there's no reason to prefer one configuration to another"; finally they tell us, "Everything is arbitrary in this choosing of yours. You take something from one pocket and pretend you're putting it into the other."

These three objections aren't very serious. Take the first objection. "You're able to do anything, no matter what" is not to the point. In one sense choice is possible, but what is not possible is not to choose. I can always choose, but I ought to know that if I do not choose, I am still choosing. Though this may seem purely formal, it is highly important for keeping fantasy and caprice within bounds. If it is true that in facing a situation, for example, one in which, as a person capable of having sexual relations, of having children, I am obliged to choose an attitude, and if I in any way assume responsibility for a choice which, in involving myself, also involves all mankind, this has nothing to do with caprice, even if no *a priori* value determines my choice.

If anybody thinks that he recognizes here Gide's theory of the arbitrary act, he fails to see the enormous difference between this doctrine and Gide's. Gide does not know what a situation is. He acts out of pure caprice. For us, on the contrary, man is in an organized situation in which he himself is involved. Through his choice, he involves all mankind, and he can not avoid making a choice: either he will remain chaste, or he will marry without having children, or he will marry and have children; anyhow, whatever he may do, it is impossible for him not to take full responsibility for the way he handles this problem. Doubtless, he chooses without referring to pre-established values, but it is unfair to accuse him of caprice. Instead, let us say that moral choice is to be compared to the making of a work of art. And before going any further, let it be said at once that we are not dealing here with an aesthetic ethics, because our opponents are so dishonest that they even accuse us of that. The example I've chosen is a comparison only.

Having said that, may I ask whether anyone has ever accused an artist who has painted a picture of not having drawn his inspiration from rules set up *a priori*? Has any one ever asked, "What painting ought he to make?" It is clearly understood that there is no definite painting to be made, that the artist is engaged in the making of his painting, and that the painting to be made is precisely the painting he will have made. It is clearly understood that there are no *a priori* aesthetic values, but that there are values which appear subsequently in the coherence of the painting, in the correspondence between what the artist intended and the result. Nobody can tell what the painting of tomorrow will be like. Painting can be judged only after it has once been made. What connection does that have with ethics? We are in the same creative situation. We never say that a work of art is arbitrary. When we speak of a canvas of Picasso, we never say that it is arbitrary; we understand quite well that he was making himself what he is at the very time he was painting, that the ensemble of his work is embodied in his life.

The same holds on the ethical plane. What art and ethics have in common is that we have creation and invention in both cases. We can not decide *a priori* what there is to be done. I think that I pointed that out quite sufficiently when I mentioned the case of the student who came to see me, and who might have applied to all the ethical systems, Kantian or otherwise, without getting any sort of guidance. He was obliged to devise his law himself. Never let it be said by us that this man—who, taking affection, individual action, and kind-heartedness toward a specific person as his ethical first principle, chooses to remain with his mother, or who, preferring to make a sacrifice, chooses to go to England—has made an arbitrary choice. Man makes himself. He isn't ready made at the start. In choosing his ethics, he makes himself, and force of circumstances is such that he can not abstain from choosing one. We define man only in relationship to involvement. It is therefore absurd to charge us with arbitrariness of choice.

In the second place, it is said that we are unable to pass judgment on others. In a way this is true, and in another way, false. It is true in this sense, that, whenever a man sanely and sincerely involves himself and chooses his configuration, it is impossible for him to prefer another configuration, regardless of what his own may be in other respects. It is true in this sense, that we do not believe in progress. Progress is betterment. Man is always the same. The situation confronting him varies. Choice always remains a choice in a situation. The problem has not changed since the time one could choose between those for and those against slavery, for example, at the time of the Civil War, and the present time, when one can side with the Maquis Resistance Party, or with the Communists.

But, nevertheless, one can still pass judgment, for, as I have said, one makes a choice in relationship to others. First, one can judge (and this is perhaps not a judgment of value, but a logical judgment) that certain choices are based on error and others on truth. If we have defined man's situation as a free choice, with no excuses and no recourse, every man who takes refuge behind the excuse of his passions, every man who sets up a determinism, is a dishonest man.

The objection may be raised, "But why mayn't he choose himself dishonestly?" I reply that I am not obliged to pass moral judgment on him, but that I do define his dishonesty as an error. One can not help considering the truth of the matter. Dishonesty is obviously a falsehood because it belies the complete freedom of involvement. On the same grounds, I maintain that there is also dishonesty if I choose to state that certain values exist prior to me; it is self-contradictory for me to want them and at the same time state that they are imposed on me. Suppose someone says to me, "What if I want to be dishonest?" I'll answer, "There's no reason for you not to be, but I'm saying that that's what you are, and that the strictly coherent attitude is that of honesty."

Besides, I can bring moral judgment to bear. When I declare that freedom in every concrete circumstance can have no other aim than to want itself, if man has once become aware that in his forlornness he imposes values, he can no longer want but one thing, and that is freedom, as the basis of all values. That doesn't mean that he wants it in the abstract. It means simply that the ultimate meaning of the acts of honest men is the quest for freedom as such. A man who belongs to a communist or revolutionary union wants concrete goals; these goals imply an abstract desire for freedom; but this freedom is wanted in something concrete. We want freedom for freedom's sake and in every particular circumstance. And in wanting freedom we discover that it depends entirely on the freedom of others, and that the freedom of others depends on ours. Of course, freedom as the definition of man does not depend on others, but as soon as there is involvement, I am obliged to want others to have freedom at the same time that I want my own freedom. I can take freedom as my goal only if I take that of others as a goal as well. Consequently, when, in all honesty, I've recognized that man is a being in whom existence precedes essence, that he is a free being who, in various circumstances, can want only his freedom, I have at the same time recognized that I can' want only the freedom of others.

Therefore, in the name of this will for freedom, which freedom itself implies, I may pass judgment on those who seek to hide from themselves the complete arbitrariness and the complete freedom of their existence. Those who hide their complete freedom from themselves out of a spirit of seriousness or by means of deterministic excuses, I shall call cowards; those who try to show that their existence was necessary, when it is the very contingency of man's appearance on earth, I shall call stinkers. But cowards or stinkers can be judged only from a strictly unbiased point of view.

Therefore though the content of ethics is variable, a certain form of it is universal. Kant says that freedom desires both itself and the freedom of others. Granted. But he believes that the formal and the universal are enough to constitute an ethics. We, on the other hand, think that principles which are too abstract run aground in trying to decide action. Once again, take the case of the student. In the name of what, in the name of what great moral maxim do you think he could have decided, in perfect peace of mind, to abandon his mother or to stay with her? There is no way of judging. The content is always concrete and thereby unforeseeable; there is always the element of invention. The one thing that counts is knowing whether the inventing that has been done, has been done in the name of freedom. . . .

The third objection is the following: "You take something from one pocket and put it into the other. That is, fundamentally, values aren't serious, since you choose them." My answer to this is that I'm quite vexed that that's the way it is; but if I've discarded God the Father, there has to be someone to invent values. You've got to take things as they are. Moreover, to say that we invent values means nothing else but this: life has no meaning *a priori*. Before you come alive, life is nothing; it's up to you to give it a meaning, and value is nothing else but the meaning that you choose. In that way, you see, there is a possibility of creating a human community.

I've been reproached for asking whether existentialism is humanistic. It's been said, "But you said in *Nausea* that the humanists were all wrong. You made fun of a certain kind of humanist. Why come back to it now?" Actually, the word humanism has two very different meanings. By humanism one can mean a theory which takes man as an end and as a higher value. Humanism in this sense can be found in Cocteau's tale *Around the World in Eighty Hours* when a character, because he is flying over some mountains in an airplane, declares, "Man is simply amazing." That means that I, who did not build the airplanes, shall personally benefit from these particular inventions, and that I, as man, shall personally consider myself responsible for, and honored by, acts of a few particular men. This would imply that we ascribe a value to man on the basis of the highest deeds of certain men. This humanism is absurd, because only the dog or the horse would be able to make such an over-all judgment about man, which they are careful not to do, at least to my knowledge.

But it can not be granted that a man may make a judgment about man. Existentialism spares him from any such judgment. The existentialist will never consider man as an end because he is always in the making. Nor should we believe that there is a mankind to which we might set up a cult in the manner of Auguste Comte. The cult of mankind ends in the self-enclosed humanism of Comte, and, let it be said, of fascism. This kind of humanism we can do without.

But there is another meaning of humanism. Fundamentally it is this: man is constantly outside of himself; in projecting himself, in losing himself outside of himself, he makes for man's existing; and, on the other hand, it is by pursuing transcendent goals that he is able to exist; man, being this state of passing-beyond, and seizing upon things only as they bear upon this passing-beyond, is at the heart, at the center of this passing-beyond. There is no universe other than a human universe, the universe of human subjectivity. This connection between transcendency, as a constituent element of man—not in the sense that God is transcendent, but in the sense of passing beyond—and subjectivity, in the sense that man is not closed in on himself but is always present in a human universe, is what we call existentialist humanism. Humanism, because we remind man that there is no lawmaker other than himself, and that in his forlornness he will decide by himself; because we point out that man will fulfill himself as man, not in turning toward himself, but in seeking outside of himself a goal which is just this liberation, just this particular fulfillment.

From these few reflections it is evident that nothing is more unjust than the objections that have been raised against us. Existentialism is nothing else than an attempt to draw all the consequences of a coherent atheistic position. It isn't trying to plunge man into despair at all. But if one calls every attitude of unbelief despair, like the Christians, then the word is not being used in its original sense. Existentialism isn't so atheistic that it wears itself out showing that God doesn't exist. Rather, it declares that even if God did exist, that would change nothing. There you've got our point of view. Not that we believe that God exists, but we think that the problem of His existence is not the issue. In this sense existentialism is optimistic, a doctrine of action, and it is plain dishonesty for Christians to make no distinction between their own despair and ours and then to call us despairing.

FREDERICK OLAFSON
Principles and Persons

ETHICAL INTELLECTUALISM

The belief that the concepts of truth and falsity are applicable to judgments of value has been a central theme of Western moral philosophy since its inception. While this view may have been first put forward by Socrates, it received an explicit philosophical interpretation at the hands of Plato; and it is not too much to say that the whole subsequent development of moral philosophy has been dominated by Plato's original statement of what may be called the intellectualistic thesis. This is the view that value predicates have meaning by virtue of standing for objective qualities or relations that are independent of our feelings and volitions; that rational beings are able to apprehend these qualities; and that true (and false) statements can accordingly be made about them. In this first formulation, as later, intellectualism was intended as a refutation of skeptical views which made the moral quality of things relative to the attitudes and aspirations of individual human beings. Against the view that values are artificial human conventions, intellectualism has always insisted that the goodness or badness of a thing and the rightness or wrongness of an action are functions of the nature of that thing or action rather than of our feelings about it. "Nature" in this context means simply the set of characteristics that an object possesses and by which it is classifiable as belonging to a certain kind or species of things. Since these characteristics define a class of things and are therefore not peculiar, at least in principle, to any single object, the natures they compose have traditionally been described as "universals."

Two features of Plato's account of moral knowledge were to play an important role in the subsequent evolution of intellectualism. First, his attribution of logical necessity to the relationship between universals suggested a similar conception of the relationship between the form of the good and other universals. Knowledge of the moral quality of things has thus often been conceived to be of a type with mathematical knowledge; and in both cases the test of truth is held to be essentially logical in character and to consist in a set of dialectical operations performed upon the definitions of the terms involved.

At the same time, however, Plato often used the language of perception and of vision to characterize our apprehension of the good as well as of other universals. He did not, of course, mean that insight into moral relationships was literally seeing, but the metaphor of sight has a unique capacity to suggest the independence or "out-there-ness" of what is known, and it was therefore natural that Plato and the whole intellectualistic tradition which followed after him should make such extensive use of it. By combining these two features of moral knowledge, Plato worked out the conception of a necessity inherent in the object of moral knowledge itself that was perhaps his principal legacy to subsequent ethical theory. At the same time, by virtue of this very association of the idea of necessity with that of a vision directed upon self-subsistent entities, he created one of the most difficult problems that the intellectualistic tradition has had to resolve.

If Plato gave Western ethical theory its initial intellectualistic bent, it was Aristotle and the medieval Aristotelians who recast his teaching into the form of a detailed doctrine of human nature. Since it was this form of intellectualism that principally stimulated—by reaction—the developments in ethical theory that eventually led to existentialism, a summary review of the main relevant features of Aristotle's moral philosophy is in order.

A theory of natural teleology and a theory of natural kinds provide the basis of that doctrine. According to the latter, each individual thing is endowed with a nature or essence that it has in common with some other individuals and by virtue of which they are classifiable as belonging to a certain genus and species and so on down to the *infima species* in the lowest tiers of the classificatory pyramid. This classification into kinds is natural in the sense that the distinction between defining traits and accidental or peripheral traits is conceived to be a real, and not a conventional, distinction. It is, in fact, a kind of prelinguistic datum that must be faithfully reproduced in language instead of being itself a pragmatically justified linguistic achievement. The metaphysical priority of the traits that constitute these "natures" generates a basic vocabulary for identifying individual things; and the way of cutting up the world that is thus imposed is emphatically not optional. To tinker with it would result not just in departures from a particular system of identifying reference but in a distortion of the natures of the things classified.

The doctrine of natural teleology can be described as a further stipulation attached to the theory of natural kinds. It asserts that the natures on which the "natural" system of classification is based are compounded in such a way as to define a function, or end, that is proper to the bearers of any given nature. According to this view, it will thus be impossible to identify a particular as having any specific nature without thereby committing oneself to a number of propositions with respect to the distinctive good of that thing; it is understood that right conduct for intelligent beings consists in doing what realizes their distinctive *telos*. A conceptual system that would enable us to identify someone as a human being, while leaving open all questions as to what he ought properly to do, is thus in effect excluded. Once again, the reason is not to be sought in any linguistic conservatism on Aristotle's part, but in his conviction that what is real, independently of all language, is a combination of actuality with a special potentiality for realizing certain distinctive ends, and that this fact must be reflected in any viable scheme of classification. In summary, then, one may say that Aristotle's normative ethic consists of a set of implications that is built into the very language he uses for the description of the subjects of that theory; and this language, in turn, is interpreted as reflecting metaphysical structures that are antecedent to language and immune to change.

If this theory is applied to human action, it is clear that principles of right action will be derivable from the *telos,* or proper end, of man; and this end will be implicit in the "nature" that is peculiar to human beings. These principles will have the status of moral or practical truths; and if we follow Aristotle, at least one of them (i.e., the principle that the end of man is the exercise of intellectual virtue), will be a necessary truth. Others that bear upon the means to this end, will be among those things "that could be otherwise." In any case, they will function as the major premises in practical syllogisms; taken together with factual premises describing a given situation as of the type to which the rule applies, they will generate a particular moral judgment that tells what action would be suitable in that situation. To this piece of moral knowledge the will is referred for guidance. Aristotle's way of putting this is to say that the conclusion in a practical syllogism is an action, but this seems to prejudge the question of whether a person may not act otherwise while knowing what he ought to do. Intellectualism, as I am using the term, is a thesis about the kind of knowledge that is involved in the apprehension of the truth of moral principles; and care should be taken to distinguish this thesis from the view that the will is somehow constrained to seek what the intellect represents to it as good. . . .

One very important effect of this doctrine of natural ends that are proper to each kind of being is the restrictions it imposes upon the concept of choice. According to Aristotle, choice is the outcome of deliberation, and deliberation is concerned with means to an end and not with the end itself. Deliberation and choice thus operate within a framework of goals over which they exercise no control; and the proper goal for any being is determined by the *kind* of being it is, i.e., by its nature. The *telos* or proper end of human beings may, of course, be misapprehended by them, and when it is, choice will be directed to means that do not realize their peculiar good. But even in this case, it would presumably not be correct, in Aristotle's view, to speak of a *choice* of the mistaken end. Ends are apprehended (or misapprehended) by human reason, and precisely because our relation to them is cognitive, they are not objects of choice. If they were chosen, then there would either have to be some ulterior end to which they were means, and then this higher end would not be chosen; or the possibility would arise that in the absence of any end that has such a status, human beings might differ in their choice of the highest end. If such difference amounted to incompatibility, Aristotle's conception of man as a social being whose *true* good is necessarily compatible with that of other human beings would have to be called into question.

The view that man has a natural end and that the moral principles in which this end is defined have the status of necessary truths became a central tenet of the medieval theory of natural law by which the Greek tradition of ethical intellectualism was transmitted to the modern world. In the classical formulation of natural law theory produced by St. Thomas, intellectualism has to accommodate itself to the Christian view that the ultimate basis of morality is the will of a personal God. Such a view has strongly anti-intellectualistic implications which were to be fully developed in the later medieval and early modern periods. To meet this difficulty, St. Thomas tried to construct a theory of the divine personality in which intellect and will were related in such a way as to render compatible with one another the demands of a theistic ethic and the intellectualistic position which makes choice and will subordinate to intellect. In constructing this theory of the relation of will and intellect in the divine personality, St. Thomas was also providing a model by which the relationship of these faculties within human personality might be understood.

The premise on which Thomas's theory of God's personality rests is that God has a nature, or essence. This divine essence differs from the essences of finite creatures in many ways, but most notably by virtue of the fact that God's essence and his existence are one, as man's are not. It also differs in that all of God's attributes are perfected or complete forms of attributes which finite beings possess only in partial and fragmentary form. In spite of these differences, there is a real sense in which St. Thomas may be said to apply Aristotle's theory of natural kinds to God, since his being is tied to a constellation of attributes. As a result, God cannot be lacking in any of these attributes that constitute his essence; for if he were, he would not be what he is, and this is to say that the law of contradiction would have been violated. This is impossible even in the case of God, who must therefore act in a manner consistent with his own nature. St. Thomas certainly did not think that by this doctrine he was denying God a power that he might possibly have had, and he would doubtless have thought it senseless to assert that he was imposing real limits on what God could do, as some of his critics were to argue. On the other hand, if any of the things which, according to his theory, God cannot do, are not obviously unimaginable, the denial that God can do them will inevitably sound as though some real incapacity were being imputed to him. This is precisely what was to happen in the case of the moral limits assigned by St. Thomas to God's action.

St. Thomas assumes further that the object of God's knowledge is his own essence, and that God knows other things only mediately, i.e., as contained in his own essence. Now, one element in this essence is God's goodness which is thus, in the first instance, an object of knowledge—a *bonum intellectum*.

Similarly, the good of each finite being that is included in the nature of God is included in the nature of that thing as it figures in the divine intellect. The crucial step in the argument is St. Thomas's assertion that the object of God's will cannot be something outside him, 'but must be his own essence. Otherwise, God would be in a state of privation, and this would be genuinely incompatible with his perfection. From this it follows that the will is addressed to the *bonum intellectum,* and that it is subject to the same law of contradiction that governs the intellect:

The will is only of some understood good. Wherefore that which is not an object of the intellect, cannot be an object of the will. Now things in themselves impossible are not an object of understanding, since they imply a contradiction. . . . Therefore things in themselves impossible cannot be an object of God's will.

God cannot, therefore, will evil; and since there cannot be any possibility of error in his apprehension of the good, he does in fact will only what is truly good and good by a standard that is independent of his will.

It is another very important thesis of the theory of natural law that the moral truths that God knows infallibly and perfectly in apprehending the goodness of his own nature are in some measure accessible to the human intellect and will. To the extent that they are, human beings are not exclusively dependent upon an unpredictable revelation for guidance in the conduct of life, but are instead in a situation vis-à-vis moral truths that is essentially similar to that of God. Both stand in a cognitive relation to the good—the *bonum intellectum*—and in both cases this good is independent of their wills. Neither makes anything good by willing it or choosing it; for both, the goodness of an end is certified by a rational insight into its relationship to the nature of the being whose end it is. God's knowledge is, of course, perfect as man's is defective and partial; but man is subject to the will of God only as this is understood to be ordered to the ends proposed by his intellect, and these ends are in some degree apprehensible by the human intellect as well. If God loses his absolute autonomy by this submission of his will to his intellect, there is a compensating gain in moral intelligibility for man. Eventually, however, this subordination, which had been held by some theologians to place effective restrictions on the power of God, also came to be felt as a limitation on the moral freedom of human beings. In that feeling, a powerful movement of reaction against Thomistic intellectualism was to find one of its strongest motives. . . .

THE REJECTION OF ETHICAL INTELLECTUALISM

The true significance of Nietzsche's contribution to moral philosophy can be understood only in the context of his general theory of truth and its special application to the area of values. In spite of a great many extreme statements that make it sound as though he had no use for truth in any form, the real thrust of Nietzsche's argument is against dualistic or "copy" theories of truth. In particular, he rejects the notion of "things in themselves," and with it the view that truth must consist in a relation of correspondence to the latter. But if our ideas and beliefs are not to be described as reflections of a self-subsistent order of things, then (he argues) they must be thought of as products of our own devising which we, in some sense, impose upon our experience of the world. All of our intellectual apparatus must be in the nature of a construction or interpretation by which we actively organize and dominate the world in a certain way. Even the law of contradiction, Nietzsche argues, represents a condition that is set by us and not an ontological truth that is read off from the nature of things. Nietzsche's term for this general view of the conceptualizing function is "perspectivism," and it clearly has many points of affinity with the pragmatism of William James and others. Like the pragmatists, Nietzsche believes that all of our knowledge and our modes of conceptualizing experience involve an evaluative component and represent a decision to construe the world in a certain way. The "will to power" is simply Nietzsche's shorthand label for the aggressive character of the relationship of human subjectivity to the world that it subjects to its categories.

At the same time as he reinterprets the general notion of truth in this pragmatic spirit, Nietzsche also recognizes a fundamental distinction between establishing the truth of a factual statement and the volitional acts by which an end, i.e., a value, is freely posited. The difference is that verification involves a certain passivity in relation to what is external to the self, although Nietzsche's general doctrine of mind requires that even here *some* element of activity be present. By contrast, evaluation is a purer expression of the human power of legislating for oneself, of assigning values and meanings without any dependence on, or need for, a supporting value-quality in the things evaluated themselves. On this distinction rests what may fairly be termed the central thesis of Nietzsche's ethical theory. This is that any conception of evaluation that makes it an apprehension of truth in the sense of a verification of some state of affairs, whether empirical or metaphysical, distorts its nature and ultimately denatures the evaluative function itself. By this emphatic repudiation of all conceptions of evaluation as knowing, and by his insistence that evaluation must be understood as a volitional act, Nietzsche aligns himself with the voluntaristic tradition against all forms of intellectualism. . . .

. . . The existentialism of Heidegger and Sartre [may be] characterized as "ontological voluntarism.". . . The distinctive achievement of these philosophers has been to introduce into the concept itself of conscious human being an interpretation of human action and evaluation which they derive from Nietzsche and from the voluntaristic tradition that culminates in his thought. By itself, this pedigree commits the contemporary existentialist to a rejection of all forms of the doctrine of ethical intellectualism. In fact, both Heidegger and Sartre emphatically deny that human beings can properly be said to *know* what is morally required of them in a way that is genuinely independent of their own individual choices; and they repudiate in principle the use of the concepts of truth and falsity in moral contexts. . . .

Fortunately, it is not difficult to identify the specific form of intellectualism against which Heidegger and Sartre direct their criticisms. Throughout *Sein und Zeit* [1] there are many references to a conception of value as a special type of property that is independent of human volition and is a possible object of cognitive apprehension. . . . It is indeed possible to interpret Heidegger's whole theory of value as growing out of his criticisms of all attempts to treat value as a quality or property. Considered in this light, his mode of argument is to show that these theories attempt to transfer to a (value) property a set of functions which *no* property is capable of discharging, and that these functions are properly assigned only to human beings. This rejection of value properties passes over virtually intact into Sartre's version of existentialism, where it is closely associated with the problem of the contingency of value which, for Sartre at least, is inseparable from its dependence on individual choice. At the same time, however, his account of value is in a real sense complementary to Heidegger's since its effect is to show that the concept of a value property, which the latter criticizes, incorporates a contradiction that springs from the attempt to fuse, in the notion of a being that has its value as a necessary adjunct of its nature, the radically opposed modes of being of things and of persons. . . .

The fundamental premise on which the existentialist critique of the notion of a value property rests is that value concepts have an essentially practical character. To describe value concepts as essentially practical is to say that the use of a value concept necessarily commits its user to a judgment that some action is to be performed and, through that judgment, to the actual perform-ance of that action in the event he finds himself in the situation to which it is declared to be appropriate. Now, if value concepts are generically practical in this sense, it follows that they designate relational attributes, i.e., the rightness or "fittingness" *of* a certain action *in* a certain situation. Accordingly, the in-tellectualist must hold that in apprehending the presence in some situation of a value property, we also come to know that some action is to be performed—namely, the action that constitutes the other term in the relational complex implicit in the value property itself. The heart of the existentialist counter-argument is simply the claim that this notion of *knowing* that some action is to be performed is a conceptual muddle, and that the practical, action-oriented character of value concepts is irreconcilable with the doctrine that they desig-nate objective properties. . . .

[1] [Martin Heidegger's major philosophical work, *Being and Time*.]

This view that ethical concepts are essentially tied to action must be explicated against the background of the existentialist treatment of possibility. . . . When we speak of acting in a certain way in a given situation, what we have in mind is a series of events which would transform that situation in certain respects and substitute for it another, presently nonexistent situation. This transformation will normally be one that is believed to be within the powers of the person or persons seeking to effect it, or at least to be the kind of thing which it is reasonable for them to attempt in the light of what they know about their capabilities, even though they do not in fact succeed in bringing it about. But the most important feature of any action, from the existentialist standpoint, is that it is always doing *this* rather than *that,* where "this" and "that" represent alternative transformations of some situation which are *both* possible. Even when our action serves only to maintain in existence a situation that already obtains, the goal of that action is to realize one of the possible alternatives before us, i.e., to see to it that things remain as they are instead of changing. When we are said to act, there is thus a range of situations, any one of which might, depending upon the effort we make, follow upon the present state of affairs. These situations are possibilities, not just in the sense that their occurrence is not logically excluded by our characterization of the present situation as the action of changing my dog into Julius Caesar would presumably be, but also in the sense that the question whether or not we will attempt to bring them about is one that is left open by the present state of our knowledge. Finally, while it is not necessary to make any special claim about what goes on in the mind of a person who acts to bring about one of these alternative possibilities, it *is* necessary, if he is to be said to act at all, that he should be able to say, or somehow to convey in response to a question about what he is doing, his awareness that he is doing *this* rather than *that.* . . .

To sum up, the crucial premise of the existentialist argument is that the actions to which reference is made by value concepts are possible actions. They are actions which there is reason to think the relevant persons *could* perform if they chose; but they are also actions that are not necessary or inevitable and that those persons can also *not* perform, if they choose. To the extent that evaluative judgment involves a reference to actions, it is to actions whose mode of logical rapport with the existing situation to which they are appropriate is neither that of being excluded as incompatible with our characterization of that situation, nor that of being a necessary entailment of it. Furthermore, this setting of actual situations within a context of possibility is not just a contingent accident of the human condition, that will be eliminated . . . with human ignorance, but a permanent and distinctive feature of our relationship to the world. Thus, precisely because human experience is essentially mediated by an uneliminable contrast between what actually exists and what might possibly exist, one central human function becomes the projection of a range of possible states of affairs that might be realized by corresponding human actions. "Things" by themselves are incapable of setting up their own ranges of possible alternatives and, *a fortiori*,[2] they are incapable of designating any one of these possibilities as giving the direction in which an actual situation should evolve. Yet the concept of a value property represents both these forms of transcendent reference to possible states of affairs as relational attributes that are independent of human consciousness, with the result that the latter must be characterized as passively registering such relationships and reproducing them in true value judgments. In other words, it is claimed that we discover, or at least *can* discover, a special relationship of rightness or fittingness between the actual situation in which we have to act and some one of the possible actions which we project out of that situation. The fact that this relationship holds between a particular possible action and an actual situation, and that it does not hold between the latter and certain other possible actions is supposed to be what entitles us to say that that one action is the morally right one for us to perform.

As I have already indicated, it is precisely the application of the concept of truth to this peculiar hybrid of actuality and possibility that creates the difficulty. The reference to a possible state of affairs and a corresponding possible action by which it would be realized is essential if the attribution of a value quality is to have any relevance to the question, "What should I do?" Moreover, the situation in which we act must be reckoned with through an identification of some relevant feature it bears if action is to be more than a blind instinctual thrust. But in what sense could we be said to *discover* a relationship in which one term is a presently existent state of affairs and the other a merely possible human action? No doubt it is unexceptionable English usage to say of value judgments that they are "true"—in that sense of "true" which is close to "ditto" and which permits us to espouse judgments that have been made by others. There is a quite different use of "true" that is distinctive of fact-stating discourse and which requires that we be able to verify by some mode of inspection the presence or absence of the quality or relation designated by the predicate term in the judgment which is said to be "true." It is this second (and surely more fundamental) sense of "truth" of which the existentialists cannot make sense when it is associated with evaluative judgments. For in the evaluative case, *ex hypothesi*, one term in the relational complex which we are said to apprehend does not exist, and if the concept of truth is coordinate with what exists, as the existentialists assume throughout, then it cannot be extended to judgments that involve an essential reference to what does not exist at the time of judgment and, as far as the agent knows, may never exist. . . .

FREEDOM AND CHOICE

[There are] two quite different senses that the term "freedom" may bear in ethical contexts. One of these [is] the freedom of causal indeterminacy, and

---

[2] [Even more strongly, as a special case of this.]

the other [is] the freedom of autonomous moral legislation. When the existentialists say that man is free, they mean that he is free in both of these senses, and they hold that both kinds of freedom can be seen to follow from the general account they have given of human being. In this chapter, I propose to examine the views of Heidegger and Sartre with respect to both kinds of freedom. This review should then make it possible to gain a better understanding of the central existentialist thesis that *man makes himself,* as well as of the equally well known definitions of human being as "care" and as a "project." This in turn will lead to an inquiry into what Heidegger and Sartre mean by choice, and to a consideration of the much-vexed topic of the relation of choice to moral rules and principles. Here again I will argue that the doctrine of the existentialists has been largely misunderstood, and that their position is not correctly described as an extreme individualism that makes no place for general rules within the structure of the moral life. Instead, it is a view of the status of general rules in their relationship to particular acts of choice; and while this view breaks sharply with the Aristotelian interpretation of the relation of choice to rules, it should not be interpreted as denying the need for consistent policies in the conduct of the moral life.

I

When the existentialists discuss causal determinism, they usually treat it as a set of methodological assumptions distinctive of the scientific study of the natural world. Their main argument is that this mode of treatment of natural phenomena not only develops out of the quite different conceptual system of common sense, but also remains dependent upon that prior mode of construing the relationship of human being to "things," and cannot be used to suppress or eliminate the latter. The familiar prescientific understanding that we have of our relationship to the world implicitly recognizes the uneliminability of alternative possibilities of action. Its characterization of human beings is organized around the notions of responsibility and choice that presuppose the reality of such alternatives. Scientific determinism, by contrast, following in the path of Spinoza, undercuts this whole set of concepts by treating the belief in alternative possibilities as a product of our ignorance of the true mechanism of nature —human nature included—and it projects a reflexive application to human beings of causal and deterministic assumptions that were originally developed for the purpose of controlling physical nature. The existentialists' counterargument, in essence, is that this mode of self-objectification is one that human beings cannot really carry out in a thoroughgoing and consistent way, and that even when the attempt is made, the more primitive nondeterministic set of concepts reasserts itself. The profound sense of their defense of human freedom is accordingly that of the Kantian argument that human beings are so constituted as to be unable to think of themselves as being causally determined; and they go on to add (as Kant did) that to be unable to think of yourself except as free is in effect to *be* free.

While this assertion may sound strange to many ears, it does not proclaim any occult metaphysical doctrine. Indeed, it would be much more accurate to regard the existentialist defense of human freedom as antimetaphysical in intent than the reverse. It is antimetaphysical just in the sense that it refuses to undercut or devaluate our profound tendency to read the world in terms of alternative possibilities of action in the interest of some preconception of what the real must be. It undertakes to show that no scientific account of human action and behavior can ever, by itself, lay down the attitudes and perspectives of action that may supervene upon it, and it goes on to point out that a determinism that attempts this task must remain, as it were, a God's-eye-view which leaves human beings to resolve exactly the same indeterminacies as before. As such, determinism is perhaps irrefutable but also gratuitous, since the assumption it makes is by no means necessary to the consistent carrying-on of scientific inquiry. While it may satisfy some deep metaphysical craving, it has the positive disadvantage of treating as a mere appearance what is in fact central to our understanding of the relation between action and knowledge. There is a kind of paradox involved in the notion that we are indissolubly committed to a concept—that of alternative possibilities—which we believe to be really inapplicable to anything. The course taken by the existentialists is that of refusing to abandon the concept of alternatives, and of interpreting scientific inquiry in such a way that it presupposes a relationship to the world in which alternatives have a place, instead of trying to fit human action into a conceptual world from which both alternatives and choice have been excised. . . . What the existentialist line of argument establishes, if it is successful, is not that from some external and absolute "God's-eye-point-of-view" man is free, but rather that within the human situation the notions of predictability and freedom are complementary and interdependent.

The way in which the existentialist argument against determinism proceeds is not difficult to grasp; it is essentially similar to forms of argumentation that have been used for the same purpose by nonexistentialists. The paradigm of all such arguments is given by the case of a prediction of the way the stock market will behave. If this prediction becomes known, speculators may well act differently from the way they would have acted if it had not; and the prediction may be falsified as a result of becoming known. If the example is changed so that the prediction not only concerns the action that some human being will take in certain circumstances but also is made in accordance with some scientific theory about human behavior, it becomes possible to make the existentialist point against determinism quite concisely. If I am informed of this prediction of my behavior, this knowledge will open up alternative possibilities of action in the situation in which it is predicted that I will act in a certain way. In existentialist parlance, the prediction as well as the theory from which it derives and the sequence of events which that theory projects, become elements in my situation to which I can react in a number of different ways that are not determined by the theory itself. But, if coming to know a predictive theory of some kind by itself modifies the situation in question in a way that is relevant to the possibilities of action in it, then the deterministic case can be saved only by expanding the original theory to take account of these modifications. There would, therefore, have to be a second law-based prediction in which my reaction to the circumstances specified in the first law, as well as to the prediction itself, would be taken into account. But the same issue arises with respect to this second law: does it predict what I will do in these circumstances if I also know of *this* new prediction? It appears that as long as I know what it is predicted I will do, a series of possibilities opens up that cannot be foreclosed by that prediction. Even if I went ahead and did what it was predicted I would do, knowing that it was so predicted, the case would be the same. Because this action that I thus perform is now only one among a number of alternative modes of reaction to my knowledge of the prediction, I will have to think of myself as having done this *rather than* something else; and this is to say that I would have chosen to do it. Thus, when the prediction is known, even the course of action that confirms it does so in a way that offers no support to determinism. For I can not be sure that I will not use my knowledge of the law cited in the prediction for the purpose of intervening to forestall the predicted outcome. . . .

It would be easy to imagine predictions made in circumstances that clearly exclude the possibility of any course of action alternative to the one predicted. Thus, if a man is falling from a building and I shout to him, "You are going to be killed," it is hardly plausible to suggest that his awareness of this prediction conjures up a range of possible courses of action by which the prediction will be falsified; nor would it be sensible to say that by continuing to fall he shows that he has chosen to do so. But to treat an example like this as fatal to the existentialist argument would be to assume—erroneously—that the latter claims some sort of effective omnipotence for human beings. *Ex hypothesi,* there is in this case no possible *action* that will keep the falling man from being killed. All the existentialist needs to claim, however, is that in every situation there is some respect in which a spread of alternatives is open, and that it is impossible for a human being to build himself and his conscious life into a predictive scientific theory in such a way as to close down all but one possibility of action. The possibilities that *are* effectively open may be insignificant ones as in the case of the falling man, or momentous ones that will affect the whole subsequent course of our lives. In any case, as long as the slightest penumbra of possibility surrounds what is unchangeable in our experience, there is no limit that can be set to the eventual difference that may be made by the actions we institute, and nothing can remain wholly immune to the contingency that is introduced into the world by the possibility of action.

It has often been pointed out, even by philosophers who would accept much of the existentialist case as presented so far, that it leaves open the pos-

sibility of a study of all human activities on deterministic principles, provided
the inquiry and the predictions it produces are somehow kept isolated from
the system of events that forms its subject matter. Since this condition is in fact
often satisfied, at least for all practical purposes, and since even when it is not,
the motive of refuting a prediction in order to demonstrate the indeterminacy
of voluntary human action is in most cases either weak or nonexistent, it can
be argued that the inability of human beings to think of themselves as determined does not really constitute a serious obstacle to the "objective" scientific
study of voluntary action. This may well be true, but it should be noted that
in one important case—that of the scientific inquirer himself—the scientific
theory cannot be kept isolated from the actions it is supposed to predict; and
here, at least, it will open up possibilities of action that do not themselves
come within the purview of the theory. From the point of view of the scientist
who formulates a theory, the behavior of all persons to whom that theory applies but who are themselves ignorant of the latter and therefore cannot make
it a premise of any of their practical deliberations, will no doubt seem "determined." At the same time, to the extent that they are conceded to be capable
of comprehending the theory in question in the way that its formulator already
does, their relation to it is potentially the same as his currently is; and if they
were to stand in this relationship to the theory, the same indeterminacy would
prevail with regard to the possibilities of action it suggests to them. . . .

II

The nature of autonomy—the second kind of freedom distinguished earlier—
can be understood by analogy with the causal freedom that I have just been
describing. . . .

This kind of freedom has to do with the analysis of the situation in which
action is to be undertaken and not with the possibility of alternative courses
of action as the first did. The function of such analysis is to select those features
of a situation by virtue of which a certain line of action becomes appropriate,
and on the basis of this determination, to characterize the situation in such a
way that it "points" to that action as its appropriate fulfillment. When I organize a situation for purposes of action in this way, I may be said to transcend
the features of it upon which I light by incorporating them into a temporal
Gestalt of which the other pole is some outcome or resolution that has yet to
take place, and the occurrence of which is at least partly dependent upon my
action. Once this analysis has been carried out and the situation has been conceptually oriented toward action in the manner described, I can speak of the
"fact" that the situation has the features in question as my "reason" for acting
in the way I propose to act, and of this state of affairs itself as calling for a
certain kind of action on my part.

The freedom human beings enjoy in structuring such situations with reference to action—the freedom of autonomy—consists negatively in the fact that a situation does not indicate by itself which of its features are criterial for what kind of action. . . . It makes sense to say that it is true that X is a feature of situation Y, but no sense at all to say that it is true that situation Y's having feature X is a reason for acting in a certain way. Positively, this notion of autonomy is intended to signify that the transformation of a situation of fact into one that is oriented toward action is itself an act that individuals perform, and for which they alone are ultimately responsible. This is an act of conceptualization through which a particular situation is characterized by reference to selected features which are thus made to function as the springboard for action of a certain sort. Thus, to characterize another person's conduct as "disrespectful" or as "cruel" is to place it in a particular perspective of action, at the same time that it states a fact about that person. The autonomous character of this act naturally requires that it should have been possible for me to conceptualize the same situation differently, but this requirement which is closely connected with my *causal* freedom is not the whole story. The more important feature of autonomy is what I have called our logical freedom in evaluation, which results from the absence of any standard of truth to which such acts of evaluative conceptualization should somehow correspond or by reference to which they might be justified.

The relationship between causal freedom and logical freedom or autonomy can now be stated. If human beings were not causally free in the sense that there always remain unreduced alternative courses of action in some sphere of their lives, there would clearly be no point in speaking of them as enjoying evaluative autonomy, since the notion of action would have lost its application. But the existentialists also contend that if human beings were causally free but not autonomous (i.e., not logically free), the concept of action would have been effectively subverted again. . . . In the full sense appropriate to human beings, action requires both a range of possible alternatives and an autonomous structuring of the action situation through which the latter is oriented toward some possible course of action as its appropriate resolution. What this comes to, in practice, is that all established and "impersonal" ways of tieing situations of fact to projects of action, however natural and rationally compelling they may seem, are in principle decomposable into the elements of fact and evaluation. . . .

III

Very little has been said up to this point about choice, and yet the concept of choice is of fundamental importance to the ethical theory of existentialism, as the writings of Jean-Paul Sartre in particular make clear. It is time now to turn our attention to this concept, and to attempt to dispel some of the persistent confusions and misinterpretations that have been characteristic of much critical discussion of its place and function within existentialist philosophy. These clarifications will in the first instance bear upon the nature of choice itself, and are intended to show that the choice of which the existentialists make so much is not, as many critics have supposed, a kind of psychological event. The positive account of choice which I will propose is one that follows quite directly and obviously from my earlier discussions of logical freedom in evaluation, once these misunderstandings are set aside; and after outlining it briefly, I will show how it can be made to yield acceptable interpretations of such characteristically existentialist uses of the concept of choice as "choice of one-self" and "total choice."

If the assumption that choice must be a psychological event is the most serious obstacle to an understanding of the existentialist position, another potential source of misunderstanding has already been dealt with in the discussions of this chapter and the preceding one. I have in mind the very wide-spread tendency to suppose that choice is not only an inner act of self-determination, but also that it can properly supervene only *after* the action-situation has been analytically laid out in such a way that its action-relevant features are made evident. This is indeed the classical, Aristotelian account of choice, and as I have already shown, it rests on the further assumption that there are independently valid moral principles by which the identification of these features of the situation is controlled. By contrast, the existentialist concept of choice is one that embraces this initial characterization of the action-situation itself. What this means is that the choices we think of ourselves as making on the basis of a certain analysis of the morally relevant features of a situation are only the visible tip of a much more radical choice which includes that analysis itself. It also means that no feature of any state of affairs can confer on itself the status of being what is called a "good-making consideration" or reason, and that it acquires this status only within the context of the very system of evaluative preferences for which it is supposed to provide some measure of independent support. The force of the existentialist thesis that to treat some feature of an existing situation as a reason is—implicitly at least—to choose or decide that it should be one, is to remind us that once we understand the underivability of our evaluative judgments from anything that could be called a truth (whether necessary or contingent), we have no alternative but to espouse them as our own choices. . . .

Turning now to the characteristic existentialist employment of the concept of "choice" in such phrases as "choice of oneself" and "total choice," I must once again begin by turning aside a mistaken conception of what the existentialists intend to convey by these locutions. They are absolutely not to be understood as denials of the patent fact of initial and continuing human passivity in the face of multiple features of our situation which we do not choose. Neither Heidegger nor Sartre has any stake in explaining away the brute fact of the innumerable natural limitations that confront every human being. Some of these are physical, such as the different degrees of strength and skill or of resistance to disease that are the lot of different individuals. Some of them are psychological, although the existentialists are not often willing to recognize the "given" aspect of such personal traits as cowardice or cheerfulness since they so strongly emphasize how often we make ourselves the accomplices of our "natural" dispositions and disingenuously seek to represent ourselves as their helpless victim. Still others are historical and cultural—our having been born into a certain kind of society at a certain place and time. All of these features of our situation produce different "coefficients of difficulty" for the various projects in which an individual in a given set of circumstances engages himself in order to realize a certain goal. Not only do the existentialists not deny or minimize the significance for human action of the historical and natural environment in which it takes its rise: they emphasize repeatedly the brute contingent givenness—the facticity—of the situation in which we find ourselves, and the necessity for every human comprehension of the world to be rooted in a specific place and a specific time. Similarly, the slave makes himself what he is by his relationship to the fact of being a slave, by his way of setting up a range of possible meanings that this condition may have, and by the selection he makes among these possibilities. It is not necessary that such a person be able to describe what he is doing as "making or choosing himself," nor is it even necessary . . . for a person to detach himself completely from some predefined system of self-characterization (e.g., I am a peasant, a noble, a worker). Nor should this notion of a "choice of oneself" be taken to mean that the object of choice is always an image of the self in some narrow psychological sense that would eliminate relationships to other human beings and the social and institutional framework within which the self develops. In fact, the existentialists believe that it is quite impossible to isolate a self that is independent of other selves, and in saying that the object of choice is always the self, they are not in any way restricting the sphere of choice. What they mean is that our moral personalities are constituted by the choices we make, and that no one can make these choices for us. To act in a certain way in a certain situation contributes to making us persons of a certain sort; and there is nothing else that can do so. It might be objected to this view that it is a truism that follows from the existentialists' definition of moral personality, but it certainly does not imply that all choice is dominated by a narcissistic image of what the (psychological) self is to be. . . .

Underlying all these conceptions of self-choice is the profound Heideggerian conception of man as the being that founds his own being. This is the notion that at least in some sphere of their lives, human beings must take alternative possibilities of action seriously in such a way that even if, as we say, they fail to act, they must think of themselves as having acted. In this sphere, what they are—the identity they bear—is sustained solely by the spectrum of possibilities they effectively entertain and by what they do or try to do, so that it is proper to say, as Heidegger and Sartre do, that human beings have to *be*, i.e., act out, what they are. . . .

IV

In its broad outline, the existentialist view of the relationship of particular choices to general rules is quite clear. It is that an individual can accept a moral rule or policy only by acting in accordance with it, and that the particular choices or actions by which such rules are effectively accepted are themselves logically prior to, and independent of, the rule itself. No verbal declaration or inner resolve, however impressive, can by itself, amount to an acceptance of a moral principle unless it is backed up by action that conforms to the rule. But if it is an action that constitutes acceptance of a moral principle, then no action can do so any more than any other; or, if it does, it is only in the sense that some actions have more extensive and more significant repercussions than others do, and therefore commit us more deeply to a certain line of action. Apart from the increasing difficulty of disengaging oneself from a policy that one has pursued over a period of time, the earlier choices we make in accordance with a moral principle do not commit us to it any more finally than do later choices. The point here is that the whole question of the acceptance of any moral principle is always "reopenable" and each choice that we make in accordance with that principle can become the occasion of a new appraisal of all the considerations bearing upon our acceptance of it. Even if we make these choices more or less mechanically, and without any re-appraisal of their ultimate bases, we are implicitly endorsing the principle. This amounts to saying that there can be no such thing as making particular choices in advance by adopting a rule that will control the decision we make in cases that have yet to arise. When the time comes, the whole matter can be re-opened if only because it cannot be shut off. If we then act in accordance with the rule laid down on a previous occasion, that decision stands on its own legs and makes exactly the same contribution to our acceptance of the principle as does the earlier choice even though the latter may have represented itself as legislating in advance for future cases. . . .

The existentialists appear . . . to be committed to what has been called the "summary" view of the relationship of moral rules to individual cases, i.e., the view that moral rules are generalizations summarizing the choices made in particular cases by the person who is said to accept the rule, and that they are thus logically posterior to these particular choices. Admittedly, this view does violence to the sense most of us have of coming into new situations requiring moral choice with a prior set of accepted policies which we assume will be controlling for this situation as it has been for others in the past. It also runs afoul of the difficulty—encountered in rule-governed activities such as games—which stems from the fact that quite often one cannot even *describe* the alternative courses of action between which one has to choose without implicitly recognizing a certain rule (e.g., the rule of promise keeping) as applicable to that case. On the other hand, when one considers less straightforward cases in

which we do not have this sense of a choice-situation's being uniquely classifiable under some single moral rubric, and are torn instead between two conflicting rules both of which seem to have some claim to control our decision
in this case, the point of the existentialist argument becomes both clearer and
more plausible. In such cases, a question arises about our relationship to the
moral rules that are in conflict, and this is not a question that can be satisfactorily dealt with by an appeal to rules of precedence stipulating which rule
is to be followed in what kinds of conflicts among rules. For what is the status
of these superordinate rules and what is involved in a person's adoption of
one of them? If a conflict of rules arises for the first time in a person's entire
moral experience, is he to deduce the proper line of action from a general
rule of precedence? This would presuppose that he already accepts the rule of
precedence before he has ever acted on it. He may of course have been taught
this principle and have given sincere verbal allegiance to it, but in this case
as in the case of primary moral rules the criterion of action is the only satisfactory index of what one really accepts in the way of moral principles. It follows
that by acting in accordance with a rule of precedence we in effect *choose* the
policy reflected in that rule, and the existentialists are saying simply that that
choice must be dictated by the end we are seeking to realize.

For purposes of illustration, let us take a person who subscribes to the
moral principle that forbids lying, and also the principle that directs us to
avoid actions that cause unnecessary suffering to others. Let us suppose further
that he is successively confronted with a number of different situations in
which telling the truth would require that he cause significant suffering to
others. It may well be that in all these cases he will choose to tell the truth in
spite of the fact that he is strongly disinclined to hurt other individuals in
the way he sees to be inevitable if he does so. How are we to describe the
relationship of these choices to the general rule against lying, when each of
them involves the necessity of a choice between lying and causing suffering?
Is the conclusion: "Tell the truth" simply deduced from the general rule by
subsuming the particular case under it and drawing the consequences? This
would require that the rule contain a rider to the effect that when circumstances
of the kind in question are present in a case when the duty of truth-telling
is applicable, they are to be ignored in favor of that duty. But surely this
would be merely an ingenious *post factum* rationalization and if the rule has
this content, then it is conferred upon it by the individual choice itself which
does override the other considerations in favor of the duty of truth-telling. A
general moral rule may serve as a formula that reminds us of what our response
is to be in situations considered simply as situations in which we have either to
lie or tell the truth, but they cannot, by themselves, tell us what to do in any
individual case. For that, a decision has to be made that this principle is to
take precedence over other considerations that might lead us to act otherwise;
and this decision is logically prior to, and independent of, the rule itself.

The point of the existentialist polemic against the domination of our understanding of morality by rules can now be stated. As has already been stated, what is at issue is not the desirability or the possibility of establishing consistent, long-range moral policies. In so far as the existentialists address themselves to this issue, their contribution is simply to point out that it is extremely difficult and often practically impossible to enunciate, in advance, principles of conduct that do not have to be successively modified and qualified by the particular choices we make. They are also concerned to make evident the dangers implicit in the sort of reliance on rules that really consists in a systematic refusal to look at the features of particular choice-situations that might lead to a modification or suspension of the rule. Perhaps the best way to characterize the existentialist attitude toward moral rules is to say that it sees them as emerging from a progressive resolution of individual cases, and as gradually increasing in stability and reliability, but also as never wholly immune from review and revision.

In a sense, however, this statement of the existentialist view of the dependence of all general moral policies on particular choices may prove misleading. It fails to bring out the degree to which every particular choice is itself general in character. I have already tried to show that every action and every choice must involve an appreciation of the relevant features of the agent's situation and that these features will normally be repeatable traits that can be designated by means of universal predicates. Similarly, the other element in choice—the projected transformation of the existing situation—can only be described as the bringing about of a certain type of situation. To use an example, I may say that I helped a neighboring family *because* everyone ought to help those who are in distress. To say this is to identify the feature of the situation by reference to which my action has to be characterized, and it may be possible to justify this criterion by showing that it is derivable from yet more general criteria of action. When I cite general rules in this way as the reasons for my action, I really only re-describe *what* I have done by laying bare the deeper intentional structure of that action. Whatever level of generality this description of my action attains, the principle so exposed can be accepted only by the action that falls under it; and each such action, logically, commits me to the principle quite as much as any other. What is meant by saying that the individual choice is logically prior to the principle it instantiates is that when I have described an action by reference to the most general criteria that apply to it, I still have to decide whether by performing that action I shall accept the principle implicit in it or not; and this decision cannot itself be derived from that principle. By acting in one way, I accept the principle and by acting in another I reject it. However automatic that policy may become with time, my acceptance of it remains contingent upon my actions in particular cases, each of which can, in principle, be made to raise all the issues of the moral life. Nothing commits one to a moral principle except an individual action, and no individual action can do so for once and for all. Like Descartes' world which has to be sustained in existence from moment to moment by the omnipotence of God, so the acceptance of moral principles is effectuated by the very actions which are subsumed under them, and remains conditional upon such future actions.

AUTHENTICITY AND OBLIGATION

Thus far, my discussion of the ethical theory of existentialism has concentrated almost exclusively on the evaluative judgments of individual human beings, and has attempted to define the nature of the freedom in which those evaluations are made. Nothing has been said about the moral relations in which such autonomous individuals stand to one another, nor about the compatibility of a general ethical theory of the type outlined in earlier chapters with a recognition of some kind of moral obligation toward other human beings. This lack of attention to the social aspect of morality, it must be admitted, reflects a corresponding neglect on the part of most of the existentialist writers; and this neglect has led many critics to conclude that the concepts used by the existentialists in the analysis of evaluation are radically incapable of dealing with the phenomenon of moral community and the complex moral relationships to other human beings which such community comports. This charge has at least a *prima facie* plausibility about it which makes it all the more necessary to explore in detail the implications of the views developed so far for the whole topic of moral relationships among human beings. In this chapter, I will attempt to show that, while the existentialists do not have a fully developed theory of obligation, they have presented in embryo at least a conception of what the basis of moral relations between human beings should be. . . .

Up to this point, moral autonomy has been described simply as a state in which human beings find themselves. Unavoidably, they see their situation in terms of possible alternatives among which they must choose; but they do not choose to see the world in this way. So conceived, moral autonomy is not itself the source of any directives for human conduct; it is, instead, the relationship to ourselves and to the world that is presupposed by any such search for specific principles of action. Quite obviously it would be pointless to urge human beings to achieve moral autonomy when it is their inescapable state of being. On the other hand, if the existentialists wish to say (as they clearly do) that we can, and also that we should, choose to be free and autonomous beings, and that the achievement of this autonomy is the proper objective of a truly human life, the autonomy that is thus to be achieved cannot be the same as the autonomy that is a datum of human life.

. . . A way out of this difficulty is provided by Merleau-Ponty's "dispositional" interpretation of moral freedom. If the latter is conceived as a capacity for envisaging one's situation in terms of alternative possibilities of action, then it is certainly possible to distinguish between having such a capacity and activating it, and also between exercising it only within a very restricted area of one's life and seeking to extend it to all aspects of life. Whether one has such a capacity at all is presumably very much like the question whether a given type of being has the capacity for learning a language. One either has it or one has not—it is not chosen or achieved. But if autonomy is understood not just as a latent capacity but as the progressive development and exercise of that capacity, then it is, at the very least, not senseless to make this development itself a goal of moral effort. Interpreted now as identifying an object of choice and purposeful effort, the concept of autonomy would generate a directive to realize in ourselves an intensified moral self-consciousness, and to subject wider and wider tracts of our experience to analysis in terms of alternatives of voluntary action. It would presumably also direct that in relation to others one should do whatever one can to encourage and facilitate the development by them of a similarly heightened moral self-awareness. It is of course not at all easy to say just what steps would be required to this end but it seems highly probable that they would involve far-reaching and radical changes in our method of moral education. In any case, the mode of life in which this distinction between choice and non-choice is rigorously enforced, and in which every choice is individual in character, is what the existentialists mean by an authentic human existence. Authenticity may indeed be regarded as the prime existentialist virtue; and it consists in the avoidance of that false relation to oneself and to others that is set up when choices are represented as something other than what they are—something for which the individual is not responsible. Inauthenticity, by contrast, is the arch-principle of mystification in the relationship between human beings and in the relationship of an individual human being to himself. As Sartre's writings make very clear, it is the main obstacle in the way of any truly human relationship based on a reciprocal recognition of one another as fully responsible moral agents. The authentic human being is one who has so thoroughly defined his relationship to the moral attitudes characteristic of the community to which he belongs—either by assimilating or by modifying or by wholly rejecting them—that he is able to make moral judgments in his own name and not just in the ventriloquistic and impersonal manner of a communal morality.

It still remains to ask whether the progressive development of this way of looking at the world—this profound moralization of the self—is a good thing and also, more importantly, whether the recognition of oneself as an autonomous moral being can provide a logically sufficient and necessary condition upon which moral relationships among human beings could be founded. . . .

It is time now to turn to the concept of obligation itself, and to take note of certain of its features before going on to ask what the special relationship between authenticity and obligation may be. We may begin by considering the way in which claims that human beings have certain general duties can be established in the face of possible challenge. As has already been pointed out, such challenges are often met by arguments intended to show that the mode of conduct that is being called for is somehow part and parcel of our human nature, and thus cannot rationally be rejected by us. Since all conceptions of what constitutes our nature are themselves open to challenge, many philosophers have come to feel that the nature to which appeal is made must be one that has somehow been recognized as such by the person to whom the argument seeking to establish the reality of the obligation is being made. In the history of political philosophy, this perception has led to the elaboration of contractarian theories of obligation like Rousseau's, which justify all limitations on what may permissibly be willed by reference to certain postulated acts of assent by the very persons who are thus subject to what are really self-imposed obligations. The effect of such theories is to base all obligations on the obligation to keep a promise, and while some of the proponents of this view have associated it with excessively literalistic conceptions of the form assumed by these contractual undertakings to which they appeal, the notion of promises as the basis of obligation generally can be separated from these irrelevancies. When this distinction has been made, the conception of promises as self-engaging acts proves to have great power and suggestiveness as a model for understanding moral relationships among human beings. I will argue that, when suitably interpreted, it can provide the elements of a theory of obligation and of moral community that can be accepted by the existentialists consistently with their commitment to the doctrine of moral autonomy.[3]

Promising is, of course, merely the clearest and most dramatic example drawn from the larger class of what might be called self-created obligations. What distinguishes obligations of this kind is the fact that the obligation is explicitly assumed by a given person at a more or less definite point in time. This assumption is often, as in the case of promising, a linguistic performance of a certain kind, and involves the public use of a form of words that has the effect of placing the person who uses them under an obligation to the person to whom the promise is made. The effect of the use of the promise-formula is to license an expectation on the part of the person to whom the promise is made. What may not be so obvious but is of great importance for our purposes is that in so licensing another's expectations I must implicitly disallow in advance an appeal to any justifications for a failure to do what I have promised to do, other than those that fall within a certain more or less precisely defined range of excuses. One "reason" for non-performance that is disallowed by this formula would certainly be any such statement as "I don't want to" or "I have changed my mind." A person who tried to justify non-performance in this way would merely show that he did not understand the promise-making formula he had used. It is thus an intrinsic feature of the latter that it does effectively "change the situation" between two or more persons in a way that cannot be canceled by just any subsequent decision *not* to do what one decided to do

[3] In the outline I give here of a theory of obligation, I have drawn at various points on the views of John Rawls as stated in "Justice as Fairness," *Philosophical Review*, Vol. 67 (1958), pp. 164–94, and in other articles.

in making the promise. The change thus made is not some magical modification of the relationships in which "objects" stand to us, but rather a linguistically effected change in the relationship between the person who makes the promise and the person to whom it is made. Given normal circumstances, once a person has put himself "on the hook" by engaging in the promise-making practice, he has bound himself in a way that carries with it all the externality and rigor that any deontologist could require.

It has sometimes been alleged that even self-created obligations require as a condition of their effectiveness that there be moral principles such as "Promises are to be kept," the truth of which is certified by an act of intellection that is logically prior to all particular acts of promise-making. In this way, the authority of special obligations is assimilated to what is assumed to be the standard case in which rational necessity is the basis of moral authority. It is perfectly possible, however, to agree with the cognitivist that "Promises are to be kept" is necessarily true; and yet, to hold at the same time that this is an analytic truth which generates an actual obligation only if we decide to engage in the promise-making activity. Thus, we come to be obliged only because we choose to use the promise formula, and if we chose never to use it, we would not be under an obligation. It would not make sense to argue that *Pacta sunt servanda* [4] means that we *ought* to engage in promise-making practices; and therefore the obligation is one that we put ourselves under when we do so engage. It is of course true that most people do not think of themselves as deciding to take part in, or not to take part in, the promise-making activity which is a going social concern into which we are in some sense "born." The established social character of this practice does not, however, imply or require that there is any corresponding "natural" obligation with respect to promises at all; and it seems much more plausible to treat the whole logically structured activity of promise-making as a human contrivance, as Hume thought, and as one which does not have to be thought of in cognitivist terms at all.

To be sure, self-created obligations are usually held to be only one type of obligation. There are many others such as the obligation to deal justly with other human beings, or the obligation to prevent unnecessary suffering, which do not seem to lend themselves so readily to an analysis along these lines, and certainly do not involve any express acts of self-commitment as promise-making does. But the case of special obligations still provides a useful clue, because it is quite possible that even where such explicit verbal performances are absent, there may be other less obvious means by which, in effect, we authorize an interpretation of what we do or say, which becomes an implicit element in our relationship with other persons and has much the same force as an obligation. For example, it can be argued that simply by speaking a language we authorize others to assume that we are saying what we believe to be true, so that when we lie, we violate an obligation accepted implicitly through our use of language.

---

[4] [Agreements are to be carried out.]

So too, when we accept what has been determined by some principles of justice as our fair share in some distribution, the other participants are justified in assuming that we accept these principles and will abide by them in like cases even when it may be more advantageous to us not to do so. In this case, we have again and by our own action (though not by any explicit linguistic performance) accepted a rule of action—in this case, a rule of justice—and have, in effect, disallowed "I don't choose to" as a defense in the case of nonperformance.

These examples suggest that the notion of a self-created obligation may be susceptible of generalization. While Hume was perhaps the first to propose a conception of rule-governed reciprocity as the basis of moral obligation generally, it is Kant's vision of the human community as a kingdom of ends that most clearly suggests the form this conception might take if pressed to the limit. In place of Hume's rather skimpy list of the possible forms of reciprocity, Kant makes the principle of reciprocity the governing norm for all relationships among human beings. If I must never, as Kant says, treat any other human beings merely as a means (i.e. as a thing), then I must judge only those actions to be morally permissible which I can justify to those affected by them, by appealing to considerations which I would be prepared to accept if the situation were reversed. What is important here is not so much the actual content of these jointly acceptable rules of conduct, nor Kant's claim that this content can be uniquely determined by purely logical tests, but rather the mode of human relationship within which this consensus emerges. Each human being recognizes all other human beings as being, like himself, morally free and as endowed with the capacity for understanding, accepting, and carrying-out jointly acceptable policies; and this recognition becomes a principle of respect for the moral freedom of others through each person's disallowing an appeal to mere disinclination or subjective preference as a ground for nonperformance of obligations deriving from those policies. A "kingdom of ends" as Kant calls it, or a "moral community" is simply a human society in which the fundamental relationship in which all the members stand to one another is that of persons to whom a rational justification by reference to considerations they can freely accept is due for all actions that significantly affect them. . . .

Now that an account has been given of both authenticity and obligation, the question of whether there is some special relationship between them must be faced. Does recognition by human beings of one another as morally autonomous beings, together with a disposition to intensify and extend wherever possible the kind of self-awareness on which this recognition rests, supply a uniquely suitable basis for a moral community characterized by binding relationships among its members? There are reasons for thinking that it does, assuming always that there is a disposition to communal living based on something other than force or fear. It must also be assumed that the human beings who are so disposed have needs and desires that are not so hopelessly disparate as to be incapable of joint satisfaction, and that the powers with which these persons are endowed are not so incommensurate as to cancel out any motive that the stronger party might have for cooperation with the weaker. These material conditions seem to be roughly satisfied by human beings as we know them; and so, too (although here, no very great assurance is appropriate) is the further condition that the kind of choice of which the persons entering into these relationships to one another must be capable is not just momentary preference, but a long-term commitment to joint policies, with all the implications for disciplinary controls over the actions of individuals that such policies involve. Even though from the existentialist point of view there can be no once-and-for-all commitment to such policies that eliminates any subsequent reconsideration of the issues they pose, no long-range commitment at all can be made by persons who are constitutionally unable to resist impulses which may run counter to a line of conduct they have adopted. Unless these conditions are met, no stable human community is likely to be founded on whatever basis. When they are, however, the special kind of selfconsciousness associated with authenticity has a contribution to make which must now be described.

Let us consider first the implications that a recognition of oneself as a morally autonomous being might have for the way one presents oneself as a candidate for moral relationships to other human beings. The most salient of these implications can be very simply stated. If a man thinks of himself as a morally autonomous being, the very nature of this character that he imputes to himself is such as to absorb any other feature of his nature which he might designate as the basis for his relationships with other human beings, and on the strength of which he might demand respect and acceptance from them. Let us suppose, for example, that a man proposes to make the fact that he is a proletarian—or a white man—or a Buddhist—the primary basis of his association with other human beings. Since he is at the same time, as I am assuming, committed to the doctrine of moral autonomy, he will be forced to admit that his being a proletarian, or a white man, assumes the criterial function he assigns to it only as the result of a choice on his part. In fact, *being* a proletarian or a Buddhist or even a white man in any sense which implies the imposition of priorities by which, e.g., being a white man takes precedence for purposes of action over being something else, inescapably turns out to involve an exercise of the same autonomy that presides over the whole moral life. If this is so, then to demand that one be respected in one's capacity as a white man or as a proletarian is to demand respect as one who "chooses himself" as a proletarian, and could have "chosen himself" as something else. This, in turn, is indistinguishable from demanding recognition as a free moral agent—with this reservation, that it is not explained why respect is to be confined to those moral agents who freely choose themselves in this one way. The relevant point here, however, is that once the agent adopts the autonomist view of his own moral activity, every subsequent role he espouses must be understood as a mode of self-determination for which he bears final responsibility. For this reason, if he is prepared at all to enter into an association based on reciprocity and mutual recognition with other human beings, he can do so only in his capacity as a free moral agent. If he is an autonomous moral being, then in every subordinate goal he sets himself, and in every principle he adopts, he is also bringing into play that fundamental capacity for self-determination. He cannot repudiate or remain indifferent to the latter without, at the same time, withdrawing the claim he makes for the subordinate goals that are its expression.

This line of reasoning can quite obviously be extended so as to yield conclusions that cast light not just on the role in which I can present myself as a candidate for moral relationships with other human beings, but also on the terms of cooperation which I can offer to my prospective partners in a moral community. If they, too, are autonomous moral agents, and if they, too, can have obligations only by placing themselves under obligations, then what *could* I offer them except respect for this freedom of self-definition and self-engagement which they, like me, enjoy? Even if they were not to share my conceptions of moral personality, which, as I am assuming, is based on the doctrine of autonomy, and were to give priority to other attributes they possess, it seems clear that from my standpoint their establishment of these priorities would have to be regarded as itself an exercise of that same autonomy. In this context, it is important to emphasize once again a point that has already been made. This is that while self-conscious autonomy absorbs our other desires, wants, and aspirations by transforming them into so many forms of self-determining choice, it does not follow that these wants must be somehow derivable or deducible from the fact that we are autonomous beings. Quite obviously, many of them will pre-date the recognition of one's autonomy as a moral being; and in any case, they are absorbed into this autonomous condition not by some process of logical derivation, but by passing through a critical review as a result of which they are put forward, if at all, as claims with which others have to reckon as *my* choices, whatever their previous history and no matter how initially passive in relation to them I may have been. They must, in other words, be *assumed*. The point that I am making here is simply that if we accept the doctrine of autonomy at all, we cannot avoid thinking of other human beings, for the purposes of possible moral relationships with them, as standing in this relationship to their own desires and wants.

This point has implications which make clearer how the aspiration to authenticity may facilitate the formation of moral relationships that can be truly binding. From what has already been said, it follows that the moral community that the existentialists project is one in which the only condition of membership is the very capacity for choice and self-commitment itself, and in which the members reciprocally recognize one another as "choosers." The force of this identification resides in the fact that it requires that each individual who is a member of such a community must regard himself, and be regarded by his fellows, as the sole and responsible arbiter of his own interests, and as controlling what may be called his "input" of claims into the public adjudicatory forum in which a common policy that resolves conflicts among claims must be formulated. Thus the *données*[5] of every moral problem are provided by the expressed preferences of human beings, each of whom speaks for himself and whose "vote" must be allowed to register as it stands, and not be interpreted out of existence or tacitly overridden by some theory of human nature that by-passes or disallows the explicitly declared preferences of the individual. Nothing is more alien to the general ethos of existentialism than the kind of moral paternalism that "knows better" than the individual moral agent what is good for the latter, or worse still, what the latter "really" wants. As often as not, this is done by appealing to some view of what is involved in moral personality as such; and when, as frequently happens, this view turns out to have substantive moral implications, these are established as antecedent premises on which subsequent joint deliberation must proceed, and which it is powerless to revise. By contrast, the existentialist insists that every element entering into the consideration of a moral problem must be "sponsored" i.e., must come in as the declared preference of one of the parties to such a deliberation; and his declaration is to be authoritative for the other participants in the sense that none of them has the right to look behind or interpret this preference in any way that is not authorized by the person whose preference it is.

Perhaps the most important feature of the relationship between authenticity and obligation remains to be described; and in order to grasp its significance, one must understand how precarious and conditional such moral community as exists at any given time appears to the existentialists. As I have already indicated, there are writers on ethical theory who seem to assume the existence of a moral community as a presupposition of any distinctively moral activity on the part of individual human beings who belong to it. On this view, it does not make any sense to speak of the defining principles of such a community as reflecting any kind of choice on the part of its members; they constitute instead a datum of the moral life antecedent to, and presupposed by, the choices of individual moral agents. I have indicated too that existentialist writers, by contrast, are typically much more strongly impressed by the fraudulence of what passes for moral consensus, and by the fragility and the partiality of such genuine consensus as does exist. Because they see so clearly the insecurity and the ambiguity of our actual moral practices as judged by the standard of true mutuality, the existentialists conceive the relation of each individual to the moral community in the volitional mode and that community itself as a *realisandum*[6] or as an "endless task" in the Kantian sense. This view in turn is inspired by the perception that our moral failures are as often due to our not recognizing certain classes of human beings as candidates for moral relationships at all, as they are to non-performance of duties within the sphere in which we do recognize the authority of moral principles. Precisely because the concept of autonomy is formal in the sense of abstracting from substantive rules of

[5] [The given factors to be taken into account.]
[6] [Something to be realized.]

conduct, it makes possible a clearer focus upon the moral relationship between persons which is the precondition for a successful resolution of questions of conduct, as well as upon the problematic and vulnerable character of such moral community as exists.

If we now consider these views in the context of the theory of obligation and of the moral community sketched out in the preceding section, it is difficult not to conclude that the existentialists have made a valid and important point. It may well be the case that natural communities like the family can continue to exist and even thrive although their members simply fulfill the duties assigned to them by their roles within these communities, and no one explicitly formulates the nature of his role to himself in such a way that it incorporates a statement of the basic relationships between human beings on which that community rests. It seems impossible, however, that a moral community such as I have described should ever exist except as it is sustained by an awareness on the part of its members of the mode of relationship to others that it involves and by a conscious determination to persevere in it. For the moment we lose the sense of ourselves and of others as "choosers" or lose our belief in the importance of this mode of identifying one another, our capability for actions and decisions that are truly shared will be affected. In a moral community, the whole corpus of rules and policies must remain in principle permanently open for reconsideration and possible revision if that community is to be completely sovereign in the sense of being able to raise and to resolve in a manner binding on all whatever issues it may face. But in order to be sovereign in this sense, the members of a human group must recognize one another as endowed with the capacities of choice and self-commitment which make it possible for them to be participants in such collective choices. To the extent that that recognition is effectively denied or is restricted by unilaterally imposed limits on the scope of choice, a moral community ceases to exist, and with it, relationships of obligation lapse. Those who might otherwise be subject to obligations will not have been permitted to act jointly with us to change our relations to one another in a way that would be binding; or perhaps not even they themselves will have fully grasped their capacity for so altering their own situation. In any case, in the absence of reciprocal recognition of one another as capable of this special kind of choice, a certain mode of human relationship becomes an unavailable option; and it is this mode of relationship that alone renders obligation intelligible.

Here then, we touch on the deep underlying motive for associating authenticity with obligation in the way the existentialists do. Because the various natural communities into which we are born only very imperfectly embody the ideal of human mutuality, we, as individuals, must continuously define for ourselves the moral community in which we effectively live. By so doing, we contribute in differing degrees to the expansion or contraction of such genuine mutuality as in fact exists; and if it is true, as I have argued, that mutuality is a condition of obligation, then we can properly speak of choosing to be obliged by choosing the mode of human relationship that makes obligation possible. Moreover, like all policies, the policy of living together with other human beings on the basis of a reciprocal recognition of one another's autonomy becomes effective *only* through corresponding choices made by individual human beings. When human beings single out their capacity for choice and self-commitment and place a value on it by seeking to extend and intensify their awareness of the choices that are open to them, and when they are able to describe these choices to themselves in such a way as to make evident the full burden of moral implication they carry, the making of such choices bearing on the constitution of a moral community will at the very least be facilitated. If, at the same time, they understand that only a similar recognition and prizing of the autonomy of other human beings can provide the framework within which the claims they may wish to make on others will have a place, they will surely perceive in the existentialists' positive evaluation of our capacity for autonomous moral choice, not just a facilitating but a necessary condition of the form of life they seek.

Supplementary Paperback Reading

A. Camus, *The Myth of Sisyphus and Other Essays* (Vintage Books, N. Y.)

A. Camus, *The Rebel: An Essay on Man in Revolt* (Vintage Books, N. Y.)

S. de Beauvoir, *The Ethics of Ambiguity*, trans. B. Frechtman (Citadel Press, Secaucus, N. J.)

N. Greene, *Jean-Paul Sartre: The Existentialist Ethic* (University of Michigan Press, Ann Arbor)

M. Grene, *Introduction to Existentialism* (University of Chicago Press)

M. Grene, *Sartre* (New Viewpoints Press, Franklin Watts, Inc., N. Y.)

K. Jaspers, *Reason and Existenz* (Noonday Press, N. Y.)

W. Kaufmann, ed., *Existentialism from Dostoevsky to Sartre*, rev. and expanded edition (New American Library, N. Y.)

W. Kaufmann, *Nietzsche: Philosopher, Psychologist, Antichrist,* fourth edition (Princeton University Press)

S. Kierkegaard, *Concluding Unscientific Postscript,* trans. D. Swenson and W. Lowrie (Princeton University Press)

S. Kierkegaard, *Either/Or,* Vols. I and II, trans. D. Swenson and L. M. Swenson (Princeton University Press)

G. Marcel, *The Mystery of Being,* trans. R. Hague (Henry Regnery, Chicago)

G. Marcel, *The Philosophy of Existentialism,* trans. M. Harari (Citadel Press, Secaucus, N. J.)

F. Nietzsche, *Basic Writings of Nietzsche,* ed. and trans. W. Kaufmann (Random House, Modern Library, Inc., N. Y.)

J.-P. Sartre, *Being and Nothingness,* trans. H. Barnes (Pocket Books, Simon and Schuster, Inc., N. Y.)

J.-P. Sartre, *Essays in Existentialism,* ed. W. Baskin (Citadel Press, Secaucus, N. J.)

J.-P. Sartre, *The Philosophy of Jean-Paul Sartre* (collected essays), ed. R. Cumming (Vintage Books, N. Y.)

R. Schacht, *Alienation* (Anchor Books, N. Y.)

P. A. Schilpp, ed., *The Philosophy of Karl Jaspers* (Open Court Publishing Co., LaSalle, Ill.)

R. Solomon, ed., *Nietzsche: A Collection of Critical Essays* (Anchor Books, N. Y.)

M. Warnock, *Existentialist Ethics* (St. Martin's Press, N. Y.)

M. Warnock, *The Philosophy of Sartre* (Hutchinson University Library, London)